WITHDRAWN

RECEIVING SØREN KIERKEGAARD

Habib C. Malik

RECEIVING SØREN KIERKEGAARD

The Early Impact

and Transmission

of His Thought

The Catholic University of America Press
Washington, D.C.

Copyright © 1997
The Catholic University of America Press
All rights reserved
Printed in the United States of America

Frontispiece: drawing by Chr. Kierkegaard. Courtesy of The Royal Danish Embassy, Washington, D.C.

The paper used in this publication meets the minimum requirements of American National Standards for Information Science—Permanence of Paper for Printed Library materials, ANSI Z39.48-1984.
∞

LIBRARY OF CONGRESS CATALOGING-IN-PUBLICATION DATA
Malik, Habib C., 1954–
    Receiving Søren Kierkegaard : the early impact and transmission of his thought / by Habib C. Malik.
        p.   cm.
    Includes bibliographical references (p.   ) and index.
    1. Kierkegaard, Søren, 1813–1855. I. Title.
B4377.M36   1996
198′.9—dc20
                                          96-23905
ISBN 0-8132-0878-5

To the memory of my dear parents
Charles H. Malik and Eva B. Malik

Without their love, this work and much else that is good in my life would not have been possible.

Contents

	Preface	ix
	Abbreviations	xv
	Introduction	xvii
1.	Kierkegaard and Some Contemporaries (i): The "Non-Reception" by Andersen and Ørsted	1
2.	Kierkegaard and Some Contemporaries (ii): Glimmerings of an Early Reception beyond Denmark	43
3.	The *Kirkekampen* and Its Immediate Aftermath: Seeds of "Misreception"	78
4.	A Foray into Drama? The Case of Ibsen	136

5. The "Tro og Viden" Controversy, or the Rise and
   Demise of "Pseudo-Kierkegaard" — 171

6. The Biographical-Psychological Approach and Its Perils:
   Georg Brandes and Criticism as Suppression — 211

7. The Kierkegaard Legacy and the *Fin de Siècle* — 283

8. The Beginnings of Serious Reception in the German-Speaking World — 339

   Conclusion — 393

   Bibliography — 397
   Index — 425

Preface

As far back as I can remember, the name Kierkegaard has buzzed around my home, thanks mainly to my late father's philosophical preoccupations and religious orientation. It was not an exclusive focus, however, for Kierkegaard was usually presented as belonging to a gallery of towering intellectual figures from the Western tradition to whom I received sustained, though often very cursory, exposure: the thinkers of ancient Greece, Augustine, Aquinas, Pascal, Kant, Dostoevsky, Nietzsche, Whitehead, Heidegger, and Buber, among others. Yet Kierkegaard always seemed somehow special, and to a novice like myself, particularly abstruse in his elusiveness. Until, that is, I read and re-read *Fear and Trembling* in my twenties and became transfixed by Kierkegaard's penetrating phenomenology of the faith of Abraham, its central character. That book served, as it has on countless occasions with so many people, as the trigger setting me on the path of a Kierkegaardian journey. As my knowledge of Kierkegaard progressed, so also did my appreciation of the tremendously valuable nudge he almost singlehandedly gave philosophy away from abstraction and in the direction of the individual person wrestling continuously with the immediate implications for his or her life of the abiding issues that intimately touch human existence in every time and place and circumstance: God, man, freedom, death, suffering, evil, faith, love, others, humor, communication, self-discovery, morality, and happiness.

Interested as I was in intellectual connections, the more deeply I delved into the Kierkegaardian corpus, the more curious I became about the impact it had on subsequent writers. I was developing a passion for the history of ideas, and Kierkegaard's fascinating influence was becoming its driving engine. Great was my delight therefore when Donald Fleming of the History Department at Harvard, in the course of surveying selected gaps in the intellectual history of modern Europe, mentioned that the early dissemination and reception of Kierkegaard's thought were largely *terra incognita*. I jumped at the opportunity to help in charting Kierkegaard's intellectual timeline with all its attendant bifurcations. One is used to seeing something by, and/or on, Kierkegaard included in nearly every philosophical anthology that appears under the heading "Existentialism." How and why this came to be the case were never made clear from a historical perspective. More specifically, the story of the slow and tortuous emergence of Kierkegaard's writings from their marginal native setting to the pivotal place they occupy today in Western thought and beyond has never been systematically told.

Fragments of the story of Kierkegaard's early reception are scattered throughout a seemingly endless string of prefaces, forewords, and afterwords to translations of his works, as well as in introductions and conclusions to a number of secondary studies on him. Of particular interest in this regard are the "Historical Introductions" to the new translations in *Kierkegaard's Writings*. They contain a wealth of information about the historical context of each work and the reactions to it when it first appeared. There exist also several studies of the diverse aspects and phases of Kierkegaard's early reception. Aage Henriksen's *Methods and Results of Kierkegaard Studies in Scandinavia: A Historical and Critical Survey* is the only attempt of its kind in English to provide some critical analysis of the early Scandinavian works on Kierkegaard. While advancing occasional useful insights, it falls far short of the desired level of excellence, both stylistically and critically. The eighth volume of the series *Bibliotheca Kierkegaardiana*, entitled *The Legacy and Interpretation of Kierkegaard*, contains several short articles by an international group of scholars dealing with Kierkegaard's reception in a variety of countries and his influence on a number of personalities during his day and in later times. The articles tend to display minimal analysis and are, for the most part, surveys of the raw highlights of reception. They are useful, however, as avenues to more substantive treatments and, on occasion, to primary sources. On Kierkegaard's early Norwegian reception, volume XIX from 1923 of the *EDDA* series has two long studies that are very useful. There is considerable overlap between the two treatments, but they remain indispensable secondary sources. Their counterpart for Sweden is Sjöstedt's comprehensive study *Søren Kierkegaard och Svensk Litteratur*. Noteworthy in this work is the long section on Strindberg and Kierkegaard.

The subject of Kierkegaard and nineteenth-century Scandinavian-Americans is virtually untouched. From the little research done for the present study, it has become clear that this is an area of great promise with potentially rewarding discoveries awaiting the diligent scholar. Trips to St. Olaf College, Luther College, and other comparable institutions in the Midwest would be indicated as a start. Thanks to the hospitality of the Hongs at St. Olaf and the superb facilities of the Søren Kierkegaard Library there, scholars interested in pursuing research on this and other aspects of Kierkegaard would find their labors greatly facilitated.

As for articles covering various facets of Kierkegaard's reception, only a handful were found to be of significance. Hans Joachim Schoeps's "Über das Frühecho Sören Kierkegaards in Deutschland," and Helen Mustard's "Sören Kierkegaard in German Literary Periodicals, 1860–1930" offer plenty of information about the more esoteric aspects of the German reception—obscure early figures like Quehl and Jörg (Schoeps), and little-known periodical reviews from the turn of the century (Mustard). Billeskov Jansen's "L'Héritage de Kierkegaard dans les Pays nordiques" was written by one of the most learned Danish scholars, an expert on both Kierkegaard and Scandinavian literature. Although brief, it manages to cover most of the highlights of Nordic reception and contains a fascinating account of *Politiken*'s Viggo Hörup and Kierkegaard. In a more specialized—though no less fascinating—vein, Bradley R. Dewey's amusing article on the use and abuse of "Diary of a Seducer" depicts a fate that has only too frequently befallen some of Kierkegaard's writings: the concentration, usually for purposes of sensation, on outward form with little regard for content or context.

For the period preceding and immediately following the First World War, extensive use was made of material relating to Kierkegaard and housed at the *Brenner-Archiv* in Innsbruck, Austria. The journal *Der Brenner*, which ceased publication in 1954 and is all but forgotten today, was widely read and highly respected early in the century. Through it some of Kierkegaard's writings made their first entry into the German-speaking world. The unpublished letters to and from Ludwig von Ficker, the journal's editor, constitute a valuable source of information about this neglected aspect of Kierkegaard's early German reception. The *Brenner-Archiv,* under the direction of Walter Methlagl, is well organized to accommodate the needs of scholars. Methlagl himself is a living resource about the history of the "Brenner Circle." He knew Ficker personally and wrote his dissertation on the early years of *Der Brenner.* It has been my good fortune on four separate occasions to have long discussions with him about Kierkegaard and *Der Brenner.*

Other knowledgeable scholars with whom I interacted (either in person or by letter, or both), and to whom I am deeply indebted, are: Donald Fleming of Harvard on Ørsted, Jacobsen, Brandes, Rilke, Rudolf Kassner, and all aspects of the project during its successive phases; Wera Hildebrand for teaching me Danish; Brita and Krister Stendahl of Harvard on the early Swedish reception and on Kierkegaard and Fredrika Bremer; Howard V. Hong and Edna H. Hong of the Søren Kierkegaard Library at St. Olaf College in Northfield, Minnesota on a variety of topics relating to Kierkegaard's Scandinavian and early North American receptions, and on the project as a whole which includes Howard Hong's invaluable and painstaking editorial comments; Rune Engebretsen of St. Olaf on the Scandinavian reception and on Rilke; Kristofer Paulson of Chicago on Rølvaag and the Scandinavian-Americans; John Hoberman of the University of Texas at Austin on Heidegger, Scheler, Jaspers, and existentialism; Allan Janik of Boston University on *Der Brenner* and Theodor Haecker; Alex Altmann and Paul Mendes-Flohr on Scheler, Buber, and early Jewish interest in Kierkegaard; Sven Rossel of the University of Washington in Seattle on J. P. Jacobsen and Kierkegaard; Niels Thulstrup of Copenhagen on diverse elements of the theological and philosophical receptions in Scandinavia and Germany and on the merits and defects of various German translations; Julia Watkin of the Søren Kierkegaard Biblioteket in Copenhagen (she is now in Tasmania, Australia) on securing books and other resources and on making contacts with key people; F. J. Billeskov Jansen of Copenhagen on Andersen, Jacobsen, and the Copenhagen of Kierkegaard's day; Herta Staub of Vienna on Kassner and Rilke; Adolf Darlap of Innsbruck on the German Catholic reception; Curt Hohoff of Munich on Haecker; and Wolfdietrich von Kloeden of Krefeld on Albert Bärthold and the early German reception in general. It must be pointed out that the footnotes throughout the text often contain critical evaluations of sources cited. All translations into English not otherwise attributed are by this author.

I wish also to offer special thanks to the Office of Information Technology at Harvard University, in particular to Zack Deal for his assistance with word processing capabilities; to Cynthia Lund and the staff of the Kierkegaard Library at St. Olaf College; to Garett S. Gentry for his invaluable editorial work; to Marie-Therese Alam of the Lebanese-American University Library staff; to the Computer Center at The Catholic University of America, in particular to Betsy Pohlhaus for her tireless help with the intricacies of word processing and text formatting; to David J. McGonagle, Director of The Catholic University of America Press, for his enthusiastic dedication to the project and his patience; and to his assistant Maryellen Tramontano; and to Elizabeth Benevides; and to Susan Needham.

Abbreviations

All references to Kierkegaard's works in English translation were made to the authoritative edition of *Kierkegaard's Writings*, edited and translated by Howard V. Hong and Edna H. Hong and published by Princeton University Press. Throughout the book this has been abbreviated as *KW* followed by a Roman numeral indicating the relevant volume number in the series. In the few instances where a new English translation of a work by Kierkegaard has not yet appeared in this series—for example, *The Book on Adler, Crisis in the Life of an Actress,* and the final articles against the Danish Lutheran Church—references were made to the earlier available translations by Walter Lowrie and Stephen Crites.

The following abbreviations were used for other works cited:

ADB	*Allgemeine Deutsche Biographie*
ASKB	*Auktionsprotokol over Søren Kierkegaards Bogsamling*
BA	*Brenner Archiv*
DBL	*Dansk Biografisk Lexicon*
EDDA	*EDDA: Nordisk Tidsskrift for Litteraturforskning*
JP	*Søren Kierkegaard's Journals and Papers*
LD	Kierkegaard's *Letters and Documents* (which is *KW,* XXV)

NBL   *Norsk Biografisk Leksikon*
NDB   *Neue Deutsche Biographie*
Papirer   *Søren Kierkegaards Papirer*
SV   *Søren Kierkegaards Samlede Værker*

In the title of Chapter 3 and thereafter, the Danish word "*Kirkekampen*" (the Church struggle) has been preceded by the definite article "the" in English. Although this risks sounding redundant to the native Danish ear, it retains the full original name given to the culminating phase of Kierkegaard's life when he confronted the state-Church in Denmark.

Introduction

The variety of elaborate excuses advanced for writing still another book on a great thinker in history is abundant, and it is not my intention to add one more to the long list. The rationale behind the present study rests on the simple fact that certain important and unanswered questions have always hovered around the historical fortunes of the thought of Søren Kierkegaard. Why did it take such a long time for his ideas to emerge as a potent force on the European intellectual scene? What are the reasons for the oft-repeated statement that Kierkegaard was ahead of his time and belongs intellectually more in the twentieth century than in his own? Phrased differently, why and how did the "genius in a market town" become the "father of twentieth-century existentialism"? Now that poets, philosophers, theologians, psychologists, literary critics, aestheticians, and a host of scholarly commentators have had their say on Kierkegaard from every conceivable angle, it is time the intellectual historian attempted to shed light on those seventy-odd years between Kierkegaard's death in 1855 and the beginnings of his serious reception following the First World War.

Although essentially true, the familiar rendition among scholars and others that little or no reception of Kierkegaard's thought occurred during that first seventy-year interval becomes highly misleading if merely left at that. Amidst a great degree of contention, many prejudices were created, others reenforced, stereotypes were set, and particular methodological approaches to Kierkegaard were born during that period, all of which renders it essential that the period be probed and pondered carefully as a prelude to understanding later more momentous developments. The "Early Reception" chronicle, which is the subject of this study, fits a definite framework: it proceeds from "non-reception," to glimmerings of reception, to "misreception," to attempts at suppression, to deliberate distortion, and finally to the beginnings of serious reception. The first chapter focuses on two of Kierkegaard's prominent Danish contemporaries, Hans Christian Andersen and H. C. Ørsted, as examples of intellectuals living in early-nineteenth-century Copenhagen who had a certain amount of personal interaction with Kierkegaard, yet who arrived at virtually no comprehension of his thought or its significance. They serve as two of the more visible indicators of the indifference that greeted Kierkegaard's writings when they first appeared. Contemporary Copenhagen attitudes toward Kierkegaard, as evidenced, for instance, by the *Corsair* Affair (the public ridicule to which Kierkegaard was exposed through the irreverent depictions and caricatures of him and his writings in the pages of Copenhagen's leading satirical paper, under the editorial direction of Meïr Goldschmidt), are not explored in detail because much has already been written about them. In the case of the relation to Ørsted, the aim has also been to use it as a convenient vehicle for exploring the controversial question of Kierkegaard's views on science.

Chapter Two discusses the first signs of contemporary reception outside Denmark, which in the late 1840s and early 1850s meant principally Scandinavia and some isolated German theological commentaries. All known instances of the earliest mention of Kierkegaard in English are traced and documented, as well as the beginnings of Kierkegaard's migration to North America via early Scandinavian-American settlers in the Midwest. Taken together, Chapters 1 and 2 constitute an extended introduction to the rest of the project, dealing as they do mostly with the period prior to 1855.

With the third chapter we enter the substance of the topic. This chapter is a detailed, in-depth investigation of Kierkegaard's final attack on the Danish Lutheran Church and the diverse reactions this attack precipitated, both during Kierkegaard's final months and in the few years that followed. It is here that specific stigmas emerged and attached themselves to Kierkegaard's posthumous reputation in such a way as to color subsequent views and assessments of him, often to the detriment of a unified and balanced picture of his intellectual and spiritual totality. The beginnings of the fragmentation of his legacy are traceable to this period, as are a number of lingering misconceptions about his position regarding ecclesiastical authority and the intended corrective nature of his polemics.

The fourth chapter focuses on Ibsen's relation to Kierkegaard and the extent to which his knowledge of certain works and concepts by Kierkegaard (the either-or motif and the Abraham theme) might have influenced the genesis of his three middle plays: *Love's Comedy*, *Brand*, and *Peer Gynt*. In itself this is a fascinating topic; however, its real significance for a history of Kierkegaard's reception lies in the fact that, rightly or wrongly, there grew with time a popular perception that Ibsen was an intellectual child of Kierkegaard, having derived most of his inspiration for the plays in question from studying Kierkegaard's writings. Thus the destinies of their two legacies became willy-nilly intertwined, and in the process Kierkegaard received something of a "free ride" on Ibsen's wings.

In Chapter 5 new and potentially grave misconceptions regarding Kierkegaard's views on the crucial relation between faith and knowledge are discussed within the context of the "Tro og Viden" Controversy that took place throughout the 1860s and early 1870s in Denmark. Some of the more difficult Kierkegaardian concepts like the paradox and the leap of faith come into play here, and the entire treatment revolves around the winding intellectual development of that onetime Kierkegaard enthusiast turned critic, Rasmus Nielsen.

As Kierkegaard's private journals became available for public perusal during the 1870s, several facts surfaced about his childhood, his early upbringing, the relations with his father, his broken engagement to Regine Olsen, and his overall idiosyncrasies, all of which led Georg Brandes to write the first critical "biography" of Kierkegaard, published in 1877. This effectively inaugurated a new method for dealing with Kierkegaard, the biographical-psychological approach. While this approach legitimately highlighted the relationship between Kierkegaard's life and his thought, it had the simultaneous negative effect of sidetracking interest in the substance of Kierkegaard's writings in favor of a preoccupation—often a morbid one—with Kierkegaard the person. Brandes's own intellectual formation and acquaintance with Kierkegaard's works, his 1877 book that was motivated by an undeclared desire to undermine the impact of its subject, and the many adverse reactions this work provoked throughout Scandinavia and Germany constitute the topic of Chapter 6.

Brandes's influence on later Kierkegaard scholarship and on the shaping of popular attitudes about Kierkegaard has been nothing less than formidable. Also covered in this chapter are the first trickles of German translations in the 1870s, thanks mainly to a thriving interest in Kierkegaard at Tübingen among the students of the theologian J. T. Beck.

Brandes's writings on Kierkegaard and Ibsen led many important writers and thinkers at the turn of the century, including Strindberg and Unamuno, to Kierkegaard. Chapter 7 opens with a look at these two men and then treats, in some detail, the elusive influence that Kierkegaard exercised on a young Brandes protégé, Jens Peter Jacobsen, who in a way was also ahead of his time as a writer. Following this, however, the treatment quickly shifts to a consideration of the accelerated pace of Kierkegaard's German reception in the 1880s and 1890s, due principally to the controversial activities of the lapsed Lutheran pastor and Kierkegaard translator Christoph Schrempf. Schrempf's own tangled view of the world played a major role in determining the kind of Kierkegaard he allowed to make its way into German. At the same time that Schrempf was busy in Germany, a new work on Kierkegaard appeared in 1892 by the Danish philosopher Harald Høffding. Its eventual translation into German contributed appreciably to the dissemination of Kierkegaard's thought, but also to the perpetuation of old misconceptions and the generation of some new ones. Despite this, Høffding's broad contacts and renown in philosophical circles made him the chief transmitter of Kierkegaard at the turn of the century. Schrempf and Høffding are analyzed in connection with their status as *fin de siècle* figures. The shifting philosophical and theological situations during the last two decades of the nineteenth century, along with the forces impacting on each, especially the swift rise of the Nietzsche vogue in the 1890s, impeded to some extent the emergence of Kierkegaard in full force onto the European stage. Although *fin-de-siècle* malaise was conducive to Kierkegaardian *Angst,* the absence of a major catastrophe delayed for a couple of decades the personal and philosophical manifestations of this *Angst*.

The final chapter takes the story up through the years of the First World War, with special attention being paid to the beginnings of serious reception on all levels—literary, philosophical, and theological—in the German-speaking world. This is preceded by a survey of rising French, Anglo-Saxon, and Italian interest in Kierkegaard before the war. The mid-1920s are used as a convenient cutoff point, since they usher in the new era of existentialism. Several German and German-educated East

European intellectuals in the early twentieth century developed a fascination for Kierkegaard through the story of his broken engagement to Regine Olsen. Their respective Kierkegaardian encounters are analyzed, as are the activities of the Austrian cultural periodical *Der Brenner*. Starting in 1914, this periodical became the central organ through which many of Europe's budding young thinkers received their first exposure to certain timely Kierkegaard texts, hitherto unavailable in German. It was here, through the labors of Theodor Haecker, that the distorted "Schrempf Kierkegaard" was overthrown in favor of a more balanced Kierkegaard. The study terminates with a brief discussion of early Catholic views on Kierkegaard and some of the issues they raise.

This study is *not* a history of the rise of twentieth-century existentialism. Instead, it is the story of a series of fumbles and missed opportunities, of unfavorable circumstances and inept mediators, and of a few shining examples of insight and dedication. Warning is given against reading too much structure and coherence into a reception that had very little of either. Emphasis is laid on the various avenues of transmission, how they came about and where they led. The foremost concern is with the early "maieutic agents," to use a Kierkegaardian term adapted from Socrates, who brought forth his writings and ideas from the relative parochial obscurity of mid-nineteenth-century Copenhagen to the center of the world's intellectual arena.

On one level, therefore, the chronicle of Kierkegaard's early reception is the account of his profound impact on the lives and thoughts of a handful of individuals. The issue often boils down to the degree of sympathy and fair-mindedness that each of these individuals managed to exercise with respect to Kierkegaard. There were those whose faith was strengthened by coming in contact with Kierkegaard, and those who were led to atheism after reading him. There were those who experienced elation at their discovery of him only to see it turn into resentment when their lives changed drastically as a result. There were those who tried to use him for their own petty polemical aims, while for others he represented a mere "stage" on their life's way to a different destination. And there were those, finally, who viewed him with admiration and respect, but declined to follow the path he had charted.

Kierkegaard's early reception necessarily places famous and influential thinkers side by side with curiously minor and intellectually peripheral figures. Not every great thinker undergoes a reception as tortuous, but also as colorful, as Kierkegaard's. The fundamental reason for this uniqueness is the very nature of Kierkegaard's thought, which *personalizes everything* to such an extent that there is no escaping its powerful and penetrating grip on the lives of those who come in contact with it. This should not surprise anyone, considering that in Kierkegaard, after all, we come face to face with the supreme spokesman and champion of the "single individual."

1
Kierkegaard and Some Contemporaries (i)
The "Non-Reception" by Andersen and Ørsted

It is not enough to be an exceptional genius in order to produce a clear-cut and sustained impact on one's surroundings and on posterity. Historical circumstances, cultural milieu, and personal idiosyncrasies often impede the recognition of genius.

In the case of Kierkegaard many factors combined to delay or prevent a just appreciation of his writings and an integrated understanding of his thought. He lived in a small and culturally peripheral European country, and wrote everything in its unfamiliar language. In many of his writings, he also deliberately engaged in convoluted attempts at self-concealment behind pseudonyms (and incidentally very much enjoyed doing this),[1]

---

1. "Then it occurred to me—what if I were to settle down to making everything difficult?" *JP* 5828 (VI A 85). Unless otherwise specified, all subsequent references to Kierkegaard's journals will be to the authoritative English translation of *Søren Kierkegaard's Journals and Papers (JP)*, volumes I–VIII, ed. and trans. Howard V. Hong and Edna H. Hong assisted by Gregor Malantschuk (Bloomington, Indiana: Indiana University Press, 1967–78), then the appropriate entry number; this will be followed by the corresponding reference in parentheses to the complete Danish edition of *Søren Kierkegaards Papirer*, 20 volumes, I–XI³, ed. by P. A. Heiberg, V. Kuhr, and E. Torsting (Copenhagen: Gyldendal, 1909–48).

in the name of his staunchly held methodological and epistemological principle of indirect communication. The result was that few among the general reading public could comprehend his works and fathom their intentions. Those who managed to penetrate the veil of pseudonymity usually became bogged down in one or two striking aspects of Kierkegaard's rich thought, and therefore ended up with a truncated view of the whole. This brings us to another important feature of Kierkegaard that affected his reception: he was a uniquely multifaceted thinker, combining several intellectual qualities simultaneously. He was a self-styled humorist, a literary writer (a kind of poet),[2] an aesthete, a philosopher, a moralist, a religious thinker, a psychologist, and a polemicist all rolled into one. He was also a believing Christian. Such complex versatility provided something for nearly everyone of his readers.[3] It also rendered a unified and balanced interpretation of the man and his works very difficult to achieve.

Complicating matters even further was the eccentric life that Kierkegaard led in the eyes of Copenhageners during the 1840s and 50s, against the backdrop of a very uncommon childhood and upbringing. The notorious stories of public ridicule and stereotyping resulting from such incidents as the affair with *Corsaren* (the *Corsair*) are well known.[4] Ordinary people could hardly take such a caricatured figure or any of his strange writings seriously. Indeed Kierkegaard himself reflects on the incomprehensibility of his writings and the difficulties they raise for his future readers. In a journal entry from 1849 he writes:

> My life, my work as an author will be explained *höchstens* [at best] as a special kind of genius by no means as serious and by no means as consistent as the lives of various others. None of my contemporaries penetrates more deeply than this. I am the only one who can explain it . . . alas, and I am silent. It is as though someone had a great treasure and hid it so securely that he threw the key away.
>
> What troubles me is whether or not I have the right to do this, whether in relation to God this silence is permissible, whether it is permissible to let

---

2. See Louis Mackey, *Kierkegaard: A Kind of Poet* (Philadelphia: University of Pennsylvania Press, 1971).

3. What adds to the complexity is the fact that there is considerable overlapping of these roles in certain single works by Kierkegaard.

4. See *The Corsair Affair, and Articles Related to the Writings*, in *Kierkegaard's Writings*, volume XIII (*KW*, XIII), ed. and trans. with introduction and notes by Howard V. Hong and Edna H. Hong (Princeton: Princeton University Press, 1982).

a productivity which is so infinitely indebted to Him for its ingenuity remain an enigma and for many somewhat odd.[5]

So it did remain for many, and for a long time after Kierkegaard's death. However, he was confident that the truth of what he was saying would impose itself eventually: "And this is why the time will come when not only my writings but my whole life, the intriguing secret of the whole machinery, will be studied and studied."[6] Elsewhere, he warns against excessive preoccupation with his personal life:

> This is the way I present myself as an author to my contemporaries—and in any case this is the way I belong to history. My thought is that here I am permitted and able to speak of myself only as an author. I do not believe that my personality, my personal life, and what I consider my shortcomings are of any concern to the public. I am an author, and who I am and what my endowments are I know well enough. I have submitted to everything that could serve my cause.[7]

Finally, in a journal note from 1850, Kierkegaard presents a prophetic assessment of the fate of his legacy:

> Frequently I find something sad in the fact that I, with all my capabilities, must always stand outside as a superfluity and impractical exaggeration. But the whole thing is very simple. Conditions are still far from being confused enough for proper use to be made of me. . . . But it will all end, as they shall see, with conditions getting so desperate that they must make use of desperate people like me and my kind.[8]

These and similar words in Kierkegaard's private journals remained unavailable to the reading public for years after his death. The way in which the eventual publication of the journals affected the course of later Kierkegaard interpretation and scholarship is an integral part of the history of his reception.[9]

Before proceeding to an examination of Kierkegaard's relations with some of his celebrated contemporaries, one must mention a crucial factor that colored his posthumous legacy and hovered around it like a curse.

---

5. *JP* 6345 (X^1 A 115). See also *JP* 5891 (VII^1 A 104) for a lengthy entry about his pseudonymity and incomprehensibility to his readers (dated March 16, 1846).
6. *JP* 6078 (VIII^1 A 424).   7. *JP* 6205 (IX A 171).
8. *JP* 6709a (X^3 A 680).
9. See chapters 6ff. below. Also, the way his interpretations of his own authorship in *The Point of View for My Work as an Author* (written in 1848, published in 1859) affected his reception will be dealt with in Chapter 4 below.

Kierkegaard's assault on the established Lutheran Church in Denmark during the final year and a half of his life left a bitter taste in many quarters. It created a fixed image of him in the popular mind and certainly in ecclesiastical and theological circles that took a long time to dissipate. The real intentions of his attack on the Church were obscured by the very polemics out of which they emerged.[10]

We are not here concerned with the popular reception in Denmark, or the lack thereof, of Kierkegaard and his works while he was still alive. That story hardly goes beyond the misunderstandings and the caricaturing alluded to above. We know, for example, that none of the sixteen books he had already published between 1838 and 1845, in editions of 525 copies each (except *The Concept of Anxiety*, 250 copies), was sold out.[11] His books on the whole received scanty attention by Danish reviewers in the press and in literary and theological periodicals before 1855. The two exceptions to this were his series of articles in *Fædrelandet* (The fatherland) (1854–55), and his nine *Øjeblikket* (The moment) articles of 1855 that caused a considerable sensation.[12]

How much was Kierkegaard known outside the borders of Denmark during his lifetime? Whom did Kierkegaard know and interact with of his famous intellectual contemporaries, both in Denmark and beyond? What impact, if any, did he have on these people? Answers to these questions would reveal the glimmerings of whatever early response to Kierkegaard and his works was under way before his death. It will be shown that among Kierkegaard's leading intellectual contemporaries, both at home and abroad, very few proved conversant with his ideas in any depth, or "received" them in a meaningful way. Most had never heard of him, and those who had (like Andersen and Ørsted) could not, for a variety of reasons to be examined, act as preliminary channels for the transmission of his ideas. The net result of this is best described as the

---

10. See Chapter 3 below.

11. See *JP*, vol. 5, p. 533, note 1276; see also Frithiof Brandt and Else Rammel, *Søren Kierkegaard og Pengene* (Copenhagen: Levin and Munksgaard, 1935), especially pp. 11–56.

12. For a list of contemporary Danish reviews of Kierkegaard's works see Jens Himmelstrup, ed., *Søren Kierkegaard International Bibliografi* (Copenhagen: Nyt Nordisk Forlag, 1962), pp. 9–13; and Aage Kabell, *Kierkegaardstudiet i Norden* (Copenhagen: Hagerup, 1948), pp. 13–18. The *Concluding Unscientific Postscript* of 1846, considered today to be Kierkegaard's principal philosophical work, received only five short critical reviews when it first appeared and a few others some years later; see Himmelstrup, p. 11. For a discussion of the impact of Kierkegaard's *Fædrelandet* and *Øjeblikket* articles, see Chapter 3 below.

phase of non-reception that preceded the slow posthumous coming to grips with Kierkegaard's complex legacy.

First a look at some of the key thinkers in Europe in Kierkegaard's lifetime and immediately thereafter.

Hegel died in 1831 when Kierkegaard was eighteen years old, and Schleiermacher died three years later. Both thinkers, particularly the former, preoccupied Kierkegaard for the rest of his life and exercised a decisive influence on his thought. Neither of them knew anything of Kierkegaard.[13] As for Schopenhauer, Feuerbach, and Marx, all three of whom outlived Kierkegaard, there exists no evidence to suggest that any of them knew anything about him and his works. Kierkegaard became acquainted with Schopenhauer's writings in 1854,[14] a few months before launching his attack on the ecclesiastical establishment and its clergy. He delighted in Schopenhauer's own denunciation of Hegel and of academic philosophers, but he disagreed sharply with Schopenhauer's misanthropic outlook on life.[15] Concerning Feuerbach, Kierkegaard's knowledge of his works came much earlier. In him Kierkegaard discerned a tactical ally whose critique of Christianity exposed the defects of a heinous Christendom that became the object of Kierkegaard's sustained attacks.[16] Thus Feuerbach was for Kierkegaard "an involuntary ally and a declared adversary at one and the same time."[17]

---

13. The literature on Kierkegaard and Hegel is vast. See, as examples, Niels Thulstrup, *Kierkegaard's Relation to Hegel*, trans. by George L. Stengren (Princeton: Princeton University Press, 1980); Mark C. Taylor, *Journeys to Selfhood: Hegel and Kierkegaard* (Berkeley: University of California Press, 1980). On Kierkegaard and Schleiermacher see Hayo Gerdes, *Der geschichtliche biblische Jesus oder den Christus der Philosophen: Erwägungen zur christologie Kierkegaards, Hegels und Schleiermachers* (Berlin: Verlag die Spur, 1974); D. T. O'Connor, "Schleiermacher and Kierkegaard: The Odd Couple of Modern Theology," in *Religion in Life* 41 (1972), pp. 8–17; and Richard E. Crouter, "Kierkegaard's Not So Hidden Debt to Schleiermacher," in *Journal for the History of Modern Theology* 1 (1994), pp. 205–25. See also *JP*, vol. 4, pp. 626–27.

14. He had heard of him as early as 1837 from his teacher and close friend Poul M. Møller, who mentions Schopenhauer in his treatise *On Immortality*. See Møller's *Efterladte Skrifter*, 3d ed., V (Copenhagen, 1856), p. 99.

15. On Kierkegaard and Schopenhauer see Villy Sørensen, *Schopenhauer* (Copenhagen: G. E. C. Gad, 1969), especially pp. 101–6; Søren Holm, "Schopenhauer und Kierkegaard," in *Schopenhauer-Jahrbuch* 43 (1962), pp. 5–14. Kierkegaard was thoroughly amused by Schopenhauer's use of the word "*Windbeutel*" (windbag) to describe Hegel and the "professor-philosophers." See *JP* 1621 (XI^1 A 183); see also *JP*, vol. 4, pp. 631–33, for a brief discussion of Kierkegaard's relation to Schopenhauer's thought.

16. See *JP* 6523 (X^2 A 163).

17. Jean Brun, "Feuerbach et Kierkegaard," in *Cahiers du Sud*, vol. 50, no. 371 (Marseilles, April–May 1963), p. 36. The Auction Catalog of Kierkegaard's book collection

Nowhere in his books or journals does Kierkegaard mention Marx. Some have found it hard to believe that he had not even heard of Marx or read anything by him, especially during the 1840s, when some of Marx's pivotal early works appeared.[18] Gregor Malantschuk, the renowned Kierkegaard scholar, has advanced an interesting though largely speculative theory regarding the possibility that Kierkegaard may have read some Marx.[19] According to Malantschuk, Kierkegaard must have come across Marx's name in *Kjøbenhavnsposten,* and he is known to have possessed a book of 1843—*Anekdota,* edited by the left-Hegelian Arnold Ruge—containing a short article under the pseudonym *"Kein Berliner"* that Marx was then using. The article was entitled "Luther als Schiedsrichter zwischen Strauss und Feuerbach."[20] Kierkegaard had no way of knowing that the author's name was Karl Marx.

In this article Marx essentially appeals to Luther as judge between two critiques of Christianity, Strauss's and Feuerbach's respectively, and sides with Feuerbach's more subtle and sophisticated treatment. From the conclusions *"Kein Berliner"* draws in this article it would be difficult to gauge his precise attitude toward Christianity, for he could be supporting Feuerbach's position in order to reveal to Christians the true nature of their religion, and such a position could conceivably coincide with Kierkegaard's.[21] In any event, Kierkegaard's possible acquaintance with this article cannot be taken as an indication that he "knew" Marx. He did not, and Malantschuk's theory establishes nothing of significance in this regard. Kierkegaard may have obtained the first detailed information about Feuerbach's *Das Wesen des Christentums* from Ruge's *Anekdota.*

---

includes the following works by Feuerbach: *Geschichte der neueren Philosophie* (1837); *Das Wesen des Christentums* (1843); *Abelard und Heloise* (1834) [*Auktionsprotokol over Søren Kierkegaards Bogsamling,* ed. H. P. Rohde (Copenhagen: Det Kongelige Bibliotek, 1967), nos. 487, 488, 1637]. On Kierkegaard and Feuerbach see also John W. Elrod, "Feuerbach and Kierkegaard on the Self," in *Journal of Religion* 56 (1976), pp. 348-65.

18. *The German Ideology* (1846) and *The Communist Manifesto* (1848) to mention two. *The Economic and Philosophical Manuscripts of 1844* were first published in 1932.

19. Gregor Malantschuk, *The Controversial Kierkegaard,* trans. by Howard V. Hong and Edna H. Hong for the Kierkegaard Monograph Series, ed. Alastair McKinnon (Waterloo, Ontario: Wilfred Laurier University Press, 1980) (first published in Copenhagen in 1976); Chapter 5 entitled "Did Kierkegaard Read Karl Marx?"

20. Ibid., p. 76. The Auction Catalog of Kierkegaard's book collection lists as no. 753 *Anekdota zur neuesten deutschen Philosophie und Publicistik,* ed. Arnold Ruge, I–II (Zurich, 1843).

21. Malantschuk, *The Controversial Kierkegaard,* pp. 79 and 81.

He purchased *Anekdota* on February 20, 1844, and got Feuerbach's book a month later.[22]

The principal figures, therefore, in German nineteenth-century philosophy who lived during Kierkegaard's time were oblivious to his existence, and could not possibly have played a role in his reception.

Of Kierkegaard's well-known intellectual contemporaries in Denmark, Hans Christian Andersen (1805-75) was perhaps the most antithetical temperamentally to Kierkegaard. He did not possess any of the philosophical training or reflective complexity of Kierkegaard. His personality was uncomplicated, and he sometimes gave the impression of sheer naiveté to people who knew him through his writings and behavior. This sense of simpleness was enhanced by Andersen's success as a writer of fairy tales for children.[23]

Kierkegaard realized early on the differences between himself and Andersen. In the late 1830s Andersen was attempting to establish himself as a novelist following his growing reputation as a fairy-tale writer. Kierkegaard meanwhile was deeply engrossed in the study of Hegel's thought and other abstruse philosophical questions. He had discussed Andersen with his admired teacher Poul Martin Møller, and both agreed that Andersen's pieces contained several flaws from a writer's point of view.[24]

In 1837 Andersen published a novel entitled *Kun en Spillemand (Only a Fiddler)*. The plot was somewhat amorphous, with two main characters, Christian the talented fiddler, and Naomi, an adventurous Jewish girl whom he had known in his childhood. Christian in many ways embodied autobiographical features from Andersen's own life. He had, for instance, left the island of Funen at an early age to travel to the big city, Copenhagen, where he hoped to become famous. Andersen had done the same at the age of fourteen. Throughout the story Christian the musical genius acts in a weak and indecisive manner in the face of life's cold realities. His ultimate fate is unclear, and the latter half of the book is mainly the

---

22. Ibid., p. 79.
23. Werner Betz, "Andersen und Kierkegaard," in *Festschrift für Walter Baetke*, ed. Kurt Rudolph et al. (Weimar: Böhlau, 1966), p. 51.
24. A. Egelund Møller, *Søren Kierkegaard om Politik* (Copenhagen: Forlaget Strand, 1975), p. 63. See also *JP* 5077 (I C 46) from 1835 containing a reference to Andersen's *Fodreise fra Holmens Canal til Østpynten af Amager i Aarene 1828 og 1829* (Copenhagen, 1829), of which P. M. Møller did not think very highly; and *JP* 5211 (II A 42) from 1837, where Kierkegaard writes: "I have read Andersen's novel *Improvisatoren* [Copenhagen, 1835] and find nothing in it, just one good observation."

story of Naomi, who is Christian's opposite in every sense. Through her, other aspects of Andersen's own experience are disclosed, principally his wide travels all around Europe. The story, taken as a whole, does not hang together very well; nevertheless, it received considerable recognition, especially in Germany, where it was translated as *Nur ein Geiger* and helped make Andersen well known.

Poul Martin Møller died in March of the following year, 1838.[25] In April, Kierkegaard began work on a piece of criticism that he hoped would embody what he had learned from Møller. He chose Andersen's *Only a Fiddler* as the object of his treatment. His short book—more like a pamphlet—appeared on September 7 under the title *Af en Endnu Levendes Papirer (From the Papers of One Still Living)* with the subtitle: *Om Andersen som Romandigter med stadigt Hensyn til hans sidste Værk "Kun en Spillemand" (About Andersen as a novelist with continual reference to his latest work: Only a Fiddler).*[26] The style was involved and the prose heavy, reflecting the considerable influence of Hegelian philosophy on the young Kierkegaard. Andersen as novelist was approached through a scathing critique of *Only a Fiddler.* Kierkegaard argued that Andersen in this particular novel was lacking in any coherent life view *(Livsanskuelse),* or even the notion that a good novelist ought to articulate one. Revealing that he himself had attained such a level of self-awareness, Kierkegaard wrote:

> For a life view is more than a quintessence or a sum of propositions maintained in its abstract neutrality; it is more than experience [*Erfaring*], which as such is always fragmentary. It is, namely, the transubstantiation of experience; it is an unshakable certainty in oneself won from all experience [*Empirie*].[27]

---

25. Kierkegaard later dedicated *The Concept of Anxiety* (1844) to "the late Professor Poul Martin Møller . . . the object of my admiration, my profound loss, . . ." For more on Kierkegaard and Poul Martin Møller see H. P. Rhode, "Poul Møller" in *Kierkegaard's Teachers,* vol. 10 of *Bibliotheca Kierkegaardiana,* ed. Niels Thulstrup and Marie Mikulova Thulstrup (Copenhagen: C. A. Reitzel, 1982), pp. 89–109.

26. This and some newspaper articles he wrote during his early university days are included in *Early Polemical Writings (KW,* I), ed. and trans. Julia Watkin (Princeton: Princeton University Press, 1990), p. 61. See the Danish edition of *Søren Kierkegaards Samlede Værker (SV)* 15 vols. ed. A. B. Drachmann, J. L. Heiberg, and H. O. Lange (Copenhagen: Gyldendal, 1920–36) [*SV,* XIII, pp. 11–100]. Unless otherwise specified, all subsequent references to Kierkegaard's works will be to the most recently available, authoritative English translation in *KW,* or to *SV* if the work has not been translated.

27. *Early Polemical Writings (KW,* I), p. 76. See also *SV,* XIII, p. 73.

Kierkegaard then proceeded to attack Andersen's notion of genius as represented by the weak-willed Christian. This supposed musical genius of Christian is actually nothing more than vanity, according to Kierkegaard, and the main purpose of its display is to attain public acclaim.[28]

Andersen had apparently heard of Kierkegaard's book before it appeared on September 7. A week earlier, on August 30, Andersen wrote the following in his diary: "Suffered torment of the soul at Kierkegaard's not yet published criticism."[29] When the book came out Andersen wrote: "A shocking letter from Commander Wulff immediately followed by Kierkegaard's criticism. Eduard gave me a sedative. Been as in a haze."[30] Years later in his autobiographical *Mit Livs Eventyr* [The fairy tale of my life] of 1855, the year of Kierkegaard's death, he related the circumstances of his "confrontation" with Kierkegaard:

> The novel *Only a Fiddler* made a strong impression for a short time on one of our country's young and highly gifted men, Søren Kierkegaard. Meeting him in the street, he told me that he would write a review of my book, and that I should be more satisfied with that than I had been with the earlier, because, he said, they had misunderstood me! A long time elapsed, then he read the book again, and the first good impression of it was effaced. I must almost believe that the more seriously he examined the story, the more faults he found; and when the critique appeared, it did not please me at all. It came out as a whole book, the first, I believe, that Kierkegaard has written; and because of the Hegelian heaviness in the expression, it was very difficult to read, and people said in fun that only Kierkegaard and Andersen had read it through. I learned from it that I was no poet, but a poetical figure that had

---

28. *Early Polemical Writings* (*KW*, I), pp.98-100. See also *SV*, XIII, pp. 96-97. According to Frithiof Brandt, a Danish scholar, Andersen actually did have an outlook on life, though in another sense than the Kierkegaardian. It came close to that of the common folk and the man in the street of his time, and it is what made Andersen a great writer understood and appreciated by the whole world. That Kierkegaard regarded such a life view as something pitiable is really another matter, says Brandt. He adds that a story writer and poet attains world renown more quickly than a philosopher of life. Andersen and Kierkegaard each had a special genius: the genius of unsophisticated spontaneity, and the genius of reflection. See Brandt's article "Søren Kierkegaard: Hans tre hovedoptagelser—Hvorfor er han saa verdensberømt?" in *Politiken*, November 10, 1955, pp. 16-17.

29. Quoted in Elias Bredsdorff, *Hans Christian Andersen: The Story of His Life and Work, 1805-1875* (New York: Scribner, 1975), p. 128.

30. Ove Kreisberg and F. J. Billeskov Jansen, "H. C. Andersen," in *Kierkegaard: Literary Miscellany*, vol. 9 of *Bibliotheca Kierkegaardiana* (1981), p. 121. See also H. C. Andersen's *Mit Livs Eventyr*, vol. 1, ed. H. Topsøe-Jensen (Copenhagen: Gyldendal, 1951), note p. 440.

escaped from my group, in which my place would be taken by some future poet or be used by him as a figure in a poem, and that thus my supplement would be created! Since that time I have had a better understanding with this author, who has always met me with kindness and discernment.[31]

Indeed, despite the many differences in temperament and interests between them, Kierkegaard and Andersen came to view each other more tolerantly as the years went by. For his part Kierkegaard expressed his softened, if somewhat patronizing, opinion of Andersen to Israel Levin (1810–83), a man of letters and a linguist who acted for a time as Kierkegaard's personal secretary. Levin reports:

> We talked about Andersen one evening in Frederiksberg garden: [Kierkegaard said] "Andersen has no idea what fairy tales are all about, and also what he is to do with poetry. He has a good heart though, and that is enough."[32]

Kierkegaard actually surprised Andersen in 1849 by sending him an autographed copy of both volumes of his *Either/Or*. Andersen wrote Kierkegaard a brief letter dated May 15 to express his gratitude. The letter went as follows:

> Dear Mr. Kierkegaard,
> You have given me really great pleasure by sending me your *Either/Or*. I was, as you can well understand, quite surprised; I had no idea at all that you entertained friendly thoughts of me, and yet I now find it to be so. God bless you for it! Thank you, thank you!
>
> Yours with heartfelt sincerity,
> H. C. Andersen[33]

In addition to the letter Andersen reciprocated Kierkegaard's gift with the first collection of his *Nye Eventyr* (New fairy tales) (1843–48) containing a personal handwritten dedication at the beginning:

---

31. Hans Christian Andersen, *Mit Livs Eventyr* (Copenhagen, 1855), pp. 198–99. The English translation quoted here comes from H. C. Andersen, *The Story of My Life*, translator unknown (New York, 1871), pp. 136–37.
32. My translation, from Israel Levin's remarks on Kierkegaard written in 1858 and 1869, and found in Steen Johansen, ed. *Erindringer om Søren Kierkegaard* (Copenhagen: Reitzel, 1980), p. 86. Throughout the book all translations not otherwise attributed are by this author.
33. Søren Kierkegaard, *Letters and Documents* (*LD,* which is *KW,* XXV), ed. Howard V. Hong and Edna H. Hong, and trans. with introduction and notes by Henrik Rosenmeier (Princeton: Princeton University Press, 1978), letter no. 206, p. 289. Andersen's surprise reflects the background of the 1838 critique by Kierkegaard of his *Only a Fiddler*.

Dear Mr. Kierkegaard! Either you will like my little ones or you will not. But I assure you they come without fear and trembling, and that at least is a beginning. Kindly, the author.[34]

The "either," the "or," and the "fear and trembling" were not accidental.

Andersen's genuine sympathy for Kierkegaard is revealed in a letter to Henriette Wulff dated October 10, 1855, a month before Kierkegaard's death. He wrote: ". . . Kirkegaard [sic] is very sick. The entire lower part of his body, it is said, has become paralyzed. He is at the hospital. A theologian, Thura[h], has written a crude poem against him."[35]

Many scholars have attempted to fathom why Kierkegaard devoted the whole of his first book in 1838 to the vehement criticism of Andersen's *Only a Fiddler*. Frithiof Brandt argues in his *Den Unge Søren Kierkegaard*[36] that Andersen and Kierkegaard were members of a group of young intellectuals who interacted frequently in the 1830s. The group included the writer Henrik Hertz, the judge P. V. Jacobsen, and P. L. Møller the womanizer. Brandt's contention is that many of Kierkegaard's pseudonyms in his later writings derived their ostensible personalities from these real characters with whom he had associated. For example, Assessor Wilhelm of *Either/Or* volume II was based on P. V. Jacobsen, and Johannes the Seducer of volume I represented P. L. Møller. Likewise, Hertz's novel *Stemninger og Tilstande* (Moods and situations) (1839), which centers on five bachelors who dine together, bases its characters, according to Brandt, on members of this same group including Kierkegaard. Brandt deduces from Hertz's book, which he regards as an authentic mirror of actual relations, that Andersen and Kierkegaard had a falling out around the time Kierkegaard was preparing his critique of Andersen's *Only a Fiddler*. Andersen then wrote his fairy tale *Lykkens Galoscher* (The galoshes of fortune), which appeared on May 19, 1838, and features an arrogant parrot allegedly intended to parody Kierke-

---

34. Ove Kreisberg and F. J. Billeskov Jansen, "H. C. Andersen," p. 124. Kierkegaard's Auction Catalog lists two volumes of Andersen's tales in his library, as well as many other collections of folk and fairy tales (Greek, Roman, Dutch, Hungarian, Irish, and German). Prominent among these are the stories of the Brothers Grimm, and *1001 Nights*. See Ernst Fr. Hansen, "Søren Kierkegaard og Danmarks Genius i Verdenslitteraturen," in *Kristeligt Dagblad*, Thursday, June 8, 1933.

35. Translated from Niels Birger Wamberg, ed., *Deres Broderligt Hengivne: Et Udvalg af Breve fra H. C. Andersen* (Copenhagen: Gyldendal, 1975), p. 168. On Thurah see Chapter 3 below.

36. Frithiof Brandt, *Den Unge Søren Kierkegaard* (Copenhagen: Levin and Munksgaard, 1929), esp. pp. 115–60.

gaard. "The only human words that the parrot could say, and which at times sounded comical, were 'Come now, let us be men.' All the rest of his chatter made as little sense as the twittering of the canary."[37] Upon reading this, it is claimed that Kierkegaard angrily decided to sharpen his critique of Andersen, published three and a half months after *Lykkens Galoscher*.

Brandt's evidence is flimsy and inconclusive at best. His controversial thesis has been challenged and rejected by several leading scholars.[38] If one examines the events in Kierkegaard's life during 1838, two things stand out that may shed light on his preoccupations as he wrote his Andersen critique. A few months after the death of his beloved teacher Poul Martin Møller, Kierkegaard experienced the loss of his father on August 8. The father in his gloom had predicted that the death of his son would precede his own death. Hence comes the phrase "one still living" in the title of Kierkegaard's work published one month after his father's death. Kierkegaard was genuinely surprised to be still alive.[39] Also, it is believed that during this period Kierkegaard was undergoing a religious transformation and essentially moving out of a phase of youthful dissipa-

---

37. H. C. Andersen, "The Galoshes of Fortune," in *Andersen's Fairy Tales*, trans. Jean Hersholt (New York: Heritage Press, 1942), p. 104.

38. F. J. Billeskov Jansen, the leading authority on Danish literature, told this author during a discussion held at the Søren Kierkegaard Biblioteket in Copenhagen on April 11, 1983, that when one reads Brandt's book one is fascinated by the beauty of the story it presents, and one wishes it were actually true; however, it has no historical basis whatsoever. "Very delightful, but all wrong," was Billeskov Jansen's last judgment. In 1847 in a journal entry (*JP* 5988 VIII¹ A 44) Kierkegaard briefly refers to *Lykkens Galoscher* in a dismissing sort of way that suggests it had little impact on him. As further examples of scholarly rejections of the Brandt thesis see Aage Henriksen, *Methods and Results of Kierkegaard Studies in Scandinavia: A Historical and Critical Survey*, Publications of the Kierkegaard Society, vol. I (Copenhagen: Munksgaard, 1951), pp. 92–106; and Aage Kabell, *Kierkegaardstudiet i Norden* (Copenhagen: Hagerup, 1948), pp. 278ff. Henriksen sums up his critique thus: "Brandt's attempt to deepen the understanding of Kierkegaard's production by shedding light on the milieu in which he lived in his undergraduate days, and by calling attention to the controversies he may have had with a couple of his acquaintances, has failed in the main, because the material brought to light has been misused" (p. 106). Søren Gorm Hansen's book *H. C. Andersen og Søren Kierkegaard i Dannelseskulturen* (Copenhagen: Medusa, 1976) provides a solid discussion of the relations between the two great Danish writers. See especially pp. 123ff. for an analysis of Kierkegaard's critique of *Only a Fiddler*, and pp. 134ff. for the author's critique of Brandt's thesis. Finally, Elias Bredsdorff in his article "H. C. Andersen og Søren Kierkegaard," in *Anderseniana*, 3d series, vol. III, no. 4 (Odense, 1981), pp. 229–54 (with an English summary), rejects outright the Brandt thesis.

39. Walter Lowrie, *A Short Life of Kierkegaard* (Princeton: Princeton University Press, 1970), p. 133.

tion. At 10:30 AM on May 19, 1838, the same day Andersen's *Lykkens Galoscher* appeared, Kierkegaard recorded in his journals a quasi-mystical feeling of "indescribable joy," something akin to Pascal's intense religious experience.[40] The jolt of his father's death hastened this process of transformation. This too reflects itself in *From the Papers of One Still Living*, where there is a constant emphasis on the need for a well-defined view of life, a thing Kierkegaard himself had been struggling to achieve. These two facts highlight the complex factors affecting Kierkegaard's development at the time, and act to dilute any angry obsession with Andersen portrayed by Brandt as the principal driving force behind Kierkegaard's first book.

The Kierkegaard-Andersen connection, however, is not yet completely exhausted. Shortly after the publication of his 1838 book, Kierkegaard wrote in his journal the following cryptic line which, as Howard Hong informs us, was intended for use in a possible confrontation with Andersen, should one develop: "An esthetic thought-bridle on knight Andersen's wild hunt through the shadowed valley of self-contradiction."[41] But Kierkegaard was convinced that Andersen was basically harmless, for in another entry he stated: "But Andersen is not so dangerous, after all; from what I have experienced, his main strength is an auxiliary chorus of volunteer arrangers and invitation distributors, a few vagabond esthetes, who perpetually protest their honesty."[42]

Two years later, in 1840, Andersen wrote a play that was performed at the Royal Theater on May 13 and caused Kierkegaard some irritation. It was called *En Comedie i det Grønne, Vaudeville i een Akt efter det Gamle Lystspil: "Skuespilleren imod sin Villie"* [An Open-air Comedy, Vaudeville in One Act after the Old Comedy: "An Actor in Spite of Himself"]. In Scene IV the main actor, a barber cast as a Hegelian, quotes incompletely one of Kierkegaard's most intricate sentences from his 1838 work.[43] This occasioned a short polemical rejoinder from Kierkegaard entitled "Et Øjeblik, Hr. Andersen" (Just a moment, Mr. Andersen), which he never published because his engagement to Regine and his work on his

---

40. *JP* 5324 (II A 228). See also Walter Lowrie, *Kierkegaard* (London: Oxford University Press, 1938), pp. 150ff.
41. *JP* 5339 (II A 768); see note 474, p. 493 in vol. 5 of *JP*.
42. *JP* 5348 (II A 781).
43. The sentence begins: "The sublimate of joy over life . . ." and goes on for half a page. See *Early Polemical Writings* (*KW*, I), pp. 65–66, and *SV*, XIII, pp. 61–62. See also O. Kreisberg and F. J. Billeskov Jansen, "H. C. Andersen," pp. 121–22.

thesis, *The Concept of Irony*, were preoccupying him at the time, and were more important to him.⁴⁴

Perhaps one reason for Kierkegaard's generally cool and unenthusiastic attitude toward Andersen's literary production was his resentment of what he regarded as Andersen's crude autobiographical orientation in his tales. Andersen's *Only a Fiddler* and his later *The Ugly Duckling*, among others, contained intimate revelations about his own person and drew on his experiences during his extensive travels in Europe. To Kierkegaard all this seemed inappropriate and lacking the subtlety of his own indirect approach to self-revelation, which he labeled the Socratic "maieutic purpose" of his writings.⁴⁵ Kierkegaard may also have been irked by the unassuming, child-like simplicity of Andersen's stories, which made them accessible to a wide range of readers and appealing to adults and children alike. Kierkegaard wished any personal disclosures about himself in his writings to be as concealed from the casual reader as the indirect method would allow, short of becoming utterly impenetrable.

Looking at the relationship from Andersen's perspective, can one speak of any Kierkegaardian influence on the fairy-tale writer? Influence would be too strong a word. We know, however, that the sting of Kierkegaard's 1838 critique was still felt by Andersen nearly a quarter of a century later. This is manifested in his little parable "The Snail and the Rose Bush" of 1861.⁴⁶ It makes a great deal of sense to read this piece with the Kierkegaard-Andersen encounter in mind, although Elias Bredsdorff disagrees and insists that Andersen's diary reveals the snail to have been intended to represent a young Danish philosopher named Viggo Drewsen, not Kierkegaard.⁴⁷ The piece could be seen as illustrating Andersen's

---

44. *Early Polemical Writings* (*KW*, I), pp. 218–22; see also *Papirer*, III B 1, pp. 105–10. See Werner Betz, "Andersen und Kierkegaard," p. 58.

45. A journal entry from 1849 entitled "N.B." makes clear the distinction between his approach and Andersen's: "That Socrates belonged together with what he taught, that his teaching ended in him, that he himself was his teaching, in the setting of actuality was himself artistically a product of that which he taught—we have learned to rattle this off by rote but have scarcely understood it. Even the systematicians talk this way about Socrates. But nowadays everything is supposed to be objective. And if someone were to use his own person maieutically, this would be labeled 'à la Andersen.' " See *JP* 6360 (X¹ A 146).

46. Reginald Spink, *Hans Christian Andersen and His World* (London: Thames and Hudson, 1972), p. 56.

47. Elias Bredsdorff, "H. C. Andersen og Søren Kierkegaard," in *Anderseniana*, 3d series, vol. III, no. 4 (Odense, 1981), p. 248. This article is very valuable since it documents all the instances in Andersen's diaries and private letters where he mentions Kierkegaard.

fixed view of philosophers in general, acquired years earlier through his encounter with Kierkegaard and now transferred onto the young Drewsen. The snail (Kierkegaard/Drewsen) says to the Rose Bush (Andersen): "No, you have never taken the trouble to think of anything. Have you ever considered yourself, why you bloomed, and how it happens, why just in that way and in no other?" "No," replied the Rose Bush, "I was just happy to blossom because I couldn't do anything else." The snail then said, "I spit at the world. It's no good! It has nothing to do with me. Keep giving your roses; that's all you can do! I retire within myself, and there I shall stay. The world means nothing to me." With that the snail crept into its shell and closed up the entrance behind it.[48]

Andersen's diaries, which are detailed daily records kept with meticulous regularity, show that he continued to read bits of Kierkegaard now and then after the 1838 incident. An entry for June 26, 1852, for instance, simply says in the course of the daily routine: "read in Kirkegaard [sic]."[49] Some years later, during a trip to Luxemburg with his friend Jonas Collin, Andersen described the hotel room in his diary, and then added: "Jonas had forgotten his Søren Kierkegaard in the train wagon. It was brought to him by the railway officer."[50] We also know that he read Kierkegaard's *Concept of Anxiety*, because an entry dated October 13, 1862, reads as follows:

> Went in rain up to Wisby; read at home in Kirkegaard's [sic] *Concept of Anxiety* where he talks of the secret way of the genius, destiny's presence, and that God in Heaven (in a certain way) does not understand the genius! I said this was unchristian, and Jonas said "God and Christianity were two different things!"—I said that God counseled; that He was the only one. This [which Kierkegaard is saying] is not Christianity; the Jews also believe in a God, but not in Christ!—I obtained in clear words God's expulsion from Christianity for the sake of the new God, Christ.[51]

This brings us to Andersen's conception of religion, and how it differed from Kierkegaard's. Although his father was an atheist, Andersen

---

48. H. C. Andersen, "The Snail and the Rose Bush," in *Hans Christian Andersen's Shorter Tales*, trans. Jean Hersholt (New York: Heritage Press, 1948), p. 314.
49. H. C. Andersen, *Dagbøger: 1825–1875*, volumes I-XII, ed. by Kåre Olsen and H. Topsøe-Jensen (Copenhagen: G. E. C. Gad, 1971–77), vol. IV: 1851–1860, ed. Tue Gad (1974), p. 105.
50. Entry from April 15, 1861, in Andersen, *Dagbøger*, V: 1861–1863, ed. Tue Gad and Kirsten Weber (1971), pp. 26–27. After this comment Andersen described how they went around to see the city.
51. Ibid., p. 256.

grew up as a deeply religious person. His religious beliefs can be summed up in three basic points: he believed in the existence of a god; in the importance of behaving decently; and in the immortality of the soul. This triad of God, Virtue, and Immortality—a sort of simplified rational theology—constituted the essence of Andersen's religion.[52] His religious position was primitive and undogmatic. He regarded Christ as the great teacher and the model for mankind. Nature was God's universal church. He himself seldom went to church, and he was unmoved by the contrasting religious philosophies of N. F. S. Grundtvig (1783–1872) and Kierkegaard. Appropriately, Andersen's favorite New Testament quotation was: "Except ye become as little children, ye shall not enter the Kingdom of Heaven."[53]

Kierkegaard's radical Christian individualism, often expressed in intellectually tortuous language, had little appeal for Andersen. His fifth novel, entitled *At Være Eller Ikke Være?* [To Be, or Not to Be?] (May 15, 1857), is the closest Andersen came to writing a philosophical essay or a religious tract. In fact it was an impossible mixture of both, with very little plot for a novel.[54] Its theme, if one can speak of a theme, was the immortality of the soul. The hero, Niels Bryde, recovers his Christian faith at the end of the novel as a result of this doctrine. Andersen's attitude in this novel toward Kierkegaard's philosophico-religious outlook is best summed up by Bredsdorff:

> Admittedly, there are some interesting and some amusing elements in the novel. The reader is left in no doubt, for instance, that the author dislikes both Grundtvig's "Edda-Christianity" and Kierkegaard's "stalactite cave spring of humour and cleverness," as the heroine [Esther] calls it; she is also fed up with [Kierkegaard's] "crawling along the pavement of language to get to the temple of thought."[55]

Kierkegaard's relationship with Andersen, although a clear example of poor reception of his ideas, marks the earliest instance of interaction between him and another major living figure in Danish intellectual life. Andersen, however, not only was unequipped philosophically to deal with Kierkegaard's complex output but never gave such an undertaking the slightest consideration. He and Kierkegaard, though natives of the

---

52. Elias Bredsdorff, *H. C. Andersen: The Story of His Life and Work, 1805–1875*, pp. 297–98.
53. Ibid., p. 298.   54. Ibid., p. 233.
55. Ibid., pp. 232–33.

same city during overlapping periods of time, lived in two entirely different intellectual worlds.

Other encounters were soon to follow. Toward the end of 1838, Kierkegaard was already busily at work on what was to be his dissertation: *The Concept of Irony, with Continual Reference to Socrates.*[56] Three years later, on September 29, 1841, Kierkegaard performed his oral defense of the completed thesis, during which he faced a set of professors and answered their questions and criticisms for over seven hours. Present at the examination was an impressive array of the learned academicians of the day in Copenhagen. In addition to F. C. Sibbern (1785-1872), Kierkegaard's principal professor and dean of the faculty of philosophy, there were two professors of Greek, Petersen and Peter Oluf Brøndsted, as well as J. L. Heiberg (1791-1860), the first great Danish Hegelian (who introduced Hegel to Denmark in the 1820s), and the German-educated Danish theologian Andreas Frederik Beck (1816-61), who was deeply influenced by the religious philosophy of D. F. Strauss.[57] The rector of the University of Copenhagen at the time was Hans Christian Ørsted (1777-1851), the celebrated physicist and discoverer in 1820 of electromagnetism.

An investigation of Kierkegaard's relationships with both Ørsted and Sibbern is in order. In the case of the former, the object would be to provide yet another example of abortive intellectual interaction, and an instance of non-reception of Kierkegaard's ideas by a leading contemporary. By contrast, the relationship with the latter is pivotal for the story of Kierkegaard's reception in Scandinavia.[58]

Before proceeding, it must first be said that Kierkegaard's reception

---

56. See Lee M. Capel's excellent "Historical Introduction" to his translation of Søren Kierkegaard's *The Concept of Irony: With Constant Reference to Socrates* (Bloomington: Indiana University Press, 1965), pp. 28 and 356-57. Capel includes a highly informative survey of the major scholarship on Kierkegaard's dissertation (pp. 351-57). See also the "Historical Introduction" to *The Concept of Irony, With Continual Reference to Socrates* (*KW*, II), ed. and trans. Howard V. Hong and Edna H. Hong (Princeton: Princeton University Press, 1989), pp. vii-xxv.

57. Capel, "Historical Introduction," to *Concept of Irony*, p. 9. Conspicuous in his absence from Kierkegaard's oral defense was H. L. Martensen (1808-84), who along with Heiberg was mentioned in the last section of the dissertation on irony. Kierkegaard later sent him a dedicated copy of the published work. On A. F. Beck see *Dansk Biografisk Lexicon (DBL)*, ed. C. F. Bricka (Copenhagen, 1887-1905), vol. II, pp. 10-11.

58. Kierkegaard's relationship with J. L. Heiberg has been discussed at length in a great deal of the secondary literature that treats either Kierkegaard's critique of Hegel or his conception of the aesthetic. It is not necessarily germane to a history of his reception.

in Germany commenced with A. F. Beck, who attended the oral defense session of the dissertation. Beck, although Danish, was steeped in German culture and the German intellectual tradition. He had studied theology at the University of Copenhagen alongside Kierkegaard in the 1830s. He completed his theological training in Kiel in Germany and received a doctorate in 1839 for a treatise about Hebrew poetry. His adherence to the Straussian form of theology came through his association with the Tübingen school. He resisted formally joining the ranks of dogmatic theologians and serving the Church, whose officials found his theological interpretations unacceptable. Instead he devoted much of his time to historical and political studies. His frequent disputes with the other theologians caused him much bitter anguish. He wrote several articles against the theology of Grundtvig, which was rooted in a sort of deified Danish nationalism. This along with his German training distanced him from the local theological scene in Denmark and enhanced his cosmopolitanism. He consequently found a more sympathetic audience among German readers, and expressed many of his ideas in their language. His style relied heavily on sharp, sarcastic humor. The final years of his life were a constant battle with sickness and poverty.[59]

Beck read Kierkegaard's published dissertation on irony carefully and wrote a review of it some months later in *Fædrelandet*.[60] Three months later, the same basic review with some minor changes appeared in German in *Deutsche Jahrbücher für Wissenschaft und Kunst*, edited by Arnold Ruge.[61] This German review by Beck of Kierkegaard's *Concept of Irony* from 1842 represents the earliest existing piece on Kierkegaard, and indeed the first printed mention of his name, in the German language. The one or two direct quotations from Kierkegaard's work translated by Beck for use in this review constitute the first bits of Kierkegaard to appear in German translation.

Beck's review was generally sober and intelligent. In his German version he omitted a refutation of Rasmus Nielsen (1809–84),[62] whose thought he

---

59. *DBL*, pp. 10–11.
60. *Fædrelandet*, no. 890, May 29, 1842; and no. 897, June 5, 1842.
61. *Deutsche Jahrbücher für Wissenschaft und Kunst* (Halle, 1842), no. 222, September 17, pp. 885–88; and no. 223, September 19, pp. 889–91. One cannot help wondering whether Marx knew of Kierkegaard through Beck's review in Ruge's publication. This could be a very interesting question if only there were sufficient historical grounds for seriously raising it. See the discussion on Kierkegaard and Marx above.
62. Beck wrote in *Fædrelandet* that in Kierkegaard's work one does not meet with "the vague and diffuse lines of reasoning, as are found in Professor Nielsen, regarding

had compared unfavorably in the *Fædrelandet* article with Kierkegaard's approach. He presumably thought that his German readers would not be interested in such an intellectually parochial comparison. He analyzed Kierkegaard's theory of irony and of Socrates as its highest representative. He took issue with Kierkegaard's unsparingly scornful critique of Xenophon, arguing it was based on inadequate observations. In the same breath, however, he praised Kierkegaard, who "earns for himself a merit which cannot be sufficiently appreciated." He pointed out that Kierkegaard neglected to discuss the relation between comic irony and social irony. Finally, he ended by describing Kierkegaard's language as "flowing, light, free of all the constraints of scholastic language," and added that "the presentation is pervaded by a certain peculiar humor."

This review by Beck elicited an ironic response from Kierkegaard in *Fædrelandet*, no. 904, on June 12, 1842.[63] He made fun of Straussians, in whose ranks Beck clearly belonged, and added sarcastically that it weighed heavily on him to see how little Beck understood him, and worse still, how in many places Beck was strongly convinced he had grasped his meaning.[64] Kierkegaard's tone effectively terminated any further public discussion of Beck's article.

A certain type of person—dogmatic theologians and academic professors—presented Kierkegaard throughout his life with frequent opportunities for polemical criticism and satirical derision.[65] Although Beck did not belong strictly to either of these two categories, he did not escape Kierkegaard's razor-sharp pen. H. C. Ørsted and F. C. Sibbern, on the other hand, were both distinguished scholars in the academic circles of Copenhagen, each in his own field. Kierkegaard was personally acquainted with both and studied under the latter. He himself never became

---

being and phenomena, phenomena and being, in complete abstraction from the historical." Kierkegaard, according to Beck, is more concrete and exact, less idealistic and abstract than Nielsen. See chapters 3 and 5 below for more on Nielsen and Kierkegaard.

63. See *SV*, XIII, pp. 433-42. Also see Søren Kierkegaard *The Corsair Affair* (*KW*, XIII), pp. 9-12.

64. *SV*, XIII, p. 440.

65. In a journal entry from 1854, for example, Kierkegaard talks directly about how in the future he will be misunderstood by these types: ". . . a future when admiring scoundrel professors and the preacher-rabble turn the life and activity and witness of those who are dead into profit for themselves and their families" [*JP* 6920 (XI^2 A 32)]. See also *JP* 1927 (XI^1 A 41) for a similar comment. There are many others in the journals. Besides giving the professors and clergy of today much food for thought, such statements by Kierkegaard reveal a profound level of awareness on his part, and a penetrating anticipation of later problems in the reception of his legacy.

a university professor but spent much of his time in the company of professors with whom he interacted intellectually as well as socially. Through these contacts from his early student days, Kierkegaard left a lasting impact on academia which antedates more recent academic interest in him. After all, Kierkegaard himself was the product of the university, and it was through that environment that he managed to influence certain professors whose names today are well recognized in Danish intellectual history, and who figured prominently in the history of the reception of his legacy.[66] As rector of the University, H. C. Ørsted's name and various titles appear on the official document conferring on Kierkegaard the Magister diploma from the University of Copenhagen in 1841 for his dissertation on irony.[67] Both Ørsted and Sibbern signed Kierkegaard's diploma. Ørsted had glanced through Kierkegaard's dissertation, which Sibbern had sent him, and commented as follows in an undated letter to Sibbern:

> Thanks dear friend and colleague for letting me have Kierkegaard's essay for examination. The brief period of time, together with other matters, have limited me to the most cursory examination. Although I clearly see expressions of considerable intellectual force in this work, I cannot deny that it makes an overwhelmingly unpleasant impression upon me, particularly by two things I abhor: prolixity and artificiality.
>
> Although I have no doubts that this essay deserves to be accepted more than many another, and that the examination of it by additional readers will

---

66. Interspersed throughout Kierkegaard's writings and particularly in his journals are several now-notorious passages exposing the limitations and shortcomings of university professors and academicians in general. Take, for instance, the place in *Fear and Trembling* (1843) where he talks about *Docents,* or assistant professors: "With security in life, they live in their thoughts: they have a *permanent* position and a *secure* future in a well-organized state. . . . Their life task is to judge the great men, judge them according to the result. Such behavior toward greatness betrays a strange mixture of arrogance and wretchedness—arrogance because they feel called to pass judgment, wretchedness because they feel that their lives are in no way allied with the lives of the great." See *Fear and Trembling and Repetition* (*KW,* VI), ed. and trans. Howard V. Hong and Edna H. Hong (Princeton: Princeton University Press, 1983), pp. 62–63. At one point in his journals, a little before his death, he called assistant professors "those animal creatures." See *JP* 1940 (XI^2 A 434). Kierkegaard particularly disliked the Hegelian orientation of the professors of philosophy, those staunch upholders of "the System." His main criticism of them was that, in their constant tendency to rationalize and conceptualize everything, they forgot what it means to exist. You simply cannot *think* personal existence as you think everything else. For more on Hegelian professors see *Concluding Unscientific Postscript to 'Philosophical Fragments'* (*KW,* XII.1 and XII.2), ed. and trans. Howard V. Hong and Edna H. Hong (Princeton: Princeton University Press, 1992), pp. 150, 211, 231–32, 280–82, 299–300.

67. *LD* (*KW,* XXV), document XVII, pp. 25–26.

not change the already established verdict, still, with respect to its form it seems necessary that either Martensen . . . or Nielsen . . . also read and vote on it.[68]

Ørsted made it clear that he did not find Kierkegaard's style of writing—what he called the "form" of the essay—appealing. Nevertheless, and despite his superficial reading, he seems to have been impressed by the solid content of the work. He was, however, displeased with the generally hurried way in which the whole matter of Kierkegaard's dissertation was being handled by Sibbern.[69]

A word about Ørsted's intellectual development is necessary as a prelude to an investigation of his relation with Kierkegaard. Hans Christian Ørsted and his younger brother Anders Sandøe (1778–1860) spent the early part of their youth teaching themselves and each other the basics of various disciplines. They entered the University of Copenhagen in 1794, and continued to live together and to impart to each other the results of their studies, even though their interests diverged, with Hans Christian going in a scientific direction, while his younger brother concentrated on the study of philosophy and law, eventually becoming a jurist and then entering politics to end as prime minister of Denmark. Despite his scientific inclination, Hans Christian never lost touch with philosophy. Indeed, during the early years of the nineteenth century there were no clear-cut divisions among what we today categorize as distinct disciplines. The title of Hans Christian's doctoral dissertation, *The Architectonics of Natural Metaphysics*, illustrates this point.[70]

---

68. The letter is quoted in Carl Weltzer, "Omkring Søren Kierkegaards Disputats," in *Kirkehistoriske Samlinger*, vol. 6, 6th series (Copenhagen, 1948-50), pp. 300-301. This article includes the texts of several letters and statements by Kierkegaard's professors regarding his dissertation, as well as the reproduction of a letter from Kierkegaard to the king requesting that he be given official permission to defend his thesis in his native language, Danish, rather than in Latin as was the custom. Permission was granted. For an English translation see *LD* (*KW*, XXV), document XV, p. 23. The present translation of the quote comes from "Historical Introduction" to Lee M. Capel's translation of Kierkegaard's *The Concept of Irony*, p. 11.

69. Weltzer, "Omkring," pp. 299 and 300. Weltzer speculates that Sibbern was aware that Kierkegaard's engagement to Regine was going through some difficulties during the summer of 1841. He was a friend of both Regine and Kierkegaard, and wanted to promote the dissertation as much as possible so that Kierkegaard could then go abroad for a while until his relationship with Regine clarified itself. Soon after, of course, the engagement was broken. Ørsted was unhappy with Sibbern's approach all along.

70. See "The Life of H. C. Oersted" by Peter Ludwig Möller at the beginning of the English translation of Ørsted's *The Soul in Nature, with Supplementary Contributions,*

From an early age the two Ørsteds were considerably influenced by Kant. In 1798 H. C. Ørsted wrote a treatise on the first principles of *Naturfilosofi* in which he discussed Kant's theoretical concepts about natural science. He subscribed in all essentials to Kant's basic methodology and this qualified to some extent the later impact on him of Schelling's philosophy.[71] The inspiration that both Ørsteds received from Kant's philosophy constituted a central intellectual bond between them that continued even after their careers had diverged.[72] As J. C. Hauch (1790–1872), the Danish poet and novelist who knew the Ørsteds personally and wrote a short biography of H. C. Ørsted, attested, Hans Christian lived in an intimate and honest relationship with his brother until his death. The two seemed to have an intellectual affinity that drew them together and dated back to their earliest childhood. This lasted throughout all the changes of their lives, and was even fortified in their later years.[73]

The other major influence in H. C. Ørsted's intellectual formation was Schelling. Ørsted was an adherent of Schelling's *Naturphilosophie*, whose vogue in Germany and the Scandinavian countries in the early nineteenth century stimulated general interest in science. Many of the ideas that Ørsted began to form about the forces in nature, which eventually proved crucial to his scientific investigations and discoveries, derived in their essence from Schelling's philosophy. For example, Ørsted held to the idealistic-cosmological view—Schellingian in origin—that a Grand Idea permeated and unified all of nature. This Idea had manifold manifestations in the world, both visible and invisible. Ørsted therefore believed that a deeper philosophical understanding of the world can be attained

---

trans. from the German edition by Leonora and Joanna B. Horner (London, 1852), pp. viii and ix-x.

71. Anathon Aall, *Filosofien i Norden: Til Oplysning om den Nyere Tænknings og Videnskaps Historie i Sverige og Finland, Danmark og Norge* (Christiania: Dybwad, 1919), p. 113. See also the section on Ørsted and Kant in C. Christiansen, "H. C. Ørsted som Naturfilosof," in *Oversigt over det Kongelige Danske Videnskabernes Selskabs Forhandlinger*, no. 4 (Copenhagen, 1903), especially pp. 473-79, where Kant's knowledge of Newtonian physics and of Descartes is discussed. Ørsted may have received his first inspirations regarding a relation between the phenomena of magnetism and electricity from a thorough study of Kant's treatises, especially his *Metaphysische Anfangsgründe der Naturwissenschaft* (1785). According to Christiansen, the other two sources of inspiration for Ørsted were Johan Wilhelm Ritter of Weimar and J. J. Winterl (pp. 479-84).

72. Vilhelm Andersen, *Tider og Typer, af Dansk Aands Historie*, II: "Goethe" (Copenhagen: Gyldendal, 1916), pp. 116-17.

73. Johannes Carsten Hauch, *H. C. Oersteds Leben*, trans. H. Sebald (Spandau, 1853), p. 45. The Danish original was published in 1843.

through scientific research into nature. Other philosophical approaches, he maintained, lacked this dimension and hence were deficient. Not only philosophical truths but genuine poetry lay hidden in the laws of nature—greater beauty than that found in many a manmade poem. Ultimately Ørsted believed that our religious views can be modified and refined through a deeper delving into nature.[74]

In 1801 Ørsted went on his first trip to Germany, where he met personally with Schelling and made the acquaintance of the two Schlegel brothers, Fichte, Schleiermacher, Tieck, and others. Fichte visited Copenhagen in 1807 in quest of some repose, and while there he frequented the gatherings of a circle of intellectuals including both Ørsteds and Oehlenschläger, Denmark's most celebrated nineteenth-century poet.[75]

An event little known outside Denmark occurred in 1814–15 involving Ørsted and Grundtvig, the Danish nationalist religious thinker. The two had a public collision over religion and science, with each proposing his own interpretation of the place of biblical exegesis and the duties of theology. This clash signaled the beginning of a long and heated debate in nineteenth-century Denmark about the relationship of religion to science, faith *(Tro)* to knowledge *(Viden)*. The later progress of this debate is intertwined with the history of Kierkegaard's reception, and therefore its genesis merits some attention.[76]

Grundtvig wrote a treatise in 1814 in which he protested against what he perceived as an erosion of traditional Christian teachings by philosophical rationalism and the rationalist theologians. Arguing from biblical texts, he embraced a form of fundamentalism claiming that the Bible, in all essentials, should be understood literally. The tone of his writing in this piece and in an earlier one entitled *Verdenskrønike* (1812) seemed to suggest that he saw himself as speaking prophetically and with divine authority. At least this was what Ørsted sensed and took strong exception to. In a literary periodical,[77] he wrote an anonymous critical article that drew a swift and biting response from Grundtvig, who called the un-

---

74. P. Hansen, ed., *Illustreret Dansk Litteraturhistorie*, 2d ed. vols. 17–18, nos. 41–42 (Copenhagen, 1902), p. 850. See also nos. 48–49, pp. 1121–24 of the same publication, where C. Christiansen discusses Ørsted's early scientific training.
75. Peter Ludwig Möller, "The Life of H. C. Oersted," pp. viii–ix and xi–xiii; and Aall, *Filosofien i Norden*, p. 114. In later years A. S. Ørsted married Oehlenschläger's sister.
76. See Chapter 5 below for a discussion of Kierkegaard's legacy and the "*Tro og Viden*" Controversy.
77. *Dansk-Litteratur Tidende*, nos. 12–13 (1814), pp. 177–208.

known author of the article "a false prophet who deludes the people." Ørsted replied with an article signed in his own name. He declared that there was no dispute over the fundamental truths of the Christian religion—faith in Jesus, love of God and neighbor. On the other hand, theology was a sphere of knowledge like all others, and was not the words of salvation. Consequently, the theological interpretation of scriptural texts was subject to the same difficulties encountered by all other forms of comprehension. Grundtvig, in his writings, had revealed, according to Ørsted, that he was a scholarly amateur, and had added further offense by claiming to speak on behalf of God. This sort of conduct, wrote Ørsted, is dangerous, and can lead to unpleasant consequences for the public. He called Grundtvig a fanatical, narrow-minded pastor who had lit a burning pyre. Grundtvig's errors and confusions should be made plain to everyone, and his unjustifiable foolishness exposed.[78] Grundtvig's reply took the form of a huge treatise attacking the present vicious generation in Europe that had been corrupted by the new education, especially Schelling's *Naturphilosophie*. This philosophy Grundtvig flatly called "unchristian, ungodly, and mendacious." From Grundtvig's standpoint, therefore, Ørsted as an adherent of *Naturphilosophie* represented an example of intellectual arrogance.[79]

The significance of this acrimonious confrontation for our purposes is that it provided Ørsted with an opportunity to express some early views on science and religion that he later developed more fully. Kierkegaard was to evaluate these critically. Ørsted's overall position, emerging in his anti-Grundtvig articles, was that scientific endeavor was a sort of religious undertaking, and indeed a duty. For him the worlds of nature and of the soul were intermeshed.[80] However, at this early period he still distinguished between sensuous, finite, and changeable reality on the one hand, and a transcendental, eternal reality on the other, to which people gained

---

78. Erik M. Christensen, "Guldalderen som idéhistorisk periode: H. C. Ørsteds optimistiske dualisme," in *Guldalder Studier: Festskrift til Gustav Albeck,* ed. Henning Høirup (Aarhus: Universitetsforlag, June 5, 1966), p. 15. For a detailed account of Ørsted's confrontation with Grundtvig, I have relied, in addition to Christensen's article, on C. I. Scharling, *Grundtvig og Romantiken: belyst ved Grundtvigs Forhold til Schelling* (Copenhagen: Gyldendal, 1947), esp. pp. 117–25; and Henning Høirup, *Grundtvigs Syn paa Tro og Erkendelse, Modsigelsens Grundsætning som Teologisk Aksiom hos Grundtvig* (Copenhagen: Gyldendal, 1949), esp. pp. 106–22.

79. Christensen, "Guldalderen," pp. 15–16; see also p. 42, n. 10, for a chronology of the confrontation.

80. Vilhelm Andersen, *Tider og Typer,* p. 118.

admission through personal striving, thereby achieving internal harmony.[81] The main thrust of Ørsted's arguments against Grundtvig was a repeated emphasis on an existing harmony of human reason with the natural order that enables man, despite his limitations, to undergo a pilgrimage from the finite realm of reality to the transcendental.[82] In God's eyes the diverse phenomena of the world and of nature are a whole—beautiful, good, and rational. This was Ørsted's fundamental optimistic hypothesis.[83]

In the years following Kierkegaard's graduation from the University, he and Ørsted became personally acquainted and were, from all indications, on friendly terms. Kierkegaard got to know both Ørsted brothers and was in the habit of taking frequent walks with them in the late 1840s, especially with the younger Ørsted, the jurist-politician, whom he seems to have known more intimately than his brother.[84] He mentions these walks in at least one letter to his friend the law professor Kolderup-Rosenvinge in 1848.[85] A short anecdote is related by Troels-Lund, a relative of Kierkegaard, concerning an incident during one of Kierkegaard's walks flanked by the two Ørsteds, one on either side. Apparently an eccentric draper named G., known to Kierkegaard and the neighborhood for his peculiar fashion of greeting people in public—with a condescending smile and two fingers raised to the brim of his hat—chanced

---

81. Christensen, "Guldalderen," pp. 18-19. Hence the basis for Christensen's designation of Ørsted's outlook as one of "optimistic dualism."

82. Ibid., p. 20.   83. Ibid., p. 27.

84. Kierkegaard sent A. S. Ørsted dedicated copies of three of his books when the latter was prime minister of Denmark: *Concluding Unscientific Postscript* (1846); *Works of Love* (1847); *Sickness unto Death* (1849). See *LD* (*KW*, XXV), "Dedications" nos. 5, p. 430; 7(b), pp. 430-31; 11(d), p. 432. F. C. Sibbern, who was a walking companion of Kierkegaard in addition to being his teacher, mentions in his reminiscences that Kierkegaard in his last days visited A. S. Ørsted often, and that the jurist enjoyed the visits: "I never knew him to be melancholy. He took many walks and visited many people, even in his [Kierkegaard's] last years the old A. S. Ørsted, who took much pleasure in him. But, I suppose, he [Ørsted] lost interest when his [Kierkegaard's] attack on Mynster's reputation came about" (Copenhagen, October 3, 1863); see Steen Johansen, ed., *Erindringer om Søren Kierkegaard*, p. 83. It is interesting that Sibbern, who supposedly knew Kierkegaard well, should reveal in his denial of Kierkegaard's melancholy how superficial his understanding of Kierkegaard's deeper moods was. In another entry Sibbern writes of Kierkegaard: "For a number of years until his death, I did not see him any more. In his last days he began to visit A. S. Ørsted, the jurist, which was something he liked. But when his attack against Mynster came, he discontinued these visits, and the other [Ørsted] also broke them off" (Copenhagen, October 2, 1863); see *Erindringer om Søren Kierkegaard*, p. 81.

85. *LD* (*KW*, XXV), letter 189.

across the three gentlemen as they were strolling along. He and Kierkegaard solemnly exchanged the curious greeting (Kierkegaard jestingly), which made the fellow appear to be more important than he actually was. The two Ørsteds, says Troels-Lund, were visibly impressed.[86]

There are no letters extant between Kierkegaard and either of the Ørsted brothers. Nor does H. C. Ørsted mention Kierkegaard by name anywhere in his entire published corpus. However, he must have followed Kierkegaard's career to some extent after the latter's dissertation on irony appeared in 1841. Ørsted maintained a keen interest in philosophical issues all his life, and Kierkegaard's works would have been easily available to him. In fact, certain passages from an 1844 lecture delivered by Ørsted at a meeting of Scandinavian philosophers in Christiania, and entitled "The Comprehension of Nature by Thought and Imagination,"[87] have Kierkegaardian undertones, and may indicate—although this cannot be proved—that Ørsted was reading some Kierkegaard at the time. He spoke of the "dread of exercising reason" that is exhibited by people who have grown accustomed to living "in the world of their own imaginations." He lamented the fact that insights obtained from the physical and natural sciences were often intermingled with, if not eclipsed by, lingering superstitions in the popular mind about the universe. Once again the imagination dictated its own fanciful conceptions of reality. Returning to the theme of "dread," Ørsted concluded:

> Hence arises that strange dread, possessed by so many, of the results of science; a dread which threatens to destroy that world which their faith and feeling for the Beautiful, had created; thus they are consigned to a vacuity and nothingness which would indeed be fearful were it unavoidable, and the triumphant conquests of natural science which give us the purest pleasure, are for such unhappy beings no less than the dangerous approaches of a conquering foe. Their greatest desire is that this foe should be driven back, and at times they entertain some faint hopes of it, which however are repeatedly destroyed by a stronger feeling of the truth, so that in reality they dare not commit themselves to the truth of their own existence, and therefore are happiest when able to forget this dangerous enemy.[88]

---

86. Johansen, *Erindringer om Søren Kierkegaard*, p. 140. The anecdote is undated.

87. This 1844 lecture was included in Ørsted's book *The Soul in Nature* (1850); see H. C. Ørsted, *Aanden i Naturen*, vol. I, (Copenhagen, 1850), pp. 57–75; which corresponds to *The Soul in Nature*, pp. 41–55.

88. H. C. Ørsted, *Aanden i Naturen*, vol. I, pp. 58–59 (*The Soul in Nature*, pp. 42–43).

Two works by Kierkegaard, *The Concept of Anxiety* and *Philosophical Fragments,* appeared in 1844, the same year Ørsted wrote this. In the first, Kierkegaard discussed in several places the limitations of science in explaining sin.[89] Ørsted may have read it and concluded that Kierkegaard's general outlook represented an antagonistic posture with respect to science. However, a direct correlation between Kierkegaard's views in *The Concept of Anxiety* and Ørsted's in his 1844 piece remains elusive, and perhaps even farfetched. The Danish word used by Kierkegaard and usually translated as "science" is *Videnskab.* Kierkegaard employed this same word in several contexts to mean different things: in *Concluding Unscientific Postscript,* for example, it referred to Hegelian speculation and the Hegelian philosophical system which Kierkegaard confronted with his notions of subjectivity and inwardness;[90] in *The Concept of Anxiety* it designated at times dogmatics and at others any scholarly discipline generally;[91] elsewhere Kierkegaard used *Naturvidenskab* directly to mean natural science. This last is the one Ørsted as a naturalist used consistently in his writings. Also, the Danish word in Ørsted's essay translated into English as "dread" is *Frygt,* which means fear.[92] Therefore connections drawn between dread (fear) as Ørsted used it and dread/anxiety in Kierkegaard's *The Concept of Anxiety* are tenuous.

Leaving the vagaries of terminology aside, it remains a fact that the Kierkegaard-Ørsted connection provides points of interest and raises questions that go beyond mere similarities in book titles. Kierkegaard's journals contain some hints of his attitude toward the great physicist and his massive 1850 book *Aanden i Naturen (The Soul in Nature),* which are worth considering. At one point in 1846 Kierkegaard was writing about how one excels in one's particular field in a small place like Denmark, and he referred to an article that had been written about him that

---

89. Søren Kierkegaard, *The Concept of Anxiety* (*KW,* VIII), trans. Reidar Thomte and Albert B. Anderson (Princeton: Princeton University Press, 1980), pp. 9, 16, 21, 50, and 182.

90. The word "unscientific" *(uvidenskabelig)* in the title was meant to emphasize Kierkegaard's dissociation from the Hegelian system, and *not* that he was in any way anti-science.

91. It is crucial to remember that in the first half of the nineteenth century the boundaries of the various disciplines were still not clearly demarcated, and the terminology used to describe these disciplines was loose.

92. "Dread" is an inaccurate translation and this is probably due to the 1852 English edition of Ørsted's *The Soul in Nature* having been translated from the first German edition rather than from the Danish directly.

same year in which the suggestion was made that he ought to be compared with and be as popular as, in Kierkegaard's words, "such a profound philosopher as H. C. Ørsted."[93] Kierkegaard meant the reference sarcastically, and his tone was a familiar one of assumed modesty. Three years later in 1849 Kierkegaard wrote: "The saying that Councillor H. C. Ørsted told me is a good one: when a lark wants to fart like an elephant, it has to blow up. And in the same way all scholarly theology must blow up, because it has wanted to be the supreme wisdom instead of remaining what it is, an unassuming triviality."[94] Ørsted probably imparted the amusing saying to Kierkegaard on one of their habitual promenades.

Around Christmas of 1849 Ørsted published *The Soul in Nature*. Following the nineteenth-century European custom, the publisher dated the first edition 1850, since it appeared at the very end of 1849. The work included several treatises written for various occasions and at different periods in Ørsted's life. Collectively these essays gave a clear and intriguing portrait of the author's world view *(Weltanschauung/Verdensanskuelse)*. The central thought of the book was that in nature, which exists as uninterrupted alternations, there are forces that stem from a basic pervasive force and laws that reveal themselves with piercing rationality. Physical reality is not the only actuality; physics is merely the outer manifestation of living activities. Body and soul are inseparably bound in the same principles. In thought the creative nature is awakened and becomes consciousness in us. We are therefore in a position to comprehend nature.[95] In fact, historical epochs are defined by the unique ways in which they conceive of nature. On this last point Ørsted quoted Heinrich Steffens, professor of philosophy and Scandinavian literature at the University of Berlin: "It is the peculiar mode of viewing nature, which especially imparts a marked peculiarity to certain periods, by which they are distinctly separated from the earlier and later periods, and stand forth as peculiar and distinguished historical phenomena."[96]

Readers of Ørsted's *The Soul in Nature* can readily see that he never completely severed his intellectual and spiritual ties to the romantic trend in early-nineteenth-century German philosophy. Although by 1811 he had developed the first principles of his own philosophy of science, combining experimental discipline with intellectual creativity, Ørsted continued

---

93. *JP* 5909 (VIII^1 A 124).   94. *JP* 4780 (X^1 A 397).
95. P. Hansen, *Illustreret Dansk Litteraturhistorie*, pp. 850–51.
96. H. C. Ørsted, *Aanden i Naturen*, vol. II, pp. 156–57 (*The Soul in Nature*, p. 258).

to derive inspiration from such sources as *Faust* and from Goethe's general interest in nature and alchemy.[97] Goethe had the idea of an intimate, organic relationship between man and nature. *The Soul in Nature* is a quest for the pervading harmony in nature, and for the spiritual unity of the human soul with this harmonious nature. Man as a microcosm reflects the macrocosm of nature with which he is ultimately bound. The laws of nature are therefore rational laws.[98] Ørsted explored this from many angles, and elaborated certain aesthetical theories of beauty as in his discussions of symmetry and musical tones, which he said were nature's lesson to us in rational harmony.[99] A distinctly noble and humane spirit radiates from Ørsted's work.

Kierkegaard familiarized himself with the contents of Ørsted's book shortly after it appeared. This is evidenced by a revealing journal entry from 1849, in which he curtly dismissed the work as insignificant:

> The *Berlingske Tidende* trumpets Ørsted's book *Aanden i Naturen* as a work which will clear up the relations between faith and science, a work which "even when it is polemical always uses the finest phrases of the cultured urbanite." One is tempted to answer: the whole book from first to last is scientifically—that is, philosophically-scientifically—insignificant, and even when it tries to be most significant it always moves in the direction of the most insignificant phrases of triviality.[100]

Kierkegaard may even have discussed the work with its author on one or more of their walks. Whether he would have been as blunt with Ørsted in person as in the privacy of his journals appears unlikely. Kierkegaard was capable of being tactful in face-to-face dealings with people whose views he did not particularly care for.

Given Kierkegaard's powerful, personal form of Christianity, it becomes evident that what he found most objectionable in Ørsted's book was its naturalistic-cosmological speculations coupled with pantheistic-

---

97. Johs. Witt-Hansen, "H. C. Örsted, Immanuel Kant, and the Thought Experiment," in *Danish Yearbook of Philosophy*, vol. 13 (Copenhagen: Munksgaard, 1976), p. 58. See also F. J. Billeskov Jansen, " 'Aanden i Naturen.' H. C. Ørsteds naturmetafysiske system," in *Oversigt over det Kongelige Danske Videnskabernes Selskabs Virksomhed* (Copenhagen, 1970-71), pp. 127-37.

98. *Aanden i Naturen*, vol. I, p. 141 (*The Soul in Nature*, p. 104.): "In short, the natural laws of chemistry, as well as those of mechanics, are laws of Reason, and both are so intimately connected, that they must be viewed as a unity of Reason."

99. *Aanden i Naturen*, vol. II, pp. 242-88 and 290ff. (*The Soul in Nature*, pp. 325-71, 375ff., and 387ff.). See also J. C. Hauch, *H. C. Oersteds Leben*, pp. 62ff.

100. *JP* 6564 (X^2 A 302).

monistic undertones and implications. Ørsted's conception of God, as expressed in the following quote for example, could not in any way have appealed to Kierkegaard: "It has been already explained in the earlier divisions of this book, how the contemplation of Nature when founded on reasonable grounds proves that all existence is an everlasting, perpetual, active work of the Eternal and Living Reason, which, when viewed in its Self-consciousness and Personality, we name God."[101]

Ørsted's use of phrases like "Eternal and Living Reason" here, and "the Infinite Whole" and "the Infinite All" elsewhere,[102] betrays an ambiguous and highly diffuse notion of God that was reminiscent of Hegelian abstractions and ran counter to the fundamental grain of all Kierkegaard's thinking. Between God's will, which is not to be understood as resembling that of man, and Nature's essence, there can be no conflict; they are *one* in Ørsted's eyes.[103] Even Hauch, Ørsted's biographer, asks whether Ørsted's discourse does not land him in pantheism at times and deism at others.[104] Hauch adds he will not pursue the issue of how Ørsted's Christian faith is reconciled with some of his other views, because he is not in full possession of Ørsted's entire thought.[105] Attempting to find such a unified position in Ørsted's religious conceptions is, of course, futile. Clearly in some places Ørsted wrote as a Lutheran Protestant who extolled the "freedom" that Christianity attained after Luther, and condemned the "superstitious" Middle Ages and "the dark ages of Catholicism."[106] However, the overall view of God remains essentially cosmological.

Kierkegaard was not the only one unimpressed with Ørsted's book. Bishop J. P. Mynster wrote a critical article on it shortly after it appeared,[107] which prompted Ørsted to supplement the work with an additional lengthy section by way of reply to Mynster.[108] On December 10, 1850, Kierkegaard received an agitated letter from a troubled young

---

101. *Aanden i Naturen,* vol. I, p. 154 (*The Soul in Nature,* p. 114). For examples of Kierkegaard's denunciations of pantheism see his *JP* 2004 (VIII¹ A 482); 2942 (IX A 294); and 3887 (II A 248).
102. *Aanden i Naturen,* vol. II, pp. 357–58 (*The Soul in Nature,* pp. 449 and 450).
103. P. Hansen, *Illustreret Dansk Litteraturhistorie,* p. 851.
104. J. C. Hauch, *H. C. Oersteds Leben,* p. 72.
105. Ibid., pp. 72–73: "I don't exactly know his views on this."
106. *Aanden i Naturen,* vol. I, pp. 91ff. (*The Soul in Nature,* pp. 65ff).
107. *Videnskabsskriftet,* vol. I (1850), pp. 291–395. For a contemporary discussion of Ørsted's confrontation with Mynster see H-t, *Striden mellem Ørsted og Mynster, eller Videnskaben og den Officielle Theologi* (Copenhagen, 1851), 54 pages.
108. *Aanden i Naturen,* vol. II, pp. 1ff. (*The Soul in Nature,* pp. 143ff.).

woman named Lodovica de Bretteville, who called herself his "confessant," and who appealed to him passionately for guidance. It turned out that this woman had read Ørsted's *Aanden i Naturen* during the summer of 1850 and found it very appealing: ". . . here expression was given to many theories that I had only felt obscurely."[109] She goes on to add that "even though there was too much physics and too little philosophy, too much religious restraint and too little dialectics in it to satisfy a searching soul, it is as if it were cloaked in a veil behind which one is supposed to divine the godhead."[110] So far so good. But then she read Bishop Mynster's critique of Ørsted's work and found herself agreeing with practically everything in the critique. She became utterly confused and decided to seek help from Kierkegaard, whom she admired and had read. Kierkegaard wrote a draft of a reply[111] in which he stated that he was no confessor, that he could do nothing for her, and that she alone had to sort things out for herself and take a decision about where she stood. He did not send the draft but merely put her letter in an envelope and wrote on it: "I cannot become involved in this."

Only a few months earlier Kierkegaard had written in his journal that he regarded Ørsted's book as "insignificant." His view of Mynster at this time had also begun to alter for the worse. To him the divergent positions they were espousing must have appeared equally erroneous. Hence his refusal to arbitrate between the two men as requested. The Mynster-Ørsted confrontation, like the Grundtvig-Ørsted one some thirty-five years earlier, must be viewed in the larger context of the ongoing debate between scientific knowledge and religious faith. It is also important to keep in mind that Kierkegaard would have disagreed with most of the positions taken by either side in the debate—which went on for years after his death—just as he did in the contemporary case of Ørsted and Mynster.[112]

Today we remember H. C. Ørsted not for his *The Soul in Nature*, with its cosmological monism and its unitary world view presented under the rubric of scientific rationalism, but rather for his epoch-making discovery in 1820 of electromagnetism.[113] Indeed, this discovery contributed

---

109. *LD* (*KW*, XXV), letter 270, p. 367.
110. Ibid.   111. Ibid., letter 271, pp. 371–72.
112. More on this in Chapter 5 below.
113. The treatise in which he announced his discovery was entitled *Experimenta circa effectum conflictus electrici in acum magneticum*. It made him instantly famous throughout Europe.

a lot to Ørsted's perceptions of the natural world. The very nature of electromagnetism inspires one with a sense of the underlying harmony in nature. Both electricity and magnetism are intangible natural forces, and to discover that they are intimately related was enough to give the discoverer a quasi-mystical experience, especially since he happened to be philosophically inclined to begin with. Ørsted expressed his findings in language rich with speculative naturalistic metaphors.

Throughout his life, Ørsted maintained an equilibrium between reflection and practical experimentation, between pure thought and actual scientific results. He was both a scientist and a thinker to the end, balancing delicately speculation and empirical verification. His constant quest was for the order in a well-structured cosmos, and the cultivation of science for him was akin to a religious exercise.[114]

The Soul in Nature had distinct Platonic undertones, but as a scientist Ørsted could not escape being Aristotelian as well. Where Ørsted and Plato part company is on the place of ideas. For Plato ideas stood in and by themselves apart from the rest of existence, while for Ørsted and Aristotle ideas were always bound up with things, with actual existents. In this respect Goethe, one of Ørsted's principal inspirers, was closer to Plato than Ørsted.[115]

Whether Ørsted regarded Kierkegaard's philosophical positions as hostile to science, and whether indeed he gave any thought to the matter, is very hard to tell. In the absence of any letters between them, and with very few references to Ørsted in Kierkegaard's journals to go by, one begins to doubt that any significant intellectual interaction took place at any time. How much oral exchange of ideas on this subject occurred during their walks becomes a matter of pure conjecture.

However one is to assess the Kierkegaard-Ørsted relationship, it does raise the important and somewhat difficult question of Kierkegaard's problematic attitude toward science. As early as 1835, in a long letter to Peter Wilhelm Lund, a relative and a natural scientist who spent time in Brazil studying the flora and fauna of that region, the then twenty-two year old Kierkegaard in expressing his views on natural science and on theology showed why he had decided to pursue the latter instead of the

114. Vilhelm Andersen, *Tider og Typer,* pp. 115–16 and 118.
115. Ibid., p. 132. *The Soul in Nature* has similarities with Plato's *Timaeus,* and also with the Platonic ideas of Tycho Brahe, the sixteenth-century Danish astronomer. See *The Soul in Nature,* pp. 122–23.

former.[116] He made a distinction between those scientists who merely collect "a great wealth of details" and seek to discover new ones, and those who go beyond their science and rise up to heights from which they are able to survey the whole of existence. About this second category of scientists Kierkegaard wrote:

> The case differs of course with respect to those scholars in the natural sciences who have found or have sought to find by their speculation that Archimedean point that does not exist in the world and who from this point have considered the totality and seen the component parts in their proper light. As far as they are concerned, I cannot deny that they have had a very salutary effect on me. The tranquility, the harmony, the joy one finds in them is rarely found elsewhere. We have three worthy representatives here in town: an Ørsted, whose face has always seemed to me like a chord that nature has sounded in just the right way; a Shouw, who provided a study for the painter who wanted to paint Adam naming the animals; and finally a Horneman, who, conversant with every plant, stands like a patriarch in nature.[117]

Thus Kierkegaard had a special admiration for Ørsted from that early period and recognized the physicist's inclination toward speculative philosophical matters. His own orientation, however, was already decided in the direction of theology, as he proceeded to inform Lund in the remainder of the letter. The precise reference to Ørsted is interesting because Kierkegaard's comparison of Ørsted's finely chiseled face to a harmonious chord of nature strongly suggests he was familiar with, and was perhaps recalling, Ørsted's 1807 early essay on tonal sounds: *Om Grunden til den Fornøjelse, Tonerne frembringer* (On the basics of the pleasure produced by musical tones), and his *Forsøg over Klangfigurerne* (Experiment on sound patterns).[118]

Although Kierkegaard followed the route of theology, he by no means remained totally out of touch with the realm of science. In a letter to his

---

116. At least one commentator on Kierkegaard's works, Emanuel Hirsch, argues that the letter is fictive and belongs to the "Faustian Letters," which were an early pseudonymous project that Kierkegaard never published as a separate book. See *JP*, vol. 5, notes 92 and 245 in the back.

117. *LD* (*KW*, XXV), letter 3 (June 1, 1835), pp. 44–45. For another translation of the same letter, see *JP* 5092 (I A 72).

118. See *Det Kongelige Danske Videnskabernes Selskabs Skrifter*, vol. II (Copenhagen, 1807-8), pp. 31ff. Also, Vilhelm Andersen, *Tider og Typer*, pp. 111-12. Ørsted's basic idea in this early essay, which stayed with him and was developed more fully in *The Soul in Nature*, is that in musical tones, as well as in natural beauty and in existence generally, there is operating a concealed rational element.

friend Kolderup-Rosenvinge, written in August 1848, and in the course of discussing the political events of that year, particularly the war between Denmark and Prussia over Holstein, Kierkegaard remarked:

> We have not been at war for a long time, but it has never impressed me as a real war. To me the whole thing seems more like a lecture (such as Ørsted's on physics) during which the presentation is illustrated with experiments. To my way of thinking this war has really always been some sort of peace making or making of peace—the most peculiar sort of war I have ever known.[119]

This suggests that Kierkegaard had attended—if only out of curiosity—some of Ørsted's lectures and observed him performing certain experiments. Does this then mean Kierkegaard maintained an interest in, let alone understood, developments in natural science? To a slight extent, yes. Yet his reference here to the method of scientific experimentation shows that Kierkegaard saw it as a very artificial and peculiar way of approaching reality. The entire remark, therefore, serves only as another clue in the sketchy relationship of Kierkegaard to Ørsted.

It is interesting to mention here by way of contrast to Kierkegaard that Hans Christian Andersen, who knew Ørsted very well and was in one sense a protégé of his, displayed constant enthusiasm for science and its discoveries. In the small world of mid-nineteenth-century Copenhagen, almost everybody who was anybody moved in the same well-defined social circles of the city's intellectual élite. This is where Andersen made Ørsted's acquaintance. When he began to write fairy tales, many of the critics castigated him and urged him not to waste his time on such trivialities. Most of them preferred the novel, and indeed so did Andersen. H. C. Ørsted was one of the few who thought otherwise, and he was neither a critic nor a literary man primarily. He predicted that Andersen's fairy tales would make him immortal, although Andersen did not agree with him at the time. Ørsted became one of Andersen's first and most loyal patrons, and a lasting friendship developed between them.[120] A sign of

---

119. *LD* (*KW*, XXV), letter 184 (August 1848), p. 253.

120. Reginald Spink, *Hans Christian Andersen and His World*, p. 55. See also Elias Bredsdorff, *H. C. Andersen: The Story of His Life and Work*, pp. 120–21. Ørsted often helped Andersen at crucial junctures in his career. He gave him letters of introduction to people abroad whom Ørsted knew. One such instance occurred in May 1831 while Andersen was in Berlin. He used a letter from Ørsted to call on Adalbert von Chamisso (Bredsdorff, p. 80). In November 1834, Andersen applied for a post at the Royal Library in Copenhagen because he was poor and needed the money. Ørsted wrote a letter supporting

Andersen's close association with Ørsted was the habit he developed of dining quite regularly on Tuesdays at Ørsted's house when he was not otherwise abroad traveling.[121] In fact in 1837 Andersen fell in love with Ørsted's daughter Sophie. He had known her since she was a child; now she was sixteen and he was in his early thirties. He hesitated to approach her because he had little money, although he desired to marry. His heart sank when one day she announced to him she had become engaged.[122]

Andersen developed a lively interest in scientific discoveries owing, among other factors, to his friendship with H. C. Ørsted. His "In Thousands of Years' Time" (1852) predicted air travel and anticipated the future stories of Jules Verne.[123] His "The Drop of Water" (1848), in which he deals with new scientific techniques, was written for Ørsted, as he later said in the comments on the origin of his tales.[124] Andersen, unlike Kierkegaard, shared Ørsted's faith in cultural progress through technical

---

the application. The librarian, however, told Andersen he was much too talented for such a post. In the autumn of 1836, Andersen wanted to go abroad again; so he wrote to Ørsted asking that he use his influence with the king to procure him a travel grant (Bredsdorff, p. 130). The two of them corresponded extensively over the years.

121. Spink, *Hans Christian Andersen*, p. 103. Bredsdorff relates an anecdote about Andersen and Ørsted: In October of 1829, Andersen sat for the two parts of the crucial *examen artium*, which allowed one to enter the University, and passed both. One of his examiners was H. C. Ørsted. Andersen answered all the initial questions satisfactorily, but then Ørsted asked, "Please tell me what you know about electromagnetism." "I don't even know the word," Andersen replied to the discoverer of electromagnetism, "there is no mention of it in your textbook of chemistry." Ørsted admitted this was true, but added that he had talked about it in his lectures. "I have attended all of them except one," said Andersen, "so you must have talked about it at the one I missed." Later, in Ørsted's house, Andersen asked him to explain electromagnetism (Bredsdorff, *H. C. Andersen*, pp. 73-74).

122. Bredsdorff, H. C. Andersen pp. 135-36. Andersen resigned himself to a celibate life and decided never to become engaged. He regarded his love for Sophie Ørsted as having been an infatuation.

123. Spink, *Hans Christian Andersen*, p. 64.

124. Bredsdorff, *H. C. Andersen*, p. 350. In "The Galoshes of Fortune," which was discussed above, Andersen alludes several times to scientific theories current in his day. He talks of meteors being "a manifestation of the Northern Lights, probably caused by electricity" (*Andersen's Fairy Tales*, p. 88). In another place he is describing how the watchman was instantly transported to the moon after wearing the magical galoshes: "All of us know how fast steam can take us. We've either rushed along in a train or sped by steamship across the ocean. But all this is like the gait of a sloth, or the pace of a snail, in comparison with the speed of light, which travels nineteen million times faster than the fastest race horse. Yet electricity moves even faster. Death is an electric shock to the heart, and the soul set free travels on electric wings. The sunlight takes eight minutes and some odd seconds to travel nearly one hundred million miles. On the wings of electricity, the soul can make the same journey in a few moments" (*Andersen's Fairy Tales*, pp. 93-94).

innovations. He believed that providence worked through man's self-confidence in improving his lot. He also believed in mankind as opposed to the individual, which was the converse of Kierkegaard's dim view of the collective and his celebration of personal existence.[125]

After travels in Sweden in 1849, Andersen produced a work he called simply *I Sverrig* (In Sweden). It was no ordinary travel book but exuded new ideas and reflections. In the final chapter Andersen seemed to hail openly the advance of science, and his view was that poets and creative writers ought to be concerned with the future and derive their inspiration from the untapped sources of science. He rejoiced, for instance, in the railways criss-crossing Europe. He entitled this last chapter appropriately "Poesiens Californien" (Poetry's California), which was evocative of the pioneering spirit of the explorers of the American West. "There can be little doubt," writes Bredsdorff, "that the direct inspiration for the ideas of this epilogue came from a book by H. C. Ørsted, *The Soul in Nature*, published in 1850." Bredsdorff continues:

> Having read Ørsted's book, Andersen wrote to him to say how much he liked it and how much he agreed with the philosophical ideas put forward in it. Andersen also said that in his religious beliefs he preferred knowledge to blind faith. "It does not do the Lord any harm to be seen through the intelligence he himself gave us. I refuse to go towards God blindfold; I want to have my eyes open, to see and to know, and even if I do not arrive at any other goal than the person who is content with just believing, then after all my thought has been enriched."[126]

The contrast with Kierkegaard's reaction to Ørsted's book is very stark.

Like many others of his time, Ørsted, in *The Soul in Nature*, incorporated evolutionary theories into his naturalistic philosophy. He was familiar with the work of the French and English naturalists Buffon, Condillac, and Darwin; and he saw in evolutionary thought a possible argument in favor of a belief in the spiritual unity of all things. His brother A. S. Ørsted, the jurist, assessed the impact of evolutionary theory on the spheres of ethics and law.[127] Perhaps Kierkegaard viewed all this as being the result exclusively of the spirit of Hegel infecting the scientists and the jurists alike—the idea of unity through Spirit as set forth in Hegel's evolutionary

---

125. Ove Kreisberg and F. J. Billeskov Jansen, "H. C. Andersen," pp. 125–26.
126. Bredsdorff, *H. C. Andersen*, pp. 226–27.
127. John W. Elrod, *Kierkegaard and Christendom* (Princeton: Princeton University Press, 1981), pp. 37ff.

philosophical idealism—and dismissed it as such without seriously bothering about the strictly biological issues.

Actually Kierkegaard was more fully aware of developments in the natural sciences than he might at first glance be given credit for. As an example, he owned in his library, and had carefully read, the work of the German physiologist Carl G. Carus entitled *Psyche: zur Entwicklungsgeschichte der Seele* (1846).[128] His attitude toward the natural sciences, however, underwent certain refinements during the twenty-year period from the mid-1830s until his death. His earlier position, as the letter to P. W. Lund of 1835 reveals, was one of uncritical positive admiration for natural scientific research. He even spoke approvingly of that class of scientists who managed to rise above the confines of their science and survey the rest of existence from their newly attained vantage point; and he named Ørsted as one of them. Yet with the passing of the years Kierkegaard grew more sensitive to the limitations of natural science in dealing with those domains of human existence whose depths he was attempting to plumb. He never abandoned his early respect for science within its legitimate boundaries; however, as he explored the complex ethico-religious questions of freedom, sin, despair, death, repentance, and salvation, he became convinced of the inherent limits of reason alone to comprehend these universal features of the human condition—hence his famous leap of faith. He therefore became increasingly impatient with people who were attempting to turn science into a new religion intended to supplant Christianity and the need for God. "The conflict between God and 'man' will therefore culminate in the withdrawal of 'man' behind natural science. And it is perhaps the trend of the future that Christianity now wants to shake off illusions, with the result that there will be hosts of people whose religion will become natural science."[129] Kierkegaard wrote this in 1853,

---

128. The Auction Catalog for Kierkegaard's book collection lists it as no. 459 and shows he bought it on November 20, 1846. He refers to it in his journals in the course of discussing the limitations of natural science. See *JP* 2809 (VII^1 A 186). Elsewhere he says it is "excellent" because "at all decisive points [Carus] makes unqualified room—for the miracle, for the creative power of God, for the absolute expression of worship, and says: This no one can grasp, no science, neither now nor ever. Then he communicates the interesting things he knows" [*JP* 2818 (VII^1 A 198)]. Carus's work is generally regarded as a prime specimen of *Naturphilosophie*, which means it is not strictly a treatise on natural science; however, in those days the boundaries between science and speculative philosophy were still murky, and pure science had not yet appeared as an independent discipline.

129. *JP* 2823 (X^5 A 73). A journal entry from 1850 went directly to the point: "What the 'race' tends toward is apparently the establishment of natural science in the place of religion" *JP* 2821 (X^2 A 362).

but he had long since come to similar conclusions about the need for science to recognize its own limitations.

The year 1846, the same in which he acquired Carus's book, appears from a survey of his journal entries to mark a turning point in his critical assessment of the place of natural science. The journals from that year are replete with comments about what Kierkegaard saw as a dangerous encroachment by natural science on the sphere of ethics: "Physiology will ultimately extend itself to the point of embracing ethics." People will treat ethics like physics, he adds, with statistical tables and averages "as one calculates vibrations in laws of nature."[130] What does the natural scientist's knowledge of blood circulation, nerve impulses, and the digestive process have to do with the ethical command "thou shalt . . ." that he as a single unique person receives, asks Kierkegaard. Nothing, he answers; and therefore he asks rhetorically, "I wonder if I am not weakening my whole ethical passion by becoming a natural scientist?"[131] He then turns to the natural scientist himself who, on the one hand, admits his inability to explain how consciousness comes into existence or how it becomes self-consciousness and God-consciousness and, on the other, ". . . skeletonizes, . . . dissects, [and] pierces with knives as far as he can, in order to show—that he cannot!"[132] All sense of wonder and of "the miracle," as Kierkegaard calls it, is lost through the scientist's delusion of self-sufficiency in his preoccupation with the minute details of his observations. "Curiosity" is Kierkegaard's label for this self-absorbed type of scientific investigation; it does not yield essential knowledge that makes a personal, existential difference.[133] He praises Socrates for totally forsaking all curious knowledge "in order in all simplicity to be ignorant before God." Goethe, however, is castigated because he was cowardly enough to cling to "that differentiating knowledge."[134]

One could go on giving examples that illustrate Kierkegaard's displeasure with what he termed "sophistical physiology."[135] What then are the

---

130. *JP* 2807 (VII¹ A 182). 131. Ibid.

132. Ibid. Kierkegaard's opinion of physiologists is unsparing: "Those mere butcher-apprentices, who think they can explain everything with a knife and with a microscope, are an abomination to me." "Physiologist" was the common term used in Kierkegaard's day to refer to biologists, evolutionists, and medical doctors.

133. *JP* 2809 (VII¹ A 186). 134. Ibid.

135. Kierkegaard exclaims: "O dreadful sophistry which expands microscopically and telescopically in volume after volume and yet, qualitatively understood, yields nothing but does deceive men out of the simple, profound, passionate wonder and admiration which gives impetus to the ethical" (ibid.).

conclusions that must be drawn from all this regarding Kierkegaard's attitude to natural science? Perhaps the following excerpt from another journal entry in 1846 will sum up his overall position:

> If there were anything by way of the natural sciences which would help define spirit, I should be the first to get hold of a microscope, and I think my perseverance would equal anyone's. But when by qualitative dialectic I easily perceive that, qualitatively understood, in 100,000 years the world will not have advanced one single step, I shall do the very opposite, preserve my soul and not waste one single second of my life on curiosity.[136]

Much is revealed by these words. Kierkegaard's primary preoccupations were ethical and spiritual; consequently, a serious involvement with natural science on his part would occur only if he were convinced it could tell him anything about his real concerns. Since he was sure that in the very nature of things natural science was incapable of such illuminations, which fall entirely outside its purview, he could not devote precious time to accumulating knowledge of secondary importance. It was a question of priorities with him. Although this is not to imply Kierkegaard saw no need for natural science, it does mean he did not share the naive optimism about man generated by scientific discoveries that people like Andersen felt so strongly. The province of natural science did not encompass the spiritual; this was a fundamental tenet of Kierkegaard's philosophy. He was therefore interested in defining the limits of the former and stressing that only a qualitative "leap" could lead to the latter. All loose bridge building over the abyss that separates the two realms of reason and spirit was not only unwarranted but dangerous. The possibility of an eternal, invisible world can be neither proved nor disproved by natural science, and so all the scientific discoveries that follow each other at a mad pace cannot decide anything regarding one's faith.

Viewed in retrospect, Kierkegaard in his comments on the natural sciences of his day was reacting to the crude beginnings of modern scientism—the presumption of science to explain everything—which has since run rampant in a world increasingly dominated by technology. Carus's 1846 book, although praised as exceptional in many respects by Kierkegaard, seems to have confirmed his growing suspicions of the exaggerated claims of natural science in making definitive statements about the origins and development of man. According to Kierkegaard, natural scientists

136. *JP* 2813 (VII¹ A 191).

should be more humble and allow greater room for the inexplicable creative powers of God. He found the materialistic biologists the most comic of all.[137] First they kill the spirit and admit only the material as the foundation of life, and afterwards they believe that out of this dead stuff they can explain life and all its multiplicity. One could smile at or ironize over these fruitless efforts, says Kierkegaard, if the matter were not so serious and the consequences so grave.

He also maintained that the evolutionists, to whom Carus loosely belonged, were unjustified in trying through their investigations to "prove" a continuous line in the history of the development of organisms and thereby to obliterate all qualitative differences.[138] Such differences between the lifeless and the living and between human beings and other creatures were not merely quantitative—because stretched over long periods of time—but qualitative, as were the transitions from life to mind to spirit.[139] For Kierkegaard, however, there is no qualitative progress taking place through the *sheer* passage of time; all such qualitative changes occur as a result of God's direct creative intervention and remain incomprehensible to unaided human reason. It is on this question of qualitative progress that Kierkegaard differed most markedly from either Andersen or Ørsted, and indeed from all nineteenth-century positivism.

The ethical and the spiritual were what mattered first to Kierkegaard, and so he focused on the undesirable consequences that would befall them because of an arrogant and uncontrolled reliance on natural science. He feared that all absolute moral obligations would be undermined and the entire scope of ethics jeopardized if the domains of nature and spirit were confused. This explains his strong judgment: "Ultimately all corruption will come from the natural sciences."[140] It also throws important light

---

137. *JP* 2809 (VII[1] A 186).

138. Ibid. Evolution as a clearly formulated theory was still unknown in Denmark during Kierkegaard's life; however, "evolutionists" of sorts existed all the same.

139. For an interesting discussion of Kierkegaard's positions on natural science, see Gregor Malantschuk, "Søren Kierkegaard og naturvidenskaberne," in *Kristeligt Dagblad*, Monday, October 22, 1951, p. 5. It must be noted that Malantschuk, who was writing in the immediate post-war period, was to some degree conditioned by skepticism about the natural sciences arising from the recent war experience. He concludes that Kierkegaard's critical remarks on the natural sciences could only with difficulty be fully understood before our time (1951). People then were blinded by their enthusiasm for scientific progress. "In our time one begins to see more clearly and soberly the problems associated with the natural sciences and their limitations. Kierkegaard's views today find more adherents."

140. *JP* 2809 (VII[1] A 186).

on his lack of enthusiasm for Ørsted's attempt to harmonize the world of spirit with that of nature. He offered on two occasions a candid and decidedly Christian response to Ørsted's enterprise. On September 10, 1851, the year Ørsted died, Kierkegaard published a work he entitled *For Self-Examination, Recommended to the Present Age,* which belonged to the series of upbuilding or edifying discourses he had been writing under his own name in tandem with his early pseudonymous body of writing and continued after it. At the end of the section discussing Christ's Ascension, Kierkegaard, with Ørsted's *The Soul in Nature* in mind, warned against skeptically making light of the fundamental miracles, such as the Ascension, on which Christianity is based:

> Oh, when you live admired, flattered, highly esteemed, in abundance, you are tempted to say many things and to take part in much that you perhaps might rather have left alone, and which you—remember this!—will still have to account for—and the Ascension also very easily slips out of your mind. You may even, if you ever think about it, doubt and say: An Ascension—that goes against all the laws of nature, against the spirit in nature—but only the nature spirit![141]

Soon thereafter, Kierkegaard wrote a piece to which he gave the name *Judge for Yourself!* (1851-52); however, it remained among his papers and was not published until 1876. Once again he made a passing reference to Ørsted's book in a heavily Christian context:

> So pay attention to the lily and the bird! Surely there is spirit [*Aand*] in nature—especially when the Gospel inspires [*beaande*] it, because then nature is pure symbol and pure instruction for man; it, too, is inspired [*indblæst*] by God and is "profitable for instruction, for reproof, for correction."[142]

Kierkegaard clearly continued to ponder Ørsted's book long after he had dismissed it in his journal in 1849, and the stand he took on it and on

---

141. Søren Kierkegaard, *For Self Examination and Judge for Yourself* (*KW*, XXI), ed. and trans. Howard V. Hong and Edna H. Hong (Princeton: Princeton University Press, 1990), p. 70.

142. Ibid., p. 182. In this same work Kierkegaard laments the scientists' indifference, in their preoccupation with their science, to moral issues. He says satirically that their kind of knowledge about human nature consists merely of "information about how we human beings *are* now or *are* at this time, a natural-scientific, statistical knowledge about the human moral state as a natural product, explained by the situation, the air currents, the wind, the rainfall, the tides, etc. Whether we human beings may have degenerated from generation to generation is of no concern to this kind of knowledge about human nature" (p. 157).

the natural sciences generally expressed itself eventually in unequivocal, Christian terms.[143]

Neither Andersen nor Ørsted can be regarded as having at any time seriously tackled Kierkegaard's philosophical and religious positions with comprehensive profundity or as having interpreted them to future generations. This is disappointing, yet understandable, given the wide differences in interests and talents among the three great Danes. In terms of a history of the reception of Kierkegaard, therefore, his encounters with both these men, fascinating as they indeed were, remain a void.

---

143. The secondary literature on the relation of Kierkegaard to science is very slight. In addition to Malantschuk's article referred to above, see Marie Mikulova Thulstrup, "Kierkegaard og naturvidenskaben," in *Kierkegaardiana*, vol. VIII, ed. Niels Thulstrup (Copenhagen, 1971), pp. 53–63, which gives a brief discussion of Kierkegaard's views of three scientist-thinkers in his day: Franz von Baader, C. G. Carus, and H. C. Ørsted. See also the section entitled "Videnskaben" in Johannes Sløk, *Kierkegaard: Humanismens Tænker* (Copenhagen: Reitzel, 1978), pp. 25–35. Sløk says that the young Kierkegaard, as his 1835 letter to Lund reveals, shared with his age a romanticized respect for scientists (p. 27). However, in later years he came to the conclusion that, fascinating as the sciences may be, they were not existential, meaning they did not address the deepest struggles and personal crises of the individual (p. 35).

2 Kierkegaard and Some Contemporaries (ii)

Glimmerings of an Early Reception beyond Denmark

Frederik Christian Sibbern was a mild-mannered and easily accessible person, much liked by his students at the University of Copenhagen, where for fifty-seven years he was professor of philosophy. He began in 1813, the year Kierkegaard was born, and became the dean in 1845. During his long academic tenure Sibbern exercised a considerable influence on whole generations of students and intellectuals in Denmark, leaving his distinct mark on the history of nineteenth-century Danish thought.

Sibbern's acquaintance with Kierkegaard dated from the winter semester of 1830–31, when Kierkegaard attended Sibbern's lectures on psychology. They lived close to each other and took frequent walks together. A friendship developed between them, and Kierkegaard often found himself an invited guest at Sibbern's house.[1] Shortly before Poul Martin Møller died in 1838, he enjoined Sibbern to look after Kierkegaard, who up to then had been under Møller's care. From that time until Kierkegaard's

---

1. Robert J. Widenmann, "Sibbern," in *Kierkegaard's Teachers*, vol. 10 of *Bibliotheca Kierkegaardiana*, ed. Niels Thulstrup and Marie Mikulova Thulstrup (Copenhagen: C. A. Reitzel, 1982), p. 81.

attack on the Church commenced in 1854, Sibbern acted as his mentor, and "their relationship was that of a fatherly teacher and advisor to a young man seeking the right path in life."[2] Except for H. C. Ørsted, Sibbern was the only figure present at Kierkegaard's oral thesis defense whose relation with Kierkegaard bears upon the history of his reception.

In many respects Sibbern's views coincided with some of Kierkegaard's more mature convictions. There is, in fact, the strong likelihood that Sibbern had a far-reaching influence on the intellectual development of Kierkegaard, a theme still inadequately explored by scholars and Kierkegaard specialists. It is known, for example, that Sibbern was politically very conservative, supporting the monarchy and advocating central authority. He was appalled by the 1848 revolutions. Kierkegaard's political views were very similar. In his later years, however, Sibbern settled for a more utopian position that advocated an idealized form of government.[3] Sibbern also began as an outspoken anti-Hegelian, and was attacking the Danish Hegelians J. L. Heiberg and H. L. Martensen at a time when Kierkegaard was starting to feel uncomfortable in his "Hegelian phase." Sibbern's attack came in 1838 in the form of a lengthy treatise entitled *Bemærkninger og Undersøgelser fornemmelig betreffende Hegels Philosophie* (Comments and studies mainly concerning Hegel's philosophy). This vigorous rejection of Hegelian philosophy by Sibbern was instrumental in transforming Kierkegaard's intense early concern with Hegel's thought into a highly critical enterprise.[4] Another unsympathetic figure for both Sibbern and Kierkegaard—this time a theologian—was N. F. S. Grundtvig. Although a personal friend of his, Sibbern did not concur with Grundtvig's theological outlook.[5] Sibbern certainly contributed to the emphasis on a personal Christianity that became a hallmark of Kierkegaard's religious thought.

These similarities, while significant, ought not to obscure the fact that Sibbern's influence had its limits, and some major features of his thought

---

2. Ibid., p. 82. According to Kierkegaard's journals, P. M. Møller at the time also asked Sibbern to tell Kierkegaard, "You are so thoroughly polemical that it is quite appalling." Kierkegaard remembered and recorded these words years later in 1854. See *JP* 6888; (XI^1 A 275).

3. See Jens Himmelstrup, *Sibbern, en Monografi* (Copenhagen: J. H. Schultz, 1934), pp. 184–219 for a discussion of Sibbern's politics. See also Widenmann, "Sibbern," pp. 74–75.

4. Niels Thulstrup, *Kierkegaard's Relation to Hegel*, pp. 33–34; pp. 150–54 and 163–65.

5. Himmelstrup, *Sibbern*, p. 231.

were unacceptable to Kierkegaard. Despite his severe critique of Hegel, Sibbern eventually formulated a speculative theology of his own. It was a cosmology, based on an evolutionary conception of God as developing toward integration with the universe. This was not altogether unlike the position of Hegel. Moreover, Sibbern tried unconvincingly to combine pantheism with a belief in a personal God.[6] By definition, Kierkegaard's transcendental conception of God precluded all such attempts. Like Ørsted, Sibbern employed various abstractions to designate God: "the All-Constitutive," "the Ideal-Real," "the All-Active," and others.[7] Sibbern, however, stopped short of creating any self-contained system of philosophy à la Hegel. Indeed, Sibbern has been correctly regarded as a rich source of unfinished ideas for others—he himself never completed anything.[8]

Kierkegaard read many of Sibbern's works over the years, but referred to them or to Sibbern himself very rarely in his journals. There is evidence that in the mid-1830s he read Sibbern's autobiographical *Efterladte Breve af Gabrielis* (The Posthumous letters of [the son of] Gabriel) which appeared in 1826 but was actually written earlier.[9] This work, augmented in 1850 by a sequel entitled *Ud af Gabrielis Breve til og fra Hjemmet* (Extracts of the letters to and from home by [the son of] Gabriel), was the fruit of a couple of disappointed infatuations Sibbern experienced while still a student at the University. There in 1806, he met the brothers Ørsted and also Grundtvig, who were living in the same dormitory. He soon got to know Albertine Ørsted, the sister of the two Ørsteds, and fell madly in love with her, only to be heartbroken when she married and left Copenhagen.[10] The parallels with H. C. Andersen's later infatuation with H. C. Ørsted's daughter are striking.[11] Sibbern, however, quickly shifted his amorous attentions to Adam Oehlenschläger's sister Sophie, who became A. S. Ørsted's wife and died young in 1818. It was Sophie

---

6. F. C. Sibbern, *Speculativ Kosmologie med Grundlag til en Speculativ Theologie* (Copenhagen, 1846), pp. 70–75.

7. Ibid., p. 14; pp. 1 and 5; pp. 3 and 8. See also Poul Lübcke, "F. C. Sibbern: Epistemology as Ontology," in *Danish Yearbook of Philosophy*, vol. 13 (1976), pp. 96 and 104. For a discussion of Sibbern's *Spekulativ Kosmologie* see Poul Kallmoes, *Frederik Christian Sibbern, Træk af en Dansk Filosofs Liv og Tænkning* (Copenhagen: Munksgaard, 1946), pp. 51–53 and 72–83.

8. Widenmann, "Sibbern," p. 77.

9. See *JP* 2206; (I C 66). The Auction Catalog to Kierkegaard's book collection does not list this book by Sibbern.

10. Himmelstrup, *Sibbern*, pp. 28–29.   11. See Chapter 1 above.

who inspired Sibbern in his *Gabrielis Breve*, in which he used a fictional correspondence to describe his love for her. The year after she died, Sibbern married Christine Margaretha Ipsen.[12]

The significance of all this for our purposes is many-sided. In addition to his romantic escapades with the Ørsted and Oehlenschläger girls, Sibbern interacted vigorously with the two Ørsted brothers on an intellectual level while studying at the University, and A. S. Ørsted's Kantian orientation exerted a strong influence on him.[13] He also benefited from H. C. Ørsted's interest in the empirical sciences, and actually studied some physics under him.[14] His trip to Germany in 1811, when he attended lectures by Fichte and Schleiermacher and met Schelling and Hegel, enriched his knowledge of continental philosophy with their emphasis on logic and epistemology. His diverse if amorphous intellectual interests are reflected in the more than sixty works he wrote during his long life, on a wide range of philosophical, religious, political, and psychological issues.[15]

Kierkegaard's regular attendance at Sibbern's lectures, and their general close association throughout the 1830s, placed Sibbern in the unique position of having some access to Kierkegaard's personal life and inner development during that period. Sibbern became one of the very few people whom Kierkegaard grew to trust. His disappointments in love and his personal revelations in *Gabrielis Breve* undoubtedly struck a responsive chord in the young Søren. It is no wonder that Kierkegaard willingly got Sibbern involved in his relationship with Regine Olsen. Sibbern ac-

---

12. Widenmann, "Sibbern," pp. 71–73. On Sibbern and Sophie Oehlenschläger see also Kallmoes, *Frederik Christian Sibbern*, pp. 9–60 (esp. pp. 29–33, 42 and 45–48).

13. Widenmann, "Sibbern," p. 72.

14. Himmelstrup, *Sibbern*, p. 82. Basically, Sibbern agreed with Ørsted's understanding of the unity of soul and body, and he raised questions about the relations between psychology and physiology. His interest in both psychology (soul/mind/reason) and biology (brain) became apparent from his book *Psychologie, indledet med almindelig Biologie* (1843), and was developed further in his *Om Forholdet mellem Sjæl og Legeme* (1849). This and other features of his thought have caused many to regard Sibbern as a transitional figure in Danish philosophy; see, for example, Anathon Aall, *Filosofien i Norden*, pp. 164–66. Aall maintains that nothing of outstanding psychological value is to be found in Sibbern's works.

15. The main reason Sibbern is not more widely known and read is that his writing style was often ridiculously complex, involving a combination of impossible Danish interspersed with many Germanisms and strung out into long sentences. Translating such a style has proven very difficult. Pastor Hans Dahl attempted to compile a lexicon of the most frequently used "Sibbernisms" in the philosopher's corpus. See Hans Dahl, *Frederik Christian Sibbern og Modersmålet, et Stykke Dansk Ordbogsarbejde* (Copenhagen, 1884). It is telling that none of Sibbern's many works have been translated into English.

companied Kierkegaard on many of his visits to Regine, and sometimes acted as messenger between them.[16] When Kierkegaard finally broke the engagement on October 11, 1841,[17] Regine sought Sibbern for solace, and Sibbern played the role of the hurt father. All this greatly suited Kierkegaard's purposes, and facilitated his plans of terminating the relationship with Regine as smoothly as possible. Sibbern continued to provide Kierkegaard with information about Regine long after everything had ended between them.[18]

On October 25, 1841, barely two weeks after breaking the engagement with Regine, Kierkegaard took off on his first trip to Germany, and indeed his first excursion outside Denmark. He stayed in Berlin until March 6, 1842.[19] Within a few days after his arrival in Germany he was writing his close friend Emil Boesen (1812–81), another of the trusted few in whom Kierkegaard confided, that he was not particularly fond of travel: "It is still my unalterable opinion that travel is foolish."[20]

This visit to Germany, followed by A. F. Beck's articles in Danish and German on *The Concept of Irony*,[21] represented the first instance in which Kierkegaard received attention, although minuscule, in the German-speaking world. It also marked an important phase in his own intellectual development, as he began his early pseudonymous writings with the completion of most of the first volume of *Either/Or* while in

16. Widenmann, "Sibbern," p. 83.

17. Kierkegaard had become convinced that he could not attain the highest religious stage and at the same time marry. So he wanted to break the engagement in such a way as to preserve the girl's reputation. This he succeeded in doing, and she went on to marry someone else.

He had actually sent back the ring to Regine on August 11, a month and a half before he completed the defense of his thesis. Sibbern had been aware of the deteriorating situation all along.

18. In a journal entry from 1849 Kierkegaard wrote that he learned from Sibbern that Regine had read "The Diary of a Seducer" in *Either/Or*, volume I. Sibbern also disclosed that Regine had told him she could not bear to see Kierkegaard after his return from Germany, but Kierkegaard discovered that this was in fact not true. See *JP* 6472; (X^5 A 149). In another entry from May 1852 we learn that Kierkegaard discovered from Sibbern that Regine had read his *Two Upbuilding Discourses* of 1843. See *JP* 6800; (X^4 A 540).

19. All in all, Kierkegaard made three other trips to Berlin in addition to this one during his short life: in May 1843 for three weeks; in May 1845 for a week and a half; and in May 1846 for two weeks. See Walter Lowrie, *Kierkegaard*, Appendix III: List of Dates.

20. *LD* (*KW*, XXV), letter 49 (October 31, 1841); also found in *JP* 5513. Emil Boesen was also privy to Kierkegaard's affair with Regine, and in this letter Kierkegaard inquired about her and expressed the hope that Sibbern would visit her and speak with her.

21. See Chapter 1 above.

Berlin. Actually, Kierkegaard got much more exposure to German thought during his stay there than the Germans got to his. Indeed, in a letter to Sibbern from Berlin dated December 15, 1841, Kierkegaard confessed how little he interacted with anyone: "On the whole I live as isolated as possible and am withdrawing more and more into myself."[22] He did attend cultural events in Berlin, and tried to absorb as much as possible of the city's rich offerings. It appears, however, that aside from the Danes in town who usually gathered at the Café Belvedere by the Opera House, Kierkegaard associated with very few people, least of all with Germans.[23]

In the same letter to Sibbern of December 15, Kierkegaard described his stay in Germany and his impressions. He told of the various lectures he was attending: "So here I am in Berlin going to lectures. I am attending lectures by Marheineke, Werder, and Schelling. I have heard Steffens a few times and have also paid my fee to hear him, but oddly enough, he does not appeal to me at all."[24] Steffens's lack of appeal was more than compensated for by the engrossing lectures of Schelling, which, according to Kierkegaard, were always well attended: "I have never in my life experienced such uncomfortable crowding—still, what would one not do to be able to hear Schelling."[25]

The Schelling lectures that Kierkegaard attended were on *Die Philosophie der Offenbarung*. He listened carefully and took extensive notes. His impressions of Schelling are scattered in many of the letters he wrote to friends back in Copenhagen during this period. In one to pastor Peter J. Spang, written on November 18, shortly after Schelling began his lecture series, Kierkegaard remarked wryly about the great German philosopher's appearance: "Schelling himself is a most insignificant man to look at; he looks like a tax collector."[26] With time, and after the initial enthusiasm wore off, Kierkegaard grew disillusioned with Schelling and exasperated by his labyrinthine philosophical speculations. He wrote irately: "Schelling talks endless nonsense both in an extensive and an intensive sense. I am leaving Berlin and hastening to Copenhagen." These were the opening lines of a letter to Emil Boesen dated February 27, 1842, one week

22. *LD* (*KW*, XXV), letter 55; also found in *JP* 5543.
23. *LD* (*KW*, XXV), letter 58 (December 28, 1841).
24. *LD* (*KW*, XXV), letter 55. Philipp Konrad Marheineke (1780–1846); Karl W. Werder (1806–93); F. W. J. Schelling (1775–1854); Heinrich Steffens (1773–1845).
25. Ibid.   26. *LD* (*KW*, XXV), letter 51.

before Kierkegaard returned to his homeland.[27] These sentiments were echoed in a letter to his brother Peter Christian Kierkegaard (1805–88), sent around the same time: "Schelling talks the most insufferable nonsense. . . . I think I might have become utterly stupid if I had continued to listen to Schelling."[28]

It is not difficult to grasp why Schelling's philosophical discourse rubbed Kierkegaard the wrong way. As with Ørsted and Sibbern, so also with their principal inspirer Schelling: the speculative cosmology, the naturalism, and the pantheism were simply too foreign to Kierkegaard's fundamental existential assumptions to have any lasting appeal.

Kierkegaard's first trip to Germany left no discernible impact on anyone in that country. Yet he seems to have been aware of his potential to find an eager reading audience among the Germans for his writings. In his December 15 letter to Sibbern he wrote:

> The longer I live in Berlin the more I realize the truth of the advice you have given me again and again out of regard for both me and my dissertation: that it be translated into German. I will wait and see about that. If it does happen, I can honestly say that you are responsible. If any good comes of this, it will be a pleasure for me to think that in this I have once more an occasion to thank you.[29]

Sibbern's advice indeed reveals his foresight and his appreciation of Kierkegaard's genius at that early stage. Yet Kierkegaard died before his dissertation or any of his works were translated into German, the most likely language outside of Scandinavia in which Kierkegaard's writings could have appeared that early. Ironically, his dissertation was one of the last works to be translated into German.[30]

The second mention of Kierkegaard in a German publication came in 1844, and once again A. F. Beck was responsible. In a thirty-nine page article in *Theologische Jahrbücher,* Beck surveyed the theological scene

---

27. *LD* (*KW,* XXV), letter 69; also found in *JP* 5552. Kierkegaard in this letter does qualify his earlier view of travel, however, and writes: "I do owe Schelling something. For I have learned that I enjoy traveling, even though not for the sake of studying. . . . I must travel. Formerly I never had the inclination for it." But in reality, as we know, Kierkegaard did very little traveling after this.

28. *LD* (*KW,* XXV), letter 70.   29. *LD* (*KW,* XXV), letter 55.

30. The translation appeared as late as 1929, well after the German edition of the *Gesamelte Werke* (1909–22) was finished. For a word on the translator, Wilhelm Kütemeyer, and the circumstances of his translation of *Der Begriff der Ironie mit ständiger Rücksicht auf Sokrates* (Munich: Kaiser Verlag, 1929), see Chapter 8 below.

in Denmark in the early 1840s. Kierkegaard is mentioned once in the context of a discussion of Grundtvigian theology.[31] Beck's stated purpose was to illustrate the intimate relationship which Danish culture, and Scandinavian culture generally, had with European, particularly German, culture.[32] His main conclusion was that German philosophical speculation prepared the way for new developments in Danish theology. With his considerable knowledge of the respective Danish and German philosophical and theological situations, and with some of Kierkegaard's writings, Beck was ideally fitted to translate Kierkegaard into German, but he did not.

A year later, in 1845, an anonymous German review of Kierkegaard's *Philosophical Fragments* (1844) appeared in a theological journal published in Berlin.[33] The review was brief and touched on the central themes of the book: the Absolute Paradox; the offense; contemporaneity with the event of the Incarnation; and the Moment (or Instant) of that event as a unique point at which the eternal pierces the temporal, both historically and in the life of the individual.[34] The anonymous writer concluded by stating that, despite Kierkegaard's "peculiar approach" to these issues, he was going to leave to someone else any judgment of whether Kierkegaard's "apologetic dialectic" was conducted seriously (i.e., in earnestness) or ironically.

The review was apparently brought to Kierkegaard's attention while he was in the thick of his work on the *Concluding Unscientific Postscript*, which appeared the following year, 1846. The *Postscript*, intended to be just a postscript to the earlier *Fragments*, in fact constituted a major philosophical work in itself and occupied a central place in the entire corpus. There are frequent references to the *Fragments* throughout the *Postscript*, and in the context of one of these, Kierkegaard mentioned this German review.[35] He conceded that the review had a couple of commendable points about it:

---

31. A. F. Beck, "Uebersichtliche Darstellung des jetzigen Zustandes der Theologie in Dänemark," in *Theologische Jahrbücher*, vol. 3, ed. E. Zeller (Tübingen, 1844), p. 501.

32. Ibid., pp. 498–99.

33. *Neues Repertorium für die theologische Literatur und kirchliche Statistik*, vol. II, 1 (Berlin, April 1845), pp. 44–48.

34. These central theological-existential categories in Kierkegaard's thought are treated at length in this book and in the other major works such as the *Postscript*.

35. Søren Kierkegaard, *Concluding Unscientific Postscript* (*KW*, XII.1 and XII.2), ed. and trans. Howard V. Hong and Edna H. Hong (Princeton: Princeton University Press, 1992), note pp. 274–77.

> The reviewer has an excellent quality: he is brief and refrains almost entirely from what is usually found in reviews, the introductory and concluding examination—ceremony of lauding the author, of citing him for special distinction or perhaps even for special distinction and congratulations.

But more substantively, Kierkegaard added:

> The reviewer . . . goes on to give an account. His report is accurate and on the whole dialectically reliable, but now comes the hitch: although the report is accurate, anyone who reads only that will receive an utterly wrong impression of the book. The mishap, of course, is not too serious, but on the other hand this is always less desirable if a book is to be discussed expressly for its distinctive character. The report is didactic, purely and simply didactic; consequently the reader will receive the impression that the pamphlet is also didactic. As I see it, this is the most mistaken impression one can have of it.[36]

It was the absence in the review of any mention or appreciation of his method of indirect communication that Kierkegaard found most lamentable. He described his art of communication paradoxically as a form of "taking away" excessive knowledge from a saturated readership "whose misfortune is that they know too much." He likened this to a man who is starving to death because his mouth is so full of food it prevents him from swallowing. Removing some of the extra food will enable the man to eat the remainder and gain nourishment. Similarly, Kierkegaard's "peculiar procedure," which the review totally misunderstood, functions by taking away rather than adding.

The concluding sentence of the review, in which the question of whether Kierkegaard was writing earnestly or ironically is left unanswered, aroused Kierkegaard's indignation. He wrote:

> In other regards, there is nothing to say about the review, except that the four last lines are again a demonstration of how in our didactic age everything is conceived didactically. . . . When the reporter leaves it up to each one whether he will look for earnestness or irony in the pamphlet, this is misleading. . . . If the presentation in a book is unmixed, pure didactic ultra-earnestness, there can be some point in saying it. . . . But the pamphlet was far from being pure and simple earnestness—it was only the report that became sheer earnestness.[37]

Here Kierkegaard was driving at the point that his *Philosophical Fragments* represented an intricate mixture of both irony and earnestness

36. Ibid., pp. 274–75. 37. Ibid., pp. 276–77.

decipherable only if his method of indirect communication was grasped. This the anonymous reviewer utterly failed to comprehend. "But the presence of irony does not necessarily mean that the earnestness is excluded," wrote Kierkegaard in conclusion, "Only assistant professors assume that."

The German review and the emphatic reaction it occasioned in Kierkegaard provide us with a rare example of Kierkegaard commenting on his own reception.[38] The obvious importance of the few instances of this sort is twofold. First, they display the rigorous criteria required by Kierkegaard of his readers in order for them to begin to understand him. Second, which is the obverse of the first, they raise the legitimate question of the place of Kierkegaard's prescriptions for how he wished to be approached and understood. The validity and relevance of such directions from the author, when it comes to his reception by others, were poignantly called into question in the case of Kierkegaard's *The Point of View for My Work as an Author* (written in 1848; published posthumously in 1859).[39] Did Kierkegaard write this "manual of instructions" for aiding the puzzled and foiling the malicious among his reading audience, and if so, must we heed his call and blindly follow the path he assigns to unlock his secrets? Or was this work intended as another enigmatic thread in the overall tapestry of Kierkegaard's convoluted writings, and should we not view it as such regardless of the author's intentions? These questions have preoccupied Kierkegaard scholars ever since his entire corpus became available to a discerning posterity.

There may not have been much of a discerning Danish audience in Kierkegaard's day for whom his works generated any sustained interest, at least not before his stormy confrontation with the Church captured the public eye, but was this also true for the rest of Scandinavia? In fact,

---

38. In a journal entry from 1845 Kierkegaard recorded the following sentences, which complement his comments in the *Postscript* about the anonymous review in *Neues Repertorium:* "The review of my *Fragments* in the German journal is essentially wrong in making the content appear didactic, expository, instead of being experimental by virtue of its polar form, which is the very basis of the elasticity of irony. To make Christianity seem to be an invention of Johannes Climacus is a biting satire on philosophy's insolent attitude toward it. And then, too, to bring out the orthodox forms in the experiment 'so that our age, which only mediates etc., is scarcely able to recognize them' (these are the reviewer's words) and believes it is something new—that is irony. But right there is the earnestness, to want Christianity to be given its due in this way—before one mediates." *JP* 5827 (VI A 84).

39. See Chapter 4 below.

some of his religious ideas began to find an echo in Norway as early as 1846, and this grew steadily with time. As Kierkegaard's feud with the *Corsair* raged furiously in Copenhagen throughout the early months of 1846, precipitated by P. L. Møller's impertinent review of *Stages on Life's Way* (1845), an extract from *Stages* was published in the same year in Norway in a literary anthology entitled *Læsebog i Modersmaalet for Norske og Danske, tilligemed en Exempelsamling af den svenske Litteratur og med æsthetiske og litteraturhistoriske Oplysninger* [Reader in the mother tongue for Norwegians and Danes, including examples of Swedish literature and with aesthetic and historical notes]. The editor of the anthology was a twenty-six-year-old classicist named Henning Junghans Thue, who had been present at Kierkegaard's oral defense of his thesis on irony in 1841; no record of Thue's participation exists. This extract from *Stages* represented the first instance of a Kierkegaard text becoming accessible to the Norwegian reading public.[40]

In the year 1846 also, a Swedish poet and publicist named Oscar Patrick Sturzen-Becker (1811–69) wrote a book containing his impressions up to that point of his two-year stay in Denmark. He departed the following year. The last section of his book *Hinsidan Sundet* (Beyond the Channel) dealt with various Danish literary writers, and five pages were devoted to Kierkegaard. Sturzen-Becker, who wrote under the fictitious pseudonym "Orvar Odd," called Kierkegaard's works "types of speculative fantasies," and branded Kierkegaard himself "a Sebastian Bach in dialectics."[41] Much of the book had already appeared in the form of letters sent to the Swedish newspaper *Aftonbladet* in 1845. Sturzen-

---

40. Paulus Svendsen, "Norwegian Literature," in *The Legacy and Interpretation of Kierkegaard*, vol. 8 of *Bibliotheca Kierkegaardiana* (1981), p. 12. Undoubtedly some copies of Kierkegaard's earlier works reached Norway and other parts of Scandinavia, but for the most part in this period they remained confined to private libraries and individual book collections.

41. See Nils Åke Sjöstedt, *Søren Kierkegaard och Svensk Litteratur: från Fredrika Bremer till Hjalmar Söderberg* (Göteborg: Elander, 1950), pp. 15–19. Sjöstedt's work has been regarded as something of a milestone in Kierkegaard scholarship. Harald Beyer, a leading scholar on the reception of Kierkegaard in Scandinavia, remarked in one of his articles that before reading Sjöstedt's book he had always believed Norway in the nineteenth century was on the whole deeper in its response to Kierkegaard than Sweden, and the Norwegian mentality accepted the radical Kierkegaardian either-or choice more readily than the Swedish, which leaned in the direction of a compromising "both-and." Sjöstedt's book on Kierkegaard's reception in Sweden changed all that. See Harald Beyer, "Søren Kierkegaard og Svensk Litteratur," in *Kirke og Kultur*, vol. 56, no. 8 (Oslo, October 1951), p. 500.

Becker's chief contribution, however, to Kierkegaard's reception in Sweden came in 1855, when he returned to Copenhagen and wrote articles in Swedish about the controversy with the Church that Kierkegaard had instigated. In one of these articles[42] he translated large portions of Kierkegaard's provocative *Øjeblikket* (The moment) articles into Swedish. He himself had definite irreligious tendencies and found in Kierkegaard a convenient ally for undermining the Church.[43] During 1855 he followed the progress of the controversy closely and wrote in a letter from Copenhagen to a friend of his that "my remarks conveyed through letters regarding the Kierkegaard struggle have been splendidly received here."[44]

Kierkegaard was more famous through hearsay than through his works in Scandinavia in the 1840s and early 1850s. Although his works did not require translation into Norwegian, few actually read him, but many, for example, had heard of the clash with the *Corsair* of 1846. In Sweden, where it was necessary for Danish books to be translated in order to reach a wide reading public, familiarity with works by thinkers like Kierkegaard was limited initially to a handful of literary and ecclesiastical savants. One of the former was Fredrika Bremer (1801–65), the celebrated Swedish writer and founder of the suffragette movement in Sweden in the nineteenth century. Bremer visited Copenhagen in the autumn of 1848 and remained there until 1849. A brief look at the curious situation that developed between Bremer and Kierkegaard while she was in Denmark, and its consequences for both, will reveal how Kierkegaard's increasingly reclusive disposition—because he was convinced his contemporaries were misunderstanding him—determined the fixed impressions people formed of him from a distance, without really having the opportunity to verify them through closer contact.

Before turning to Bremer, however, two instances of German reception should be mentioned. The first involved a package of books that Christian Molbech (1783–1857), the accomplished Danish historian and philologist and one of Kierkegaard's professors at the university, sent in April 1847

---

42. The article was entitled "Den officiella Kristendomen är icke det Nya Testamentets Kristendom. Fremställning af Dr. Søren Kierkegaards polemik mot Statskyrkan i Danmark"; Sturzen-Becker wrote it anonymously. See Sjöstedt, *Søren Kierkegaard*, pp. 17–18. See also Aage Kabell, *Kierkegaardstudiet i Norden*, p. 18 (no. 97). Many of his articles appeared in *Öresundposten* in 1855.

43. Sjöstedt, *Søren Kierkegaard*, p. 19; Kabell, *Kierkegaardstudiet i Norden*, p. 104.

44. See the letter to F. Borg from 1855 in Ragnar Sturzen-Becker, *Oscar Patrick Sturzen-Becker (Orvar Odd)*, vol. I (Stockholm, 1911), p. 201.

to his friend Dr. Edmund Zoller in Stuttgart. Among the books was a copy of the first edition of Kierkegaard's *Either/Or*, which had appeared in February 1843 and sold out by 1845. Molbech had asked Kierkegaard for a copy of the scarce first edition, and Kierkegaard had willingly dispatched one with a note saying: "I hasten to comply with your wish for one or two of my books for that German friend of the Danish language [i.e. Zoller]."[45] The incident is one example of how, through personal connections, some of Kierkegaard's works could have made it to particular individuals in Germany, or elsewhere abroad, in the 1840s and later.

The second instance was a paragraph on Kierkegaard included in a massive German survey of European poetry and literature since the sixteenth century published by Johan Georg Theodor Grässe in Leipzig. In a section near the end dealing with Danish poetry and fiction, Grässe reserved a few lines for Kierkegaard's *Either/Or*.[46] Kierkegaard is labeled "a Hegelian" by Grässe, who gives the entire first volume of *Either/Or* the title of "a seducer's diary." In it, he says, everything that should make a man holy is undermined and derided, especially the institution of marriage, depicted as totally useless. The second volume presents a long treatise pointing out the drawbacks of a purely aesthetic view of marriage. The whole enterprise, concludes Grässe, "is composed with such objective originality," and it is unfortunate that in Germany people do not know this work, "the finest product of modern Danish literature." For the first time Kierkegaard makes his way into an encyclopedic survey in the German language and finds himself comfortably situated in the company of other representatives of Danish literary excellence—Blicher, Heiberg, Winther, Hertz, and Andersen.

These two instances illustrate the embryonic and chancy nature of Kierkegaard's "impact" on the German intellectual world during the 1840s. An incident that occurred in 1849 involving Fredrika Bremer highlights another aspect affecting Kierkegaard's flimsy reception abroad: his growing social self-isolation and intellectual aloofness. While in Denmark, Bremer tried unsuccessfully to meet Kierkegaard. She made the personal acquaintance of many of the country's leading thinkers during her stay in Copenhagen. She had known Andersen from before and met Ørsted,

---

45. *LD* (*KW*, XXV), letter 169 from 1847. Kierkegaard wrote that the copy of *Either/Or* he was sending "is certainly in respectable condition, nevertheless it is not quite new."

46. J. G. Th. Grässe, *Geschichte der Poesie Europas und der bedeutendsten aussereuropäischen Länder vom Anfang des 16. Jahrhunderts bis auf die neueste Zeit* (Leipzig, 1848), p. 979.

Oehlenschläger, and Grundtvig for the first time. Her excitement was heightened by H. L. Martensen's 1849 theological work *Christelige Dogmatik*, which she read carefully and discussed with the author on several occasions. Martensen impressed her greatly, and Bremer went about extolling the merits of his book and his erudition. In May 1849, just before she was to depart Copenhagen for a visit to America that would last nearly two years, she sought a meeting with Kierkegaard. She had read his *Stages on Life's Way* and wished to exchange her impressions of it with the author himself. To that end she sent him a letter addressed to Victor Eremita, Kierkegaard's pseudonym and the fictitious editor of *Either/Or*:

> A recluse, like you (even though she lives in the midst of society), sincerely wishes to meet you before she leaves this country—partly to thank you for the heavenly manna in your writings and partly to speak with you about *Stages of Life,* the metamorphoses of life, a subject that at present is more profoundly interesting than ever to her.[47]

The letter went unanswered, and so on May 15 Bremer again sent a brief note to Kierkegaard inquiring if he intended to comply with her request for a meeting.[48] At that point he answered with a very polite letter refusing her request and begging that she not misunderstand his position.[49]

Outwardly, the matter ended there.[50] Kierkegaard's journals, however, contain revealing entries on Fredrika Bremer from that period. These entries explain Kierkegaard's reluctance to meet with her, but also shed light on his attitude toward others at the time, particularly women. In one entry Kierkegaard reacted vehemently to a characterization of him by Bremer in her book *Lif i Norden* (Life in the North), written while she was in Copenhagen but appearing in September 1849 after she had left for America. Bremer praised Martensen at length in her book and then continued:

> While the richly talented Martensen enlightens the circumference of all existence and all the phenomena of life from his central point of view, Søren Kierkegaard stands like Simon Stylites on his lonely pillar with his eyes focused steadily on a single point. He holds the microscope over it, he scruti-

---

47. *LD* (*KW*, XXV), letter 201.   48. Ibid., letter 203.
49. Ibid., letter 204.
50. For accounts of the Bremer-Kierkegaard correspondence see Sjöstedt, *Søren Kierkegaard och Svensk Litteratur*, pp. 56–60; and Elisabeth Hude, *Fredrika Bremer og Hendes Venskab med H. C. Andersen og andre Danske* (Copenhagen: Gad, 1972), pp. 161–67.

nizes it down to the least of its atoms, he researches its most fugitive motions, its innermost alterations, he makes speeches about it, and again and again he writes endless folios about it. . . . Inasmuch as he does say divine things during his tiresome dialectical wanderings, he has gained a not inconsiderable audience, especially among the ladies in gay and merry Copenhagen. . . . He lives in solitude, this man who writes for "that single individual," inaccessible and really known by no one. During the day one sees him walking up and down the most heavily trafficked streets by the hour in the midst of the crowd; at night his lonely house is said to be shining with lights. It is not so much being rich and independent that makes him behave in this way as a sickly and irritable disposition that finds occasion to be annoyed with the sun itself when its rays fall in a direction other than that he might wish.[51]

Kierkegaard definitely found occasion to be annoyed with these very words, and he released a barrage of anger in the privacy of his journals:

> Fredrika Bremer will become popular in various circles because of this interpretation. . . . Fredrika's version is that I am so sickly and irritable that I can become bitter if the sun does not shine when I want it to. You smug spinster, you silly tramp, you have hit it! Various circles that are perhaps not so different will be united by this interpretation. On the one side Martensen, Paulli, Heiberg, etc., on the other Goldschmidt, P. L. Møller.[52]

At the time these words were written Kierkegaard had already been subjected to numerous bouts of public abuse and ridicule as a consequence of the highly publicized *Corsair* affair during which he bitterly confronted both Meïr Goldschmidt (1819–87) the editor, and the writer P. L. Møller. Bremer's careless assessment, he felt, would only add fuel to an already-smoldering fire. Also, by 1849 Kierkegaard had retired into semi-seclusion and was dodging repeated attempts to draw him out. He was busy tackling the question of how one becomes a Christian through a personal

---

51. Fredrika Bremer, *Lif i Norden* (Stockholm, 1849), pp. 53–55. The book was translated into Danish as *Liv i Norden*, and published the same year in Copenhagen. In 1850 Mary Howitt produced an English translation entitled *Life in the North*, which was published in *Sartain's Union Magazine of Literature and Art*, vol. VI, ed. Mrs. C. M. Kirkland and Prof. John S. Hart (Philadelphia, January–June 1850), pp. 157ff. and 329ff. The reference to Kierkegaard is on p. 332. Howitt's translation is the first reference to Kierkegaard to appear in English. In 1853 the first German translation was put out by the Brockhaus publisher in Leipzig under the title *Leben im Norden, Eine Skizze*. The second German edition appeared in 1858. The English translation of the passage quoted here is by Henrik Rosenmeier; see *LD* (*KW*, XXV), pp. 482–83.

52. *JP* 6493 (X^2 A 25) from 1849.

relationship with God, and all his energies were devoted to that endeavor. He had nothing but scorn for the prevailing theological notions of his day exemplified by Martensen's speculative pontifications. Martensen's *Christelige Dogmatik,* appearing that year, elicited several sarcastic jabs from Kierkegaard's pen and set the stage for his final outburst against official religion. Bremer's fuss over the book and its author appalled Kierkegaard. He wrote derisively:

> It was a wonderful old world—Martensen may witness "for God and his conscience"; did he not become Bishop and swathed in velvet and did not Fredrika run to him every day and read his *Dogmatik,* of which she got proof sheets (this is a well-known fact). And Goldschmidt may declare: It was a wonderful old world, I always had 3,000 subscribers. Tutti, it was a wonderful world; only Magister Kierkegaard was so sickly and irritable that he could get bitter if the sun did not shine when he wanted it to.[53]

Bremer's determined fraternizing with the principal intellectuals of Copenhagen Kierkegaard regarded as uncouth and even suggestively lewd. He described her with caustic graphicness as "having lived here a long time and had sexual intercourse with famous people; she also wanted to have sexual intercourse with me, but I remained virtuous."[54] He found her intimation that he was a ladies' author highly offensive.[55]

Of all the irritations associated with Bremer, none seems to have struck a more sensitive point in Kierkegaard than her incessant doting on Martensen's *Christelige Dogmatik.* In her behavior Kierkegaard detected something of the intellectual upstart clamouring nervously for recognition. While criticizing speculative theology he wrote the following in his journals in 1849 and signed it "a disciple of Johannes Climacus:"[56]

> Johannes Climacus has shown that the fundamental confusion in all modern speculation is to have pulled back the essentially Christian one whole sphere, down into the esthetic. . . . For example, Martensen, the profound M., who has already found a connoisseur in the no less profound Fredrika Bremer, who profoundly prophesies that Martensen's *Dogmatik* will regenerate all scientific scholarship in the North, perhaps also in *North* America, where the forerunner, the traveling Fr. B. has now gone. . . . This involves nothing less

---

53. Ibid.   54. *Papirer,* X^1 A 658 from 1849.
55. Ibid.
56. Johannes Climacus is the pseudonym Kierkegaard used for the *Concluding Unscientific Postscript* (1846).

than—as Fredrika B. prophesies—the rebirth of theological scholarship in the North, and to which we add (what modesty no doubt has prevented Fredrika B. from adding) in North America.[57]

Bremer continued her hobnobbing with the well known of Denmark even from America. In a long letter written in Swedish from New Jersey and dated August 10, 1850, Bremer informed H. C. Ørsted that she had read the first volume of his *The Soul in Nature,* which had recently come out.[58] She wrote how she had been greatly impressed by its "clear logical thought." Her attitude toward the book was diametrically opposite to the disdain Kierkegaard expressed for it in his journals.[59] Clearly Fredrika Bremer would have had very little understanding of the criteria by which Kierkegaard judged a work like Ørsted's. Despite her deeply held religious views and her intellectual interests—in the late 1840s and 1850s Bremer's head was buzzing with issues and impressions—she operated on an entirely different level from Kierkegaard. In a sense this was unfortunate because, had she been in a better position to comprehend him, and had they met, she might have been instrumental in spreading his reputation or disseminating his works on her many foreign travels. In the same letter to Ørsted, after describing in detail her voyage across the Atlantic and her stay in America, Bremer concluded with the assertion that the country was "a hospitable land not only for men, but also for ideas."[60] She could have served perhaps as an early transmitter of Kierkegaard's thought to America had she been able to penetrate his elaborate defenses and, more important, grasp the fundamental thrust of his philosophy.

Bremer, however, did have an indirect hand in introducing Kierkegaard to the English-speaking world. The unwelcome words she wrote about him in *Lif i Norden* were indeed the first impressions of Kierkegaard the person to appear in the English language. This came about through the translation of her book in 1850 by Mary Botham Howitt (1799–1888), the wife of William Howitt (1792–1879).[61] The literary fame that these

---

57. *JP* 6475 (X^6 B 105). The following year, 1850, Kierkegaard was still thinking about Bremer in connection with Martensen's *Christelige Dogmatik.* See *JP* 6636 (X^6 B 137), where he wrote essentially the same thing we have quoted.

58. Ørsted himself gave her a copy. See Elisabeth Hude, *Fredrika Bremer,* pp. 135–36.

59. See Chapter 1 above.

60. For the full text of Bremer's long letter to Ørsted see *Breve fra og til Hans Christian Ørsted,* ed. Mathilde Ørsted, second collection (Copenhagen, 1870), pp. 285–96.

61. See note 51 above.

English Quakers sought eluded them, and they remained on the periphery of the Victorian literary landscape; they did, however, leave a rich legacy of translations and assorted writings—compilations, journals, letters, literary surveys, travel accounts—entitling them to a modest place among the various commentators and cultural transmitters of their day. Most significant were the abundant connections they cultivated among some of nineteenth-century Europe's celebrated writers, particularly in Scandinavia.

Mary Howitt informs us in her autobiography that she and her husband William learned Swedish while in Heidelberg in the early 1840s. They studied it with a German woman married to a Swede, and found it to be "a delightful employment, which might be called a relaxation rather than a labour." Soon, through the same woman, they were introduced to Bremer's novels and were impressed by their "originality, freshness, and delicate humour," and they decided to make them available to the English reading public. They commenced by translating *The Neighbours* and *The Home* from the German versions and revising them from the Swedish originals. Apparently these two stories met with immediate and wide recognition both in England and America. This prompted a surprised Fredrika Bremer to write Mary Howitt a letter from Stockholm dated February 21, 1843, in which she expressed her pleasure at the English translations and urged the Howitts to continue their fine work. "Sweden," wrote Bremer, "is a poor but noble country, England is a rich and glorious one; in spirit they are sisters, and should know each other as such. Let us, dear Mrs. Howitt, contribute to that end." "To the best of my ability I united with her in so doing," writes Howitt in her autobiography.[62]

The letter of 1843 marked the beginning of a long and mutually rewarding association between Bremer and the Howitts, one result of which was Mary Howitt's translation of *Lif i Norden* into English in 1850 while Bremer was in America. Howitt's extraordinary flair for languages also led her to learn Danish, and in 1847 she translated some of H. C. Andersen's fairy tales into English for the first time. Andersen was naturally pleased as he had longed to become known and read in England, and despite the initial poor sales of his stories there he insisted that Mary

---

62. Mary Howitt, *An Autobiography*, in two volumes edited by her daughter, Margaret Howitt (Boston and New York, 1889), vol. II, pp. 22-24.

Howitt translate all his tales. This she could not do, but she and her husband remained good friends with Andersen and invited him to be their guest in England.[63]

The Howitts never met Kierkegaard but apparently knew about him and his works. The general information they had probably came from Bremer initially. This was enough to guarantee Kierkegaard a few lines in the first comprehensive English-language history of Scandinavian literature, which William and Mary Howitt produced in two volumes in 1852. They constructed a long survey of the literature of the North by piecing together translations and excerpts spanning several centuries of Nordic literary lore. The result was *The Literature and Romance of Northern Europe,* in many respects a shallow, uncritical effort sacrificing nuance for the sake of superficial inclusiveness. Several of Denmark's leading contemporary authors, for example, were lumped together and their often widely disparate works combined under misleading general descriptions. The very different writings of Sibbern, Mynster, Grundtvig, Martensen, and "the brothers Kierkegaard" (Peter and Søren) evoked the following remark: "In these works we have a profoundly interesting history of the progress of a human spirit through all the sorrows and troubles of sceptical doubt and fear, to victory and peace." Directly after these words comes a brief paragraph on the Kierkegaards:

> Peter Christian Kierkegaard made himself intimately acquainted in his youth, not only with the writings, but the persons and living thoughts of the German moral philosophers, of however differing views—Hegel, Schleirmacher [*sic*], Neander, etc.; and has shown his own convictions, not only in his writings, but by his long and zealous friendship and cooperation with Grundtvig. Sören Aaby Kierkegaard, "the solitary philosopher," has also probed the depths of the same metaphysic systems in the society of the great advocates of them, having especially devoted himself to the study of Schelling; and in his singular but remarkable works, "Enten-Eller:" that is, "Either-Or," a Life's Fragment, by Victor the Hermit; "Reiteration;" "An Attempt in Experimental Psychology;" "Fear and Trembling," a Dialectic Lyric, by John de Silentio; and his "Instructive Tales," dedicated *To That Individual,* has with wonderful eloquence, and with the warmth of an actual experience of the "Fear and Trembling" and the "Gospel of Suffering" of which he speaks, proclaimed his firm adhesion to that true spirit of the North, which of old

---

63. Amice Lee, *Laurels and Rosemary: The Life of William and Mary Howitt* (London: Oxford University Press, 1955), pp. 176–77.

saw, in the myth of Valhalla, combat and death as leading only to victory and life.[64]

It is interesting to observe that the remark quoted earlier describing the heterogeneous works of a number of Danish writers applies best, despite its general nature, to Kierkegaard's writings. In the minds of the Howitts at least, who had a most cursory knowledge of the works of Kierkegaard, this overcoming of "doubt and fear" in man and the attainment of "victory and peace" characterized the Nordic spirit ever since ancient times. Also of interest in the passage about the Kierkegaards is the emphasis placed on Søren's mastery of Schelling's philosophy. The manner in which this is put suggests the Howitts knew of and had in mind Kierkegaard's trip to Berlin in 1841-42 when he attended Schelling's lectures. In spite of its glaring shortcomings, *The Literature and Romance of Northern Europe* by William and Mary Howitt remained the standard history of the subject in English for most of the rest of the nineteenth century.

Kierkegaard, therefore, owes his first two inadvertent and barely noticeable forays into the English language indirectly to Fredrika Bremer. Bremer's connection with Kierkegaard did not end there. After her return from America in 1851 Bremer decided to devote much of her energy to improving the condition of women in Sweden. In America she had witnessed a mounting tide in favor of emancipation from slavery, and she drew the appropriate conclusions with regard to the status of women back in her homeland. She began to develop the more universal concept in her mind of an educating and redemptive mission that women were providentially called upon to fulfill in the world. In her own life she now saw a double purpose: on the one hand to awaken this sense of mission in women around her, and on the other to participate actively as a woman in accomplishing her share of the mission. She rejected the radical equality proposed by the St. Simonians and favored instead a vision of women as possessing a purifying and softening power capable

---

64. William and Mary Howitt, *The Literature and Romance of Northern Europe: Constituting a Complete History of the Literature of Sweden, Denmark, Norway and Iceland, with Copious Specimens of the Most Celebrated Histories, Romances, Popular Legends and Tales, Old Chivalrous Ballads, Tragic and Comic Dramas, National and Favourite Songs, Novels, and Scenes from the Life of the Present Day*, in 2 volumes (London, 1852), vol. II, pp. 239-40. See also Carl Ray Woodring, *Victorian Samplers: William and Mary Howitt* (Lawrence, Kansas: University of Kansas Press, 1952), p. 156. Woodring wrote his thesis at Harvard on William and Mary Howitt (1949).

of enhancing domestic harmony, provided they were liberated from society's prejudices.[65]

Bremer quickly set to work recording her observations from her American trip and outlining the implications for women. The result was a two-volume work that Mary Howitt promptly translated into English.[66] Bremer also wrote several newspaper articles for the Swedish press on the same subject. But she did not stop there. Already she was conceiving plans for a novel with a leading heroine who would embody many of her ideas about women. Her plans germinated eventually in the novel *Hertha* (1856), for which she is perhaps most famous.[67]

In the autumn of 1854 Bremer made a brief visit to Copenhagen during which she met again with Martensen, now the bishop primate of the Danish Church in place of Mynster, who had died earlier in the year. Shortly after her return to Sweden, on December 18, Kierkegaard published his well-known article against Martensen in *Fædrelandet*—the opening shot that signaled the start of his attack on "Christendom" as he called it.

Bremer followed the controversy from Sweden, and she read the articles that Kierkegaard wrote in the course of 1855. On March 2 of that year Bremer's mother died, and she began work on *Hertha* with a deep feeling of sorrow that lasted throughout the year. She also read Kierkegaard's *Øjeblikket* articles as they appeared and was considerably affected by them. Being a religious person herself, she understood the significance of the issues raised and the critiques leveled by Kierkegaard, and she was both attracted and repelled by his position. Undoubtedly the depth of her comprehension and degree of her personal involvement in what Kierkegaard was now expressing had increased and become more genuine,

---

65. For the influence, or lack thereof, that Bremer's writings had on the emancipation reforms for women in the 1840s and 1850s in Sweden, see Gunnar Qvist, *Fredrika Bremer och Kvinnans emancipation: Opinionshistoriska studier* (Göteborg: Läromedelsförlaget [Akademiförlaget], 1969).

66. Fredrika Bremer, *Homes of the New World: Impressions of America*, 2 vols., trans. Mary Howitt (New York, 1853). Following Bremer's return from America Howitt noted the change in her: "Her religious and social views had, in America, been materially influenced. An intense desire animated her to aid in the liberation of every oppressed soul; above all, to rescue her country-women from the dark and narrow sphere allotted them; and Sweden listened to her pleadings for women." See Mary Howitt, *An Autobiography*, vol. II, p. 85.

67. Working from manuscript sheets Bremer sent her, Mary Howitt produced an English translation of *Hertha* that appeared simultaneously with the first Swedish edition in 1856. That same year the first German translation was also published.

and her thinking had matured appreciably since the episode of 1849.[68] This is evident in part from a couple of letters she wrote shortly after Kierkegaard's death in the fall of 1855. To H. C. Andersen she wrote on December 14 from Stockholm:

> As God wills, I say with S. Kierkegaard, we must only know that we are to follow His exhortation and carry out His commandments to us! As far as your Danish Simon Stylites is concerned, he has also awakened a good deal of interest here. Most people here—and I among them—believe that he is correct on many points and incorrect on many others. He is not a pure manifestation of the truth, and his sickly bitterness has, I suppose, impeded the soundness and fairness of his judgments.[69]

Despite her tedious refrain about Kierkegaard's "sickly bitterness," the guarded ambivalence that Bremer displayed here with respect to his attack on the Church shows she had kept closely in touch with the developments of the controversy and had read Kierkegaard's articles carefully. This was essentially true for his *Øjeblikket* pieces, which made a lasting impression on her—so much so that she seriously considered quoting long excerpts from them in her novel *Hertha*. The reasons why she eventually decided against this idea are not entirely clear; however, we do know that several drafts for sections of *Hertha* containing Kierkegaard extracts were revised and discarded. In a letter to Mary Howitt dated March 27, 1856, Bremer, writing in English as she always did to Howitt, instructed her to ignore a fragment by Kierkegaard which was among the proofs she had sent her for translation:

> I have made a very prosaic but litteral [sic] translation of the 4 lines of Tegnér. As to the fragment of Kierkegaard you may as well omit it as it is an anachronism to have it at the time. Kierkegaard is a mystical religious philosopher recently dead in Denmark [he was only 43 years old] [sic] whose strong protest against the Statechurch and the clergy as *"wholly unchristian institutions"* and his violent *assault* on Bishop Martensen has made an immense sensation in Denmark and even in Sweden. He is deep but ambiguous in his writings, and must be almost incomprehensible to foreigners. It will be best

---

68. E. Hude, *Fredrika Bremer*, p. 173. See also Sjöstedt, *Søren Kierkegaard och Svensk Litteratur*, pp.60ff.

69. Letter from Bremer to Andersen (Stockholm, December 14, 1855) in *Fredrika Bremers Brev*, ed. Klara Johanson and Ellen Kleman in 4 volumes (Stockholm: Norstedt, 1917), vol. III: 1846–57, p. 417. Three days after writing this letter, on December 17, she sent another one to Per Johan Böklin, an old friend, in which she expressed the same views on Kierkegaard's final struggle using nearly identical words. See vol. III, p. 421.

to let the young chivalric friend of Hertha (a personal memory has made me call him forth) give her some pretty flowers from the banks of the canal (or wild berries) instead of a book; and she will not fling them in the fall. This all can very well be omitted.[70]

Curiously enough, a small piece by Kierkegaard did find its way into the final version of Howitt's English translation of *Hertha*, although it was not from his *Øjeblikket* articles. It came from a short tract entitled "This Must Be Said; So Let It Now Be Said" that Kierkegaard published on May 16, 1855. The Swedish edition substitutes an extract from J. O. Wallin's "The Angel of Death" in place of the Kierkegaard. In the English version, however, Hertha is handed "a little printed tract" by the gentleman she meets on the boat during her journey to Trollhätta. She reads a few paragraphs from the tract depicting the inner torments of a suffering Christian soul.[71] Then the narrator continues:

> Hertha did not inquire by whom this heart-rending confession was made; but she felt that a combating and suffering heart throbbed here in unison with her own, embittered, bleeding, loving, and still, though as in the midst of the flames, seeking to lay hold upon God; and she felt less solitary in the world.[72]

Howitt indicates in a footnote that Kierkegaard is the author of the tract, and erroneously ascribes it to his *The Moment (Øjeblikket)* set of articles.

---

70. The letter is quoted in Greta Wieselgren, *Fredrika Bremer och Verkligheten: Romanen Herthas tillblivelse* (Stockholm: Norstedt, 1978), pp. 198–99. Bremer terminated the letter to Howitt about the Kierkegaard fragment with the following: "I am sure you would translate them beautifully. But the thing is not of importance" (p. 199). For a detailed discussion of Kierkegaard's place in Bremer's *Hertha*, see in Wieselgren's book the whole of chapter 4, entitled "Fredrika Bremer och Sören Kierkegaard." Apparently Klara Johanson, the editor of Bremer's correspondence, did not have access to all of Bremer's letters to Mary Howitt, but fortunately Howitt preserved them, and Wieselgren uses them to follow Bremer's completion of *Hertha* step by step and to outline the many changes she made during the last phase of composition.

71. Fredrika Bremer, *Hertha*, trans. Mary Howitt (New York, 1856), pp. 241–42. The full text in English translation of the Kierkegaard tract from which the excerpt translated by Howitt comes can be found in Walter Lowrie's translation of Kierkegaard's last polemical articles against the Danish Lutheran Church and other related writings, which Lowrie published under his chosen title, "Attack upon 'Christendom.' " See Søren Kierkegaard, *Attack upon "Christendom,"* translated with introduction and notes by Walter Lowrie (Princeton: Princeton University Press, 1944), pp. 63–65. For more on this Kierkegaard excerpt and its absence from the 1856 German edition of *Hertha*, see Karin Carsten Montén, "Zur Rezeptionsgeschichte Fredrika Bremers in Deutschland," in *Scripta Minora*, ed. Berta Stjernquist (Lund, 1976), pp. 57–58.

72. *Hertha*, pp. 242–43.

A little later, and again in violation of Bremer's wishes as expressed in the March 27 letter, Howitt includes in her translation the scene of Hertha tossing the Kierkegaard tract in the waterfall:

> When the steamer burst forward through the locks of Trollhätta on its way into the beautiful river, Hertha was sitting alone on Gull, or Gold Island, with the thundering falls roaring around her, and the words of Kirkegaard [*sic*] in her hand. . . . The words of Kirkegaard [*sic*] no longer consoled her. The spirit which spoke to her in them was too much absorbed by the combat, had not yet passed victoriously through it. In the dark tumultuous state of mind in which she then was, she threw the printed tract into the foaming waters. It whirled round for a moment, sank, and vanished from sight. How beautiful to sink thus, to vanish in the cool depths, and forget, and rest;—the thundering, whirling waters would be heard there no longer![73]

Once again, thanks to Mary Howitt—and to Fredrika Bremer indirectly and unintentionally—we encounter another first in the unfolding story of Kierkegaard's early reception beyond Denmark: the appearance in English translation, and in a rather unlikely context, of his name and a snippet of his writing as far back as 1856. Admittedly, its stimulation of any serious interest in Kierkegaard in the English-speaking world at the time was utterly negligible.

Hertha caused a sensation in Sweden during its first year and led to much debate about women's rights. Although its effect on actual legislation was almost nil, it was the first novel of its kind in the history of Swedish literature. Bremer's vacillation with respect to Kierkegaard's relevance for the views she was setting forth in *Hertha,* and her ultimate rejection of him, show that, notwithstanding her interest in his last religious writings, she felt their usefulness for the central preoccupation of her book was minimal. Some have suggested that her attitude toward Kierkegaard, both in her book *Lif i Norden* and in her deliberate omission of his passages from the *Hertha* manuscript, far from being dictated by revenge for his refusal to see her in 1849, were the result of her disagreement with his position on women as gleaned from several of his books.[74]

---

73. Ibid., pp. 244–45.
74. See, for example, G. Wieselgren, *Fredrika Bremer och Verkligheten,* p. 208, where the suggestion is made that Hertha's character and development were intended to be a counterattack on what Bremer perceived as a misogynistic depiction of women by Kierkegaard in *Either/Or* and *Stages on Life's Way*. This argument is developed at length in

In fact Kierkegaard was very sceptical about the emancipation of women, which had begun to emerge as a social issue in his day. Judge William of *Either/Or*, volume II (1843), rejects emancipation for women unequivocally. After declaring that woman's task is within finitude while man chases after the infinite, he adds:

> But because woman thus explains the finite in this way, she is man's deepest life, but a life that is supposed to be hidden and secret, as the life of the root always is. That is why I hate all that detestable rhetoric about the emancipation of women. God forbid that it may ever happen. I cannot tell you with what pain the thought can pierce my soul, nor what passionate indignation, what hate, I harbor toward anyone who dares to express such ideas.[75]

These are powerful words, and according to Gregor Malantschuk the position taken by the conservative pseudonymous Judge on women, whether in relation to emancipation or marriage or equality, mirrors that of Kierkegaard in real life.[76] With the passing of years Kierkegaard's views of women only increased in their polemical nature, and the sharpness of their sarcasm became more acute. As he concealed himself deeper in his own seclusion and geared up for the fight with the Church, Kierkegaard grew even less tolerant toward women. "But it is precisely from this plane of the solitary hermit that Kierkegaard now looks not only at pastors but also at women," says Malantschuk.[77]

Bremer's overriding concern in the 1850s was with the patriarchal order of society and its adverse effects on the status of women. She could not possibly accept the position advocated by Kierkegaard's Judge William. Although Hertha's religious development is vaguely suggestive of a progression through Kierkegaard-like stages, her entire personality was intended by Bremer as a defiant protest against precisely those views on women set forth by the Judge. One reason she attained such a good friendship and smooth working relationship with Mary Howitt was that

---

Wieselgren's book. It would be interesting to know just how much Kierkegaard Bremer did read, and whether, for instance, she was familiar with his earliest publication, a satirical article on the emancipation of women published in December 1834 in *Kjøbenhavns flyvende Post* (*SV*, XIII, pp. 11–13).

75. Søren Kierkegaard, *Either/Or*, vol. II (*KW*, IV), ed. and trans. Howard V. Hong and Edna H. Hong (Princeton: Princeton University Press, 1987), p. 311.

76. Gregor Malantschuk, *The Controversial Kierkegaard*, pp. 47–48. For an insightful analysis of Kierkegaard's attitude toward women, see all of Malantschuk's third chapter, pp. 37–61.

77. Ibid., p. 59.

they both agreed on women's rights.[78] Bremer's authentic, though passing, interest in Kierkegaard's *Øjeblikket* in 1855 did not deflect her from her main purpose of improving women's lot in the world, starting with her own country. Everything, including any spiritual nourishment Kierkegaard could offer, was harnessed by her to this end.

One woman who had greater reason than Fredrika Bremer to be personally offended by Kierkegaard was the Norwegian novelist Camilla Collett (1813-95), also a feminist. While in Copenhagen in 1852, she tried to see Kierkegaard by actually visiting his house. She was told at the door by the servant that he was not in, but as she emerged into the street she chanced to glance up at one of the windows and to her surprise saw Kierkegaard standing there with a sarcastic smile looking back down at her.[79]

Collett was the daughter of Nicolai Wergeland and the sister of the romantic and unconventional Norwegian poet Henrik Wergeland (1808-45). She fell madly in love with the main literary rival of her brother, J. S. Welhaven (1807-73), but was repeatedly rejected by him. Her infatuation created an odd situation for her brother, who became locked in a vigorous literary feud with the more rational Welhaven in the early 1830s. Their confrontation was widely felt throughout literary circles in Norway, and had repercussions in Denmark.

In 1839 Camilla Wergeland became engaged to Peter Jonas Collett, a professor of jurisprudence whom she respected but could not really love. He wrote her a letter in July 1843 in which he said he intended to get hold of Kierkegaard's *Either/Or*, which he described as a book that entirely stirs up something deep in the emotions.[80] This may have been the first time that Camilla heard of Kierkegaard. She had aspirations to become a writer, for she believed in women's intellectual equality with men. Like many other educated Norwegians in her generation—usually men—

---

78. They were both religious also, which strengthened their bond. In later life, Mary Howitt moved to Rome and eventually converted to Catholicism in the spring of 1882, six years before her death. See Amice Lee, *Laurels and Rosemary*, p. 314.

79. Harald Beyer, "Søren Kierkegaards betydning for Norsk Aandsliv," in *EDDA: Nordisk Tidsskrift for Litteraturforskning*, ed. Gerhard Gran and Francis Bull, vol. 19, 10th year, copy 1 (Christiania, 1923), p. 4. For another account of the visit and rebuff see Clara Bergsøe, *Camilla Collett, et livsbillede* (Copenhagen, 1902), p. 92. Bergsøe was a Danish friend of Collett. See also Sejer Kühle, "Sören Kierkegaard und die Frauen," in *Orbis Litterarum* 10 (1955), pp. 127-28.

80. Ellisiv Steen, *Diktning og Virkelighet: En Studie i Camilla Colletts Forfatterskap* (Oslo: Gyldendal, 1947), pp. 159-60.

she desired to travel to Copenhagen, the nineteenth-century cultural hub of Scandinavia, to become personally acquainted with as many of the literary personalities there as possible. This she did in 1852, and managed to meet with the poet Christian Winther (1796–1876) and with the celebrated J. L. Heiberg. She also saw Orla Lehmann, an old friend of hers from youth and a man whom Kierkegaard despised. It was in response to attacks by the liberal Lehmann that Kierkegaard published some of his earliest newspaper articles during his university days in the 1830s. Finally, she was outmaneuvered in her attempt to meet Kierkegaard himself.[81]

Collett too, like Bremer, was preoccupied with the women question as it related to conditions in Norway, and in 1854, around the time when Bremer was formulating strategies for *Hertha,* Collett was already busy at work on a novel which she published anonymously in Norway the following year.[82] *Amtmandens Døtre* (The governor's daughters) embodied all the author's frustrations as a woman living in a male-dominated Norwegian society. The realism was so stark that at first the book was denounced as ugly, but eventually it achieved the recognition it deserved and came to occupy an important place in Norwegian feminist literature.[83]

There is no doubt that Collett read some Kierkegaard and found it to be stimulating, although how much she read is unclear. In *Amtmandens Døtre* one of the main characters, Margrethe, keeps a diary which sounds very much like something that Cordelia in "The Diary of a Seducer" could have written, had Kierkegaard intended to give us a glimpse into her personal thoughts. What enhances the similarities is the presence in the story of a character, Georg Cold, who in many respects resembles Johannes the Seducer. And Cold also writes strange and "seductive" letters to Margrethe. In one of them Cold unabashedly describes to Margrethe the young women he has courted. Here one can detect unmistakable echoes of Welhaven's poem "Den første Kjærlighed" (The first love),

---

81. Ibid., p. 230.
82. A second edition, also anonymous, was published in Copenhagen by Gyldendal in 1860. Most Norwegian books during this period were published in Copenhagen as well, which signified the close literary relationship between Norway and its politically and culturally dominant neighbor, Denmark. See P. M. Mitchell, *A History of Danish Literature,* 2d ed. (New York: Kraus-Thomson Organization, 1971), p. 172.
83. B. J. Hovde, *The Scandinavian Countries, 1720–1865: The Rise of the Middle Classes* in 2 volumes (Boston: Chapman and Grimes, 1943), vol. II, pp. 686–87. For a sampling of newspaper reviews of the book from the period and other primary and secondary sources see Sigurd Aa. Aarnes, *Søkelys på Amtmandens Døtre* (Oslo: Universitetsforlag, 1977).

and Kierkegaard's "Diary of a Seducer" from *Either/Or,* volume I.[84] Margrethe, in her own character, combines elements from Cordelia, Marie Beaumarchais, and Margaret, three of Kierkegaard's women in *Either/Or.*[85] There appears to have been a conscious attempt on Collett's part to borrow from this work by Kierkegaard and even to imitate his style in certain places.

If indeed Collett had the story of Kierkegaard's seducer in mind as she wrote *Amtmandens Døtre*—and admittedly this is only a hypothesis, because she had ample material to draw on from her personal experience with disappointed love—then she would be the first in a long line of female writers to have reacted creatively to the issues posed by that strangely alluring figure in the Kierkegaardian gallery: Johannes the Seducer. The line stretches all the way into the twentieth century, where its most celebrated representative would be Isak Dinesen (Karen Blixen) (1885-1962), the writer and African traveler, who was influenced by her fellow Dane Kierkegaard and wrote a little story called *Ehrengard* that some have viewed as the woman's response to Kierkegaard's "Diary of a Seducer." It must be stressed that in Camilla Collett any connection stems from an unproven assumption, based in turn merely on a few clues and suggestive parallels. Nowhere in her entire corpus does Collett mention Kierkegaard by name.

The similarities between Collett's relation to Kierkegaard and Bremer's, if any are to be found, would be exclusively in the issue of women's emancipation. This was the primary focus for both as pioneers of female emancipation in their respective countries. Kierkegaard's views on women aroused interest in each, but he did not provide them with a chance to discuss and perhaps air their criticisms in person. The result was that their interest in Kierkegaard inevitably decreased with time as they became more absorbed in women's issues, and any traces of Kierkegaardian ideas in a couple of their novels were minimal and very indirect. They differed, however, in their attitudes to Kierkegaard's religious writ-

---

84. See Ellisiv Steen, *Diktning og Virkelighet,* p. 291. Collett's fascination with Welhaven's character apparently did not wane after she was rejected by him and went on to marry the conventional Peter Jonas. She may very well have come to regard Welhaven as a kind of living representative of Kierkegaard's seducer.

85. Valborg Erichsen, "Søren Kierkegaards betydning for Norsk Aandsliv," in *EDDA,* vol. 19, 10th year, copy 2 (Christiania, 1923), p. 277. Marie Beaumarchais and Margaret are two of the three women discussed by Kierkegaard in the section entitled "Shadowgraphs" in *Either/Or,* vol. I.

ings, with Collett remaining virtually impervious to any influence from that direction,[86] while Bremer took a more serious look at the controversy with the Church. On the whole Bremer and Collett have been regarded as transitional figures in the history of Scandinavian literature, forerunners of the realism of the 1870s and 1880s. Their involvement with the topical social issues that constituted the themes of their stories contributed to the further distancing of the Scandinavian novel from the romanticism of the early nineteenth century. Kierkegaard was for them at best a source of passing inspiration, and on the women question a negative stimulus.

The early 1850s saw a few more noteworthy instances of the dissemination of Kierkegaard's ideas and reputation outside the borders of Denmark. In the summer of 1850 another article in German by A. F. Beck appeared in the *Nordisches Telegraph,* signed only "B". It was just two pages long, and had the title "Martensen und Kierkegaard."[87] It discussed Martensen's *Dogmatik* of 1849 and Kierkegaard's criticisms of it. Danish-German systematic theology, deriving from Hegel and represented in Denmark by Martensen, had been entrenching itself in the universities at the time and had become a favorite target of Kierkegaard's attacks.

The year 1851 brought two unrelated developments in the reception of Kierkegaard, and on two separate continents. In Sweden, Albert Theodor Lysander (1822–90), a professor of Latin in Lund, published an article in *Tidskrift för Litteratur* entitled "Sören Kierkegaard, Litterärhistorisk teckning" [Søren Kierkegaard, a literary-historical sketch].[88] Lysander was an expert on Swedish literary history and an all-round man of culture as well. He made a careful study of Kierkegaard's writings and also read Sturzen-Becker's brief treatment of him in *Hinsidan Sundet.* Like Sturzen-Becker he believed that the important thing was to understand the Kierkegaard of the works and not Kierkegaard "the stroller" ("den promenerande"), presumably a reference to popular perceptions of Kierkegaard as he appeared to people on his famous habitual walks caricatured in the *Corsair.*[89] Consequently, Lysander's analysis avoided irrelevant gossipy details and concentrated on Kierkegaard's ideas. This in itself marked a new departure and an important step in the direction of serious Kierkegaard scholarship. Although Lysander aimed to present a balanced

---

86. Erichsen, "Søren Kierkegaards betydning," p. 279.
87. *Nordisches Telegraph,* II, no. 89 (June 14, 1850), pp. 1095-96.
88. *Tidskrift för Litteratur,* ed. C. F. Bergstedt, no. 10 (Uppsala, 1851), pp. 227-52.
89. Sjöstedt, *Søren Kierkegaard och Svensk Litteratur,* p. 20. On Lysander see pages 19-25 in Sjöstedt.

picture of Kierkegaard's works as a whole, his main focus was on *Practice in Christianity* of the previous year. He provided a short biographical sketch of Kierkegaard and plunged straight into the works, discussing among other things Kierkegaard's relation to Martensen. In later years Lysander made several references to Kierkegaard in various essays on literary criticism.

Thousands of miles away from Lund in the frontier parsonage at Spring Prairie, Columbia County, Wisconsin, someone else was reading Kierkegaard in 1851 . . . and writing about him too! This was Linka Keyser Preus (1829-80), the wife of a Norwegian emigrant pastor named Herman Amberg Preus (1825-94). He became the pioneer pastor at Spring Prairie in 1851, and later, in 1862, the president of the Norwegian Synod. Linka was born Caroline Dorothea Margrethe in Christiansand, Norway, and became motherless at the age of ten. Her father was a pastor and subsequently a theology professor at the University of Christiania. He died seven years after his wife, leaving Linka an orphan at seventeen. Her grandmother took her and five other sisters into her home. Eventually she married Herman Preus, who in 1851 was summoned by J. W. C. Dietrichson (1815-83), the pastor of the Norwegian immigrant community at Koshkonong, Wisconsin, to come from Norway and serve the parsonage at Spring Prairie. He and his wife Linka made the transatlantic crossing in the same year.[90]

Herman Preus was among the tens of thousands of Norwegian immigrants to the United States in the nineteenth century. They left Norway seeking better economic opportunities in the New World and fleeing political and religious persecution at home. They were mostly of lower-class rural stock, namely farmers. Their attachment to their native homeland remained great, and consequently they were torn between the lure of opportunity and freedom across the ocean and their roots in Norway. Many returned to Norway later, and some went back to America for a second time. Religiously they were mostly followers of the Norwegian pietist revivalist Hans Nielsen Hauge (1771-1824), the Norwegian counterpart of Grundtvig in the sense that, as Grundtvig did for Denmark, he left a lasting imprint on Norwegian spirituality, especially among the

---

90. See Caroline Dorothea Margrethe (Keyser) Preus, *Linka's Diary: On Land and Sea, 1845-1864,* trans. and ed. Johan Carl Keyser Preus and his wife Diderikke Margrethe, née Brandt (Minneapolis: Augsburg Publishing House, 1952), p. viii of the foreword, and p. xii of the introduction.

country peasants. Because of his pietistic orientation, he got into trouble with the official Lutheran Church authorities and his followers, known as Haugians, suffered many hardships as a result. This was one factor contributing to the steady stream of Norwegian emigration to America.

The church authorities in Norway, while they were opposed to emigration and tried to dissuade people from leaving, soon realized that there was religious chaos in the American wilderness and on the Midwestern prairies. Pastors were dispatched to minister to budding parishes and to try to maintain some order, both administratively and doctrinally. One of these was Dietrichson, who had strong Grundtvigian leanings and became the first Norwegian-trained pastor to arrive in 1844 in Koshkonong. The task awaiting him was not easy since there were many deep divisions in the community; nevertheless, he managed to struggle along and organize the pioneer parishes in Wisconsin and Illinois. In 1850 he wrote to his friend Herman Preus in Norway requesting that he come to Wisconsin and discharge his pastoral duties.[91]

Linka began keeping a diary in 1845. To it she committed her intimate reflections during times of loneliness. Contained in her diary are several references to Kierkegaard, whom she read off and on over the years. Though fascinating, this is not necessarily surprising, because a number of clergymen throughout Scandinavia in the mid-nineteenth century had in their private libraries copies of Kierkegaard's works, particularly his devotional writings (i.e. his *Upbuilding Discourses*). Many of them who emigrated to America took their libraries with them and in that way Kierkegaard was transported across the ocean, although when he reached the other side he still lacked active spokesmen in the New World for years to come.[92] Clergymen of the official Church avoided his works for a long time following his stormy break with the Church in 1855.

---

91. The literature on Norwegian emigration to the United States is sizable and growing rapidly. As examples see Arlow W. Andersen, *The Norwegian-Americans* (Boston: Twayne Publishers, 1975); Nicholas Tavuchis, *Pastors and Immigrants: The Role of a Religious Elite in the Absorption of Norwegian Immigrants* (The Hague: Nijhoff, 1963), esp. pp. 12–37; and E. Clifford Nelson, ed., *A Pioneer Churchman: J. W. C. Dietrichson in Wisconsin, 1844–1850*, trans. Malcolm Rosholt and Harris E. Kaasa (New York: Norwegian-American Historical Association by Twayne Publishers, 1973), esp. the introduction.

92. The existence of references to Kierkegaard in Linka's diary is the kind of proof Lewis A. Lawson would have needed to support his guess that Kierkegaard had made it across the Atlantic in the 1850s. Lawson writes: "No doubt there were Danes who brought Kierkegaard's works with them when they settled in Wisconsin or Minnesota or Iowa, but I know of no reference in a diary or a letter to confirm my speculation." See Lawson's

These facts render the few references to Kierkegaard in Linka's diary all the more valuable. She stopped writing the diary in 1864 because she became too preoccupied with housework, her family, and extensive correspondence with friends in Norway.[93] The diary remained untranslated and unpublished for a hundred years, and was finally edited, translated, and sent for publication in 1952 by Linka's grandson. In one entry written on New Year's Day, 1851, in Fredrikshald, Linka describes how she and Herman first learned that they were being called to America. They were reading in Kierkegaard[94] when the letter from Dietrichson arrived:

> This forenoon I went to church, and after our return Herman read us a funeral sermon by Kierkegaard. During the reading, a letter was brought in—for Herman—but neither he nor the rest of us would allow ourselves to be disturbed—apparently, perhaps I should add, as far as Herman and I were concerned. It did distract both of us, as the letter was of great importance to us. Finally the reading was at an end, and Herman and I took hold of the letter—and what a New Year's gift the Giver of all good gifts had sent us! These lines from Dietrichson brought to Herman a letter of call to become the minister at Spring Prairie.[95]

At the time Linka and Herman had not yet married. They did marry just before departing for America. On April 17, 1851 (Maundy Thursday), Linka wrote:

> A recent letter from Herman informs me that on Palm Sunday, April 13, our bans were published for the first time in the church at Halden. Perhaps in three weeks I shall be Herman's wife. My resolutions to be a good wife are of the best, according to my judgment—O God, help me to carry them

---

article: "Small Talk on the 'Melancholy Dane' in America," in *The Legacy and Interpretation of Kierkegaard,* in *Bibliotheca Kierkegaardiana,* vol. 8 (1981), pp. 178–79. It is interesting that while in America Fredrika Bremer visited a Swedish immigrant colony at Pine Lake, Wisconsin, in 1851, right around the time when Linka and her husband were settling in Spring Prairie. There Bremer apparently read aloud to the people from H. C. Andersen's "The Fir Tree." See E. Hude, *Fredrika Bremer,* p. 248. There was no comparable messenger of Kierkegaardiana to be found trumpeting Kierkegaard anywhere in the New World at this time.

93. *Linka's Diary,* postscript, p. 277.

94. This was before Kierkegaard's rupture with the Church and while he was still quoted by pastors on particular occasions. His brother Peter, who later became a bishop, never had a problem in this respect. We know from the diary, for instance, that Herman Preus possessed a copy of P. C. Kierkegaard's 1841 and 1842 *Nordisk Tidskrift for Christelig Theologi,* which he edited jointly with Th. W. Oldenburg.

95. *Linka's Diary,* p. 116.

through! In mentioning the word "resolution", I am reminded of an address by Kierkegaard which I read today. It discussed the subject *Resolutions,* how to preserve one's soul in patience, and how a resolution springing from a "preserved soul" shall be carried out through patience. I did not get to church today, the roads were too muddy to walk, and I would not ask for a horse.— Herman, have you preached in Halden today?—Good Night.[96]

On the ship during the voyage to America, Linka was more specific about a particular book by Kierkegaard. She wrote this on May 2, 1851:

> Today we arrived in Halden. . . . When I no longer could see Christiania and the surrounding places I love so well, when I had said fare-thee-well to everything dear to me in those parts, I joined in the conversation of my fellow travelers, and shared their cheerfulness, not indeed within myself, but rather on the surface. . . . As we were passing Næsodden, I wrote [Pastor Fredrik Waldemar] Hvoslef asking him to accept a copy of Kierkegaard's *Works of Love* as a remembrance of me and my English lessons. Otherwise the time was spent in conversation, knitting and reading.[97]

The ship arrived in New York in mid-July, and after a few days there Linka and Herman proceeded to Wisconsin. The following winter, when they had settled in their new surroundings, Linka was still reading in Kierkegaard:

> Sunday, February 1, 1852. . . . This morning I have read a great deal in Kierkegaard's *Works of Love.* I am sure I do not understand one half of what he says, but I do grasp enough so that the book has aroused within me an intense interest. I catch some of it, and it seems to adhere to my cranium. I might compare myself to a twirling-stick used in stirring up a velvety butter-pudding: a little butter sticks to it.[98]

Linka was not an exceptionally gifted writer—she lacked the subtlety and sophistication of the urbane Fredrika Bremer and Camilla Collett. The feminist issues in which they were actively engaged would not have interested her in the least. She was content with the simple life of a pastor's wife, and her diary radiates the values of solid country folk: simplicity, honesty, transparency, and sincerity. She read in Kierkegaard's devotional

---

96. Ibid., p. 121. As preparation for her own wedding, could Linka have been reading Kierkegaard's discourse entitled "On the Occasion of a Wedding," in which he discusses the spiritual significance for both partners of life-long resolutions? See Søren Kierkegaard, *Three Discourses on Imagined Occasions* (*KW*, X), ed. and trans. Howard V. Hong and Edna H. Hong (Princeton: Princeton University Press, 1993), pp. 41–68.

97. *Linka's Diary,* p. 126.   98. Ibid., p. 211.

writings as a believer would read any devotional literature: with the humility and openness of real faith. Perhaps had she read some of the more controversial pseudonymous works of Kierkegaard, in particular his views on women, her attitude might have been altered. But one suspects that even then Linka would not have metamorphosed into a feminist activist; in her simplicity she would probably have been able to penetrate Kierkegaard's secrets better than many a cultured and socially aware woman.

The point of dwelling on Linka is to demonstrate a whole new dimension of Kierkegaard's reception hitherto unexplored: the presence and influence of Kierkegaard among the immigrant Scandinavian colonies on the American prairies.[99]

Back in Europe a book of travels appeared in 1852 in London called *Sixteen Months in the Danish Isles*. The author was a certain Andrew Hamilton, a young Scotsman, who had stayed in Denmark sixteen months in 1849–51 and traveled all over the peninsula. While there he learned to read and speak Danish and associated daily with artists, poets, writers, professors, and clergymen.[100]

Hamilton observed that the lovely tree-lined streets and narrow lanes of Copenhagen lent themselves to promenading all over the city.[101] Like the Danes, he did a lot of walking around Copenhagen and predictably came across Kierkegaard. Their frequent encounters provided Hamilton with many opportunities to observe Kierkegaard closely:

> The fact is *he walks about town all day,* and generally in some person's company; only in the evening does he write and read. When walking, he is very communicative, and at the same time manages to draw everything out of his companion that is likely to be profitable to himself. I do not know him. I saw him almost daily in the streets, and when he was alone I often felt much inclined to accost him, but never put it into execution. I was told his 'talk' was very fine. Could I have enjoyed it, without the feeling that I was myself being mercilessly pumped and sifted, I should have liked very much.[102]

---

99. The story of Kierkegaard's dormant years in nineteenth-century America has yet to be written. I am indebted to Edna H. Hong of the Kierkegaard Library at St. Olaf College for bringing *Linka's Diary* to my attention. Any serious research into this fascinating side of the Kierkegaard reception must inevitably lead one to the Norwegian-American Archives at St. Olaf College in Northfield, Minnesota, and to Luther College in Decorah, Iowa, as well as to other Scandinavian-American centers and communities in the Midwest.

100. Villads Christensen, *Peripatetikeren Søren Kierkegaard* (Copenhagen: Graabrodre Torvs Forlag, 1965), p. 9.

101. Ibid., p. 10.

102. Andrew Hamilton, *Sixteen Months in the Danish Isles,* vol. II (London, 1852), pp. 269–70. See also Christensen, *Peripatetikeren,* p. 12.

Kierkegaard was presumably oblivious to Hamilton's existence. Although the *Corsair* had effectively deprived him of interaction with the common folk, he continued to take his cherished walks in the city silently by himself, or with a select companion. Hamilton had obviously read some of Kierkegaard's works, because he offers a description of the style of writing: "He [Kierkegaard] writes at times with an unearthly beauty, but too often with an exaggerated display of logic that disgusts the public."[103] Hamilton also mentions by name *Works of Love, Either/Or,* and *The Sickness unto Death.*[104] His amusing impressions of Kierkegaard were summed up in the following perceptive and sobering statement: "There is no Danish writer more in earnest than he, yet there is no one in whose way stand more things to prevent his becoming popular."[105]

Who then was this Andrew Hamilton? From the British embassy, the Royal Archives, and the Royal Library in Copenhagen, the scholar Villads Christensen managed to find out that Hamilton was born on December 15, 1826, as the youngest son of the Scottish pastor William Hamilton and his wife Jane. In the Royal Library there are six letters from Hamilton to various people, including one to H. C. Andersen and one to Bishop J. P. Mynster. Hamilton had dedicated his book to Mynster and wrote to him on March 18, 1852, expressing his thanks for the bishop's approval of the dedication.[106] Hamilton appears to have returned to Copenhagen in 1855 for a brief visit, but concerning his later fate no information is available.

Hamilton's sketch of Kierkegaard has significance not only because it was the earliest direct and independent assessment in English, coinciding as it did with the brief second-hand reference in the Howitts' survey of Scandinavian literature. It also presented Kierkegaard to the English-speaking world as the Danish peripatetic philosopher.[107] Hamilton pragmatically followed a middle course between the *Corsair*'s malicious exploitation of Kierkegaard's walking habits and idiosyncracies and the avoidance of the subject altogether by Lysander and Sturzen-Becker. For Hamilton, Kierkegaard was indeed "Kierkegaard the stroller," as Lysander put it; and he simply chose to watch him walk.

103. Hamilton, *Sixteen Months*, p. 269.   104. Ibid.
105. Ibid.
106. V. Christensen, *Peripatetikeren*, pp. 49–50.
107. Ibid., p. 54.

3 The *Kirkekampen* and Its Immediate Aftermath

Seeds of "Misreception"

To a significant degree the history of the Lutheran Church in nineteenth-century Denmark was determined by an interplay between two opposing currents: popular pietism and established ecclesiastical authority. Kierkegaard's attitude toward this Church and the consequences of his open attack on it occupy a pivotal place, both in the history of his own reception and in the broader framework of modern Scandinavian church history.

Pietism began in eighteenth-century Germany as a Protestant religious movement stressing the practice of godliness and generally laying greater emphasis than traditional Lutheranism on the need for good works. It spread northwards into Scandinavia in the late eighteenth century as the rationalism of the Enlightenment anchored itself more firmly in central Europe. The seat of Nordic pietism became Norway, where the movement rallied around the charismatic revivalist preacher H. N. Hauge. The Haugians rejected the notion of an organized clergy and were repeatedly persecuted by the official Church authorities. As a result, many chose to emigrate to the New World.¹ For those who opted to remain behind, persecution, far from dampening their zeal, caused them to assert more forcefully their rugged Nordic individualism, further enhanced by the harsh climate and difficult geography of Norway. People tended to cluster in small isolated groups interspersed among the valleys and fjords, a situation which bred a rigorous form of pietism with a strong scriptural emphasis. As people struggled with the elements, they also battled one another's popular forms of religion, and consequently many localized revivals sprang up.

In Sweden the Lutheran Church was more centralized and there was less room for popular expressions of individual piety. Although Nordic Lutheranism was on the whole not as clerical and intellectual as its counterpart in Germany, the laity played an even less active role in the affairs of the Swedish church than in Norway.

Denmark occupied a middle ground ecclesiastically between the radical individualism of Norway and the hierarchical structure of Sweden. The community, through the parish, represented the center of religious life in Denmark. The Danish Lutheran Church, however, was a state-Church, that is, its clergy received a government salary and it was financed by a special tax, with a government minister—the cultus minister—overseeing its affairs. In order to preserve one's rights as a Danish citizen in the first half of the nineteenth century, one had to belong to the state-Church. Even those Danes who had no faith were bound to the Church and went through its religious functions: baptism, confirmation, communion, marriage, and burial.²

A revival in the Danish Lutheran Church began to occur at the outset of the nineteenth century; in time it combined elements of official reform from the top with popular renewal from below. Yet these two tendencies were not always in harmony with each other. The reaction against the pantheism of romanticism was best exemplified by H. Steffens's lectures in 1802-3, in which he assailed the romantics for having diverted the focus of religion from moral life and the New Testament to an "immediate feeling of the presence of the eternal metaphysical world." The reaction

---

1. It is to the ranks of these Norwegian settlers that Linka and Herman Preus belonged; see Chapter 2 above.

2. J. Oskar Andersen, *Survey of the History of the Church in Denmark* (Copenhagen: O. Lohse, 1930), p. 42.

was later continued with the theology of N. F. S. Grundtvig. Bishop J. P. Mynster (1775-1854) in the 1840s carried on the revival from within the ecclesiastical establishment and was concerned with preserving the position of the clergy in the official state-Church. He was not very keen about the beginnings of a popular, parish-centered movement that was to coalesce around Grundtvig and challenge the privileges of the clergy in the Church.[3]

By the mid-nineteenth century the Danish Lutheran Church was passing through a period of turmoil the core of which was a struggle between Grundtvigianism and the ecclesiastical authorities.[4] Much fragmentation resulted, with many new "parties," "societies," and "trends" cropping up and deepening the general discord. The disputes now revolved around specific theological questions such as infant baptism and the place of the Church and its clergy in Christian life.

After the 1848 upheavals in Europe, which quickened the pace of every ongoing movement of a revivalistic or liberating character, a new and more liberal era set in. In Denmark the Grundtvigian revival received a boost as did demands for political and social freedom. Absolutism ended and a "Constitution" was introduced. A law was enacted the following year that came to be called the great liberalizing law [*Grundloven*] of 1849. This law granted greater freedom to the Church and to religious schools, but at the same time it legally established the bond between the Church and the state by declaring that "the evangelical Lutheran Church as the national church of Denmark [*Folkekirken*] shall be supported by the state."[5] Among the denominations that breathed easier in Denmark was Catholicism, and particularly the Jesuit order. Soon, however, a new friction was added to the inter-Protestant divisions, namely that between a more active Catholicism and the various Protestant groupings already vying for preeminence.[6]

It is against this background that Kierkegaard's audacious open critique of the established Lutheran state-Church in Denmark ought to be

---

3. Ibid., pp. 44-47.
4. The latter were known as the "Scripture-theologians"; see ibid., pp. 56ff.
5. Ibid., p. 57. Kierkegaard's hated "Christendom" now became a formally and legally sanctioned entity.
6. See Hal Koch and Bjørn Kornerup, eds., *Den Danske Kirkes Historie* [8 volumes], vol. VII (Copenhagen: Gyldendalske Boghandel, 1958), pp. 14-20, the section entitled "Grundloven og Kirken."

viewed. And this is also the milieu from which emerged the diverse reactions to his attack, many of which appeared in the form of articles in the press during the last months of his life and continued in the immediate years following his death.

Kierkegaard preferred to define his role from the start as that of a "corrective," and he actually detested the approach of the "zealous" reformers of his period, including Grundtvig, with his secure passionless faith and his compromises with the state-Church.[7] Indeed Grundtvig, being descended from an old Danish family of pastors, was naturally predisposed toward accepting the idea of a collective spiritual life within the Church, even though his relations with both Mynster and Martensen were not very good.[8] His movement was a nationalistic one within the ecclesiastical domain and generated much communal appeal. Kierkegaard was very critical of Grundtvig's "people's church" and his "objectified" Christianity: ". . . we have tried to abolish or supplant what is truly Christian—namely, that Christianity is related to the single individual [*den Enkelte*]—and thus we have produced a lower state of religion, 'national religion and a national God,' corresponding to paganism and Judaism."[9] That Kierkegaard had Grundtvig in mind when writing this is all but certain.

For Kierkegaard the corrective of the "single individual" was necessary as a dialectical counterbalance to "the established" [*det bestaaende*], and had to go to the opposite extreme from what the establishment stood for in order to fulfill its purpose as corrective: "The person who is to provide the 'corrective' must study the weak sides of the established scrupulously and penetratingly and then one-sidedly present the opposite—with expert one-sidedness."[10] Yet according to Kierkegaard, once the corrective begins to take on some of the features of the established order that it set out

---

7. See Howard A. Johnson's "Kierkegaard and the Church: A Supplement to the Translator's Introduction" in Søren Kierkegaard, *Attack upon "Christendom,"* trans. Walter Lowrie, p. xxiii. See also Ed. Lehmann, "Deux réformateurs du Protestantisme danois: Kierkegaard et Grundtvig" in *Révue d'Histoire et de Philosophie Religieuses* 11 (1931), pp. 499-500.

8. Lehmann, "Deux réformateurs," p. 502.

9. *JP* 2045 (X^5 A 97). For direct statements by Kierkegaard on his view of the absurdity of concepts like a "state-Church," a "folk church," and "Christian countries" see his *JP* 2057 (XI^1 A 190) and 4503 (XI^2 A 373) and 6932 (XI^2 A 206).

10. *JP* 6467 (X^1 A 640). The references in Kierkegaard's journals to his activity as a "corrective" are abundant; see as examples: *JP* 708 (X^4 A 15) and 710 (X^5 A 106).

to correct, it ceases to be the corrective and is itself transformed into that same established order.[11] This is what happened with Lutheranism in Kierkegaard's view: it ended by replacing the Catholic establishment with a new order instead of merely acting as corrective in its time. He was emphatic about this in his journals: ". . . what nonsense, what dishonesty, and what corruption Protestantism is—if it is supposed to be religion, to be Christianity, rather than a necessary corrective at a given time."[12] Kierkegaard therefore regarded his own reaction to the Danish state-Church as being conducted in an *authentically* Lutheran spirit—that of the corrective—against an increasingly "Catholic" Lutheranism.

None of Kierkegaard's contemporaries was in a position to grasp the complex nuances underlying his attack on "official Christianity." Those few who appeared to stand by him and defend his actions later proved disappointing in their sincerity and depth of comprehension. In fact the general shock and incredulity produced by his first article in *Fædrelandet* [The fatherland], which appeared on December 18, 1854, but which had actually been written ten months earlier, was a testimony to the superficiality and ignorance of a reading public who did not detect the obvious signs of Kierkegaard's displeasure with the ecclesiastical establishment expressed as early as 1850, and the radical direction his thought had been taking since then. No one had access to his private journals, where the background to the attack lay clearly delineated; but a careful reading of *Practice in Christianity* (begun in 1848 and published in 1850) would have revealed the author's sustained critique of certain basic concepts such as "established Christendom" and the "Church Triumphant" (i.e., the state-Church) that were to become the targets of his open assault four years later.[13] By "Christendom" Kierkegaard meant the modern phenom-

---

11. "Nothing is easier for the one providing the corrective than to add the other side; but then, right there, it ceases to be the corrective and itself becomes established order" *JP* 6467 (X^1 A 640).

12. *JP* 2763 (XI^1 A 198). See also *JP* 711 (XI^1 A 28), where Kierkegaard says Luther's message became the *status quo:* "Luther's emphasis is a corrective—but a corrective made into the normative, into the sum total, is *eo ipso* confusing in another generation (where that for which it was a corrective does not exist)." For an in-depth discussion of Kierkegaard's concept of "corrective" and its relation to Luther, see Per Lønning's excellent article, "Kierkegaard's 'Corrective'—a Corrective to Kierkegaardians?" in *Liber Academiæ Kierkegaardiensis Annuarius,* vols. II-IV, 1979-81, ed. Alessandro Cortese and Niels Thulstrup (Copenhagen, 1982), pp. 105-19.

13. As examples see Søren Kierkegaard, *Practice in Christianity (KW,* XX), ed. and trans. Howard V. Hong and Edna H. Hong (Princeton: Princeton University Press, 1991), pp. 35-36, 201-32, and 252-57. Kierkegaard's dialectic of "Church Triumphant" and

enon that witnesses Christianity in all its aspects, institutionally, clerically, even doctrinally, becoming "at home in" and "comfortable in" the world to such an extent that, in his view, it ceases to be authentic Christianity. The state-Church in Denmark, and more generally the modern liberal state, represented for Kierkegaard two external manifestations of this pervasive Christendom.[14]

The attack proper, coming as a culmination of a steady development in Kierkegaard's thinking rather than a sudden eccentric departure from the norm,[15] was brought into the open by Martensen's eulogy of the deceased Bishop Mynster on Sunday, February 5, 1854, two days before the burial. During the oration Martensen used the phrase "a genuine witness for the truth" [*Sandhedsvidne*] to describe Mynster; Kierkegaard was among those listening to Martensen. Although Mynster had been an old friend of the family, much admired by Kierkegaard's father, and a teacher of the young Søren at one time, he had in recent years come to embody for Kierkegaard the loathsome figure of worldliness attired in clerical apparel. For him now to hear Mynster called a witness for truth by another unappealing prelate was too much.

Quickly Kierkegaard wrote a scathing denunciation of Mynster but refrained from publishing it right away. He did not wish to impede Martensen's chances of succeeding Mynster in the bishopric, much as he disliked Martensen's Hegelian orientation and his brand of worldly self-satisfaction. Also, public attention during the coming months and especially in the summer of 1854 became concentrated on the growing opposition to A. S. Ørsted's government, which finally fell on December 12. Having already delayed publication, Kierkegaard now felt that a premature appearance of his article would not generate sufficient interest in his views. More importantly, Kierkegaard wished to plan his strategy for the

---

"Church Militant" distinctly echoes the Augustinian dichotomy of the Two Cities (see St. Augustine's *The City of God*), although a strict correlation would be inaccurate.

14. John W. Elrod, *Kierkegaard and Christendom*, p. 78. Elrod's analysis tends at times to place excessive emphasis on economic factors such as class conflict and the material benefits of privilege, power, and wealth accrued by bourgeois liberalism. Doubtless these were highly objectionable features of Christendom for Kierkegaard, but to concentrate on them as causes rather than outcomes of a deeper spiritual confusion runs the risk of cloaking Kierkegaard's revolt in quasi-Marxist garb. Kierkegaard's fundamental concerns were theological, and the root of the problem for him was a distortion of the true meaning and practice of Christianity in the modern world.

15. An "explosion of S. K.'s pent-up indignation," Lowrie calls it. See Walter Lowrie, *Kierkegaard*, p. 565.

attack carefully, and his journals from 1854 are brimming with entries which he later incorporated into several newspaper articles at the height of the attack.[16]

Why did Kierkegaard employ the very medium, the press, which had been so malicious toward him in the mid-1840s and for which he had reserved some of the harshest words in his journals,[17] in order to wage his battle against Christendom and the established Church? Precisely because he had come to appreciate from painful personal experience the immense power of the press in transmitting ideas and shaping opinion. The *Corsair*'s attacks and cheap quality of satire had given Kierkegaard a deep insight into the possibilities of the daily press for influencing the public. While under the impact of the *Corsair* affair, Kierkegaard in 1846 had written: "Together with the passionlessness and reflectiveness of the age, the abstraction 'the press' . . . gives rise to the abstraction's phantom, 'the public,' which is the real leveler."[18] The highly polemical nature of what he now intended to publish suited the chosen medium perfectly. He too, using the press, could play the same game and create his own phantom public.

His choice of *Fædrelandet* was an interesting one. The Copenhagen-based paper was founded in 1834 as a weekly by Christian Georg Nathan David (1793–1874), but became a daily in 1840 when two gifted journalists, Jens F. Giødwad and Orla Lehmann, joined its editorial staff after leaving *Kjøbenhavnsposten*.[19] In May of the following year Carl Ploug (1813–94) was recruited by Lehmann and the other editors to join *Fædrelandet*. He became its chief editor for the next forty years and is considered a principal figure in the history of the Danish press.[20]

---

16. Johannes Hohlenberg, *Sören Kierkegaard: A Biography*, trans. T. H. Croxall (New York: Pantheon, 1954), pp. 234–35. See also the "Postscript" to Kierkegaard's first article in *Fædrelandet* (December 18, 1854) in Søren Kierkegaard, *Attack upon "Christendom,"* trans. Walter Lowrie, p. 8. Two of the *Fædrelandet* articles were written in 1854 and published a year later in 1855: no. 6 was written on March 31, 1854, and published March 20, 1855; no. 7 was written in May 1854 and published March 21, 1855.

17. See, for example, *JP* 2955 (X^3 A 21); 2168 (X^3 A 280); 2171 (X^5 A 138); 2173 (XI^1 A 232); and 6886 (XI^1 A 242). Ulf Kjær-Hansen, in his *Søren Kierkegaards pressepolemik: Søren Kierkegaards Meninger om Dagpressen* (Copenhagen: Berlingske Forlag, 1955), gives a large selection of Kierkegaard's statements about the press.

18. Søren Kierkegaard, *Two Ages: The Age of Revolution and the Present Age, A Literary Review* (*KW*, XIV), ed. and trans. Howard V. Hong and Edna H. Hong (Princeton: Princeton University Press, 1978), p. 93.

19. Chr. Kirchhoff-Larsen, *Den Danske Presses Historie*, in 3 volumes, vol. III: 1827–66 (Copenhagen: Levin and Munksgaard, 1942–43), pp. 197–98.

20. Ibid., p. 214.

Orla Lehmann was the same person who had occasioned a few of Kierkegaard's early newspaper articles against liberalism during his student days in the mid-1830s,[21] and it is somewhat ironic that Kierkegaard should now adopt as his mouthpiece a paper with which Orla Lehmann was affiliated. Indeed *Fædrelandet* was regarded as a liberal journal and supported the policies of the National Liberal Party, but as its name suggests it also exhibited an undisguised streak of Danish nationalism; the combination made for very popular reading. In a political sense, Kierkegaard's choice of *Fædrelandet* as the organ through which he would launch his attack on the established Church may be seen to represent a "liberalizing" tendency in an otherwise very conservative person who had consistently supported the authority of the monarchy and the traditional political establishment. The reasons for the choice, however, were pragmatic, and were spelled out by Kierkegaard himself in a journal entry dated April 8, 1855, some months into the attack:

> Still I did want to achieve an approximation of preaching in the streets or of placing Christianity, thinking about Christianity, right into the middle of life's actuality and in conflict with its variants, and to that end I decided to use this newspaper [*Fædrelandet*]. It is a political paper, has completely different interests, concerns itself with a great variety of subjects—but not with Christianity. Having these little articles printed in this daily paper got them a hearing in a medium quite different from what they deal with. . . . Another advantage was that I could communicate my thoughts in small doses. . . . Furthermore, I managed in a simple way to maintain an independence, free from the possibility of becoming a party. . . . In a daily paper utterly unassociated with me and my cause, I live, if you please, as a tenant. . . . Thus I also succeeded in using the daily press without contradicting my own views of the press. Part of my objection to the daily press is its being used in such a way as to become a sensate power itself, also to its being used anonymously.[22]

---

21. *SV*, XIII, pp. 7–44. See also *JP* 5116 (I B 2).

22. *JP* 6957 (XI³ B 120). In at least two *Fædrelandet* articles Kierkegaard mentioned the reasons for his choice of the newspaper. He wrote in article no. 17 (May 10, 1855): "In order to make the contemporaries take notice, and in order to preclude the clergy from the evasion that this was something nobody read, I have made use of a political journal with a wide circulation." Five days later in article no. 19 (May 15), he wrote: "It was for religious reasons I decided to use a widely circulated political journal—to make people take notice. This I have religiously understood as my duty, and I do it also with joy, even though it is very distasteful to me. . . . I shall guard myself well against too much chumminess with everyone who writes some sort of a thing in a newspaper." See *Attack upon "Christendom,"* pp. 49–50 and 53–54 respectively.

86   Kirkekampen: *Seeds of "Misreception"*

The appearance of Kierkegaard's article in *Fædrelandet* on Monday, December 18, 1854, under the title "Was Bishop Mynster a 'witness to the truth,' one of 'the genuine witnesses to the truth'—is this the truth?" precipitated immediate and diverse reactions in the form of newspaper articles; thus the *Kirkekampen* (The Church struggle), as it came to be called, was on.[23] In his article Kierkegaard argued that a genuine witness to the truth in the Christian sense must experience suffering, poverty, and ultimately martyrdom—none of which applied in the case of Bishop Mynster. He added that one reason for not making his protest earlier, while Mynster lived, was his desire to honor the memory of his dead father, who had brought him up on Mynster's sermons. This had been his misfortune, but now that Mynster had passed away he was free to speak out.

Three days later an anonymous article signed simply "A" appeared in another Copenhagen paper under the title "Et Angreb paa Biskop Mynster" (An attack on Bishop Mynster).[24] The writer's point was to question Kierkegaard's "filial piety" that bade him remain silent about the living and allowed him to speak about the dead. This is difficult to comprehend, he writes, and more incomprehensible is how Kierkegaard could let his actions be determined by such motives. Has he forgotten, asks "A" somewhat affectedly, that he who said "I am the Way and the Truth and the Life" also said "He who loves father and mother more than me is not worthy of me"? He concludes that Kierkegaard's alleged loyalty to his father's admiration for Mynster was a contrived excuse invented to conceal the fact that Kierkegaard had actually altered his opinion of Mynster from uncritical acceptance to outright rejection. Such a change raised doubts about Kierkegaard's "infallibility" which, according to "A," Kierkegaard was in earnest to maintain, since he regarded himself as a prophet.

The following day two more articles came out in two separate newspapers. *Berlingske Tidende* featured an anonymous piece signed "L" and entitled "En Karrikaturtegning af Dr. S. Kierkegaard" (a caricature sketch

---

23. Other names that were used were: *Kirkestorm, Sandhedsvidnestriden, Øjebliksstriden, Øjeblikskampen, Øjebliksstormen, Statskirkefeindskab,* and other similar combinations.

24. *Dagbladet,* December 21, 1854. The paper (The daily sheet), was started in 1851 by Carl Steen Andersen Bille (1828–98) at a very young age. It was national-liberal and oriented toward European issues with a wide range of subject matter. Denmark's leading newspaper on certain current topics, it was read by the cultured upper classes. Bille, who was otherwise for Grundtvigianism, felt sympathetic toward Kierkegaard while the struggle was raging (see Kirchhoff-Larsen, *Den Danske Presses Historie,* III, pp. 451–52).

of S.K.).[25] It involved a critique of Kierkegaard's conception of "witness to the truth." This conception, contended the writer, is false because Kierkegaard equates it with "martyr." The phrase has only an etymological significance, whereas martyr implies an additional historical dimension. Not all witnesses to the truth are martyrs, but all martyrs are witnesses to the truth, declared the writer solemnly. His conclusion was that Kierkegaard had merely managed to caricature the truth. The second piece, signed "B," was actually a long letter to the editor of *Dagbladet*.[26] It picked up on the point made by "A" in the previous day's article, namely the charge that Kierkegaard was inconsistent in his attitude toward Mynster before and after the bishop's death. To illustrate this, a couple of examples are quoted from Kierkegaard's writings, notably *For Self-Examination* (1851), where he speaks highly of Mynster's sermons and appears to concur with their fundamental orientation. The writer then urges Kierkegaard to clarify not only to his opponents but, more importantly, to his admirers and followers the position such laudatory utterances occupy in relation to his later attacks on Mynster. Thus those who accept Kierkegaard's views unquestioningly must learn from his inconsistency here to be more distrustful of "the Master" and to apply to him the same critical standards of judgment they apply to everyone else.[27]

Already in these initial replies to Kierkegaard's first article one is able to catch a glimpse of the polemical course which the rest of the press debate in the *Kirkekampen* was to follow. At times it would get harsher, while in some rare instances the tone of the retorts was mild, even sympathetic to Kierkegaard's position. The debate afforded an opportunity for many to send anonymous contributions to the leading dailies of the day, resulting in a lively and rich exchange of a variety of outlooks. There were those who simply wished to experiment, to try their hand at journalism; they did not arrive at any important or meaningful results within the context of the debate itself. Others, however, were genuinely concerned

---

25. *Berlingske Tidende*, December 22, 1854. This is Denmark's oldest and most prestigious newspaper. It was founded by Carl Berling (1812–71) and was named after him (Berling News). Walter Lowrie incorrectly translates it as "Berlin News" throughout *Attack upon "Christendom,"* pp. 6, 10, 15, 16, etc. The chief editor of *Berlingske Tidende* from 1838–58 and 1865–66 was Mendel Levin Nathanson (1780–1868).

26. *Dagbladet*, December 22, 1854.

27. A few days after this letter by "B" another appeared signed "C" (*Dagbladet*, December 28), in which the author declared that he agreed with "A" (*Dagbladet*, December 21) but not with "B," whose poor choice of quotations from Kierkegaard's works was inadequate as a counterpoise to Kierkegaard's recent assault on Mynster.

88   Kirkekampen: *Seeds of "Misreception"*

with the wide-ranging implications of Kierkegaard's assault on the established Church. They were usually theologians, professors of religion, or members of the clergy who felt particularly put on the spot by Kierkegaard's increasingly anticlerical posture. People did not realize it at the time but Kierkegaard's virulent open critique was to have far-reaching significance for the subsequent history of the Lutheran state-Church in Denmark. F.-J. Billeskov Jansen does not exaggerate when he writes: "In Denmark in particular, the evolution of the Church since 1855 is explained to a great extent by the efforts of the state-Church to formulate a response to the arguments of Kierkegaard."[28]

As for Kierkegaard's own reactions to what was being published in response to him, they varied according to the nature and severity of the reply. For the most part, however, he ignored the views of others and proceeded to spew forth relentlessly one article after another for *Fædrelandet*. In a few cases he did react openly, but on the whole his reactions were confined to the privacy of his journals. For example, a week after his first article appeared, *Kjøbenhavnsposten*—a liberal newspaper which had become the standard-bearer of liberalism in Denmark since the early 1830s following the July Revolution in France[29]—printed on two successive days two nasty pieces, a poem and an article, mocking Kierkegaard for his attack on the deceased Mynster. The poem was signed "1127," and in one line said of Kierkegaard that he "belonged to the devil's family."[30] The article was signed "æsculap", and concluded: "Possibly next time he [Kierkegaard] will not confine himself to flogging a dead person, but will even beat a human being to death. This, it appears, must become his next form of mortification."[31] To this sort of abuse Kierkegaard had the following to say:

> When a newspaper, in both prose and poetry, has pronounced a man insane, then this man might venture to expect that, in all fairness, the paper will quit

---

28. F. J. Billeskov Jansen, "L'Heritage de Kierkegaard dans les pays Nordiques," in *Cahiers du Sud* 50, no. 371 (Marseilles, April–May, 1963), p. 18.

29. *Kjøbenhavnsposten* was a daily ed. J. P. M. Grüne (1805–78) from 1839 to 1859. Grüne was highly critical of Kierkegaard during the latter's final years. Kierkegaard for his part despised *Kjøbenhavnsposten* and had questioned the meaning of its imitation liberalism back in the mid-1830s [see *JP* 5116 (I B 2)]; see also Ulf Kjær-Hansen, *Søren Kierkegaards Pressepolemik*, pp. 14ff., and Kirchhoff-Larsen, *Den Danske Presses Historie*, III, pp. 105ff.

30. *Kjøbenhavnsposten*, December 23, 1854. Another translation would be "you are a kinsman of the devil."

31. *Kjøbenhavnsposten*, December 24, 1854.

talking about him; and it betrays contempt for its readers when, after declaring a man insane, it goes on chatting with them about him as if he were not insane. This kind of conduct is talking on and on, is babbling. This is the relation of *Kjøbenhavnsposten* to me.³²

On the whole Kierkegaard throughout the press debate was expecting more substantial opposition. He was actually surprised at the generally poor quality of response his articles received, and the knee-jerk reactions they provoked.³³ Instead of engaging him in meaningful debate over specific points, most of the early protests against his articles did not go beyond personal invective. Whenever an attempt at sustained argumentation was made, it usually proved too tediously convoluted or too frail and shallow to merit a rejoinder from Kierkegaard. Take, for instance, the article in *Flyveposten* written by a certain "J. L." in reaction to Kierkegaard's opening article against Mynster. After nearly an entire column in which hardly anything significant is said, the author labels Kierkegaard's article "scandalous" and adds that it "portrays Mr. Kierkegaard himself in his basic inner character."³⁴ J. L.'s main point, a little further on, is that Kierkegaard is a man lacking seriousness. What is one to make of Kierkegaard waiting until Mynster had died to launch his objection in the form of a measly article: "Is this Christian seriousness, or is it a scandalous joke?" he asks acidly. Finally, J. L. questions Kierkegaard's definition of "witness to the truth," and concludes that Luther would not qualify since he did not live in degradation, was not laughed at, was not roasted on a grill, and was not tortured by the executioner. Little did J. L. suspect that by this time Kierkegaard had developed certain fundamental reservations regarding Luther's posture as reformer-corrective.³⁵ Since Luther had not been martyred, his qualifications as witness for truth were being called into question by Kierkegaard during this final phase of his complex relationship to the great Protestant reformer. Thus Kierkegaard

---

32. *JP* 6964 (XI² A 411).
33. J. Hohlenberg, *Sören Kierkegaard: A Biography*, p. 236.
34. *Flyveposten*, December 27, 1854. *Flyveposten* [The flying post] was a Copenhagen newspaper founded in 1845 by Edvard Meyer (1813-80). It was supported by political conservatives and various opponents of the National Liberal Party policies. Under the editorship of Jacob Davidsen and Gottlieb Siesby the paper violently attacked Kierkegaard during the *Kirkekampen*. On Meyer see Kirchhoff-Larsen, *Den Danske Presses Historie*, III, pp. 253ff.
35. See the discussion earlier on Kierkegaard's concept of "corrective," and see note 12 above. Kierkegaard's references to Luther in his journals are numerous and become increasingly critical with time.

felt no compulsion to reply to objections of this sort coming from anonymous writers who were in the habit of framing their arguments in webs of cheap sarcasm; J. L. ended his tirade mockingly: "Thank you, thank you, oh noble Mr. Kierkegaard that you held back your little article for so long!"[36]

The same objection to Kierkegaard's apparent confining of the title "witness to the truth" to martyrs came from a more prominent personality who was directly concerned with the debate underway. H. L. Martensen finally broke his silence and published a long article in *Berlingske Tidende* on December 28 which he called, "I Anledning af Dr. S. Kierkegaards Artikel i 'Fædrelandet' nr. 295" (With reference to S. K.'s article in *Fædrelandet* no. 295).[37] Martensen, at one point, declared that "S. Kierkegaard, whose Christianity is without church and without history, and who only seeks after Christ in the deserts and in the chambers," is incapable of understanding that truth is transmitted from one generation to the next by teachers in the community. As for witnessing to the truth necessarily entailing suffering, it need only be remarked that there have been many zealots and fanatics who have undergone great sufferings without meriting to be called witnesses to the truth; and besides, "what entitles him [Kierkegaard] to ignore that there are also sufferings other than tangible persecution?" For a "well-trained sophist like Dr. S. Kierkegaard" to have such "fixed ideas" is very disappointing, remarked Martensen ruefully. Furthermore, he accused Kierkegaard of harboring base motives and of having betrayed his father's memory. His Christianity was a private religion with little relation to the faith of the community, and it omitted altogether the action of the Holy Spirit within the Church.

Parallel to the running criticisms of Kierkegaard, praise was lavished on Mynster throughout Martensen's article. Like the good preacher that he was, Mynster never said more or less than what the Spirit had charged him with. Yet not only his preaching but his life and character as well were calumniated by Kierkegaard, who displayed "the unscrupulous falsehood

---

36. This is a reference to Kierkegaard's having waited some months before publishing his first *Fædrelandet* article. In his second *Fædrelandet* article of December 30, 1854, Kierkegaard wrote the following in passing: "It will be understood then that I cannot take account of what every anonymous writer, every 'Æsculapius' brings out in a newspaper, or what a serious-minded man from Nørrebro [J. L.] with all the seriousness of the *Flying Post* says to explain to people that I lack seriousness." See *Attack upon "Christendom,"* p. 14.

37. *Berlingske Tidende,* December 28, 1854.

and injustice, . . . the impure and undisciplined spirit, [and the] wantonness which plays with what is venerable, plays with people's own better feelings." "Indeed," concluded Martensen sarcastically, "this mask which was cast off in *Fædrelandet* will surely remain safeguarded for a long time in the history of our public morals, and will enhance S. Kierkegaard's renown."

Perhaps the most outraged reaction to Kierkegaard's initial attack on Mynster came from Caspar Paludan-Müller (1805–82), a Danish historian and poet, and a generally conservative person, well-grounded in the classics and in German philosophy.[38] His article, appearing in *Berlingske Tidende*[39] the same day that Kierkegaard's second article was published in *Fædrelandet*, had the tone of an apologetic for Mynster. The author declared indignantly that Kierkegaard's assault on Mynster "is a slap in all the faces" of those who have been inspired by the bishop's sermons, and who have had many a Christian seed planted in their hearts as a result. For Kierkegaard to call Mynster "weak" and "self-indulgent" is quite excessive; "these are hard words to hear," writes Paludan-Müller, " . . . least of all was I expecting to hear him [Mynster] called a weak man." Elsewhere, Paludan-Müller reiterates the point made earlier by "J. L." concerning the relationship between martyrdom and being a witness to the truth: should Kierkegaard's necessary linkage of the two prove valid, then both Augustine and Luther would not qualify.

With this article round one of the *Kirkekampen* came to a close.[40] It was to be followed by no fewer than thirty others, if one counts the remaining twenty articles in *Fædrelandet* and the ten issues of *Øjeblikket*. In certain cases Kierkegaard did address the objections of his critics directly, although for the most part he was simply content to repeat his points with more emphasis. In a long footnote in his second article of December 30, for instance, Kierkegaard mentions that he was surprised to see Martensen's article in *Berlingske Tidende*—"an article which properly does not require an explicit reply, since it does not alter the case in the least."[41] The remainder of the note, however, comprises a brief retort to Martensen, particularly on the question of the identification of "witness

---

38. *DBL*, vol. XVII, pp. 607–12.   39. *Berlingske Tidende*, December 30, 1854.

40. Kabell lists in his bibliographic work the following additional articles for 1854 that were of lesser importance: *Berlingske Tidende*, December 22, signed "L"; December 29, by pastor H. F. Binzer; *Corsaren*, December 22 and 29. See Aage Kabell, *Kierkegaardstudiet i Norden*, p. 15.

41. *Attack upon "Christendom,"* p. 10.

to the truth" exclusively with "blood-witness" (i.e. martyr), which Kierkegaard argues is a misunderstanding of his position.

His third article of January 12, 1855, was an exception, as he himself admits, since it was devoted solely to answering a sharp counterattack on him in the form of a twenty-two-page brochure written in defense of Mynster.[42] The author was Jens Paludan-Müller (1813-99), a pastor and the brother of Caspar. He had obtained a degree in theology before his ordination, and had also come briefly under Sibbern's influence philosophically. In 1850 he published a sympathetic appraisal of Martensen's *Christelige Dogmatik,* a work regarded with contempt by Kierkegaard; and in 1854 he wrote a thorough analysis of Mynster's art of preaching, focusing mainly on its apologetic ingredients.[43]

J. Paludan-Müller's tract was an involved attempt—packed with numerous scriptural citations and abstruse theological reasoning—to come to the defense of Mynster by challenging Kierkegaard to prove his case with similar references from the New Testament. The answer Kierkegaard offered was typical. He argued that to do what Paludan-Müller was demanding would be tantamount to changing the subject and diluting the real issue at hand, since it would plunge the entire discussion into an endless spiral of theological "prolixity," as he termed it. The matter is very clear and does not require lengthy learned treatises; Mynster's preaching never leads to the breach with this world that would render it authentically Christian: "Bishop Mynster's preaching is related to the Christianity of the New Testament as Epicureanism is to Stoicism, or as cultivation, refinement, education, is related to a fundamental change of character, to a radical cure."[44]

Late in 1855, J. Paludan-Müller published a long study of Kierkegaard's concept of Christianity, based on an examination of his *Practice in Christianity,* which appeared in a new edition in April of that year.[45] The study was generally characterized by its sobriety of tone and its balanced evaluations.[46] Although the author's declared intention was to

---

42. "Dr. Søren Kierkegaards Angreb paa Biskop Mynsters Eftermæle" (S. K.'s assault on Bishop Mynster's reputation) (Copenhagen, 1855).

43. *DBL,* vol. XVII, pp. 624-26.   44. *Attack upon "Christendom,"* p. 17.

45. Kierkegaard's article no. 20 in *Fædrelandet* (May 16, 1855) was written on the occasion of the appearance of this new edition, and related the work to the ongoing strife with the Church; see *Attack upon "Christendom,"* pp. 54-55.

46. J. Paludan-Müller, "Dr. Søren Kierkegaards Indøvelse i Christendom" (S. K.'s practice in Christianity), in *Nyt Theologisk Tidsskrift* 6 (1855), pp. 318-405.

resume the dispute with Kierkegaard by contending that his later behavior had been at variance with the way he would make Christianity dissimilar from the world, Paludan-Müller did make an interesting observation. Having apparently done a closer reading of Kierkegaard's explicitly religious writings, Paludan-Müller finally came to the perceptive conclusion that the climaxing struggle against the established Church was but a dramatic recapitulation of a Kierkegaardian life-view *(Livsanskuelse)* founded from the beginning on a radical personal approach to the Christianity of the New Testament.[47] In this sense Kierkegaard's entire life-view rested on one continuous training in Christianity, and a progressive deepening of oneself in accordance with the notion of the stages.[48] This was an insightful "discovery" on Paludan-Müller's part, since it was not based on knowledge of either Kierkegaard's journals or his as yet unpublished *The Point of View for My Work as an Author,* in both of which Kierkegaard spells out unequivocally the connection between his religious writings and the culminating attack upon the Church. As the *Kirkekampen* proceeded, Kierkegaard widened his attack from its initial focus on Mynster and Martensen to encompass other, more general questions: the position and role of the clergy in the Church, the relationship of New Testament Christianity *(Christendommen)* to official Christianity or "Christendom" *(Christenhed),* and the relationship of Church and state.[49] Paludan-Müller detected the roots and saw the implications of this shift, and was therefore one of the very few of Kierkegaard's contemporaries who managed, despite basic disagreements with him, to arrive at a somewhat integrated picture of the successive phases of Kierkegaard's intellectual and spiritual output.[50]

Another participant in the *Kirkekampen,* and one who at least claimed an intellectual affinity with Kierkegaard, was Rasmus Nielsen (1809-84).

---

47. Ibid., pp. 326 and 328.

48. Ibid., p. 330. A detailed discussion of Kierkegaard's philosophy and concept of communication followed; see pp. 389ff.

49. A definite transition to the larger issues began to occur as early as the fourth and fifth *Fædrelandet* articles (both appearing on the same day: January 29, 1855), and Kierkegaard's polemical style started to become highly charged with passion; see *Attack upon "Christendom,"* pp. 18-24.

50. He had begun writing his long article before Kierkegaard's sickness, but did not publish it until after his death. He wrote that since Kierkegaard's passing away he had found no cause to alter anything in his understanding of him; see J. Paludan-Müller, "Dr. Søren Kierkegaards Indøvelse i Christendom," p. 405. For a brief discussion of J. Paludan-Müller's treatise see A. Kabell, *Kierkegaardstudiet i Norden,* pp. 54-55.

In 1841, when Kierkegaard submitted his dissertation on irony to his professors,[51] Ørsted desired an additional expert opinion philosophically, and so referred it to Martensen and to Nielsen, who had just been appointed in the department of philosophy. Martensen read it but Nielsen declined to do so, or to give an evaluation. Whether it was because he had been too busy, or out of caution as a new appointee, is difficult to determine.[52]

During the late 1840s Nielsen and Kierkegaard became intimate friends, seeing each other regularly and having frequent exchanges of ideas, usually over long walks.[53] This was also the period when Kierkegaard was assessing closely his literary endeavors, and wrestling with the question of direct versus indirect communication.[54] He was becoming increasingly concerned about the fate of his ideas after his death, and his friendship with Nielsen was partly motivated by a hope that the professor would be capable of understanding him more deeply than others, and would somehow carry on in his intellectual footsteps.[55] Initially Nielsen had shown promise in this regard. After reading the *Postscript* he renounced his earlier Hegelianism and radically altered his philosophical orientation in order to embrace Kierkegaard's anti-idealistic and person-centered position. However, despite this apparent conversion to Kierkegaard's standpoint, Nielsen never appreciated the importance for Kierkegaard of the difference between direct and indirect communication. A tract he wrote in 1849 against Martensen,[56] although containing many

---

51. See Chapter 1 above.

52. Carl Weltzer, "Omkring Søren Kierkegaards Disputats," in *Kirkehistoriske Samlinger* 6 (1948–50), p. 286. Weltzer speculates that Nielsen's hesitation was due to Kierkegaard having mocked his philosophical abilities and qualifications for the position in front of Sibbern during those same months.

53. In a journal entry from 1852 (*Papirer*, X^6 B 99, not translated into English in the Hong edition) Kierkegaard describes how, after a long period of coolness, Nielsen finally approached him and they became friends and began to take regular Thursday walks together.

54. Between 1848 and 1851 Kierkegaard wrote *Armed Neutrality, An Open Letter, The Point of View for My Work as an Author,* and *On My Work as an Author.* His journals from this period are full of reflections on the two forms of communication; see, for example, *JP* 658–81.

55. Kierkegaard's confidence in Nielsen was quite a development from his skepticism a decade earlier. Yet Rasmus Nielsen was later to justify Kierkegaard's view that a disciple is the greatest of all calamities; see Walter Lowrie, *Kierkegaard,* p. 381. For a discussion of Nielsen's distortions of Kierkegaard's views on faith and knowledge, see Chapter 5 below.

56. Rasmus Nielsen, *Mag. S. Kierkegaards "Johannes Climacus" og Dr. H. Martensens "Christelige Dogmatik", en undersøgende Anmeldelse* (Copenhagen, 1849).

criticisms Kierkegaard would subscribe to, had the net effect of angering Kierkegaard since in it Nielsen expounded pedantically certain themes that Kierkegaard had taken pains to present indirectly and through the stratagem of the pseudonyms. After having spent countless hours and great pains attempting to impart to Nielsen the intricacies of his thought and methodology (with much by way of intimate revelations about his private life to boot), Kierkegaard now became convinced that the effort had been a waste. Thus the hitherto warm and familiar friendship between them soon came to an end.

Nielsen wrote two articles for *Fædrelandet* in January 1855 that dealt with Kierkegaard's attack on official Christianity.[57] Both sum up neatly Nielsen's personality and disposition with respect to Kierkegaard and the issues he raises. In the first,[58] Nielsen analyzed Kierkegaard's objections to Mynster's being designated a witness to truth. He called Kierkegaard's protest "a good deed" (which is also the title of the article), and went on to add:

> In his rich works, Kierkegaard has, from the first to the last, as he himself says, "willed only one thing"; . . . and what then is this one thing, S. Kierkegaard has willed in his entire authorship? I understand that the answer to this question is like this: What is a witness to the truth?[59]

According to Nielsen, no other author has consistently "willed one thing" throughout his diverse writings as Kierkegaard has. If, therefore, one were to assert that Kierkegaard's conception of what it is to be a witness to truth is false, then by implication his entire work and indeed his very existence would be false as well: "Against such a perception of this man I must for my part hereby protest," stated Nielsen emphatically. We see here that, despite his break with Kierkegaard in 1850, Nielsen remained loyal to his former friend and mentor, and continued to appreciate the intellectual worth of his works. In fact this first article consisted of a defense of Kierkegaard's position on the Church. Nielsen objected, as a Lutheran Protestant, to the accusation that Kierkegaard was "un-

---

57. Actually a short review by Nielsen of Kierkegaard's *For Self-Examination* (1851) appeared in *Fædrelandet*, December 29, 1854. Most of it was a direct quote from Kierkegaard's book, and Nielsen's scanty comments at the end are insignificant.

58. "En god Gjerning" (A good deed), in *Fædrelandet*, January 10, 1855.

59. Ibid. The phrase 'willed only one thing' is taken from part one of Kierkegaard's *Upbuilding Discourses in Various Spirits* (1847) on the theme: "Purity of Heart Is to Will One Thing." See (*KW*, XV), p. 154.

churchly" and that his outburst was "a private affair." As Nielsen saw it, the *Kirkekampen* precipitated by Kierkegaard was an ecclesiastical struggle to a high degree, and concerned the Church as a whole. He also tried to show that Kierkegaard admired Mynster and thought highly of his opinions while he was still alive, but that Mynster never granted Kierkegaard the personal recognition he deserved and expected from a Church official who had read his Christian writings. Nielsen concluded that Kierkegaard's present protest, far from being motivated by vanity and self-love, had sprung from a genuine regard for safeguarding Christianity and the Church; it was done "to clarify the unclear."

In this article Nielsen included a personal touch that underscored his abiding devotion to Kierkegaard. After calling him "a master of reflection in a reflective age," Nielsen qualified his judgment by adding that with all his reflectiveness Kierkegaard remained a man of feeling: "When I read him, when he talked to me (even when he teased me) I had a feeling for him, that there in the thin man with the shattering words there still was, nevertheless, a soft and child-like temper."[60]

The second article[61] was actually an open letter addressed to Martensen. In a polite—even servile—tone Nielsen defended his support of Kierkegaard in the previous article as not in contradiction to his high esteem for "your Eminence," or for the late Bishop Mynster: "[It was never my] intention either to cut down the honor which appropriately belongs to Bishop Mynster, or to act in hostile opposition against your [Martensen's] very frank and unreserved judgment pronounced in your article in the *Berlingske Tidende.*"[62] Nielsen then timidly asked Martensen to respond if he felt Nielsen's position was incompatible with his own.

The impression gained from reading both the first article and the open letter is that Nielsen was hedging his bets in the *Kirkekampen.* On the one hand, he exhibited a degree of intellectual faithfulness to Kierkegaard by attempting to view the strife against Mynster and Martensen in the larger context of the whole authorship, but on the other hand, knowing that as a professor of philosophy and theology he was in a more vulnerable position than Kierkegaard vis-à-vis the ecclesiastical and academic author-

---

60. Unlike some others who knew Kierkegaard personally, Nielsen did not leave us any written reminiscences of him except a few bits like this one interspersed here and there in his prolific writings.

61. "Til Høivelbaarne Høiærværdige Biskop Martensen: Et Spørgsmaal" (To the honorable and very reverend Bishop Martensen: a question), in *Fædrelandet,* January 16, 1855.

62. The reference is to Martensen's article of December 28, 1854; see note 37 above.

ities, he declared his solemn allegiance to these same authorities in no uncertain terms. He wanted to have it both ways, and this best describes Rasmus Nielsen.[63] Kierkegaard had long before detected these very tendencies in his friend and had ceased to take him seriously. On at least two occasions in his *Fædrelandet* articles, Kierkegaard indirectly rebuked Nielsen for his extra caution about not wanting to cause a scandal, and for misrepresenting him in terms of "a Christian severity as opposed to a Christian leniency."[64]

One important result of Nielsen's open letter, however, was that, by asking Martensen to reply, it had raised the question of his conspicuous silence since his first and only article, and in the face of repeated provocations from Kierkegaard. In fact two days after Nielsen's open letter an anonymous contribution to the same paper signed "X" had urged Martensen to maintain his silence, because an answer would serve only to make the situation worse and would benefit no one.[65] Thus Nielsen's clear, though cautious, challenge to Martensen, coupled with this latter's stubborn silence, provided Kierkegaard with the ammunition he needed for his final *Fædrelandet* article of May 26, 1855.[66] Here Kierkegaard released all his pent-up frustration at Martensen's protracted silence and avoidance of a public confrontation. He reminded Martensen of Nielsen's challenge and assured him that his public reputation was diminishing with every day of continued silence.

63. See Chapter 5 below.
64. Article no. 4 in *Fædrelandet*, January 29, 1855, and article no. 12 in *Fædrelandet*, March 31, 1855; see *Attack upon "Christendom,"* pp. 22 and 37. Both references are to Nielsen's January 10 *Fædrelandet* article in defense of Kierkegaard. A week later an article criticizing Nielsen appeared in *Berlingske Tidende* (January 17, 1855) written by a certain pastor B. F. Fog. Much later, in the fifth issue of *Øjeblikket* (July 27, 1855), Kierkegaard referred to Fog's article and rejected his view that there are two types of Christianity, as he had claimed. See *Attack*, p. 162. In his final *Fædrelandet* article (May 26, 1855) Kierkegaard lamented Nielsen's unfortunate application of the term "Christian resignation" to Martensen in his January 10 article. See *Attack*, p. 69. In the tenth and last issue of *Øjeblikket*, which did not make it to the press before his death and was published posthumously in 1881, Kierkegaard had a few words of appreciation for Nielsen: "The only man who occasionally has said a fairly true word about my significance is Professor R. Nielsen; but it is true perception he got from private conversation with me." See *Attack*, pp. 284-85.
65. *Fædrelandet*, January 18, 1855.
66. Article no. 21 entitled: "That Bishop Martensen's silence is, Christianly, (1) unjustifiable, (2) comical, (3) dumb-clever, (4) in more than one respect contemptible," in *Attack upon "Christendom,"* pp. 67-72. Actually, Kierkegaard had brought up the issue of "this significant silence" of the clergy in his 17th *Fædrelandet* article (May 10, 1855); see *Attack*, p. 47.

Throughout the *Kirkekampen* there were divided views on Martensen's silence among his supporters. Some believed Martensen had given Kierkegaard a satisfactory answer in the one article he wrote, and that no more was needed. Others thought Kierkegaard's attack could best be met with total silence, and that Martensen had therefore already taken up his pen once too often.[67] Still others were satisfied neither with the answer nor with the ensuing silence, and began to write agitative articles. Most articles of this type appeared in *Kjøbenhavnsposten,* whose editors were already predisposed against Kierkegaard, and they included a lot of personal abuse hurled at Kierkegaard. For some reason it pleased a couple of these anonymous writers to conjure up the odd image of Kierkegaard as a hypocritical pharisee or a base scribe. In the words of one, Kierkegaard resembled the pharisee who throws himself on his knees before the eyes of the multitude in the temple of "the Fatherland" (i.e., on the pages of *Fædrelandet*) and thanks God that he is not "one of these publicans," meaning Martensen and the clergy![68] The other anonymous writer, who signed cryptically "2pp," put it as follows: ". . . by grossly abusing, deriding, persecuting and casting dirt on the Bishop . . . he himself [i.e. Kierkegaard] descends to the level of the pharisees, the scribes, and the crucifiers, and [assumes their] deplorable role. Poor, miserable Søren! Must you end like this?"[69] Such malicious abuse in the press continued through the rest of that year.[70]

From his correspondence of the period and from his autobiographical reminiscences entitled *Af Mit Levned* (Of my life), published in 1883, one

67. One anonymous writer signing "D" in *Dagbladet,* February 20, 1855, called upon Martensen to reply, but in a different manner: he would let the court decide the matter, and in this way he could obtain a declaration from the court that the whole thing was null and void. His silence, the article argued, could be mistaken for his inability to get such a court order declaring the affair terminated.

68. Anonymous article entitled "Mod S. Ks 'aphoristiske' artikler i 'Fædrelandet' " (Against S. K.'s aphoristic articles in *Fædrelandet*) in *Kjøbenhavnsposten,* May 12, 1855; clearly this refers to Luke 18:11.

69. Article entitled "Nr. 120 af 'Fædrelandet' 1855" (Number 120 of *Fædrelandet* 1855) in *Kjøbenhavnsposten,* May 30, 1855. Kierkegaard is also accused by the author of harboring "a vain craving after theological fame."

70. An anonymous article suggested that, whereas Kierkegaard had made a masterful debut with his attack, his luck had begun to run out (*Kjøbenhavnsposten,* August 23, 1855). Another anonymous one entitled "Et Rygte om S. Kierkegaard" (A rumor about S. K.) made the damaging suggestion that Kierkegaard was secretly in league with the atheists and was out to undermine religion by presenting Christian faith as a paradox, something opposed to reason (*Kjøbenhavnsposten,* September 5, 1855).

can see that Martensen had felt very deeply the personal aspects of the Kierkegaardian strife. He regarded the whole matter as a personal insult and a scandal. He expressed this in his letters to his friend the pastor L. Gude in Hunseby, particularly in a letter dated January 11, 1855.[71] In his reminiscences Martensen defended his solitary reply in *Berlingske Tidende* as the only reasonable course to have taken at the time. He could have chosen an attitude of meekness, he wrote, but Kierkegaard's "moral wickedness made me indignant. And I had always assumed that a righteous wrath is also something permitted, an indignation, which has its right to a statement."[72] After making his statement he found that silence would be the most proper policy: "I maintained silence. He [Kierkegaard] deserved no other answer than that, and it was given him."[73]

Martensen's silence did not deter other prominent representatives of what was termed "the Church party" in the debate from coming forward with articles of their own denouncing Kierkegaard's protests. Among these—and also an admirer of Grundtvig—was Jørgen Victor Bloch (1812-92), a provost (dean) of three districts in the Church since 1851, and the holder of some secular posts in the people's assembly as well—an archetypal embodiment of Christendom.[74] In a series of newspaper articles and in a separate essay, Bloch attacked Kierkegaard from the position of a spokesman on behalf of the Church. Although Bloch stopped short of actually calling Kierkegaard "the Antichrist himself,"[75] he strongly hinted this. He argued in Grundtvigian fashion against Kierkegaard's emphasis on the "single individual" as the starting point of becoming a Christian, and in favor of a congregational/communal focus highlighting "the community of the faithful," or the Church.

71. Bjørn Kornerup, ed., *Biskop H. Martensens Breve,* in 3 volumes (Copenhagen: Gad, 1955), vol. I: Letters from 1848 to 1859, letter no. 66, pp. 133-35.

72. H. L. Martensen, *Af Mit Levned,* in 3 volumes (Copenhagen, 1882-83), vol. III, p. 16.

73. Ibid. Martensen's reminiscences reveal the extent to which he took Kierkegaard's attacks personally. He called them a "low blow" and could view them only as a "simple, personal enmity, not to say hatred" (see p. 13).

74. *DBL,* vol. III, pp. 268-69. Bloch got involved in the Grundtvigian idea of *Friskolen* (the free school) for which Grundtvig is best remembered in Denmark today. Bloch wrote a treatise on it in 1857 and defended the idea against repeated criticisms in the 1860s. Eventually Bloch became a full-fledged Grundtvigian and wrote treatises on the notion of Christian communal fellowship through a common national education.

75. J. Victor Bloch, "Guds Kirke er bygget for Evigheden: Et kirkeligt Vidnesbyrd mod Dr. S. Kierkegaard" (God's church is built for eternity: an ecclesiastical testimony against S. K.) (Odense, 1855), p. 25. See also A. Kabell, *Kierkegaardstudiet i Norden,* p. 56.

Bloch's newspaper articles were even more virulent than his essay. He took strong exception to a proposal made to Kierkegaard by an anonymous writer in *Fædrelandet* that Kierkegaard cease the "clangs and shouts . . . the lightning and thunder," and instead show people the way out of their dead relationship with God by providing an exposition of the teachings of the New Testament.[76] This infuriated Bloch, who could not imagine that someone as hostile as Kierkegaard appeared to be toward the Church would be called upon to show people the right way of the Gospels. In an indignant article he self-righteously accused Kierkegaard of questioning the very existence of the Church and denying its eternal spiritual character, and concluded that so long as Kierkegaard had effectively placed himself beyond the walls of the Church, the Church should in turn lock her doors in his face.[77] Kierkegaard's sixteenth *Fædrelandet* article (April 27, 1855) was a sarcastic reply to Bloch's "excommunication" of him. By now Kierkegaard had so distanced himself from the Danish Lutheran Church, its public worship, and its sacraments that such attacks had no effect on him except perhaps to stimulate him in a comical way.[78]

This derisive reply by Kierkegaard did not satisfy Bloch, who proceeded to publish further attacks on him. In one of these[79] Bloch declares confidently that not for a moment did he fear the Christian Church would

---

76. "N-n" [whom some have speculated was H. N. Clausen (1793-1877), professor of theology and colleague of Martensen; see A. Kabell, *Kierkegaardstudiet i Norden*, no. 81, pp. 16-17], "Forslag til Hr. Dr. S. Kierkegaard" (Proposal to S. K.), in *Fædrelandet*, April 3, 1855. The author states that Kierkegaard's "convulsive outburst" served a good purpose to the extent that it awakened more seriousness, caused deeper self-examination, and introduced into Danish Christianity some of that necessary "calm unrest" *(stille uro)* required for spiritual renewal. Kierkegaard's reply to the proposal resembled in its caution the one he had given to J. Paludan-Müller's similar suggestion (see earlier discussion above). It came in his 13th and 14th *Fædrelandet* articles (April 7 and 11, 1855), where he said he feared the proposal was "a trap" designed to divert the discussion and dilute the power of his critique. As on other occasions he merely pointed to his earlier works, especially *Practice in Christianity*, where ample treatment of Christian themes occurs. See *Attack upon "Christendom,"* pp. 40-43.

77. J. Victor Bloch, "I Anledning af 'Forslaget' til Dr. S. Kierkegaard" (on the occasion of "the proposal" to S. K.), in *Fædrelandet*, April 24, 1855.

78. By devoting an entire article to replying directly to one of his attackers Kierkegaard was again departing from his oft-stated pledge not to answer his denigrators. He replied to specific critics in at least five *Fædrelandet* articles (see numbers 13, 14, 16, 19, and 21) and intermittently throughout *Øjeblikket*.

79. J. Victor Bloch, "Ikke Navnet, men Sagen!" (Not the name, but the issue in question), in *Berlingske Tidende*, June 1, 1855.

be rocked in its eternal foundations by Kierkegaard. He adds, however, that he is worried about believers being plunged into doubts about the Church as a result of Kierkegaard's campaign. In view of this fear, he reaffirms his earlier point that the Church has nothing to do with someone like Kierkegaard, who has as much claim to membership in "the Danish People's Church" as a Mormon does.[80] Much effort was expended by Bloch in singing the praises of this Church and its pious servants.

To the likes of Bloch and the representatives of ecclesiastical officialdom, Kierkegaard dealt his decisive blow in a statement he published on May 16, 1855 and called "This Must Be Said, So Let It Now Be Said." The statement was addressed to any reader and was very blunt: whoever refrains from taking part in the public worship of God is thereby no longer making a fool of God by pretending that what passes as Christianity is actually the Christianity of the New Testament. This brief and powerful message[81] marked the end of the first phase of the *Kirkekampen*, and the beginning of the second and last phase, characterized by the appearance of *Øjeblikket*.

From the end of May to the end of September, Kierkegaard published nine issues of this journal, of which he was both sole writer and editor. He did not terminate his dealings with *Fædrelandet* because of any falling out with the editors; he and they continued to be friends through the rest of the year. Kierkegaard simply wanted to move one step further in his utilization of the press and create his own independent organ so as to broaden the scope of his critique of "Christendom," from its initial preoccupation with the shortcomings of particular clerics to an assault on the clergy as state employees and the intertwining of church and state. He also wished to elaborate further his running theme that contemporary Christianity bore little resemblance to what the Gospels prescribe.

The term *"Øjeblikket"* is significant as a Kierkegaardian category. *"Et Øjeblik"* (an instant, a moment; literally, the blink of an eye) meant for Kierkegaard the event of eternity piercing through time.[82] It was not an

---

80. "Den danske Folkekirke" is a Grundtvigian designation of the Lutheran Church in Denmark, which Bloch here employs. Grundtvigians in particular, and the entire clerical establishment generally, were very hostile to fringe sects such as the Mormons.

81. It appeared 10 days before Kierkegaard's last article in *Fædrelandet* dealing with Martensen's silence and was put out in a separate tract by Bianco Luno Press, which also published his *Øjeblikket* articles. See *Attack upon "Christendom,"* pp. 57–65.

82. ". . . the Moment, this breaking through of the eternal, . . ." as Kierkegaard says in *Ojeblikket*, no. 10, published posthumously; see *SV*, XIV, p. 349; see also *Attack upon "Christendom,"* p. 281. In at least two of his major works Kierkegaard includes discussions

ordinary temporal concept, but rather pointed to a flash of the timeless and the unchangeable (i.e. Christian truth, and specifically the Incarnation with its consequences for each person) in our fleeting and imperfect world.

Not surprisingly, the more vocal members of "the Church Party" during the *Kirkekampen* paid little attention to the substance and intricacies of such Kierkegaardian religious categories. Their primary objective was to discredit Kierkegaard in the eyes of the public as one who had no legitimate claim to speak out against the Church. Hence their strategy entailed magnifying the radical aspects of Kierkegaard's critique to assume grotesque proportions.

A principal proponent of this approach was F. L. B. Zeuthen (1805–74). He was a pastor and the son of the youngest sister of the philosopher Henrich Steffens. After receiving his theology degree he went to Berlin, where he attended lectures by Schleiermacher, Neander, Hegel, and Marheineke. In 1833–34 he heard Schelling's lectures; soon realizing that Schelling was the thinker he had been seeking, he became his disciple philosophically. In the theological realm Zeuthen came under Mynster's influence, and to a lesser extent Grundtvig's. Using Schelling's philosophy as Martensen had done with Hegel, he eventually led a vigorous polemical campaign against Grundtvigianism in 1840 that involved, among other things, a dispute between him and P. C. Kierkegaard, Søren's brother, who was a Grundtvigian pastor.[83]

Kierkegaard's explosive articles in *Fædrelandet* (1854–55) incited Zeuthen, who was a polemicist by nature, to take action. At first he made a few contemptuous references to Kierkegaard in passing in a series of articles he wrote for *Evangelisk Ugeskrift* early in 1855.[84] Later, after *Øjeblikket* began to appear, with its penetrating jabs against the Church's

---

of "the Moment" as a religious/existential category. Its relation to Greek thought and to the religious view of man as a synthesis of the temporal and the eternal is discussed in *The Concept of Anxiety* (1844) (see the translation by Reidar Thomte and Albert B. Anderson in *KW*, vol. VIII, esp. pp. 82–91). In *Philosophical Fragments* (1844) Kierkegaard also treats the concept, particularly in its relation to "the Eternal," "the Paradox," the Incarnation, "new birth," personal decision, and leap. [See *Philosophical Fragments* (*KW*, XIV), ed. and trans. Howard V. Hong and Edna H. Hong (Princeton: Princeton University Press, 1985), especially pp. 13, 19, 25, 28, 30, 43, 51–52, 56, and 58–64.]

83. *DBL,* vol. XXVI, pp. 460–62.

84. See *Evangelisk Ugeskrift* (Evangelical weekly) (1855), nos. 6–7, p. 90; nos. 11–12, pp. 177ff; no. 22, pp. 342 and 350ff. In his 19th *Fædrelandet* article (May 15, 1855), Kierkegaard alludes to Zeuthen's remarks about him; see *Attack upon "Christendom,"* pp. 52–53.

sacraments and clergy, Zeuthen was further provoked to write a long tract in three parts, which he entitled *Polemiske Blade imod Dr. Søren Kierkegaard* (Polemical sheets against S. K.).[85] He commenced by stating that Martensen's silence had been a dignified and meaningful silence *(en talende Taushed)*, but that he, Zeuthen, wished to speak out.[86] The tone thence quickly lapsed into personalized polemics—somewhat cheap at times—with Zeuthen going after Kierkegaard's "proud self-esteem,"[87] and heavy-handedly applying the words in John 4:20 ("He who says: I love God, and hates his brother, he is a liar") to Kierkegaard: "Dr. K. talks now more than before about his love for God, but also now more than before about his own genius."[88] The remainder of Part I of Zeuthen's tract argued against Kierkegaard's radical understanding of the New Testament's call to leave everything and follow Jesus. In the course of the discussion, Zeuthen defended the clergy against Kierkegaard's charge that, instead of the uncompromising either-or between God and Mammon which the New Testament demands, they represented a worldly both-and.[89]

In Part II, Zeuthen depicted Kierkegaard as a belligerent renegade with a contentious interpretation of religion: "Dr. S. K. calls his Christianity the New Testament's Christianity, but its real name is polemical Christianity . . . his passionate blindness and polemical lust lead him out beyond all the boundaries of truth."[90] Kierkegaard was described as one who would put any Christian precept to use in the service of his unrestrained polemics.[91] At one point Zeuthen accused him of desiring to foment rebellion among the people rather than being content with merely admonishing those who "unworthily" call themselves Christians.[92] This line of criticism was slightly ironic in view of Zeuthen's own proclivity toward polemics even in the title of his tract.

The third part began by conceding to Kierkegaard a few moments of truth in an otherwise unreasonable and falsely contrived critique.[93] But Zeuthen's point here was that this mixture of a little truth with a lot of falsehood produced confusion and generated doubts in souls already wavering. He concluded that according to Kierkegaard's rigid either-or

---

85. F. L. B. Zeuthen, *Polemiske Blade imod Dr. Søren Kierkegaard*, I-III (Copenhagen, 1855).
86. Ibid., I, p. 3.
87. Ibid., I, pp. 4–5.
88. Ibid., I, p. 6.
89. Ibid., I, pp. 14–16.
90. Ibid., II, pp. 6–7.
91. Ibid., II, p. 9.
92. Ibid., II, p. 12.
93. Ibid., III, p. 3.

demands one could be either a human being, or a Christian, but not both simultaneously.[94] The obvious implication was that this was a ridiculous position to espouse.

Sentiments similar to Zeuthen's were voiced by another warrior for the Church, Andreas Daniel Andresen (dates unavailable), a provost like Bloch. In a three-part tract called *Dr. Søren Kierkegaards falske Paastande* (S. K.'s false assertions),[95] Andresen argued that official Christianity has its own legitimacy and justification, and that the clergy can with a clear conscience live by evangelizing. He frequently gave the example of the Apostles and how they made their living evangelizing.[96] He based his position on a literal reading of 1 Corinthians 9:14: "Even so hath the Lord ordained that they which preach the gospel should live by the gospel." He also defended the sacraments of the Church—particularly infant baptism—which had repeatedly been the butt of Kierkegaard's derision.[97] His conclusion was that Kierkegaard had worked much evil by weakening people's respect for the divine and eternal, and by doing all he could to demolish confidence in the living words of Scripture, which remain the only comfort and guide in life; Kierkegaard was a concrete example of what happens when one speaks shamelessly about all that is sacred.[98]

One of the more amusing responses to Kierkegaard (though he hardly viewed it as such at the time), and one that stirred a whirlwind of discussion in the press, came from a young theology student named Christian Henrik Thurah (1830–98). In addition to studying theology Thurah cultivated many talents including drawing and poetry writing. He gravitated toward Grundtvigianism theologically, and was eventually ordained.[99] Toward the end of 1855 he published a couple of short essays and poems against Kierkegaard. Their tone was extreme to the point of cruelty, though when read today they can have a wickedly witty and entertaining ring to them. A poem entitled "Riimbrev til Johannes Forføreren alias Dr. Søren Kierkegaard" (Rhymed epistle to Johannes the Seducer alias

---

94. Ibid., III, p.11.

95. A. D. Andresen, *Dr. Søren Kierkegaards falske Paastande,* I–III: I and II in 1855, III in 1856 (Copenhagen, 1855-56).

96. Ibid., I, pp. 10–15; II, pp. 27–42; III, pp. 3–21.

97. Ibid., II, pp. 35ff. Kierkegaard's critique of infant baptism antedates the *Kirkekampen*. For his views on it during the church strife, see his *Øjeblikket* no. 7 in *Attack upon "Christendom,"* pp. 205f.

98. Andresen, ibid., III, p. 40.   99. *DBL,* vol. XXIV, p. 90.

S. K.) appeared on September 27, three days after Kierkegaard's ninth issue of *Øjeblikket* was published. It began with the lines:

> Oh hear this you sweet bastard
> With this unequaled tongue
> So smooth like any slimy eel
> So sharp like some cutting steel . . .

and proceeded to apply a string of violent adjectives to Kierkegaard's person and views.[100]

There is no mention of Thurah anywhere in Kierkegaard's journals, yet we do know that he owned a copy of this poem, read it, and was considerably upset by what he read. This comes to us from one who can be regarded as Kierkegaard's closest lifelong friend, the pastor Emil Boesen.[101] Kierkegaard was admitted to Frederik's Hospital on October 2 after having collapsed in the street a few days earlier—the same day, in fact, that Thurah's poem appeared in print.[102] He died on November 11, 1855. During those final days that Kierkegaard spent at the hospital, Boesen visited him regularly and the two of them entered into some highly illuminating exchanges, which Boesen later had the presence of mind to record in the form of a chronological account. For Sunday, October 21, Boesen wrote the following brief words: "I was only in there with him for an instant: he said, it was an inopportune time. He talked about

---

100. C. H. Thurah, "Riimbrev til Johannes Forføreren alias Dr. Søren Kierkegaard" (Copenhagen, 1855). A little further on (p. 9) Kierkegaard is called "Satan's sweet monkey," and after that (p. 14) Thurah writes the following verses to imply that Kierkegaard *is* Satan: "Hear this! When we shall all duly gather / It is the Ancient One, the Murderer / Whose role you in this play / Will at last be sure to assume. . . ." Relating Kierkegaard to one of his characters, Johannes the Seducer of *Either/Or* I, was not an original idea of Thurah's. See the piece "Taler Dr. Søren Kierkegaard ikke om sig selv?" (Is not S. K. speaking of himself?) in *Flyveposten,* June 4, 1855, where the anonymous author simply quotes a long passage from Kierkegaard's "Diary of a Seducer."

101. On Kierkegaard's relation with Emil Boesen see Carl Koch, *Søren Kierkegaard og Emil Boesen, Breve og Indledning med et Tillæg* (Copenhagen, 1901). For other brief accounts in English translation of Boesen's last conversations with Kierkegaard at the hospital see J. Hohlenberg, *Sören Kierkegaard: A Biography,* pp. 268ff., and Regis Jolivet, *Introduction to Kierkegaard,* trans. W. H. Barber (New York: Dutton, 1946), pp. 36–39.

102. Carl Weltzer speculates that the two events were not pure coincidence but causally related; that is, Thurah's ugly poem had a hand in worsening Kierkegaard's already failing health to the point of inducing his collapse; see Weltzer's *Peter og Søren Kierkegaard,* in 2 volumes (Copenhagen: Gad, 1936), vol. II, p. 262. Pages 257–63 are on Kierkegaard and Thurah.

Thurah and Martensen."[103] Thurah, then, was definitely on Kierkegaard's mind.

It is also possible that in talking about Thurah to Boesen, Kierkegaard brought up another short piece by the theology student which was dated October 6 and appeared as an independent tract on, or slightly after, that day.[104] Although Kierkegaard was in the hospital by then, someone might have brought the piece to his attention. This would only have added to his distress, since in it Thurah says that Kierkegaard mocked the Lord by calling himself God's tool; he mocked the Church and the entire profession of Christian teaching; and he mocked humanity by declaring marriage to be fornication and infant baptism an abomination in God's eyes.[105] More interesting is Thurah's self-justifying statement that he used Kierkegaard's "own weapons"—mockery, ridicule, unprincipledness, venom—against him: "precisely in these weapons lay his [Kierkegaard's] strength; . . . he attacked on a personal level, for he battled everyone without exception; I fought him personally in turn. He made fun of marriage and pointed fingers at all children; I mocked his celibacy and pointed fingers at his [thin] legs . . ."[106]

Reactions to Thurah's libelous campaign[107] inundated Copenhagen's publishing houses and daily papers that October; and they indicated the public's mood in the *Kirkekampen* on eve of Kierkegaard's death. The reactions came from various quarters and were mostly ones of shock and

103. See Boesen's account in Steen Johansen, ed., *Erindringer om Søren Kierkegaard*, p. 155.

104. C. H. Thurah, "Hvorfor netop saaledes? Præmisserne i Sagen C. H. Thurah contra Dr. S. Kierkegaard" (Why just like this? Premises in the matter of C. H. T. versus S. K.) (Copenhagen, October 6, 1855).

105. Ibid., p. 3.

106. Ibid., p. 4. Thurah ended by saying that, should Kierkegaard's behavior thereafter become customary in Denmark, he, Thurah, would only wish he had never been born and raised there.

107. Thurah was not satisfied with the two pieces mentioned above and soon added a third to them: "Mester Jakel. En Dyrehavs-Scene, gjengivet efter Virkeligheden" (Punch and Judy show. A Deer Park scene presented as reality) (Odense, 1855). This was published by Milo Forlag in Odense instead of by the Copenhagen-based C. G. Iversen Forlag that had hitherto published Thurah's attacks on Kierkegaard. The uproar caused by Thurah's first two pieces, and the criticism of Iversen for printing them (see *Dagbladet*, October 2, 1855) had made it impossible for Thurah to use the same publisher again. In this latest piece Thurah maintained Kierkegaard's "either-or" is actually a "both-and," that is, Kierkegaard wanted to be both Christian spokesman and Johannes the Seducer, both the water of life and filthy slush, both Christ and the devil. See A. Kabell, *Kierkegaardstudiet i Norden*, p. 57.

outrage, but there were a few noteworthy exceptions. Another young theology student, Peter Vilhelm Grove (1832-93)[108]—who in 1857 became a journalist and a correspondent for *Dagbladet*—wrote a swift reply to Thurah that was characterized by its good-tempered tone. Grove agreed that Kierkegaard had been excessive in his attacks on the Church and clergy, but he took Thurah to task for the extreme language he had used. In Grove's opinion, Thurah's savage counteroffensive had done him and other theologians more harm than it had done Kierkegaard, because it would be regarded as a dismal expression of the moral standpoint of theologians generally: in short, an eye for an eye is not the Christian way.[109] Thurah was also criticized by the author Thomas Lange (1829-87) in a poem that focused on the impropriety of such personal attacks.[110]

Yet the most consistent critic of Thurah was the newspaper *Dagbladet*.[111] In a couple of brief and anonymous reviews Thurah's brutality and coarseness were laid bare and denounced. One reviewer wrote that some theologians have defended the established Church against Kierkegaard's onslaught:

> The author of the new "Rhymed Epistle", however, goes in this respect beyond all boundaries; the Danish literature, which has its share of smut to exhibit, hardly has anything so vile, so filthy, so outrageous as this poem from a student of theology who appears to have caught exclusively the coarseness of Grundtvigianism. The author deserves the most serious chastisement for this indecent product.[112]

A second reviewer wrote that the question was not whether Kierkegaard was right, but whether such conduct as Thurah's was permissible under any circumstances: "There is a certain kind of combat which does injury only to the one who uses it, and not to the one against whom it is

---

108. *DBL*, vol. VIII, p. 337.
109. P. V. Grove, "Thurah og Søren Kierkegaard. Nogle Bemærkninger af en theologisk Student" (T. and S. K. Some remarks from a theology student) (Copenhagen, 1855). For brief, anonymous reviews of Grove's piece and Thurah's anti-Kierkegaard writings, the latter of which the reviewer says "have met deserved disapproval from all sides," see *Dagbladet*, October 12, 1855. See also C. Weltzer, *Peter og Søren Kierkegaard*, pp. 262-63; and A. Kabell, *Kierkegaardstudiet i Norden*, p. 63.
110. Thomas Lange, "Riimbrev til 'defensor fidei' alias stud. theol. Thurah" (Rhymed epistle to "the defender of the faith" alias T.) (Copenhagen, 1855).
111. This was mainly due to its editor C. S. A. Bille's friendly disposition toward Kierkegaard and his struggle.
112. Anonymous, "Et Indlæg i den Kierkegaardske Strid" (A contribution in the Kierkegaardian strife) in *Dagbladet*, October 2, 1855.

applied.[113] Even *Flyveposten,* a paper not known for its sympathy with Kierkegaard or his cause, found Thurah's poetry "disgraceful," and called it "in a word . . . one of the dirtiest and most vulgar writings that have ever been printed in Danish."[114]

It might appear reasonable to conclude that Thurah was fast becoming an embarrassment to Grundtvigians, given the outcry he was causing and the repeated emphasis of his Grundtvigian links. But no such thing is apparent from reading Hans Friedrich Helweg's article on Thurah in *Dagbladet.*[115] Helweg (1816–1901) was a pastor and a staunch disciple of Grundtvig, from whom he learned the organic relationship between Christianity and the historical tradition. He even imitated Grundtvig's abstruse style of writing, with the end product best described as "affected" analysis.[116] In his article he maintained that both *Dagbladet* and *Flyveposten* had overreacted to Thurah's poem. Kierkegaard liked to view his relation to the established order as analogous to that of Socrates with respect to the Athens of his day, wrote Helweg. But Socrates had his Aristophanes, and no one today labels the satirical Greek playwright's works "profane literature" or "smut." And was Helweg therefore making of Thurah an Aristophanes? "By no means," he answered his own rhetorical question, since "our modern Socrates," namely Kierkegaard, is not just that but also an Aristophanes of sorts, and a notorious satirist. Helweg's point was that a fine line separates the poetic from the debased in literature, and the writings of both Thurah and Kierkegaard combine elements of the two.

There were some exceptions to the overwhelming chorus of condemnation that Thurah's slander of Kierkegaard met with. As one would expect *Kjøbenhavnsposten,* for example, published an anonymous article on Thurah's poem, which argued that he was merely making use of the same linguistic devices as Kierkegaard and resorting to the same severity of expression as in many of Kierkegaard's own writings. Then the writer became less reserved in his defense of Thurah:

> Mr. Kierkegaard has driven his noxiousness to such a high degree of shamelessness; he has by his paradoxes, insane interpretations of a few stray texts

---

113. *Dagbladet,* October 12, 1855.

114. *Flyveposten,* October 5, 1855. Thurah is described as displaying "a self-styled Grundtvigian arrogance," and being out "to revolt the feelings of all readers."

115. Fr. Helweg, "Et Ord om Thurahs Riimbrev" (A word on T.'s rhymed epistle) in *Dagbladet,* October 26, 1855.

116. *DBL,* vol. X, pp. 34–36.

and of a single aspect of Christianity's teachings, sought to show the impossibility of combining Christianity with the life of the religious community, and has by this so openly intended the disgrace of the Church's teachers that a Christian theologian who was truly permeated by eagerness and zeal for his vocation could only reply with the harshness and outspokenness which Mr. Thurah has used, and which alone could be expected to exert some effect.[117]

Although Thurah was a Grundtvigian, he did not really reflect the mainstream attitude of the followers of Grundtvig toward the *Kirkekampen* instigated by Kierkegaard. Most of those belonging to "the Church party" who responded to Kierkegaard were influenced in varying degrees by Grundtvig.[118] There was a core of die-hard Grundtvigians, however, who cannot be classified in the same category with speculative theologians like Martensen and Zeuthen. In fact they tended to be critical of that form of theology, as well as of the ease with which church and state were combined in Denmark. To this extent they shared common targets with Kierkegaard, but as Kierkegaard's attacks on the Church and her sacraments mounted, the Grundtvigians reacted sharply. The main organ through which they presented their views was the periodical *Dansk Kirketidende*. Many of the articles written on Kierkegaard in 1855 reflect this mixture of approval and criticism. In one, for example, L. N. Boisen (1803-75), while defending the established Church and the clergy by resorting to frequent scriptural references in refutation of Kierkegaard's charge that true Christians no longer existed, conceded that it was good of Kierkegaard to strive to awaken that inner unrest which a proper reading of the Gospels ought to evoke.[119] Boisen also agreed with Kierkegaard that the disputed concept "truth witness" cannot be applied indiscriminately to members of the clergy. Kierkegaard's problem, in Boisen's view, was that he went further and denied the clergy the general calling to

---

117. *Kjøbenhavnsposten*, October 18, 1855.

118. It must be kept in mind that Grundtvigianism was not a separate sect outside the Danish Lutheran Church, but rather a movement within the Church emphasizing the centrality of the sacraments, the tradition, and the national character and communal life of the faithful in the Church. However, the Grundtvigians and "the Church Party" of the *Kirkekampen* were not the same—and indeed were often at odds—even though a few members of one group belonged to the other also.

119. L. N. Boisen, "Indlæg i Sagen: S. K. contra 'det bestaaende' " (Contribution to the matter: S. K. versus "the established") in *Dansk Kirketidende,* no. 20, ed. L. Helveg and C. J. Brandt (Copenhagen, May 6, 1855), pp. 313-17. Boisen was a pastor and an expert on ancient biblical languages. In 1833-34 he met and became a follower of Grundtvig; see *DBL,* vol. III, pp. 392-93.

become witnesses to truth; he even denied to everyone, including himself, the title "Christian," which, said Boisen, was too extreme.[120] He terminated his article, however, on a positive note with respect to Kierkegaard: "I regard S. Kierkegaard's action to be important and momentous . . . he has undertaken this step in heartfelt seriousness and not without a severe struggle within himself." In any case, concluded Boisen optimistically, the whole affair will undoubtedly lead to the awakening of greater seriousness.[121] Boisen's article summarized the Grundtvigian attitude toward Kierkegaard: very critical of his position regarding the Church, yet genuinely approving of the seriousness with which he took the relationship to God.

Among those also publishing in *Dansk Kirketidende* was a curious young student who had been gripped by Kierkegaard's outspoken writings on the Church. This was Jacob Christian Martin Ørum (1823–1905), and to what extent, if any, he was a Grundtvigian is unclear.[122] Ørum's first piece came in the form of a critique of J. Paludan-Müller's response to Kierkegaard.[123] He termed as baseless Paludan-Müller's charge that Kierkegaard was falsifying Christianity, and in a brief discussion of Kierkegaard's view of Mynster's sermons, Ørum arrived at the conclusion that Kierkegaard and Paludan-Müller agreed that these sermons were hardly penitential ones designed to arouse "fear and trembling." Several months later, Ørum published another article dealing this time with Kierkegaard's *Øjeblikket*.[124] After pressing Kierkegaard's call for a separation of church and state, and the two realms of God and Caesar—a theme which found favorable echoes in Grundtvigian circles—Ørum made the following courageous declaration: "It is my full and firm belief, that *Øjeblikket* was written in the service of the truth, and with the warmest feelings for Christianity."[125] He added that only by keeping in mind Kierkegaard's basic guiding thought—Christianity as an absolute truth utterly

---

120. Boisen, "Indlæg i Sagen," pp. 321–22. The recurring criticism that Kierkegaard was too extreme is the best indication of how little aware people were of his role as a corrective, and the need for extremes in precisely such a role.

121. Ibid., p. 325.

122. Ørum eventually became a teacher and the director of a school in Vordingsborg from 1861–97. See *DBL*, vol. XXVI, p. 590.

123. J. C. M. Ørum, "Forespørgsel til Pastor J. Paludan-Müller i Aalborg" (Enquiry to pastor J. P-M in Aalborg) in *Dansk Kirketidende*, nos. 7–8, February 25, 1855, pp. 142–44.

124. J. C. M. Ørum, "Om S. Kierkegaards 'Øjcblikke'" (On S. K.'s "Moment") in *Dansk Kirketidende*, no. 45, November 4, 1855, pp. 742–44.

125. Ibid., p. 743.

irreconcilable with the world—will all the pieces in his attack coalesce to constitute "an organic whole" *(et organisk Hele)*.[126] We do not know whether these words of support, a few days before Kierkegaard's death and in the wake of Thurah's vicious assault, ever came to his attention.

A regular contributor to *Dansk Kirketidende* was the Grundtvigian Friedrich Helweg. His articles on Kierkegaard tended to be long-winded and involved. In one of these he attempted a comprehensive discussion of Kierkegaard's concept of faith as found throughout his writings, both signed and pseudonymous.[127] As an early attempt of its kind, it did offer a few interesting insights,[128] but on the whole it fell short of being an adequate treatment of such a complex subject. Helweg then wrote a study of Hegelianism in Denmark, which after the first few pages became a treatment of Kierkegaard's relation to Hegel. He began by stating that Hegelianism came to an end with Kierkegaard, even though the latter, in Helweg's view, did not completely repudiate Hegel.[129] He then proceeded to discuss their relationship, starting with the *Concept of Irony*, and showed in what ways Hegel had been surpassed by Kierkegaard's philosophy. Kierkegaard's critique of Martensen's Hegelianism and how it served to wean Rasmus Nielsen away from Hegel were also covered. The significance of Helweg's survey is that it underscored another common area between the Grundtvigians and Kierkegaard: both were highly suspicious of speculative theology and critical of its Hegelian philosophical underpinnings.

Grundtvig himself did not participate in the daily press debates of the *Kirkekampen*, and generally eschewed writing for the dailies. He tried deliberately to maintain a distance from the controversy that was raging. In April 1855, someone signing "en Lægmand" (a layman) had written in *Flyveposten* that Grundtvig was "a man with apostolic authority," and

126. Ibid., p. 744.
127. See Fr. Helweg, "Dr. S. Kierkegaards og Bibelens Beskrivelse af den Christne Tro" (S. K.'s and the Bible's accounts of the Christian faith) in *Dansk Kirketidende,* no. 29, July 1, 1855, pp. 457–72. Helweg continued to write on Kierkegaard's Church struggle and the question of separating church and state in *Dansk Kirketidende* during 1856 and 1857.
128. For example Helweg's breakdown of those elements in Kierkegaard's concept of faith that revealed a Lutheran tendency (inwardness and personal appropriation), those that pointed in a Catholic (Roman) direction (the importance of the demand "thou shalt," that is works oriented), and those that were peculiarly Kierkegaard's (faith as suffering and faith's relation to paradox, or the *credo quia absurdum*).
129. Fr. Helweg, "Hegelianismen i Danmark," in *Dansk Kirketidende,* no. 51, December 16, 1855, p. 829.

then quoted from a talk Grundtvig gave before the Danish Parliament *(Rigsdag)* in which he said that the clergy are called to be witnesses to the truth and the Lord has granted all his messengers the same standing in his eyes; he also mentioned "the icy scoffer, who always dangles like icicles under the Church roof."[130] Kierkegaard made a direct reference to Grundtvig's supposed apostolic authority in his sixth issue of *Øjeblikket,* and dismissed it out of hand. The only freedom Grundtvig ever fought for, wrote Kierkegaard, was freedom for himself and his followers from "the yoke which the state-Church laid upon him;" he never fought for the Christianity of the Apostles.[131] The possible allusion to him as an "icy scoffer" undoubtedly contributed to Kierkegaard's anger.

For his part Grundtvig, although staying aloof from the public debate, did not disagree totally with Kierkegaard's stand. He too believed, for instance, that Mynster hardly merited the title "truth witness." He was also encouraged indirectly by Kierkegaard's open confrontation with the state-Church to begin to demand a separation of the two, and to call for a national or people's Church having an autonomous status with guarantees for the freedom of its pastors.[132] As the nineteenth century progressed, it was the Grundtvigians who benefited the most from the legacy of the *Kirkekampen* initiated by Kierkegaard in terms of reforms within the Danish Lutheran Church.

Only after Kierkegaard's death did Grundtvig actually make a direct reference to the *"Kirke-Storm,"* as he called it, and to "him who awakened it," without mentioning his name. This came in an article he wrote for *Dansk Kirketidende.*[133] In it he also predicted the dust would settle by

---

130. En Lægmand, "Et Ord i den Kierkegaardske Sag" (A word in the Kierkegaard affair), in *Flyveposten,* April 16, 1855.

131. *Attack upon "Christendom,"* pp. 184–85. Like Mynster and Martensen, Grundtvig was accused by Kierkegaard of being too lukewarm and indifferent to the radicalness of the Christian message.

132. J. Osker Andersen, *Survey of the History of the Church in Denmark,* pp. 58–59.

133. N. F. S. Grundtvig, "Om en christelig Skilsmisse fra Folke-Kirken" (On a Christian separation from the people's church), in *Dansk Kirketidende,* no. 49, December 2, 1855, pp. 798f. Kierkegaard was also referred to as "the recently deceased storm-awakener." On several occasions during Kierkegaard's attack on the Church, Grundtvig reacted in his Sunday sermons to specific criticisms and theological points made by Kierkegaard, without, however, injecting himself directly in the public combat. For a compilation of Grundtvig's Sunday sermons from the period see P. G. Lindhardt, *Konfrontation* (Copenhagen: Akademisk Forlag, 1974). See also by the same author an overview of Kierkegaard's attack entitled *Søren Kierkegaards Angreb paa Folkekirken* (Aarhus: Aros, 1955).

itself on the whole affair now that the one who started it was gone. In Grundtvig's eyes Kierkegaard had always been too ascetically inclined, and it was therefore time to get on with the business of securing greater freedoms for a national church unencumbered either by state control or by speculative theology.

Indeed both "the Church party" and the followers of Grundtvig were firmly opposed to Kierkegaard's person-oriented Christianity, his focus upon "the single individual's" direct relation to God as the centerpiece of Christian faith. In this sense Kierkegaard was closer to the evangelical revivalists and the pietists, even though he did not join any sect or found one. This, however, did not deter many among his adversaries from circulating rumors to the effect that Kierkegaard was on the verge of establishing a new party, or that he already belonged to a fanatic sect. Some, especially Grundtvigians, led an anti-Kierkegaard campaign after his death, mostly in outlying rural areas where pietist tendencies were strong and where they feared Kierkegaard cults might begin to emerge. This action was not surprising, considering that *Dansk Kirketidende,* the Grundtvigian mouthpiece, spent much ink polemicizing against various sects, particularly the Mormons.

Kierkegaard's Christian individualism did cause reverberations in pietist circles, mainly in Norway. These reverberations predated the *Kirkekampen* and were galvanized by it. Some of Kierkegaard's religious writings, notably *Works of Love* (1847), were being read in Norway long before 1855.[134] With the appearance of *Øjeblikket,* interest in Kierkegaard's earlier writings, especially *Practice in Christianity* (referred to repeatedly by the author in his articles), was heightened. By covering developments extensively during the *Kirkekampen* in neighboring Denmark, the Norwegian press played a decisive role in bringing Kierkegaard's views to a broad reading public. *Christianiaposten* led the way with a series of articles containing long commentaries on and excerpts from Kierkegaard's *Fædrelandet* and *Øjeblikket* articles as they appeared.[135] The tone was

---

134. Valborg Erichsen, "Søren Kierkegaards betydning for norsk Aandsliv," *EDDA: Nordisk Tidsskrift for Litteraturforskning,* vol. 19, 10th year, copy 2 (Christiania, 1923), p. 231.

135. Ibid., pp. 231–32; see also Harald Beyer, "Søren Kierkegaards betydning for norsk Aandsliv," *EDDA,* vol. 19, 10th year, copy 1 (Christiania, 1923), p. 3. *Christianiaposten,* no. 2317 (1855), named many of Kierkegaard's earlier aesthetic and philosophical works, pointing out that a proper understanding of his relation to Christianity entailed delving into these writings in order to see how he paved the way to his present position. See Erichsen, "Søren Kierkegaards betydning" (2), p. 234.

generally supportive, and this was characteristic of most Norwegian papers that covered the *Kirkekampen*.[136]

Øjeblikket was truly a watershed for Kierkegaard's reception in Norway. It acted as a catalyst, both by popularizing Kierkegaard's critique of official Christianity and by arousing interest in his earlier works. Its overall impact on Norwegian religious life would be difficult to exaggerate; one can actually speak of a "pre-*Øjeblikket*" and a "post-*Øjeblikket*" phase in the history of religious development in Norway. This phenomenon merits closer investigation.

Tensions between an established institutional clergy and free-roving revivalist preachers has always been a feature of Church history. The first half of the nineteenth century in Norway was dominated by such tensions, and they eventually transcended the narrow confines of the Norwegian religious scene to take on an added political dimension that stemmed from a mounting national desire to become independent of the Kingdom of Denmark. Thus the concept of the state-Church, for instance, hitherto firmly ensconced in Denmark and Nordic life generally, began to come under increasing fire from several quarters, including the outspoken pietists of Norway. The deep spiritual cleft between the Danish and Norwegian temperaments expressed itself in the two opposing religious camps: the Grundtvigians and the official Church hierarchy on the one hand, and the pietist Haugians on the other. In Norway the open struggle with the state-Church began about 1850, long before *Øjeblikket*, and centered around several cities that were the traditional seats of pietism: Skien, Tromsø, Fredrikshald, Kragerø, Trondhjem, Stavanger, Grimstad, Bergen, and even the capital, Christiania (later Oslo). The struggle usually took the form of defiant and enthusiastic public revivals in which the state-Church was denounced, Scripture was quoted extensively, and a call for a radical personal conversion was made by the revivalist preacher.

A leading figure of the pietist revival in Norway in the mid-nineteenth century, one who came to be regarded as the successor of Hauge, was Gustav Adolph Lammers (1802–78), a tall and stately man with a thunderous voice and an arresting eloquence. Lammers was Danish by birth, the son of an officer from Copenhagen, but he moved to Norway for his

---

136. A good indication of this was the outpouring of articles in defense of Kierkegaard following Thurah's attack, which received wide coverage in Norway; see, for example, the article by "xy" entitled "Protest med Mere til C. H. Thurah," in *Christianiaposten*, no. 2708 (March 20, 1856).

education and in 1849 took up residence in Skien, where, as a pastor, he began to exercise great authority through his revivalistic preaching. His influence spread to many Norwegian towns, and he acquired a massive following. He commenced his crusade with a battle against indecisiveness and moral laxity, but toward the mid-1850s his sermons took a sudden radical turn and he became an outspoken enemy of the state-Church and its sacraments. There was only one reason for this new change: Lammers was reading Kierkegaard's *Øjeblikket* at the time. It was *Øjeblikket*—and especially the seventh issue, where infant baptism is condemned—that led Lammers to a direct confrontation with the state-Church. Lammers's fiery sermons were full of direct quotations from *Øjeblikket*, with whole passages read verbatim sometimes. He attacked infant baptism and the confirmation of children, even writing his own treatise against baptism, before finally leaving the Church and ceasing to be a pastor. This occurred on March 19, 1856, and as a result many of his supporters stormed out of the Church and began to agitate openly against it. *Øjeblikket* spread among these revivalists like wildfire. At times the agitation took on strange forms. In Tromsø, for example, Kierkegaard's name was even used in a Catholic pamphlet entitled *Jesu Kjærlighet* (1856) in order to foment rebellion against the Lutheran Church. Everywhere among the Norwegian pietists, Kierkegaard was seen as a prophet.[137]

Lammers had many aesthetic interests in his youth, and it is not inconceivable that his readings would independently have led him to Kierkegaard. It is more likely, however, that he was pointed in that direction by another great name in Norwegian pietism, Gisle Johnson (1822–94).[138] Johnson had definitely read *Practice in Christianity* and *For Self-Examination* before 1855. Several Kierkegaardian themes informed Johnson's spirituality, themes such as the uncompromising either-or motif, the paradoxical in faith, and a personal relationship with God.[139] Yet Johnson was also known for his strict Lutheran orthodoxy, and indeed as a theologian he represented the leading spirit in the new synthesis of pietism, puritanism, and orthodoxy during the second half of the nineteenth cen-

---

137. On Lammers see Paulus Svendsen, "Norwegian Literature," in *The Legacy and Interpretation of Kierkegaard*, in vol. 8 of *Bibliotheca Kierkegaardiana* (1981), pp. 18–19. See also H. Beyer, "Søren Kierkegaards betydning for norsk Aandsliv," *EDDA*, vol. 19, 10th year, copy 1, pp. 11–13; and V. Erichsen, "Søren Kierkegaards betydning for norsk Aandsliv," *EDDA*, vol. 19, 10th year, copy 2, pp. 290ff.

138. Erichsen, "Søren Kierkegaards betydning" (2), p. 283.

139. Ibid., pp. 280–82.

tury in Norway. He became a lecturer in theology at Christiania University in 1849, and full professor in 1860.[140]

Johnson was initially entranced by *Øjeblikket,* which opened his eyes to many defects in the state-Church. He supported Lammers in 1855, and wrote some articles in agreement with his positions early in the following year.[141] Things began to change between them, however, after Lammers left the Church in March 1856. Johnson drew a clear line between criticizing the Church with a view to improving it and quitting it altogether. He rethought his earlier Kierkegaardian orientation and decided it had been flawed. In 1857 he wrote a treatise against Lammers and in defense of infant baptism which he entitled "Nogle Ord om Barnedaaben" (A few words on infant baptism). He traveled to Skien and Tromsø from Christiania to counteract Lammers's growing influence, but his greatest impact in this regard came through his activities in the theological student societies at Christiania University, where many of the young men preparing to enter the ministry were having second thoughts after being exposed to *Øjeblikket* in 1855 and 1856. Heated debates raged about whether it was Christianly justifiable to remain or become a pastor in the state-Church.[142] Kierkegaard's ideas were being tossed back and forth among the theology students, and Johnson found much to keep him busy. It was common to hear Kierkegaardian catchwords in student circles: the single individual, the aesthetic stage, the paradox, either/or, and so on. This vocabulary only increased in currency with time and seeped into various student publications.[143] Johnson preached to the students that it was a wonderful calling to be a minister of the Church, but even his sermons retained some Kierkegaardian themes, such as his emphasis on commitment and attack on complacency, and his view of faith as an inward relation with God.[144] In this way Johnson acted to temper some of the radical influence that *Øjeblikket* was having on Norway's youth.

The combined effects of *Øjeblikket* and Lammers's revivalism precipitated a mass exodus from the state-Church in Norway during the latter

140. Svendsen, "Norwegian Literature," pp. 19–20.
141. See, for example, *Norsk Kirketidende* (February 1856), nos. 6–10.
142. Beyer, "Søren Kierkegaards betydning" (1), pp. 6–7 and 15. The author lists some of the prominent participants in the debates. With most of these students the period of doubts turned out to have been a passing phase, and they went on to be ordained. For more on Norwegian theology students and Kierkegaard in the 1850s see Erichsen, "Søren Kierkegaards betydning" (2), pp. 316ff.
143. Erichsen, ibid., pp. 319–22.
144. Beyer, "Søren Kierkegaards betydning" (1), p. 7.

half of the 1850s. This "Laymen's Movement" involved the departure of both pastors and members of their congregations. A number of these became Baptists, and the movement took on a definite schismatic and sectarian character. Toward the end of the fifties, however, the movement began to diminish and even be reversed. Many returned to the Church; the frequency and intensity of the revivals receded. In Skien, Lammers himself re-entered the Church in 1860 and with him a host of the movement's original leaders. Lammers was not reappointed pastor, and he lived on painting altar pieces and triptychs until his death on May 2, 1878.[145] Although the outer furor was over, Kierkegaardian influences remained and left a lasting imprint on the Norwegian religious consciousness, both lay and clerical. The awakening that *Øjeblikket* had caused resulted in a fresh appreciation for the message of the New Testament with its implications for the life of the individual.

Nordic pietism's attraction to Kierkegaard rested chiefly on two foundations: his Christian individualism based on personal decision, and his critique of the established state-Church. One can add to these a certain implied emphasis in his religious writings on living a sanctified life (the practice of godliness, or the *imitatio Christi*), which leaned in the direction of "good works" as essential for salvation and was correspondingly uncharacteristic of Lutheran Protestantism. This last feature appealed to the mystical streak in pietism. These affinities, however, do not make of Kierkegaard a pietist, although during his formative years he read and was deeply influenced by the writings of the great eighteenth-century German pietists, many of whose books he owned.[146]

If Kierkegaard's strife with official Christianity and the Church had such wide repercussions in Norway, what were the echoes a little closer to home, in the Danish countryside? They certainly were not as pronounced or tumultuous as in Norway; nevertheless, the *Kirkekampen* was definitely felt beyond the city limits of Copenhagen, and for an assessment of that one must turn to the provincial press. The first thing one notices is the proliferation of articles in support of Kierkegaard's action. This

---

145. Ibid., pp. 14–15.

146. Kierkegaard's relation to pietism is complex. For a discussion of Kierkegaard's knowledge of Brorson and the German pietists Spener, Francke, and Tersteegen see Marie Mikulova Thulstrup, *Kierkegaard og Pietismen,* published in the Søren Kierkegaard Selskabets Populære Skrifter, no. 13 (Copenhagen: Munksgaard, 1967), available also in English translation as the section entitled "Pietism" of *Kierkegaard and Great Traditions,* in *Bibliotheca Kierkegaardiana,* vol. 6 (1981), pp. 173–222.

was significant and gave many Grundtvigians and members of "the Church party" plenty to worry about.

The influential newspaper of southern Jutland, *Dannevirke*,[147] published in the town of Haderslev in Schleswig, was consistently on Kierkegaard's side and provided sustained coverage of the debate in Copenhagen with frequent extracts from Kierkegaard's articles. The tone of the writers was candid and aggressive. They did not hesitate, for instance, to make fun of those Copenhagen papers championing the anti-Kierkegaard crusade: you read one, you have read them all, was the way one writer aptly summed it up.[148] Another who signed "UK-d" and was a frequent contributor to the paper had nothing but praise for *Fædrelandet*, in whose pages Kierkegaard waged the first part of his fight: "the most distinguished paper in the land," he called it.[149] This writer was of the opinion that Kierkegaard had correctly depicted the distinction between the Christianity of the New Testament and official Christianity or Christendom. He reflected the sincere feelings of many writers during the *Kirkekampen* who hoped the present strife would lead to the reemergence of a more personal Christian life among believers.[150]

A perceptible anticlerical—and specifically anti-Grundtvigian—streak pervaded *Dannevirke*'s treatment of the *Kirkekampen*. The newspaper was in the habit of printing comments sent in by pastors questioning the propriety of the *Dannevirke*-Kierkegaard connection, and then providing

---

147. Originally, Dannevirke was the name of the boundary rampart in southern Jutland (Danne refers to Denmark). The word "Dannevirke" translates roughly into "activity of cultivation," which suggests a paper designed to educate the public and fashion opinion. Its founder and editor was Peter Christian Koch (1807–80). It began as a bi-weekly, and its first issue appeared on July 20, 1838. It became a daily in the summer of 1851. It had the unique and controversial feature of using popular colloquial language in many of its articles in order to counteract the influence of German in the region. It played an active role in the national question of Schleswig-Holstein and battled separatist tendencies. For more on *Dannevirke*, see Kirchhoff-Larsen, *Den Danske Presses Historie*, III, pp. 138ff.; on P. C. Koch see pp. 131ff.

148. Anonymous, "S. K. og Hans polemiske Modstandere" (S. K. and his polemical opponents) in *Dannevirke*, January 11, 1855. The writer singled out specifically *Flyveposten* and *Berlingske Tidende* for criticism.

149. UK-d, "Dr. S. Kierkegaards Kamp," in *Dannevirke*, April 7, 1855.

150. In this he was in agreement with some of the contributors to *Dagbladet*, a paper that showed much sympathy to Kierkegaard's positions during the *Kirkekampen*. See, for example, the anonymous article "Den Kierkegaardske Strid" in *Dagbladet*, April 25, 1855, in which it is suggested that the best way to rectify the spiritual situation would be to reintroduce home devotion: "Christ is a stranger in our homes," laments the writer.

a reply, usually by the editor P. C. Koch, either in the same issue or on the following day. Koch had come under the spell of Kierkegaard's powerful thrusts against the state-Church; he decided to make the pages of his publication available for discussion of the issue. He himself, however, was sympathetic to Kierkegaard's position, and made no attempt to disguise his feelings. In one of his replies to a piece by the Grundtvigian cleric F. E. Boisen that *Dannevirke* printed, Koch began thus: "*'Dannevirke'* considers Dr. S. Kierkegaard's treatises in *'Fædrelandet'* very timely, necessary, and beneficial for the nation's spiritual welfare."[151] He added that *Dannevirke's* task was to render Kierkegaard's writings accessible to a wider circle of readers. On another occasion Koch wrote that Kierkegaard "is a reformer, and as such must have alarmed the clergy."[152] He was responding to an anonymous Schleswigian pastor's protests that *Dannevirke*, which has battled all separatist tendencies in the political arena, ought not to promote Kierkegaard's anti-Church doctrines. Such a paper, continued the pastor, is not the place where views like those of Kierkegaard should get an airing.[153]

Actually the real anti-Grundtvigian at *Dannevirke* was not Koch but "UK-d," who wrote freely that Grundtvigians initially rubbed their hands with glee when Kierkegaard fired his opening salvos at Mynster. But they took up arms against Kierkegaard when they perceived the edifice of the established Church starting to crumble under the force of his attacks.[154] Elsewhere, the same writer summed up his point dramatically: "The

151. See P. C. Koch in *Dannevirke*, April 12, 1855. Boisen, writing in the previous day's edition under the title " 'Dannevirke' og Dr. S. Kierkegaard," said he commended the paper's coverage of the affair, and he, for one, was not caught off guard by Kierkegaard's attack, and even considered Kierkegaard's cry of protest as one made by "a friendly voice," until the moment when Kierkegaard declared that Christianity and true Christians no longer existed. Boisen criticized *Dannevirke* for continuing to support Kierkegaard after that statement.

152. See P. C. Koch in *Dannevirke*, July 12, 1855.

153. See the same issue of *Dannevirke* as in the previous note. The pastor insinuated that Kierkegaard should sell all his possessions and give the money to the poor in order to set an example. Koch, in his reply, defended Kierkegaard on this score.

154. "Kierkegaard has overthrown the Christendom of our time," wrote the author; see UK-d, "Grundtvigianerne—S. Kierkegaard: Strøtanker" (Grundtvigians—S. K.: aphorisms) in *Dannevirke*, April 28, 1855. The article prompted a reply from J. V. Bloch, which tried to dissociate totally the Grundtvigians from Kierkegaard and claimed that, if anything, Kierkegaard was closer to the Catholics; see *Dansk Kirketidende*, no. 27, June 17, 1855, pp. 436-40.

state-Church and her servants should now ... begin to experience their 1848."[155]

Of the provincial newspapers, *Dannevirke* was the one that concerned itself the most with the *Kirkekampen,* but there were others. An example of straightforward factual reporting at the outset of the debate can be obtained from *Holbæk Amts Avis,* the daily paper for the district of Holbæk, a town in Zeeland west of Copenhagen. Their reporter in Copenhagen wrote on January 3 that Dr. Kierkegaard had suddenly launched "a strong and bitter" attack on the deceased Mynster, and he predicted correctly that "this will very likely give rise to an entire cycle of literature."[156] A little further to the south, the main paper for the Diocese of Lolland and Falster presented a mixed assortment of articles on the events as they unfolded in Copenhagen. Some were critical of Kierkegaard and did not believe his attack could be justified as "a good deed," as Rasmus Nielsen had argued.[157] Others termed his words about Mynster "severe, hard accusations" coming from one who was no longer a young theology candidate but had been around for some time and "gained a distinguished literary name."[158] There were those, on the other hand, who felt that Kierkegaard had put his finger precisely on the basic problem, and it had become a known fact that official Christianity was no more than a matter of appeasement and compromise; Christians were taking Christianity for granted and then having nothing to do with its substance.[159]

Whether in the capital, in the provinces, or across the sea in Norway, the issues raised by Kierkegaard during the *Kirkekampen* did not die with him; his death, however, did rob the onslaught of much of its momentum. Both his supporters and his adversaries were sobered by his death, and many among them began to reflect more profoundly on the significance of his tempestuous final years. To some his death was a relief, even though

---

155. See UK-d, "Kirkespørgsmaalet i Kongeriget" (The church question in the Kingdom of Denmark), in *Dannevirke,* July 20, 1855. Not even Thurah was spared. Someone signing "-d-n" wrote a long poem about his "impression" of Thurah's slanderous verse; see *Dannevirke,* October 22, 1855.

156. *Holbæk Amts Avis,* January 3, 1855.

157. See en Lægmand, "Kan Dr. phil. Søren Kierkegaards Angreb paa Biskop Mynsters Eftermæle kaldes 'en god gjerning'?" in *Lolland-Falsters Stiftstidende,* January 25, 1855. The reference in the title is to Rasmus Nielsen's article in *Fædrelandet* of January 10; see discussion earlier.

158. See "X," "Om Sandhedsvidnestriden" in *Lolland-Falsters Stiftstidende,* January 1, 1855.

159. See the letter to the editor from "f" in *Lolland-Falsters Stiftstidende,* February 14, 1855, in reply to another anonymous piece in the same paper dated January 31.

they would learn with time that the aftereffects were not going to fade quickly. To others, however, death was an occasion to look back on the life of this strange man and attempt to make fuller sense of his enigmatic writings.[160]

Kierkegaard died on November 11, 1855. All the major newspapers in Copenhagen and beyond carried obituaries on him the following day and accounts of his funeral on November 18. Here again a spectrum of reactions can be observed. While, for instance, *Fædrelandet* called him "Denmark's greatest religious author," *Kjøbenhavnsposten*, in a curt, six-line notice, wrote condescendingly: "He will certainly be judged after his death more mildly and better than he himself has judged others who were deceased ... as a consequence of his bodily sufferings, he cannot be considered during his later life to have been a complete master over his own thoughts and words."[161] *Morgenposten*, a paper that hitherto had covered the *Kirkekampen* only peripherally, now wrote an obituary extolling Kierkegaard's virtues and ending with the words: "Therefore Søren Kierkegaard's works will not sink into oblivion with his death."[162] *Dagbladet*'s dispassionate analysis made the point that one can correctly contemplate Kierkegaard's enterprise as a consequence of Protestantism in that he detached himself from the established Church and turned exclusively to the single individual.[163] *Flyveposten*, in a vein similar to that of *Kjøbenhavnsposten*, wrote snidely that now that Kierkegaard was dead, people would not follow the example he set in his attack on the deceased Mynster.[164]

---

160. Six of his works came out in second editions during his lifetime. These were: *Either/Or* (1843; 2d ed. 1849); *Works of Love* (1847; 2d ed. 1852); *The Lily in the Field and the Bird of the Air* (1849; 2d ed. 1854); *Practice in Christianity* (1850; 2d ed. 1855); *Two Discourses at the Communion on Fridays* (1851; 2d ed. 1852); and *For Self-Examination* (1851; 2d ed. 1852). Many of his writings were published simultaneously in Copenhagen and Christiania. See J. Himmelstrup, *Søren Kierkegaard International Bibliografi*, pp. 9–13. For an interesting and systematic account of Kierkegaard's attacks on the Church, its officials, and Christendom, and the connection between these attacks and the sociopolitical makeup of Denmark at the time, see the chapter entitled "The Attack on Christendom" in Bruce Kirmmse, *Kierkegaard in Golden Age Denmark* (Bloomington, Indiana: Indiana University Press, 1990), pp. 449–81. Kirmmse devotes only five pages at the end of his huge and informative study to reactions to Kierkegaard's attack. See "Epilogue: The Response to the Attack on Christendom," pp. 482–86.

161. *Fædrelandet*, November 12, 1855; *Kjøbenhavnsposten*, November 13, 1855.

162. *Morgenposten* (Morning post), November 14, 1855. The same point was made at the conclusion of another article on Kierkegaard; see *Morgenposten*, November 20, 1855: "Søren Kierkegaard's works will not die with him."

163. *Dagbladet*, November 14, 1855.   164. *Flyveposten*, November 16, 1855.

Of significance was the announcement of Kierkegaard's death in the prestigious Swedish newspaper *Aftonbaldet* (Evening paper) on November 22:

> One of Denmark's most intelligent and profound thinkers, who is also the greatest religious author in Scandinavia . . . has died in Copenhagen. . . . His literary work is well known to the educated world in Sweden. We have already given an account of the attack he recently began against official Christianity and its prelatical lords with their coats of arms. . . . The passing of such a talented, honest, courageous, and self-sacrificing fighter for truth will certainly call forth feelings of sorrow in all the three northern kingdoms.[165]

Although Sweden did not experience anything resembling the religious upheavals in Norway caused by *Øjeblikket,* a number of Swedish intellectuals and theologians followed the *Kirkekampen* avidly and concurred with Kierkegaard on many of the points he raised.[166] More important for them than the accounts of the attack in the Swedish press were the translations of all nine *Øjeblikket* articles into Swedish, which appeared in 1855 and were reissued in 1858.[167] Thus Fredrika Bremer's assessment that "Kierkegaard's 'Moment' has awakened here a considerable though passing sensation," written to her friend Bishop Martensen some months after Kierkegaard's death, was only partly true: the sensation was indeed

---

165. *Aftonbladet,* November 22, 1855. The quote is taken from a translation of the Swedish obituary by T. H. Croxall in his *Glimpses and Impressions of Kierkegaard* (London: Welwyn Herts-J. Nisbet, 1959), pp. 84–85. Croxall's book is the first and only source that provides English translations of a mere handful of the documents pertaining to the *Kirkekampen.* Some of the selections are impressive, though many are rather obscure. There is a brief discussion of Thurah, pp. 96–98. Also, a selection from *Holbæk Amts Avis* (November 21, 1855) warns against the dangers of forming "a new religious society in a Kierkegaardian spirit." The book, however, contains quite a number of inaccuracies and mistakes; one glaring example is found on p. 44, where Croxall says erroneously that *Either/Or* was translated into German as early as 1856.

166. See "Dr. Søren Kierkegaards Dødsfald" (S. K.'s death) in *Dagbladet,* November 21, 1855, where reactions in Sweden, especially *Aftonbladet,* are discussed.

167. In Swedish *Øjeblikket* becomes *Ögonblicket.* Some other works by Kierkegaard appeared in Swedish translation during his lifetime. These were: a number of the *Upbuilding Discourses* (1843, 44, 52, 53); *The Lily in the Field* . . . (1852 and 53); *For Self-Examination* (1852); parts of *Practice in Christianity* (1853); "This Must Be Said . . ." (1855); "Christ's Judgment Upon Official Christianity" (1855). The dates are those of the first Swedish editions; see J. Himmelstrup, *Søren Kierkegaard International Bibliografi,* pp. 24–25.

considerable, but to regard it as "passing" was wishful thinking on Bremer's part.[168]

As for the Norwegian press, the news of Kierkegaard's death elicited overwhelming sympathy. "A martyr for the truth," wrote *Bergensposten*, and the eulogist in *Folkevennen*, a small local publication, wrote as follows:

> We may not share Søren Kierkegaard's views in everything, but it cannot be denied that the above-named broadsheets *Øjeblikket* contain irrefutable truths; and for many centuries there has scarcely been any Dane who dared to tell us such sweeping truths as Søren Kierkegaard has done.[169]

A dramatic scene took place at Kiekegaard's funeral. The details were carried by all the papers and traveled swiftly across Scandinavia, adding to the commotion already in progress. At the cemetery, after a solemn service at the Church of Our Lady attended by a large crowd and including an oration by Søren's brother Peter, a young medical student and relative of Kierkegaard who looked after him at the hospital, Henrik Lund (1825–89), suddenly interrupted the burial and launched into an emotionally charged tirade about the deceased. The gist of Lund's outburst—which included excerpts read from *Øjeblikket* and the New Testament—was that the state-Church had no right to take someone and bury him as one of her own when she knew very well that while he lived he had dissociated himself from her totally.[170]

Lund came under the influence of Kierkegaard's later writings in a sentimental fashion. Many of those present at the funeral were young students who appeared to be in agreement with Lund's position. They were a motley assortment of loud and disgruntled misfits to whom the

---

168. See Bremer's letter of April 28, 1856 to Martensen in Klara Johansen and Ellen Kleman, eds., *Fredrika Bremers Brev*, vol. III: 1846–57, p. 448. Bremer here and in other letters calls Kierkegaard "the new Simion Stylites"; see her letter of December 14, 1855, to H. C. Andersen, p. 417.

169. *Bergensposten* quoted in Beyer, "Søren Kierkegaards betydning" (1), p. 3. *Folkevennen*, November 23, 1855, trans. T. H. Croxall, *Glimpses and Impressions of Kierkegaard*, p. 90.

170. Lund argued that a baptized Jew would not be buried as a Jew, and a Turk who had left his religion would not be buried as a Mohammadan; similarly must it be with Kierkegaard and the state-Church, the representative of that official Christianity he had renounced. For the full text of Henrik Lund's monologue see Steen Johansen, ed., *Erindringer om Søren Kierkegaard*, pp. 167–69. See also Skat Arildsen's article "Protesten ved Søren Kierkegaards Begravelse," in *Kierkegaardiana*, vol. VIII (1971), pp. 80–102.

name "Kierkegaard's Party" was inappropriately applied by the newspapers.[171] The spectacle of Lund's intervention at the burial was exactly the kind of sensationalism the press was after as the grand finale to a singular affair that had captured the public's imagination for a year. Consequently, every paper related the story in its own way, thus engraving the theatric peculiarity of the entire event upon people's minds. This prompted Lund to write an article for *Fædrelandet* complaining of the misleading newspaper accounts of what he had actually said. He also took the opportunity to set the record straight and related in detail what had happened. He appeared to retreat somewhat from the radical elements in his oral declamation, and he took individual newspapers to task for their inaccurate reporting.[172] A few days later, however, he reverted to his contentious nature and published a highly polemical piece in an attempt to carry on in Kierkegaard's footsteps by mimicking the style of *Øjeblikket*. The resulting product fell short of the mark.[173] Hans Christian Andersen was correct in calling the attempt "a caricature" of Kierkegaard, and the anti-Kierkegaard press lost no time in seizing on this and playing it up.[174]

A milestone was reached in the German reception of Kierkegaard through an interesting occurrence: the Royal Prussian consul general to the Danish monarchy, Ryno Quehl (?-1864), was present at Kierkegaard's funeral and kept a written record of his impressions. Quehl was consul in Copenhagen from 1853 until his sudden death in 1864, during which time he moved in literary circles and partook of Danish cultural life. He also translated some Danish works of literature into German.[175]

---

171. See, for example, *Kjøbenhavnsposten*, November 21, 1855, which referred unfortunately to the pathetic bunch at the funeral as "his present rowdy followers or party members." If anything, they were a complete parody of someone's disciples.

172. Henrik Lund, "Min Protest: Hvad jeg har sagt og ikke sagt" (My protest: what I have said and did not say) in *Fædrelandet*, November 22, 1855.

173. Henrik Lund, "I næste Øjeblik—hvad saa? En Opbyggelig Tale—Samtiden anbefalet til Overveielse" (In the next instant—what then? An edifying discourse—the age recommended for reflection) in *Fædrelandet*, November 26, 1855. At one point Lund writes: "But against 'the official state-Church' we will—with God's help—struggle." His feeble attempt to "carry on" Kierkegaard's struggle was largely ignored.

174. See Andersen's letter of November 26, 1855, to Henriette Wulff, quoted in Niels Birger Wamberg, ed., *Deres Broderligt Hengivne: Et Udvalg af breve fra H. C. Andersen* (Copenhagen: Gyldendal, 1975), p. 169. Andersen attended Kierkegaard's funeral and described it to Wulff, including Lund's scene at the grave. In a letter dated October 10, also to Wulff, Andersen mentioned Kierkegaard's sickness and the fact that a theologian, "Thura [*sic*]," wrote a "crude poem against him"; see p. 168.

175. Frithiof Brandt and Else Rammel, *Søren Kierkegaard og Pengene*, p. 100.

He had been sent away as consul to Denmark because his influence at the department of information in Berlin was growing, and certain officials were unhappy about it. With his journalistic flair Quehl kept the authorities in Berlin satisfied by supplying them with a steady stream of reports on Denmark and the Schleswig-Holstein situation.[176]

In a book he wrote about Denmark, Quehl devoted some thirty pages to a discussion of Kierkegaard's controversial views, and to speculation concerning the significance of his last writings for the Danish state-Church as well as for Prussia.[177] The incident with Henrik Lund at the graveyard was described at length, and some biographical information on Kierkegaard was provided. Included also were German translations of selections from the nine *Øjeblikket* issues, the first such translations of their kind.[178] Quehl found support in *Øjeblikket* against the concept of a "Christian state" in Prussia. Being the son of a pastor and having had some theological education in his youth, Quehl understood the significance of Kierkegaard's critique of Christendom and regarded it as very timely. He noted that despite Kierkegaard's lack of interest in politics, which for Quehl was the natural arena where people attained recognition, he had in recent months achieved a widespread reputation, due purely to his unsparing attack on the Danish state-Church. Quehl wrote:

> It is certain that with the news of Kierkegaard's death many clergymen breathed more freely in Denmark, but it is also more certain that the interest and sympathy which his writings evoked are not extinct with his death. It is also certain that their good as well as bad effects will endure, and that the name Kierkegaard will not be forgotten in the history of the development of Danish church life.[179]

176. On Ryno Quehl see the article by Wippermann in *Allgemeine Deutsche Biographie* [*ADB*], vol. 27, ed. the Historical Commission of the Royal Academy of Sciences, vol. 27 (Berlin and Leipzig: Duncker & Humblot, 1970), pp. 31-32; see also Eugen Stamm, *Konstantin Frantz, 1857-1866: Ein Wort zur Deutschen Frage* (Berlin and Leipzig: Deutsche Verlag, 1930), pp. 56-62; and Hans Joachim Schoeps, "Über das Frühecho Søren Kierkegaards in Deutschland," in *Meddelelser fra Søren Kierkegaard Selskabet*, vol. 3, no. 2 (Copenhagen: Munksgaard, 1951), pp. 96-98.

177. Ryno Quehl, "Dr. Sören Kierkegaard wider die dänische Staatskirche, mit einem Hinblick auf Preussen," in *Aus Dänemark* (Berlin, 1856), pp. 277-306.

178. For a long time these translations by Quehl remained unknown to Kierkegaard researchers. The first complete, though clumsy, German translation of the nine *Øjeblikket* issues appeared under the title *Christentum und Kirche* (Hamburg, 1861). A German reviewer writing in 1862 in *Literarischen Central-Blatt für Deutschland*, no. 12, expressed disbelief that Kierkegaard would at any time attain significance in Germany. See H. J. Schoeps, "Über das Frühecho Søren Kierkegaards in Deutschland," p. 96.

179. Quehl, "Dr. Sören Kierkegaard wider die dänische Staatskirche," p. 281.

With every sentence he wrote about Kierkegaard, Quehl had one eye on Prussia and the possible implications of the *Kirkekampen* for future developments there. He was aware that the Church in Prussia had defects similar to those assailed by Kierkegaard in Denmark, and he knew that Kierkegaard's significance would eventually extend beyond his homeland to wherever there was an interest in political-ecclesiastical questions.

Another early and detailed account in German of the *Kirkekampen*, which has escaped most scholars, can be found in the bi-weekly *Kopenhagener Zeitung*. This paper came out in Copenhagen on Mondays and Thursdays and catered to the German-speaking community in Denmark, with subscriptions also possible for Germans living beyond the borders. It enjoyed broad circulation and provided informed articles on current events. Politically, it could be regarded as the adversary of a paper like *Dannevirke* on the explosive issue of Schleswig-Holstein.

In a series of thirteen long articles published between January 24 and March 31, 1856, *Kopenhagener Zeitung* provided its readers with a thorough account of the successive phases of the *Kirkekampen* and inserted several sizable excerpts from *Øjeblikket* in German translation. The treatment was not uncritical, and Kierkegaard was continually taken to task for not having expounded at length his notion of the rigorous demands that an authentic Christianity places on its adherents; he dwelt too much on the negative aspects of official Christianity and paid little attention to offering a constructive alternative. The criticism is a familiar one, voiced by writers in the Danish press on various occasions during the heat of the *Kirkekampen*. Also familiar is the suggestion, at one point, that the "negative elements of society, doubters and presumed atheists" will rejoice over some of Kierkegaard's careless and inconsiderate statements. The anonymous writer, however, added that he intended to give prominence in his discussion to the less nihilistic and more truth-laden pronouncements of Kierkegaard, and proceeded to translate extensively from *Øjeblikket*.[180] When he came to the sections attacking marriage, the author labeled them "extravagant," an exaggerated interpretation of St. Paul's call to celibacy and indicative of a basic confusion in Kierkegaard's thinking between the letter and the spirit of a text, "which we ought not to follow."[181] The author's approach entailed a methodic and critical survey

---

180. "Die dänische Staatskirche, der Angriff Sören Kierkegaards," II, in *Kopenhagener Zeitung*, January 28, 1856.

181. Ibid., V, February 7, 1856.

of *Øjeblikket* and a sifting of the "true" from the "confused" in Kierkegaard's concept of the church. It used essentially conservative criteria and maintained throughout that Kierkegaard's ecclesiology was basically defective.

In Germany proper the Danish *Kirkekampen* received direct attention on at least two occasions. These came in the form of two articles written by the theologian A. F. Beck, an old-time observer of Kierkegaard. They appeared in the *Darmstädter Allgemeine Kirchenzeitung* (September 22, 1855, and January 31, 1856). Once again, Beck's main concern was that Kierkegaard's negative critique of the Church played into atheist and sectarian hands and suited their purposes. This theme seems to have been an obsession of the initial German commentators on Kierkegaard's final polemical writings.

Regarding Denmark itself, attention must be called to an important article that *Fædrelandet* ran on December 1, 1855. It was signed "-r"; however, scholars agree unanimously that the author was the philosopher Hans Brøchner (1820-75).[182] Brøchner possessed an impressive knowledge of the Kierkegaard corpus and had interacted with him over a period of twenty years. Curiously, however, he is not mentioned anywhere in the works or journals. Intellectually, Brøchner was influenced by Strauss and Feuerbach—he had translated Strauss's *Die christliche Glaubenslehre* (1843). He was something of a freethinker, yet his admiration for Kierkegaard was genuine and their relationship friendly, as attested by Brøchner's reminiscences of Kierkegaard (an invaluable source for scholars).[183]

Following Kierkegaard's death, his significance became fully apparent to Brøchner, who undertook to produce a synthesis of the works based on Kierkegaard's own instructions about how he should be read. These Brøchner gleaned from the appendix at the end of *Concluding Unscientific Postscript* (1846) and from a small tract entitled *On My Work as an Author* (1851). He published the synthesis as an article in *Fædrelandet*[184] soon after

---

182. See S. V. Rasmussen, *Den Unge Brøchner* (Copenhagen: Gyldendal, 1966), p. 126. See also A. Kabell, *Kierkegaardstudiet i Norden*, no. 81, p. 17; and J. Himmelstrup, *Søren Kierkegaard International Bibliografi*, no. 2110, p. 59.
183. See Hans Brøchner, *Erindringer om Søren Kierkegaard*, ed. Steen Johansen (Copenhagen: Reitzel, 1953); for a reprint see also the compilation with the same title, ed. Steen Johansen, pp. 91–117. On Brøchner see Kalle Sorainen, "Brøchner," in *The Legacy and Interpretation of Kierkegaard*, in vol. 8 of *Bibliotheca Kierkegaardiana*, pp. 198–203. For more on Brøchner see chapters 5 and 6 below.
184. "-r" (Hans Brøchner), "Om Søren Kierkegaards Virksomhed som religiøs forfatter" [On S. K.'s activity as a religious author], in *Fædrelandet*, December 1, 1855.

Kierkegaard passed away, because he was upset about the proliferation of misinterpretations then filling the pages of the newspapers as a result of the *Kirkekampen*.

The article is an admirable exercise in fidelity to the wishes of Kierkegaard that his works be regarded as fundamentally religious and as embodying an inner unity throughout. Brøchner also strove to show the intrinsic connections between Kierkegaard's last writings of the *Kirkekampen* and his previous intellectual production. He discussed the early works successively and, following Kierkegaard's own classification, singled out *Postscript* as the decisive mid-point in Kierkegaard's career as an author.

Among early posthumous writings on Kierkegaard, Brøchner's article stands out conspicuously, not only in its faithfulness to the subject matter but also in its logical reasoning and erudition. Coming from one who was not religious, and not particularly in agreement with Kierkegaard philosophically, the article acquires added weight. Brøchner truly grasped the intellectual significance of Kierkegaard for posterity, and his article makes refreshing reading in the panoply of writings on the *Kirkekampen*. And Brøchner sincerely liked Kierkegaard personally, as his reminiscences reveal.

He did not stop at one article but decided to write a review of Ørum's book of 1856 on the *Kirkekampen*.[185] Ørum had examined critically the various responses to Kierkegaard during the previous year—ones like Zeuthen's and Andresen's—and decided they all left much to be desired. Brøchner agreed and went farther: since no clergyman has so far empirically (i.e., through actions in his own life) demonstrated the utter incompatibility between Christianity and the world, all could be considered Kierkegaard's opponents. At this time only Brøchner and Ørum insisted emphatically on making connections between Kierkegaard's earlier works and his last writings. Brøchner, in a letter to his friend and later heir C. K. F. Molbech, warned prophetically against interpreting Kierkegaard exclusively through the pages of his *Either/Or*.[186] Neither the Kierkegaard of *Either/Or* nor the one of *Øjeblikket*, taken in isolation, represents a sound portrait of the versatile thinker; Brøchner knew this well.

In 1856 Kierkegaard's library was auctioned, and his brother got custody of his private papers. Brøchner bought many of the books at the

---

185. J. C. M. Ørum, *Sandhedsvidnestriden* (Copenhagen, 1856); see Brøchner's review in *Fædrelandet*, December 20, 1856.

186. See T. H. Croxall, *Glimpses and Impressions of Kierkegaard*, pp. 41–44 for a translation of the letter dated February 17, 1856.

auction.[187] Tremors from the *Kirkekampen* persisted and familiar names continued to publish now and then, while new voices were raised in support of Kierkegaard's later actions. Rasmus Nielsen held a series of twelve public lectures on Kierkegaard's thought, and a weekly religious periodical, *Brevbærer mellem Kristne til Oplysning af Forbindelse*, began to print extracts from Kierkegaard's religious writings—mostly *Practice in Christianity*.[188] This periodical circulated among clergymen and their parishes throughout the countryside. In this way *Practice in Christianity* and a number of the *Upbuilding Discourses* quickly joined the ranks of popular devotional literature in Danish congregations.

Many newspapers gave up all references to Kierkegaard with the onset of the new year. *Berlingske Tidende* published only one article on January 17 praising Andresen's piece against Kierkegaard. In *Flyveposten*'s case there was no letup in the pressure on Kierkegaard and his friends. Victor Bloch wrote an article for *Fædrelandet* (February 13) in which he tried to appear fair toward the deceased Kierkegaard, insisting that along with his condemnations of Kierkegaard's positions the previous year he had also pointed out whatever was legitimate in his conduct. The article contained an apologetic for Grundtvig as well. Worthy of mention too is a tract by P. C. Zahle (1825-98), a young politician and a Kierkegaard enthusiast, comparing Kierkegaard to the German philosopher Johan Georg Hamann (1730-88), whom Kierkegaard admired.[189] Zahle stressed the centrality of life as opposed to ideas for Kierkegaard's philosophy.[190] He wrote that it was not Kierkegaard but the clergymen who scared people away from the Church, and he ended excitedly with the words: "Read Søren Kierkegaard!"[191] Finally, the earliest reference to Kierkegaard in French occurred

187. For a contemporary reflection on the auction see *Morgenposten*, April 4, 1856. See also Sejer Kühle's article in *Berlingske Aftenavis*, February 24, 1943; H. P. Rohde, ed., *The Auction-Catalog of Søren Kierkegaard's Book Collection* [*Auktionsprotokol over Søren Kierkegaards Bogsamling (ASKB)*] (Copenhagen: Det Kongelige Bibliotek, 1967); Robert L. Perkins, "Søren Kierkegaard's Library," in *American Book Collector* 12 (1961), pp. 9-16; and Ronald G. Smith, "Kierkegaard's Library," *Hibbert Journal* 50 (1951), pp. 18-21.

188. See the issues of *Brevbærer* (Letter-bearer), ed. Niels Johansen, for the months of May and June 1856, and April 1858.

189. P. C. Zahle, *Til Erindring om Johan Georg Hamann og Søren Aabye Kierkegaard* (Copenhagen, 1856). For more on Hamann and Kierkegaard see Isaiah Berlin, *The Magus of the North: J. G. Hamann and the Origins of Modern Irrationalism*, ed. Henry Hardy (New York: Farrar, Strauss and Giroux, 1993), esp. pp. 19-20.

190. Zahle, *Til Erindring*, p. 32.

191. Ibid., p. 45 and 48. In 1857 Zahle wrote some articles for *Fædrelandet* attacking the approach the theologians took toward Kierkegaard's final views.

in 1856 in the *Annuaire des deux Mondes*.[192] It was a short note about his death in the context of an article on Denmark.

The year 1857 saw the gathering and publication of all Kierkegaard's newspaper articles, including the twenty-one from *Fædrelandet*, in a single volume. This was done painstakingly with an annotated bibliography and references by Rasmus Nielsen, and it helped to disseminate Kierkegaard's protest against Mynster and official Christianity throughout Scandinavia. The *Bladartikler*, as they were called, were announced by all the major Norwegian and Swedish newspapers. In Denmark, *Øre-Sund* reviewed the collection and praised Nielsen for the service that he had rendered. Thanks to Nielsen's efforts, wrote the reviewer, people can now follow step by step Kierkegaard's intellectual development over a period of twenty years.[193]

Fallout from the *Kirkekampen* continued in 1857. The first Scandinavian church conference *(Kirkemøde)* was held in Copenhagen between July 14 and 16. As might be imagined, extensive discussions about the *Kirkekampen* took place, and most opinions did not favor Kierkegaard. He was accused of having been out "to subvert everything," and having propagated "colossal lies" about the Church.[194]

During this period a remarkable man rushed to the defense of Kierkegaard in the face of renewed hostilities against him from ecclesiastical quarters. H. P. Kofoed-Hansen (1813-93) was a farmer's son from Zeeland who studied theology and showed strong leanings toward philosophy, but not Hegel's. His teachers were Sibbern and H. C. Ørsted. The decisive turn in his life was brought about by his discovery of Kierkegaard.[195] In particular, *Either/Or* kindled the first spark of a prolonged enchantment. He wrote reviews of *Either/Or* when it first appeared and of several other works by Kierkegaard. He also published many books of his own

---

192. Anonymous, "Etats européens—Le Danemark. Questions religieuses," in *Annuaire des deux Mondes, Histoire génerale des divers états*, vol. VI (Paris, October 20, 1856), p. 489.

193. *Øre-Sund*, vol. 1, no. 47, November 22, 1857. P. C. Koch of *Dannevirke* became editor of *Øre-Sund* from 1857 to 1859.

194. See the article on the conference in *Flyveposten*, July 24, 1857. Two other Scandinavian church conferences were held, in 1859 and 1861. At both, Kierkegaard was discussed and, for the most part, condemned.

195. See the massive study of Kofoed-Hansen by P. P. Jørgensen, *H. P. Kofoed-Hansen med Særligt Henblick til Søren Kierkegaard* (Copenhagen: Gyldendal, 1920), pp. 24 and 109. Kofoed-Hansen knew Kierkegaard personally; see *JP* 4029 (X^2 A 429) and 6673 (X^3 A 422).

containing plenty that smacked of Kierkegaard. Despite his ordination as a pastor, he saw fit in 1856 and 1857 to publish two small books attacking Martensen and the establishment in Kierkegaardian fashion and employing ample quotations from Kierkegaard in the process.[196] In the second book, Kofoed-Hansen argued that Kierkegaard did not reject communal worship although emphasizing individual faith. He also wrote on a more personal note: "I am neither Søren Kierkegaard's successor nor his disciple . . . [but] I shall confess I have learned from him not only the way one learns from an author, but also through a personal relationship, and I learned what Christianity is all about."[197] Years later, in 1887, Kofoed-Hansen converted to Catholicism. He was the first of many whose interest in Kierkegaard eventually led them along the road to Rome.

One person already viewing the world from the perspective of Rome was Joseph Edmund Jörg, the German Catholic historian and conservative politician. He found out about Kierkegaard through the three independent German sources discussed earlier: Quehl's book, Beck's articles, and *Kopenhagener Zeitung*, all in 1856. He cites the first two repeatedly, and he quotes from Quehl's translations of *Øjeblikket*.

Jörg, who was interested in the study of Protestantism, wrote an article in 1856 on the religious movements in Scandinavia. Two years later he revised and expanded it and had it published in a German history of Protestantism.[198] Ninety percent of the article dealt with Kierkegaard's attack on the Danish Lutheran Church, which Jörg rejoiced at. He wrote that Kierkegaard had flashed "like a meteor through the sky of the Nordic church."[199] He pictured him as an aloof recluse who was correct in his critique of the Lutheran Church, except that he failed to draw the appropriate conclusion and seek a fuller expression of the Christian Church.[200] What Jörg was driving at was that Kierkegaard, while single-handedly

---

196. H. P. Kofoed-Hansen, *Dr. S. Kierkegaard mod Dr. H. Martensen* (Copenhagen, 1856); and *S. Kierkegaard mod det bestaaende* (Copenhagen, 1857).

197. Kofoed-Hansen, *S. K. mod det bestaaende*, p. 49.

198. J. E. Jörg, "Streiflichter auf die neueste Geschichte des Protestantismus: Die religiöse Bewegungen in den scandinavischen Ländern," in *Historisch-politische Blätter für das Katholische Deutschland*, ed. G. Phillips and G. Görres, no. 38 (Munich, 1856), pp. 1–30; and "Dr. Kierkegaard und seine Kritik des protestantischen Kirchenthums," in *Geschichte der Protestantismus in seiner neuesten Entwicklung*, vol. 2: "Die Schwärmerkirche und ihre Bedingungen" (Freiburg, 1858), pp. 336–50.

199. Jörg, *Historisch-politische Blätter*, p. 30.

200. Jörg, "Dr. Kierkegaard und seine Kritik des protestantischen Kirchenthums," p. 337.

exposing the shortcomings of Protestantism, ultimately remained a tragic-pathetic case since he did not, as a consequence of his attack, make the indicated move toward Catholicism.[201] On the question of celibacy and the renunciation of marriage, Jörg argued that Kierkegaard was very close to the Catholic position.[202] Besides being an early Catholic interpreter of Kierkegaard—the first German Catholic to take a serious look at him—Jörg was the inaugurator of a special disposition toward Kierkegaard that is peculiar to certain Catholics. Others were to imitate Jörg's attempts at appropriating Kierkegaard for Catholicism, particularly during the early decades of the twentieth century in southern Germany and Austria.[203]

While Jörg in Germany was engaged in lamenting Kierkegaard's failure to enter the Catholic fold, a familiar Danish sympathizer with Kierkegaard was busy comparing him to Martin Luther, the father of the Protestant Reformation. This was Ørum, who in 1858 published a treatise on the relation between Kierkegaard and Luther.[204] Although the comparison had been made before, Ørum's piece was the first lengthy and exclusive discussion of the subject. Ørum was motivated, among other things, by the desire to establish the legitimacy of Kierkegaard's controversial stands during the *Kirkekampen*. What better way of doing this than to depict him as a contemporary Luther and show how Luther himself would have agreed not only with the thrust of Kierkegaard's critique but also with his use of polemics?

The *Kirkekampen* and its predecessor, the *Corsair* Affair, represented the two instances in which Kierkegaard received public exposure during his life. In both cases Kierkegaard burst onto the scene with fanfare, and the public was treated to a peculiar, eccentric, contentious, and ultimately puzzling mixture of polemics, caricature, and serious substance. The net result was a definite conditioning of the public mind with respect to Kierkegaard destined to have far-reaching consequences for his personal and intellectual legacy. While the *Corsair* Affair, taken in its most positive light, alerted the general public to the existence in their midst of a curious

---

201. Ibid., pp. 341–42. 202. Ibid., p. 348.
203. See the final chapter below. For more on Jörg and Kierkegaard see H. J. Schoeps, "Über das Frühecho Søren Kierkegaards in Deutschland," pp. 98–100; and Maria Poll, *Edmund Jörgs Kampf für eine christliche und grossdeutsche Volks- und Staatsordnung* (Paderborn: Ferdinand Schöningh Verlag, 1936), esp. pp. 37–40.
204. J. C. M. Ørum, *Om Forholdet imellem Søren Kierkegaard og Luther: Iagttagelser af en Lægmand* (On the relationship between S. K. and Luther: observations of a layman) (Copenhagen, 1858).

and highly unusual man, that "genius in a market town," the *Kirkekampen* revived, confirmed, and often compounded certain images and identifiable character traits, effectively branding Kierkegaard with an indelible stigma.

It would not be unjustifiably facetious to call the *Kirkekampen* a *"Pressekampen,"* for Kierkegaard's last attack was not only a media event but also the occasion for vigorous dueling among politically opposed newspapers, competitive editors, anonymous writers, aspiring critics, renowned figures, and an unavoidable quota of practical jokers. Even comparing it to a carnival, with each vendor shouting at the top of his voice to attract the crowds to his wares, would be in order. The overriding quality of this cacophony was unbridled polemics. Both Kierkegaard and his opponents used strong verbal weapons to execute their attacks and counter offensives, making them both guilty of a not inconsiderable amount of viciousness. Those among Kierkegaard's enemies who argued that he had "asked for it" were correct in that polemics invariably breed counterpolemics, and substantive issues often become submerged in a maelstrom of recriminations and countercharges. Kierkegaard anticipated that his contemporaries would not grasp his self-consciously assumed disposition as a corrective, with one-sided severity as its inevitable product if the exercise was to have penetrating effect. He saw this and determined to go ahead anyway. Yet his very foresight somehow turned into a self-fulfilling prophecy, and despite the stray Brøchner or Ørum with their sympathetic insights and their genuine desire to accommodate the whole, seeds of future "misreception" were sown. Add to this Kierkegaard's natural penchant for combativeness, using the sophisticated weapons of irony and sarcasm, which made it difficult for him to stick to his frequently repeated principle of avoiding the temptation of a run-in with every anonymous detractor. We find him getting sucked into the fray again and again, with the result that a perpetual sense of outrage on all sides pervaded the *Kirkekampen.* Reading the sources one gets the feeling that at times it was hardly a debate, but rather a group of people, each with his axe to grind, talking past one another instead of engaging in a constructive exchange of opinions.

Amid all this babel our primary concerns remain the tint and flavor that the *Kirkekampen* cast on Kierkegaard's literary output and intellectual legacy. There is no doubt that the sensationalism of the *Kirkekampen* conditioned decisively the manner in which his entire writings have been received, particularly during the first few decades following his death.

Øjeblikket, in this sense, was a double-edged sword. On one level it served to enlarge his readership and increase his popularity, but on another it fostered a warped impression of him in many circles. To peer at Kierkegaard exclusively, or even predominantly, through the prism of *Øjeblikket,* or, for that matter, the narrow lenses of the *Corsair* Affair and the "Diary of a Seducer," would be to run the risk of distortion; this is exactly what happened.

We have seen how the established Church, the custodian of official Christianity in Kierkegaard's view, handled his attack: no formal and conclusive answers to his charges were advanced by the ecclesiastical authorities then or later. There were condemnations galore and half-baked attempts at refuting specific points, but no official pronouncements. The "Church party" was content with this state of affairs, and used the devious tactic of secretly prompting anonymous writers to publish in praise of the Church and Mynster in order to nurture the illusion of overwhelming popular support for their position. However, the more thoughtful among them did not deceive themselves about the massive appeal Kierkegaard's protests were eliciting everywhere. They finally devised a method to deal with the problem. Given the Lammers phenomenon and the widespread defections from the Church that were associated with Kierkegaard's articles, it was relatively simple for the religious hierarchy to accuse Kierkegaard of furthering unbelief and "being in league with the atheists." There may have been something to this, although inadvertently and certainly not in the deliberate conspiratorial sense that some of Kierkegaard's adversaries would have us believe. Intersection of interests and coincidence of objectives, regardless of differences in motivation, have made strange bedfellows: Kierkegaard himself derived great inspiration from Feuerbach. The converse is also true: diverse types of freethinkers have been attracted to Kierkegaard, based purely on a calculated and selective reading of his anti-Church writings. (Brøchner is an exception.) That Kierkegaard lent himself to this sort of use—or abuse—is undeniable. Whether one would go so far as to say, with Karl Löwith, that Kierkegaard, through his radicalism, actually "contributed ... to the destruction of the Christian tradition" becomes another matter.[205]

Attracting freethinkers and repelling churchgoers is a direct outcome

---

205. Karl Löwith, "On the Historical Understanding of Kierkegaard," in *Review of Religion* 7 (March 1943), p. 228.

of the *Kirkekampen*, and represents one facet of "misreception" for which Kierkegaard is not entirely lacking in responsibility. This, along with a dozen other factors to be investigated throughout this study—some originating in the *Kirkekampen*, others being inherently idiosyncratic, still others belonging to the category of historical givens—contributed to the fragmentation that Kierkegaard's intellectual bequest suffered after his death. It is as though with his death, and against the explosive backdrop of the *Kirkekampen*, Kierkegaard's writings entered straight into a "chop shop" to be dismantled, at times beyond recognition: "Deeper analysis of the fate of Kierkegaard reveals that he has been broken up all too much like Humpty Dumpty. All too few of the king's men have even tried to put him back together again."[206]

206. Mallary Fitzpatrick, Jr., "Kierkegaard and the Church," in *Journal of Religion* 27 (1947), p. 256.

4 A Foray into Drama? The Case of Ibsen

After Kierkegaard's death, and with the passage of time, the outward rumblings of the *Kirkekampen* gradually subsided. The issues he had raised, however, were by no means settled, and the sting they had caused left its telltale mark on the Church and in the public mind. A peculiar reputation outlived him as a result, usurping for a long time the place of any budding interest in seriously tackling his corpus in its entirety. His works did not sink into oblivion following his departure from the scene; rather they went collectively into a prolonged period of hibernation, being picked at now and then by a stray writer here or a theology professor there. Indeed what characterized the early reception of Kierkegaard was precisely this nibbling, which usually entailed latching onto a single idea or theme in the works to the exclusion of others. Whether it was the demand for personal authenticity, the anti-Christendom position, the notion of paradox, or the either-or motif, Kierkegaard for many came to mean *one* of the diverse concepts in his writings. This natural development was not due solely to the monolithic posthumous reputation suppressing the diversity of the works, for the unsystematic quality inherent in the Kierkegaard corpus precluded any early and meaningful assessment of the whole. It was instead conducive to fragmentation.

Then, in 1859, Kierkegaard's brother Peter Christian, who had custody of his papers, saw fit to publish *The Point of View for My Work as an Author*, eleven years after it had been written, along with two short pieces on "the Individual," written in 1846 and 1847 respectively. Considering the reigning confusion—compounded by the havoc of the final outburst against the Church—which plagued readers of Kierkegaard's works, *The Point of View* and the two accompanying pieces could not have appeared at a better time. They were to have the eventual effect of diluting the prejudiced reputation and arousing interest in more serious explorations of the complex gallery of passions and thoughts which made up Kierkegaard, but not before generating some polemics of their own.

In this book, Kierkegaard undertook to communicate directly to his readers and to posterity the hitherto concealed meaning of his writings (the early pseudonymous works as well as the *Upbuilding Discourses*)—that they had had a religious purpose all along, of showing the way to "becoming a Christian."[1] He reviewed his pseudonymous writings and claimed that as a religious author he had been compelled to resort to duplicity and indirection (a sort of teleological suspension of direct communication) because he was also a dialectical author through and through, and because the age, with its mediocrity and its reflectiveness, had to be met initially on its own level.[2] We are told, for instance, that his *Either/Or* was actually postulating a deeper choice than the surface one between an aesthetic and an ethical existence: it was, in reality, a choice between both of these, on the one hand, and the religious life. Kierkegaard, we learn, had already chosen the cloister, and this significant fact had been hinted at in the pseudonym Victor Eremita (Victor the Hermit).[3]

There were, in addition, veiled autobiographical allusions throughout *The Point of View*, such as the break with Regine, and the repeated references to people having misunderstood him to the point of persecuting him publicly (the *Corsair* Affair), both of which had caused him to endure

1. Søren Kierkegaard, *The Point of View for My Work as an Author*, trans. Walter Lowrie (New York: Harper and Row, 1962), pp. 5-6.
2. Ibid., p. 10 and p. 15. Kierkegaard had to descend to the age's own level in order to be effective: ". . . if you can find exactly the place where the other is and begin there, you may perhaps have the luck to lead him to the place where you are" (p. 29). For more on "the age" and the events of 1848 see pp. 44-45, 54ff., 74, 88-89, 112ff., and 129-30.
3. Ibid., p. 18.

much suffering.[4] What must have appeared striking to readers in 1859—though hardly surprising when one considers the extraordinary nature of the writer—was Kierkegaard's effusive self-confidence in his exceptional intellectual abilities, coupled with a sincere attitude of humility and gratitude before divine providence for the bountiful gifts bestowed upon him.[5] A genius like Kierkegaard, fully cognizant of his superiority, could not refrain, therefore, from calling his countrymen to task for failing to appreciate him, and at the same time dialectically anticipate their failure and use it to provide a profound and timeless description of "the present age."[6]

The Point of View revived public interest in and stimulated renewed discussion of Kierkegaard's oeuvre. The press, as usual, was swift to provide long reviews of the book and happy to speculate on its author's childhood, abortive engagement, and attitude toward Christianity, concerning all of which new revelations were surfacing. *Berlingske Tidende* ran a sizable review that acknowledged, among other things, the error of many during the *Kirkekampen* who interpreted Kierkegaard's stormy conduct toward the Church as a desertion of his earlier position.[7] As it turned out, "the single individual" had been his focus all along. *Dagbladet* also featured a front-page review of *The Point of View*, continued in the

---

4. For examples see ibid., p. 5, 7, 8, 18, 21, 41, 48–63, 76–92, 94–95, 121, and 125–26.

5. "I say that it never remotely occurred to me that in my generation there lived or was to be born a man who had the upper hand of me . . . that, even if I were to attempt the most foolhardy enterprise, I should not be victorious," ibid., p. 78. See also pp. 82 and 98.

6. The "provincial town" of Copenhagen (ibid., p. 100), and the "little land" of Denmark (p. 125) became frequent targets for Kierkegaard's vented frustration following the *Corsair* Affair. Journal entries from 1848, the year *The Point of View* was written, contain many reproachful comments about his country and its citizens; for example, "Even if Denmark would do it, it is highly questionable whether it could rectify the wrong it has done me. That I am an author who definitely will bring honor to Denmark is indisputable" [*JP* 6204 (IX A 169)]. See also 6254 (IX A 288); 6282 (IX A 432); 6285 (IX A 458); 6288 (IX A 471); and 6290 (IX A 484). Kierkegaard, however, was not unwavering in his bitterness, and one comes across such declarations as "I love my fatherland. . . . I am proud of my mother tongue whose secrets I know, . . ." even in 1848 [*JP* 6259 (IX A 298)]. See also Frater Taciturnus's praise for Copenhagen and Denmark at the end of *Stages on Life's Way* (*KW*, XI), ed. and trans. Howard V. Hong and Edna H. Hong (Princeton: Princeton University Press, 1988), pp. 489–91; this was written before the *Corsair* incident. For an interesting discussion of Kierkegaard's relation to Denmark see Holger Hansen's article "Søren Kierkegaard og Danmark," in *Berlingske Aftenavis*, September 6, 1940.

7. *Berlingske Tidende*, July 27, 1859.

following day's edition.⁸ The reviewer described the public's reaction to the sudden appearance of the book as one of surprise. At first some had maintained it was a hoax, or the work of another author using Kierkegaard's name as a pseudonym to present his own version of an "indirect communication." More substantively, the reviewer rejected Kierkegaard's claim that the aesthetic works had been intended from the beginning to serve a religious purpose. This claim, he wrote, was advanced in a short piece entitled *On My Work as an Author*, which Kierkegaard had published in 1851, but which few readers paid much attention to at the time. Although it was possible some religious motivations were at work in the aesthetic works, Kierkegaard's claim, according to the reviewer, was made largely with the benefit of hindsight. Furthermore, he bestowed on Kierkegaard the odd label of a "thought machine" and said his intellectual make-up was totally lacking in freshness and immediacy. The reviewer congratulated himself on having demonstrated, as he put it, that the famous deceased was, after all, not free of errors, and he added patronizingly that "Kierkegaard's errors do not preclude greatness."

As a testimony to the abidingly controversial nature of Kierkegaard, and the latent high emotions still present four years after the *Kirkekampen*, an anonymous article signed "67" appeared in *Fædrelandet* a month later. Entitled "En Antikritik," it was intended as a rebuttal to *Dagbladet*'s negative review.⁹ The writer was highly sympathetic toward Kierkegaard and engaged in a point by point refutation of the articles in *Dagbladet*.

Nor was the proclamation of *The Point of View*, with the disputes it engendered, confined to the Copenhagen press. The book rekindled interest in Kierkegaard in the provinces and beyond Denmark. The *Flensburger Zeitung*, for instance, a biweekly German-language paper from the town of Flensburg in Schleswig, carried a report about the book that called it "a key" to the understanding of Kierkegaard's works, his conduct, his aims, and his outlook.¹⁰ Kierkegaard, wrote the paper, still had "zealous followers and admirers" who placed him in the same class with Socrates and Luther. Despite the continued turmoil between Denmark and Prussia over Schleswig-Holstein, considerable attention, the paper said, has been accorded this newly uncovered piece from Kierkegaard's literary inheritance. Short excerpts from the book were quoted in German translation. The report ended by designating Kierkegaard as "one of the greatest

---

8. *Dagbladet*, September 21 and 22, 1859.
9. *Fædrelandet*, October 22, 1859.   10. *Flensburger Zeitung*, May 11, 1859.

spirits ... to have come out of Denmark." In Norway too, *Christianiaposten* was quick to announce the appearance of *The Point of View*. Other Norwegian papers soon followed suit.[11]

Ever since it became available to a discerning reading public, *The Point of View* has raised more questions about Kierkegaard than it has answered. Much hinges on whether the reader decides to take seriously Kierkegaard's own prescriptions concerning how he wishes to be read and interpreted. In *The Point of View,* Kierkegaard makes the claim of writing as a religious author, and also the corollary claim to wholeness and consistency within a diversified yet ultimately integrated set of works. These claims raise interesting and perplexing questions: Is this the sincere opinion of the author about his corpus, and does it truly reflect his intentions from the very beginning? Is he not playing another game with his readers, setting them up for the supreme irony of receiving directions on how to write critically about him from his own pen? Was it not an afterthought, or perhaps the result of a significant personal conversion experience in the author's life around 1848, that caused him to insist in retrospect that his entire writings be viewed in a religious light? Is it not simply a necessary step in his intricately self-conscious posture as a *dialectical* author to write something like *The Point of View*? These and many more questions have surfaced again and again in critical appraisals of this fascinating and enigmatic work, and the answer is probably a combination of all the elements they allude to, and others as well. Whether *The Point of View* is to be taken as a clue or as a ruse (and whether it really matters), one cannot deny that the work reveals its author's uncanny preoccupation with his readers, which sets him apart from other nineteenth-century thinkers, with the exception of Nietzsche.[12]

---

11. *Christianiaposten,* no. 152 (1859).

12. The difficulty of neatly categorizing Kierkegaard's *The Point of View,* and his writings generally, is driven home—albeit in a singular fashion—by today's "deconstructionists," who are the latest product of the seemingly endless self-entanglements of contemporary language philosophy and its derivatives in literary criticism. Two essays exemplify this recent growing interest in Kierkegaard and *The Point of View* among these latter-day so-called "textual demystifiers": Christopher Norris, "Fictions of Authority: Narrative and Viewpoint in Kierkegaard's Writing," in his *The Deconstructive Turn: Essays in the Rhetoric of Philosophy* (London: Methuen, 1983), pp. 85–106; and Carl Pletsch, "The Self-Sufficient Text in Nietzsche and Kierkegaard," in *The Anxiety of Anticipation,* in the biannual *Yale French Studies,* number 66, ed. Sima Godfrey (New Haven, 1984), pp. 160–88. Norris, for instance, writes in his preface: "The undecidability of Kierkegaard's text is such as to engender suspicions of fictional and figurative sense even in 'authentic' productions like *The Point of View for My Work as an Author*" (p. 4; see also pp. 95 and

It has been argued that *The Point of View* contributed to the polemical streak informing early treatments of Kierkegaard, insofar as it promoted a natural resistance among critics to being told by the author how they ought to read him.[13] The frustration of the critics, however, was compounded by their knowledge that they could not simply dismiss Kierkegaard's "point of view" and get on with their critical interpretations. Aage Henriksen has stated their dilemma quite succinctly:

> It will appear . . . that whether or not we follow Søren Kierkegaard's directions, we shall have reason to regret both procedures. . . . A point of view which neither violates the totality nor the separate parts does not seem to have been attained by anybody. The core of the authorship has not been penetrated.[14]

The way many of the early critics handled this situation was to come up with a counteremphasis to Kierkegaard's religious one, and to construct their evaluations around that. Usually the most convenient course to follow has been a kind of biographical-psychological approach to the interpretation of the idiosyncratic Dane and his strange works.[15]

Writing in 1848, long before his public assault on the ecclesiastical establishment, Kierkegaard was fully aware that a religious author—which he was arguing had been his status all along—had, in the nature of the case, to be polemical:

> Every religious author is *eo ipso* polemical; for the world is not so good that the religious man can assume that he has triumphed or is in the party of the majority. A victorious religious author who is *in the world* is *eo ipso* not a religious author. The essentially religious author is always polemical, and hence he suffers under or suffers from the opposition which corresponds to whatever in his age must be regarded as the specific evil.[16]

---

100). At the end of his involved discussion, however, Norris recoils in deference and admits: "In Kierkegaard [deconstruction] meets perhaps the highest and most resourceful challenge to its powers of textual demystification" (p. 106). Indeed Kierkegaard always seems one step ahead of such critics; he manages to anticipate and subvert in advance—and with satirical finesse far surpassing their own bids at cleverness—all newfangled attempts to "demystify" or reduce him. Consequently, such "demystification" attempts on Kierkegaard, performed in the "deconstructive" vein, are producing evaluations more mystifying than ever.

13. See Aage Henriksen, *Methods and Results of Kierkegaard Studies in Scandinavia*, pp. 7–8.
14. Ibid., p. 10.
15. For more on this and the problems it raises see Chapter 6 below.
16. *The Point of View*, p. 59.

This meant that Kierkegaard had been completely prepared for the public opposition, particularly as evidenced in the press, which greeted his eventual open attack in 1854-55. He also foresaw that the polemics would not cease with his death, but would go on indefinitely. *The Point of View*, coming as it did in 1859, virtually guaranteed a revival of the contentions associated with the *Kirkekampen*. Although years after the event, some continued to eulogize with moving words the passing of a great figure in Scandinavian intellectual history—"It was like a shudder went over all the north on that November day in 1855," was the compelling way in which the Norwegian Lorentz H. S. Dietrichson (1834-1917) put it in a lecture at Uppsala in 1860[17]—certain periodicals, especially ecclesiastical ones, could not refrain from reminding their readers of the affront Kierkegaard had offered to the Church five years earlier. A religious weekly called *Pilegrimen* ("the Pilgrim"), for example, edited by M. A. Sommer, published a series of informal discussions of Kierkegaard's *Øjeblikket* that allegedly took place at a clergyman's house in May 1855.[18] At one point in the conversation a lady interrupts the speaker and asks:

> Thank you! my dear doctor, that was very good; but I would like to ask: Is this Dr. S. K. a crazy man? Has he been in an insane asylum, or will someone soon lead him over there? A man who talks in this manner about the official divine service must be either a great mocker, or a mad person. If the official worship of God is not the true Christianity, what should that be then?[19]

And she proceeds to launch into a tirade about how uplifting it is to see people young and old gather in the church on Sunday morning at the striking of the clock in order to worship God. Readers of this in 1860 would begin to wonder, and some would be bound to experience a recurrence of the revulsion from Kierkegaard that they may have felt at the height of the *Kirkekampen*.

Popular reactions to the life and works of a great thinker are only part of the story of his reception. Every truly outstanding figure in the history of thought must at some point, whether while living or posthumously, and in some fashion, either through attraction or repulsion, stimulate

---

17. Lorentz Dietrichson, *Indledning i Studiet af Danmarks Literatur i vort Aarhundrede: Literærhistoriske forelæsninger holdne i Uppsala vaarterminen* (Uppsala, 1860), p. 156.

18. See "Samtaler i Præstens Huus over Dr. S. Kierkegaards 'Øjeblikke,' " in *Pilegrimen*, 1st year, nos. 25-40 (1860).

19. Ibid., no. 25, p. 399.

another significant mind. The reception of one eminent writer's works is never more meaningful or more lasting in its impact than when it occurs at the hands of another remarkable writer. It is precisely this kind of one-to-one creative intellectual interaction that builds a cumulative tradition of thought in history.

It was to be some time before Kierkegaard's works found a major thinker, or set of thinkers, to discover them, become engrossed in them, be seized by a few of their themes, and act as transmitters of these, usually in the mantle of a new critical interpretation. Perhaps the earliest posthumous instance of this came about with Henrik Ibsen (1828–1906). Ibsen's "appropriation" of Kierkegaardian themes, however, was not without its problems, and this fact would lead the scholar to conclude that with Ibsen, Kierkegaard's time had really not yet arrived.

Barely ten years after Kierkegaard's death we find Ibsen, who had then moved to Italy from Norway, completing his play *Brand* (published in 1866)—a play that exhibits curious affinities with the ideas of the famous Danish philosopher and has since occasioned much discussion concerning the precise intellectual relationship between the two Scandinavians. Earlier, in 1862, Ibsen's *Love's Comedy* appeared, and subsequent speculation by biographers, literary critics, and scholars was to focus on the extent to which its author was aware of Kierkegaard's views on love and marriage as he created the play. Kierkegaard's personality and doctrines were starting to be widely discussed in intellectual circles throughout the North by the early 1860s, yet how much and in what way this affected Ibsen's thinking at the time remains problematical.[20]

Certain issues and themes that are central to both *Love's Comedy* and *Brand* and suggest a Kierkegaardian influence recur at intervals throughout the entire Ibsen corpus, making it crucial to establish the nature of the playwright's acquaintance with the thoughts of Kierkegaard.[21] The question relevant to the story of Kierkegaard's reception is whether Kierkegaard's influence, which according to every major scholar does exist

---

20. Brian Downs, in his book *A Study of Six Plays by Ibsen* (London: Cambridge University Press, 1950), p. 15, interprets the character Falk in *Love's Comedy* as a Kierkegaardian aesthete. While this makes interesting dramatic criticism, it tells us nothing about whether and how Ibsen might have received impulses from Kierkegaard which had an input in the creation of Falk. See also pp. 13–14.

21. Some examples of these themes would include love, marriage, the individual versus the community, compromise versus faithfulness to one's perceived calling, personal versus institutional religion, the relationship of art to life, the nature of tragedy, and the power of the human will.

in some form or other, came about directly as a result of Ibsen's having read his works, or indirectly through Ibsen's reacting to the popular reputation of Kierkegaard that spread swiftly over Scandinavia soon after his death. Although this reputation was unbalanced and gave a lopsided picture of the totality of Kierkegaard's thoughts and positions, it could have served as an inspiration for some of Ibsen's ideas in the plays under consideration. The question is not how much he managed to penetrate to the essence of Kierkegaard's intellectual and spiritual views and integrate them into a coherent understanding of the man (Ibsen did not do this and was not interested in doing it), but rather which of Kierkegaard's ideas, even if in truncated form, made an impact on the playwright's works, how that came about, and how they were possibly transmitted via the dramatic medium.

Ibsen, with his diverse literary interests and contacts among leading intellectuals of his time, could hardly have escaped being exposed to Kierkegaardian ideas during his formative years, especially since Kierkegaard was "in the air," certainly the *Scandinavian* air, in the mid-nineteenth century.[22] It is not easy to determine precisely the nature of indirect influences in intellectual history; nevertheless, most scholars are in agreement that educated Scandinavians of Ibsen's generation were impregnated with Kierkegaardian concepts and modes of thinking.[23]

---

22. "It is inconceivable that any student who traveled in the literary circles of Oslo in the forties and fifties could have been untouched by the work of Soren [*sic*] Kierkegaard. Norway was still dependent culturally on Denmark, though she had begun to declare her independence." See Wendell Q. Halverson, "Ibsen and Kierkegaard," in *Union Seminary Quarterly Review*, I1 (November 1946), p. 16.

23. Maurice Muret, "Un Précurseur d'Henrik Ibsen; Soeren Kierkegaard," in *La Revue de Paris* (July–August 1901), p. 100. This article is more important for the discussion of Kierkegaard's introduction into France than it is for illuminating the question of his influence on Ibsen. Many of Muret's and others' overly anxious detections of similarities between Kierkegaard's ideas and Ibsen's, ascribed to tangible influences, are debunked in P. G. La Chesnais's seminal article "Ibsen Disciple de Kierkegaard?" in *EDDA*, vol. 34 (1934). Muret compares the diffusion of Kierkegaard's ideas in Scandinavia and their creation of an intellectual climate with the similar occurrence in France brought about by Renan's doctrines. Michael Meyer, in his monumental three-volume biography of Ibsen, makes the same point with respect to Proudhon, and implies that Ibsen would have to have been feebleminded for nothing of the prevailing intellectual atmosphere around him to have rubbed off on him and manifested itself in his works [vol. II, *Henrik Ibsen: The Farewell to Poetry, 1864–1882* (London: R. Hart-Davis, 1971), p. 144]. Brian Downs, in *Ibsen: The Intellectual Background* (London: Cambridge University Press, 1946), p. 79, says, somewhat optimistically, that Northern Europe appreciated Kierkegaard's originality even while he was still alive; and his doctrines "passed into general currency very soon after his premature death in 1854 [*sic*]." For an article in French on Ibsen—earlier than

Ibsen was the sort who read few books and picked up many ideas from people he knew, such as the celebrated Danish literary critic Georg Brandes (1842–1927) and the Norwegian dramatist Bjørnstjerne Bjørnson (1832–1910), who were themselves voracious readers, and from plays he attended. He was one of the few writers who worked without a library.[24] He was also generally reluctant to acknowledge the influence of others on him, and underlying this attitude one may detect traces of vanity in his character. An example of this can be seen in connection with his earliest play *Catiline* (1849). There were strong similarities between some parts of it and Shakespeare's *Julius Caesar*, yet Ibsen insisted that at the time he wrote it he had not read any Shakespeare.[25]

Concerning Kierkegaard, in a letter to his publisher Fredrik Hegel dated June 9, 1866, Ibsen categorically denied using the Danish philosopher as a prototype for his Brand.[26] In two more letters, one to his publisher (March 8, 1867) and the other to Peter Hansen, one of his biographers (October 28, 1870), Ibsen repeated the denial and declared he had read very little of Kierkegaard and understood even less.[27] The striking similarities between some of Ibsen's ideas and those of Kierkegaard, even in their nearly identical wording in places, suggest that somewhere, somehow, Ibsen must have come in contact with Kierkegaardian ideas phrased in Kierkegaardian language. As F. L. Lucas puts it, since mere coincidence as an explanation of the resemblance is too

---

Muret's—which mentions Kierkegaard's influence as having permeated Scandinavian intellectual life in Ibsen's day, see M. Prozor, "Un drame de Henrik Ibsen, *Brand*, drame philosophique," in *Revue des deux Mondes*, 4th series, 126 (Paris, 1894), pp. 129–61 (see pp. 130–31, and p. 160).

24. Meyer, *Henrik Ibsen: The Making of a Dramatist, 1828–1864* (London: R. Hart-Davis, 1967), vol. I, p. 140. In some of Ibsen's early poems there occur "turns of phrase from Kierkegaard" along with eclectic collecting from various authors, poets, and playwrights—for example, Wergeland and Oehlenschläger; see Halvdan Koht, *The Life of Ibsen*, 2 volumes, trans. from Norwegian by Ruth Lima McMahon and Hanna Astrup Larsen (New York: B. Blom, 1931), vol. I, p. 45.

25. Koht, *The Life of Ibsen*, vol. I, p. 41. Koht says: "Such statements should not be taken too literally, however. Ibsen was always unwilling to acknowledge the influence of others, and, because he was personally absorbed in his themes, it was not easy for him to recognize his debt to earlier writings."

26. Laurvik and Morison, trans., *Letters of Henrik Ibsen* (New York: Duffield & Company, 1908), p. 119.

27. Ibid., pp. 135–36, and 198–99. According to Richard Hornby, the denial that the character of Brand is intended to depict the *life* of Kierkegaard does not preclude his *philosophy*'s providing "the structural underpinning for the play." See his *Patterns in Ibsen's Middle Plays* (Lewisburg: Bucknell University Press, 1981), pp. 64–65.

remote a possibility, and since it is difficult to believe that Ibsen was lying or had forgotten, we are left with only one alternative: "he did not realize what he owed . . . the indebtedness was mainly unconscious, and often at second or third hand."[28] This, along with not a small tinge of the stubborn pride that constituted a visible component of Ibsen's temperament, is the most plausible explanation for his seeming unawareness of the glaring parallels in thoughts and wording between himself and Kierkegaard.[29]

The little reading that Ibsen did in Kierkegaard occurred in the late 1840s when he was still in Grimstad. There he made the acquaintance of an English spinster named Miss Crawfurd, who had come to settle in Grimstad in the 1820s. She owned a sizable private library containing a copy of Kierkegaard's *Either/Or* (1843). Ibsen used to borrow books from her library occasionally, and in addition to reading some Kierkegaard he also had exposure to Dickens and Walter Scott.[30] Michael Meyer, Ibsen's most comprehensive biographer and translator, believes that Miss Crawfurd "may well have provided Ibsen with his first introduction to Kierkegaard's work."[31]

While at Grimstad, Ibsen formed an intimate circle of friends who shared similar literary interests. He and his two closest companions, Christopher Due and Ole Carelius Schulerud, studied Kierkegaard's books. This is mentioned in a book that Due later wrote, and the two works by Kierkegaard he specifically cited as having been read are *Either/*

---

28. F. L. Lucas, *The Drama of Ibsen and Strindberg* (New York: Macmillan, 1962), pp. 91–92. Downs, years earlier in his *Ibsen: The Intellectual Background*, p. 90, says roughly the same thing: ". . . a very deep-rooted conception may have passed altogether out of his [Ibsen's] conscious recollection of its origin." One therefore ought not to take Ibsen's denials very seriously, observes Downs, echoing Koht (p. 79). It should be mentioned that Lucas's treatment of Kierkegaard is very negative and shows little appreciation for the complexity of his thought.

29. Another consideration that might have been a factor in Ibsen's vehement denials of Kierkegaardian affinities is his fear of the possible charge of plagiarism. He wished at all costs to be regarded as an original thinker. See Hornby, *Patterns in Ibsen's Middle Plays*, pp. 24–25. Hornby speaks of Ibsen's "technique of characterization," in addition to "certain plot elements" and "much of the symbolism," as being particularly Kierkegaardian (p. 27). He also insists that it would be a mistake to press the Kierkegaardian approach to Ibsen too far (pp. 28 and 70).

30. Koht, *The Life of Ibsen*, vol. I, p. 33.

31. Meyer, *Henrik Ibsen*, vol. I, p. 51. On Ibsen and Crawfurd, see also H. Eitrem, *Ibsen og Grimstad* (Oslo: H. Aschehoug, 1940), pp. 40–41.

Or and *Works of Love* (1847), which, he added, it was fashionable in those days to read.[32]

In 1850, Ibsen left Grimstad and went to the University in Christiania. There he may have read some Hegel, and also the Danish Hegelian Johan Ludvig Heiberg.[33] Did he pursue his readings of Kierkegaard? We do not really know much about what exactly he was reading at this time.[34] In February 1852, Ibsen, then newly affiliated with the theater at Bergen, made his first trip abroad: he visited Copenhagen, where he was introduced to the famous Danish actress Johanne Luise Heiberg, wife of the noted Hegelian. She was later to arrange for the staging of Ibsen's plays in Denmark. Ibsen met her husband as well; the circumstances of their encounter, however, were very formal, with little room for the exchange of ideas.[35] He also managed to make the acquaintance of H. C. Andersen on this trip, but he did not meet Kierkegaard.

One person who did meet Kierkegaard in her youth was Magdalene Thoresen (1819–1903), the step-mother of Ibsen's wife and a Dane by birth. She became in later years an enthusiastic follower of Kierkegaard as "interpreted" by Rasmus Nielsen.[36] In the 1850s she conducted a literary *salon* into which Ibsen, who was then courting her daughter, was introduced. It is more than likely that Kierkegaard was discussed at these gatherings. In 1858 Ibsen also joined the newly established group of literary critics revolving around Paul Botten-Hansen that later came to be known as the Holland Circle. He may have been present at some of their debates that dealt with Kierkegaard's ideas.[37]

---

32. Christopher Due, *Erindringer fra Henrik Ibsens Ungdomsaar* (Copenhagen, 1909), p. 38. Due also mentions that at the time the three of them, in contrast to their other friends, were "as poor as church mice" (p. 38).

33. Koht, *The Life of Ibsen,* vol. I, pp. 60–61. For a discussion of Hegelian elements in Ibsen's early plays see Brian Johnston, *To the Third Empire: Ibsen's Early Drama* (Minneapolis: University of Minnesota Press, 1980).

34. Meyer, *Henrik Ibsen,* vol. I, p. 81.

35. Koht, *The Life of Ibsen,* vol. I, pp. 78–79. Koht informs us that Copenhagen offered little that was new to Ibsen, for "with Danish intellectual life he was intimately allied before." The implication here is that by the time he made his trip to Copenhagen, Ibsen had become acquainted to some degree with Kierkegaard's writings, among others.

36. Or misinterpreted as is shown in Chapter 5 below. For more on Thoresen and Nielsen see Clara Bergsøe, *Magdalene Thoresen, Portrætstudie* (Copenhagen, 1904), pp. 38–43.

37. Downs, *Ibsen: The Intellectual Background,* p. 80. See also *A Study of Six Plays by Ibsen,* p. 14 (footnote) by the same author.

In a letter to Hanna Wiehe, a close friend of hers, Thoresen reveals that Wiehe had first recommended Kierkegaard to her. She began to read him, and Shakespeare, unceasingly. She briefly contrasts them in the letter. She also singles out *Either/Or,* calling the first volume "mysteriously tempting," but admits that she found the work as a whole difficult to read: " . . . oh, certainly, certainly one does not grasp this [work] during the years of youth."[38] In her memoirs Thoresen wrote a short comparison between Ibsen and Kierkegaard that ran as follows:

> Outwardly the resemblance was small; Søren Kierkegaard was long-striding and gangling, while Ibsen took short paces and had the squat build of a miner. What similarity there was must, therefore, have lain deeper; and so it was. I have never seen in any other two persons, male or female, so marked a compulsion to be alone with themselves.[39]

Perhaps Ibsen's revolt against attempts to affiliate him with Kierkegaard stemmed, in part, from constant associations his mother-in-law kept making between them in the early 1860s as *Love's Comedy* and *Brand* were taking shape.

From the preceding brief survey of Ibsen's erratic exposure to Kierkegaard, it becomes evident that his knowledge of Kierkegaard's works and the broad themes informing his thought was sketchy at best and entirely unsystematic. One can therefore readily rule out the view expressed by Georg Brandes in an essay on Ibsen written in 1867 and subsequently entitled "First Impression," that the playwright was consciously aspiring to be regarded as "Kierkegaard's poet." Brandes himself, in a "Second Impression" written in 1882, altered his position and called it a "misapprehension" to say that Ibsen had had Kierkegaard in mind when writing *Brand*.[40]

---

38. Letter from Magdalene Thoresen to Hanna Wiehe dated June 4, 1857, in *Breve fra Magdalene Thoresen: 1855-1901,* ed. Jul. Clausen and P. Fr. Rist (Copenhagen: Gyldendal, Nordisk Forlag, 1919), pp. 36-37.

39. Quoted in Meyer, *Henrik Ibsen,* vol. I, p. 148.

40. Both "Impressions" plus a third written in 1898 are included in one book by Brandes entitled *Henrik Ibsen and Bjørnstjerne Bjørnson,* trans. Jessie Muir (New York, 1899), p. 21 (First Impression reference) and pp. 70-71 (Second Impression reference). For a discussion of why Brandes shifted his position from a belief in a direct Kierkegaardian influence on Ibsen to one of indirect impact, see P. G. La Chesnais, "Ibsen Disciple de Kierkegaard?" pp. 355-56. See also Chapter 6 below for a treatment of Brandes's views on Kierkegaard and how they developed. In the "Third Impression," Brandes remarks that the ending of *An Enemy of the People* (1882)—"the strongest man in the world is he who stands alone"—is very Kierkegaardian, and that not since *Brand*

In addition to the irritation Ibsen felt upon hearing his name repeatedly allied with Kierkegaard's, his sense of indignation may also have resulted, consciously or unconsciously, from a deep-rooted idealistic-romantic streak of Norwegian nationalism and contempt for all forms of Danish hegemony, whether political or cultural-intellectual. It must not be forgotten, however, that Ibsen himself went through many changes in his attitude toward the Danes and toward his own people and their culture. In the 1850s he was involved with Norwegianism; then, in the 1860s, he castigated his people and the Swedes for not aiding the Danes in their war with Prussia.[41] Later, he began to embrace a form of Scandinavianism that included Swedes, Norwegians, and Danes; still later, the Germans came to consider him a Germanic playwright. As he became more famous, his cosmopolitanism increased.[42]

The entire controversy about the influence of Kierkegaard's philosophical and religious ideas on Ibsen's works centers primarily on three plays he produced roughly in the middle of his career as a dramatist: *Love's Comedy*, *Brand*, and *Peer Gynt*.[43] Of the three, *Brand* has been most consistently linked to Kierkegaard. The issue chiefly disputed among scholars has been to what degree Kierkegaard's life and thoughts were the sources from which Ibsen molded the personality of his Brand. We know that two men who crossed paths with Ibsen at the time he was

---

had Ibsen expressed himself with such Kierkegaardian terminology. In using the term "Kierkegaard's poet" to describe Ibsen, Brandes had in mind Kierkegaard's own words about a future person, "my poet," who "when he comes will assign me a place among those who have suffered for the sake of an idea." See the conclusion of *The Point of View*, pp. 100–103; see pp. 62–63 in the same work by Kierkegaard for similar references to "my lover."

41. The bitterness Ibsen experienced as a result of what he perceived to be his countrymen's betrayal of their fellow Scandinavian brothers was one of the factors that caused him to create *Brand*.

42. For a while Ibsen wavered between Norwegian nationalism and Scandinavianism, but finally supported the latter as attested, among other things, by his zeal for language reform to bring Danish, Norwegian, and Swedish closer together (see Koht, *The Life of Ibsen*, vol. II, pp. 73ff.). In the mid-nineteenth century Ibsen took part in the Norwegian nationalist movement that sought political and cultural independence from Denmark. He played his role in the specific area of drama, particularly as director of the Christiania Norwegian Theater in 1857 (Koht, *The Life of Ibsen*, vol. I, chap. 11). In the late 1860s, after the appearance of *Brand*, Ibsen, then living in Italy, became very critical of all forms of Norwegian exclusivism and national self-satisfaction (ibid., vol. II, pp. 19–20).

43. Scholars have argued to a lesser extent about Kierkegaardian influences in other Ibsen plays as well, notably *Emperor and Galilean* (1864–73) and *An Enemy of the People* (1882).

formulating his ideas about *Brand* left a distinct mark on the character of the play's religious hero, and both can be loosely described as having been "Kierkegaardians" of sorts. These men were Gustav Adolf Lammers and Christopher Arnt Bruun (1839–1920).

Lammers, the fiery revivalist and onetime admirer of Kierkegaard, became the successor in Norway of Hauge, initiator of a religious movement that quickly took a puritanical turn and displayed open hostility toward cultural and artistic endeavors, in particular the theater. Lammers established himself in Ibsen's hometown of Skien, where he succeeded in 1856 in attracting members of Ibsen's family, particularly his sister Hedvig, as his followers. They soon "counted their Henrik as one of the damned" because he refused to abandon his love for the theater.[44]

The openly proclaimed positions of Lammers on spiritual matters in the mid-1850s were a mixture of pietism and a certain interpretation of Kierkegaard that derived largely from the latter's biting offensives against the Christianity of his day in Denmark. Lammers, after coming in contact with *Øjeblikket*, "went out into the fields" to preach his new message. Ibsen had probably read in *Christianiaposten* about the *Kirkekampen* raging in Copenhagen in 1855. He may even have perused issues of *Øjeblikket*, which would have been easily available to him in Norway. In fact, according to one of the many biographies of Ibsen written while he was still alive, Ibsen was familiar with Kierkegaard's *Øjeblikket* and with Lammers's sermons inspired by it. However, Henrik Jaeger, the biographer in question, plays down the significance of Kierkegaardian influences on Ibsen's *Brand*:

> Danish critics, Brandes among them, and, following in his footsteps, the majority of the German writers who have dealt with Ibsen of late, have treated him in connection with Søren Kierkegaard, and assumed the poem [*Brand*] to have been suggested by the writings of the latter, and by the agitation led by him against the established church. It is easy to understand how this misconception has arisen among foreigners, not intimately acquainted with Norwegian conditions, for the points of resemblance are obvious. When Kierkegaard bewails the pitiable character of the age, when he exalts the individual,

---

44. Downs, *Ibsen: The Intellectual Background*, p. 46. Downs says that the doubts and questions this revivalism provoked in Ibsen found their modified expression in *Brand*. For a discussion of the impact of Lammers on Ibsen and the shaping of the character of Brand, see Oskar Mosfjeld, *Henrik Ibsen og Skien: En Biografisk og Litteratur-Psykologisk Studie* (Oslo: Gyldendal, 1949), pp. 176–77 and 237–46. See also Koht, *The Life of Ibsen*, vol. I, pp. 277–78; and Wendell Q. Halverson, "Ibsen and Kierkegaard," p. 15.

and pours his scorn upon society, when he attacks official Christianity from the standpoint of a broad humanity, and when he, a theologian who had even been a preacher *sic*], declares, at the close of his life, that, sooner than enter a church, he would commit the grossest of crimes, the analogy which he offers to Brand is sufficiently apparent.

In spite of this, we are but crossing the stream to fetch water when we look to Kierkegaard for the actual model upon which *Brand* was based. At the time *Brand* was written Ibsen knew almost nothing of Søren Kierkegaard; he had not read half a dozen sheets of his writings,—a little of *Either/Or,* and *The Moment* [*Øjeblikket*] that was all. The course of Kierkegaard's last agitation was followed in Norway, and naturally aroused certain interest there, but it made little impression upon Ibsen, and he never felt called to be "Kierkegaard's poet," although the term has been applied to him.

On the other hand, his attention has been very strongly held by the agitation which Pastor G. A. Lammers had aroused, towards the close of the fifties, in Ibsen's native town of Skien.[45]

Jaeger was Ibsen's close friend and biographer. It is understandable that he should support Ibsen's claim of there being no direct influence on him from Kierkegaard. Jaeger, however, does mention Lammers as one who had a strong impact on Ibsen's thinking. Ibsen himself once remarked to Jaeger that "Kierkegaard was too much of a closet agitator; Lammers, on the other hand, was an open-air agitator like Brand."[46] On a different occasion, Ibsen said to William Archer, his first English translator, that "it is all nonsense to say that Brand had anything to do with Kierkegaard . . . a man who formed a sort of model for Brand was a Pastor Lammers."[47] Clearly, judging by these straightforward admis-

---

45. Henrik Jaeger, *Henrik Ibsen, 1828–1888, A Critical Biography,* first published in 1888 and translated from the Norwegian by William Morton Payne (Chicago, 1890), pp. 180–82. Jaeger is right about rejecting the term "Kierkegaard's poet" for Ibsen, which Brandes coined in his "First Impression" of 1867, but seems unaware of Brandes's change of view expressed in the "Second Impression" (1882). See note 40 above.

46. Jaeger, *Henrik Ibsen,* p. 186. The word "brand" in Danish means fire or conflagration. Lammers's "fire and brimstone" style of preaching may have provided the inspiration for the name of the play's hero.

47. Quoted in Lucas, *The Drama of Ibsen and Strindberg,* p. 76. Lucas concludes that Brand was really a mixture of Lammers and Bruun. At times Ibsen would insist that one of them acted as a model for Brand; then, on other occasions, he would say it was the other. P. G. La Chesnais makes the interesting argument that Lammers acted as a prototype more for Einar than for Brand, although he does not completely rule out similarities with Brand (see his "Ibsen Disciple de Kierkegaard?" pp. 368 and 375). Lucas picks up on this argument and says that Lammers, like Einar, began as a painter, then lost the woman he loved (Agnes, in the play), and finally ended up as a revivalist preacher.

sions on Ibsen's part, Lammers played a crucial role in shaping Brand's personality. This should not be taken to mean, however, that Brand is therefore an accurate, if indirect, representation of Kierkegaard and his ideas, for Lammers himself conveys only a very superficial and one-sided Kierkegaardian sensibility.[48]

In addition to the self-styled preacher Lammers, there was another "Kierkegaardian" who left a distinct impression on the author of *Brand*. Christopher Bruun was a young Norwegian theology student from Christiania who joined the Danish army in its ill-fated war with Prussia in 1864. He later visited his family in Italy, where he met Ibsen when the latter was engaged in the creation of *Brand*. Bruun had studied Kierkegaard's works zealously and from them had acquired an idealistic loathing of compromise. Kierkegaard's notion of martyrdom for the truth achieved a firm grip on his soul. He was a man with set convictions and a strong sense of duty. His Kierkegaard-inspired idealism had led him to fight on the side of the Danes and this impressed Ibsen greatly, especially in view of the fact that the trend among Norwegians and Swedes had been to avoid getting involved. Their apathy considerably irked Ibsen, but in Bruun he saw before him a living example of the sort of Scandinavian he so admired and longed for. They spent many hours discussing the war and the implications of the humiliating defeat of the Danes for Scandinavia. Kierkegaard's philosophy was also the topic of exchange at several of their encounters.[49]

---

48. Walter Lowrie, in the introduction to his *Kierkegaard*, pp. 10-11, makes this point and then states that Brand's total lack of a sense of humor represents a basic difference between him and Kierkegaard. Brand was also a fanatic, says Lowrie, whereas Kierkegaard's satirical posture, in the midst of his attacks on the Church, saves him from such an accusation. Lowrie, however, mistakenly uses "Lamme" for Lammers. Downs succinctly expressed a similar view as follows: "If the ascription of Kierkegaardianism to *Brand* be only very partially tenable, to see in its hero, as some writers have done, a portrait of Kierkegaard himself is wild error." See his *A Study of Six Plays by Ibsen*, pp. 62-63.

49. On Bruun see Klaus Sletten, *Christopher Bruun: Folkelæraren—Stridsmannen* (Oslo: Gyldendal, 1949), especially the part entitled "Under Kierkegaards Åndsmakt," pp. 30-51, which discusses Bruun's relation to Kierkegaard and offers extracts from his diary; also pp. 154-63, which treat his impact on the shaping of *Brand*. See also Meyer, *Henrik Ibsen*, vol. I, pp. 197-99; Downs, *Ibsen: The Intellectual Background*, p. 83, where he states that the character of Brand was modelled largely on that of Christopher Bruun; F. J. Billeskov Jansen, "L'Héritage de Kierkegaard dans les Pays Nordiques," in *Cahiers du Sud* 50, no. 371 (Marseilles, April-May 1963), p. 19; Wendell Q. Halverson, "Ibsen and Kierkegaard," pp. 15-17. P. G. La Chesnais makes several references to Bruun in his article, including long quotes from letters that La Chesnais, who apparently knew Bruun personally, had received from him. La Chesnais says that Bruun was a partisan of the

Bruun's peculiar variety of Kierkegaardian idealism, and his own stern nature, left their mark on the temperament of Ibsen's Brand. They were perhaps best displayed in the hero's abhorrence of compromise. This raises yet again the much-disputed question of whether Brand's unyielding battle cry, "All or Nothing," is derivative of or a variant upon Kierkegaard's "Either-Or." Ibsen scholars have disagreed on the precise connection. One such scholar put it bluntly: "Kierkegaard's 'either-or' in Ibsen becomes 'all or nothing.'"[50] Another maintained the opposite: "The slogan 'All or Nothing' to which Brand subscribes has sometimes been looked upon as Kierkegaard's, but that is not so."[51] Between these two extremes lie the cautious scholars, like Michael Meyer, who argue that the evidence is simply too scanty to deduce from it a clear-cut connection between Kierkegaard and Ibsen on this point. For Meyer, Kierkegaard acted as a catalyst who crystalized ideas already present in Ibsen's mind.[52]

That the two phrases "all or nothing" and "either-or" imply decision—even radical choice—in fundamental matters is not sufficient to render them identical. They represent two distinct forms of the rejection of compromise. Semantics aside, it has to be acknowledged that the Kierkegaardian "either-or" exists in a rich philosophical context and carries an enormous load of ethico-religious baggage which Ibsen's simplistic "all or nothing" lacks. Add to this Ibsen's apparent ignorance of Kierkegaard's assertion in *The Point of View* that in fact he had already made the decision in favor of the religious even as he was presenting his "either-or" alternatives to his readers.[53]

Yet "all or nothing" and "either-or" highlight the fact that, for both Brand in the play and Kierkegaard in real life and in his writings, the importance of the *will* and of one's faithfulness to an inward ideal of duty

---

separation of church and state, and that he had come to this position after reading Kierkegaard's *Øjeblikket* (La Chesnais, "Ibsen Disciple de Kierkegaard?" p. 379; see also p. 367). But La Chesnais's central argument remains that any Kierkegaardian influence on Ibsen was minimal and largely deformed through indirect transmission via avenues such as Bruun (p. 379). In later life Christopher Bruun made significant contributions to the high school system in Norway. He entered into the service of the state-Church in 1893, and became editor of *For Kirke og Kultur*, an ecclesiatical publication.

50. Koht, *The Life of Ibsen*, vol. I, p. 274.
51. Downs, *A Study of Six Plays by Ibsen*, p. 56. In his *Ibsen: The Intellectual Background*, p. 84, published four years earlier in 1946, Downs appears to have held the view that Ibsen's "All or Nothing" did indeed come from Kierkegaard's "Either-Or."
52. Meyer, *Henrik Ibsen*, vol. I, pp. 115 and 197.
53. *The Point of View*, p. 18.

are paramount.[54] In 1899 an article appeared in the *Fortnightly Review* written by a certain Mrs. Mabel Annie Stobart (1862-1954) and entitled "New Lights on Ibsen's 'Brand.' " According to at least two sources, Stobart enjoys the distinction of being "the first English critic to reveal a genuine interest in Kierkegaard and his influence."[55] Stobart emphasizes throughout her article the central role that willpower, which she identifies with "that subjectivity, that inwardness essential to the sacrifice of *'all,'* " plays in *Brand,* and the very Kierkegaardian nature, as she sees it, of that willpower.[56] This Kierkegaardian connection is the "New Lights" of the article's title. She refers to Kierkegaard's famous dictum that "Truth is Subjectivity," which he develops in detail in the *Postscript,* and she declares that this subjectivity is precisely the inwardness and willpower which manifest themselves in Brand's convictions and deeds.[57] In her view, Kierkegaard's "either-or" is identical in its meaning and implications with Brand's "all or nothing."[58] Furthermore, she maintains that Ibsen has "truthfully impersonated" Kierkegaard in his Brand.[59] Despite the pioneering nature of her article, none of Stobart's claims are historically founded or the result of research on her part into the history of Ibsen's intellectual relationship to Kierkegaard.[60]

54. "The ruling characteristic in [Brand] is will," says Downs, adding that Brand's "All or Nothing" is the cornerstone of his doctrine of will (*A Study of Six Plays by Ibsen,* pp. 51-52). The necessity for inwardness and the idea of attaining self-realization, Koht suggests, are unmistakable echoes of Kierkegaard in Ibsen's *Brand.* "Time and again, even constantly, as one reads *Brand,* one seems to hear Kierkegaard" (*The Life of Ibsen,* vol. I, pp. 273-74).

55. Lewis A. Lawson, editor, *Kierkegaard's Presence in Contemporary American Life: Essays from Various Disciplines* (Metuchen, N.J.: Scarecrow, 1970), Introduction, p. vii; and Downs, *A Study of Six Plays by Ibsen,* p. 58. Downs says that Stobart's article "gave the general British public its first introduction to Kierkegaard." If this is true, then Kierkegaard first became known to the English-speaking world in the context of his impact on Henrik Ibsen. Downs sees in the article's line of argument "one of the completest alignments of *Brand* to Kierkegaard's philosophy." In his discussion of her article, however, Downs mistakes the author for a man! Another interesting early connection in English between Kierkegaard and Ibsen can be found in the small paragraph on Kierkegaard in the famous eleventh edition of the *Encyclopedia Britannica,* vol. 15 (London, 1910-11), p. 788, where the author (unfortunately unknown) declares of Kierkegaard that "to him Ibsen owed his character Brand."

56. Mabel Annie Stobart, "New Lights on Ibsen's 'Brand,' " in *Fortnightly Review,* LXVI (August 1, 1899), p. 230.

57. Ibid., pp. 228-30. 58. Ibid., p. 229.

59. Ibid., p. 236.

60. In her article Stobart displays a knowledge of Kierkegaard that is rudimentary at best. It would be interesting to investigate how she came about this knowledge at such

Tracing similarities in ideas can be a very tenuous exercise from an intellectual historian's perspective. Such a historian usually prefers to avoid, as much as possible, the comparative approach of the literary critics and to concentrate instead on the genetic one. This said, an attempt may nevertheless be made to place Brand in one of the three main Kierkegaardian stages: the aesthetic, the ethical, or the religious. The historian justifies such an attempt as further illuminating the precise nature of the Kierkegaardian influence that he has already determined does exist precariously in Ibsen's *Brand*. To which of Kierkegaard's categories does Brand belong, or to which one can he be approximated? It seems obvious that he has moved beyond the aesthetic level of existence, and so the question becomes, did he make it all the way to the religious, or did he end up somewhere in the ethical?

There are many obstacles to regarding Brand as equivalent to the Knight of Faith of the religious stage. Although Brand appears superficially similar to Abraham, the prototype of the Kierkegaardian Knight of Faith, crucial differences manifest themselves upon closer scrutiny. Brand, like Abraham, has a son, Alf, whom he dearly loves and whom he proceeds to sacrifice in answer to a "higher calling." However, in Brand's case this calling is not from God, as for Abraham, but from Brand's own will.[61] Brand actually loses Alf because he believes in himself, while Abraham gains Isaac because of his faith in God.[62] Brand comes

---

an early period in the Anglo-Saxon reception. Lawson, in his *Kierkegaard's Presence in Contemporary American Life*, p. viii, says about Stobart: "No doubt Mrs. Stobart would be more widely recognized as an early admirer of Kierkegaard, if she had continued to publish such studies. But her interests soon turned to a much more active life. She was founder of the Women's Sick and Wounded Convoy Corps, a detachment of which she took to Thrace in the Balkan War of 1912-13. Early in World War I she organized hospitals in Belgium and France until she was captured by the Germans and sentenced to be executed as a spy. After her release, she served in Allied hospitals in Serbia. Her writing after the war most often dealt with spiritualism, and she served as Chairman and Leader of the Spiritualist community from 1924 to 1941. Before her death in 1954, at the age of ninety-two, she must often have reflected upon the wide popularity in England of the thinker whom she had introduced over fifty years before."

61. See the perceptive article by John M. Hems, "Abraham and Brand," in *Philosophy*, XXXIX (April, 1964), p. 137. Hems correctly labels Brand's reasoning for sacrificing his son "the logic of Caiphas: 'It is expedient for us that one man should die for the people' " (pp. 137-38). This is very different from Abraham. Downs also argues that the Brand-Abraham parallel does not hold all the way. See his *Ibsen: The Intellectual Background*, pp. 84-85.

62. Hems, "Abraham and Brand," p. 138. In this sense Brand is closer to an inverted or failed Abraham.

much nearer to Kierkegaard's description of the tragic hero who succumbs to the Universal, i.e. the ethical, than he does to Abraham, who transcends the Universal through his teleological suspension of the ethical and operates on a religious plane unintelligible to those around him.[63]

The theme of child sacrifice in *Brand* strongly suggests that Ibsen had Kierkegaard's *Fear and Trembling* (1843) in mind at the time of the play's composition. Whether he had actually read the work, or was present during a discussion of its contents, or perhaps heard about it through Bruun, is impossible to tell. The fact remains that Brand, at one point, even refers directly to Abraham's sacrifice:

> AGNES: Yes! There is one sacrifice which God dare not demand.
> BRAND: But if He should dare? If He should test me as He tested Abraham?[64]

In reality it was Brand's inward sense of duty that tested him and not the God of Abraham, as this exchange suggests; hence, Brand can best be identified with Kierkegaard's ethical stage. Though he may have been striving for higher religious goals, he never quite makes it to the religious stage as conceived by Kierkegaard.[65] But what does an identification of

---

63. Ibid., pp. 138ff. Brand's faith is an ethical faith, for which *duty* toward his community comes before *duty* toward his son. Stobart, in her "New Lights on Ibsen's 'Brand,' " p. 229, wrongly makes a complete identification of Brand with Abraham.

64. Quoted from Michael Meyer's translation of Ibsen's *Brand* (New York: R. Hart-Davis, 1960), p. 98. Meyer, in the preface to his translation (pp. 16–17), explains his belief that Kierkegaard's *Fear and Trembling* was much more likely to have been an influence on the play than *Either/Or*. See Downs, *A Study of Six Plays by Ibsen*, p. 61, for an assessment similar to Meyer's.

65. The clearest and most convincing argument for relating Brand to Kierkegaard's ethical stage is made by Forrest Wood, Jr., in his article "Kierkegaardian Light on Ibsen's Brand," in *The Personalist* 51 (1970), pp. 393–400. Wood refutes W. H. Auden's claim, made in his Foreword to Meyer's translation, that Brand fits Kierkegaard's category of the Apostle. This would elevate Brand to Kierkegaard's religious stage, which Wood rejects. Downs too concludes that Brand belongs in the ethical stage (*Ibsen: The Intellectual Background*, p. 84), and he sees in Einar a portrait of the aesthete, especially in the beginning. In Act V, Einar is transformed and becomes a caricature of Brand, according to Downs. Contrary to both Wood and Downs, Richard Hornby, in *Patterns in Ibsen's Middle Plays*, p. 72, maintains that Brand moves from the ethical to the religious stage at the end of the play. Among Ibsen scholars, however, he remains in the minority. P. G. La Chesnais, in "Ibsen Disciple de Kierkegaard?" pp. 399–400, surveys various scholars' views on the question of Brand and the Kierkegaardian stages, and declares that the association of Brand with any stage is false because Ibsen and Kierkegaard had very different conceptions in their minds. With particular reference to the ethical stage, La Chesnais says that none of Ibsen's characters is analogous to Judge William of *Either/Or*, vol. II. Unlike Wood, La Chesnais does not associate Brand with Kierkegaard's Knight

Brand with the ethical stage mean historically; was Ibsen consciously intending an association of this kind? Not if what has been established earlier about Ibsen's sparse acquaintance with Kierkegaard's philosophy is to be believed. Ibsen could not, from his meager exposure to Kierkegaard, have had a lucid conception of the three Kierkegaardian stages. Much less could he have cared to represent such categories dramatically.

Fitting Brand into some tenable Kierkegaardian mold could have the benefit of clarifying the amorphous influence Kierkegaard exercised on Ibsen. It should not make one forget, however, the glaring differences between, say, Ibsen's understanding of religion as expressed through Brand and Kierkegaard's own conception of the religious. A surface similarity exists, for example, between Kierkegaard's reluctance to call himself a Christian and Brand's words to Einar: "I do not speak for the Church. I hardly know if I'm a Christian."[66] Even assuming that Brand here mirrors Ibsen's views, the resemblance remains merely verbal and probably coincidental, because the two positions issue from, and presuppose, totally different givens. Basically, the difference lies in the attitudes toward Christian faith that Ibsen and Kierkegaard respectively exhibited. Through Brand's words, Ibsen's own skeptical position regarding Christianity comes out. He had lost his faith before the age of nineteen, but retained throughout his life an ambiguous religious disposition, which was reflected in many of his plays.[67] Kierkegaard, on the other hand, never questioned the faith but rather mounted an open crusade to replace what he considered to be a sham Christianity with his interpretation of the authentic one.

---

of Infinite Resignation, who could be taken to represent the ethical in some of its dimensions. La Chesnais concedes that Ibsen was at least familiar with the title of Kierkegaard's book *Stages on Life's Way* (1845).

66. Quoted from Meyer's translation of *Brand*, p. 60.

67. La Chesnais, "Ibsen Disciple de Kierkegaard?" p. 360. Religiously, says La Chesnais (p. 370), Kierkegaard's focus is the New Testament, while Ibsen invokes the Old, notwithstanding the final words of the play "Han er *Deus Caritatis*" (He is the God of Love). La Chesnais is very wary about drawing hasty conclusions from dubious similarities between Ibsen and Kierkegaard, whether in their lives or in their works. He especially singles out Harald Beyer's book *Søren Kierkegaard og Norge* (Christiania: H. Aschehoug, 1924) as an example of an unjustified listing of intricate "parallels" between Ibsen and Kierkegaard (see pp. 357–60 of La Chesnais's article). Downs, in *Ibsen: The Intellectual Background*, p. 85, writes: "Early in the play Brand says he scarcely knows whether he is a Christian or not: the same, I fancy, Ibsen would have said of himself. He never approached what Kierkegaard calls the religious *stadium*. He reverenced the person of Jesus Christ but his love of the Bible seems mainly to have been literary."

What emerges from the entire preceding discussion of *Brand* is a very patchy picture of the main character in the play. Brand is really a composite personality made up of part Lammers, part Bruun, part Kierkegaard mediated through both Lammers and Bruun, and part Ibsen himself.[68] The result is a very un-Kierkegaardian hybrid containing ethical, religious, pietistic, and idealistic elements all eclectically jumbled together to form one personality. Not without reason has the character of Brand been called "a travesty of Kierkegaard."[69]

That Brand reflects to some degree the temperamental qualities and life experiences of his creator is beyond any doubt. In his letter to Peter Hansen,[70] Ibsen states, "Brand is myself in my best moments—just as certainly as it is certain that by self-analysis I brought to light many of both Peer Gynt's and Stensgaard's qualities." Ibsen did indeed exhibit a marked intolerance for compromise and an insistence upon radical choices in his own life. This began to be apparent in his relations with his parents during his youth in Skien. He avoided them as he grew older, with religious and temperamental differences separating them. He retained close contacts only with his sister Hedvig.[71] He also possessed a certain "power of indignation" that, as in Brand's case, constantly urged him on to higher things.[72]

Perhaps the most significant trait that Brand and his creator shared with Kierkegaard was a rugged, often bleak, Nordic individualism. Koht quotes Ibsen speaking to a German about life in Norway:

---

68. See Otto Heller, *Henrik Ibsen: Plays and Problems* (Boston and New York, 1912), pp. 60–62. Heller, who was a professor of German language and literature in Washington University, arrives at this conclusion and says: "At all events, Brand must be classed as a composite portrait, not a strictly true copy from life" (p. 62). In his view, Kierkegaard "left unquestionable marks of influence in the great poem [i.e. *Brand*]" (p. 60). Examples of this influence given by Heller are: renunciation of the "official" Christianity of the churches; emphasis on a "gospel of sorrow" and a renunciation of the world; emphasis on direct—even contractual—relations between the Deity and the individual; and consistent conformity to the demands of an absolute ideal.

69. T. H. Croxall, *Glimpses and Impressions of Kierkegaard*, p. 98.

70. Laurvik and Morison, trans., *Letters of Henrik Ibsen*, p. 199. Koht, in *The Life of Ibsen*, vol. I, pp. 275–76, says the character traits of Brand are "deeply and firmly rooted in [Ibsen's] own being."

71. Koht, *The Life of Ibsen*, vol. I, p. 26. Ibsen is portrayed throughout Koht's two-volume work as a person with a strong temper that was slow to anger, but that exploded against the falsehoods around him.

72. Ibid., vol. I, p. 34.

The people up there are indeed different from you here, and he who would know me fully, must know Norway. The grand but austere nature with which people are surrounded in the North, the lonely, isolated life—their homes often lie many miles apart—compel them to be indifferent to other people, and to care only about their own concerns; therefore they become ruminative and serious-minded; they ponder and doubt; and they often despair. With us every other man is a philosopher! Then there are the long, dark winters, with the thick fog about the houses—Oh, they long for the sun![73]

The same, with slight modifications, can be said of Denmark, although geographically and climatically it differs from Norway and is more hospitable.

Coupled organically with this Nordic individualism is the likewise Nordic brand of Lutheran Protestantism, whose fiber permeated Ibsen's personality to its core, regardless of whether he was actually a religious believer. It would have been natural for Ibsen, therefore, to respond to similar threads permeating Kierkegaard's personality and writings.[74] In *Brand*, Ibsen poses fundamental questions in relative isolation from tradition and the actual living communities of thought and spirit that embody it. In many of his religious writings, particularly his critique of "Christendom," Kierkegaard does the same. Ibsen displays a contempt for "the majority" in some of his plays (*An Enemy of the People*, for instance), which reverberates with discernible Kierkegaardian overtones. The same theme also comes up in *Brand*, with the Mayor and the Provost each representing hostile majorities that Brand had to face. The Provost, in particular, was a depiction of the loathsome ecclesiastical figure who had so irritated Kierkegaard and now Ibsen as well.[75]

It is interesting to read in a letter Ibsen sent to Bjørnson dated Septem-

---

73. Ibid., vol. II, pp. 11–12. For a discussion of the impact of Nordic traits on the thinking of Ibsen and Kierkegaard, presented with a distinct climatic and geographic determinism, see Maurice Muret, "Un Précurseur d'Henrik Ibsen; Soeren Kierkegaard," pp. 108 and 110–11.

74. On the Protestant Lutheran individualism that Ibsen shared with Kierkegaard see Muret, "Un Précurseur," pp. 116–17 and 119–20. See also Koht, *The Life of Ibsen*, vol. I, p. 37.

75. Koht, *The Life of Ibsen*, vol. II, p. 180. Ibsen's concern with assertive personalities—a gallery of egoists—reveals the thin line between individualism and subjectivism-egotism. Dr. Stockman of *An Enemy of the People* is convinced he is right even though he is in a minority and the majority of people are opposed to him. This is reminiscent of Kierkegaard's "Truth is in the minority" and "A single individual is the highest power."

ber 12, 1865, that while writing *Brand* he read nothing except the Bible.[76] Given *Brand*'s subject matter, given the Nordic temperament of its author, and given Kierkegaardian individualism infused with the Protestant ingredient of nonconformity, there could not have been a more natural thing to do than steep oneself exclusively in Scripture while writing a play like *Brand*.

Through Ibsen's *Brand*, more than through any other literary creation, Norway entered into the European intellectual arena of the 1860s. All the plays Ibsen published during that decade, especially *Brand*, appeared at a time when liberalism and individualism were in the ascendant in Europe. It was the era of *laissez-faire*, of the quest for personal freedom, and of philosophical reflections on the nature of liberty. It was a time when "the Individual, the Ego, the I was the subject with which modern thought was concerned."[77] Philosophically, another chapter in the unfolding story of modern subjectivism was being written everywhere and in diverse forms:

> No other time has known such faith in the will and powers of the individual. . . . If we seek to know what gave reality to Norway's participation in the movement, we can find no one thing of greater importance than Ibsen's *Brand*. Individualism has not created a mightier work of literary art. It is deeply rooted in the age that fostered it, and at the same time it exalts the fundamental thought of that age with such power as to infuse into it new ideals. Individualism becomes an ethical principle. With the appearance of *Brand* we may mark the beginning of a new period in Norwegian intellectual life.[78]

Ibsen's plays contributed a uniquely Nordic perspective on the individual that blended well with the *Zeitgeist*, and significantly enriched it. Kierkegaard's shadow loomed conspicuously in the background of this contribution.

In the case of the two other plays that bear some Kierkegaardian hallmarks, *Love's Comedy* (1862) and *Peer Gynt* (1867), it is more difficult to pinpoint actual influences. The situation that obtains in *Love's Comedy*

---

76. Cited in La Chesnais, "Ibsen Disciple de Kierkegaard?" p. 374.

77. Angelo S. Rappoport, "Ibsen, Nietzsche, and Kierkegaard," in *New Age*, III (1908), p. 409. Rappoport makes an important observation: "It must not be forgotten that the ideas of Kierkegaard, as of Ibsen, are those of the age in which they lived" (p. 409). This means that, in addition to having enriched the individualism of the age, their ideas were also products of it.

78. Koht, *The Life of Ibsen*, vol. I, p. 290; see also p. 289.

between the two lovers, Falk and Svanhild, and their subsequent disengagement have been likened successively to Kierkegaard's own relation with Regine, to Johannes and Cordelia in the "Diary of a Seducer" in *Either/Or,* volume I, and to *Repetition: An Essay in Experimental Psychology* (1843).[79] That resemblances exist there can be no doubt, and they have been thoroughly tabulated and discussed by literary critics. But almost nothing concrete supports a direct and conscious borrowing by Ibsen of ideas from Kierkegaard. Ibsen nowhere has anything to say about a possible connection between his *Love's Comedy* and Kierkegaardian concepts. From the little reading he did of Kierkegaard off and on, and the occasional discussions he took part in, it is possible that certain ideas such as the disdain for marriage and the breaking of an engagement in order to elevate love to a religious level stuck in Ibsen's mind and subsequently appeared in this play.

With *Peer Gynt* the links between its themes and Kierkegaard's philosophy are even more rarefied. One can argue that inasmuch as Peer represents the antithesis of Brand—someone utterly given to compromise and with no personal vision or will to assert his individuality—he belongs on the aesthetic level in the Kierkegaardian scale of existence. Whether or not Ibsen had such an idea in mind is really anybody's guess. Brian Downs is uneasy about the view that Peer indeed depicts the tragic consequences of not fully being a Kierkegaardian. He says that *Peer Gynt* is a good example of the difficulty of matching Ibsen's philosophy with Kierkegaardian categories. It is not a tragedy at all in his opinion, and the supposed Kierkegaardian condemnation of Peer for remaining on the aesthetic level just does not come across in the play.[80] Once again, whether or not Ibsen intended Peer to exemplify the failures of a man who has rejected the Kierkegaardian demand to "be oneself" is not and cannot be known. Yet Downs qualifies his position somewhat by declaring that "... the dissociation must not be carried too far. The kernel of the thought implied in *Peer Gynt* is not only a Kierkegaardian notion, but even phrased in the language of Kierkegaard."[81] Downs, however, is unable to provide solid proof of this.

---

79. See Downs, *Ibsen: The Intellectual Background,* pp. 81–82, and his *A Study of Six Plays by Ibsen,* pp. 15–16; Lucas, *The Drama of Ibsen and Strindberg,* pp. 56–57; and La Chesnais, "Ibsen Disciple de Kierkegaard?" pp. 379–85.

80. Downs, *Ibsen: The Intellectual Background,* pp. 88–89.

81. Ibid., p. 89.

If the manner in which Kierkegaardian themes found their way into certain plays by Ibsen is not altogether clear, their presence, nevertheless, though in greatly modified form, seems to be established. Here the historian must ask the crucial question: Was Ibsen, therefore, a transmitter of Kierkegaardian ideas, and if so, how and to whom? This question, in turn, suggests another that should be addressed prior to it—Is Kierkegaard transmissible via the dramatic medium?

A few preliminary observations are in order. To begin with, Kierkegaard was no stranger to the dramatic arts. He was an established patron of the Royal Theater in Copenhagen, attending countless performances and interacting personally with some of the most famous actors and actresses of his day, including Johanne Luise Heiberg, about whom he wrote the essay entitled *The Crisis and a Crisis in the Life of an Actress* (1848).[82] Nor was this the only piece on the performing arts by Kierkegaard, for in the first volume of *Either/Or* we find a long section on Mozart's opera *Don Juan;* a discussion of Scribe's *The First Love;* a comparison of ancient and modern tragedy; countless references to Sophocles, Aristophanes, Shakespeare, Moliere, and Holberg; and the "Diary of a Seducer," which approaches the dramatic genre and evokes a kind of stage setting all its own. Moreover, in his journals Kierkegaard often made references to and wrote short pieces on drama, the theater, plays, playwrights, and actors. These include essays like "Herr Phister as Captain Scipio," dedicated to a well-known actor named Phister, whose performances Kierkegaard greatly enjoyed.[83]

Kierkegaard's flair for the dramatic extended well beyond his occasional writings on the subject. His "histrionic sensibility," as it has been called,[84] encompassed his entire repertoire of pseudonyms, even finding

---

82. It first appeared as four articles in *Fædrelandet,* July 24–27, 1848, under the pseudonym "Inter et Inter," and represented Kierkegaard's last aesthetic work. It was published as a single essay following Kierkegaard's death in 1855 by J. L. Heiberg, the husband of the actress in question.

83. For English translations of both *The Crisis* and "Herr Phister," see Søren Kierkegaard, *Crisis in the Life of an Actress, and Other Essays on Drama,* trans. Stephen D. Crites (New York: Collins, 1967). In scouring the works for evidence of dramatic expression one must not overlook the significant subtitle Kierkegaard gave to his principal philosophical work, the *Concluding Unscientific Postscript: A Mimical-Pathetical-Dialectical Composition, An Existential Contribution.* The word "Mimical" is a deliberate invocation of a dramatic metaphor.

84. See Jane Ellert Tammany, *Henrik Ibsen's Theatre Aesthetic and Dramatic Art: A Reflection of Kierkegaardian Consciousness—Its Significance for Modern Dramatic Interpretation and the American Theatre* (New York: Philosophical Library, 1980), p. 87.

expression in his own idiosyncratic, and often purposely enigmatic, conduct in public. The section in *Stages on Life's Way* entitled "The Banquet," for example, comes closest to being a theatrical display. The "dramatis personae"—a collection of pseudonyms from previous works—gather at a banquet to exchange views on diverse subjects in philosophy and aesthetics. Moreover, in one sense *The Point of View* represents the author/dramatist's survey of his own "dramatic" creations (the early pseudonymous works), and interpretation of them to his audience. In his own public life, which he intended to be an extension of his literary endeavors, Kierkegaard was, as Stephen Crites puts it, "quite self-consciously on the stage in the impression which he made in person."[85] "[T]he mystique of his 'indirect communication,' " continues Crites, "required that he should appear to the public eye in a guise which he regarded as necessary for the reception of his works in a dialectically correct manner."[86] Kierkegaardian "indirect communication" can thus assume the aesthetic-dramatic form of pseudonymity, or it can occur through the more tangible spectacle of a deliberately cultivated flippancy and aesthetically oriented external existence—a trick Kierkegaard liked to play on the citizens of Copenhagen. The converse is also true: drama can serve as a suitable—even ideal—medium for Kierkegaardian "indirect communication." Through the device of theatrical indirection, therefore, it becomes possible to transmit Kierkegaard.

Yet in fact what we have is a dearth in nineteenth- and early twentieth-century European literature of dramatic representations of Kierkegaardian themes. This should not surprise us, considering the slow and tortuous route that Kierkegaard's reception followed for decades after his death. Ibsen, despite the problematic nature of Kierkegaard's input in his plays, was the earliest playwright to point in the direction that Sartre, Beckett, and many others would follow much later. As for Ibsen's being a transmitter of Kierkegaard, it can be said that, insofar as people read or attended performances of those plays of his that embody traces of

---

Tammany's book, although not intended to be historical, is an interesting yet somewhat belabored argument in favor of a running parallelism between the lives and works of Kierkegaard and Ibsen. The section entitled "Kierkegaard and the Theatre," pp. 83–115, is perhaps the most useful.

85. See the excellent introduction by Crites to his translation of Kierkegaard's *The Crisis*, p. 44.

86. Ibid. Crites says Kierkegaard "engaged throughout his career in a remarkable kind of theatrics in fulfilling his very vocation as a Christian author" (p. 38). See also Tammany, *Henrik Ibsen's Theatre Aesthetic and Dramatic Art*, p. 85.

Kierkegaard's philosophy, he did indeed serve as an agent of transmission. For the vast majority of Ibsen's audience, however, these Kierkegaardian elements were not readily perceived as originating with the Danish thinker. A notable exception was Ibsen's specifically *Danish* audience, where many did recognize echoes of the familiar ideas of Kierkegaard. Kierkegaard's philosophy and the final public climax of his career had prepared the soil in Denmark well for the reception of a powerful psychological play like *Brand:* "It is not in the least strange, therefore, that when *Brand* appeared, people, especially in Denmark, regarded it, so to speak, as Kierkegaard in verse form, and thought that Ibsen had meant to picture Kierkegaard's own life struggle."[87] Brandes, the leading Danish literary critic of his day, was the first to write, in *Dagbladet*, extolling the energy of the work; soon other critics followed suit in the Copenhagen press, hailing *Brand* as a breakthrough in Norwegian literature.[88] The reaction of such critics is an indication of the extent to which Kierkegaardian categories were influencing the standards of critical assessment in the arts during the late 1860s and early 1870s in Denmark. But in the 1870s Brandes launched what amounted to a revolution in literature and the arts based precisely on a rejection of Kierkegaardian categories.[89]

At the time of its first appearance in Denmark, *Brand* fitted in well with a trend already in progress—a trend that derived some of its animating spirit from Kierkegaard—which magnified the inner life as a reaction to the disgraceful defeat of 1864.[90] The play, in turn, acted as a stimulant for Kierkegaardian passions and helped to keep up their popular momentum. Thus, a symbiotic relationship developed in Denmark in the 1860s between the already circulating and controversial ideas of Kierkegaard and those of his concepts reverberating through Ibsen's plays, principally *Brand*. According to Meyer, "*Brand* was . . . discussed and debated as no previous book had ever been in Scandinavia—including Kierkegaard, for *Brand* was written in more accessible and less abstract language."[91]

On many of Ibsen's contemporaries, his plays left a distinct Kierkegaardian impression. But his friend and fellow playwright Bjørnstjerne

---

87. Koht, *The Life of Ibsen*, vol. I, p. 275. It was *Brand* that made Ibsen known to the Danish people, writes Koht (p. 227).
88. Hans Heiberg, *Ibsen: A Portrait of the Artist*, trans. Joan Tate (London: Allan & Unwin, 1969), p. 134.
89. For more on this see Chapter 6 below.
90. Koht, *The Life of Ibsen*, vol. I, p. 291.
91. Meyer, *Henrik Ibsen*, vol. II, p. 53.

Bjørnson remained unaffected. The son of an orthodox Lutheran clergyman, Bjørnson in the 1850s came in contact with the doctrines of Kierkegaard independently of Ibsen. Eventually, under the influence of Brandes, he decided that Kierkegaard's rigorous moral demands were simply beyond man's powers. This conclusion he later expressed in the title of one of his plays: *Beyond Our Power* (1883). Because of his position on Kierkegaard he disliked *Brand*; however, he seems to have sensed no implied criticism of moral rigidity and extremism in Brand's fate. Bjørnson finally became a follower of Grundtvig, which confirmed him, though on a different basis, in his antagonistic attitude toward Kierkegaard.[92]

The situation was different with another contemporary of Ibsen, the Swede August Strindberg (1849-1912). Strindberg admits, in one of his autobiographical novels, that at the time he first read *Brand* in the late 1860s he felt a spiritual kinship to its "pietist" and "fanatic" protagonist.[93] Shortly thereafter, as a student at the University of Uppsala in the fall of 1870, Strindberg made his first acquaintance with Kierkegaard's writings. He began by reading *Either/Or* and some *Upbuilding Discourses,* and subsequently read *Practice in Christianity*. They made a profound impression on him at the time, and this lasted through the 1870s until he fell under the spell of Brandes's much-publicized freethinking posture and critique of religion. Writing his autobiographical sketch in the mid-1880s while passing through an irreligious phase, Strindberg betrays a bitterly contemptuous attitude toward his early pietist inclinations. Hence the coupling of the terms "pietist" and "fanatic" to describe Brand; hence also his claim, a little further on, that at the time he became excited about Kierkegaard he did not know that Kierkegaard was a Christian.[94] Strindberg's retrospective irreligiosity notwithstanding, it remains true that his early readings of Ibsen's *Brand* and Kierkegaard complemented one another and served to reinforce the pietism of the young Swede during a crucial period of his intellectual formation.

That the impact of Kierkegaardian ideas appears to be confined mostly to a compact and well-defined period of Ibsen's career, the 1860s or

---

92. Downs, *Ibsen: The Intellectual Background,* pp. 121-22. See also Georg Brandes, *Henrik Ibsen and Bjørnstjerne Bjørnson,* p. 147 and the whole section on Bjørnson.

93. August Strindberg, *Jäsningstriden: En Själs Utvecklingshistoria* (Stockholm, 1886), p. 165. Strindberg calls the play "dark and austere."

94. Strindberg, *Jäsningstriden,* p. 204. See also Martin Lamm, *Strindberg och Makterna* (Stockholm: Svenska Kyrkans diakonistyrelses Bokförlag, 1936), pp. 38ff., who makes this point about Strindberg's irreligious position in the mid-1880s having influenced his autobiographical glimpse at his initial encounter with Kierkegaard's works.

what has been termed the "middle period" of his literary production, has suggested to some that Ibsen later consciously departed from Kierkegaard under the influence of prevalent radicalizing factors in the intellectual life of nineteenth-century Europe.[95] Foremost among these factors for Scandinavian intellectuals was Georg Brandes, who played perhaps the most decisive role in altering the course of Ibsen's thinking. He influenced Strindberg in the same direction ten years later. In 1870, Brandes, an avowed iconoclast, began to introduce radical ideas from other parts of Europe into Denmark, through a series of essays he wrote. Ibsen read some of these and was greatly agitated by them. Brandes wrote to Ibsen, reproaching him for his lack of interest in modern science.[96] This same critic, who had hailed *Brand* as a remarkable achievement when it first appeared, now strongly disapproved of the style of moral preaching that Ibsen had employed in the play; he ultimately persuaded Ibsen to abandon it in favor of a more "modern" style.[97] Ibsen had displayed radical and agnostic tendencies ever since his youthful days in Grimstad, when he read Voltaire and dabbled in deism and pantheism.[98] The post-*Brand* period in his life, initiated by Brandes's critique, saw a reawakening of the challenges to religion. This had the effect of drawing him further away from anything that smacked of Kierkegaardian spirituality. The inner tension experienced by Ibsen on the issue of religion is described by Brandes in his "Second Impression" of 1882:

> Ibsen follows in Kierkegaard's footsteps. Brought up like the rest of his generation in the north, under the influence of romanticism, his attitude towards religion is at first uncertain, confused. In his own nature there was a double bias, certain to give rise to inward conflict—an inborn tendency to mysticism,

---

95. The chief proponent of this argument is the German scholar Werner Möhring, in his article, "Ibsens Abkehr von Kierkegaard," in *EDDA,* vol. 28 (1928), pp. 43–71. Möhring considers *Brand* the turning point in Ibsen's career, after which he negated all idealism and, under the influence of radical ideas such as Darwinian evolution, abandoned himself to open skepticism. This, according to Möhring, had to involve the renunciation of Kierkegaard's philosophy. The Möhring thesis is challenged by P. G. La Chesnais, "Ibsen Disciple de Kierkegaard?" p. 401, where the author argues that Ibsen had actually lost his faith long before Darwin published his evolutionary theory. Möhring's and La Chesnais's positions need not be regarded as mutually exclusive if one maintains that there was a turning away by Ibsen from Kierkegaard, but not exclusively for the reasons Möhring gives.

96. Koht, *The Life of Ibsen,* vol. II, pp. 88–89.

97. Downs, *A Study of Six Plays by Ibsen,* p. 68. Ibsen's *Emperor and Galilean* (1873) was to be his last play in the old forceful and expressive style. Downs laments this change and terms Brandes's influence on Ibsen "negative."

98. Meyer, *Henrik Ibsen,* vol. I, p. 56.

and an equally strong natural tendency towards hard, dry rationality. In few other men does one find such almost morbid flights of fancy alternating with such quiet acceptance of the prose of life.[99]

Ibsen's internal struggles were compounded as he began to encounter, one after the other, the main currents of European intellectual ferment: Hegel's idealism, Schopenhauer's pessimism, Darwinian evolution, Eduard von Hartmann's *Philosophie des Unbewussten* (1869), and biblical criticism. Of these, the newly enunciated theory of evolution captivated Ibsen's interest at once. He had dealt with the theme of inherited guilt in some of his plays, notably *Brand*, and it was to recur in such later plays as *Ghosts* (1881). He most probably did not read Darwin's *Origin of Species* (1859) until after the first Danish translation was made available by Jens Peter Jacobsen in 1872.[100] His later so-called "social plays," like *A Doll's House* (1879) and *Hedda Gabler* (1890) for instance, derived their inspiration, in part, from John Stuart Mill's *The Subjection of Women* (1869), which Brandes translated into Danish in the same year it appeared, and which created a stir throughout Scandinavia concerning the question of the emancipation of women.[101]

These diverse impulses swirling around Ibsen augmented the eclectic quality of his beliefs and anchored them firmly in the intellectual soil of the nineteenth century. While the moralizing tone of *Brand* was eclipsed, along with any intimations of a budding spirituality in his works, the familiar human states of being (the existential themes) such as anxiety, anguish, dread, fear, even nausea and absurdity, continued to find vigorous and ingenious expression in Ibsen's later dramas. For this reason Ibsen has been regarded by some as a pioneering precursor of contemporary existentialism—presented, in his case, through the vocabulary of drama.[102] If this is accepted, then it follows that Ibsen is one of the many links between Kierkegaard and this new existentialism. This remains true even though Ibsen denied or suppressed all visible associations with Kierkegaard.

99. Brandes, *Henrik Ibsen and Bjørnstjerne Bjørnson*, p. 69. Brandes calls *Brand* "pure and simple mysticism."
100. La Chesnais, in "Ibsen Disciple de Kierkegaard?" p. 362, is certain Ibsen had not read Darwin before 1872.
101. Koht, *The Life of Ibsen*, vol. II, p. 139. Ibsen also acknowledged his indebtedness to Collett's *Amtmandens Døtre* (1855), especially in planting the seeds for *A Doll's House*.
102. Mary Graham Lund, "The Existentialism of Ibsen," in *The Personalist* 61 (Summer 1960), pp. 310 and 314–15.

Ibsen ultimately remained an artist.[103] One question raised by Kierkegaard haunted Ibsen to the end of his days—the relationship of art to life, of aesthetics to existence. He longed for deeds instead of just literature, and experienced a sinking feeling of unfulfillment every time he completed a new play.[104] This basic dissatisfaction with himself as a mere artist points to a latent existential yearning in him that never fully came to fruition. He wrestled with the issue throughout his life and finally made it the central theme of his last play *When We Dead Awaken* (1899).[105] By doing this he demonstrated his inability to overcome the problem existentially, and ended by writing about it artistically, thus perpetuating it.

Kierkegaard's philosophy aims at overcoming an aesthetic existence, or the aestheticizing of life. He did not deny a legitimate place to aesthetics, even in the life of a believing Christian;[106] however, he was emphatic about designating any purely aesthetic existence as inferior to a religious one. The fact that the aesthetic level is the lowest stage in the Kierkegaardian scheme—with the implication that it ought to be transcended—appears to have become a source of permanent anxiety for Ibsen in his later years. One can assume that by then he had read a little more Kierkegaard, or at least had heard of the Kierkegaardian stages. In *When We Dead Awaken*, Rubek, who loved Irene very much, renounced his love for the sake of his statue; his art was ultimately more important to him than living out his human love. This is perhaps an accurate portrait of Ibsen's long life as an artist and the sacrifices such an "aesthetic" existence necessitates. But it may also reflect Ibsen's skeptical view, in his old age, of the Kierkegaardian renunciation of love within the confines of marital bliss for the sake of a higher ideal: "Becoming a Christian." One cannot help being reminded here of Kierkegaard's broken engagement to Regine.

---

103. Koht, *The Life of Ibsen*, vol. I, p. 1. Koht emphasizes at the outset of his biography that Ibsen was first and foremost a poet, an artist: "Too many have attempted to make him a thinker or a philosopher, a social critic or a social reformer." Richard Hornby, in *Patterns in Ibsen's Middle Plays*, p. 75, calls Ibsen a perfect example of Kierkegaard's "ironic" man, torn between the aesthetic and the ethical modes of existence.

104. Koht, *The Life of Ibsen*, vol. II, p. 296.

105. Ibid., Epilogue, vol. II, pp. 321ff.

106. See *The Point of View*, p. 12, where Kierkegaard says about his writings: "The religious is present from the beginning. Conversely, the aesthetic is present again at the last moment." He is referring to the fact that he wrote the aesthetic essay on drama (*The Crisis and a Crisis in the Life of an Actress*) two years after he had commenced his strictly religious works. See pp. 12–14. For a discussion of the place of aesthetics in a religious oeuvre see the section entitled "The Role of the Aesthetic in the Religious Life and in a

In conclusion, is it valid to say that with Ibsen certain features of Kierkegaard's intellectual legacy made a foray into the realm of drama? Not exactly. Kierkegaard was certainly *not* dramatized by Ibsen, and even those supposedly shared aspects that have excited much debate among scholars and critics fall considerably short of constituting a basis for such an assertion. In the end, Brand's "all or nothing" is *not* Kierkegaard's "either-or," nor even a variation thereof.

Yet of all the European philosophers of the nineteenth century, it is Kierkegaard who lends himself the most to dramatic presentation, as regards both his own life and some of the themes in his works. The sheer intellectual seductiveness of this proposition, coupled with Ibsen's ambivalent and curiously elusive relationship to Kierkegaard, has been enough to arouse repeated speculation by scholars, and this, in turn, has contributed indirectly to the dissemination of Kierkegaard and has stimulated interest in him. Very often contemporaries (in this case Brandes) and later scholars (Stobart and others) *think* there is an influence or a transmission of ideas when in reality there is no such thing, or at best there are feeble hints at distant similarities. When this happens the real truth usually becomes irrelevant, since so many have convinced themselves and others that there was indeed an influence. Thus a myth is born and spreads, and the ingredients composing it are willy-nilly popularized. This occurrence ultimately renders the convoluted question of influence historically immaterial. In short, Kierkegaard's legacy received something of a "free ride" as a result of its often unwitting association with Ibsen, and Ibsen's legacy eventually benefited from this linkage as well.

The fact remains, however, that Kierkegaard's frequent use of amusing anecdotes and short fable-like parables, which are interspersed throughout his prose,[107] moves him closer to the fairy tale form of Andersen or the dramatic genre of Ibsen, and may point to a distinctive Nordic literary trait. It is therefore not unwarranted to investigate the generic affinity among these three writers, not only comparatively, but also—where it

---

Christian 'Authorship' " in Stephen Crites's introduction to his translation of Kierkegaard's *The Crisis*, pp. 37–47.

107. For a collection of these see Thomas C. Oden, ed., *Parables of Kierkegaard* (Princeton: Princeton University Press, 1978). Oden's collection does a great service to Kierkegaard studies in English by highlighting an important talent and mode of articulation in Kierkegaard that often gets submerged in his otherwise heavy prose. For a discussion of the relation of this kind of Kierkegaardian style to drama see Tammany, *Henrik Ibsen's Theatre Aesthetic and Dramatic Art*, pp. 89f.

exists—historically. Kierkegaard's triple role as spectator (eager theatergoer and astute observer of actual life situations), dramatist (storyteller, creator of fictional settings and characters, and possessor of an acute awareness of his readers as an audience), and actor (his self-conscious projection of a definite image in public life), renders a probe of the intertwining of his legacy with Ibsen's very rewarding for intellectual history.

5 The "Tro og Viden" Controversy, or the Rise and Demise of "Pseudo-Kierkegaard"

The 1860s in Scandinavia witnessed a renewed interest in theological debates, especially regarding the complex issue of the relation of faith to reason. Given the successive breakthroughs in science on the one hand, and the irreconcilable philosophical cleavage between Right- and Left-Hegelians on the other, European theologians at mid-century had their hands full attempting to keep Christianity not only afloat but intellectually respectable. Hence apologetics became the order of the day in the face of an increasingly assertive secularism. Paralleling this was the ongoing assimilation of Hegel's philosophical idealism into what emerged as the rational or speculative theology that dominated the religious scene in Germany and northern Europe for most of the remainder of the century.

Ever since Kant's *Die Religion innerhalb der Grenzen der blossen Vernunft* (1793), the problematic of faith and reason, and the corollary question of subjectivity, became the focal concerns of modern theologians and philosophers of religion. With Hegel, "the process of consciousness comes to be viewed as an integral part of a spiritual process," and religious faith is inseparably entwined with philosophical self-understanding, thus becoming "objectified."[1] Many of Kierkegaard's efforts were spent combating this Hegelian tendency and its theological derivatives in favor of a restoration to faith of its autonomous realm, which, he held, is based not on ideas but on the personal encounter of the individual with the "Absolute Paradox" of the God-Man. Furthermore, as a counterbalance to prevailing trends in speculative theology, Kierkegaard can be construed as advocating a return to the Augustinian position of faith as a gift from God ("the paradox gives itself")[2] that in turn evokes a free response in man (the leap).

Some have erroneously maintained that Kierkegaard's revolt against Hegel represents merely a reformulation of the Kantian position of absolute dichotomy between faith and knowledge.[3] In fact the situation is considerably more complicated than this and requires an elaborately involved explanation that would fall outside the scope of the present discussion. The originality of Kierkegaard surfaces through his view of faith as an inward passion in the realm of subjectivity that defines the believer's personal relation to God. Passion and subjectivity are two technical terms in the specialized Kierkegaardian vocabulary. This radical existential dimension of faith as presented by Kierkegaard constitutes its novelty and its power. Kierkegaard's concept of faith and its relation to reason does include ingredients from Schleiermacher (faith as a yearning, and as an expression of absolute dependency), Kant (a separation between the objective and subjective domains of knowledge, though with Kierkegaard not to the point of a radical duality), Aquinas (both provide a "phenome-

---

1. Louis Dupré, *A Dubious Heritage: Studies in the Philosophy of Religion after Kant* (New York: Paulist Press, 1977), pp. 1 and 53.

2. Søren Kierkegaard, *Philosophical Fragments; Johannes Climacus* (*KW*, VII), ed. and trans. Howard V. Hong and Edna H. Hong (Princeton: Princeton University Press, 1985), p. 59.

3. See, for instance, Jerry H. Gill, "Kant, Kierkegaard, and Religious Knowledge," in *Philosophy and Phenomenological Research* 28 (1967), pp. 188–204. Gill presents a more balanced, though very brief, account of Kierkegaard's relation to Kant in the section entitled "Kantianism" of *Kierkegaard and Great Traditions*, vol. 6 of *Bibliotheca Kierkegaardiana* (1981), pp. 223–29. Gill makes the point that, despite similarities in their epistemologies, Kierkegaard and Kant differ in their conceptions of the ethical and the religious; however, Gill continues to err in stating that with Kierkegaard the domains of knowledge and faith are entirely separate (p. 228). For a recent and more rigorous treatment of Kierkegaard's relation to Kant's philosophy see Ronald M. Green, *Kierkegaard and Kant: The Hidden Debt* (Albany: State University of New York Press, 1992). Green argues strongly in favor of an extensive Kantian influence on Kierkegaard and maintains that both concurred on the question of faith and knowledge being fundamentally opposed; see pp. 133–39.

nology of faith," yet neither bases his own belief on it), and Augustine (faith as gift); however, it stops short of fully, or exclusively, embracing any one of these positions.[4] Ultimately, Kierkegaard posits neither a total harmony between faith and reason along the lines of Hegel's system, nor an utterly unbridgeable chasm as with Tertullian's *credo quia absurdum,* although on certain occasions his paradox comes very close to the second. The discussions of faith as passion, paradox, and gift; its relations with reason and freedom; and the shortcomings of a purely rational theology, are not to be found in a single work, but are dispersed through Kierkegaard's writings over a period of twelve years from 1843 until his death.

This fact, coupled with the inherent difficulty of the subject matter and the unavailability of Kierkegaard's private journals, made it virtually impossible for people in the late 1850s and the 1860s to grasp the precise nuances, or the full import, of his position on the crucial topic of faith and reason. On the contrary, snippets from the writings were denuded of their context, their relations with other portions ignored, and they were either crudely employed in support of views that were foreign to Kierkegaard's convictions and purposes, or turned against their own author with the aim of exposing alleged contradictions and inconsistencies in his thought. Kierkegaard's writings were subjected to this kind of abuse repeatedly during the early years following the *Kirkekampen,* and nowhere more so than in the strife that raged throughout the 1860s in Denmark and was dubbed by thinkers and theologians the "Tro og Viden" (Faith and Knowledge) Controversy.

The debate was not an isolated incident in Danish theological and intellectual history but was related to the broader European background. Sporadic clashes between theologians and scientists, for instance, occurred in the first half of the nineteenth century. An example in Denmark is

---

4. The secondary literature about Kierkegaard's views on faith and reason is substantial. See, as examples, James Collins, *The Mind of Kierkegaard* (Chicago: H. Regnery, 1953), pp. 137–74 and 264–68; Louis Dupré, *Kierkegaard as Theologian: The Dialectic of Christian Existence* (New York: Sheed and Ward, 1963), pp. 115–46; James Collins, "Faith and Reflection in Kierkegaard," and Cornelio Fabro, "Faith and Reason in Kierkegaard's Dialectic," both in *A Kierkegaard Critique,* ed. Howard A. Johnson and Niels Thulstrup (New York: Harper, 1962), pp. 141–55 and 156–206 respectively. For more recent treatments see Steven M. Emmanuel, *Kierkegaard and the Concept of Revelation* (Albany: State University of New York Press, 1996), esp. chap. 3, "Reason, Faith, and Revelation," pp. 39–60, and chap. 5, "Grace and Will in the Transition to Faith," pp. 77–93; and David J. Gouwens, *Kierkegaard as Religious Thinker* (Cambridge: Cambridge University Press, 1996), esp. chap. 4; "Becoming Christian I: Responding to Christ in Faith," pp. 122–52, and chap. 7, "Witness in Faith, Hope, and Love," pp. 209–29.

the dispute between Grundtvig and Ørsted in 1814–1815. Kierkegaard's own reflections on natural science constitute another step in the direction of the eventual debate about faith and knowledge. He argued that the legitimate exercise of reason through science provides objective knowledge or partial truth, whereas faith penetrates the inner domain of subjectivity and yields more essential truths for man's existence. Consequently, faith is our only avenue to crucial yet rationally unclarifiable truths.[5]

The appearance of Martensen's *Christelige Dogmatik* in 1849 touched off a new round of controversy over faith and knowledge that would have mushroomed and attracted a greater number of participants had it not been quickly overshadowed by the *Kirkekampen* and delayed for a decade. Two treatises, one by Rasmus Nielsen and the other by an assistant professor at the University named P. M. Stilling (1812–69), were published in response to Martensen's Hegelian speculative position, and both appealed to Kierkegaard's *Postscript* for support.[6] The point under consideration was Martensen's Hegelian-inspired claim of complete harmony between faith and knowledge. Nielsen and Stilling disputed this and referred to Kierkegaard's discussion of the differences between believing and understanding, and the rift between the believer and the speculative philosopher, in his principal philosophical work.[7] During the *Kirkekampen*, Kierkegaard attacked Martensen's silence, which, he said, had begun with Martensen's refusal to reply to the objections put forth by Nielsen and Stilling back in 1850.[8]

Following Kierkegaard's death, people's attention remained focused on the shock precipitated during his final months; however, the attention of some began to shift gradually to a consideration of the problem of faith and knowledge. Speculative theologians—usually Right-Hegelians—con-

---

5. See Chapter 1 above for a discussion of Grundtvig and Ørsted, Kierkegaard and science.

6. Rasmus Nielsen, *Mag. S. Kierkegaards "Johannes Climacus" og Dr. H. Martensens "Christelige Dogmatik", en undersøgende Anmeldelse* (Copenhagen, 1849); and P. M. Stilling, *Om den indbildte Forsoning mellem Tro og Viden med særligt Hensyn til Martensens "Christelige Dogmatik"* (Copenhagen, 1850). See Chapter 3 above.

7. See especially the section entitled "Truth is Subjectivity" in Søren Kierkegaard, *Concluding Unscientific Postscript* (KW, XII.1), pp. 189–251; on Kierkegaard's view of faith as infinite passion being opposed to objective knowledge see pp. 203 and 29–30. For a contemporary account of the dispute with Martensen, written by a Martensen supporter, see C. E. Scharling's reviews in *Nyt Theologisk Tidsskrift* 1 (1850), particularly pp. 358–59.

8. See the *Fædrelandet* article dated May 26, 1855, in *Attack upon "Christendom,"* p. 69.

tinued, in Martensen's footsteps, to attempt to harmonize the two. Even a writer of fiction like H. C. Andersen published a novel in 1857 that he called *To Be, or Not to Be?* as his contribution to the controversy shaping up between science and freethought on the one hand and religious faith on the other. Andersen had always been fascinated by scientific discoveries, and he retained a simple faith in God throughout his life. Not surprisingly, therefore, he aimed to show in his book that both science and religion could be combined in a meaningful way.

Before treating the "Tro og Viden" Controversy of the 1860s and Kierkegaard's impact on it, consideration should be given to a young Norwegian preacher who wrote in 1864 an article in German on Kierkegaard that was both pioneering and comprehensive, although not uncritical.[9] This was Johan Christian Heuch (1838–1904), who later became bishop of Kragerø, in 1889. His mother was descended from an old French family that had emigrated to the north, while his father was the son of a well-known Norwegian patron of literature and the arts. During Heuch's early school days in Kragerø, the headmaster, a certain H. G. D. Barth, first introduced him to the works of Kierkegaard and Grundtvig. This proved to be decisive in the young Heuch's intellectual formation, as did the interest he soon developed in the sermons of Gisle Johnson, himself an avid reader of Kierkegaard's *Øjeblikket* in the mid-1850s. What most attracted Heuch to Johnson was the latter's ability in his sermons to transform abstract theological principles into fruitful guidelines for the religious life.

Heuch studied theology in the University of Christiania and passed his exams in 1861. Shortly thereafter he went to Germany, where he pursued his theological studies for a year in Leipzig and Erlangen before returning to Norway. His visit to Germany deepened his attachment to the Lutheran Church, and he became a staunch religious conservative, waging several polemical campaigns against liberal theologians and acting as apologist for the faith in the face of secularists and atheists.[10]

The 1864 article on Kierkegaard was his first publication of any consequence. It appeared as a contribution to the journal *Zeitschrift für*

---

9. A. Kabell is certainly not justified in calling it "a paltry treatise," marking "an all-time low" in terms of articles on Kierkegaard; see Kabell's *Kierkegaardstudiet i Norden*, p. 97.

10. On J. C. Heuch see *Norsk Biografisk Leksikon* (*NBL*), ed. Einar Jansen, vol. 6: 1923 (Oslo: Aschehoug, 1932), pp. 80–84. See also Knut Rygnestad, *Johan Christian Heuch: Apologet og Stridsmann* (Trondheim: Globus Forlag, 1966), pp. 15, 18, and 20.

die gesammte lutherische Theologie und Kirche.[11] Despite some inaccuracies in chronology,[12] Heuch managed, in the space of a few pages, to touch on a number of crucial Kierkegaardian themes, displaying a broad though not particularly profound knowledge of the major works. He dealt, for instance, with "the single individual," the three stages of existence, Kierkegaard's religious purpose behind his writings as stated in *The Point of View*, indirect communication, how one becomes a Christian, despair, and sin, and he ended with an overview of the *Kirkekampen*. He did all this with considerable dispassion and, as a biographer put it, did not allow himself to be blindly led by Kierkegaard's apron-strings.[13]

On the question of faith, Heuch wrote, quoting Kierkegaard, that it is not as easy as " 'putting one's foot in a sock,' " and that what is required "is not an understanding of faith, but an existence in faith, which can only be won through an independent breach with the [understanding]."[14] Heuch deplored the trend in nineteenth-century theology whereby faith and knowledge were "reconciled" by reducing faith to a form of knowledge, thus rendering the vital realm of life experiences superfluous.[15] He repeated Kierkegaard's definition of faith as given in *The Sickness unto Death* (1849): " 'Faith is: that the self in being itself and in willing to be itself rests transparently in God.' "[16] The careful attention Heuch paid to

---

11. J. C. Heuch, "Sören Aaby Kierkegaard," in *Zeitschrift für die gesammte lutherische Theologie und Kirche,* ed. A. G. Rudelbach, H. E. F. Guericke, and Fr. Delitzsch, 25th year (Leipzig, 1864), pp. 295–309.

12. Heuch gives the date of Kierkegaard's death as November 10, 1855, one day too early ("Sören Aaby Kierkegaard," pp. 296 and 309); also, Mynster's death is erroneously said to have occurred in the spring of 1855 (p. 308). Climacus is written "Elimäus" by Heuch (p. 302), which suggests that he had only heard the name and not read the work.

13. Jens Tandberg, *Biskop Heuchs Liv og Virke* (Christiania, 1905), pp. 14–15. Tandberg insists that Heuch managed to liberate himself totally from Kierkegaard's "one-sided" emphasis on the individual to the exclusion of the religious community [*Samfundet*], or the Church (p. 16). Tandberg's scholarship is unfortunately tainted by an emotional element—Norwegian nationalism; consequently, his deliberate minimizing of the impact of Kierkegaard on Heuch has to be approached critically.

14. Heuch, "Sören Aaby Kierkegaard," p. 298. For the reference to "putting one's foot in a sock" see Søren Kierkegaard, *Practice in Christianity* (*KW,* XX), p. 95.

15. Heuch, "Sören Aaby Kierkegaard," pp. 296–97.

16. Ibid., p. 304. The translation quoted here is from Søren Kierkegaard, *The Sickness Unto Death* (*KW,* vol. XIX), ed. and trans. Howard V. Hong and Edna H. Hong (Princeton: Princeton University Press, 1980), p. 82.

"the offense of the Paradox" and to "the Absurd" underscores the extent to which he was aware of the nonrational elements in Christianity as depicted by Kierkegaard.

Appended to Heuch's piece was a short extract on Kierkegaard in German translation taken from the writings of a Swedish philosopher named Kristian Claëson (1827-59).[17] He was a student of Sweden's leading idealistic philosopher of the early nineteenth century, C. J. Boström, and as such belonged to the philosophical camp opposing Kierkegaard's thought. Claëson had already displayed his opposition when he confronted Zacharias Göransson (1823-81), who published a book in 1859 entitled *Om möjligheten af Christlig Philosophi* (On the possibility of Christian philosophy). Göransson argued against such a possibility, and in so doing was one of the very few thinkers in Sweden to maintain a position similar—though not identical—to Kierkegaard's.[18] Claëson died shortly after the disagreement with Göransson, and his collected works were published in Swedish the following year, 1860. Among these was a review of a Swedish translation of a book by a certain Karl Schwarz called *Beitrag zur Geschichte der neuesten Theologie* (1856).[19] Claëson, in the course of discussing various nineteenth-century philosophers and religious thinkers, touches on Kierkegaard, and it is this section of his review that is translated into German and attached to Heuch's article of 1864. Claëson's point is that Kierkegaard's uncompromising critique of the state-Church and "objective faith" in favor of individual faith and subjectivity, in addition to opening the door for every conceivable sect to appear and flourish, has the logical consequence of leading one to the final conclusion that only a single true Christian existed: Christ himself.[20] In this way Claëson misunderstands Kierkegaard's concept of subjectivity by equating it crudely with subjectivism. At the same time he anticipates similar future misinterpretations, which became partly responsible for

---

17. See Heuch, "Sören Aaby Kierkegaard," pp. 309-10. The translator is the Erlangen theologian Gustav Plitt (1836-80). For the Swedish original see Kristian Claëson, *Skrifter*, vol. II (Stockholm, 1860), pp. 24-25.

18. N. Å. Sjöstedt, "Swedish Literature," in *The Legacy and Interpretation of Kierkegaard*, vol. 8 of *Bibliotheca Kierkegaardiana* (1981), p. 40. See also Sjöstedt's *Søren Kierkegaard och Svensk Litteratur*, pp. 45-49.

19. See Claëson, *Skrifter*, II, pp. 3-38.

20. Ibid., p. 25; for the German version see the appendix to Heuch, "Sören Aaby Kierkegaard," p. 310. On Claëson see Sjöstedt, *Søren Kierkegaard och Svensk Litteratur*, pp. 48-51.

the strong streak of subjectivism-relativism in certain forms of twentieth-century existential philosophy.

The opinions about Kierkegaard expressed by Heuch and Claëson, though dissimilar, were not unrelated to the "Tro og Viden" Controversy that went into full swing in the mid-1860s in Denmark. Both concentrated on Kierkegaard's concept of faith and on the paramount role he assigned to the individual, and these two themes constituted pivotal items of discussion in the aforementioned debate.

A single person could be viewed as the instigator of the debate and the central figure around whom it revolved. This was Rasmus Nielsen. During a brief but intense period between 1848 and 1850, Nielsen became the person closest to Kierkegaard. Their relationship was peculiar from the start, motivated on each side by somewhat selfish desires: Kierkegaard, afraid he would die soon, was searching for a custodian for his papers who understood the basic orientation and purpose of his thought; Nielsen, for his part, having been deeply influenced by the *Postscript,* was hungering for recognition and sought intellectual stimulation from the master himself. In this sense both used, and abused, each other's friendship. With time, Kierkegaard came to experience a deep disappointment with Nielsen and realized that he had made a mistake in placing such high hopes in him as an intellectual commentator on his works, not to mention a possible "successor."

Kierkegaard's disappointment had several causes. Nielsen's *Evangelietroen og den moderne Bevidsthed* (Christian faith and the modern mind) of 1849, his first book after their newly developed friendship had taken root, angered Kierkegaard because it contained a host of his ideas without acknowledging their source and because its pedagogic presentation of these ideas lacked the necessary subtlety demanded by the dictum of indirect communication. To Kierkegaard, Nielsen appeared to bask in intellectual sunshine that was not really his. Kierkegaard also felt that Nielsen's reply to Martensen's *Christelige Dogmatik,* although agreeing with the main thrust of Kierkegaard's critique of speculative theology, fell short of being satisfactory, especially since it seemed as if Nielsen was merely using Kierkegaard to settle a score with Martensen and was, in places, setting himself up arrogantly as arbiter between them. In the final analysis Kierkegaard's disappointment with Nielsen stemmed from his realization that Nielsen had no intention of translating the significant intellectual impact Kierkegaard had had upon him into tangible manifestations in his own personal life. As far as Kierkegaard could tell, he had only served as an occasion for Nielsen to philosophize, and any consequent existential implications of this philosophizing were missing. Simply put, Nielsen was utterly lacking in passion.[21]

As later developments were to demonstrate, Kierkegaard's disappointment with Nielsen, of which there is ample expression in the form of journal entries from 1849 and 1850, had been neither misplaced nor unfair.[22] It is true Nielsen possessed a rare quality that Kierkegaard admired: he had been an "attentive" listener, which, as Kierkegaard admitted, is not insignificant when one is an older man (Nielsen was four years Kierkegaard's senior).[23] Nielsen's interest in Kierkegaard in 1848 was genuine; however, seen in retrospect, it represented a mere phase in the winding, and often erratic, course of his intellectual development. The fact that Nielsen could start out as a Right-Hegelian and a follower of Martensen in the early 1840s, only to undergo a complete reversal upon reading the *Postscript* and being attracted to Kierkegaard's concept of paradox, reveals a deep-seated intellectual restlessness. Nielsen turned against his own former Hegelian outlook with a vengeance and attacked Martensen's speculative theology, embracing the Kierkegaardian emphasis on personal existence. Yet even at the height of his enthusiasm for Kierkegaard, Nielsen began to depart from him in crucial areas, thus betraying further instability, and perhaps insecurity. He espoused, for instance, a communal sense of the congregation despite the strong orientation toward the individual that he received from Kierkegaard. Also, the tension between Christianity and philosophy depicted by Kierkegaard was carried to its extreme with Nielsen such that one became the complete opposite of the other. On ethics Nielsen began to maintain, unlike Kierkegaard, that man experienced a conflict between what he called "fate" and "providence," the first being governed by egotism and the second by conscience. Nielsen also stressed the role of the will in religious faith, whereas Kierkegaard balanced human free will (the leap) with God's grace (faith as gift). Most importantly, Nielsen soon arrived at the dualistic view that

---

21. On Kierkegaard's views of his relation with Nielsen after 1848 see the abundant entries in his journals. See also Johannes Hohlenberg, *Sören Kierkegaard, a Biography*, pp. 210–17; and chap. 4, entitled "Skuffelsen med Rasmus Nielsen," of Carl Jørgensen's *Søren Kierkegaards Skuffelser* (Copenhagen: Nyt Nordisk Forlag, 1967), pp. 35–40; and Helge Hultberg, "Kierkegaard og Rasmus Nielsen" in *Kierkegaardiana*, vol. XII, ed. Niels Thulstrup (Copenhagen, 1982), p. 12.

22. See in particular *JP* 6342 (X^1 A 111); 6630 (X^3 A 146); 6663 (X^6 B 94); and 6664 (X^3 A 381).

23. Søren Kierkegaard, *Papirer*, X^6 B 114 (not translated in the Hong edition).

faith and knowledge stemmed from two utterly unrelated principles, and therefore could not possibly come into conflict with one another. Having erected such a dualism Nielsen, in the late 1850s, devoted his energies to logic, mathematics, and the sciences, thus commencing another new phase in his tortuous intellectual journey.[24]

After being rebuked by Kierkegaard back in 1849 for using his ideas without authorization, Nielsen had promised to correct his mistake in his future writings. He subsequently tried to keep his promise, but his attempts only acted as the two faces of Janus with respect to the reception of Kierkegaard's thoughts. It must not be forgotten that Nielsen was one of the few who stood by Kierkegaard during the *Kirkekampen* when it seemed as though all of Copenhagen had taken up arms against him.[25] It was Nielsen who lectured on Kierkegaard in 1856, and who edited his last articles for publication the following year. And it was Nielsen again who rushed to Kierkegaard's defense in 1858 in the face of allegations by a Martensen supporter, C. E. Scharling, that Kierkegaard had not been in full possession of his mental faculties during the last years of his life.[26] Nielsen countered with an essay he entitled "Om S. Kierkegaards 'Mentale Tilstand' " (On S. K.'s mental condition), in which he argued that Kierkegaard's entire life's work comprised a unity. Given such a harmony between the first and last works, those like Scharling who claim to be unable to pronounce "any certain verdict" on Kierkegaard's mental condition in his final years, must also extend their reservation to include the

---

24. Nielsen wrote treatises on mathematics and logic, such as *Philosophie og Mathematik* (1857) and *Mathematik og Dialektik* (1859). On Nielsen's early divergence from Kierkegaard see P. A. Rosenberg, *Rasmus Nielsen: Nordens Filosof* (Copenhagen, 1903), pp. 48–49, 52, and 54–56. Rosenberg, who was Nielsen's student in the latter part of the century, exhibits a biased admiration for his teacher that often implicates him in errors of judgment. He is wrong, for example, when he declares that Kierkegaard's insinuations against Nielsen in his journals were "entirely disgraceful" and unfair (see pp. 45–46 in Rosenberg's book). See also Eduard Asmussen, *Entwicklungsgang und Grundprobleme der Philosophie Rasmus Nielsens* (Flensburg: Laban & Larsen, 1911), p. 52, for a brief assessment of Rosenberg's book. For more on Rosenberg and Kierkegaard see Chapter 8 below.

25. As a result of his close association with Kierkegaard in the late 1840s and his stand during the *Kirkekampen* some years later, Nielsen effectively isolated himself from his colleagues at the University and was forced to sever contacts with many people. His wife never looked with favor on his friendship with Kierkegaard, which she regarded as a hindrance to her husband's career. See Asmussen, *Entwicklungsgang*, p. 25.

26. See *Nyt Theologisk Tidsskrift* 8 (Copenhagen, 1857), pp. 203–4 for Scharling's article.

earlier writings as well. Nielsen's point was that Kierkegaard ought to be assessed in his entirety if any judgment is to be made about his mental state shortly before his death.[27] Coming as it did one year prior to the appearance of *The Point of View,* in which the claim of a unified literary corpus is made by the author himself, Nielsen's article underscores his intimate acquaintance with both Kierkegaard's writings and Kierkegaard's views of his works. Commenting on Kierkegaard's self-assigned task as an author, Nielsen wrote:

> It was Kierkegaard's plan to carry out a revision of the categories of existence and liberate them from all confusion. . . . He solved this problem with a certainty, thoroughness and versatility that will warrant him a place among thinkers of the first rank in the coming ages.[28]

Nielsen continued to lecture on Kierkegaard's works into the 1860s, and his lectures were usually sprinkled with extensive quotations from the writings themselves.[29]

Yet Nielsen's incessant efforts at invoking Kierkegaard and his ideas—as a way of compensation after their breakup—eventually backfired. The result was an unintended disservice to Kierkegaard's legacy. With time Nielsen's strained appropriations of Kierkegaardian concepts ended by confusing matters, implicating him—and Kierkegaard by association—in self-contradictions and drawing fire from several quarters. The basic problem with Nielsen's treatment of Kierkegaard's thought was that he continued to employ loosely categories like subjectivity and paradox long after he had effectively ceased to be a true follower of Kierkegaard—when he had, in fact, departed considerably from him.

In the 1860s Nielsen embarked on yet another philosophical venture regarding faith and knowledge. As a Hegelian in the early 1840s he had felt no hesitation about unifying the two. Later, under Kierkegaard's influence, he experienced serious doubts about such a combination and reversed himself so radically that he posited a dualism not unlike the one

---

27. Rasmus Nielsen, "Om S. Kierkegaards 'Mentale Tilstand,' " in *Nordisk Universitets-Tidsskrift,* IV (Copenhagen, 1858), p. 29.

28. Ibid., p. 8.

29. A good example would be the collection of Nielsen's lectures published in 1860 under the title *Paa Kierkegaardske "Stadier": Et Livsbillede* (On the Kierkegaardian "stages," a portrait of life). The collection consisted of four lectures: two dealing with sections of *Stages on Life's Way,* one on marriage, and one on *Fear and Trembling.*

Kant makes between the noumenal and phenomenal realms. Now, after more deliberation and a few mathematical and scientific treatises, Nielsen decided to harmonize Hegel and Kant, that is, to try and have it both ways. One key proposition found in the introduction to his two-volume magnum opus entitled *Grundideernes Logik* (1864 and 1866) summarized his attempt, and with it the "Tro og Viden" Controversy of the 1860s was born. After formulating a Kantian interpretation of the chasm between subjectivity and objectivity, which Kierkegaard enunciates in his famous statement "subjectivity is truth," Nielsen adds the following:

> As the struggle between faith and knowledge is driven in this way to its extremes, the intellectual reconciliation is at the same time inaugurated: the absolutely heterogeneous principles could not, in an essential sense, be separated from each other. . . . Faith and knowledge could then without contradiction be combined in one consciousness.[30]

The rest of Nielsen's massive work proceeds to "show" how these two totally dissimilar elements, faith and knowledge, can coexist jointly in one consciousness and not result in a perverse and unacceptable antagonism.

The two-volume work represented the first investigation of its kind in Scandinavia to offer a self-sufficient philosophical system, and one that simultaneously claimed to be antagonistic to speculative theology.[31] As a systematic treatise, the work violated a basic Kierkegaardian precept, namely the aversion to all philosophical system-building. As a work purporting to be anti-speculative theology, it peddled a thin, pseudo-Kierkegaardian emphasis on interiority that was, in reality, a species of pedagogic formalism and not authentically personal. Nielsen now attacked the theologians, not from the standpoint of faith as he had done during his brief Kierkegaardian phase, but from that of knowledge. The problem with the theologians, according to him, was that they desired to know scientifically (i.e., rationally) things in their relation to their ultimate source, yet that source lay beyond the boundaries of human knowledge.[32] It is as though all Nielsen was able to conclude in the end from Kierkegaard's crusade against "the System" and against rational theology was a type of Kantianism that reduced itself to a rudimentary dualism. But Nielsen did not stop there. Being incapable of overcoming

---

30. Rasmus Nielsen, *Grundideernes Logik*, vol. I (Copenhagen, 1864), p. xxiii.
31. Rosenberg, *Rasmus Nielsen: Nordens Filosof*, p. 101.
32. Ibid., pp. 102–3.

the lure of speculation, he desperately sought to reconcile his dualism with a lingering Hegelianism by situating it in a single consciousness.[33]

Grundideernes Logik provoked swift reactions from two disparate sides in 1866: the secular intellectuals and critics like Georg Brandes, and the speculative theologians represented by Martensen. Brandes had been a student of Nielsen, but in the mid-1860s he was experiencing a significant transformation of outlook in the wake of exposure to scientific and evolutionary thought and to certain radical thinkers.[34] In a short but incisive essay entitled *Dualismen i vor nyeste Philosophie* (Dualism in our contemporary philosophy) Brandes leveled a sustained critique at Nielsen's fundamental thesis that the two absolutely heterogeneous principles, faith and knowledge, can without contradiction be joined in one consciousness.[35] How can Nielsen maintain such a position, Brandes asks, when according to orthodoxy (as Brandes calls it) death, for example, came into the world through sin and the world was created in six days, while science teaches that death is a part of the organism's life and the world came into being over millions of years?[36] Brandes commences his essay by declaring: "There is nothing in professor R. Nielsen's understanding of the relationship between science and biblical faith that may necessarily win him many hearts."[37] Nielsen's ideas are presented throughout the essay as anachronisms running counter to scientific progress in the nineteenth century. In fact a recurring theme in the essay, and in later writings by Brandes, is his constant comparison of the dynamic scientific and philosophical situation in the rest of Europe with what he perceived to be its relative stagnation in Denmark.

Without bothering to probe more deeply, Brandes flatly states that Nielsen's type of thinking derives from Kierkegaard, "this great genius." Although by now Brandes had completely emerged from an early and fleeting religious phase in his development, he retained a respect for Kierkegaard as a brilliant figure.[38] In his view, Nielsen was able, with such apparent ease, to hold fast to his basic proposition because of his

---

33. Hultberg, "Kierkegaard og Rasmus Nielsen," pp. 12-13. See also Rosenberg, *Rasmus Nielsen,* pp. 84-85.

34. For details of Brandes's intellectual formation see Chapter 6 below.

35. Georg Brandes, *Dualismen i vor nyeste Philosophie* (Copenhagen, 1866), p. 25. For information on the background leading up to this work by Brandes see Chapter 6 below.

36. Ibid., pp. 30-31.   37. Ibid., p. 7.

38. Ibid., p. 9.

unquestioning adoption of a radical dualism. As Brandes saw it, "Absolute heterogeneity is absolute dualism," and such a dualism is "a masquerade farce" *(en Maskeradespøg)* and "a trap."[39] In Brandes's monistic vision of the world, this dualism could only be obscuring an underlying unity and uniform homogeneity of being. Moreover, the advocates of Nielsenian dualism are by definition anti-rationalist, because they believe in paradoxes. Falling back on Hegel, Brandes asserts that since the real is the rational, the anti-rational cannot be real.[40] It follows that no science can be built on the basis of the anti-rational.

At the time he wrote on Nielsen, Brandes was reading extensively in the works of Hippolyte Taine, the French philosopher and critic, in particular his book *Les philosophes francais du XIXe siècle* (1857), from which he quotes.[41] Brandes also makes frequent references to a work by a Danish professor of philosophy named Sophus Heegaard (1835–84). The book is entitled *Indledning til den rationelle Ethik* (Introduction to rational ethics) (1866), and in it Heegaard expounds a position close to Nielsen's. Curiously, however, Heegaard published the following year a scathing attack on Nielsen's doctrine of faith and knowledge from a purely rationalist point of view. The work, which he called *Prof. Rasmus Nielsens Lære om Tro og Viden* (Prof. R. N.'s doctrine of faith and knowledge) (1867), provided additional ammunition to the freethinkers and secular rationalists in their battle with Nielsen over the question of "Tro og Viden."[42] Another book Brandes utilizes is Ørsted's *The Soul in Nature*. He praises Ørsted as a natural scientist and discoverer, pointing to his optimistic dualism; however, he criticizes Ørsted's philosophy as unpractical.[43] Kierkegaard's *Postscript* is mentioned a few times, usually as the source and inspiration for Nielsen's ideas. Toward the end of the essay Brandes makes an interesting observation about Nielsen's approach: "[His] entire doctrine consisted essentially in the following: that one took Kierkegaard's *Øjeblikket* in the one hand, Ørsted's *Aanden i Naturen* in the other, clapped them together and bound them into one bundle."[44] Brandes adds, however, that the net result with Nielsen

---

39. Ibid., p. 34.   40. Ibid., pp. 52–53.
41. Ibid., p. 65.
42. On Heegaard see Søren Holm, *Filosofien i Norden før 1900* (Copenhagen: Munksgaard, 1967), pp. 141–42.
43. Brandes, *Dualismen,* pp. 36, 42, and 67.
44. Ibid., p. 67.

was that he effectively "cut Ørsted away and retained Kierkegaard."[45]

The other reaction to Nielsen's work came from Bishop Martensen, who, after reading Brandes's response and a few tracts by some minor authors, decided that the Church had to put forth its case on the issue of faith and knowledge from the standpoint of dogmatic theology as he understood it. He regarded a project of this sort as both vital and pressing, particularly in light of what he felt was an open attack by Nielsen on theology as such. Lingering memories of his previous confrontation with Nielsen in 1849 acted as an additional incentive for him to state his position clearly and repel the assault on speculative theology. The resulting treatise appeared in March of 1867 under the title *Om Tro og Viden, et Lejlighedsskrift* (On faith and knowledge, an occasional work).

Martensen argues in favor of an organic unity between faith and knowledge, the latter being "knowledge of the highest, of God and the divine matters," namely metaphysics.[46] He asks rhetorically, at the outset of the book, what Kierkegaard would have said about Nielsen's "absolutely heterogeneous principles" of faith and knowledge being crammed into the same consciousness. As he sees it, Kierkegaard would go along "if not arm in arm, then still side by side with professor Nielsen's 'knowledge' as with his absolute heterogeneity principle."[47]

In the section devoted to a historical review of the problem of faith and knowledge, Martensen looks back at what he calls early "Christian gnosis" in order to lay the foundations for his refutation of Nielsen's heterogeneity thesis. He appeals only in passing to the Church Fathers, the medieval scholastic thinkers, and the Protestant Reformers. His argument is that all these figures in the history of Christianity upheld "Christian gnosis," which he claims is at the basis of modern speculative theology. Knowledge and faith, therefore, have been intimately related and intertwined throughout the entire Christian tradition.[48] From the nineteenth century Martensen selects his favorite theologian, Schleiermacher, and the Right-Hegelian Guizot, to support his contention of unity between faith and knowledge. He invokes from Guizot's *Méditations sur*

---

45. Ibid. For a collection of Brandes's assorted writings on the question of "Tro og Viden" see Georg Brandes, *Samlede Skrifter*, vol. XIII (Copenhagen, 1903), pp. 5-136. His essay *Dualismen* is reproduced on pp. 43-84.
46. H. L. Martensen, *Om Tro og Viden, et Lejlighedsskrift* (Copenhagen, 1867), p. 2.
47. Ibid., p. 6. 48. Ibid., pp. 10 and 15-16.

l'essence de la religion chrétienne (1864) what the author calls "[l']harmonie entre le philosophe et le chrétien."⁴⁹

Having provided some historical legitimacy for his position, Martensen then proceeds to reject both Nielsen's heterogeneity concept and his subterfuge of combining the two principles in one consciousness. Like Brandes, he detects a dualism in the first and self-contradiction in the second. He says, at one point, that Nielsen's dualism leads to the suggestion that the God of faith is totally other than the God of knowledge: "[It] must undoubtedly be assumed that the author [Nielsen] does not intend to teach two gods."⁵⁰ Similarly, Nielsen is guilty of positing a new dualism between knowledge *(Viden)* and power *(Magt)*, and of ascribing each to a separate notion of the divine, thus opening the way once again for two deities.⁵¹ "His teaching," writes Martensen, "leads unavoidably into a personal double-existence."⁵²

To Martensen, Nielsen's compromise of localizing faith and knowledge in the same consciousness is a sham form of harmonizing them, since it merely pays lip service to their underlying fundamental unity. Only speculative theology is able to bring out that real harmony. Considered historically, Nielsen's philosophy, according to Martensen, is best viewed as an attempt at a concordance between Hegel and Kierkegaard.⁵³ Such an undertaking could hardly be appealing to a speculative theologian like Martensen.

Nielsen's overall position is declared by Martensen to be "not only a-theological, but anti-theological philosophy."⁵⁴ His animosity toward theology boils down to his claim that theology is not a science. But Martensen hastens to ask why Nielsen should single out theology for such a criticism when all the reasons he gives for not calling theology a science also apply to philosophy.⁵⁵ Nielsen's main objection is that theology sees itself as "the science of miracles" *(Mirakelvidenskaben)*, namely it seeks to "clarify miracles," which is impossible.⁵⁶ Martensen, however, denies this, calling theology instead "the science of Revelation" *(Aabenbaringsvidenskaben).*⁵⁷

For Martensen, as for Brandes before him, Kierkegaard seemed to lurk conspicuously in the background of Nielsen's philosophical outlook. In

49. Ibid., quoted on p. 28. See also pp. 18ff.
50. Ibid., p. 42.
51. Ibid., pp. 55–56.
52. Ibid., p. 86.
53. Ibid., pp. 130–31.
54. Ibid., p. 8.
55. Ibid., pp. 99 and 104.
56. Ibid., p. 106.
57. Ibid., p. 112.

fact Martensen says in one place that Nielsen is in the habit of trying to pose as Kierkegaard's intellectual heir.[58] How much such contrived posing distorted the original was, on the whole, of little concern to Brandes and Martensen. They often did not hesitate to implicate Kierkegaard in Nielsen's follies, and at times even holding him somehow responsible for them. Martensen, however, does point out a crucial difference between Kierkegaard and Nielsen: the Kierkegaardian concept of faith as a passion of the solitary individual is not the same as Nielsen's.[59] Martensen makes it very clear that he himself disagrees with Kierkegaard's view, which he designates as "anti-social," but insists the disagreement is entirely independent of Kierkegaard's role in the *Kirkekampen*.[60] He takes this opportunity to advance a few long-harbored criticisms against Kierkegaard, and concludes that Kierkegaard's conceptions of God, eternity, and the unchangeable are borrowed more from Greek sources, especially Plato, than from Revelation. Kierkegaard was too interested in a personal relationship with God to find the time to come up with a theologically sound conception of God; he could not see that his favorite expression, "the eternal, essential Truth," was nothing but an abstract Greek notion.[61]

A beleagured Nielsen responded in the summer of 1867 to Martensen's criticisms. He accused Martensen of confusing divine knowledge with human knowledge, and of being totally blind to the absolute limits of the latter. The central emphasis, however, in this latest piece by Nielsen involved a new concept intended to overcome the allegation of self-contradiction that both Brandes and Martensen had made against him. According to Nielsen, the fact that faith and knowledge are combined in a single consciousness, yet remain two absolutely heterogeneous principles, is "an absolute mystery."[62] The key word here is "mystery," which now begins to supplant the Kierkegaardian term "paradox" in Nielsen's lexicon. His infatuation with the Kierkegaardian paradox had been short-lived, and although he had continued to employ it here and there in his writings, he was developing greater misgivings about it with time. The

58. Ibid., p. 130. 59. Ibid., pp. 132–33.
60. Ibid., p. 134.
61. Ibid., pp. 136–37. For a detailed discussion of Martensen's participation in the "Tro og Viden" Controversy of the 1860s and his critique of Nielsen see Skat Arildsen, *Biskop Hans Lassen Martensen, Hans Liv, Udvikling og Arbejde* (Copenhagen: G. E. C. Gad, 1932), esp. chap. 16, entitled "Striden om Tro og Viden," pp. 325–406.
62. Rasmus Nielsen, *Om "Den gode Villie" som Magt i Videnskaben* (Copenhagen, 1867), pp. 33–34. See also Arildsen, *Biskop Hans Lassen Martensen*, pp. 381–88; and Rosenberg, *Rasmus Nielsen: Nordens Filosof*, pp. 109–12.

"Tro og Viden" Controversy persuaded him to terminate this agonizing love-hate relationship with the paradox and abandon it in favor of "mystery."

Kierkegaard's paradox was too dialectical and possessed distinct rationalistic undertones with which Nielsen no longer felt comfortable. To "comprehend that faith cannot be comprehended,"[63] and to say that "reasons can be given for the impossibility of giving reasons,"[64] as Kierkegaard declares, still leaves room for reason to operate with respect to faith and the unknowable in a manner that Nielsen could no longer accept. Yet for Kierkegaard a paradox remains rationally unresolvable. It is like a mental problem that perpetually seduces the mind to seek to unlock it, even though the mind knows it cannot do so by the powers of logic alone. (This differs from the meaning of paradox in conversational English where, according to the dictionary, it is only a seeming contradiction, implying it can be resolved rationally.) The concept of mystery, on the other hand, has a certain finality about it that puts the mind in a mood of wonder and resignation. It is thus more in keeping with the absolute limits Nielsen sets on human knowledge.[65] Given the radical dualism of Nielsen's two separate spheres of faith and knowledge, mystery was for him the more suitable term to describe their simultaneous presence in one consciousness: "Instead of paradox, therefore, *the mystery*—not as a foggy and vague expression, but as a clear and comprehensible category."[66]

In the fall of 1867 Nielsen gave a series of six lectures at Christiania University in Norway that were gathered into one volume and published the following year under the title *Om Hindringer og Betingelser for det aandelige Liv i Nutiden* (On the obstacles and conditions for the spiritual life of the present). He was introduced in the Norwegian press principally through his relation to Kierkegaard.[67] In one of these lectures Nielsen

---

63. *JP* 3564; (X^1 A 561). 64. *JP* 4896; (X^4 A 356).

65. This is not to imply that Kierkegaard believed in boundless human knowledge capable of solving all mysteries and doing away with wonder. On the contrary, Kierkegaard insisted on the need for "a leap of faith" as the essence of his paradox; however, he was by no means a fideist in that he did not subscribe to the position of faith alone to the exclusion of reason.

66. Quoted from one of Nielsen's lectures in Hultberg, "Kierkegaard og Rasmus Nielsen," p. 16. The notion of mystery has always appealed to the temperament of Eastern Christians, who never speak in terms of "paradox," or use rationalistic words like "contradiction".

67. *Aftenbladet*, nos. 213, 214, and 217 (1867); see Valborg Erichsen, "Søren Kierkegaards betydning for norsk aandsliv," in *EDDA*, 19 (2) (Christiania, 1923), p. 235.

discusses briefly Kierkegaard's idea of paradox as presented by Johannes Climacus in the *Postscript*. He concludes as follows:

> We admit that Kierkegaard is absolutely correct in the assertion that faith for the unbeliever has to be a paradox. . . . But now the question recurs—and it is this question that has been stirring throughout our investigation—namely: Is faith then a paradox unto itself? Is the believer so blind to his own instances of thought that they cannot possibly develop themselves for him into clear coherent conceptions? This must be denied.[68]

At first glance it may appear as if Nielsen, by saying this, is discarding his dearly guarded dualism of faith and knowledge. In reality it is nothing more than the same old dualism with an allowance for a loophole whereby faith and knowledge can be united in the believer's rational consciousness. Nielsen's uneasiness with the notion of paradox is clear. It continued to elude his attempts to fit it into the "coherent" scheme he was striving to produce. His way out, as before, was to resort to "mystery" as a safe substitute for "paradox." The magic word is invoked with mounting frequency in his lectures as a way of dealing with the complexities of the questions raised by faith and knowledge. Faith itself is defined by Nielsen in his lecture as "an act of will,"[69] yet no mention is made of Kierkegaard's "leap of faith." By now Nielsen's conception of faith had diverged significantly from Kierkegaard's, and had lost much of its previous subtlety in the process.

To Nielsen's secular contemporaries, particularly some of his colleagues at the University, his shift from paradox to mystery suggested that fantasy was stepping in to replace passion as the authentic expression of religious sentiment. Mystery at best sounded like a half-solution, an ambiguous vacillation, and at worst smacked of self-delusion and even escapism.[70] One person to whom Nielsen's entire dualistic position appeared untenable from the beginning was Hans Brøchner, a professor of philosophy since 1857, the year he completed a book on Spinoza.

Brøchner was a Left-Hegelian, greatly influenced by the writings of D. F. Strauss and Ludwig Feuerbach. In 1842 he translated Strauss's *Die*

---

68. Rasmus Nielsen, *Om Hindringer og Betingelser for det aandelige Liv i Nutiden* (Copenhagen, 1868), p. 234.
69. Ibid. Nielsen writes on the same page: "The principle of faith is, in its deepest meaning, a principle of will." See also Rosenberg, *Rasmus Nielsen: Nordens Filosof*, chap. XI, pp. 121–33, esp. p. 132.
70. Carl S. Petersen and Vilhelm Andersen, *Illustreret Dansk Litteratur-Historie*, no. 14 (Copenhagen: Gyldendal, 1924), pp. 710–11.

christliche Glaubenslehre into Danish. He had commenced his education in 1836 with the study of theology, but declared five years later that he could not accept the Church's dogmas. He wrote a treatise in 1843 entitled *Nogle Bemærkninger om Daaben* (Some observations on baptism) in which he criticised Martensen's teachings on baptism. He then turned to philosophy, but did not cease to be interested in religion. As a philosopher he retained an acute ethico-religious sensitivity that manifested itself in his writings.[71]

The "Tro og Viden" Controversy interested Brøchner greatly, and he gave several lectures in 1867 that were critical of Nielsen's position in the debate. They appeared as a book the following year under the title *Problemet om Tro og Viden, en historisk-kritisk Afhandling* (The problem of faith and knowledge, a historical-critical treatise). Like Martensen's work, this book begins with a historical survey of the problem; however, Brøchner's is more thorough in its treatment of the philosophical side of the question, particularly within the German tradition.[72] From Leibniz and Spinoza, through Schelling, Schleiermacher, and Hegel, to Feuerbach, the relation of faith to knowledge and the various attempts at harmonizing them are traced. Feuerbach is said to have conducted his search for a solution to the problem from the standpoint of "the interests of knowledge." Simultaneously with Feuerbach's endeavors, Kierkegaard in Denmark was steering the issue down a new path. Agreeing with Feuerbach's distinction between the two spheres of faith and knowledge, Kierkegaard soon made the break decisive. This says Brøchner, is the origin of Nielsen's view.[73]

Feuerbach and Kierkegaard are compared repeatedly throughout Brøchner's work. The comparisons are significant not only as being the earliest of their kind, but also as coming from one who was intimately familiar with the philosophies of both men and influenced by each in a special way.[74] Brøchner declares in the foreword that Kierkegaard is in

71. See the articles on Brøchner by K. Kroman and S. V. Rasmussen respectively in the *DBL,* 1st ed., III (Copenhagen, 1889), pp. 202–6; and *DBL,* 2d ed., IV (Copenhagen, 1934), pp. 286–92.

72. One of Brøchner's strengths was as a historian of philosophy. His magnum opus, *Philosophiens Historie i Grundrids* [The history of philosophy in outline], 2 vols. (1873–74), was the first general history of philosophy of its kind in the Danish language.

73. Hans Brøchner, *Problemet om Tro og Viden, en historisk-kritisk Afhandling* (Copenhagen, 1868), p. 26.

74. Nielsen too alludes to Kierkegaard and Feuerbach in one of his lectures. He says that, although they were diametrically opposed to each other in outlook, they were united

basic agreement with Feuerbach's contrasting of knowledge and faith, but that he parts company with Feuerbach on the reasons for such a contrast and the conclusions to be drawn from it. According to Brøchner, Kierkegaard essentially distinguishes between religion and philosophy in religion's favor. He maintains that the human soul's deepest interest lay in attaining a subjective existential certainty that can come only through faith, since the realm of knowledge is limited and cannot satisfy the spirit's yearning for eternal happiness. Hence, only through a recognition of the subordination of knowledge to faith can a compatability between them be achieved, and a sense of certainty within the realm of knowledge itself be attained.[75]

With Feuerbach, although the spheres of faith and knowledge are differentiated, the right of reason over against faith is established, and religion is declared to be irrational. This results in a major difference between Feuerbach's and Kierkegaard's understandings of religion, particularly Christianity. Yet despite this, insists Brøchner, there is no other contemporary with whom Kierkegaard has more points of similarity in terms of a determination of the nature of Christianity.[76] It is without a doubt Feuerbach, he says, whom Kierkegaard had in mind when writing in *Postscript* about the confusion of the theologians concerning what is Christianity: "On the other hand, a scoffer attacks Christianity and at the same time expounds it so creditably that it is a delight to read him, and the person who is really having a hard time getting it definitely presented almost has to resort to him."[77] Brøchner was the first to make this association that has since been adopted by all major Kierkegaard scholars.[78] He also enumerates a long list of points that Kierkegaard and Feuerbach have in common regarding Christianity.[79]

On Nielsen and Kierkegaard, Brøchner dwells at length. He says they both recognized built-in limitations to human knowledge and posited the

---

in proclaiming the characters of religion and science to be "incompatible" [*uforenelig*]. See R. Nielsen, *Om Hindringer og Betingelser for det aandelige Liv i Nutiden*, p. 273.

75. Brøchner, *Problemet om Tro og Viden*, p. 3.

76. Ibid., p. 124.

77. Ibid., quoted on p. 125. See Søren Kierkegaard, *Concluding Unscientific Postscript* (*KW*, XII.1), p. 614.

78. Walter Lowrie, for example, in his earlier translation of the *Postscript*, mentions Feuerbach in a footnote to the passage in question. See Søren Kierkegaard, *Concluding Unscientific Postscript*, trans. Walter Lowrie (Princeton: Princeton University Press, 1941), p. 573, note 8. See also *Concluding Unscientific Postscript* (*KW*, XII.2) p. 270, note 862.

79. Brøchner, *Problemet om Tro og Viden*, pp. 125-26.

need for faith as the highest form of certainty for existence. With Nielsen the two realms are separate and distinct. Yet contrary to appearances, claims Brøchner, Nielsen's dualism actually subordinates knowledge to faith in the same way that Kierkegaard's concept of relative and finite knowledge renders it subordinate to faith. Despite Nielsen's intention to have the two realms absolutely heterogeneous, in fact one is subservient to the other as in Kierkegaard. Brøchner concludes that on all the fundamentals Nielsen's position derives from Kierkegaard's. Still, Brøchner believes there is room to distinguish their respective views and to illuminate certain peculiarities in Nielsen's outlook on faith and knowledge that stem from his own psychological and metaphysical theories. It is these that, according to Brøchner, have resulted in the many contradictions plaguing Nielsen's philosophy, contradictions that Kierkegaard manages to avoid.[80] In Brøchner's eyes, Kierkegaard is absolved of Nielsen's fallacies, although he is not without a few of his own.

Brøchner expounds Kierkegaard's philosophy in some detail, emphasizing his divergence from Hegelian speculative idealism in the direction of personal existence and greater inwardness. According to Kierkegaard, he says, such idealism is based on objectivity that at best yields uncertain knowledge. The individual can base his eternal happiness neither on the uncertainty of objective knowledge, nor on the approximations of a purely historical knowledge, nor on the abstractions of mathematical understanding. Only through the passion of faith can certainty be attained by the subject regarding the eternal. Hence, truth resides in subjectivity alone. Objective truth exists but remains chimerical unless it is appropriated by the individual through subjectivity. This subjective appropriation *(tilegnelse)* of truth is achieved through faith in the Absolute Paradox (the God-Man), something unintelligible to reason. A break with objective knowledge is made at this point, and one enters the realm of faith, where thought is the servant of faith and submits unquestioningly to the Paradox. Thus all attempts to grasp the Paradox through the understanding are thwarted in the domain of faith. For Kierkegaard, therefore, as Brøchner sees it, the "reconciliation" of faith and knowledge is based on the distinction of the two spheres and the subordination of knowledge to faith.[81]

Turning to Nielsen, Brøchner sees a similar distinction to Kierkegaard's between faith and knowledge, except that here the cleavage is so

---

80. Ibid., pp. 29–30.
81. Ibid., pp. 118–23. Brøchner obviously relies heavily on the *Fragments* and the *Postscript* for his exposition.

total that its outcome is a dualism. He agrees with Nielsen's other adversaries that the absolute heterogeneity principle is self-contradictory when Nielsen proposes to combine faith and knowledge in one consciousness. (While Brøchner was writing this book Nielsen had still not published his concept of mystery as a means of dispelling the alleged contradiction in his position.) Brøchner also detects, like Martensen, several other dualisms in Nielsen's philosophy: will and knowledge, power and knowledge, subjectivity and objectivity, personal and impersonal truth, and so on.[82] Nielsen, on the one hand, radically contrasts each component of these pairs, and on the other, engages in all sorts of convoluted psychological and metaphysical ploys designed to bridge the gap he himself has erected. The most prevalent contrast is the one between will and knowledge, yet in the final analysis knowledge is subordinated to will, which, for Nielsen, is the operating force in the ethico-religious domain. It emerges, therefore, that in Brøchner's view the difference between Kierkegaard and Nielsen is one of degree: Kierkegaard, although separating faith and knowledge, does not go so far as to posit a dualism, and thus escapes the pitfall of self-contradiction.[83]

For Brøchner this difference is important; to some extent it frees him to take on Nielsen independently of Kierkegaard. There is a certain amount of arbitrariness and ambiguity, he says, in Nielsen's understanding and use of Kierkegaardian concepts. This not only serves as a basis for a critique of Nielsen, it also helps to clarify the relationship between him and Kierkegaard. According to Brøchner, Nielsen borrows Kierkegaard's notion of the difference between existence and knowledge and twists it around by changing its basic assumptions. Instead of a personalized concept of existence, Nielsen develops an abstract (theoretical) one that at times has an *a priori* nature, and at others is described as the "practical" manifestation of being. Brøchner sees another one of Nielsen's contradictions here.[84]

In a similarly arbitrary fashion, Nielsen adopts Kierkegaard's distinction between subjective and objective. The problem is compounded with Nielsen when "subjectivity" and "the subjective" assume an egotistical meaning and degenerate into subjectivism. Brøchner recognizes that for Kierkegaard subjective truth signifies appropriated *(tilegnede)* truth; i.e., despite being interiorized by the individual believer through subjectivity,

---

82. Ibid., p. 126. 83. Ibid., pp. 127–29.
84. Ibid., pp. 130–31.

it retains its independent otherness and universal objective character within itself. The danger with Nielsen, Brøchner astutely points out, is that his position easily lapses into subjectivism, entailing the notion of self-concocted truth. This is so because, unlike Kierkegaard, Nielsen does not conceive of subjectivity as a process of appropriation. He posits an abstract contrast between the general (objective) and the particular (subjective), and the dichotomy becomes so great that the particular is locked within its own psychological and metaphysical ego-centered world. Nielsen's subjectivity is in fact a form of egotism.[85]

With this point about egotism/subjectivism Brøchner has placed his finger on an extremely significant (and infamous) distortion of Kierkegaardian subjectivity—namely, its confusion with, or degeneration into, crude subjectivism. If Brøchner's accusation is correct, Nielsen would represent one of the earliest instances of this kind of philosophical sophism that reaches epidemic proportions in the twentieth century.[86] Such a basic misconception has tremendously far-reaching consequences with respect to the very nature of truth. In the end, Brøchner is pointing to the fact that there exists a fundamental ontological difference between Kierkegaard's and Nielsen's conceptions of subjectivity.

Of all the participants in the debate against Nielsen over "Tro og Viden," Brøchner does Kierkegaard the most justice. This may seem remarkable, given Brøchner's freethinking Left-Hegelian orientation and an underlying pantheistic-monistic streak that he gets partly from Spinoza, and partly from Hegel. In all his philosophical writings, Brøchner aimed at a grand rationalistic synthesis not unlike that of Hegel; in some respects it is reminiscent of the harmony Ørsted strove for between soul and nature.[87] Brøchner approached the "Tro og Viden" Controversy

85. Ibid., p. 132.
86. The relativistic-subjectivistic implications of Sartrean existentialism would be a good example. For a concise discussion of the secondary literature on Kierkegaard's theory of truth and his concept of subjectivity in its relation to subjectivism, see chap. 4 in David R. Law, *Kierkegaard as Negative Theologian* (Oxford: Clarendon Press, 1993), esp. pp. 90–99. Law lists both groups of opposed scholars, calling them respectively "the subjectivist camp" (those who hold that Kierkegaard's concept "Truth is Subjectivity" lands him in subjectivism), and "the non-subjectivist camp" (those who maintain that Kierkegaard's thesis does not dispense altogether with objectivity). Law believes that "Kierkegaard has a much broader conception of truth than the subjectivist camp gives him credit for" (p. 94). The present writer agrees with Law.
87. On Brøchner's relation to Hegel's philosophy, and on his uniting of soul and nature see S. V. Rasmussen, *Den Unge Brøchner,* chap. 21, pp. 198–212, and chap. 22, pp. 213–28, respectively. Rasmussen concludes that Brøchner's conception of the relation

from a typically nineteenth-century, Straussian angle—that of biblical higher criticism—which operates on the assumption that Scripture and Christian doctrine can and should be studied scientifically and critically, as one investigates everything else. It is precisely this outlook, stressing historical-critical knowledge, that Kierkegaard assails in his *Philosophical Fragments* as bearing no relation to the nature of faith. For Brøchner, however, the only valid form of religious relationship is what he calls "the absolute relationship to the Absolute."[88] By this he means a full participation of the human essence (thought, feeling, will) in an experience of the Absolute that he designates as *our* Absolute, namely, one who shares our essence with us. Echoes of Feuerbachian anthropomorphism and Hegelian immanence are evident here. Brøchner, therefore, rejects the God of Abraham, because in his view an arbitrary and condemnatory deity cannot be man's God.

Although Brøchner was worlds apart from Kierkegaard philosophically and religiously, he always felt a curious affinity toward him. This was mostly due to a twenty-year friendship between them that produced a subtle and elusive influence—more like a strong impression—by Kierkegaard on Brøchner. Kierkegaard's final attack on the Church, for instance, appeared to Brøchner as a courageous and honest exposure of the confusion and mediocrity of an institution gone astray and no longer true to its original calling. Yet it was only after Kierkegaard's death that his significance became clear to Brøchner.[89] The obituary he wrote for *Fædrelandet* on the occasion stands out as the most profound and comprehensive assessment of the deceased and his writings to appear among the plethora of articles during the *Kirkekampen*.[90]

Now, some thirteen years later, Brøchner's sensitivity to sham and contradiction, sharpened by Kierkegaard's example, is employed against Nielsen and his misuse of Kierkegaardian categories in the "Tro og Viden" Controversy. Nielsen's grand effort at upholding simultaneously a strict dualism and a synthesis of sorts is finally designated by Brøchner to be "a thought-experiment" and a "psychological amphibium" that remains on the abstract level of theory, notwithstanding all Nielsen's

---

between philosophy and religion contains both transcendent and immanent elements joined together (p. 230).

88. Brøchner, *Problemet om Tro og Viden*, pp. 211–12.

89. See Kalle Sorainen, "Brøchner," in *The Legacy and Interpretation of Kierkegaard*, vol. 8 of *Bibliotheca Kierkegaardiana* (1981), p. 201.

90. See Chapter 3 above.

claims to the contrary.⁹¹ As for Kierkegaard, he is not to be saddled with Nielsen's contradictions. In fact, attests Brøchner, Kierkegaard's ideas have a certain "irresistible power" that lures the spirit when confronted by them.⁹² They focus on the existing person's relationship to the eternal through faith in the Paradox. Brøchner then surveys briefly Kierkegaard's concepts of the eternal and the paradox, both of which define the limits of human knowledge. However, he is unable to accept either, for he regards the eternal as too abstract,⁹³ and the paradox as an intellectualism that precipitates a conflict in man's consciousness, causing it to split within itself.⁹⁴ For Brøchner the Kierkegaardian paradox is ultimately conducive to a self-contradiction all its own, since it is at the same time the product of reason and a constant cause for reason to rebel. Brøchner, therefore, while freeing Kierkegaard of Nielsen's contradictions, believes he has uncovered some that are uniquely Kierkegaard's. From Brøchner's rational monistic standpoint, Nielsen and Kierkegaard disturb, albeit in different ways, the harmony and equilibrium that he maintains exist in the world, in man, and in man's relation with the world.⁹⁵

Nielsen was quick to reply to Brøchner in a short and terse piece he called *Hr. Prof. Brøchners filosofiske Kritik gjennemset* (B's philosophical critique reviewed). Nielsen's chief objection was that throughout his book Brøchner assumes precisely what he supposedly sets out to demonstrate: that the principle of knowledge has validity over the domain of faith.⁹⁶ To this Brøchner responded with a thirty-page essay entitled *Et Svar til Professor R. Nielsen* (A reply to R. N.) in which he makes the unfortunate statement that since Nielsen's theory enjoys an intimate relationship with Kierkegaard's ideas, a refutation of the latter would also apply to the former.⁹⁷ Brøchner, however, does not proceed to do this, but instead attacks Nielsen's dualism directly. It is, in fact, surprising that Brøchner should say this, given the care he took, in his initial critique of Nielsen, to disentangle Kierkegaard as much as possible from the errors of his pseudo-follower.

At one point in the essay Brøchner mentions the various phases and intellectual changes Nielsen had gone through since first becoming a professor. What is interesting is the latest turn Nielsen's peculiar develop-

91. Brøchner, *Problemet om Tro og Viden*, p. 214.
92. Ibid., p. 215.   93. Ibid., pp. 216–18.
94. Ibid., p. 219.   95. Ibid., pp. 224–26.
96. Rosenberg, *Rasmus Nielsen: Nordens Filosof*, pp. 115–16.
97. Hans Brøchner, *Et Svar til Professor R. Nielsen* (Copenhagen, 1868), note pp. 4–5.

ment appears to have taken: by 1868 he was well on the road to Grundtvigianism.[98] After failing to convince anyone with his dualism and after his desperate attempts, as Martensen had put it, to combine Hegel and Kierkegaard, Nielsen sought refuge in the safe haven of the Grundtvigian Folk Church, where the entire issue of faith and knowledge is "settled" (or skirted, as the case may be) through one's belonging to a spiritual community of believers. Actually, Nielsen had begun to move closer to the Grundtvigians in the early 1860s. He received sustained support from them throughout the ensuing "Tro og Viden" Controversy, mostly in the form of sympathetic articles published in the Grundtvigian church periodical *Dansk Kirketidende*, whose editor between 1860 and 1872, Niels Lindberg (1829–86), was an intimate personal friend of Nielsen.[99]

Psychologically, Nielsen's isolation during the "Tro og Viden" Controversy conditioned him to become increasingly receptive to the communal dimension of Grundtvigianism. He craved fellowship as he passed the lonely years of the heated debate he had precipitated, and he finally found it in the ranks of Grundtvig's followers. The radical individualism of Kierkegaard had lost all its appeal, and in its place Nielsen substituted what he felt was a more balanced view of the individual's relationship with his spiritual congregation. Thus the individual ceased to be an end in himself for Nielsen, and became an important point of departure toward the life of the community.[100] Whether there were other hidden motives for embracing Grundtvigianism, such as Nielsen's desire to escape the rigors of the Controversy and the assaults of secular intellectuals, or his wish to make a name for himself independently of Kierkegaard's legacy and Martensen's rival theology, is very difficult to determine. It has been suggested that Nielsen was in fact embarking on a new venture: to unite Kierkegaard and Grundtvig in one overall view. If so, he would be the first to have taken on a challenge that Danish culture has been attempting unsuccessfully to meet ever since. The proposed combination is indeed close to impossible.[101]

98. Ibid., p. 23.
99. Arildsen, *Biskop Hans Lassen Martensen*, p. 335.
100. Rosenberg, *Rasmus Nielsen: Nordens Filosof*, pp. 54–55. Eduard Asmussen, *Entwicklungsgang und Grundprobleme der Philosophie Rasmus Nielsens*, p. 57, follows Rosenberg in suggesting that the roots of this communal tendency in Nielsen go back to his early Kierkegaardian phase, when he exhibited signs of it in his writings.
101. The suggestion that Nielsen attempted a harmonization of Kierkegaard and Grundtvig came from the scholar Vilhelm Andersen; however, Helge Hultberg thinks it

In 1869 both Brøchner and Nielsen published works that showed how far apart their respective positions on faith and knowledge really were. Neither attacked the other, and their actual direct confrontation had, for the most part, come to an end. Brøchner's *Om det Religiøse i dets Enhed med det Humane* (On the religious in its unity with the human) was a supplement to his *Problemet om Tro og Viden* of the previous year. It constituted the "positive" side of Brøchner's contribution to the debate over "Tro og Viden," the "negative" having been his critique of Nielsen. Brøchner offers a detailed investigation of the rational principles behind the proposed unity of the understanding *(den Erkjendelse)* and the ethico-religious sensibility. There are long sections on his concept of the Absolute, on Feuerbach, on Hegel, and on the problem of evil. Kierkegaard is mentioned a few times here and there, especially in connection with his concept of the religious as paradoxical, and its relation to the ethical. The author concludes vaguely that Kierkegaard's understanding of Christianity is "absolutely spiritualistic".[102]

On the whole, Brøchner's treatises had very little impact beyond the immediate academic and philosophical environment in which they were conceived and received. He has been regarded as a transitional figure in the history of Danish philosophy,[103] the last and most prominent of the Danish Left-Hegelians. With his passing a new era of rationalism and positivism was ushered in.

Nielsen's 1869 book, entitled *Religionsphilosophie,* is, in many respects, antithetical to Brøchner's work of the same year. It embodies an emphatic reproclamation of his two polar propositions: the heterogeneity of faith and knowledge, and their concurrent reconciliation through "the mystery." Indeed, the book is one litany of praise for the concept of mystery as a panacea for unresolved problems in theology. A statement just after the title page summarizes what is to follow:

> Faith and reason are, as principles, absolutely heterogeneous. The heterogeneity of the principles does not break the universal laws of thought, but shows the impossibility of any intellectual crossing over either from knowledge to faith, or from faith to knowledge. . . . The proposition that truth in religion is not truth in science, is no longer a paradox, when the absolute limits of

---

is not possible to achieve such a union. See Hultberg, "Kierkegaard og Rasmus Nielsen," p. 20.

102. Hans Brøchner, *Om det Religiøse i dets Enhed med det Humane* (Copenhagen, 1869), p. 43; see also pp. 35–37, 41–42, and 120–21 for references to Kierkegaard.

103. See the article on Brøchner by S. V. Rasmussen in *DBL,* IV (1934), p. 291.

knowledge collapse with the mystery, from which the understanding of faith emerges, and to which it comes back.[104]

Thus mystery replaces paradox and all contradictions disappear so that despite the existing heterogeneity a synthesis is possible.

Nielsen begins by presenting two standard positions regarding faith and knowledge: the first he calls "negative criticism," that is the point of view of science, which views religion as an absurdity and proceeds to analyze it on that basis. The second is what Nielsen terms the Kierkegaardian position, in which religion proclaims itself as an absurdity and, by doing so, once and for all excludes science and all objective knowledge. Nielsen concludes from these two perspectives that religion and philosophy are not only heterogeneous but absolutely so.[105] The question then arises: Is a "philosophy of religion" *(en Religionsphilosophie)* possible? The rest of the book is Nielsen's endeavor to show that it is.

Gradually, the unwieldy and discordant concepts of "paradox" and "absurdity" are phased out in favor of "mystery" in each of the three major sections of the book dealing with the Father, Son, and Holy Ghost consecutively. For instance, Nielsen defines mystery with respect to God the Father as a unifying component: "The mystery is, in its fatherly self, the original unity of essence and will, of necessity and freedom."[106] A little further on, he adds: "The mystery is . . . the unity of the idea in the form of necessity with the idea in the form of freedom, the original unity of nature and soul."[107] Hegelian idealism and Ørstedian *Naturphilosophie* appear as the guiding inspirations behind Nielsen's latest attempts at forging unities. The boundary where knowledge and faith presumably separate is, at the same time, their meeting place. This is the mystery according to Nielsen, who defines it as follows: "The mystery is the absolute limit of knowledge and faith; the mystery is the absolutely heterogeneous principles' secret unity; the mystery is dualism's resolution." He continues: "The reconciliation is brought about only by this, that the determinations of the boundary be shown so that the contradictions dissolve into the mystery."[108]

All along, the reader gets the feeling that Nielsen is very conscious of Kierkegaard's concept of paradox and is trying his best to dissociate his

---

104. Rasmus Nielsen, *Religionsphilosophie* (Copenhagen, 1869), unnumbered page after title page.
105. Ibid., pp. 6–7.
106. Ibid., p. 100.
107. Ibid., p. 102.
108. Ibid., p. 174.

philosophy from it. This is reinforced by his repeated declarations that the mystery is not the paradox.[109] However, it comes across most vividly when Nielsen discusses God the Son. He says that Kierkegaard's designation of the God-Man as "the Absolute Paradox" has its share of truth, yet for the believer this does not signify an absurdity, but rather a mystery: "Mystery dissolves the contradiction, while absurdity [or paradox] retains it."[110] It is as though Nielsen is tossing the accusation of self-contradiction, which was directed at him from all sides at the height of the "Tro og Viden" Controversy, straight onto Kierkegaard's shoulders. After a while, one also has the impression that Nielsen is engaging in a game of semantics as he cavalierly substitutes mystery for paradox at every turn: "The Son's God-manhood itself is not a Paradox; rather it is a Mystery."[111] The spiritual self is not a paradox but an unfathomable mystery, as are the sacraments of rebirth through baptism and sanctification.[112] Kierkegaard is called "the representative of the dialectic of the paradox" *(Paradoxdialektikens Repræsentant)*,[113] and the paradox is equated throughout with the absurd.

Religionsphilosophie can be said to belong to the genre of speculative theology. Oddly enough, it resembles Martensen's *Christelige Dogmatik* of 1849, the work that both Nielsen and Kierkegaard disliked and reacted against. After twenty years of eclectic experimentation, Nielsen appears to have returned to the method of establishing rational harmony among philosophy, science, and theology. His desire may have been to supplant Martensen's rationalistic system with one of his own that would revolve around the pervasive concept of mystery. The scholar Helge Hultberg is not off the mark when she states that the difference between Martensen's book and Nielsen's is merely formal, and at times purely verbal.[114] In one place Nielsen even talks of mediations and accommodations *(Forhandlingerne)* between religion and science.[115] He also mentions a "science of limits" *(Grændsevidenskab)*.[116] His book represents one of the last attempts to save the crumbling pieces of a systematic theological presenta-

109. An example would be ibid., p. 34.
110. Ibid., pp. 302–3.   111. Ibid., p. 304; see also p. 295.
112. Ibid., pp. 452–458, 510–11, and 515–17 respectively.
113. Ibid., p. 515.
114. Hultberg, "Kierkegaard og Rasmus Nielsen," p. 14.
115. Nielsen, *Religionsphilosophie*, p. 157. The Danish word even suggests negotiations and bargaining.
116. Ibid., p. 9.

tion of Christianity in the face of the mighty onslaught of positivism and freethought. In his case the approach combined a blend of speculative theology and Grundtvigianism. Concepts like "mystery," "wonder," and "the miraculous" worked conveniently to form links between a Martensen-like theological synthesis and Nielsen's own Grundtvigian leanings. In short, Nielsen ended by trying to harmonize Martensen and Grundtvig, a task that was a very far cry from anything Kierkegaardian.

In the years following *Religionsphilosophie,* Nielsen drifted farther into Grundtvigianism and into his own peculiar theories. The works he wrote in the 1870s, such as *Natur og Aand* (1873), *Om Fantasiens Magt* (1876), and *Om Aandsdannelse* (1877), reveal how alien Kierkegaard's philosophy had become to him. He also put up increasing resistance to certain new scientific views, mainly the theory of evolution. Beginning in *Religionsphilosophie,* he had denied that the theory could explain the origins of the world and all other things. Creation, its coming into existence, and the preservation of its natural processes are and remain a mystery.[117] A few years later, in one of his popular lectures, Nielsen had this to say about evolution:

> All the alarm about people's animal descent arises from the fact that a famous naturalist has forgotten that there is something in nature called design. It is through the power of his divine design that man appears as God's image on earth.[118]

For all practical purposes the "Tro og Viden" Controversy came to an end in 1869 with the two divergent publications of Brøchner and Nielsen. Lest it be thought, however, that the debate involved only Nielsen on the one side, and Brandes, Martensen, and Brøchner on the other, a glance at a few other participants is necessary. A host of lesser figures took part in the debate for and against Nielsen on faith and knowledge. They often used the occasion to refer to Kierkegaard's views as they analyzed Nielsen's controversial positions.

Supporting Nielsen, in addition to the Grundtvigians, was an aesthetician and philosophical essayist named P. C. Rudolf Schmidt (1836-99), who was convinced that Nielsen had found the only satisfactory solution to the problem of faith and knowledge. He wrote several polemical articles in Nielsen's defense. Also on Nielsen's side was the critic Clemens C. M.

---

117. Ibid., pp. 157-66, and pp. 174ff.
118. Quoted in Carl Jørgensen, *Søren Kierkegaards Skuffelser,* p. 39.

Petersen (1834–18), whose articles were sharp and caught the attention of many.[119]

One of the earliest negative reactions to Nielsen's *Grundideernes Logik* came from a Norwegian Hegelian professor of theology and philosophy teaching in Copenhagen, E. F. B. Horn (1829–99), who wrote a ninety-six page tract in 1866 called *Tro og Tænkning, en indledende Undersøgelse* (Faith and thought, an introductory investigation). He attacked Nielsen's heterogeneity principle, calling it "a misunderstanding," and he criticized Kierkegaard's concept of paradox as well. Both faith and thought, he argued, were God's gifts, and faith surrounds thought in the same way that the sky surrounds the earth. Only when thought loses sight of its limits does faith oppose it, but this normally does not happen. Horn, like Martensen, utilized the speculative approach in theological writing.[120]

Martensen's entry into the fray in 1867 encouraged many Right-Hegelians to speak out against Nielsen. One of these was the Norwegian philosopher and publicist M. J. Monrad (1816–97), who attended Nielsen's lectures on faith and knowledge in 1867 at the University of Christiania. He wrote a critique of Nielsen's dualism for *Morgenbladet* shortly after the lecture series was over. The article was subsequently expanded and published separately in 1869 as *En Episode under Forhandlingerne mellem Tro og Viden* [An episode in the debates between faith and knowledge]. Monrad tried to maintain a separation between faith and knowledge, and at the same time mediate them dialectically in a Hegelian fashion. Abrupt transitions from one sphere to the other were not congenial to his way of thinking. He also discussed Kierkegaard's category of "the single individual" in the course of his essay. He called it "one-sided" and said the emphasis on inner subjectivity led to "isolation." In his view, Kierkegaard's excessive preoccupation with the individual derived from pietism. It interfered with the Christian call to love one's neighbor, and turned everyone in on himself, in a quest for personal salvation, to the point of fragmenting community.[121]

---

119. See Arildsen, *Biskop Hans Lassen Martensen*, pp. 334–35.

120. On E. F. B. Horn see *NBL*, vol. 6, pp. 335–39. See also Harald Beyer, "Søren Kierkegaards betydning for norsk Aandsliv," in *EDDA*, 19 (1), p. 22. Thirty years later, in 1896, Horn gave a series of 12 lectures at the University of Christiania on the same theme of "Tro og Tænkning."

121. On M. J. Monrad see *NBL*, vol. 9, pp. 315–33. See also Harald Beyer, "Søren Kierkegaards betydning" (1), pp. 18–21. Like Horn, Monrad returned to the subject of faith and knowledge many years later and published *Tro og Viden* in 1892. Once again he discussed Kierkegaard, in whom he detected both an attraction and a repulsion toward

An old foe of Kierkegaard from the *Kirkekampen* days, the pastor F. L. B. Zeuthen, got himself involved with Nielsen over "Tro og Viden." In 1866 Zeuthen reacted to Nielsen's newly proclaimed views by sending him a long letter. In it he argued against dualism and in favor of a harmony between religion and thought. Nielsen wasted no time in replying to Zeuthen's letter, and his answer contained many of the ingredients—wonder, miracle, mystery—that constituted the nub of the position he was tending toward. When Zeuthen responded with another letter, Nielsen did not bother to answer.[122]

Three years later, in 1869, Zeuthen published a short autobiography. Kierkegaard is mentioned in it, but interestingly, the reference is neither to the "Tro og Viden" Controversy, nor, as one might have expected, to the *Kirkekampen*. Instead, it concerned a brief and friendly correspondence the two had exchanged in 1848. At that time, Zeuthen wrote Kierkegaard a laudatory letter telling him how much he had enjoyed reading the then recently published *Christian Discourses,* and Kierkegaard replied with a cordial note (which Zeuthen includes in his autobiography) expressing gratitude for Zeuthen's admiration.[123] Viewing this incident in retrospect, it is slightly surprising to see them clash so fiercely some years later in the *Kirkekampen*. Zeuthen's decision to publish the letter in 1869 may indicate a softening of the animosity he had once displayed toward Kierkegaard, and a recognition perhaps that Kierkegaard's posthumous reputation merited a more serious global evaluation than it had received during the last two years of his life.

The attention Nielsen's writings received during the "Tro og Viden" Controversy, and the tenuous links his ideas had to Kierkegaard's, generated comparisons of one or both of them with Kant. Martensen, in his critique of Nielsen, brought up the point that Nielsen's dualism must have had Kant's distinction between the theoretical and the practical as its model.[124] In Nielsen's case the comparison makes sense, because in many respects his philosophical conclusions have Kant far more than Kierke-

---

combining faith and knowledge. This interpretation of Kierkegaard's position reflected the ambivalence of Monrad's own dialectical Hegelian perspective. As for Kierkegaard's "truth is subjectivity," Monrad continued to consider it a sophism.

122. On Zeuthen's correspondence with Nielsen over "Tro og Viden," see Arildsen, *Biskop Hans Lassen Martensen,* pp. 344–48.

123. See F. L. B. Zeuthen, *Et Par Aar af mit Liv* (Copenhagen, 1869), pp. 22–23. For English translations of Zeuthen's letter and Kierkegaard's reply see *LD* (*KW,* XXV), letters 174 and 175, pp. 241–43.

124. Martensen, *Om Tro og Viden,* p. 141.

gaard as their intellectual source. With Kierkegaard, however, one has to be careful, and not everyone was. In 1869, the Danish theologian and editor of *Evangelisk Ugeskrift* since 1864,[125] Henrik Scharling (1836–1920), gave two lectures at the University of Christiania, one of which was a comparison of Kierkegaard and Grundtvig in favor of the latter. The lecture appeared in print the following year, and in it Scharling called Kierkegaard a Kantian.[126] He did so perhaps under the impact of the perceived Kierkegaardian connections with Nielsen's widely disputed dualism of faith and knowledge. He also accused Nielsen of "subjectivism," as Brøchner had done in 1868. Consequently, in his lecture we find Kant, Fichte, and Kierkegaard lumped together as "one-sided subjective thinkers." The only distinction made between Kierkegaard and the other two was that Kierkegaard "derived the ethical from the religious," whereas Kant and Fichte performed the derivation in reverse.[127] Scharling's interpretation was thus typical of the warped reading Kierkegaard received through the distorted Nielsenian prism of the "Tro og Viden" Controversy.[128]

It was not until 1874 that someone openly undertook to set the record straight on behalf of Kierkegaard. This was an obscure pastor from Aarhus named A. F. Schiødte (dates unavailable). In a short, twenty-four page piece on Kierkegaard's concept of paradox, Schiødte found room to dissociate Kierkegaard from both Nielsen and Brøchner:

> [Kierkegaard] in his totality has become very little understood and to a great extent misunderstood. The entire R. Nielsenian connection to Søren Kierkegaard is a complete misunderstanding. . . . Those who know professor Dr. H. Brøchner's great composure and thoroughness in the interpretation of strange philosophical systems would know in advance that his exposition of Søren Kierkegaard's doctrines in his treatise *Problemet om Tro og Viden* cannot but signify a glaring misunderstanding.[129]

---

125. After 1865 *Evangelisk Ugeskrift* changed its title to *Ugeblad for den danske Folkekirke*.

126. Henrik Scharling, "Søren Kierkegaard og Grundtvig," in *Dansk Tidsskrift for Kirke- og Folkeliv, Literatur og Kunst*, I (Copenhagen, 1870), p. 12.

127. Ibid., pp. 12–13, and 18.

128. This is not to belittle the importance and complexity of Kierkegaard's relation to Kant's philosophy quite independently of Nielsen. For more on Kierkegaard and Kant see note 3 above. On Scharling see *DBL*, 2d edition, vol. 21, pp. 62–66. Scharling's lecture also asserted that the key to understanding Kierkegaard was to know that he was foremost a polemicist. This view was probably the result of the predominance of the *Kirkekampen* in Scharling's mind, and that of most theologians like him.

129. A. F. Schiødte, *Om de dialektiske Grundbegreber hos Søren Kierkegaard* (Copenhagen, 1874), pp. iv–v.

In the little space he permitted himself the author was unable to expound greatly on his assertions, but he did point out that in place of Kierkegaard's "faith and reason" *(Tro og Forstand)* Brøchner had substituted "faith and knowledge" *(Tro og Viden),* and had approached Kierkegaard with his own preconceived assumptions. According to Schiødte, Kierkegaard never pitted faith and knowledge against one another, but he did distinguish between faith and reason.[130] Schiødte's observation actually applies to a great many of the writings of the "Tro og Viden" Controversy; in most of these the terms "knowledge" and "reason" were used synonymously and interchangeably. In setting faith against "science" *(Videnskab)* in some of his works, continued Schiødte, Kierkegaard was alluding to the prevailing Hegel-oriented philosophy of the time, which he called the pure immanent science as opposed to something transcendent. This is evident, for instance, in *Concept of Anxiety.*[131]

The rest of the essay is a lively rebuttal of many misconceptions about Kierkegaard's paradox generated by the debate over faith and knowledge. In Schiødte's view, paradox simply does not fall within the domain of reason *(Forstanden).* This flies in the face of Brøchner's criticism that paradox is "an intellectualism"; it also preempts all attacks on the concept from a purely rational standpoint. Schiødte insisted, moreover, that Kierkegaard does not teach "faith in nonsense," and that it is a gross error to label his position anti-philosophical or anti-scientific (except in the sense of anti-Hegelian). In fact it is both philosophical and theological.[132] Schiødte held Nielsen responsible for identifying the Kierkegaardian paradox with faith in nonsense. He specifically mentioned an 1857 book by Nielsen, in which the author equates the paradox with such a faith in nonsense.[133] This confirms Nielsen's discomfort with the concept throughout the 1850s.

Schiødte's essay brought to a close a public debate over faith and

130. Ibid., pp. vi and vii. In fact his point about Kierkegaard never having opposed faith and knowledge is not accurate; see note 4 above.

131. Ibid., p. vi. 132. Ibid., pp. 9, 10, and 12.

133. See Rasmus Nielsen, *Philosophiske Propædeutik i Grundtræk* (Copenhagen, 1857), p. 80. Schiødte's attack on paradox as faith in nonsense calls to mind an amusing article by Henry E. Allison that first appeared in *The Review of Metaphysics* (March, 1967), entitled "Christianity and Nonsense"; it represented an interpretation of Kierkegaard's *Postscript* from a Wittgensteinian analytic point of view. Nearly a hundred years earlier, a simple pastor from Aarhus had seen through such linguistic sophisms. For a reprint of the article, see *Kierkegaard: A Collection of Critical Essays,* ed. Josiah Thompson (New York: Anchor Books, 1972), pp. 289-323.

knowledge that had preoccupied Scandinavian professors, intellectuals, and theologians across the board for nearly ten years. Once again, as with the *Kirkekampen,* momentous issues were raised only to be left unresolved. At the center of this debate was Rasmus Nielsen, not an original thinker by any standard. His lack of clarity about his intellectual objectives, the successive and sometimes confusing phases of his philosophical and religious development, and the oppressive eclecticism characterizing his voluminous and pedantic writings, did not present his contemporaries with a very appealing picture to admire, much less emulate. Consequently, Nielsen remained a solitary figure despite the sustained attention his problematic writings received, and the responses they provoked.

In view of where he finally ended (Grundtvigianism), and the crooked road he followed to get there, it may be irrelevant, if not misleading, to speak of Nielsen in retrospect as having been, at one time, a follower of Kierkegaard, a Kierkegaardian. It would be equally misleading, and indeed erroneous, to deny the presence, throughout his many works, of nondescript Kierkegaardian threads that were woven into and out of his thinking all along. The constant direct references to Kierkegaard, strewn in most of his books, articles, and lectures from 1849 well into the 1870s, are themselves an indication of the extent to which Nielsen was preoccupied with the man at practically every turn of his own peculiar development. In fact this preoccupation assumed the form of a relentless wrestling with particular Kierkegaardian concepts, notably the paradox.

If applying the adjective "Kierkegaardian" to Nielsen seems inappropriate, then "pseudo-Kierkegaardian" might be deemed pure affectation. However, in the context of tracing the reception of Kierkegaard, the term serves a useful purpose. Given the extent to which Nielsen invoked Kierkegaard in his writings, the running parallelism he tried to erect between his own evolving philosophy and certain features of Kierkegaard's thought—such as the category of subjectivity—the often deliberate opportunism marking his appeals to or criticisms of Kierkegaard, the relative ease with which he substituted one concept for another to suit the demands of his increasingly contradictory positions, and the well-known history of his onetime close association with Kierkegaard personally, then "pseudo-Kierkegaardian" presents itself as a highly suitable description. More important than all these reasons for designating Nielsen a "pseudo-Kierkegaardian" may be the conscious or subconscious identification his critics kept making between him and Kierkegaard, certainly between specific ingredients in his philosophy and a Kierkegaardian influence that suggested itself unavoidably. It is as though these adversaries of Nielsen recognized in him—rightly or wrongly—a continuation of the kind of philosophy, initially encountered in Kierkegaard, that had produced in them a profound discomfort, not to say outright hostility. It is as though they regarded Nielsen as the embodiment of an unsettling Kierkegaardian spirit they wished to stifle, or at least to curtail. In reality, they were only doing battle with pseudo-Kierkegaard; however, the fortunes of the true Kierkegaard and his legacy were inevitably caught in the crossfire and affected by the fallout.

It is not surprising that Nielsen, who wrote many books in later life, never again received the kind of attention he got during the "Tro og Viden" Controversy. The reason is simple; people took serious notice of his writings in the 1860s and felt challenged by their controversial positions mainly because of the links these works evoked with a far more novel and potent set of themes that were in the air and only slowly beginning to have an impact on the intellectual and spiritual concerns of the times: the themes of Kierkegaard. The debate over "Tro og Viden" in Scandinavia signaled the last gasp of a theological-philosophical order that was fast giving way to the new age of positivism. Seen in this light, Nielsen represented a bold yet ultimately clumsy attempt to uphold the old order. His error was that he fought the new forces by trying to assimilate them, employing in the process flawed devices like "mystery" and "wonder" to smooth over the rough edges of disagreement. Furthermore, he did this while at the same time pathetically clinging to his pet dualism. Nielsen lacked the crucial Kierkegaardian qualities of existential depth, decisiveness, and consistency: the ability to adopt, and stick to, a carefully formulated critique of the age that, through the very nature of its personal-existential anchor, would be able to stand up to the counteroffensive of that age. Instead, Nielsen wavered and wanted to have it both ways. As he had done during the *Kirkekampen,* when he tried to support Kierkegaard without angering Martensen and the Church hierarchy, so now, with the dispute over faith and knowledge, he erected a "both-and" position on the issues that inevitably landed him in trouble. In the end his critics were correct about the charge of self-contradiction.

Yet these very same critics shared with Nielsen a tendency abhorrent to Kierkegaard: the Hegelian urge to mediate and reconcile opposites abstractly and ideationally. If in Germany Left- and Right-Hegelians were bitter enemies, in Denmark they seem to have combined forces against Nielsen, who himself had started as a Right-Hegelian and never really broke out of that mold. In other words, the "Tro og Viden" Controversy was, on one level at least, an extended exercise in inter-Hegelian squabbling. Nielsen found himself in the awkward and unenviable position of having to do battle on two fronts against Left- and Right-Hegelians, and this was due principally to the Kierkegaardian "contamination" that both sides detected in his philosophy. Also, old and current professorial rivalries at the University between Martensen and Nielsen, and between Nielsen and Brøchner, must not be overlooked as a contributing factor.

Where does all this leave Kierkegaard? Where did he actually stand on the question of the relation between faith and knowledge? In the *Kirkekampen,* Kierkegaard's involvement had been direct, whereas this time it was indirect, allowing greater room for misrepresentation and abuse. A brief consideration of some of the problems the debate raises with respect to Kierkegaard's own position is indicated.

One may be tempted to dismiss the entire debate as nothing more than a futile exercise in verbal acrobatics, since it seems to have involved merely plenty of word switching: knowledge in place of reason, and mystery in place of paradox. Actually, these terminological differences are not as trivial as they may sound, and ought to be situated in the historical context in which they arose. As a fundamental reaction primarily against Hegel, Kierkegaard preferred to formulate the problem not so much in terms of faith and reason in the abstract, but rather as the relation between existence (the authentic domain of faith) and pure thought (reflection).[134] For Kierkegaard the question of faith can be approached satisfactorily only if it is approached *existentially*, as pertaining to the life of the individual believer. None of the participants in the "Tro og Viden" Controversy did this (with the possible exception of Schiødte, and he only to the extent that he pointed to the proper way fleetingly and from a distance). The debate was thus too skewed in an epistemological direction to bring out the central existential element in faith that Kierkegaard was convinced makes it what it is. The radical novelty of Kierkegaard's approach to the question of faith was lost on that first generation of intellectuals debating the issue after his death. They were all caught up in the epistemological labyrinth of post-Kantian German philosophy. This significant historical

---

134. James Collins, "Faith and Reflection in Kierkegaard," in *A Kierkegaard Critique,* p. 141.

fact helps to explain, in part, the delay experienced by Kierkegaard's existential emphasis in making its impact on the European philosophical and religious scenes.

It would be incorrect to apply Brandes's charge of "anti-rationalism," leveled against Nielsen, to Kierkegaard's conception of faith. For Kierkegaard, faith was neither anti-rational, nor irrational, nor a-rational; it was *supra-rational,* above reason. Brøchner comes closest to comprehending this when he speaks of the subordination of reason to faith in Kierkegaard. The two realms of faith and reason are distinct, and are hierarchically related. Moreover, faith is never attained through rational demonstration. Reason, therefore, has definite limitations, and Kierkegaard agrees with Nielsen on this point. However, the distinctiveness of the two realms does not result in a dualism, and the limitations of reason do not imply that the believer is irrational. By performing his "leap of faith," the believer does not abandon his reason. He retains it in a submissive state in which it relinquishes itself totally and obediently to the dictates of faith. Thus the sphere of faith enjoys its own thought content and understandability.[135] On this point Kierkegaard's position is not unlike the *credo ut intelligam* of Anselm, Aquinas, and the Scholastics: understanding follows faith, and faith is arrived at independently of the understanding.[136] Far from erecting a dualism, Kierkegaard ultimately aspires to a harmony of faith and reason on faith's terms, but not to a Hegelian mediation on reason's terms.

A peculiar feature of the "Tro og Viden" Controversy was that all those taking part, once again with the exception of Schiødte, were opposed, in one form or another, to the paradox. One may view the debate as a general war from all sides, including Nielsen, on Kierkegaard's concept of paradox. There was something about the paradox that profoundly agitated mid-nineteenth-century Scandinavian intellectuals of every ideological strain. In some cases Kierkegaard was named as the source of the troublesome concept and criticized directly; in others, such as the attacks

---

135. Ibid., pp. 149–50. See also N. H. Søe, "Kierkegaard's Doctrine of the Paradox," in *A Kierkegaard Critique,* p. 221.

136. See the sections pertaining to St. Thomas in Cornelio Fabro's "Faith and Reason in Kierkegaard's Dialectic," in *A Kierkegaard Critique,* pp. 156–206. See also James Collins, *The Mind of Kierkegaard,* pp. 264–68. Louis Dupré, in *Kierkegaard as Theologian,* p. 142, says that Kierkegaard's purpose was basically apologetic, and that he was out to rediscover the compatability of faith with reflection. This places Kierkegaard in the same camp with the Scholastics.

on Nielsen, there were frequent roundabout insinuations about Kierkegaard as the one who had imparted the paradox to Nielsen in the first place. In Nielsen's own convoluted development over the years, the only consistent trend was his gradual renunciation of the Kierkegaardian paradox. For his part, Brøchner was sincerely anxious to separate Kierkegaard from Nielsen's errors, but at the same time he was not in agreement with many of Kierkegaard's views, particularly his concept of paradox, which Brøchner singled out for special criticism.

For an age desperately striving after rational clarity, comprehensive wholeness, and harmonious unities in every field of human endeavor, and among the fields themselves, the Kierkegaardian paradox, with its defiance of reason and its suggestion of absurdity, was anathema. Nobody wanted it. Yet nobody made the effort to probe beneath the surface to discover for himself Kierkegaard's reasons for espousing it, and the manner by which it operated in the life of the person of faith. Such a difficult investigation might have yielded confusing results, for in some instances Kierkegaard's use of paradox is without question against reason *(contra rationem)*. In the vast majority of instances, however, including the more important ones, the paradox for Kierkegaard signifies beyond or above reason *(super rationem)*, and thus falls in the same category as faith.[137] Brøchner was perhaps right about Kierkegaard's paradox being ultimately "an intellectualism," but that is because it too is singularly the product of its times and bound up with the Hegel-dominated philosophical context of the early and mid-nineteenth century. Unfortunately, it and other elements of Kierkegaard's thought were not given adequate exposure and a fair hearing on the platform of the "Tro og Viden" Controversy. This fact, more than the inconclusiveness of the debates themselves, renders the Controversy a historical disappointment.

137. Per Lønning, "Kierkegaard's 'Paradox'," in *Orbis Litterarum*, vol. X, ed. Steffen Steffensen and Hans Sörensen (Copenhagen, 1955), pp. 157 and 162. See also Søe, "Kierkegaard's Doctrine of the Paradox," pp. 209 and 219–20.

6 The Biographical-Psychological Approach and Its Perils

Georg Brandes and Criticism as Suppression

Two important developments for the future of Kierkegaard scholarship were taking place in the 1860s and early 1870s, in conjunction with the "Tro og Viden" Controversy. A preliminary attempt was being made to gather, edit, and publish Kierkegaard's journals and private papers, and the first full-length German translations of some of his works were starting to make their appearance.

Shortly after Kierkegaard died, his papers were moved to the home of his brother-in-law, J. C. Lund, where they remained for about two years. While there, they were catalogued by Kierkegaard's nephew, Henrik Lund, the same person who had caused the scene at the funeral. Lund did not complete his catalog, and in 1858 the papers were transferred to Aalborg in Jutland to be in the custody of Søren's brother, Bishop Peter Christian Kierkegaard.[1] Seven years later, in 1865, the bishop engaged a young man and former newspaper editor to be his assistant and treasurer of the diocese at Aalborg. This was Hans Peter Barfod (1834–92), who

---

1. See "Translator's Preface" to *JP*, vol. I, p. xv. For an account of Henrik Lund's intervention at Kierkegaard's funeral, see Chapter 3 above.

was also assigned the task of arranging Kierkegaard's papers for eventual publication. He completed Lund's catalog, and in the fall of 1867 received permission to prepare the material for the printers.[2]

P. C. Kierkegaard had begun to read through his brother's papers following Denmark's disastrous war with Prussia in 1864. He became convinced of the need to publish them, although he felt himself too tired and busy to carry out the work singlehandedly. He had been bishop for eight years, during which time his life was hectic because of his many duties, and his health was weakened as a result. Barfod was thus hired to accomplish the job that Peter felt would have to be done sooner or later.[3] He had never been on good terms with his brother, and he had criticized his works in public on more than one occasion. Back in 1849, for example, during a lecture he gave at the Roskilde Clergy Convention in Ringsted, Peter compared Martensen's newly published *Christelige Dogmatik* with Kierkegaard's writings by declaring that while Martensen's book stood for "sober-mindedness" [*Besindigheden*], Kierkegaard's works advocated "enthusiasm" [*Ekstasen*].[4] Søren Kierkegaard never forgot this, and the very journals whose publication Peter was now about to sponsor contained several entries critical of his character and religious disposition. Peter was a peculiar blend of stiff orthodoxy and Grundtvigianism that considerably irritated his brother. He was also a bishop in the same Church that Kierkegaard did combat with at the end of his life.[5] Peter did not take part in either the *Kirkekampen* or the debate over "Tro og Viden." The first event embarrassed him, as his oration at Søren's funeral reveals, and the second does not seem to have concerned him much.

As Barfod set to work on Kierkegaard's papers in 1865, he soon discovered a sealed and undated manuscript in which Kierkegaard states unequivocally that it is his wish that Rasmus Nielsen take charge of publishing his papers after his death. Barfod brought it to the bishop's attention, who felt consternation at the unwanted discovery. Nielsen and Henrik

---

2. On Barfod see *DBL*, 2d ed., vol. 2, pp. 156–57. See also Hong's preface to *JP*, vol. I, pp. xvff.

3. Carl Weltzer, *Peter og Søren Kierkegaard*, vol. II, pp. 311–12.

4. For a translation of Peter's speech see T. H. Croxall, *Glimpses and Impressions of Kierkegaard*, pp. 118–19. See also the entire section on Peter and Søren, pp. 116–29, which includes excerpts from Kierkegaard's journals relating to his brother.

5. Otto Holmgaard, *Extaticus: Søren Kierkegaards sidste Kamp, derunder hans Forhold til Broderen* (Copenhagen: Nyt Nordisk Forlag, 1967), p. 9.

Lund had been angling separately throughout the 1860s for possession of the papers and the rights to publish them.[6] Peter was not an admirer of Nielsen. In 1849 he had made some unfavorable remarks about Nielsen at the Roskilde Convention; he was clearly unimpressed by *Evangelietroen og den moderne Bevidsthed*, which Nielsen published that same year. Nielsen's intimacy with Søren at the time did little to endear him to Peter. In 1859, at a gathering in honor of the queen, Nielsen and Peter Kierkegaard clashed publicly over Søren's views on faith, on suffering, and on the established Church, with Nielsen finally conceding grudgingly that Peter had more occasion to delve into Søren's papers at home than he did.[7] During the 1860s, Nielsen's anti-theological pronouncements in connection with the "Tro og Viden" Controversy discredited him further in Peter's eyes, and it was a long time before his eventual move in a Grundtvigian direction rehabilitated him with the bishop.

For these reasons Peter decided in 1865 to conceal the inconvenient manuscript and proceed with his own plans to publish Kierkegaard's papers. Thus the existence of the document remained a secret for ten years, that is, until two large volumes of the papers had been published by Barfod under Peter's supervision, and the third was almost ready for printing. In 1875 Peter donated the papers to the University library in Copenhagen, where they were placed for a time in the care of an archivist named Thorsen before being moved to their permanent home in the Royal Library. At the same time he wrote Rasmus Nielsen informing him of the manuscript and explaining why he had deliberately overlooked it. Peter's explanation made no reference to his feelings about Nielsen except to say that based on certain liberties Nielsen had taken in 1849 and 1850 in his use of some of Kierkegaard's views, especially those regarding the accounts of miracles in the Old and New Testaments, Peter could not bring himself to comply with the instructions of the manuscript, which he apparently felt had been the product of a temporary phase in his brother's development.[8] Peter took sick before the letter to Nielsen was

6. Weltzer, *Peter og Søren Kierkegaard*, vol. II, pp. 311 and 317. Some of Lund's correspondence with Peter about Kierkegaard's papers is reproduced in Weltzer's book. On Nielsen and the papers see also P. A. Rosenberg, *Rasmus Nielsen, Nordens Filosof*, pp. 43-44.

7. Otto Holmgaard, *Peter Christian Kierkegaard: Grundtvigs Lærling* (Copenhagen: Rosenkilde og Bagger, 1953), p. 93.

8. The letter from P. C. Kierkegaard to Rasmus Nielsen is dated "February 23 or 25, 1875" and has the heading "confidential" at the top. It is published, along with three other letters from Peter to Nielsen, by Ernst Heilmann in *Søren Kierkegaards hidtil fortiede*

finished, and the task of completing it fell to Barfod, who expressed the bishop's regret for the incident and asked, on his behalf, for Nielsen's forgiveness.[9]

At first Nielsen was naturally very upset, but after the initial shock wore off and the apology was repeated, he pardoned the bishop.[10] Nevertheless, he refused Peter's offer to take over the task of editing and publishing the remainder of Kierkegaard's papers from Barfod, who was quitting after ten years of working for the bishop.[11] Nielsen, however, had little ground for feeling insulted by this offer even though it came ten years late. Barfod and the bishop had been correct in their decision to bypass Nielsen and to regard Kierkegaard's request—written most likely in 1848, soon after he made Nielsen's acquaintance—as indicative of a state of mind in which he was convinced his death was imminent. Given the subsequent erosion of Kierkegaard's intimacy with Nielsen, the innumerable critical references to him in later journal entries, and Nielsen's own philosophical and theological development in the 1860s as pertains to the "Tro og Viden" Controversy, the bishop's decision was fully justified, although the handling of the matter might have been more tactfully executed.[12]

---

testamentariske Villie angaaende hans literære Efterladenskaber (Copenhagen: Bertelsen, 1909), pp. 9–13.

9. Ibid., pp. 12–13. This conclusion to Peter's letter, written by Barfod, is dated March 5. For the excerpt from Peter's diary that mentions this correspondence with Nielsen see Weltzer, *Peter og Søren Kierkegaard*, pp. 338–39.

10. Peter repeated his apology to Nielsen in two letters dated April 24, 1875 and November 10 and 11, 1879; see Heilmann, *Søren Kierkegaards hidtil . . .*, pp. 14–16. For an indication of Nielsen's frustration at the new revelation see Weltzer, *Peter og Søren*, pp. 340–42.

11. See A. B. Drachmann, "Søren Kierkegaards Papirer, I," in *Tilskueren*, I (January–June 1910), p. 142.

12. Ibid., pp. 141–42. Drachmann, who was one of the editors of the first and second editions of Kierkegaard's *Samlede Værker* (Collected works), takes Peter's side in the issue of the problematic manuscript, but says the entire incident was blown out of proportion by both parties. He admits that Peter's conduct, though basically sound, was lacking in propriety. Drachmann's position is diametrically opposite to Heilmann's, which is expressed in his brief introduction to the four letters from Peter to Nielsen that he published in 1909. Heilmann claims that Peter's conscience bothered him, and this caused him to write Nielsen about the manuscript (*Søren Kierkegaards Hidtil fortiede testamentariske Villie angaaende hans literære Efterladenskaber*, pp. 4–5). He adds that, had Nielsen been allowed to publish the journals, this would have been in keeping with Kierkegaard's expressed wishes because "hardly any other knew or understood Søren Kierkegaard as R. Nielsen did [!]" (p. 5). Peter, according to Heilmann, knew nothing about the relationship between his brother and Nielsen (p. 5). Of the two scholars, Drachmann is obviously the more accurate historically, and the more faithful to the facts.

It could be argued that, due to his own disagreements with his brother, Peter's sponsorship of the editing and publication of the journals ran potential risks of distortion similar to those he wished to avert by not allowing Nielsen to direct the project. In fact some mishandling of the material in question did occur, but this had less to do with the bishop than with his assistant, Barfod.

Kierkegaard once reflected on the future publisher of his journals and concluded that "anyone could publish my remaining papers."[13] It was Barfod's lot to be that "anyone," and his efforts had both positive and negative effects on early Kierkegaard scholarship. On the beneficial side, Barfod managed to penetrate beyond Kierkegaard's eccentricities and fasten on his abiding significance as few others of his generation were able to do. As the scholar Aage Henriksen has put it, Barfod "possessed a feeling for Kierkegaard's greatness, even in its more bizarre expressions, a feeling which was foreign to most of his contemporaries."[14] He devoted over ten years of his life to Kierkegaard's personal papers, which constituted in itself a unique scholarly privilege and experience. Barfod also made a lasting contribution to Kierkegaard studies by soliciting information and letters from a number of Kierkegaard's acquaintances and schoolmates. The response he received was impressive and provided him with broad new sources on which to base his notes to the first volume of the papers. Every scrap of information from these people who knew Kierkegaard was invaluable, and the letters to Barfod have become a permanent part of the Søren Kierkegaard Archives at the Royal Library in Copenhagen. They supplement Kierkegaard's own memoirs of his early youth, presenting us with a wealth of anecdotal material that has helped shape our image of Kierkegaard the person.[15] We learn too from some of these letters about Kierkegaard's final days at the hospital and about his death.[16]

Despite Barfod's sensitivity to Kierkegaard's genius and the dedication and precision with which he went about his work on the papers, his record as the first editor of Kierkegaard's journals will always remain

13. *Papirer*, IX A 228. The translation is not found in Howard Hong's edition of the *Journals and Papers*, but comes from his article "The Kierkegaard Papers," in *Tri-Quarterly*, no. 16 (Fall 1969), p. 118.
14. Aage Henriksen, *Methods and Results of Kierkegaard Studies in Scandinavia*, p. 16.
15. Ibid., p. 21. Henriksen observes that "among the enterprising Barfod's many ideas the recovery of this important psychological material is the only thing which later enquirers have been ready to appreciate."
16. See Robert J. Widenmann's article on Kierkegaard's death in *Kierkegaard as a Person*, vol. 12 of *Bibliotheca Kierkegaardiana* (1983), p. 176.

tarnished in the eyes of posterity by inexcusable blemishes. His gravest fault was the utter carelessness he displayed in his handling of the actual documents themselves: he sent the original copies to the printers; he underlined, corrected, cut, and pasted various sections of the papers in the process of editing them; he deleted or changed words and omitted whole sentences in places; he even lost a few of the earliest manuscripts in the confusion.[17] Barfod also adopted a chronological rather than a thematic strategy in his editing. This necessitated determining the precise dates of entries, which was not an easy job since Kierkegaard often did not bother to attach a date to what he was writing. The entries, however, were arranged by Kierkegaard in thirty-six successive notebooks, thus facilitating the dating process somewhat; nevertheless, Barfod committed grave errors in chronology that were subsequently discovered and corrected. The first two volumes of Barfod's edition covering the years 1833–43, which he called Kierkegaard's *Efterladte Papirer* (Posthumous papers), appeared in 1869. In the Foreword, Barfod defended his plan favoring a chronological compilation over a thematic one.[18] Apparently he had in mind arranging the material for an extensive biography of Kierkegaard that was yet to be written.

Among the people in 1869 replying to Barfod's requests for additional information about Kierkegaard was Emil Boesen, Kierkegaard's close friend and now the archdeacon of Aarhus. Boesen urged Barfod not to publish any attacks on Martensen that might be among Kierkegaard's papers. He argued that everything Kierkegaard wished to say publicly about Martensen had already appeared in print and was enough.[19] Many reviewers of the first two volumes of the *Efterladte Papirer* echoed similar sentiments and criticized Barfod for publishing material that was offensive to people still living.[20] As a result Barfod felt compelled to defend his policy of not omitting any references to those persons with whom Kierkegaard had had a less than smooth relationship—for example, Goldschmidt of the *Corsair,* and Regine. He maintained simply that his timing was fair to the reputations of these individuals since it allowed them to

---

17. Drachmann, "Søren Kierkegaards Papirer, I," pp. 143–44. See also Henriksen, *Methods and Results of Kierkegaard Studies in Scandinavia,* p. 17.

18. H. P. Barfod, "Udgiverens Forord," in *Søren Kierkegaards Efterladte Papirer,* vols. I–II: 1833–43 (Copenhagen, 1869), pp. X–XII. See also Henriksen, *Methods and Results,* pp. 18–19.

19. Weltzer, *Peter og Søren Kierkegaard,* p. 323.

20. Henriksen, *Methods and Results,* pp. 19–20.

speak out for themselves. Rejecting the notion of omissions for so-called diplomatic purposes would avoid creating a distorted picture of Kierkegaard's personal development.[21]

The appearance in 1869 of the first installment of Kierkegaard's journals aroused renewed interest in the man and his achievements. Now, at last, it was possible to peer behind the perplexing works and catch an unadulterated glimpse of the private life and inner thoughts of their author. It became quickly apparent that the works and the life were, to a considerable degree, organically interrelated, so that an understanding of one was often enhanced by a knowledge of the other. The journals constituted the indispensable key to unlocking this complex interdependence. Furthermore, whatever exterior eccentricity and enigmatic behavior had been displayed before the inhabitants of Copenhagen by Kierkegaard during his life, were now, it seemed, partially accounted for by revelations of a gloomy childhood, the overarching shadow of a stern father, and an intensely introspective upbringing. As the journals were gradually converted into public property throughout the 1870s, it became almost impossible henceforth to write anything about Kierkegaard without recourse to them in one form or another. Thus was born what can be described as the biographical-psychological approach to Kierkegaard and his oeuvre, and along with it came the strong temptation to dwell on the strange and morbid in his life as a means to explaining away the works and purposely compromising the inherent autonomy of certain universal themes in them that would otherwise be perfectly capable of standing their ground independently of the idiosyncrasies of their author. In other words, the sensational aspects of Kierkegaard's personal life and the inner workings of his mind, as delineated in his journals, became convenient tools in the hands of those who wished to deflect attention from the substantive significance of his works, thereby undermining their potential intellectual and spiritual influence.

One of the earliest examples of this form of abuse came at the hands of Erik Bøgh (1822-99), a Danish playwright and poet who also became a theater director and newspaper editor.[22] In the preface to a short book

21. See the preface to the third volume of H. P. Barfod's edition of *Søren Kierkegaards Efterladte Papirer,* vol. III: 1844-46 (Copenhagen, 1872), pp. xii-xiii. See also Henriksen, *Methods and Results,* pp. 20-21. Drachmann concludes his discussion of the pros and cons of Barfod's work by declaring that on balance his merits outweighed his shortcomings; see "Søren Kierkegaards Papirer, I," p. 144.

22. On Erik Bøgh see *DBL,* vol. IV, 2d ed. (Copenhagen, 1934), pp. 441-44.

written in 1870 and given the caustic title *Søren Kierkegaard og St. Sørens-Dyrkelsen* [S. K. and the Saint Søren Cult], Bøgh admits he had once in his early years admired Kierkegaard.²³ The remainder of the book, however, seethes with venom. Basically, Bøgh felt indignant at the rising interest in Kierkegaard following the 1869 publication of two volumes of his journals. He belonged to a class of Danish writers whose literary snobbery prevented them from viewing Kierkegaard as anything but an upstart in their ranks. What is noteworthy about Bøgh is the "clinical" and pseudo-medical vocabulary he employs to describe in graphic detail Kierkegaard's "diseased" condition: "Søren Kierkegaard was not merely a man of genius, but he was unfortunately a sick man as well. Those of his works published by himself during his own life witness to an abundance of both parts of his person."²⁴ Bøgh relies on revelations in the journals for his descriptions, but says condescendingly, at one point, that his "hatred for the disease is certainly not hatred for the diseased person. . . ."²⁵ Yet his depiction of Kierkegaard throughout is anything but attractive, and portrays a very sick man both physiologically and psychologically: "Søren Kierkegaard was, as is well known, both a hypochondriac and an affected man."²⁶ He also speaks of Kierkegaardian "insensitivity," "vanity," and "self-worship" as character traits in his subject, adding harshly, a little later, that Kierkegaard's "entire intellectual career was a confused sisyphus-battle in order to reflect the fervor within himself. . . . [He] drove his melancholy to the edge of madness!"²⁷

Concerning the journals, on which he repeatedly fell back for information about Kierkegaard's private life, Bøgh dismissed them strangely as "in general unreliable. . . . Now they are an expression of self-deception, and now an experiment in the deception of others. Most often it is both parts together."²⁸ He reserved some praise for Barfod's efforts in gathering and publishing Kierkegaard's posthumous papers, and urged those future authors, who would seek to write Kierkegaard's biography, to be grateful to Barfod for his indefatigability and precision.²⁹

Bøgh's treatise foreshadowed some of the problems that would arise from the increasing pursuit of the biographical-psychological avenue to the understanding of Kierkegaard. Once the journals were out, this be-

---

23. Erik Bøgh, *Søren Kierkegaard og St. Sørens-Dyrkelsen* (Copenhagen, 1870), p. v.
24. Ibid., p. 4.   25. Ibid., p. vii.
26. Ibid., p. 6.   27. Ibid., pp. vi, and 4.
28. Ibid., p. 5.   29. Ibid., p. 7.

came the easiest and most popular method to follow when writing about him. The publication of the journals during the 1870s, however, was not the only event that focused renewed attention on Kierkegaard. The appearance of a steady stream of German translations of his works contributed its share to broadening the already heightened interest in Kierkegaard beyond Scandinavia. The journals and the translations complemented each other, which set the stage for a lively flurry of critical and scholarly writing toward the end of the 1870s that encompassed Danes, Norwegians, Swedes, and Germans. It seemed as though the floodgates of serious reception were opening at last—or were they?

The earliest full-length German translation of "a work" by Kierkegaard appeared in 1861; it comprised the first nine *Øjeblikket* articles. A second edition followed in 1864. It was translated anonymously under the conspicuous title *Christentum und Kirche. "Die Gegenwart." Ein ernstes Wort an unsere Zeit, insbesondere an die evangelische Geistlichkeit.* Significantly, the publishing house—Oncken Verlag of Hamburg—was a Baptist center, which may explain the initial scanty response to the work in broader German theological circles. Many German theologians viewed Kierkegaard with suspicion, seeing him as a convenient ally for certain sects interested in subverting the established ecclesiastical order. Nevertheless, in 1862, a young theology student from Schleswig named Christian Hansen published a translation of Kierkegaard's *For Self-Examination* (1851), which he called *Zur Selbstprüfung der Gegenwart empfohlen.* It appeared in a second edition in 1869; further editions followed some years later. Hansen's purpose in selecting and translating this work was to present another side of Kierkegaard from the nonconformist one suggested by *Øjeblikket:* here it is not the polemically contentious Kierkegaard confronting the Church, but the more serene and homiletic Kierkegaard, exhorting his readers to heed the words of Christ and anchor their lives in Scripture. Thus someone in the early 1860s made a conscious attempt to offer German readers a religiously balanced picture of Kierkegaard. The use of the word *"Gegenwart"* (the present) in the translated titles of both works underscores the special interest there was in emphasizing the relevance of Kierkegaard's religious writings to theological concerns in Germany at the time of the translations.[30]

30. For the complete references to these translations and a list of the few and generally insignificant reviews they received, see J. Himmelstrup, *Søren Kierkegaard International Bibliografi,* p. 25.

These translated works illustrate the strictly *theological* preoccupation that the Germans had initially with Kierkegaard. It was not the philosophical implications of his attack on Hegel that first caught their eye, but rather his rejection of speculative theology and his devastating critique of Christendom and the mediocrity of a worldly church. This resonated favorably in many quarters, notably Tübingen, where it was taken up by the theologian Johann Tobias Beck (1804-78). Beck was professor of systematic theology at Tübingen from 1843 until his death. He possessed a certain personal magnetism and managed, during the period he was there, to gather a sizable following among the students. He founded no definite theological school, yet his appeal stemmed precisely from the streak of nonconformity in his theology, which expressed itself in the dim view he took of the ecclesiastical hierarchy and of modern culture in general. In his sermons and letters he lashed out at the contemporary theology of his day, particularly its Hegelian speculative features and its affinities with Schleiermacher. The outspoken confrontations he repeatedly had with various church officials derived their inspiration from Kierkegaard: as Karl Barth informs us, "there is a direct link with Kierkegaard, and indeed with Kierkegaard of the last years, who was the only distinguished theologian of the time of whom Beck had a good opinion."[31] In this way Beck served as an agent for the dissemination of Kierkegaard at Tübingen during the 1860s and 1870s. Beck's impact on German theology, however, remained minimal and diminished drastically after his death. Sweden and Finland were the only countries where his influence continued to be strongly felt.[32]

Of Beck's students, one in particular became intensely fascinated by Kierkegaard and decided to delve deeper into his writings. His name was Albert Bärthold (dates unknown), and he came from Magdeburg and later became a pastor in Halberstadt. Bärthold felt so drawn to Kierkegaard's works that he resolved to learn Danish and made a few trips to Denmark. It is to this little-known man that we owe scores of the earliest

31. See Karl Barth, *Protestant Theology in the Nineteenth Century: Its Background and History*, trans. Brian Cozens and John Bowden (Valley Forge, Pennsylvania: Judson Press, 1975), p. 618.

32. For additional information on Beck see [*ADB*], vol. 46/supplement (Berlin, 1902), pp. 297-302; and *Neue Deutsche Biographie* [*NDB*], ed. Franz Schnabel and Walter Goetz, vol. I (Berlin: Duncker & Humbolt, 1953), p. 703. See also Karl Barth, *Protestant Theology*, pp. 616-24. Barth discloses that his father, Fritz Barth, was one of those who manifested signs of Beck's influence in his life-work (p. 622).

German translations of Kierkegaard, along with some noteworthy commentaries on them.[33] For instance, in 1872 Bärthold published his first translation, consisting of selections from *Practice in Christianity*. In a short note at the beginning he referred to Kierkegaard as one who purified the spiritual atmosphere from all illusions and was the wise counselor.[34] Every year thereafter, during the 1870s, Bärthold put out a translation, a commentary, or both.

There were others besides Bärthold who were thinking and writing about Kierkegaard in those years, and who still had the acrimony of the *Kirkekampen* on their mind. The appearance in 1872 of the third volume of Barfod's edition of the journals spurred fresh interest in Kierkegaard. The volume covered the years 1844-46 and contained, among other things, a large section on Goldschmidt of the *Corsair* and some interesting references to Bishop Mynster.[35] These latter drew the attention of Martensen, who was curious to discover Kierkegaard's attitudes toward the deceased bishop prior to the *Kirkekampen*. In a letter he wrote to Bishop Otto Laub of Viborg informing him of the volume's appearance, Martensen explained Kierkegaard's shift from admiration to bitterness as having been the result of not receiving the expected acknowledgment of his talents from Mynster. He had reacted therefore by ruthlessly caricaturing the bishop, a behavior that Martensen labeled euphemistically as a "highly remarkable psychological phenomenon." In Martensen's opinion, Kier-

---

33. Unfortunately, we have only scraps of information about Bärthold. They come principally from a section written by Barfod of the foreword to *Søren Kierkegaards Efterladte Papirer*, vol. V (1848), ed. H. P. Barfod and H. Gottsched (Copenhagen, 1880), pp. vii–viii. Bärthold remains a neglected figure in the history of Kierkegaard's German reception. Two possible routes could be pursued by scholars in their search for more clues about this elusive person, but neither is very promising. The first would entail investigating the parishes in Halberstadt for any surviving records of his life and work there. Halberstadt, in what not too long ago was East Germany, was subjected to heavy allied aerial bombardment during the Second World War and was badly destroyed, including, probably, any such records that might have existed. The second route would involve searching the archives at Tübingen for documents relating to his student days there as a pupil of J. T. Beck. What useful information this would yield regarding Bärthold's early excitement about Kierkegaard remains to be seen. One thing seems certain, however: our knowledge of Bärthold's personal life is not likely to increase substantially, and vital material that might have made a difference appears to be irretrievably lost.

34. Albert Bärthold, editor and translator, *Einladung und Aergerniss. Biblische Darstellung und christliche Begriffsbestimmung von Sören Kierkegaard* (Halberstadt, 1872), p. iv.

35. See Barfod, ed., *Søren Kierkegaards Efterladte Papirer*, vol. III, pp. 219ff. on Goldschmidt; pp. 548–56 and 814–20 on Mynster.

kegaard had greatly overestimated himself and regarded his understanding of Christianity as the exclusive truth.[36] Laub wrote back saying he read with great interest, though without satisfaction, Kierkegaard's soliloquy-like statements on his relation with Mynster: "Nothing more than what you said can essentially be added to explain this sad and cheerless reversal."[37] According to Laub, Kierkegaard from the beginning saw Mynster as his ideal, but was repeatedly frustrated in his attempts to communicate with him because of the bishop's unapproachable disposition. The final change in attitude was thus entirely Kierkegaard's and had nothing to do with Mynster's character.[38]

Whatever one might think of Martensen's views on Kierkegaard's beliefs or conduct, one cannot accuse him of complete unfairness. This becomes evident when we examine Martensen's massive three-volume *Christelige Ethik* (1871–78). It seems that during the fifteen years between the death of his adversary in the *Kirkekampen* and the publication in 1871 of the first volume of his huge work, Martensen had come to accept the validity of some of Kierkegaard's fundamental concepts. In fact he devotes no less than twenty-five pages of his book to a critical discussion of Kierkegaard's emphasis on the individual.[39] This "spokesman for individualism," as Kierkegaard is designated, opposes the individual to the universal or the abstract realm of ideas. In so doing he reenacts, in modern terms, the medieval controversy between realists and nominalists, the opposition between Leibniz and Spinoza, and the differences between Hegel and Schelling.[40] Martensen sides with Kierkegaard in his battle against all forms of pantheism resulting from the dilution of the individual through concepts, and he accepts Kierkegaard's emphasis on concrete personal existence as a basis for an ethico-religious interpretation of Christianity.[41] Already these represent substantial concessions to Kierkegaard by the principal spokesman for Hegelian speculative theology in Denmark. Martensen, however, stops short of endorsing Kierkegaard's anti-church and anti-communal positions; he maintains that while the focus on the individ-

---

36. See Martensen's letter to Laub dated December 30, 1872, in F. L. Mynster and G. Schepelein, *Biskop Otto Laubs Levnet,* part I: 1855–82 (Copenhagen, 1886), pp. 298–99.
37. Laub's letter to Martensen dated January 11, 1873 in ibid., p. 302.
38. Ibid., pp. 303–5. Martensen replied to Laub in a letter dated January 13 in which he agreed with his friend and concluded that despite Kierkegaard's early liking for Mynster, he had even then begun to exhibit signs of antagonism. See pp. 306–7.
39. See H. L. Martensen, *Den Christelige Ethik,* vol. I (Copenhagen, 1871), pp. 275–300, and 383–90.
40. Ibid., pp. 277–80.   41. Ibid., p. 279 and 298.

ual is sound, it need not conflict with the social dimension. He posits a "higher unity of universalism and individualism, of idea and existence."[42] For him, Kierkegaard's corrective to the excesses of abstract idealism itself requires some moderating correction.[43]

Like his *Christelige Dogmatik* of 1849, Martensen's *Christelige Ethik* was promptly translated into German. Martensen, unlike Kierkegaard, always saw to it that German translations were made of his works. This difference, coupled with his personal connections among German theologians and prelates and his enthusiasm for the most renowned figures in the German theological tradition, helped spread his name to German readers with an interest in theology much quicker than Kierkegaard's. When the brand of speculative theology he embraced exhausted its appeal in Germany at the beginning of the twentieth century, his name swiftly faded into oblivion and Kierkegaard's began to emerge on the scene and gain attention. Therefore the brief and straightforward account of Kierkegaard's thought, which is presented in Martensen's *Christelige Ethik* of 1871, becomes all the more valuable, given the circulation of the work in Germany and the concomitant scarcity of material on or by Kierkegaard in German at the time.

Attitudes toward Kierkegaard's role in the *Kirkekampen* continued to diverge sharply during the early 1870s, and the stigma of those final years of his life did not cease to haunt his intellectual reputation or determine the manner in which he was looked upon by people. His name showed up in odd places, but perhaps the most singular context to date was in the third volume of a massive unfinished work of science fiction, of the speculative utopian genre, published in 1872 by none other than F. C. Sibbern, Kierkegaard's old friend and teacher, who died that same year. Sibbern had distanced himself from Kierkegaard during the *Kirkekampen* because he could not comprehend the deeper corrective motives behind Kierkegaard's outburst. He even thought of writing an article against Kierkegaard, but discarded the idea when he saw the torrent of attacks on him that, he felt, said all there was to say.[44] Of particular interest to

42. Ibid., p. 277.
43. For a brief analysis of Martensen's discussion of Kierkegaard in *Christelige Ethik*, see Howard A. Slaatte, "Kierkegaard's Introduction to American Methodists: A Tribute," in *The Drew Gateway*, XXX (spring 1960), pp. 163-64.
44. Letter from Sibbern to an unknown woman dated March 26, 1855, in *Breve til og fra F. C. Sibbern*, vol. II: "Breve fra Sibbern," ed. C. L. N. Mynster (Copenhagen, 1866), p. 224.

Sibbern was the concept of "witness to the truth"—under so much dispute throughout the *Kirkekampen*—which he regarded as having been misrepresented by Kierkegaard in his assault on Mynster.[45]

Years later, in 1869, when the first volumes of the journals appeared, Sibbern wrote Barfod admitting that throughout his long personal association with Kierkegaard he had not detected outward signs of Kierkegaard's internal torments:

> I have not found K. in the least 'lonesome', and would never have applied such an epithet to him. He walked abroad a great deal, visited A. S. Ørsted, who enjoyed his company greatly, but became estranged when K. besmirched Mynster's memory. I can honestly say that he was never heavy and broody in all the long time I have known him, and it was only in the last two or three years of his life that I ceased to see him. To be a cross-bearer, and to preach the cross, are two very different things; the latter one can do to entire satisfaction. In my house we think a lot of K.'s writings.
>
> It astonishes me that one who throughout all the time I have known him hated agitation, should himself become an eager agitator. That makes me realize that a man can carry on a deep broodiness within him alongside much vivacity.[46]

One wonders whether to ascribe Sibbern's myopia to his weak powers of observation or to Kierkegaard's exceptionally clever ability of concealment, or perhaps to both.

Since delivering a series of lectures on politics and religion in 1846 and 1847, Sibbern had been busy at work developing his vision of an ideal futuristic society that would arise from the ashes of the present European one and remedy all the social ills and religious abuses of its predecessor. He produced three volumes in the form of a fictional account of such a utopia where perfect justice would reign, and he gave it the name *Meddelelser af Indholdet af et Skrift fra Aaret 2135* (A report on the content of a writing from the year 2135). The entire project was long-winded, nebulous, and strange. The third volume, appearing in 1872, contained a curious reference to Kierkegaard. In the course of an exchange about Christian witness between the two principal characters, Klitov and Adelaide, the subject of "truth witness" comes up. Klitov

---

45. Ibid., p. 225. See also Poul Kallmoes, *Frederik Christian Sibbern Træk af en Dansk Filosofs Liv og Tænkning* (Copenhagen: Munksgaard, 1946), p. 242.

46. Letter from Sibbern to H. P. Barfod, dated September 19, 1869, quoted in P. A. Heiberg, *Søren Kierkegaard i Barndom og Ungdom* (Copenhagen, 1895), pp. 9–10, and trans. T. H. Croxall in *Glimpses and Impressions of Kierkegaard*, p. 70.

asks Adelaide not to confuse "blood witnesses" *(Blodvidner)* with "truth witnesses" *(Sandhedsvidner):* a person can belong to the latter category without being physically martyred. At this point Sibbern interjects a long footnote relating how once in Copenhagen a man named Kierkegaard had dismally mixed the two categories together. Sibbern wonders in amazement at the brilliant mind that was capable of slandering eminent clergymen like Mynster and Martensen and stooping to such "a miserable level of philistinism." He urges people to remember the earlier Kierkegaard, and to prevent the final unfortunate twist in his development from distorting his previous lofty accomplishments.[47] It is clear that Sibbern never overcame his acute disappointment over the *Kirkekampen*, and this haunted him until his death.[48]

Further south, in Germany, a different and far more sympathetic view of Kierkegaard's position in the *Kirkekampen* was prevailing. In 1873 Bärthold produced German translations of *The Point of View*, "My Position as a Religious Writer in 'Christendom' and My Tactics" (1851), "An Open Letter" (1851), and several of Kierkegaard's last *Fædrelandet* articles, along with some of the replies they provoked. These translations were bound in one volume and interconnected with commentaries and explanations written by the translator.[49] The result was the first attempt of its kind in German to present an integrated organic picture of the crucial years 1848–51 and 1854–55 of Kierkegaard's life, with the aim of supporting his claim, made in *The Point of View*, that he had always been, and remained to the end, a religious author.[50] Bärthold's choice of texts and his accompanying comments reveal several things about him: an in-depth familiarity with Kierkegaard's writings; a posture antagonistic to ecclesiastical officialdom derived, no doubt, from his theology professor J. T. Beck and reinforced by Kierkegaard; an interest in Kierkegaard's uses of the methods of direct and indirect communication; and an emphasis on concrete individual existence as the antidote to all murky collectives or abstractions. From the very outset the collection is given a polemical

47. F. C. Sibbern, *Meddelelser af Indholdet af et Skrift fra Aaret 2135*, in 3 vols.: 1858–72, vol. III (Copenhagen, 1872), pp. 720–21.
48. For more on Sibbern's enigmatic *Skrift fra Aaret 2135* see J. Himmelstrup, *Sibbern, en Monografi*, pp. 197–219; and Kallmoes, *Frederik Christian Sibbern*, p. 59.
49. Albert Bärthold, ed. and trans., *Sören Kierkegaard, Eine Verfasser-Existenz eigner Art: Aus seinen Mittheilungen zusammengestellt* (Halberstadt, 1873).
50. At the end of his book Bärthold asserts that Kierkegaard's last Discourse, "God's Unchangeableness," of August 1, 1855, was written in the style and spirit of the early *Upbuilding Discourses*, which is proof that he had always been a religious author (p. 173).

flavor when Bärthold refers to Kierkegaard as "a strong fortress in the midst of enemy territory."[51] Kierkegaard's readers are asked to approach his works with good intentions and allow "the breath of his spirit" to speak for itself.[52]

Although Bärthold's translations are generally of good quality and faithful to the original, his rendering of *The Point of View* from the 1859 Danish first edition leaves out several sections; the end product thus looks more like extended selections from the work than a full translation. In some places Bärthold adds explanatory notes containing quotations from other works by Kierkegaard, usually for purposes of illustrating transitions from indirect to direct communication that Kierkegaard talks about in *The Point of View*.[53] Following the translation, Bärthold undertakes a survey of the early writings—the aesthetic pseudonymous ones and the *Upbuilding Discourses*—up to and including *Postscript,* after which Kierkegaard commences his religious works proper. The idea is to corroborate Kierkegaard's assertion of a religious intention from the start, and to highlight the centrality of the individual as he moves through the stages of existence toward the religious life. When treating *Postscript,* Bärthold mentions Martensen's cool reception of it in 1849 and Nielsen's subsequent defense.[54] The concern with Kierkegaard's shift in mode of communication leads Bärthold to focus upon two short pieces published in 1851 that display a candid and unconcealed Kierkegaard, far from the circumlocutions of the pseudonyms. The first, about his status as a religious author, appears in *On My Work as an Author,* and belongs strictly to a project for a book Kierkegaard had intended to publish under the title *Armed Neutrality*.[55] The second is an article written for *Fædrelandet* against a certain Andreas Gottlob Rudelbach (1792–1862), whom Kierke-

---

51. Ibid., "Vorwort," p. i.   52. Ibid., p. ii.
53. As an example see ibid., p. 34, where Bärthold, in a footnote, quotes from *Postscript*. On the whole inaccuracies are few, but one nagging error keeps cropping up throughout: Victor Eremita, the pseudonymous editor of *Either/Or*, is repeatedly designated "Emerita!"
54. Ibid., p. 92.
55. Ibid., pp. 109–17. For an English translation see Søren Kierkegaard's "My Position as a Religious Writer in 'Christendom' and my Tactics," in Lowrie's translation of his *On My Work as an Author* (New York: Harper and Row, 1962), pp. 159–64. For *Armed Neutrality* (1848–51), the related work that remained unpublished among Kierkegaard's journals, see *Papirer*, X^5 B 107. It is translated into English by Howard V. and Edna H. Hong as Kierkegaard's *Armed Neutrality and an Open Letter* (Bloomington, Indiana: Indiana University Press, 1968), pp. 33–46.

gaard attacked for politicizing and rendering sectarian the reform of the Church.[56]

Bärthold's choice of these two essays as preludes to his discussion of the *Kirkekampen,* which he accompanies with assorted translations from the articles of the period, speaks highly of his insight into the inner mechanics of Kierkegaard's transition to direct communication. Kierkegaard's open critique of Rudelbach in 1851 presaged his later attack on Mynster; in both cases the press was utilized as the medium of direct communication. In the last section of his book, Bärthold quotes extensively from Kierkegaard's *Fædrelandet* articles, as well as from Martensen's initial reply of December 28, 1854, and Nielsen's supportive article of January 10, 1855.[57] He succeeds in conveying to his German readers an overview of the *Kirkekampen* that was previously unavailable to them in such detail. His intention is to supplement the already translated *Øjeblikket* articles with material from the earlier phase of the *Kirkekampen,* and so he ends his survey appropriately with a translation of Kierkegaard's "The Midnight Cry" of April 11, 1855.[58]

Far from being a random patchwork of translations and running commentaries, Bärthold's book represents a definite theological interpretation of Kierkegaard in the nonconformist tradition, and one that offered Germans an elaborate sketch of his restless yet piquant spirit. Bärthold's eagerness to translate and present the religious Kierkegaard to the Germans continued unabated, but now it assumed a more clearly defined goal: to counteract certain new depictions of the man and his thought that originated from a decidedly non-Christian secular perspective and were motivated by a desire to stifle specifically the appeal of the religious component in his life and writings. Bärthold's battle with ecclesiastical officialdom was not over, but a new front was opening up alongside it: a confrontation with the freethinkers. This is made apparent in the Foreword to a book he published in 1874 entitled *Aus und über Sören Kierkegaard. Früchte und Blätter.* He mentions, as the occasion for this latest

---

56. Bärthold, *Søren Kierkegaard, Eine Verfasser-Existenz,* pp. 119–31. See Søren Kierkegaard, "Foranledigt ved en Yttring af Dr. Rudelbach mig betræffende," [An Open Letter, prompted by a reference to me by Dr. R.] in *Fædrelandet,* January 31, 1851. See also *SV,* XIII, pp. 436–44. For an English translation see the one made by the Hongs in Kierkegaard's *Armed Neutrality and an Open Letter,* pp. 47–55.

57. Bärthold, *Søren Kierkegaard, Eine Verfasser-Existenz,* pp. 132ff. See also Chapter 3 above.

58. Ibid., pp. 171–72.

compilation of translations and interpretive comments, two books that were rapidly attaining a wide popularity in Germany: Martensen's *Christelige Ethik* and a book published the previous year by a certain Adolf Strodtmann (1829–79) called *Das geistige Leben in Dänemark*. Both of these works and what they had to say about Kierkegaard guided Bärthold's selections for his 1874 book.[59]

Strodtmann's book has an interesting story behind it that is germane to the history of Kierkegaard's German reception in the 1870s. In it Strodtmann treated a variety of aspects in Danish cultural and intellectual life during the period 1848–73. The author had been a prisoner of war in Copenhagen in 1848 and subsequently wrote his reminiscences and impressions of the architecture (Tivoli), the art scene, the literature and literary criticism, the press, the diverse political currents, and the religious movements, and he even added three sections at the end on Norwegian literature, two of which dealt with Ibsen. Kierkegaard was covered in about thirty pages under the section on literary criticism.[60] The real significance of these pages on Kierkegaard lay in the source who inspired them: Georg Brandes.

In 1871 Brandes, fresh out of the University of Copenhagen with a doctorate in French aesthetics, went on an extended trip abroad that took him, among several places, to Berlin. There he made the acquaintance of Strodtmann, a scholar and cultural historian with an interest in Scandinavia and a penchant for translation. The two soon became close friends and colleagues, and Brandes stayed at Strodtmann's house near Berlin for long stretches of time. As it turned out later, there had been an added attraction there for Brandes besides his intellectual association with Strodtmann. On July 29, 1876, Brandes married Henriette (Gerda) Strodtmann, the former wife of his friend. Brandes had been having an affair with her for four years, and had finally induced her to obtain a divorce from her aging husband. This development, however, did not affect his relationship with Adolf, who had acquiesced in the arrangement.[61] Several of Brandes's letters to close friends from that period con-

---

59. Albert Bärthold, ed. and trans., *Aus und über Sören Kierkegaard. Früchte und Blätter* (Halberstadt, 1874), p. v.

60. Adolf Strodtmann, *Das geistige Leben in Dänemark. Streifzüge auf den Gebieten der Kunst, Literatur, Politik und Journalistik des skandinavischen Nordens* (Berlin, 1873), pp. 95–125.

61. The details of the story went as follows: In 1866, at the age of nineteen, Henriette married a much older Strodtmann. It was an arranged marriage, reflecting all the dismal qualities of the oppressed status of women that are vividly depicted in some of Ibsen's

tain amorous references to Henriette, who had become a principal reason for his frequent visits to Germany.[62]

Intellectually and politically, Brandes and Strodtmann held similar views and cooperated in the preparation of *Das geistige Leben in Dänemark*. In fact it was more than cooperation in some places, especially the section on Kierkegaard, where many of Brandes's own ideas are presented in such a way as to suggest that Strodtmann was merely serving as his mouthpiece. Strodtmann states at the beginning of the book that it is mainly intended as a contribution to efforts at mutual understanding between Denmark and Germany now that the debate over the north Schleswig question, suspended during the Franco-Prussian war, has resumed in the Danish and German presses.[63] That may be so, but on another level the book appears to have been designed to promote Brandes's personal reputation as a critic in the German-speaking world. Not only was it packed with his ideas, but an appendix contained Strodtmann's translation of a long piece by Brandes on H. C. Andersen as a writer of fairy tales.[64] And directly following the section on Kierkegaard, Strodtmann makes a very interesting declaration: "The authentic intellectual heir to

---

social plays, and that J. S. Mill speaks about in his *The Subjection of Women*, which Brandes translated into Danish in 1869. Upon falling in love with her, Brandes discovered that her husband had a serious case of syphilis which he had contracted as a young man after a trip to Paris, and which had resulted in blindness in one eye. After consulting with a doctor friend of his and questioning Henriette about her feelings toward Strodtmann, Brandes was relieved to find out that she had never engaged in sexual relations with her husband, and lived in the house more as a daughter than as a wife. Brandes then set to work arranging a divorce, and Strodtmann did not object. For more on this affair see Bertil Nolin, *Den Gode Européen, Studier i Georg Brandes's idéutveckling 1871–1893* (Stockholm: Svenska Bokförlaget, 1965), pp. 21–27; see also Nolin's *Georg Brandes* (Boston: Twayne Publishers, 1976), pp. 45–47.

62. Writing from Berlin to his friend Emil Petersen on October 11, 1872, Brandes declared: "I live with Strodtmann and his charming wife." This seemingly innocent remark later developed into outright love allusions to Gerda, as she was called. See Morten Borup, editor, *Georg Brandes og Emil Petersen, en Brevveksling* (Copenhagen: Lademann, 1980), p. 157. On another occasion Gerda is referred to by Brandes as "the one who now controls my heart." See Brandes's letter from Munich to C. J. Salmonsen dated August 1, 1873, in Morten Borup, ed., *Georg og Edvard Brandes: Brevveksling med nordiske Forfattere og Videnskabsmænd*, vol. I (Copenhagen: Gyldendal, 1939), p. 291.

63. Strodtmann, *Das geistige Leben in Dänemark*, pp. v and vii.

64. See "H. C. Andersen als Märchendichter. Ein literarisches Charakterbild," in ibid., pp. 269–339. Parts of the long essay first appeared in Danish in *Illustreret Tidende* (July 1869), and is regarded as the first serious piece of scholarship devoted to Andersen's literary art. For more on Brandes and Andersen see Elias Bredsdorff, *H. C. Andersen: The Story of His Life and Work*, pp. 253–54.

Søren Kierkegaard is Georg Brandes, . . . the shrewdest and most sensible critic" since the days of Lessing.[65]

Brandes is quoted at length in Strodtmann's discussion of Kierkegaard. Strodtmann cites an article by Brandes in *Dagbladet* in which the author calls Kierkegaard "an enormous genius, who comes once every hundred years." Brandes adds, however, that Kierkegaard is also "the Tycho Brahe of our philosophy": like Brahe he was great, yet also like Brahe he failed to pinpoint the sun as the center of our solar system; and the sun, in Brandes's analogy, represents reason.[66] This brief description of Kierkegaard, quoted by Strodtmann, summarizes Brandes's view very neatly, and the remainder of Strodtmann's treatment amplifies on it. Kierkegaard is described as the last and most important of the early-nineteenth-century romantics.[67] His religious orientation is compared to that of Pascal, the comparison being the earliest of its kind and coming from Brandes.[68] The bulk of the discussion thereafter is devoted to a survey of the three main Kierkegaardian stages of existence; however, Strodtmann dwells inordinately on the aesthetic stage and quotes extensively from the first volume of *Either/Or*, particularly the "Diapsalmata" and the "Diary of a Seducer."[69] Once again the direction of the emphasis is Brandesian in origin.

On Kierkegaard's Christianity, Strodtmann offers what was increasingly to become Brandes's proclaimed position: Kierkegaard's genius will outlast his indefensible orthodoxy. The clear strategy behind this view is to denude Kierkegaard of all his Christian spiritual components and appropriate his remaining powerful literary attributes for secular humanism and freethought. Although Strodtmann acknowledges the importance of Kierkegaard's category of the "single individual" and the influence it has had, he adds that an intensive study of Kierkegaard results invariably in hyper-reflection and self-preoccupation to the point of inhibiting action. Those who admire Kierkegaard, therefore, must eventually wrench themselves free of his grip in order to win back their original nature and be able to act again.[70] In the end, Strodtmann spells out the real source of inspiration for his and Brandes's critique of Kierkegaard's Christianity:

---

65. Strodtmann, *Das geistige Leben*, pp. 125–26. The precise degree of Brandes's input into Strodtmann's book is not easy to determine, but it is clear from the style and detailed information on Denmark and on Kierkegaard that he played a major role in shaping the work.

66. Ibid., p. 101.
67. Ibid., p. 123.
68. Ibid., p. 97.
69. Ibid., pp. 103–12 and 113–17.
70. Ibid., p. 102.

Feuerbach's *Das Wesen des Christenthums* (1841).[71] Kierkegaard's attack on "Christendom" is interpreted as an admission of the practical impossibility of Christianity, and his entire life's work is seen as a demonstration of the ultimate untenability of Christian faith.[72] In this way Strodtmann/ Brandes deliver the final blow by turning Kierkegaard's own corrective arsenal against what it was intended to rehabilitate.

The radical nature of Strodtmann's book did not go unnoticed by the critics. One of these, writing for *Dagbladet*, branded the work "a party platform, inspired by the clique of 'freethinkers.' "[73] In light of what Strodtmann has to say about Kierkegaard, it becomes clear why Bärthold makes specific selections from Kierkegaard's writings for translation and inclusion in his 1874 book. He too is reacting to the dechristianizing of Kierkegaard; in fact, he takes issue openly with Strodtmann's conclusion that Kierkegaard's case proves the impracticality of Christianity.[74] For this reason Bärthold returns to a couple of the early pseudonymous works, avoiding the strictly "aesthetic" elements in them as much as possible and concentrating instead on their religious features. He begins with a word about inwardness and the "single individual"; this is followed by a translation of fragments from *Fear and Trembling* on Abraham as the "Knight of Faith."[75] He then turns to Johannes Climacus, the pseudonymous author of *Postscript*, whom he depicts as walking the thin line between finite (temporal) and infinite (eternal) existence, or teetering on the edge of the leap of faith.[76] Selections from *Postscript* come next, focusing on humor, the religious existence, the individual, inwardness, and the part on "truth is subjectivity." Also included is the final section of *Postscript*, where Climacus talks about the various pseudonyms and their place in the overall scheme of the writings.[77] Bärthold's aim behind all this, once again, is to bolster Kierkegaard's claim in *The Point of View* that he had been a religious writer from the start.[78] If Strodtmann meant to imply that Kierkegaard had a proud, unyielding, and ambitious nature, capable of attaining self-fulfillment through tackling and surmounting the difficulties of Christianity, then Bärthold says he concurs.[79] The translations he provides from *Fear and*

---

71. Ibid., p. 124.   72. Ibid., p. 123.
73. *Dagbladet*, March 25, 1873.
74. Bärthold, *Aus und über Sören Kierkegaard. Früchte und Blätter*, pp. vi-vii.
75. Ibid., pp. 3-19.   76. Ibid., pp. 22 and 53-54.
77. Ibid., pp. 23-52, 57-96, and 99-132.
78. Ibid., p. 53.   79. Ibid., p. 55.

Trembling and *Postscript*, in response to the challenge of the freethinkers, were the first of their kind in German.

At the time Bärthold was unaware that he was actually confronting, and reacting to, the ideas of Brandes as set forth indirectly through Strodtmann. By 1873, when Strodtmann's book appeared, Brandes had experienced and overcome a religious crisis of profound proportions. Kierkegaard was at the vortex of this crisis. As a consequence of this experience Brandes permanently lost all feeling for religion, discarded any lingering attachments to the romantic school in literature, and paved the way for "the Modern Breakthrough" [*det moderne Gennembrud*] that was founded on a new secular realism and a radical positivism.

Brandes's religious crisis began in 1861 when he was nineteen and lasted for a couple of years. He had been reading extensively in Kierkegaard's works during the previous two years since entering the University, and had found himself before a superior genius:

> I felt, face to face with the first great mind that, as it were, had personally confronted me, all my real insignificance, understood all at once that I had as yet neither lived nor suffered, felt nor thought, and that nothing was more uncertain than whether I might one day evince talent. The one certain thing was that my present status seemed to amount to nothing at all.[80]

Brandes's first exposure to Kierkegaard, particularly the ethical and religious writings, jolted him deeply.[81] He had grown up in an irreligious home, and even though both his parents were Jewish, they were not practicing.

During his first year at the University, Brandes read the entire Bible and attended the lectures of Rasmus Nielsen, which contained frequent

---

80. Georg Brandes, *Reminiscences of My Childhood and Youth,* translator unknown (New York: Arno Press, 1906), p. 59; see also p. 82. This is a translation of the first volume of Brandes's three-volume autobiography entitled *Levned* (Copenhagen: Gyldendal, 1905-8). For the Danish original see *Levned, Barndom og Første Ungdom* (Copenhagen, 1905), vol. I, p. 64; see also p. 91.

81. Paul V. Rubow, in his thorough study of Brandes's early intellectual development entitled *Georg Brandes's Briller* (Copenhagen: Levin & Munksgaard, 1932), pp. 104-6, relies on Brandes's extensive diary to list the books by Kierkegaard that Brandes was reading at the time. He began with *Either/Or* and was impressed by Judge William's ethical alternative in the second volume. Then, in 1860, he read *Øjeblikket* on September 8; *Fear and Trembling* on September 14; *From the Papers of One Still Living* and *The Point of View* on September 20; *For Self-Examination* on October 12; and *Stages on Life's Way* shortly thereafter. Rubow quotes a few entries in the diary with enthusiastic references to Kierkegaard.

citations from Kierkegaard. He also heard Hans Brøchner lecturing on Hegel. At the same time, Brandes joined a group of students who met regularly to read and discuss. In this context he befriended a certain Julius Lange (1838–96),[82] who later became an important art historian. Lange, himself a Christian, observed his bright young friend wrestling with the diverse, and often conflicting, impulses he was receiving from his professors and his readings, and he resolved to lead Brandes to Christianity. On the night of August 1, 1861, while on a trip together to the island of Møn in southern Denmark, Lange and Brandes had a heated personal discussion in which Lange insisted that Brandes convert to Christianity because his life, already steeped in rationalism, was lacking the vital spiritual ingredient that would make it complete. Lange then solemnly prayed aloud for Brandes's conversion. At first the episode surprised, and then angered Brandes, as he relates in his diary,[83] but he soon found himself making efforts to believe in Christianity. His efforts met with eventual failure, but not before accentuating the struggle already raging within him between the lure of pantheism as manifested in thinkers like Hegel, Goethe, and Spinoza, and the Christian impulses he was receiving from Kierkegaard.

Brandes's feelings toward Lange were not diminished as a result of Lange's clumsy attempt at evangelism. On the contrary, he was actually quite dismayed when on December 17 of that year Lange announced to him his plans to visit Italy for five months. The prospect of being separated from his best friend for such a period, while he was in the throes of a spiritual crisis, frightened Brandes.[84] Following that fateful summer night, he had continued to share his inner torments with Lange, and in a revealing diary entry he mentions that Lange once told him, "it is crazy to have Kierkegaard as the single source from which one knows Christianity."[85]

Looking back on that period many years later in his autobiography,

---

82. Brandes, *Reminiscences,* p. 87.

83. For all the diary entries relevant to Brandes's religious crisis of 1861–63, see the third chapter of Henning Fenger's *Den Unge Brandes: Miljø, Venner, Rejser, Kriser* (Copenhagen: Gyldendal, 1957), pp. 59–94. On the incident with Lange see Rubow, *Georg Brandes's Briller,* pp. 111–12; and Henning Fenger, "Georg Brandes and Kierkegaard," in *The Activist Critic: A Symposium on the Political Ideas, Literary Methods and International Reception of Georg Brandes,* ed. Hans Hertel and Sven Møller Kristensen (Copenhagen: Munksgaard, 1980), pp. 50–51.

84. Brandes, *Reminiscences,* pp. 112–13.

85. Entry for August 3, 1861; see Fenger, *Den Unge Brandes,* p. 61.

Brandes gives the impression that, as early as 1861 when Lange tried to convert him, he had already become a thoroughgoing freethinker and was unmoved by the incident: "I was made of much harder metal than they [Lange and other friends of his], and their attempts to alter my way of thinking did not penetrate beyond my hide." He adds: "To set my mind in vibration, there was needed a brain that I felt superior to my own; and I did not find it in them. I found it in the philosophical and religious writings of Søren Kierkegaard, in such works, for instance, as *Sickness unto Death*."[86] In fact, the diary entries from those months tell a different tale. Brandes then was anything but a confirmed self-confident atheist; he was genuinely grappling with religious questions, including the possibility of being baptized. Kierkegaard continued to be the main pivot around whom his religious experience revolved: "Kierkegaard is for me . . . qualitatively different from all others. . . . I have felt inexpressible exhilaration, knelt and prayed, but there is a duplicity in me. . . ."[87] This poignant wavering went on through the winter of 1862 and beyond, fueled by intensive readings in *Postscript* and in Hegel's works.[88] In a spectacular diary passage from 1863 full of self-denunciation, Brandes, who was then still in the grip of Kierkegaard's concept of sin, writes:

> I must separate myself from everyone, especially from Jul. Lange, so as to read Kierkegaard again and again. Finally—I must be ashamed of myself, like a dog, for wanting to pass myself off as a thinker, I, a feeble mind, a miserable mind, a weak, wretched, powerless and pitiable man. Kierkegaard is the only person, before whose greatness I feel myself like a nothing.[89]

Throughout those months of intense internal conflict, the opposing influences of professors Nielsen and Brøchner were in competition over Brandes's soul. With time, however, Brøchner monopolized Brandes's

---

86. Brandes, *Reminiscences*, p. 105. Brandes's opinion of Lange's character was not really as condescending as this passage in his autobiography suggests. They remained friends for life, and Brandes wrote an appreciative book on Lange after his death. In a letter to Ellen Key dated December 22, 1898, Brandes thanked her for liking his book on Lange, adding that it was the first of his books to find favor in Denmark. He declared: "I have not loved any man more than him, and the book is a book about friendship". See *Georg og Edvard Brandes: Brevveksling*, ed. Morten Borup, vol. VII, p. 183.

87. Entry for October 27, 1861; see Fenger, *Den Unge Brandes*, p. 65.

88. See the entries for November 18, 20, 28; and December 15, 22, 31, 1861 in Fenger, *Den Unge Brandes*, pp. 66–68. See also Rubow, *Georg Brandes's Briller*, pp. 107–8. In 1862 Brandes read *Philosophical Fragments, Sickness unto Death, Concept of Anxiety*, and *Repetition* and reread *Either/Or*.

89. Entry dated simply May 1863; see Fenger, *Den Unge Brandes*, p. 92.

attention and began to direct his interests toward thinkers like Strauss and Feuerbach, in addition to the already familiar Heiberg, Hegel, and Spinoza. As the 1860s wore on, Brandes became fairly close to Brøchner, attending his lectures and having long intellectual conversations with him, often over a meal at Brøchner's house. They also corresponded regularly between 1862 and 1875. Kierkegaard remained a frequent topic of discussion, and Brøchner shared many anecdotes about him with Brandes. Brandes, in turn, began to distance himself from the religious individualism he had encountered in his readings of Kierkegaard as he became increasingly absorbed in his professor's pantheism. Brøchner, for instance, calmly disabused Brandes of belief in the possibility of human immortality, a question that had been on Brandes's mind for some time.[90] It soon became clear to Brandes that the only meaningful way he could continue to appreciate Kierkegaard's genius would be to isolate it from the religious "trappings" (as he conceived of them) surrounding it. He began to experience a strong reaction against Kierkegaard's religious writings, and the reaction quickly turned into resentment.

This resentment manifested itself initially in the context of the "Tro og Viden" Controversy of the 1860s, and was directed at Rasmus Nielsen. Brandes had a face-to-face meeting with Nielsen in May 1864, during which he was annoyed to hear Nielsen speak confidently about the future prospect of science proving the possibility of miracles. Brandes notes that Nielsen at the time had begun his renunciation of Kierkegaard and his slow shift toward Grundtvigianism.[91] Based on his newly acquired Straussian and Feuerbachian approaches to biblical criticism and religion, Brandes produced in 1866 his first substantive work, *Dualismen i vor nyeste Philosophie*, which was a critique of Nielsen's views on the relationship of science to religion and knowledge to faith.[92] Although he knew better, Brandes did not hesitate to link Nielsen's questionable positions to the legacy of Kierkegaard. This is all the more regrettable when we read, in a letter Brandes wrote to Brøchner in 1865, the following comment about Rudolf Schmidt, a Nielsen enthusiast: "What does one say about the followers of Nielsen, like Schmidt, who place Nielsen on the same level

---

90. Brandes, *Reminiscences*, pp. 102, 109–10, and 114–16. See also Paul V. Rubow, "Georg Brandes og Hans Lærere," in *Studier fra Sprog- og Oldtidsforskning*, published by the Philological-Historical Society, no. 144 (Copenhagen, 1924), pp. 3–24.

91. Brandes, *Reminiscences*, p. 142.

92. See Chapter 5 above.

as Kierkegaard? Is this to diminish Kierkegaard's honor?"[93] In the same letter Brandes even proceeds to tell Brøchner that he is preparing a treatise *(Dualismen)* in which he intends to challenge the notion that Nielsen represents an authentic interpretation of Kierkegaard![94] Somewhere along the way Brandes lost sight of that worthy goal.

Brandes's attack on Nielsen's philosophy aroused a great number of people, especially among conservative intellectuals and members of the ecclesiastical establishment. Brandes became marked as an enemy of religion, and his long feud with "orthodoxy," as he liked to call it, commenced. In 1867 Bjørnson reacted sharply to Brandes's comparison of Kierkegaard with Tycho Brahe by declaring that whoever wrote like that "had no views in common with other Danes, no Danish mind."[95] That same year Rudolf Schmidt, furious at the criticisms made against Nielsen, began an anti-Brandes campaign that went on for years. He, Nielsen, and Bjørnson started a periodical in 1869 that they jointly edited and called *For Ide og Virkelighed* (For idea and reality). Its purpose was to further the philosophical views of Nielsen by providing them with a regular public platform. It also catered to the Grundtvigian positions that he was swiftly embracing. Brandes was repeatedly attacked in its pages.[96] The periodical lasted until 1873, serving as both outlet and refuge for Nielsen during the closing years of the "Tro og Viden" Controversy when he was beset from all sides by the angry cries of opponents. Some eminent literary names were induced to contribute to it, including H. C. Andersen, Carsten Hauch, Magdalene Thoresen, Carl Ploug, H. P. Kofoed-Hansen, the Norwegian Jonas Lie, and Grundtvig himself. There were several articles by Nielsen treating a variety of topics and touching occasionally on Kierkegaard, usually with a view to enlisting him on the side of Nielsen's causes whenever suitable, or criticizing him from their peculiar stand-

---

93. Letter from Brandes to Brøchner dated September 21, 1865, in *Georg og Edvard Brandes: Brevveksling,* vol. I, p. 11.

94. Ibid., p. 13. P. V. Rubow, in *Georg Brandes's Briller,* p. 120, says the big difference between Brøchner's and Brandes's attacks on Nielsen's abuse of Kierkegaard during the "Tro og Viden" Controversy is that in Brøchner's *Problemet om Tro og Viden* the author "wants to spit out the parasite," whereas in *Dualismen* Brandes fights against ideas he has long held in high esteem. Rubow adds that with Brandes the case is not clear-cut, since it is Nielsen, and not Kierkegaard, he is really battling. But the problem is precisely that this supposed targeting of Nielsen rather than Kierkegaard is not as obvious as Rubow would have us believe.

95. Brandes, *Reminiscences,* p. 220.

96. Ibid., pp. 221–22. See also Rubow, *Georg Brandes's Briller,* p. 123.

points if that proved more opportune.⁹⁷ Brandes loathed the periodical and all that it stood for.

As Brandes delved deeper into the works of the French positivists Taine, Sainte-Beuve, and Renan, he became convinced beyond a doubt that Kierkegaard's religious writings represented the last vestiges of a romantic world view incompatible with the "new realism" of modern scientific discoveries and social criticism. J. S. Mill's *The Subjection of Women* caused Kierkegaard's views on marriage and the relations between the sexes, as set forth in the second volume of *Either/Or*, to appear outmoded, even reactionary, in Brandes's eyes.⁹⁸ Yet despite the ever-widening intellectual and spiritual gulf separating Brandes from Kierkegaard's religious philosophy in the late 1860s, Brandes continued to admire the literary genius, the wit and irony, and the powerful imagination of Kierkegaard. He clearly recognized in Kierkegaard a great man, and realized that with such potent literary talents his dangerous spiritual and social views would continue to exert an influence long after their fundamental assumptions had been refuted by the "new realism."⁹⁹

The 1871 lectures at the University of Copenhagen, delivered by Brandes upon returning from a long European excursion, inaugurated the "Modern Breakthrough" in literature and constituted the basis for the first volume of his six-volume critical study entitled *Hovedstrømninger i det nittende Aarhundredes Litteratur* [Main currents in nineteenth-century literature]. Not only Christianity but all forms of idealism and post-romantic aesthetics were openly assailed in this volume, which appeared in 1872 under the title *Emigrantlitteraturen* and was promptly translated into German by Strodtmann. Brandes even charged that the national patriotism displayed by the Danes, following the 1864 defeat of their country at the hands of Prussia over Schleswig, had encouraged an un-

97. See, for instance, Nielsen's opening article entitled "Ide og Virkelighed," in the first issue of *For Ide og Virkelighed*, ed. R. Nielsen, B. Bjørnson, and R. Schmidt (Copenhagen, 1869), pp. 1–39, esp. pp. 4–5, where Kierkegaard's conservative political outlook is invoked. See also Nielsen's article "Karakter og Villie," in *For Ide og Virkelighed* (Copenhagen, 1872), pp. 489–517, esp. pp. 505–8 and 510.

98. See Rubow, *Georg Brandes's Briller*, pp. 125–27.

99. Brandes's admiration for Kierkegaard the "great man" is attested in a letter he sent his parents from Berlin during a trip through Germany in 1868. He writes enthusiastically that he visited the place where Kierkegaard attended lectures by Schelling, and ate breakfast at Spargnapani, the place Kierkegaard alludes to in *Repetition*. See *Georg Brandes's Breve til Forældrene: 1859–71*, ed. Morten Borup (Copenhagen: C. A. Reitzel, 1978), vol. I, pp. 185 and 188.

healthy isolation, particularly from German cultural and intellectual influences.[100] The few scattered references to Kierkegaard in this work reveal Brandes's increasing preoccupation, at this time, with Kierkegaard's childhood and his relation to his father, as portrayed in the newly published journals. His attachment to his father is compared to that of Mme. de Stael to hers, and one gets the impression from other comparisons that Brandes intends to depict Kierkegaard as an irrepressible aesthetic genius, longing to break out into freedom, yet hopelessly shackled by the gloomy religious upbringing he had received at home. Brandes points predictably to Johannes the Seducer, whom he compares to Chateaubriand's René, as the fictional embodiment of this trait.[101]

Equally provocative anti-religious themes were treated in another series of lectures that Brandes gave in 1873. His subversive streak was intentionally unsubtle, thus confirming his notoriety in conservative Danish theological and philosophical circles. The book that came out of the lectures, *Den romantiske Skole i Tydskland* (The romantic school in Germany), contained several comparisons between Kierkegaard and a host of early-nineteenth-century literary figures and religious conservatives: Frederik Schlegel, Joseph de Maistre, Bonald, Novalis, Tieck, and others. Brandes's aim was to place Kierkegaard firmly and unmistakably in the company of "romantic" writers—nebulous as the term may be—with the clear message that his time, like theirs, had passed.[102] For Brandes these so-called romantics were political and ideological anachronisms representing a curious, backward-looking diversion and fleeting interlude in the onward historical march of reason and science. The great achievements of the eighteenth-century Enlightenment in all fields, especially literature, were once again being celebrated, and Denmark had to join the rest of Europe in this and move with the times.

Ideas like these found few sympathetic ears in Copenhagen. Several voices were raised in protest, through conservative newspapers like *Dagbladet* and *Berlingske Tidende*, and concerted efforts prevented Brandes

100. J. Oskar Andersen, *Survey of the History of the Church in Denmark*, pp. 62–63.
101. For the relevant references to Kierkegaard see Georg Brandes, *Hovedstrømninger i det nittende Aarhundredes Litteratur*, vol. I: "Emigrantlitteraturen" (Copenhagen, 1872), pp. 25, 69, 100, and 150. It is significant that Brandes dedicates this volume to his teacher Hans Brøchner, whose intellectual influence over him was undisputed.
102. See ibid., vol. II: "Den romantiske Skole i Tydskland" (Copenhagen, 1873), pp. 17, 51, 67–68, 72, 79–80, 146, and 191–95. Strodtmann produced a German translation of this volume that same year. See also Rubow, *Georg Brandes's Briller*, pp. 128–39 for a discussion of the references to Kierkegaard in both volumes by Brandes.

from receiving a much-coveted appointment as professor at the University. Seeing that none of the major periodicals would publish anything with his signature beneath it, Brandes and his younger brother Edvard collaborated in establishing their own monthly journal for history and criticism that they called *Det nittende Aarhundrede* (The nineteenth century). The first issue appeared in October 1874, and the publication continued regularly until September 1877. No doubt Brandes, in creating his new monthly, had in mind the recent demise of Nielsen's and Schmidt's *For Ide og Virkelighed,* which had been less than receptive to his views. A small group of talented young writers congregated around the Brandes brothers. These latter, in turn, made available the pages of their publication to the articles, essays, and poems of this group. The aspiring writers all shared a liberal-positivist outlook that it was Brandes's policy to promote. Making their debut in Brandes's journal were such budding literary names as Holger Drachmann, Harald Høffding, Jens Peter Jacobsen, Otto Borchsenius, and C. K. F. Molbech. Ibsen also contributed, as did Bjørnson, who made peace with Brandes after renouncing his previous association with Nielsen and Schmidt, and adopted wholeheartedly the program of the "Modern Breakthrough." Philosophically, the periodical tended to peddle a mixture of English utilitarian and evolutionary thought (J. S. Mill, Darwin, Herbert Spencer, and the outspoken atheist Shelley), certain French thinkers (Taine and Comte), the ideas of the German socialist Lassalle, and the new theories of the German evolutionist Ernst Haeckel. All were high on the list of Brandes's intellectual interests at the time.[103]

Kierkegaard, however, was not neglected by Brandes, and became in fact the subject of a series of lectures Brandes gave in Sweden in the fall of 1876. That year Kierkegaard's *Judge for Yourself!* (1851–52) was published posthumously for the first time and had the effect of boosting general interest in him. Brandes states in his autobiography that, having been deeply influenced by Kierkegaard at one point in his youth, he now wished to approach him more dispassionately in order to reevaluate his earlier conclusions.[104] The lectures in Stockholm, at the Science Academy's lecture hall, were well attended and generated much discussion. *Aftonbladet,* in its November 18 issue, ran an article on them featuring a brief synopsis. Brandes's intention was to travel to Norway next, and present his lectures at Christiania University; however, the senate of the

103. See Brandes, *Levned,* vol. II, pp. 165ff.
104. Ibid., vol. II, pp. 202–4.

University refused to allow him to speak publicly in any of its official forums. His reputation as a freethinker had preceded him, and reports reaching Christiania about his lectures in Sweden caused the more conservative members of the University senate to oppose his appearance under official auspices. To them, Brandes appeared less of a scholar than a propagandist and polemicist. Despite this, however, Brandes showed up defiantly before the student society at the University, where he was met with applause and cheers orchestrated by a group of radical supporters. His four ensuing lectures were also deliberately defiant, with the speaker declaring himself a freethinker, calling Christianity "dark and superstitious," and even preaching free love. He described Kierkegaard's output in the context of Danish letters as "a peculiar literature within the literature," and proceeded to spew forth his provocative views on the man and his work.[105] Shortly after concluding his controversial lecture tour, Brandes in early 1877 published these views on Kierkegaard in his famous work *Søren Kierkegaard: En Kritisk Fremstilling i Grundrids* (S. K.: a critical exposition in outline).

The year 1877 marked an important watershed in the history of Kierkegaard's reception, leaving a lasting impact on subsequent Kierkegaard scholarship. To begin with, the third installment of Kierkegaard's private journals, from the year 1847, was published by Barfod. Appearing also was a second edition of Kierkegaard's nine *Øjeblikket* articles against the Church and the clergy. Two crucial documents containing personal recollections of Kierkegaard made their way to the printers that year as well. One was the autobiography of Meïr Goldschmidt (1819–87), the former editor of the *Corsair* and onetime nemesis of Kierkegaard. Goldschmidt relates his first meeting with Kierkegaard in 1837 and describes Kierkegaard's appearance at the time: thin body, protruding shoulders, and intelligent lively eyes possessing a blend of good-nature and malice.[106] In another section Goldschmidt briefly goes over the events of Kierkegaard's clash with P. L. Møller and the *Corsair;* he supplies valuable information about several encounters he had with Kierkegaard on the streets of Copenhagen at the height of their confrontation. One of these meetings, at which

---

105. The Norwegian paper *Morgenbladet,* in its December 15 issue, carried a long, three-part, front-page article on Brandes's lectures. It wrote that no one could remember an occasion quite like this: "Dr. Brandes unfurled the red banner of the freethinkers. . . . There was no talk of mediation or compromise, only of war."

106. Meïr Goldschmidt, *Livs Erindringer og Resultater* (Life's reminiscences and results), in two volumes (Copenhagen, 1877), vol. I, p. 214.

Kierkegaard did not say a word but gave Goldschmidt a penetrating look and proceeded on his way, apparently had such a profound effect on the editor of the *Corsair*, by his own admission, that soon thereafter he sold the publication and became a literary writer.[107] These revelations from Goldschmidt augmented Kierkegaard's own side of the story as found in the journals that Barfod published in 1872.

The second document in question comprised a series of discrete paragraphs, numbered one through fifty, which contained an assortment of personal reminiscences and anecdotes about Kierkegaard. It was found among the posthumous papers of Hans Brøchner, who wrote it over the Christmas holiday in 1871–72. Apparently, Brøchner received a letter that fall from Barfod requesting clarification of certain puzzling journal entries among Kierkegaard's papers that Barfod was editing. Brøchner replied from memory as best he could, and then decided to commit to paper for posterity everything he was able to recall from the nineteen years he had been personally acquainted with Kierkegaard. Upon his death in 1875, Brøchner's papers were bequeathed to his friend Molbech, and the document of recollections was discovered shortly thereafter. Since Brøchner had been on intimate terms with Brandes and his group of followers to whom Molbech belonged, the manuscript was turned over to Brandes, who published it on March 1, 1877, in *Det nittende Aarhundrede*.[108] He did so only after editing it and deleting certain references to people then still alive. He also attached the name of the young philosopher and student of Brøchner, Harald Høffding (1843–1931), to the document as its publisher. Brandes's choice of Høffding seems to have been motivated by the fact that the philosopher was already known to the public as Brøchner's intellectual heir and successor.[109] The choice also shows Brandes's eagerness to contain the interpretation of Kierkegaard's legacy as much as possible within a line of rationalist and non-religious thinkers.[110]

---

107. Ibid., pp. 411ff.

108. This and the publication in the January issue of three hitherto unpublished letters from Kierkegaard to his cousin Julie Thomsen (in one of which Brøchner is mentioned) have earned Brandes's magazine a special distinction in the annals of Kierkegaard's reception.

109. Høffding wrote a moving obituary of Brøchner, which appeared in the weekly *Nær og Fjern*, no. 182 (December 26, 1875).

110. For the first edition of Brøchner's "Reminiscences," ed. Brandes and published under Høffding's name, see *Det nittende Aarhundrede*, vol. V (March 1, 1877), pp. 337–74. Brøchner gives the dates of their composition as December 27, 1871 to January 10, 1872. They were later published without omissions and with explanatory notes by Steen

Brøchner's "Reminiscences" have been rightly hailed as a major contribution to Kierkegaard studies. They are written in an attractive style by a man who admired Kierkegaard and retained a sincere respect for him all his life, although he differed from him drastically on basic philosophical and religious questions. Soon after Kierkegaard's death in 1855, Brøchner wrote to Molbech:

> He had meant a great deal to me, both in his writings and in our personal relationship. There is no one whose personality has inspired and stimulated me to such an extent as his. The friendly disposition he always showed towards me often gave me courage when I was in danger of losing it.[111]

These candid words assume added significance when one considers the often irreconcilable disparities between Brøchner's philosophy and Kierkegaard's. Brøchner's objectivity and sense of fairness toward Kierkegaard were demonstrated in his *Fædrelandet* article of December 1, 1855,[112] and again in his "Reminiscences."

With so many diverse writings by and on Kierkegaard surfacing simultaneously in 1877, the "Reminiscences" of Brøchner could not have come at a better time. They provided detailed information from an independent source about Kierkegaard's appearance, eating habits, walks, and views of certain contemporaries. Brøchner first met Kierkegaard in 1836 and was struck by his dishevelled appearance.[113] He used to observe Kierkegaard dining luxuriously at an expensive restaurant and ordering meats and wine.[114] Kierkegaard occasionally played cards at the house of Brøchner's

---

Johansen as *Erindringer om Søren Kierkegaard af Hans Brøchner* (Copenhagen: Gyldendal, 1953). See esp. pp. 5 and 7–10 of Johansen's introduction to his edition. An English translation of Brøchner's "Recollections of Søren Kierkegaard," as they are called, was made by T. H. Croxall in 1959 and appeared with an introduction in his collection of translated documents entitled *Glimpses and Impressions of Kierkegaard*, pp. 3–39. See Croxall's introduction, pp. 3–6. The original manuscript at the Royal Library still shows Brandes's corrections and deletions done in the margins in his own handwriting.

111. Letter from Brøchner to Molbech dated December 2, 1855, and published originally by Høffding in *Hans Brøchner og Chr. K. F. Molbech: En Brevveksling, 1845–1875* (Copenhagen, 1902), p. 174. The same letter, and another dated February 17, 1856, in which Brøchner gives Molbech a brief sketch of Kierkegaard's life and intellectual development, are published as an appendix to Johansen's edition of Brøchner's *Erindringer*, pp. 66–70. The quoted excerpt comes from a translation of the letter made by Croxall and included, along with the February 17 letter, as an appendix to his translation of Brøchner's "Recollections" in *Glimpses*, pp. 40–44.

112. See Chapter 3 above.

113. Brøchner, *Erindringer*, no. 1 (Johansen, pp. 15–16; Croxall, p. 7).

114. Ibid., no. 3 (Johansen, pp. 18–19; Croxall, pp. 8–9).

aunt (he and Brøchner were second cousins).[115] Outwardly, Kierkegaard in those days betrayed little of the inner gloom that is usually associated with his early upbringing. Brøchner tells how difficult it was to walk in the street alongside Kierkegaard: "because of his crooked figure . . . you could never walk straight when he was with you."[116] This seems to be further proof that Kierkegaard suffered from a physical deformity, perhaps a congenital spinal malformation. Brøchner also encountered Kierkegaard in Berlin during the latter's last trip there in 1846. They used to meet at a restaurant that was the common gathering place for Danes, and would take long walks after meals or go to Kierkegaard's hotel suite for wine.[117] Brøchner found great solace in his friendly association with Kierkegaard while abroad.

Throughout the years of their acquaintance, Kierkegaard frequently talked with Brøchner about celebrated thinkers and about various contemporaries. The subjectivism inherent in Hegel's exposition of the history of philosophy, the earthy sensuousness underlying Feuerbach's *Das Wesen des Christenthums*, and the strengths and limitations of Heiberg's aesthetics were but a few of the issues and philosophers discussed.[118] Closer to home, one of those discussed was Rasmus Nielsen. Brandes, in his editing of the manuscript, made sure to omit Brøchner's section on Kierkegaard's opinions of Nielsen. According to Brøchner, Kierkegaard once toyed with the idea of actively enlisting Nielsen on his side in his prospective attack on the Church, but refrained from doing so with the remark: " 'No, Nielsen is a self-advertiser.' " At other times, however, Kierkegaard had kinder words for Nielsen: " '[He] is the only one of the younger talented authors risen up among us who will achieve anything.' " Brøchner adds ruefully that it was Nielsen's intellectual capacity, not his character, which Kierkegaard admired.[119] Another figure alluded to in the "Reminiscences" was Sibbern, and in particular his poor judgment of true inner feelings versus deceptive external appearances. Brøchner writes:

> Kierkegaard set great store on Sibbern, though he was not blind to his weaknesses. Among these weaknesses, Kierkegaard once mentioned Sibbern's complete lack of irony; and also—this is a psychological point—his lack of

115. Ibid., no. 2 (Johansen, pp. 16–18; Croxall, p. 8).
116. Ibid., no. 8 (Johansen, pp. 23–25; Croxall, pp. 12–13).
117. Ibid., no. 26 (Johansen, pp. 40–43; Croxall, pp. 23–24).
118. Ibid., nos. 19, 17, and 11 respectively (Johansen, pp. 33–34, 32–33, and 27–28; Croxall, pp. 18–19, 17–18, and 14–15).
119. Ibid., no. 21 (Johansen, p. 36; Croxall, p. 20).

perception for disguised passions, and for the way one passion takes the form of another, doubling up on it, so to speak.[120]

Ironically, Sibbern's reading of Kierkegaard's outward mirth at its face value is a case in point.[121] Since Sibbern had already died, Brandes did not censor this section.

On religion, Brøchner made no secret of his divergence from Kierkegaard. When, on one occasion, he explained to Kierkegaard that he was reading the New Testament with the aim of tracing the development of dogma purely from a critical-anthropological perspective—the influence of Strauss and Feuerbach is evident here—Kierkegaard was not pleased: "For him such research was almost offensive."[122] Brøchner acknowledges the power and appeal of Kierkegaard's conception of Christianity, but he adds that many were put off by the way in which Kierkegaard went about defining Christianity: "the separation [he] postulated between Christianity and nature, and Christianity and concrete life."[123] Echoes of Brøchner's positions on the debate over "Tro og Viden" reverberate in these sections. Finally, two prominent religious personalities were regular topics of discussion: Grundtvig and Mynster. Brøchner reports that Grundtvig was usually reduced to a comic figure in Kierkegaard's eyes whenever he came up in a conversation.[124] As for Mynster, Kierkegaard gave Brøchner in 1852 a foretaste of his subsequent open attack on the bishop by speaking ironically of him as "a man of the world." Brøchner explains that Kierkegaard delayed the public expression of his true feelings about Mynster out of deference to his father's friendship with the prelate.[125]

The "Reminiscences," despite their somewhat patronizing tone in places, were written with true benevolent feeling and represented Brøchner's deep sense of gratitude to Kierkegaard for the friendly attention he gave him over the years. In the introductory paragraph Brøchner expresses the hope that his recollections will be useful to a future "competent biographer" of Kierkegaard.[126] As it has turned out, Brøchner had a surprisingly accurate memory, and many of the events and dates

120. Ibid., no. 35 (Johansen, p. 49; Croxall, p. 29).
121. See his letter to Barfod quoted earlier.
122. Brøchner, *Erindringer,* no. 40 (Johansen, pp. 54-55; Croxall, p. 32).
123. Ibid., no. 42 (Johansen, pp. 56-57; Croxall, pp. 33-34).
124. Ibid., no. 46 (Johansen, p. 60; Croxall, pp. 36-37).
125. Ibid., no. 48 (Johansen, pp. 61-63; Croxall, pp. 37-38).
126. Ibid., introductory paragraph (Johansen, p. 15; Croxall, p. 7).

he mentions have since been independently verified by scholars using other sources, principally Kierkegaard's complete journals and papers.

Recollections of the sort found in Goldschmidt's autobiography and Brøchner's "Reminiscences" belonged to a genre of writing on Kierkegaard that, in the nature of the case, was bound to be finite—as Kierkegaard's contemporaries and colleagues aged, they left their memoirs before passing on. It soon became possible to view certain controversial aspects of Kierkegaard's life from diverse external perspectives, all of which added to the rich texture of the posthumous tapestry slowly being woven around his intellectual legacy.[127] Brandes's 1877 book, on the other hand, represented a totally different approach that signaled a new departure in Kierkegaard studies: the critical, biographical-psychological plan of attack, which was guided, in Brandes's case, by a set of firmly held presuppositions regarding religion that had the undeclared purpose of inhibiting the growing popularity of its subject matter.

Søren Kierkegaard: En Kritisk Fremstilling i Grundrids is composed of twenty-eight chapters preceded by a short introduction. It adheres to a rough chronological scheme throughout, despite an immoderate amount of attention paid to the early years and the aesthetic works. At one point Brandes declares that the "Diary of a Seducer" and the "Drinking Party" of "In Vino Veritas" in *Stages on Life's Way*—both being pieces that depict the life of pleasure—are, from a linguistic point of view, Kierkegaard's most outstanding creations.[128] Brandes, in a literary sense, is mainly interested in studying the nature of the progressional development that guides Kierkegaard from one thought and one work to the next. The successive stages through which Kierkegaard passed in his life, and which were reflected in his writings, are the central concern of Brandes. For him it is not very instructive to investigate the extent to which the aesthetic works constitute a prelude to the later religious ones, although he admits he is fascinated by the way the "paradoxical-religious idea"

---

127. An example of two different perspectives on a single issue would be Goldschmidt's understandable focus on the *Corsair* feud with Kierkegaard compared to Brøchner's deliberate downplaying of the same event in his "Reminiscences." According to Brøchner, Kierkegaard exaggerated the significance of the incident in his own mind because of his "enormous reflective powers," and thus remained out of touch with the actuality of the situation as it was perceived by the general public in Copenhagen. See ibid., nos. 22 and 23 (Johansen, pp. 36–39; Croxall, pp. 20–22).

128. Georg Brandes, *Søren Kierkegaard: En Kritisk Fremstilling i Grundrids* (Copenhagen, 1877), p. 160.

evolves out of these earlier writings,[129] and he advances a definite theory on this process.

Brandes's fairly simplistic thesis hardly bothers with the subtle layers of complexity informing the interconnections between Kierkegaard's life and works; instead it uses highly selective evidence to make its case. Kierkegaard, so the argument goes, was immersed at an early age in the gloomy piety of his father, from which he never managed to recover. His physical frailty and introverted disposition made him the object of much abuse among his schoolmates, and this, in turn, sharpened in him the faculties of irony and sarcasm, which he employed as defense mechanisms to ward off his tormentors. His recourse to indirect communication through the use of pseudonyms, and a general sublimation of his sufferings in the form of literary art, came about also in response to threats of derision.[130] Thus, according to Brandes, two fundamental passions or drives, defining Kierkegaard's personality and attitude toward the world, developed and coexisted uneasily in him throughout his life: *Pietet* (reverence, veneration, respect), and *Foragt* (contempt, disdain, scorn).[131] During the early years, the reverence took the form of submission to his father's wishes and an ingrained respect for rules and authority, which in time resulted in a curtailing of creativity and a stultifying of the critical powers. Parallel to this, the contempt was directed initially at everything that opposed religion, and was also turned inwardly in the form of guilt.[132]

129. Ibid., pp. 100-102.

130. Ibid., pp. 18-22, and pp. 79-80. Brandes cannot conceive of a work of art as an autonomous creation capable of standing on its own, but has to search for its historical, biographical, and psychological underpinnings.

131. Ibid., p. 35. See also pp. 31-33. *Pietet,* says Brandes, is different from *Fromhed* (piety, devoutness), of which Kierkegaard, in his opinion, had little. *Pietet* signified a general disposition toward conformity with and subservience to authority.

132. Ibid., Chapters I-VI. Already a Taine-like approach is discernible in Brandes's strategy, which concentrated on locating Kierkegaard's main determining faculty (*faculté maitresse*): reverence and contempt. Scholars have disagreed on the extent to which Taine's critical methodology influenced Brandes's assessment of Kierkegaard. P.TV. Rubow, in "Georg Brandes's Forhold til Taine og Sainte-Beuve," in *Litterære Studier* (Copenhagen, 1949), p. 75, and Bertil Nolin, in his *Georg Brandes,* p. 83, maintain that Brandes was operating very much under the influence of Taine. On the other hand, Aage Henriksen, in *Methods and Results of Kierkegaard Studies in Scandinavia,* p. 27, and René Wellek, in *A History of Modern Criticism: 1750-1950,* vol. IV: "The Later Nineteenth Century" (New Haven: Yale University Press, 1965), the section entitled "The Lonely Dane: Georg Brandes," pp. 359 and 369, argue against such an influence and place greater emphasis on Sainte-Beuve. For a detailed study of French influences over Brandes's early intellectual formation see Henning Fenger's *Georg Brandes et la France: La Formation*

Three main nodal points in Kierkegaard's life are isolated by Brandes and inflated, in conjunction with the dual notion of reverence and contempt, to a degree that renders them responsible for the entire course of Kierkegaard's development. These are: his relation with his father; his engagement to Regine; and his clash with the *Corsair*.[133] In order to do this, Brandes makes diligent use of Barfod's as yet incomplete edition of the *Efterladte Papirer*, attempting to discover the connective tissue that binds one event and one work to another, and then presuming to piece together Kierkegaard's winding story. Kierkegaard's father, for example, stimulated his son's powers of imagination at a young age by taking him on walks in their living room, pretending all the while that they were outside seeing trees and greeting imaginary passersby. On the other hand, contends Brandes, the father's morbid melancholy and rigid puritanical religiosity, which he imparted to his son, stifled this latter's imagination by channeling it into unproductive, theological directions. Brandes here compares Kierkegaard with the young Mill, who also received much of his early education from his father. Mill's education, claims Brandes, was richer and more all-round than Kierkegaard's.[134] The tension between submissiveness (reverence) and freedom (contempt), as Brandes sometimes calls them,[135] took root in Kierkegaard during those years.

This tension manifested itself spectacularly in *Either/Or* as the glaring contrasts between the life of enjoyment and the moral life. Such contrasts, says Brandes, were outlined at the end of the *Concept of Irony*, whose "Rococo style" is neither Greek nor Socratic, but prefigures the dreary gloom of subsequent writings.[136] *Either/Or* was also the first work to exhibit the tension between reverence and contempt resulting from Kierkegaard's abortive engagement. This event in Kierkegaard's life receives extensive and generally unsympathetic treatment in Brandes's book. Like Fredrika Bremer before him, Brandes cannot help invoking the analogy with Simeon the Stylite, this time to describe Kierkegaard's posture in

---

de son Esprit et ses Goûts Littéraires, 1842–1872, vol. VIII of the publications of the Faculty of Letters and Human Sciences (Paris, 1963), especially chaps. VII, VIII, and IX.

133. Each of these is accorded several chapters in the book: the relationship with his father takes up the better portions of chaps. I–IX; the engagement is treated in chaps. X–XV; and the *Corsair* Affair and its repercussions occupy chaps. XXIII–XXVIII.

134. Brandes, *Søren Kierkegaard*, pp. 11–14.

135. Ibid., p. 19.

136. Ibid., pp. 51–53, and 59. In discussing *Either/Or* and *Concept of Irony*, Brandes amplifies on comparisons he had made in his *Hovedstrømninger* between Kierkegaard on the one hand, and Chateaubriand and Schlegel on the other. See pp. 57–59.

the engagement.[137] Based on an examination of journal entries, Brandes speculates inconclusively that Kierkegaard's "Thorn in the Flesh" must have been a sexual infirmity of some kind—impotence perhaps.[138] This situation, and a religious obsession with suffering, are what caused Kierkegaard to break the engagement.

For Brandes the episode of the engagement was the most decisive event in Kierkegaard's youth; the entire corpus of pseudonymous works was a direct result of it. In each work Kierkegaard repeated the attempt to express indirectly his guilt at having deceived the young girl. The high point of these experiments in self-purgation through indirect communication came with the Abraham story in *Fear and Trembling*, where the Old Testament figure acts as another of the many instruments on which Kierkegaard plays the same melody of his relation to Regine.[139] Earlier, Kierkegaard had embodied in Johannes the Seducer all the sleazy qualities that the town's gossip had attributed to him following the breaking of the engagement.[140] Brandes himself regarded Johannes as a character lacking in beauty and devoid of that "happy sensuality that existed under the bright sky of ancient Greece," or the "noble sensuality" in Goethe's writings and the "wildly blooming sensuality" of Byron. All that Brandes could see in Johannes was a smug spirit of "aristocratic pride" and "insatiable vanity."[141]

Even Kierkegaard's critique of the age is ascribed by Brandes to the agonies experienced after the engagement was broken. As a result of the terminated engagement, Kierkegaard attained a sharpened sensitivity and depth of feeling surpassing anything in the generation around him. His

---

137. Ibid., pp. 61–62. Brandes also compares Kierkegaard to an Egyptian sphinx! The Stylite and the sphinx metaphors were clearly intended by Brandes to allude respectively to masturbation and sexual impotence. On Bremer see Chapters 2 and 3 above.

138. Ibid., pp. 68–73. See note 137 above.

139. Ibid., pp. 103ff., and pp. 110ff.

140. Ibid., p. 78. Brandes, employing his psychological analysis, also sees Antigone in *Either/Or*, vol. I, as representing Kierkegaard himself, with Oedipus being Kierkegaard's father and Antigone's bridegroom being Regine (pp. 89ff.). He views the grieving women in *Either/Or*, vol. I, as Regine motifs, and Judge William in vol. II as enshrining the good husband type (p. 79). Later scholars have dubbed these interpretations "ingenious," although not a few of them also regretted Brandes's psychological reductionism. See, for example, R. Wellek, *A History of Modern Criticism: 1750–1950*, vol. IV, p. 363; and Oskar Seidlin, "Georg Brandes," in *Journal of the History of Ideas*, III (October 1942), p. 437.

141. Brandes, *Søren Kierkegaard*, p. 154. See all of chap. XIX. Brandes, in criticizing Johannes for being a shadow of a seducer, was perhaps measuring him with the yardstick of his own abundant sexual exploits.

eyes were opened to the impersonality, the mediocrity, and the passionlessness of his age, which thrived on philosophical mimicry and inauthenticity. He lamented the leveling tendencies of the age with its nameless crowds, its chatter, and its superficiality. He felt very isolated and cultivated this isolation in a philosophical and religious celebration of the "single individual."[142] Interestingly, Brandes rejoices in Kierkegaard's discovery of the individual, "the most precious pearl he had brought his time,"[143] yet he deplores Kierkegaard's continued association of the individual with traditional religious notions. Brandes resorts to a graphic metaphor to put across the point: "[Kierkegaard's] unmistakable greatness is that he discovered this America; his incurable madness was that he stubbornly continued to call it India."[144] By equating the newly-arrived-at concept of the individual with "the Christian," Kierkegaard was reaffirming, with much veneration, the familiar piety instilled in him by his father. His reverence was thus directed to the past, while his contempt was aimed at the present age, and although he had stumbled upon the great modern idea of the independent and self-sufficient human person, he blindly insisted on viewing it as a rediscovery of "the old wonderland."[145] Brandes's dismay is readily understood when it is recalled that several years after his book on Kierkegaard he embraced, with full conviction, Nietzsche's conception of the egotistical individual—proudly scaling the summits, powerful and free. Kierkegaard's "single individual" had left an indelible impression on Brandes, who proceeded forthwith to dechristianize it and then use it as a steppingstone to the Nietzschean Superman.

In the 1870s Brandes was the leading spokesman in Denmark for a positivist-utilitarian outlook that derived inspiration from the evolutionary theories of Darwin and the socialist politics of Lassalle. Due to a number of factors that included a generally unfavorable reception of his views in Denmark, a gradual disillusionment with democratic and socialist ideals, and a new exposure to thinkers like Schopenhauer, Edward von Hartmann, and Nietzsche, Brandes shifted his attention in the 1880s and beyond to a greater focus on famous historical personalities—those great individual peaks of the past.[146] Brandes's critique of Kierkegaard's

---

142. Ibid., pp. 102–4, and 132ff.   143. Ibid., p. 108.
144. Ibid., p. 107.   145. Ibid., pp. 105–6.
146. See Bertil Nolin, *Den Gode Europén*, pp. 137–82. Shakespeare, Goethe, Napoleon, and Caesar are a few examples.

individualism in 1877 must therefore be viewed against the backdrop of this slow change in perspective that had already begun.

Brandes rejected Kierkegaard's notion of the individual's hereditary guilt, which Kierkegaard not only obtained from the doctrine of original sin but also tied in with the assumed consequences, for himself and his entire family, of his father's "secret"—having cursed God as a young shepherd on the heaths of Jutland. Using current social and biological theories, Brandes argued that family and society had to be accorded their due share of guilt, and that the individual is never fully responsible for his actions.[147] Furthermore, a transmission of individual guilt was something Brandes could not accept. Yet Brandes was a determinist and scoffed at Kierkegaard's concept of freedom of the will.[148] His definition of freedom was ultimately very different from Kierkegaard's: it was a freethinker's view of freedom as freedom *from* religion and the dictates of traditional values, and it eventually became the Nietzschean freedom of unlimited and unconditional self-assertion. As Oskar Seidlin perceptively points out, Brandes remained ambivalent toward individual free will and harbored a secret yearning for it that clashed with his naturalistic determinism.[149] This situation mirrored itself in his interpretation of Kierkegaard, whom he saw as burdened with religious melancholy and supposed paternal guilt on the one hand, while at the same time experiencing a burning longing to cast aside all his restraints and enjoy himself freely. Brandes describes the stark choice presented by Kierkegaard's legacy in the following words that constitute an epilogue to his book: "With him [Kierkegaard] the spiritual life in Denmark is driven to the extremity from which a leap has to occur: the leap down into the black abyss of Catholicism, or out to the point from which freedom beckons."[150] Once again it is the freedom of the freethinkers that Brandes has in mind, and that for him is the only real freedom. On one level Brandes's words were prophetic, and it is interesting to read them retrospectively in the light of later developments involving many people who began as Kierkegaardians only to end up as Catholics.[151]

The *Corsair* Affair was for Brandes the third decisive turning point in Kierkegaard's life, after his relations with his father and his fiancée.

---

147. Brandes, *Søren Kierkegaard,* pp. 26ff., 88ff., and chap. XV.
148. Ibid., p. 198.
149. Seidlin, "Georg Brandes," p. 428.
150. Brandes, *Søren Kierkegaard,* p. 271.
151. See Chapter 8 below.

Following his bitter experience with the *Corsair,* Kierkegaard formulated a conception of Christianity as essentially a martyrdom of the individual believer. Just as he saw himself directly face to face with the sacrificing Abraham upon breaking the engagement, so, argues Brandes, Kierkegaard identified with the sufferings of Christ and associated them with his loss of respect among Copenhagen society as a result of the scandal sheet's persecution.[152] The bleak features of his father's religious melancholy were reinforced in him and surfaced anew. Being martyred for the truth now acquired a far greater appeal for Kierkegaard than it had before, and Brandes quotes several journal entries from 1848 and after that indicate Kierkegaard was actively flirting with the prospect of his own "martyrdom." The *Upbuilding Discourses* from that period, especially the "Gospel of Sufferings," and the heightened preoccupation with Christ's Passion, are a further confirmation, says Brandes, of the dark theology that was coming into play in Kierkegaard's mind.[153] All this produced a firm martyr complex in Kierkegaard, who now expanded the range of his weapons of irony and sarcasm beyond their initial defensive purpose of retaliating against the slanders of the *Corsair,* to take on an offensive mission: the exposure of falsehood and complacency in the so-called Christian country of Denmark, and in the Danish Church itself. In short, his contempt was starting to eat into the domain of his reverence.[154]

The first concrete signs of this new approach appear in *Practice in Christianity,* where Brandes sees the outlines of Kierkegaard's later attacks in *Øjeblikket* clearly delineated. Curiously, Brandes calls *Practice in Christianity* "one of Kierkegaard's best books," adding that it is clever and reveals the author's love for truth. Brandes suggests that if someone has little time to read Kierkegaard, he should begin with this work, because in it one encounters Kierkegaard's most intimate feelings and thoughts.[155] Here, according to Brandes, Kierkegaard depicts the Christ figure in several idealized forms whose ingredients he extracts from his own life: he is the Single Individual and the Truth, who goes on to become a martyr; he is indifferent to all worldly purposes and embraces suffering voluntarily; and he renders the false spirituality of Christendom, with its Sunday preachers, an abomination.[156] Thus, when the time came

---

152. Brandes, *Søren Kierkegaard,* p. 242.
153. Ibid., pp. 243-45.
154. Henriksen, *Methods and Results,* p. 25.
155. Brandes, *Søren Kierkegaard,* p. 245.
156. Ibid., pp. 248-51.

for *Øjeblikket,* Kierkegaard directed his reverence toward the Christianity of the New Testament as the only norm of truth, and unleashed his contempt at the clerics and their phony religiosity. Brandes correctly points out that, of Kierkegaard's writings, *Øjeblikket* most fathomed and captured the Danish psyche and left a lasting impression on it.[157] After writing a long book characterized by continuous tension between author and subject, Brandes at the end identifies with Kierkegaard's rebellion against the Church; however, he does so on his own terms as a freethinker, and their agreement is a purely surface one. Alas, Kierkegaard's death was premature, for Brandes believed that, had he lived a little longer, Kierkegaard would undoubtedly have arrived at Brandes's own radical and irreligious position. At that point contempt would have triumphed over reverence.

It does not require a highly sophisticated religious sensibility or an intricate knowledge of Christianity in particular to realize that Brandes had very little idea what he was talking about when purporting to treat the subject of religion in connection with Kierkegaard. Simply put, Brandes did not understand Kierkegaard's Christianity. His reverence/contempt dichotomy, while disarming in its simplicity and alluring in the way it seems to relate key biographical events to relevant works, fails ultimately in probing the deeper enigmas of Kierkegaard's religious faith, let alone in presenting any coherent picture of his conception of Christianity. Brandes has been acclaimed by many scholars as a pioneer in critical studies of Kierkegaard; however, few of them have cited his one-track, reductionist interpretation of Kierkegaard's religion as an outstanding contribution.[158] One reason has to do with Brandes's utter inability to comprehend Kierkegaard's category of the paradoxical, which he consigns to the realm of absurdity. He confidently reiterates a conviction he had expressed in his essay *Dualismen i vor nyeste Philosophie* that the time will come when philosophers will talk about the paradox and the role it has played exactly the way chemists nowadays speak of phlogiston.[159] Kierkegaard's incessant dwelling on the paradox was, for Brandes, a sure sign of a disturbed mind. All that Brandes could make of the paradox

---

157. Ibid., all of chap. XXVII entitled "Agitationen," pp. 254–64, deals with *Øjeblikket.*
158. An example of the majority of scholars concurring on this point would be Aage Henriksen, *Methods and Results,* pp. 28–29. Henriksen says that Brandes was bound to arrive at "fallacious conclusions" having started out from "erroneous premises."
159. Brandes, *Søren Kierkegaard,* pp. 115-16.

was to regard it as the desperate and twisted resolution of the dialectical conflict between reverence and contempt. "Dialectical" is a poor choice of words here: if anything, Brandes completely missed the pervading dialectical purpose of much of Kierkegaard's writing and its bearing on, or reflection of, his life. The "dialectic" of reverence and contempt—if one wishes to call it that—is contrived and tells us more about Brandes's own prejudices leading to his choice of these terms than about the person to whom they are supposed to apply.

Having said this, one must not underestimate Brandes's realization of the potential danger for his radical program of secular humanism posed by an unchecked rise in the popularity of Kierkegaard's religious message: the return to authentic New Testament Christianity. It has been pointed out correctly that Brandes's book on Kierkegaard was a shrewd defense of freethought involving a clever strategy to choke a rival outlook by robbing it of its most brilliant and inspiring spokesman.[160] In fact this is precisely what Brandes had been attempting for over ten years, starting with his attack on Nielsen's dualism in 1866, moving on to the despiritualizing of Kierkegaard through the indirect medium of Strodtmann's book in 1873, and culminating in a direct and elaborate statement of the case in his 1877 book. The portrait that Brandes intended to sketch was one of a genius who was on the verge of freeing himself from the last traces of religion's suffocating grip when he was tragically overtaken by death. This was the silver lining that Brandes discerned in the otherwise sordid and pathetic tale of Kierkegaard, and he offered it as both a warning and a sign of hope to the young men of the modern age.

Very little speculation has to be done about Brandes's real motives with respect to Kierkegaard, since he spells them out unequivocally in a now-famous letter he wrote to a then-not-so-well-known personality, Friedrich Nietzsche. To Brandes goes the honor of "discovering" Nietzsche in the late 1880s and contributing significantly to his dissemination. He is also credited with being the first and only person to have brought Kierkegaard to Nietzsche's attention. In 1886 Nietzsche's publisher sent Brandes *Beyond Good and Evil*, and a year later, after receiving more of his works, Brandes initiated a correspondence with Nietzsche that lasted

160. See as examples Henriksen, *Methods and Results*, pp. 23 and 25; and F. J. Billeskov Jansen, "Brandes," in *The Legacy and Interpretation of Kierkegaard*, vol. 8 of *Bibliotheca Kierkegaardiana* (1981), p. 207. See also the section in P. V. Rubow's *Georg Brandes's Briller*, pp. 140–54, for an interesting analysis of Brandes's book.

until the latter's sudden onset of mental illness in 1889.[161] The correspondence is rich with information about their common intellectual interests and their attitudes toward various writers and movements of their day. A letter Brandes wrote to Nietzsche from Copenhagen on January 11, 1888, contained the following illuminating paragraph:

> There is one Scandinavian writer whose works would interest you, if only they were translated: Sören Kierkegaard. He lived from 1813 to 1855, and is in my opinion one of the profoundest psychologists that have ever existed. A little book I wrote about him (translated, Leipzig, 1879) gives no adequate idea of his genius, as it is a sort of polemical pamphlet written to curb his influence. But in a psychological respect it is, I think, the most subtle thing I have published.[162]

The key word is "curb," which is a translation of the German *hemmen* in the original, meaning to hamper, curb, check, or impede.[163] In his reply Nietzsche wrote from Nice: "On my next visit to Germany I propose to take up the psychological problem of Kierkegaard."[164] One of the extremely regrettable facts of modern European intellectual history is that this never came about.

By alerting Nietzsche to Kierkegaard's exceptional psychological mastery and indicating simultaneously that his influence needed to be inhibited, Brandes was hoping to unleash a kindred free spirit who, he felt, would prove to be a powerful adversary against any Kierkegaard-inspired

---

161. Nietzsche's final communication with Brandes was in the form of a two-line note, unstamped and undated (the postmark said: Turin, January 4, 1889) with no return address. It was written in large handwriting on a paper ruled in pencil, like the ones children draw on. It read: "To the Friend Georg: When once you had discovered me, it was easy enough to find me; the difficulty now is to get rid of me...." It was signed "The Crucified." This English translation is included in Georg Brandes's *Friedrich Nietzsche*, trans. A. G. Chater (London, 1914), p. 97.

162. The translation is this writer's in consultation with two other translations: A. G. Chater's translation in Brandes, *Friedrich Nietzsche*, pp. 69–70; and the translation of Peter Fuss and Henry Shapiro in their edition of *Nietzsche: A Self-Portrait from His Letters* (Cambridge, Massachusetts: Harvard University Press, 1971), p. 108 note.

163. For a copy of the original letter in German see *Correspondance de Georg Brandes*, comp. and ed. Paul Krüger (Copenhagen: Rosenkilde og Bagger, 1966), vol. III, Letter no. 611, p. 447.

164. Letter from Nietzsche to Brandes dated February 19, 1888, and trans. A. G. Chater in Brandes, *Friedrich Nietzsche*, p. 71. In his reply to this letter, dated March 7, Brandes acquainted Nietzsche with Ibsen in the following fashion: "Ibsen will certainly interest you as a personality. Unfortunately as a man he does not stand on the same level that he reaches as a poet. Intellectually he owes much to Kierkegaard, and he is still strongly permeated by theology" (p. 74).

religious revival. As things turned out, however, Brandes merely managed to leave us with solid proof of the agitational intention of his 1877 book on Kierkegaard, and to provide additional confirmation that the impact of Kierkegaard's writings was on the increase.

Reactions to Brandes's book on Kierkegaard were swift and plentiful, pouring in from all over Scandinavia. Whatever the author's purpose may have been in writing his book, the result was that it stimulated unprecedented discussions of Kierkegaard in the North. In Norway, as we have seen, Brandes met with strong opposition from the academic and clerical communities when he delivered his Kierkegaard lectures in the fall of 1876. The opposition quickly translated itself into hostile responses in print.

Morgenbladet, the conservative Norwegian daily, published an analysis of the lectures containing many favorable comments about Kierkegaard's works but few compliments for their interpreter. Kierkegaard's production was "so rich, so comprehensive, so deep, so original in thought and form" that no other literature could occupy a place next to it—certainly not the drab books of devotion currently in the hands of the general public. Yet Brandes, the nature of whose investigation the paper found it difficult to define beyond calling it "a psychological study," aimed at portraying Kierkegaard as a mental case, a sick man from a sick family. This, wrote the paper, was reminiscent of Voltaire's attempt to characterize Pascal in a similar way. The religious orthodoxy of Kierkegaard's childhood plagued him all his life and prevented him from joining the ranks of the modern warriors for free thought, to whom Brandes prided himself on belonging. It was obvious to *Morgenbladet* from the blunt anti-Christian tirades of the lectures—which were toned down somewhat and rendered more subtle in the ensuing book—that Brandes wished to destroy, or at least impair, the Christian character and thrust of Kierkegaard's thought. Brandes, explained the paper, is the product of a well-defined tradition going back to Heine and Börne. Moreover, it is the outlook of this tradition that increasingly holds sway in modern society in the form of positivist-Darwinist convictions. Although Brandes's point about Kierkegaard's limitations in the areas of science and history had some validity, the paper chided Brandes for parroting the popular phrases and catchwords of science without himself either being a scientist or knowing much about natural science. He is like a wholesaler who receives his merchandise by railway, employing steam in the service of commerce and chemicals to facilitate mercantile transactions, and thereby believes he has entered the world of science and can lay claim to its treasures: "No error is in our time more widespread than this." Brandes even poked his nose into cellular pathology, concluded the paper indignantly, by comparing Kierkegaard's first work (the critical essay on Andersen) to the first cell of a cancer. Brandes here became the concerned pathologist, who perhaps ought to have prescribed Quinine or salicylic acid as treatments for the afflicted writer.[165]

Attacking Brandes's scientism was only one of the tactics used in response to his lectures and book on Kierkegaard. Another approach common among clergymen (with potentially uglier and more damaging consequences) involved unsparing character assassination that focused attention on Brandes's Jewishness. The leading spokesman in Norway for this line of opposition was pastor J. C. Heuch.[166] *Morgenbladet*'s article had alluded to Brandes's use in his last lecture of the phrase "unbaptized reason" to describe his own mind as being free of Christian infestation; however, the paper stopped short of relating this to the fact that Brandes was of Jewish extraction, and simply dismissed it as a "slightly unfortunate expression." Nor was placing Brandes in the same tradition as Heine necessarily intended to invoke racial connotations. With Heuch, on the other hand, it was a different story. He was professor of practical theology at the University of Christiania from 1875 to 1880, and was well known for his outspoken defenses of the Church and its doctrines in the face of "the age's unbelief." His policy was simply that Christians ought to fight back in self-defense. In 1875 Heuch took over the editorship of *Luthersk Kirketidende,* where he displayed excessive zeal in his apologetics. Since the Lutheran foundation sponsoring the publication desired a more cautious and circumspect course, Heuch started his own weekly in 1877 that he called *Luthersk Ugeskrift.*[167] He turned it into a platform for combating all forms of religious liberalism and modern secularism. Brandes became

165. *Morgenbladet,* December 15, 1876. See also note 105 above.
166. On Heuch see Chapter 5 above.
167. See L. Selmer, "J. C. Heuch i Kamp mot Vantroen" (Heuch in confrontation with unbelief), in *Norsk Teologisk Tidsskrift,* ed. Lyder Brun, Oluf Kolsrud, and Hans Ording, 4th series, vol. 9 (Oslo, 1938), p. 186. In 1876 Bjørnson had published, under Brandes's influence, an article in *Oplandenes Avis,* no. 42, maintaining that Christian preaching needed to change because it was no longer relevant to the modern consciousness. Heuch countered with a set of candid articles in *Luthersk Kirketidende* against "modern apostasy," declaring that in fact the modern consciousness had to change to accommodate the Christian message. The articles were later published as a book (Selmer, pp. 189–90).

one of its earliest targets. Heuch used Brandes's lectures on Kierkegaard at the Student Union as the occasion for a series of articles in which Brandes was personally denounced as "an anti-Christian Jew," "the first open denyer of Christ," and "the spokesman for manifest apostasy."[168] With regard to Brandes's treatment of Kierkegaard, Heuch wrote:

> [A]n infidel Jew must of necessity lack the preconditions to understand a personality like Søren Kierkegaard[.] How could someone who cannot grasp the meaning of the faith and the fervency involved in the religious relationship with God understand Kierkegaard's significance? To accentuate the religious intensity, to bring anyone to the point of becoming 'the single individual' upon which he repents [and moves] away from perdition in externals, these were indeed the great purposes of his entire work as a writer.

Heuch proceeds to explain the real reasons behind Brandes's choice of Kierkegaard as the subject of his lectures:

> One ought to have comprehended that the agitator Dr. Brandes did not just accidentally choose Kierkegaard out of the rich assembly of Denmark's famous literary figures, but that he did this because, better than anyone else, Kierkegaard provided him with the opportunity, under the protective shield of literary history, to lead the battle against the Christian view of life.[169]

Heuch terminates this section of his article by calling Brandes "a malicious dwarf" in comparison with Kierkegaard.

It is fascinating to observe how two people with completely opposite and antagonistic views could derive so much inspiration from the polemical weapons of a single source: Kierkegaard. Brandes's unabashed defiance of the conservative authorities at Christiania University and his militant offensive against the established religion drew much of their strength from *Øjeblikket*'s fiery style and Kierkegaard's *Kirkekampen* polemics. By the same token, Heuch's combative spirit and his fierce assaults on Brandes received substantial stimulation from the irony and sarcastic wit of Kierkegaard's writings.[170] Heuch's injurious anti-Semitic outbursts, how-

---

168. See as an example J. C. Heuch's untitled article on Brandes's lectures in *Luthersk Ugeskrift*, no. 5 (Christiania, February 8, 1877), pp. 103-12. The phrase "anti-Christian Jew" occurs three times and "infidel Jew" once in the article. Heuch also published a separate tract entitled *Dr. G. Brandes's Polemik mod Kristendommen* (Christiania, 1877), 73 pages, in which he attacked Brandes as a Jew.

169. Heuch's article in *Luthersk Ugeskrift*, p. 107.

170. On Brandes's polemics and Kierkegaard's influence see Rubow, *Georg Brandes's Briller*, p. 110. On Heuch's ironic style and its Kierkegaardian undertones see Selmer,

ever, were unfortunate and unnecessary, because they detracted from the otherwise well-founded criticisms he made of Brandes's crude campaign against Christianity. Brandes *was* anti-Christian; he *was* irreverent; he *was* hypocritical in assuming an air of false objectivity on some occasions when dealing with religious topics; and from the standpoint of the Church, he *did* represent a clear danger to Scandinavian youth and had to be dealt with. But Brandes was all these things *because* he was himself irreligious, an admitted atheist and agitator. Ascribing them to his being Jewish is not only cheap, but impairs Heuch's legitimate complaints by making it too easy for Brandes's supporters and for later scholars to dismiss out of hand, and on the basis of its bigoted anti-Semitism, his entire case against Brandes, thus liberating Brandes from rigorous critical scrutiny. By invoking Brandes's background as the root of the problem, Heuch was doing his own cause a disservice, not to mention hardly displaying the proper Christian spirit. Brandes's relationship to his Jewishness and to Judaism in general is a complex issue that he wrestled with all his life in spite of his frequent public denials of its relevance. Yet he was by no means a believing and practicing Jew, but a secular intellectual disciple of men like Mill, Spencer, Darwin, Comte, and Taine, none of whom was Jewish.[171] As Ernst Sars, a leading liberal spokesman and supporter of Brandes, put it incisively at the time: "Shall it now be wrong to account for Kierkegaard's conduct by saying that he or his father was a Jutlander, but correct to explain Dr. Brandes's behavior on the basis that he is Jewish?"[172] These few words capture the essence of the perils involved in an exclusive reliance on the biographical-psychological ap-

---

"J. C. Heuch i Kamp mot Vantroen," p. 188; and Jens Tandberg, *Biskop Heuchs Liv og Virke*, p. 19.

171. On Brandes's Jewish identity see the interesting and informative article by Henry J. Gibbons entitled "Georg Brandes: The Reluctant Jew," in *The Activist Critic*, ed. Hans Hertel and Sven Møller Kristensen (Copenhagen, 1980), pp. 55–89. The extent to which Brandes's Jewishness may have played a role in inducing his outspoken anti-Christian positions is something that neither Heuch nor any other opponents of Brandes could possibly have had a way of determining.

172. Quoted in Knut Rygnestad, *Johan Christian Heuch: Apologet og Stridsmann*, p. 73; On Heuch's attacks against Brandes and their anti-Semitic flavor see pp. 68–74. See also Tandberg, *Biskop Heuchs Liv og Virke*, pp. 45–53; and Selmer, "J. C. Heuch i Kamp mot vantroen," pp. 190–92. Many subsequent writers on Brandes have concentrated on the theme of his Jewishness. Maurice Muret's *L'Esprit juif: Essai de psychologie ethnique* (Paris, 1901), has a chapter on Brandes (pp. 214–58), in which Muret states unequivocally that the motivating force behind all of Brandes's writings was his hatred of Christianity (pp. 254 and 257).

proach, whether it be Brandes writing on Kierkegaard or Heuch on Brandes.

Heuch was not alone in harping on Brandes's Jewish background. Back in Denmark this was a favorite theme among Brandes's enemies and friends alike, and haunted him constantly. The general feeling was that Brandes, despite his culture and his urbane manners, remained essentially foreign, an outsider, and was not a genuine Dane. This feeling assumed prominence in the early 1870s, when Brandes launched his program for the "Modern Breakthrough" in literature and castigated the Danes for not keeping up with European developments. Carl Ploug, the editor of *Fædrelandet,* repeatedly reminded Brandes of his status as an alien in Danish society. Earlier, during the "Tro og Viden" Controversy in the 1860s in which Brandes had participated, no one brought up the topic of his Jewishness.[173] Sir Edmund Gosse (1849–1928), the English poet and critic who knew Brandes and paid a visit to Denmark in 1877, wrote the following observations:

> Brandes was a Jew, an illuminated specimen of a race little known at that time in Scandinavia, and much dreaded and suspected. That a scion of this hated people, so long excluded from citizenship, should come forward with a loud message of defiance to the exquisite and effete intellectual civilization of Denmark, this was in itself an outrage. Scandinavians were only just beginning to tolerate the idea of Jews in the community, and here was a wholly impenitent and unchristianized example of the race standing up in the midst of the national ideals, and breaking them with his irony and ridicule.[174]

This illustrates the rapid change in Danish attitudes toward Jews in the space of a decade. It is worthy of mention that Gosse was aware of Brandes's book on Kierkegaard, although he never read anything by Kierkegaard himself. In a letter to Brandes, Gosse praised his book and added: "It exposes the man and the work admirably even to one who, like myself, knows nothing of his writings".[175]

---

173. Gibbons, "Georg Brandes: The Reluctant Jew," p. 59, and 64–65. On Carl Ploug see pp. 62–63 and 66–67.

174. Edmund Gosse, *Two Visits to Denmark* (London, 1911), pp. 165–66.

175. Letter from Gosse to Brandes dated July 30, 1877, in *Correspondance de Georg Brandes,* ed. Paul Krüger, vol. II, p. 63. Two years after his 1877 trip to Denmark, Gosse produced a book on Nordic literature he called *Studies in the Literature of Northern Europe* (London, 1879); he dedicated it "with admiration and affection" to Brandes, "the most distinguished of Scandinavian critics." The book touched on practically every major Scandinavian writer, yet Kierkegaard's name was conspicuous in its absence. It seems strange that such an astute foreign critic as Sir Edmund, who knew about Kierkegaard

The spearhead of early reactions to Brandes's lectures and book on Kierkegaard, however, continued to be Norwegian. Two treatises from 1877 merit attention. The first was an independently published, fifteen-page essay by Ibsen's biographer P. Hansen, which he called *Noter til Dr. G. Brandes's "Søren Kierkegaard"*. It attempted, using the recently published journals of Kierkegaard for the year 1847 (Barfod's *Efterladte Papirer*, volume IV), to disqualify Brandes's interpretation by showing that Mynster, the state-Church, and the theologians were never at any time the "idols" that Brandes alleged they had been for Kierkegaard before he turned on them and smashed them "with an axe" at the end of his life.[176] The journal entries Hansen cites appeared too late for Brandes to consult in preparing his book. Hansen also takes issue with Brandes's disregard for Kierkegaard's plea that he and his pseudonyms be separated in the reader's mind. The essay further indicates the widespread irritation that Brandes's lectures and succeeding book aroused in the North.

The second treatise was a three-volume monstrosity (897 pages in all) by an ordained professor of theology at the University of Christiania named Frederik C. Petersen (1839–1903). It was entitled *Dr. Søren Kierkegaards Christendomsforkyndelse* (S. K.'s proclamation of Christianity); coming out soon after Brandes's book, it appeared to have been written specifically in response to that work. In fact the bulk of the work consisted of pieces written years earlier and only then assembled into the enormous tomes in question. Petersen had attended Brandes's lectures in the fall of 1876 in Christiania; shortly thereafter he gave his own set of lectures on Kierkegaard at the University, intended to counteract Brandes. Only the introductory note and conclusion to his ensuing work on Kierkegaard were written with Brandes in mind; the rest was a compilation of previous material.

Petersen was born in the Norwegian town of Stavanger, traditionally a Haugian pietist stronghold. His mother was Danish from Copenhagen. Both the emotional revivalist pastor Lammers and the calmer theologian Gisle Johnson exercised an impact on the young Petersen, but eventually Johnson's more systematic approach to Scripture and apologetics got the

---

through Brandes, should have neglected him in a survey of Nordic literature. Once again the Anglo-Saxon world missed a rare chance in the nineteenth century to make the acquaintance, though fleetingly, of someone who would nevertheless be destined to call on its shores.

176. P. Hansen, *Noter til Dr. G. Brandes's "Søren Kierkegaard"* (Christiania, 1877), pp. 13–15.

upper hand. Petersen was also exposed to Kierkegaard at an early age through his *Works of Love*. While still a student in 1857, he read *Øjeblikket* and then delved into a wide range of the remaining writings. He quickly became a Kierkegaard enthusiast, and it was Kierkegaard who led him to the rigorous study of theology.[177] His subsequent theological development can be characterized as a prolonged and convoluted attempt at harmonizing Kierkegaard with the later Johnson, who himself had started out as a Kierkegaardian but moved increasingly in the direction of systematic theology and became critical of his initial orientation.[178]

In 1866–67 Petersen undertook a trip to Germany that brought him to Tübingen, where he made the acquaintance of the theologian Johann Tobias Beck and attended his lectures. Petersen felt himself immediately drawn to Beck as a person, but less so to his theology. Under Kierkegaard's influence, Beck was not simply lashing out at the lukewarm faith or outright unbelief of the age; he was also critical of the impotent orthodoxy of the Lutheran Church in Germany. Petersen called Beck "the only theologian among them who wishes to adhere to the faith as Kierkegaard knows it."[179]

A degree of ambivalence toward Kierkegaard began to surface in Petersen at this time, and upon his return to Norway he lectured on Kierkegaard's works and published around a hundred pages on him in 1869 in *Theologisk Tidsskrift for den evangelisk-lutherske Kirke i Norge*.[180] He was also reacting, in part, to Rasmus Nielsen's lectures two years earlier in Christiania, in which Nielsen expounded his controversial position in the debate over "Tro og Viden." On the whole, Petersen's approach to this problem was more philosophical than Nielsen's, in that he viewed revelation as a necessary substitute for knowledge lost after the Fall, rather than as an exclusive avenue to truth and salvation.[181] As Kierkegaard's journals started to appear in 1869, Petersen decided to write reviews of Barfod's edition for the Norwegian press and periodicals. A series of these reviews

---

177. The most comprehensive source on Petersen remains Ludvig Selmer's book *Professor Fredrik Petersen og Hans Samtid* (Oslo: Land og Kirke, 1948); see pp. 11–19 and 20–28. See also Harald Beyer, "Søren Kierkegaards betydning" (1), pp. 22–23; and Paulus Svendsen, "Norwegian Literature," in *The Legacy and Interpretation of Kierkegaard*, vol. 8 of *Bibliotheca Kierkegaardiana* (1981), pp. 22–23.

178. See Chapter 3 above.

179. Quoted in Selmer, *Petersen*, p. 38; see also pp. 37–38.

180. See *Theologisk Tidsskrift for den evangelisk-lutherske Kirke i Norge* (Christiania, 1869), pp. 489–583. See also Selmer, *Petersen*, p. 41.

181. Selmer, *Petersen*, pp. 76–80; see also Chapter 5 above.

came out in 1870 in *Morgenbladet* and in *Luthersk Kirketidende,* then under the editorship of Gisle Johnson. They dealt mostly with Kierkegaard's childhood years and the melancholy that marked his early development, and contained many quotations from the journals. Interestingly, Petersen seemed anxious to downplay the importance of these journals for an overall understanding of Kierkegaard's works, perhaps because he was afraid that what he had already written on Kierkegaard would have to be reevaluated in the light of the new documents. He wrote emphatically in *Luthersk Kirketidende:*

> I do not believe that any one of Kierkegaard's works will become better understood by the help of these papers. I believe the entire corpus is, to a degree, a whole that is conclusive in itself. Nothing better can interpret them or a part of them than they themselves.[182]

He added that whatever relevant revelations about Kierkegaard's personal life were necessary for comprehending his works had already been made available in *The Point of View:* "I stress explicitly this little work by Kierkegaard." These declared views about the journals notwithstanding, Petersen remained very interested in them, as Bishop P. C. Kierkegaard, in whose possession they were, attests in his diary. In August of 1872 Petersen came especially from Christiania to Denmark to pay the bishop a visit.[183]

Petersen's large work of 1877 has been neglected by many Kierkegaard researchers, and in a sense not without good reason. It is cumbersome, prolix, and unimaginative, and adds little to our knowledge of Kierkegaard, and raises few exciting questions. The fundamental flaw of the work, according to Ludvig Selmer, is the author's persistent attempt to "systematize" Kierkegaard theologically.[184] In 1875, Petersen took over Johnson's chair as full professor of systematic theology at the University. He continued to write little articles on Kierkegaard for *Theologisk Tidsskrift* throughout the 1870s, and most of them found their way, in one form or another, into the book. The outcome was an amorphous treatise, written in the style of dogmatic apologetics, and aiming inconclusively at a critique of Kierkegaard from the standpoint of an ill-defined "official" theology that Petersen felt he represented. This becomes apparent, for

---

182. See *Morgenbladet,* January 23, 30; February 6, 13, 27; and March 6, 1870; and *Luthersk Kirketidende,* new series II (Christiania, January 15, 1870), pp. 56–57.
183. See Carl Weltzer, *Peter og Søren Kierkegaard,* vol. II, p. 332.
184. Selmer, *Petersen,* p. 43.

instance, in his treatment of Kierkegaard and Hegel. Petersen, himself an anti-Hegelian and a dissenter in the ranks of speculative theologians of his day who derived their inspiration from the German philosopher, nevertheless gives the impression of wavering between Kierkegaard's rejection of Hegelian implications for theology, and the position of those theologians, like Martensen, who erect their entire system on Hegelian foundations. His point seems to be that while Kierkegaard is justified in criticizing the pagan aspects of Hegel's thought, he commits an error when he transfers the same criticisms onto Martensen, who, after all, is a Christian.[185]

In an effort to transcend his earlier infatuation with Kierkegaard, Petersen now rejects the paradox, severely qualifies the claim of *Postscript* that "truth is subjectivity," refuses the interpretation of Abraham's sacrifice in *Fear and Trembling,* detects in the concept of the "single individual" an isolation from both God and man, and all along defends the Church against the accusations of *Øjeblikket*.[186] He devotes about 350 pages to a lucid but tedious chronological account of Kierkegaard's major writings, and regards *Either/Or* as Kierkegaard's principal work, because in it the vital notion of freedom of choice is presented.[187] He avoids any detailed discussion, à la Brandes, of Kierkegaard's personal life, which he covers in six pages.[188] In his conclusion, Petersen softens his previous criticisms by acknowledging Kierkegaard's importance for both the Church and culture as a whole. He views Kierkegaard, in the final analysis, as a transitional figure ["*en Overgangsskikkelse*"] in an age that is quickly abandoning Christianity to wallow in its own emptiness.[189] Kierkegaard points to the right way, yet because of his own unclear status, friends and enemies of Christ alike can consider him as the foundation of their opposing viewpoints, for in the case of the latter they too "inherited Kierkegaard's costume, his outer garments."[190] Petersen had to be thinking of Brandes when he wrote these words.

Even though it was not a direct response to the perceived shortcomings of Brandes's book, Petersen's work did circumvent the biographical-psychological method and made a conscious attempt to be comprehensive,

---

185. F. C. Petersen, *Dr. Søren Kierkegaards Christendomsforkyndelse* (Christiania, 1877), pp. 517–19. See also Selmer, *Petersen*, pp. 44–49.
186. Petersen, *Dr. Søren Kierkegaards Christendomsforkyndelse,* pp. 574ff., 465–69, 704–32, and 633–43 respectively.
187. Ibid., p. 881.   188. Ibid., pp. 459–64.
189. Ibid., pp. 894–95.   190. Ibid., p. 897.

albeit within the confines of a pervading theological emphasis. However, the net product, intended primarily for clergymen and learned scholars, did not really have the effect of encouraging the reader to pursue the study of Kierkegaard much further.[191] Like Brandes, the author was shaking off a youthful enthusiasm for Kierkegaard, but his conclusions were very different from Brandes's and were not propelled by tendentious, ulterior motives.

If Brandes caused such a stir in Norway with his radical views and supercilious style, in Denmark outright consternation greeted his book on Kierkegaard. So unfavorable was the general reaction that all Brandes's hopes of acquiring a professorship at the University were dashed, and he departed that year for Germany, where he remained until 1883. The degree of hostility generated by his book is reflected in a dispatch that the Copenhagen correspondent for the Swedish paper *Aftonbladet* sent home: "By throwing his entire critical apparatus against Christianity, [Brandes] has aroused strong opposition, and in this way the book has defeated its own purpose."[192]

The climate of intolerance that was building up as a reaction not only to Brandes's unreserved attacks on religion, but to the entire freethinking temper of the age, led Sophus Heegaard[193] to publish in 1878 a book entitled *Om Intolerance* in which he advocated the right of every individual to hold and proclaim his own personal beliefs free of persecution. Differing points of view could then coexist and interact in a true liberal atmosphere of mutual respect. The book caused a considerable sensation and was adopted as a manifesto by the champions of free thought all over Scandinavia. An open showdown between orthodoxy and free thought was at hand. Brandes had gingerly removed himself from the melee just in time; however, others like Bjørnson, marching in his radical footsteps, became the butt of retaliation from ultra-conservative clergymen.[194] Foremost among these religious warriors was J. C. Heuch, who regarded all attempts at being "tolerant" and "objective" as a sin against truth. Faith

191. Svendsen, "Norwegian Literature," p. 26.
192. *Aftonbladet,* May 23, 1877.
193. On Heegaard see Chapter 5 above.
194. Brandes wrote the following cryptic comment from Berlin to a friend: "I read Heegaard's book *Om Intolerance:* well-meaning and brave, but it seems to me Kierkegaardian in its thoughts and consequently elementary in its contents." See letter from Brandes to Emil Petersen dated April 7, 1878, in *Georg Brandes og Emil Petersen, en Brevveksling,* ed. Morten Borup, p. 236.

cannot be tolerant of apostasy, he wrote, because faith is not merely another idea, but a life-experience that penetrates the inner depths of a man's soul and alters his entire outlook on existence.[195] This put Heuch on a direct collision course with Bjørnson, who was an influential force in Norwegian cultural life of the late 1870s. Bjørnson had gradually renounced an earlier unquestioning faith in order to link arms with the freethinkers, liberals, and biblical critics in their fight against the Church's doctrines and apologists. In an article in *Dagbladet* from 1879, Bjørnson referred to Heuch's views as "pure humbug." Heuch angrily countered with a series of attacks on Bjørnson, which were later collected and published in book form. Soon others joined in on both sides, and Scandinavia was ablaze with renewed controversy.[196]

Significant for our purposes here is the manner in which Kierkegaard was resorted to and utilized by various individuals representing a variety of viewpoints with the aim of bolstering their opposing positions. There were those like Christopher Bruun who seized the opportunity to criticize the official Church for not being Christian enough. *Øjeblikket* was their main source of inspiration, and they were not spared by Heuch.[197] Others like Petersen were also the object of Heuch's disdain for not doing enough to rush to the Church's defense. They were perceived as liberal theologians who preferred to watch from the sidelines.[198] In the camp of the freethinkers, *Øjeblikket* was transformed into a weapon against all organized religion and religious belief. It is interesting to note that Bjørnson derived much inspiration from a book by the Swedish writer Viktor Rydberg (1828–95) entitled *Bibelns lära om Kristus* (1862, reissued 1880). Rydberg had waged a campaign against compulsory membership in the Swedish state-Church, along the lines of Kierkegaard's final confrontation

---

195. See the series of articles by Heuch entitled "Om Troens Intolerance og Tolerance" in *Luthersk Ugeskrift* for the years 1878 and 1879. See also Tandberg, *Biskop Heuchs Liv og Virke*, pp. 55–59; and Selmer, "J. C. Heuch i Kamp mot Vantroen," pp. 192–93.

196. On the confrontation between Heuch and Bjørnson see Selmer, "J. C. Heuch," pp. 193–95. See also Selmer's *Petersen*, pp. 98–99; Tandberg, *Biskop Heuchs Liv og Virke*, pp. 59–68; and Rygnestad, *Johan Christian Heuch*, pp. 74–84.

197. On Bruun and Heuch see Harald Beyer, "Søren Kierkegaards betydning" (1), pp. 34–38. On Bruun's high regard for Petersen see Selmer, *Petersen*, pp. 258–60. For more on Bruun and Kierkegaard see Chapter 4 above.

198. Lyder Brun, "Professor Fredrik Petersen," in *Norsk Teologisk Tidsskrift*, vol. 10, 4th series (Oslo, 1939), p. 68. Heuch did not specifically mention Petersen by name, but according to Brun, the implication of his words against liberal theology were clear to Petersen.

with the Danish ecclesiastical authorities.[199] Bjørnson, however, insisted in a letter to Brandes that he had ceased to read Kierkegaard long ago.[200] Finally, Heuch himself espoused an experiential-existential orientation in his defense of the faith, while at the same time drawing on his powers of irony, all of which stemmed, in part, from Kierkegaard and Johnson.[201]

Thus Brandes, through his provocative book on Kierkegaard, had ignited the first spark of a conflagration, and then had taken his leave . . . for a while.

In Germany, Brandes found a more hospitable environment for his ideas, and this helped promote his book on Kierkegaard. Strodtmann made a translation of it that he published in 1879, but not before preparing the German reading public through a series of preview extracts put out the previous year in the *Allgemeine Zeitung* of Munich.[202] Strodtmann also wrote a laudatory review of the Danish edition for the *Augsburger Allgemeine Zeitung* of March 10, 1878. With the appearance of the book in German, readers in that language had their first glimpse at some of the peculiar features of Kierkegaard's private life. For many years thereafter, this German edition of Brandes's book remained the principal source of biographical information on Kierkegaard, in the absence of a German translation of the journals. It received a few brief German reviews in addition to Strodtmann's that were not overly enthusiastic but rather condescending.[203]

199. Selmer, *Petersen*, pp. 94–100. Rygnestad, *Johan Christian Heuch*, p. 78. For a treatment of Viktor Rydberg's relation to Kierkegaard see Nils Å Sjøstedt, *Søren Kierkegaard och Svensk Litteratur*, pp. 74–131.

200. Letter from Bjørnson to Brandes dated May 29, 1881, in Bjørnstjerne Bjørnson, *Kamp-Liv, Brev fra Aarene 1879–1884*, ed. Halvdan Koht, vol. I: 1879–1881 (Oslo: Gyldendal, 1932), p. 253. Bjørnson congratulated Brandes on his Kierkegaard book and wrote highly of it to the publisher Frederik Hegel. See letter from Bjørnson to Brandes of January 24, 1879 (p. 2), and letter from Bjørnson to Fr. Hegel of January 11, 1879 (p. 1).

201. Selmer, "J. C. Heuch i Kamp mot Vantroen," pp. 200ff. See in particular Heuch's books *Vantroens Væsen* (1883), and *Kirken og Vantroen* (1888) for a full account of his views.

202. Georg Brandes, *Sören Kierkegaard: Ein literarisches Charakterbild*, trans. Adolf Strodtmann (Leipzig, 1879). See also Adolf Strodtmann, "Sören Kierkegaard: Nach einer Charakteristik seiner literarischen Thätigkeit von G. Brandes," in the *Beilage zur Allgemeine Zeitung* 81 (Munich, October 3, 5, 6, and 10, 1878), pp. 4069–70, 4101–4, 4118–20, 4143–44, and 4173–75.

203. See Hans Herrig in *Magazin für die Literatur des Auslandes* 48 (1879), pp. 105–8; P. Keppler in *Literarische Rundschau* 5 (1879), pp. 184–86; and an anonymous reviewer signing "V" in *Deutsche Rundschau* 21 (1879), pp. 163ff.

Notice was taken of the book in *The Saturday Review* of London, where a few lines were devoted to it in a survey of recent German literature. The reviewer, a certain R. Garnett, is skeptical about Kierkegaard's prospects in countries other than his own. He writes:

> Sören Kirkegaard [*sic*] has been pronounced the first prose writer of Denmark in point of style, and is undoubtedly entitled to the elegant tribute which Dr. Brandes has paid to his memory, and perhaps all the more so as it is likely to remain his sole passport to a European reputation. . . . In a series of books neither strictly belonging to the domain of philosophy nor of *belles-lettres* he propounded original ideas bearing on questions of morality and aesthetical criticism in a style which produced a great impression in Denmark, but which, if we may judge by Dr. Brandes's too scanty examples, will hardly bear transplantation to the soil of another literature. . . . Dr. Brandes's substantial tribute to his memory after nearly a quarter of a century is a sufficient proof that he will not be forgotten by his countrymen, although foreigners must always take his merits upon trust.[204]

The reviewer also compares Kierkegaard to Pascal, Carlyle, and Hazlitt and calls him "a writer exceedingly difficult to class." Some biographical highlights are mentioned, all drawn from Brandes's book. One can appreciate the dim view the English reviewer took of Kierkegaard's future popularity in foreign cultures. Basing his judgment purely on what he read in Brandes's book, the reviewer could not help concluding that Kierkegaard was too bizarre a character for anyone's interest beyond the parochial bounds of Danish society.

Back in Germany at least one knowledgeable voice was raised in protest against Brandes's book shortly after it appeared in translation in 1879. This was Albert Bärthold, who had not been idle during the preceding several years but was producing translations of, and writing treatises on, Kierkegaard at the rate of one a year at least. In 1875 translations of twelve of the *Upbuilding Discourses* were reviewed enthusiastically in the *Theologischer Jahresbericht* of Wiesbaden.[205] The following year Bärthold put out three more "Discourses,"[206] and a remarkable piece that amounted

---

204. *The Saturday Review of Politics, Literature, Science and Art* 47 (London, February 15, 1879), pp. 219–20.

205. Albert Bärthold, ed. and trans., *Zwölf Reden von Sören Kierkegaard* (Halle, 1875). The anonymous review was in *Theologischer Jahresbericht*, ed. Wilhelm Hanck, vol. 10, no. 8 (Wiesbaden, 1875), pp. 386–87.

206. Albert Bärthold, ed. and trans., *Von den Lilien auf dem Felde und den Vögeln unter dem Himmel, Drei Reden Sören Kierkegaards* (Halberstadt, 1876).

to the first substantial biographical treatment of Kierkegaard in German: *Noten zu Sören Kierkegaards Lebensgeschichte*. In this, Bärthold was even ahead of Brandes's first Danish edition by one year, but he was using an approach diametrically opposed to that of Brandes, both in the conclusions it led to and in its format, which relied heavily on direct quoting from Kierkegaard's works. Unfortunately, however, his book did not possess enough aggressive verve or provocative stimulus to propel it to a wider audience than a few specialists and some theologically inclined readers.

In the foreword to the book, Bärthold states explicitly that his purpose in assembling the biographical work was his belief that it was "desirable" for Kierkegaard to become better known in Germany. Kierkegaard's life was like "a delightfully put-together play," and one must read his works "as expressions of his life."[207] Bärthold proceeds to do just that, using, in addition to *The Point of View* and Barfod's edition of the *Efterladte Papirer*, a small and unfinished piece from 1842-43 that Kierkegaard entitled *Johannes Climacus or De Omnibus Dubitandum Est, A Narrative*. The essay provides an abundance of autobiographical material by the author in the form of a sketch of the early life and development of the "deeply serious young man" Johannes. From this Bärthold reconstructs in his first chapter Kierkegaard's own relation to his stern father, their imaginary strolls in the woods together, the oppressively somber atmosphere at home, and the ceaseless taunting at school. He concludes that two forces were released in Kierkegaard at an early age and appear in his writings: the powerful dialectic, and the heavy melancholy.[208] Elsewhere Bärthold elaborates on this, writing that by 1838 the young Kierkegaard had at his disposal "immediate passion, boundless irony, ethical earnestness, melancholic humor, solemn religiosity, . . . [and the] burning energy of the Christian spirit in its yearning and eager love."[209]

The basic assumption underlying Bärthold's book was that Kierkegaard had actually written his own autobiography in scattered journal entries and numerous enigmatic references throughout his pseudonymous works, and that he left the piecing together of the puzzle to the reader. In order for the reader to do this, Kierkegaard must be allowed

---

207. Albert Bärthold, *Noten zu Sören Kierkegaards Lebensgeschichte* (Halle, 1876), p. iii.

208. Ibid., p. 8. For an English translation of Kierkegaard's autobiographical essay see *Johannes Climacus or De Omnibus Dubitandum Est, and A Sermon*, trans. T. H. Croxall (Stanford: Stanford University Press, 1958), esp. pp. 101-55.

209. Bärthold, ibid., p. 88.

to speak for himself—hence Bärthold's method of selecting, translating, and stringing together long quotations from the writings with minimal analytical commentary. The same three milestones (father, engagement, *Corsair*) that Brandes's book was to revolve around were highlighted by Bärthold, using Kierkegaard's own words. As a result of Kierkegaard's early upbringing, according to Bärthold, an opposition developed between flesh and spirit, the temporal and the eternal, and this opposition assumed the form of a struggle between doubt and faith.[210] Following his father's death, these two tendencies in Kierkegaard's life took two distinct and conflicting turns: a Faustian one, in Bärthold's words, and one toward religion. Kierkegaard became increasingly preoccupied with "medieval personifications" like Faust, Don Juan, and the Wandering Jew.[211] At the same time he shunned the option of the cloister and decided to remain in the world.[212] He soon arrived at the discovery that the idea for which one lives and dies—the truth—is truth "for me." Thus Kierkegaard's concept of subjectivity entails a personal relationship to a universal truth; the *Credo* begins with the words "I believe."[213]

Bärthold devotes his third chapter to Kierkegaard's engagement to "the beloved"—Bärthold did not know Regine's name and confesses he tried to ascertain it without success.[214] The reason Kierkegaard broke the engagement, in Bärthold's view, was his realization that his deep melancholy made it impossible for him to marry. Bärthold quotes at length from the journals to support this explanation.[215] He also compares Kierkegaard's *Liebesgeschichte* with Goethe's and says there is an absolute difference: while both wrote poetically about their loves, Kierkegaard, unlike Goethe, did not aim to cover up his guilt through poetic expression; rather, he focused on his own unconditional responsibility for breaking the engagement and amplified it. Instead of rationalizing his role, he totally incriminated himself. He continued to love her, but he could not saddle her with his melancholy.[216] All the pseudonymous works that followed were centered, in part, on the experience of the broken

210. Ibid., pp. 21 and 46.
212. Ibid., pp. 23–24.
211. Ibid., pp. 48, 50, and 57–58.
213. Ibid., pp. 53–55.
214. Ibid., p. 82. It is lovely, writes Bärthold, that Abelard and Heloise have been bound together for all these hundreds of years, but Kierkegaard's beloved will have to remain unknown! Apparently he believed there was no way of finding out her name.
215. Ibid., pp.64–70.
216. Ibid., pp. 61–63. Bärthold frequently compares Kierkegaard to German writers and mentions the names of many German thinkers who influenced him: Strauss, Bauer, Hamann, and others.

engagement, and were written pseudonymously so as to guard the reputation of the beloved. Employing medieval imagery, Bärthold likens these pseudonymous works to valiant deeds performed by Kierkegaard with lance in hand and then laid before his beloved, who was the only person capable of understanding them.[217]

Kierkegaard's sufferings at the hands of the *Corsair* are treated with the utmost concern and sympathy by Bärthold. In such a small place as Copenhagen, he writes, the effects of a confrontation with a scandal sheet of this kind are bound to be detrimental. Kierkegaard stood alone in his fight and was abandoned by everyone because the paper succeeded in arousing the public against him. Bärthold quotes Kierkegaard's condemnations in his journals of Copenhagen and her citizenry.[218] Despite its demoralizing effect, the incident with the *Corsair* ennobled Kierkegaard in reality and was a test of Christian self-denial for him. Both the journals and *Practice in Christianity* elaborate on this theme.[219]

Finally, Bärthold was aware of the "Tro og Viden" Controversy that had been indirectly triggered by Kierkegaard's writings, and he touched briefly upon Kierkegaard's concept of faith. Faith has a different scope from knowledge, because it ranges over the territory of uncertainty. In this domain, writes Bärthold, knowledge and rational probability "cannot breathe." Faith is thus a personal decision arrived at through a leap into the uncertain. This is inimical to the teachings of dogmatic theology and belongs to the province of paradox.[220] It only makes sense for the single individual in his subjective relationship with God.[221]

Less than a year after producing this biographical work on Kierkegaard, Bärthold put out a small book containing translated excerpts from *Postscript* with some analysis. It centered primarily on the section about Lessing in *Postscript,* but it also treated themes like Kierkegaardian irony, the choice between the aesthetic and the ethical, the question of personal decision, Socrates and Christ, and Christian art.[222] Added as an appendix was a translation of Rasmus Nielsen's reply to Martensen's *Om Tro og Viden* of 1867.[223] Although Bärthold states in his foreword that Nielsen and Kierkegaard were in fact wide apart on several issues, his inclusion

217. Ibid., pp. 81 and 84.
218. Ibid., pp. 106–13.
219. Ibid., pp. 115–18.   220. Ibid., pp. 104, and 94–95.
221. Ibid., pp. 121 and 124.
222. See Albert Bärthold, *Lessing und die objective Wahrheit* (Halle, 1877), pp. 36ff.
223. Ibid., pp. 82–98.

of the piece by Nielsen seems to indicate he closely identified their views on faith and knowledge and was pulling Nielsen into the picture as additional backing for Kierkegaard.[224] Bärthold dedicates the book to his theology professor at Tübingen, J. T. Beck, whom he praises for his deep understanding of Kierkegaard and thanks for having transmitted that understanding to him. Beck is in no way responsible for the content of the book, writes Bärthold, since his endorsement of Kierkegaard is not without its reservations; nevertheless, to him must go all the credit for everything Bärthold has gained from Kierkegaard.[225] The *Theologische Literaturzeitung* of Leipzig reviewed this work along with the biographical one of the previous year and the collection of "Discourses" Bärthold had translated. The reviewer, an H. Lindenberg, referred to Kierkegaard as "an amazing phenomenon," who not only caused an uproar in the Scandinavian Church while still alive, but continued to do so after his death. He expressed gratitude to Bärthold for making Kierkegaard accessible to the German reader.[226] In actuality, Bärthold's translations and commentaries received little attention initially outside theological circles in Germany, which put them at a disadvantage with respect to the wider popularity of Brandes's more controversial writings being translated during the same period.

In 1878 Bärthold translated *Practice in Christianity*.[227] That summer he traveled to Denmark, where he met Barfod for the first time. Barfod informs us that Bärthold first came to his attention in 1874. Two years later he received a letter from Bärthold, but it remained unanswered for over a year. In 1877 Barfod, for personal reasons, quit his work on Kierkegaard's papers, which by then had been transferred from the bishopric in Aalborg to the University Library archives in Copenhagen. At their first meeting in the summer of 1878, Bärthold introduced Barfod to a young theology student from Tübingen named Hermann Gottsched (1849-?), who like Bärthold was a pupil of J. T. Beck and had been led to Kierkegaard by Beck through a reading of *For Self-Examination* in the 1862 German translation by Christian Hansen. Gottsched became so engrossed by his new discovery that he set to work learning Danish in

---

224. Ibid., p. vi.
225. Ibid., p. v.
226. See H. Lindenberg's review in *Theologische Literaturzeitung*, ed. Emil Schürer, vol. 3, no. 8 (Leipzig, 1878), pp. 186-87.
227. Sören Kierkegaard, *Einübung im Christentum*, trans. Albert Bärthold (Halle, 1878).

order to read more of Kierkegaard. That fortuitous meeting, mediated by Bärthold, resulted in good news for Kierkegaard's legacy. The two became close friends, with the result that Barfod agreed to hand over the unfinished work on the journals to the eager Gottsched and help him get started. Gottsched moved to Denmark in 1879 and completed the job of editing and publishing the remaining journals of Kierkegaard in two years.[228]

Much well-deserved praise has been lavished on Gottsched for his role in preparing the first edition of Kierkegaard's journals. He was meticulous and methodical, treating the manuscripts with greater care than his predecessor had done. This was easier to accomplish, in part, because the nature of the material he was dealing with from Kierkegaard's later years was less chaotic than the earlier entries. However, Gottsched displayed a diplomatic sensitivity in the editing process not unlike Barfod's; he was particularly careful, for example, to leave out some of Kierkegaard's more candid references to Regine (now Mrs. Schlegel), or his often extreme self-assessments arising from the challenges and frustrations of the *Kirkekampen.* Moreover, Gottsched did not provide the reader with a list of the omissions he felt he needed to make—on the whole he was more frugal in his explanatory notes than Barfod had been. Gottsched performed his task admirably, which is all the more commendable when we recall that he was not a native speaker but belonged to a culture whose national and territorial aspirations brought it repeatedly into conflict with those of Denmark. Gottsched was well aware of this as indicated by his foreword to the fifth volume of the *Efterladte Papirer,* where he congratulates himself as a foreigner for undertaking the publication of the posthumous papers of a writer who was very closely bound to his homeland and its capital city.[229]

---

228. Our information about these developments comes largely from Barfod's foreword to the fifth volume of Kierkegaard's *Efterladte Papirer,* comp. and ed. H. Gottsched (Copenhagen, 1880), pp. viii–ix. This volume comprised journal entries from the year 1848. Two additional volumes for the years 1849 and 1850 appeared in 1880, and the last two volumes for the years 1851–53 and 1854–55 respectively appeared in 1881. With this, the first Danish edition of Kierkegaard's journals and papers was complete.

229. See ibid., pp. x–xi. On Gottsched see Henriksen, *Methods and Results,* pp. 16, 21, and 22; Carl Weltzer, *Peter og Søren Kierkegaard,* p. 345; and A. B. Drachmann, "Søren Kierkegaards Papirer, I," pp. 144–45. Barfod, it should be mentioned, performed one last service for the Kierkegaard family when, upon the death of Bishop Peter Kierkegaard in 1888, he compiled a small book of essays and poems by and about the bishop under the title *Til Minde om Biskop Peter Christian Kierkegaard* (Copenhagen, 1888).

A few months after Bärthold returned to Germany from his trip to Denmark (where he was instrumental in ensuring the continuation of work on Kierkegaard's posthumous papers) Brandes's controversial book on Kierkegaard appeared in German translation. The book did not appeal to Bärthold, and may indeed have infuriated him. He was distressed by its hostility to Kierkegaard's religious faith and the distortions arising from that hostility, but he also must have felt indignant that Brandes should now monopolize the spotlight of publicity by usurping what was really his accomplishment three years earlier: illustrating the interrelationship between Kierkegaard's life and his works. Add to this Brandes's reverence/contempt dichotomy, which paralleled uncomfortably the two conflicting tendencies of faith and doubt that Bärthold discerned in the young Kierkegaard, although it was only superficially similar to them. In response Bärthold put together a calm and well-argued essay dealing mainly with Kierkegaard's aesthetic writings—the principal focus of Brandes's treatment. It was his intention to refute the methods and conclusions of Brandes by pointing out subtle flaws in his biographical-psychological interpretation.

Bärthold begins by admitting that he had previously misunderstood many things in Kierkegaard's writings and by giving credit to Brandes's book for making this clear to him. He had also taken much in the journals at face value, he confesses, and now realizes that Barfod was right in warning the reader to be extra cautious with these journals.[230] Having said this, Bärthold takes a closer look at some of Brandes's claims and offers intelligent qualifications of them that testify to his vast knowledge of the Kierkegaard corpus and his desire for balance and wholeness in any treatment of Kierkegaard. The guilt that tormented Kierkegaard's father, for instance, was primarily religious in nature, going back to the days of his youth, rather than merely the result of his having seduced the woman who became Kierkegaard's mother.[231] With regard to Brandes's discussion of Kierkegaard's first critical piece against Andersen—to which Brandes devotes an entire chapter in his book[232]—Bärthold is unimpressed. He challenges Brandes's description of the fairytale writer as "poor and defenseless," arguing that the story "The Rose Bush and the

---

230. Albert Bärthold, *Die Bedeutung der ästhetischen Schriften Sören Kierkegaards, mit Bezug auf G. Brandes: "Sören Kierkegaard, ein literarisches Charakterbild"* (Halle, 1879), p. 5.
231. Ibid., pp. 5-6.
232. See Brandes, *Søren Kierkegaard*, chap. VII, pp. 33-41.

Snail" was Andersen's way of striking back at Kierkegaard after he had died.²³³ And when Brandes declares metaphorically that, while Kierkegaard was busy defending the fortress against speculative theologians like Martensen, the freethinkers Strauss and Feuerbach, whom he had neglected, slipped in the back way and conquered the castle, he overlooks crucial statements about these very same thinkers made through the pseudonymous Taciturnus and Climacus, which show Kierkegaard's awareness of their powers and even their usefulness for religion.²³⁴ Selecting a few of the aesthetic works, Bärthold then analyzes each briefly, with the aim of demonstrating that genuine religious concerns were operative in their composition and were not just the fallout from the broken engagement, as Brandes alleges. The essay is a compact corrective to the one-sided emphasis of Brandes's biographical-psychological perspective, and Bärthold obviously takes Kierkegaard's own religious self-interpretation in *The Point of View* seriously.

For a work that truly strives to be the definitive Christian corrective to Brandes's book on Kierkegaard, attention must turn to Sweden. It was the last significant response to Brandes, and appeared in 1880 under the title *Sören Kierkegaards Person och Författarskap, ett Försök* [S. K.'s person and works, an investigation]. The author, Waldemar Rudin (1833–1921), was professor of theology at the University of Uppsala from 1877 to 1900. His interest in Kierkegaard was first awakened by Zacharias Göransson, who eventually became one of Kierkegaard's translators into Swedish.²³⁵ He closely followed developments in the *Kirkekampen* in 1855, particularly through reading *Øjeblikket*, and made the acquaintance of pastor Lammers, who visited Sweden that same year.²³⁶ Additional reinforcement for his Kierkegaardian orientation came from J. T. Beck, whose theology he carefully studied.²³⁷

Rudin was present at Brandes's lectures in Uppsala in the fall of 1876, and like Petersen in Norway he resolved to deliver a series of "corrective" lectures of his own designed to emphasize features of Kierkegaard that Brandes had either ignored or undermined. The lectures were given in

233. Bärthold, *Die Bedeutung der ästhetischen Schriften*, pp. 6–7.
234. Ibid., pp. 7–9.
235. Sjöstedt, *Sören Kierkegaard och Svensk Litteratur*, pp. 27–28. Rudin wrote many introductions to Göransson's Swedish translations of Kierkegaard.
236. Ibid., p. 34. See also Gunnar Hultgren, "Mysteriet Kierkegaard," in *Vår Lösen* 31 (Stockholm, 1940), pp. 320–21.
237. Sjöstedt, *Sören Kierkegaard*, p. 37.

1877, the year Brandes's book appeared and was translated into Swedish[238]; they formed the basis for Rudin's book of 1880.

In the introduction to that book, Brandes's treatment is labeled a caricature that sketched Kierkegaard as a misfit with a malformed personality. Brandes's greatest defect, writes Rudin, is his portrayal of Kierkegaard as "a pure natural product of circumstances." He has not the slightest inkling of the finger of divine providence or the bounty of God's grace at work in the formation of the young genius.[239] If, therefore, Brandes is guilty of stressing one-sidedly the factors of milieu and psychological makeup, Rudin goes to comparable extremes in the opposite direction, acknowledging almost exclusively the spiritual components. He sincerely believes the best guide to Kierkegaard's writings and life is Kierkegaard himself, and so, of all the early Scandinavian commentators on Kierkegaard, Rudin is the one who takes the self-elucidations in the corpus with the greatest seriousness, making no attempt to deal with their puzzling internal contradictions. As Henriksen put it: "Søren Kierkegaard's own interpretation is then not only the subject of Rudin's work but also its limit."[240] His book thus becomes an extended description of Kierkegaard's own point of view, and is characterized by a heavily Christian bias throughout. *Postscript*, *The Point of View*, the journals, and *Øjeblikket* are the chief writings he draws on, and his final chapter contains direct translations of several articles by a host of writers from the *Kirkekampen*.[241]

Impressive, however, are the clear style and abundance of detail his book offers. Despite his stated aversion to interpretations other than Kierkegaard's own, Rudin was well-read in the available Scandinavian and German tracts on Kierkegaard and gives a brief survey of them in his introduction. In addition to Brandes, writers such as Nielsen, Martensen, Heuch, Bärthold, Petersen, Pape, Dietrichson, and Lysander are mentioned.[242] Of these, Rudin appears to have gleaned the most information

---

238. See G. Brandes, *Sören Kierkegaard*, trans. O. A. Stridsberg (Stockholm, 1877). Stridsberg also translated Kierkegaard into Swedish.

239. Waldemar Rudin, *Sören Kierkegaards Person och Författarskap, ett Försök* (Stockholm, 1880), pp. 4-5.

240. Henriksen, *Methods and Results*, p. 41

241. Rudin regards *Practice in Christianity* as Kierkegaard's most important work, religiously speaking (*Sören Kierkegaards Person och Författarskap, ett Försök*, p. 203), and considers *For Self-Examination* to be "a splendid introduction to the study of Kierkegaard" (p. 238).

242. Rudin, *Sören Kierkegaards Person*, pp. 10-12. W. Pape was a German pastor from Hildesheim, who wrote "S. Aa. Kierkegaard: Skizze seines Lebens und Wirkens," in *Der Beweis des Glaubens* 14 (Gütersloh, 1878), pp. 169-89.

from Brandes, Nielsen, Bärthold, and Petersen, as well as Brøchner's "Reminiscences," which are cited frequently in the book. Bärthold, for example, is treated with respect, because he wished that Kierkegaard should speak for himself and not be drowned out by the swelling din of critical analysis. Rudin emulates Bärthold's attitude. For him Kierkegaard, like Scripture, ought not to be criticized, but rather listened to. The less the critical content of a work on Kierkegaard, the better it was in Rudin's eyes. Petersen, for instance, was too critical; however, according to Rudin, his graver fault lay elsewhere. Although presenting us with "an entirely honest, serious, and accurate work," Petersen is disappointing in the scanty treatment he allots the most important of Kierkegaard's Christian writings.[243]

Most theological circles in Scandinavia gave Rudin's book a favorable reception when it first appeared. The religious establishment had come a long way since the stormy days of the *Kirkekampen* in accepting Kierkegaard, but it was an acceptance based not so much on a detached evaluation of his spiritual views as on motives of expediency. In the 1850s the assault on the Church had come largely from within the Christian fold; now, however, the forces attacking the Church were those of atheism, secularism, and modernism, whose real target was all religion as such. If these alien outlooks could obtain convenient ammunition from twisted versions of Kierkegaard's critiques—so the reasoning went—then why could his more sedate spiritual meditations and discourses not be pressed into service for the Church and used to counter the onslaught of unbelief? To many, Rudin's book seemed to be written with precisely this in mind.

The secular press, however, with a few isolated exceptions,[244] was predictably not as sympathetic toward Rudin as the theologians and clerics were. *Aftonbladet*, in a long review of the book, accused Rudin of indulging in the same type of reprehensible caricaturing, through his harsh judgment of Brandes, that he had criticized Brandes for doing with respect to Kierkegaard.[245] And *Stockholms Dagblad*, while admitting that Brandes's presentation of Kierkegaard was one-sided, saw the same onesidedness on the other end in Rudin's book. It is true, wrote the paper, that Rudin's Christian treatment fills a gap left by Brandes's work, which

---

243. Rudin, *Sören Kierkegaards Person*, p. 11.
244. *Berlingske Tidende*, the conservative Danish daily, printed a positive review of Rudin's book; see the issue for June 29, 1880.
245. *Aftonbladet*, July 24, 1880.

he was "by nature" incapable of filling; however, the tendency among readers who reject one extreme has been to seek refuge in the other, rather than to strive for a balanced interpretation that takes both positions into account.[246] One-sided or not, Rudin's book remains a major landmark in early Swedish Kierkegaard research, and it has since exercised a considerable influence on many in that country.[247] Perhaps its very extremism is an indication that the author has captured the essence of the Kierkegaardian corrective and, more importantly, has known when to apply it as an antidote in the face of the unbridled excesses of freethought.

The year that Rudin's book came out in Sweden also saw other scattered developments in the reception of Kierkegaard. The first fruits of Gottsched's editorial skills made their appearance as volumes five, six, and seven of Kierkegaard's *Efterladte Papirer*; as the previous four had, they occasioned renewed discussions about the man and his works. Writing from Berlin to his friend Emil Petersen, Brandes commented: "Have you read the latest installment to appear of Kierkegaard's papers? What things he says of the Danes!" His thoughts then turned to his own situation and he lamented: "Is it not a shame on Denmark that it has barred me from every actively radical occupation, and withdrawn from me all external influence, indeed all the favor and support that every other Danish scholar has?"[248] As a matter of fact, the anti-Brandes campaign in Denmark had not abated in 1880. *Fædrelandet* of July 30 carried a long front-page review, by someone signing "A.S.," of Gottsched's recent editions of the journals, of Rudin's book, and of a new book by Bärthold entitled *Zur theologischen Bedeutung Sören Kierkegaards*. The reviewer complains that both Brandes and Petersen had drawn warped pictures of Kierkegaard, even though certain isolated sections in their works deserve praise. Until today, he writes, there cannot be found, nor is there contemplated, a comprehensive in-depth treatment of Kierkegaard in his totality. Bärthold and Rudin come closest to this because they apply the correct standards of evaluation, which for Kierkegaard will always be the religious. This fact is amply shown by Gottsched's latest volumes of the journals for the years 1848-50, where Kierkegaard's journey toward a full personal relationship with God is depicted in his own pen. Bärthold's

246. *Stockholms Dagblad*, November 16, 1880.
247. See Holger Ahlenius, "Sören Kierkegaard, en dansk och en svensk diskussion," in *Vår Lösen* 20, no. 4 (Stockholm, April 1929), pp. 82-87.
248. Letter from Brandes to E. Petersen dated November 11, 1880, in *Georg Brandes og Emil Petersen, en Brevveksling*, ed. Morten Borup, p. 261.

new book is important, writes the reviewer, because it describes how Kierkegaard "has charted the channel that theologians will henceforth have to navigate."[249] Rudin's accomplishment is that he stresses Kierkegaard's "universal validity," as well as his significance for Protestantism in general and for the Swedish Church in particular. Rudin is not in the least polemical; he is sympathetic to the point that in his book "the eyes of the seer are of the same makeup as the eyes of the one being seen." It is hoped the book "will act here in Denmark as a necessary corrective to Brandes, who has received a greater share of credit than he really merits."[250]

That "channel" that, in the reviewer's words, Kierkegaard charted for later theologians was what Bärthold calls in his book *"Persönlichkeit"* (personality). It is evident from this work that Bärthold was the first in a long line of Germans to be profoundly seized by the Kierkegaardian religious-existential category of personality. The book is significant as a contribution to the growing theological literature on Kierkegaard in Germany. It is also important because it put the German reader in touch with developments in Denmark such as the "Tro og Viden" Controversy and its aftermath, in an attempt to make them relevant to the local theological debates in Germany in the latter part of the nineteenth century. At one point Bärthold compares and contrasts Kierkegaard with the German theologian Albrecht Ritschl (1822–89), the author of a massive work on pietism.[251] Bärthold also covers a wide range of religious issues, all revolving around Kierkegaard's emphasis on personality, inwardness, and the paradox. Several names of Kierkegaard interpreters are mentioned, including Petersen (critically) and Rudin (favorably); Bärthold reveals that he had also read Brøchner's "Reminiscences," to which he refers now and then. One name, not surprisingly, fails to come up: that of Brandes, whom Bärthold felt he had adequately disposed of in his essay of the previous year.

---

249. The metaphor is Bärthold's; see his *Zur theologischen Bedeutung Sören Kierkegaards* (Halle, 1880), p. 21. The same metaphor is quoted in another review in German by H. Lindenberg in *Theologische Literaturzeitung* 5, no. 24 (Leipzig, 1880), p. 594.

250. *Fædrelandet*, July 30, 1880. Gottsched's volumes of the journals were reviewed in several other newspapers and periodicals. In one of these the analysis was made in conjunction with a review of a Danish translation of Alexander Vinet's book on Pascal. The reviewer, a pastor Christen Møller, compared Kierkegaard and Pascal in both their lives and thoughts. See *Sædmanden* 50 (Copenhagen, Sunday, December 12, 1880), pp. 794–800.

251. Bärthold, *Zur theologischen Bedeutung Sören Kierkegaards*, pp. 53–54.

But if Bärthold could now choose to ignore Brandes in a theological discussion, did this mean that Brandes had really been "disposed of" with respect to Kierkegaard studies? Far from it, if one looks beyond 1880, or surveys the course, from today's vantage point, that Kierkegaard research has followed over the past one hundred years. The ramifications of Brandes's interpretation of Kierkegaard have been immense.

Two related ironies characterize the Kierkegaard-Brandes connection: that the posthumous intellectual and spiritual legacy of the one thinker, whose fundamental orientation ran counter to the pervading positivism of his century, should, at a critical moment, fall into the hands of a true child and representative of that very same positivism; and that this latter, a pure product of the new "liberated" age, should end up serving, in spite of himself, as popularizer of the very same thinker he had intended to suppress. Indeed, Brandes's book on Kierkegaard, whether or not one agrees with its approach, has proved sufficiently provocative to have released a torrent of writing on the man. Instead of being the work to settle all questions and end all curiosity, as its author originally conceived it, the book generated a spiral of debates that significantly enhanced interest in Kierkegaard throughout Scandinavia and Germany. The simultaneous appearance of the journals, with all their rich ideas and intimate revelations, did its share to sustain this interest.

Generally speaking, the early reactions to Brandes's book were marked either by a streak of mediocrity and bigotry or by a degree of provincialism that in each case precluded their having a wide and lasting impact, despite the many legitimate arguments they advanced. Their sheer diversity and vehemence are testimony to the strength of their adversary. It is not a historical accident that most of these works and views did not possess sufficient staying power, often sinking into oblivion as quickly as they appeared, whereas Brandes's book continued to exercise a far-reaching influence long after 1877. As an eloquent and cosmopolitan critic given to no small amount of self-aggrandizement, Brandes was already in possession of the necessary tools for his success. He cleverly rode the wave of the times, tapped into the temper of the age, and contributed to setting the intellectual fashion and defining the cultural taste of Denmark from the 1870s onward. He fought long and hard for the recognition of the merits of literary criticism as both an art and a scholarly endeavor, and the literary critic as a worthy member of society. In this he was a real pioneer in Scandinavia. His undisguised biases and excesses notwithstanding, he was able to unravel much of the mystery that had surrounded Kierkegaard's writings. This alone assured his book its measure of durability.[252]

Alongside Brandes's positive qualities of hard work, attention to detail, and an inquisitive mind with a healthy tinge of skepticism, were to be found a manipulative opportunism and an arrogance with an inclination toward cunning agitation. He brought these latter traits to bear on his treatment of Kierkegaard and thereby caused himself much trouble both at home and abroad. He exploited to the full what were perhaps Kierkegaard's greatest points of vulnerability—the singular features of his life— in order to formulate an indictment of Kierkegaard's Christian philosophy. In doing this Brandes was guilty of what Howard Hong has called the "genetic fallacy" in Kierkegaard interpretation, or what is commonly termed the *argumentum ad hominem*.[253] In fact, Brandes is responsible for starting this trend in Kierkegaard research in the first place, and the number of those following his lead continues to grow. He was the first to use Kierkegaard's journals in an original way, and he is right in stating that, once sensitive personal papers have been published, they become public property and it is the critic's duty then to use them as he sees fit.[254] Yet this ought not to be taken as an excuse for tailoring the evidence to accommodate a preconceived scheme of interpretation. The fact that Kierkegaard's literary and religious production is not easy to disentangle from his personal life must be an inducement to the investigator to employ extra care when resorting to his private papers, lest objectivity be compromised in the effort to dispel unintelligibility. Hong makes the point as follows:

> The journals and papers are not diaries; they are essentially intellectual journals and records of a keen mind and profound spirit centrally concerned with reflections upon existence for the existing subject. Kierkegaard cannot be either the primary subject for us or the proper object for us. The reader is

---

252. A. B. Drachmann, writing thirty five years after Brandes's book first appeared, declares it unrivaled among scholarly works on Kierkegaard. See his "Brandes og Søren Kierkegaard," in *Tilskueren*, no. 2 (Copenhagen, 1912), p. 148.

253. To the best of this writer's knowledge, this comes from an unpublished and undated piece by Howard Hong entitled "Kierkegaard Interpretation and the Genetic Fallacy," which he gave me in person. For other critiques of the "genetic fallacy" in the biographical-psychological approach to Kierkegaard see Paul L. Holmer, "On Understanding Kierkegaard," in *A Kierkegaard Critique*, pp. 40–53; and Stephen Crites, "The Author and the Authorship: Recent Kierkegaard Literature," in *Journal of the American Academy of Religion* 38, no. 1 (March 1970), pp. 37–54.

254. Brandes, *Søren Kierkegaard*, pp. 99–100.

the primary subject, and the substance is the proper intermediate object, and Kierkegaard, like Socrates, is a vanishing point.[255]

A historian cannot be satisfied with mere admonition, but must produce a plausible justification for using the "ought." The purpose here has not been entirely prescriptive; it has had the descriptive function of putting into relief the inception of an important tendency that has permeated Kierkegaard scholarship and determined the course of his reception for over a century. Numerous benefits and complications have resulted from the biographical-psychological approach, and it all began with Brandes.

Brandes was the nearest thing to a committed ideologue. As such, his attitudes and actions with respect to Kierkegaard were consistent with his fundamental outlook. He could not remain true to his beliefs and, at the same time, abide by Kierkegaard's instructions in making his critical analysis, or take Kierkegaard's religious explanations and positions seriously. A kind of pre-Freudian psychoanalysis was his only recourse when faced with a phenomenon like Kierkegaard. On one level, the strong disagreements between him and his opponents over Kierkegaard boiled down to the question of whether, and how much, to accept Kierkegaard's self-interpretation about his own place in relation to the substance of his writings. Taken in isolation from the seething tempers and personal grudges of the late 1870s, this question represented the beginnings in early Kierkegaard scholarship of a healthy debate, and one that has continued to be chiseled at and refined to our day.

Brandes's answer to this question was an unqualified rejection of all Kierkegaard's prescriptions. He remained oblivious to any possible hazards arising from an indiscriminate application of the biographical-psychological method that might jeopardize wholeness, fairness, balance, substance—ultimately the truth about Kierkegaard. On the contrary, such considerations were totally out of keeping with his determination to despiritualize his subject. By embracing the Kierkegaardian "single individual," shorn of his Christian mantle, Brandes distantly foreshadowed the atheistic existentialists and demythologizers of the twentieth century: Sartre, Bultmann, and others. The Kierkegaardian individual, wrenched from his Christian context, becomes a sure recipe for subjectivism-egotism.

255. Howard V. Hong, "The Kierkegaard Papers," in *TriQuarterly*, no. 16 (Fall 1969), p. 120.

Yet it would be misleading to place Brandes in the same class with some of this century's prominent secular thinkers.[256] Brandes was far from being a philosopher; he was an articulate and prolific literary critic, who wrote, for the most part, horizontally not vertically. None of his works on the great men of the past has been considered by more knowledgeable experts as a definitive pronouncement or a last word, and that includes the book about Kierkegaard. As a literary critic he experienced constant tension between his staunchly held opinions and the need to strive for impartiality and for that famed but elusive objectivity of all critics. Like the coarse Erik Bøgh, he did not hesitate to indulge in pathological and pseudo-medical descriptions of Kierkegaard.[257] And he lacked the graciousness of the more sensitive Brøchner, himself a freethinker, yet a respectful admirer of Kierkegaard all the same.

Self-proclaimed agitator turned willy-nilly advertiser for Kierkegaard—this was Georg Brandes in the 1870s. Apparently the agitation had not been very cunning.[258]

---

256. A more appropriate association would be with someone like Walter Kaufmann, who resembles in certain respects a latter-day pale reflection of Brandes, though a considerably cruder one. For an example of crude agitational writing on Kierkegaard by Kaufmann see his introduction to Alexander Dru's translation of extracts from Kierkegaard's *Two Ages* entitled *The Present Age* (New York: Harper Collins Torchbooks, 1962), pp. 9–29.

257. In a review from 1877 of Brandes's book on Kierkegaard, Fr. Helveg actually compares Brandes's analysis with that of the obnoxious Bøgh. See Fr. Helveg, "Søren Kierkegaard og Nutiden," in *Nordisk Månedskrift for folkelig og kristelig Oplysning*, II (1877), pp. 293–94.

258. For a critical survey of early works on Brandes see Sven Møller Kristensen, "Georg Brandes Research: A Survey," in *Scandinavica* 3, no. 2 (November, 1964), pp. 121–32.

7 The Kierkegaard Legacy and the *Fin de Siècle*

The first twenty-five years following Kierkegaard's death saw a steady growth of interest in him throughout Scandinavia and Germany that tended to fall into two broad categories: either it centered on the study of particular phases in his development and writing, such as the *Kirkekampen,* or it attempted a more ambitious overview, but in so doing adopted a narrow plan of approach, dictated usually by certain preassumed prejudices, and this, in turn, precipitated equally biased reactions at the opposite extreme. Brandes's book and the responses to it from Petersen, Bärthold, and Rudin belong to the latter genre. Whether it was the use of *Øjeblikket* for polemical purposes, the indiscriminate application of the biographical-psychological method, or the reduction of the corpus to a mere tool for religious devotion and personal-spiritual edification, the results were invariably the heightening of confrontation among intellectuals and theologians and the increasing fragmentation of Kierkegaard's posthumous legacy. A comprehensive, balanced, and sufficiently detached treatment of Kierkegaard still belonged to the future.

With Brandes the sphere of interest in Kierkegaard was enlarged beyond the strictly theological, surpassing also the traditional Danish audience that his works had hitherto attracted—a few sincere individuals among an otherwise motley group of the gossipy, the curious, and those hungry for sensationalism. Many thinkers and young writers around Europe began to take serious notice of Kierkegaard as a result of Brandes's lectures and book. The book itself, in addition to being translated into Swedish in 1877 and German in 1879, appeared in Czech in 1904 and Yiddish in 1918, and was reissued in German in 1902. Extracts from it made their way into several Slavic journals in the 1880s as Brandes traveled and lectured on literature in Eastern Europe and Russia. Moreover, one observes that practically every early work on Kierkegaard to appear after Brandes's book, and after the completion of the first edition of the journals, embodied substantial biographical allusions or, in some cases, a full biographical section somewhere in its structure, usually at the beginning. Thus there developed a distinct tendency among researchers to explain *why* Kierkegaard thought as he did instead of concentrating on *what* he actually thought.

Brandes said of Kierkegaard that, had he written in one of Europe's main languages, he would have become instantly world famous.[1] Failing this, Kierkegaard required active promoters in order to achieve wide renown in Europe and exert an impact. As an "intermediary among several literatures,"[2] a prolific critical analyst, and a cosmopolitan traveler, Brandes was well suited for the role, and had in fact been serving as publicist for such writers as Ibsen, Strindberg, Nietzsche, and even Dostoevsky, whose Christianity profoundly irritated him. In spite of his own personal aversion to Kierkegaard's Christianity and his desire to minimize its appeal, Brandes also acted as transmitter of Kierkegaard to a number of celebrated European intellectuals. The Brandesian avenues of transmission were both direct and indirect and took on several forms. One interesting example illustrating the variety of ways in which Kierkegaard was broadcast by Brandes is that of the Spanish writer-philosopher Miguel de Unamuno (1864–1936). Writing in 1900 to a friend, Unamuno

---

1. Georg Brandes, *Søren Kierkegaard, en Kritisk Fremstilling i Grundrids*, p. 156. Brandes was actually thinking specifically of Kierkegaard's "Diary of a Seducer" when he wrote this.

2. René Wellek, *A History of Modern Criticism: 1750–1950*, vol. 4: "The Later Nineteenth Century," p. 368. Brandes's reputation as a critic eventually reached as far as Japan, where his *Main Currents of Nineteenth Century Literature* was translated into Japanese and he was initially regarded as an interpreter of Andersen, Kierkegaard, and Ibsen. See Toshihiko Sato, "Scandinavian Literature in Japan," in *Scandinavica* 4, no. 1 (May 1965), p. 22.

states that he is about to plunge into the works of "the theologian and thinker Kierkegaard," about whose influence he had been reading in an essay by Brandes on Ibsen.³ A few years later, in March of 1907, Unamuno was in Salamanca and wrote an essay he called "Ibsen and Kierkegaard," in which he spelled out exactly how he came to learn of Kierkegaard, who was then almost unknown among Spaniards:

> It was the Ibsenian critic, Brandes, who introduced me to Kierkegaard, and if I began the study of Danish translating Ibsen's *Brand*, it has been the works of Kierkegaard, his spiritual father, that have made me especially glad to have learned it.⁴

Unamuno, it seems, studied Danish to read Ibsen and was rewarded with gaining access to Kierkegaard in the original. A problem arises, however, when one looks more closely at the nature of the association he makes between Kierkegaard and Ibsen and at the extent of his knowledge of Kierkegaard's works. Relying on hints from Brandes, Unamuno had formed his early impression of Kierkegaard as someone whose theology and faith were accurately mirrored in Ibsen's Brand: "*Brand*, Ibsen's *Brand*, is [Kierkegaard's] reflection in dramatic art, and as long as *Brand* endures Kierkegaard will endure."⁵ This impression lingered with Unamuno. From other references to Kierkegaard in the 1907 essay and in Unamuno's principal philosophical work of 1913, *The Tragic Sense of Life in Men and in Peoples*, it can be inferred that, *Postscript* and maybe *Fear and Trembling* excepted, he had not done much serious reading in the remaining works. His adulation of Kierkegaard appears to have been based at least as much on second-hand knowledge and an undefined feeling of kinship with "our brother Kierkegaard," the melancholy and solitary fighter for truth, as on an actual reading of him.⁶ One person who

---

3. See *Epistolario á Clarin* (Madrid, 1941), vol. I, p. 82. Clarin was a pseudonym for Unamuno's friend Leopoldo Alas. The Brandes piece in question is his "Second Impression" of Ibsen from 1882; see Chapter 4 above.

4. Quoted from a translation of Unamuno's "Ibsen and Kierkegaard" in a collection of his essays entitled *Perplexities and Paradoxes*, trans. Stuart Gross (New York: Philosophical Library, 1945), p. 51.

5. Ibid., p. 52.

6. The references to "our brother Kierkegaard" in Unamuno's book of 1913 are all in the form of quotations from *Postscript*. See *The Tragic Sense of Life in Men and in Peoples*, first English edition trans. J. E. Crawford Flitch (London: Dover Publications, 1921), pp. 109–11, 115–16, 123, 153, 178, 198, 257, 287, and 327. Scholars have differed about the extent of Kierkegaard's influence on Unamuno, and many have questioned the previously held opinions that there indeed was a deep influence from Kierkegaard. Leading among

visited Unamuno in 1915 reports that the philosopher had a preference for reading books in their original language: "Don Miguel showed me his library where [there] were books in fifteen languages. He could not stand translations, so he always learned to read in the original any writer who interested him."[7] Unamuno's vast library did indeed contain all fourteen volumes of the first Danish edition of Kierkegaard's complete works, published between 1901 and 1906, as well as a 1910 Spanish translation of the "Diary of a Seducer" and Brandes's 1898 essay on Ibsen (though not his book on Kierkegaard).[8] Yet there are indications, for instance, that only relatively late in life did he read *Either/Or* with any great depth. In the preface, dated February 1924, to his *San Manuel, Bueno, mártir y tres historias más* of 1933, Unamuno calls *Either/Or* his favorite work by Kierkegaard.[9]

Any search for Kierkegaardian influences on Unamuno should be conducted while keeping sight of the other sources—in addition to what is typically Spanish—that contributed to the formation of his unsystematic,

---

these skeptics is François Meyer in his "Kierkegaard et Unamuno," in *Revue de Littérature Comparée* 29 (1955), pp. 478–92. Some have argued in favor of a limited Kierkegaardian influence, more formal than substantive, on particular works of Unamuno; see, for example, Ruth House Webber's article "Kierkegaard and the Elaboration of Unamuno's *Niebla*," in *Hispanic Review* 32 (1964), pp. 118–34, in which Webber maintains that *Either/Or* was used in the creation of Unamuno's *Niebla* [Mist] of 1914. See also Donald D. Palmer's "Unamuno's Don Quijote and Kierkegaard's Abraham," in *Revista de Estudios Hispanicos* 3 (1969), pp. 295–312, where Palmer tries to show that the concept of the "Knight of Faith" in *Fear and Trembling* influenced Unamuno's *Vida de Don Quijote y Sancho* (The life of Don Quixote and Sancho) of 1905.

7. John A. Mackay, "Miguel de Unamuno," in *Christianity and the Existentialists,* ed. Carl Michalson (New York: Scribner, 1956), pp. 45–46. Mackay, who later became the president of Princeton Theological Seminary, was a student in Madrid in 1915 and writes that "it was from his [Unamuno's] lips that I heard for the first time the name of Sören Kierkegaard." He adds enthusiastically: "Before German scholars had discovered Kierkegaard, before Karl Barth had come under his influence, that great Danish thinker, father of modern existentialists, was known to a Spaniard who lived quietly by the slow-flowing Tormes, in a medieval city on the Castilian plain."

8. For a detailed list of the holdings of Unamuno's huge library see Mario J. Valdés and Maria Elena de Valdés, *An Unamuno Source Book: A Catalogue of Readings and Acquisitions with an Introductory Essay on Unamuno's Dialectical Enquiry* (Toronto: University of Toronto Press, 1973). Despite what the authors tell us about volumes five and eight of Kierkegaard's complete works being the only ones "not marked and annotated with occasional extensive commentary" (note p. xx), Unamuno's readings in Kierkegaard appear to have been spotty, erratic, and mostly impressionistic.

9. See Oscar A. Fasel, "Observations on Unamuno and Kierkegaard," in *Hispania* 38 (1955), p. 449. Fasel belongs to those scholars skeptical about Kierkegaard's influence on Unamuno.

non-rational, and vitalist philosophy. He was a strong admirer of Socrates, Pascal, Schopenhauer, Nietzsche, and William James; he was critical of Spinoza and attacked Descartes's *cogito;* he was well read in nineteenth-century German Protestant theology; he attacked the evolutionists, rationalists, and positivists of that century; and he was a supporter of the vitalism of Henri Bergson.[10] Tormenting him constantly was his inability to find a rational justification for his desire to believe in personal immortality. His affinities with Kierkegaard derive mainly from a hazy image he had of him as a passionate individualist and a rebel against the authority of philosophical systems and ecclesiastical institutions. Although Unamuno always considered himself a Catholic, he was unorthodox in many of his religious positions, and his rocky relations with the Catholic Church parallel to some degree Kierkegaard's opposition to the Lutheran Church in Denmark. Furthermore, Unamuno's abhorrence of mass society and his criticisms of the depersonalizing aspects of fascism in Spain of the 1930s are of the same character as Kierkegaard's views in his *Two Ages* (1846). Whether there is a direct Kierkegaardian input into Unamuno's thinking in both these cases remains a difficult matter to determine, but it would not be implausible. In any event, Unamuno's 1907 essay, despite the unsubstantiated associations and speculative parallels it draws between Kierkegaard and Ibsen based primarily on a reading of Brandes, remains important in the context of any discussion of Kierkegaard's introduction into Spain.

An early instance of Kierkegaard's introduction into France and to French-speaking readers came about also in connection with Brandes. This time it was his 1877 book on Kierkegaard that was quoted in a collection of essays from 1894 about a number of Scandinavian "revolutionary" figures including Brandes, Bjørnson, Ibsen, Strindberg, and the Norwegian composer Edvard Grieg. In the chapter on Brandes, Kierkegaard is mentioned as one who protested against the "idealistic enthusiasm" of Hegel and its appropriation by official Protestantism. He is described in words that leave a negative taste with the reader: "a measly man, thin and queer, sneaky, with a puny look and a disconcerting character."[11] Parallels with Pascal are drawn, and Brandes's book is quoted at length, in particular the part where he extols the idea of the free individual that

---

10. This brief synopsis of Unamuno's fundamental likes and dislikes derives, in part, from a reading of his main philosophical work *The Tragic Sense of Life.*
11. Maurice Bigeon, *Les Révoltés Scandinaves* (Paris, 1894), p. 6.

Kierkegaard offered to his age. Obviously the author's only source on Kierkegaard is the book by Brandes, and his unappealing description is the result of impressions gathered from that book.

Eight years earlier, in 1886, a French translation was published of Kierkegaard's essay "On the Difference between a Genius and an Apostle" (1847), the first piece by Kierkegaard to appear in the French language. The translation was prefaced by a few pages of biography—again the first of their kind in French—written by a onetime personal friend of Kierkegaard, the pastor H. P. Kofoed-Hansen, who had published two short tracts back in 1856 and 1857 defending Kierkegaard in the wake of the *Kirkekampen*.[12] It was not Brandes's book that Kofoed-Hansen relied on, but rather information from Kierkegaard's journals, in addition to his own recollections of Kierkegaard and an intimate acquaintance with his works. At the time he wrote this biographical sketch in French, Kofoed-Hansen was in a phase of spiritual flux, having left the Danish Lutheran Church in 1883. The following year, 1887, he converted to Catholicism.[13]

Closer to home, Brandes's radical ideas caused many writers to reevaluate, and often renounce altogether, any earlier attraction they might have had to Kierkegaard, especially to his religious views. This was the case with Bjørnson and Strindberg in the 1880s. Strindberg, however, underwent a strange religious experience in the 1890s that he labeled the "Inferno Crisis"; he later recounted it in a book of the same name published in 1897. This experience caused him to reject Brandes's freethinking influence and reverse the irreligious course he had begun to follow under its guidance.[14] It also rekindled his interest in Kierkegaard. Although there was no basis for him to claim that he had at any time seriously immersed himself in natural science, Strindberg wrote somewhat resentfully of his skeptical period: "Dedicated from my childhood to the natural sciences, and later on a disciple of Darwin, I had discovered how unsatisfactory the scientific method is, which accepts the mechanism of the universe without presupposing a Mechanician."[15]

In a letter from Paris in 1898 to his friend the Swedish writer Gustaf af Geijerstam (1858–1909), Strindberg explained that his recently com-

12. See the preface by H. P. Kofoed-Hansen entitled "Notice sur la vie et les oeuvres de S. A. Kierkegaard" (pp. 3–8) to Søren Kierkegaard's "En quoi l'Homme de Génie Diffère-t-il de l'Apotre?" trans. Johannes Gøtzsche (Copenhagen, 1886), 32 pages.

13. On H. P. Kofoed-Hansen see Chapter 3 above.

14. Brandes had made Strindberg aware of Nietzsche's writings and put the two in touch with one another in the late 1880s.

15. August Strindberg, *Inferno*, trans. Claud Field (New York, 1913), pp. 34–35.

pleted play *To Damascus* was intended to symbolize in its structural arrangement Kierkegaard's theme of "repetition."[16] Apparently unsatisfied with a factual prose account of his religious reconversion as presented in *Inferno*, Strindberg wished to enhance the effect by dramatizing the experience. It is significant that he should turn to Kierkegaard's "repetition" for inspiration. Understood religiously, that concept characterized the process of repentance and forgiveness that a sinner goes through in becoming reconciled with God. It represents the reversal of the despair into which the sinner has sunk, and Strindberg's play tries to depict precisely this reversal. In doing so, however, Strindberg, in the guise of the play's hero, transcends the role of Paul the persecutor turned apostle on his journey to Damascus, and assumes that of the martyr—Christ himself—who atones for all of humanity. The details of his life reveal that an ingredient of self-flagellation was undoubtedly operative in Strindberg's play; nevertheless, any purely psychological explanation of his motivation would not do justice to its complexity.[17] *To Damascus* was followed by several other plays, all of which revolved around the theme of spiritual rehabilitation and leaned precariously on Kierkegaardian concepts and religious categories.[18] An article written in the year of his death testifies to the nondescript obsession he had developed with Kierkegaard: "I have gone through Inferno and Purgatory without having seen Paradise; therefore Kierkegaard with his non-confessional Christianity has again become my banner, which in reality I have never given up, since for me existence itself has merely been a great suffering."[19] Despite this declaration, it is safe to say with Billeskov Jansen that Strindberg cannot be thought of as having transmitted any Kierkegaardian ideas to anyone.[20]

16. Letter from Strindberg to Geijerstam dated March 17, 1898, in *August Strindbergs Brev*, ed. Torsten Eklund, vol. 12: "December 1896–August 1898" (Stockholm: A. Bonnier, 1970), p. 279. Geijerstam himself, under the influence of *Øjeblikket*, wrote in 1887 a satire on a clergyman he entitled *Pastor Hallin*.

17. One such psychological interpretation of Strindberg's "Inferno" experience is provided in Gunnar Brandell's *Strindberg in Inferno*, trans. Barry Jacobs (Cambridge, Massachusetts: Harvard University Press, 1974); see pp. 270–71.

18. The play *To Damascus* of 1898 turned out to be the first in a trilogy of plays that went under the same name and were written between 1898 and 1904. See also the post-Inferno religious plays *Advent* (1899), *Easter* (1900), and *A Dream Play* (1901).

19. See Strindberg's article for the Danish newspaper *Politiken* of January 22, 1912, reprinted in August Strindberg, *Samlade Skrifter*, vol. 53 (Stockholm: A. Bonnier, 1919), p. 557.

20. F. J. Billeskov Jansen, "L'héritage de Kierkegaard dans les Pays nordiques," in *Cahiers du Sud*, 50, no. 371 (Marseilles, April–May 1963), p. 25. For more on Strindberg's

For Strindberg, Kierkegaard was like an ocean in which he took a dip now and then, but he made sure to dry himself thoroughly once he was back on the shore.

Of the many young writers who constituted the vanguard of Brandes's "Modern Breakthrough" in the 1870s, it is worthwhile pausing to consider one in particular, in his interesting and subtle relation to Kierkegaard. This is Jens Peter Jacobsen (1847–85), who created through his novel *Niels Lyhne* (1880) an early fictional prototype of a familiar twentieth-century character: the atheist existentialist. What does such an accomplishment have to do with Kierkegaard? Plenty, since it could, among other things, shed light on ways in which certain Nordic predispositions toward a brooding melancholy, which received vivid expression in the life and works of men like Kierkegaard, Ibsen, and Jacobsen, were found to be so relevant—even appealing—by both the *fin de siècle* generation and the interwar generation that succeeded it.

Jacobsen's name is commonly associated with the school of naturalist realism in late-nineteenth-century Danish literary history and with the Danish translations he made of Darwin's *Origin of Species* and *Descent of Man* in 1872 and 1875 respectively, but rarely, if at all, with Kierkegaard. In addition to being a poet and writing a couple of novels toward the end of his short life, Jacobsen was a botanist by training and a confirmed atheist by conviction—two facts that hardly suggest any significant relationship to Kierkegaard. Yet the meager knowledge we possess would enable us to speak not only in terms of general temperamental affinities and shared Nordic traits or themes between the two men, but also of a direct Kierkegaardian impact on Jacobsen in a couple of instances, and the strong likelihood of a deeper and sustained, though more diffuse, influence.

In his correspondence Jacobsen reveals that he read Kierkegaard as early as 1867, at the age of twenty. Shortly afterwards, while studying botany, he also read Feuerbach and Heine, and the Bible twice.[21] By the

---

relation to Kierkegaard see Sjöstedt's *Søren Kierkegaard och Svensk Litteratur*, pp. 146–291; and the unpublished doctoral dissertation by Loftur L. Bjarnason entitled "Categories of Søren Kierkegaard's Thought in the Life and Writings of August Strindberg," at Stanford University, 1951.

21. Letter from Jacobsen to Vilhelm Møller dated January 13, 1881, in J. P. Jacobsen, *Samlede Værker: Romaner, Noveller, Digte, Breve*, edited with introduction and commentary by Frederik Nielsen (Copenhagen: Rosenkilde og Bagger, 1974), vol. 6: "Breve: 1877–1885," p. 137. Jacobsen and Møller collaborated on a life of Darwin that appeared in 1893, eight years after Jacobsen's death. In this letter Jacobsen also says he read Goethe

time he read Kierkegaard, Jacobsen had already broken with Christianity, which had not been strong in him to begin with. Kierkegaard, therefore, did not have any spiritual effect on the young poet-botanist; however, he does seem to have struck a familiar chord in him, for Jacobsen was given to introspective brooding at an early age, and a pervasive melancholy marked his character. Kierkegaardian echoes are audible in his poems and scattered writings from the late 1860s, the most conspicuous being the reference to the "copper bull of Phalaris" (found at the beginning of the "Diapsalmata" in Kierkegaard's *Either/Or*, volume I) in the poem from 1868 entitled "Saa er nu da Jorden en Kobbertyr" (Thus is the world now a copper bull). This title of the poem is also its first verse, and is followed by: "a cruel Phalaris 'God the Father'." The poem proceeds to depict God as a tyrant who sits in heaven and hears the cries of a suffering humanity in the form of sweet music.[22]

Working with Jacobsen's unpublished papers at the Royal Library of Copenhagen in the early 1950s, the scholar Frederik Nielsen uncovered a long and unfinished poem under the name "Phalaris" that was written around 1866 and placed in a notebook dated 1865. It had never been published and appears for the first time in Nielsen's massive study of Jacobsen.[23] Apparently Jacobsen had intended to write the story in epic form and had commenced with an elaborate description of the majestic court of the ruthless Phalaris, "dressed in purple" and "sitting among the gods." He hears the "whining of an anxious girl / the wailing of a tortured youth / and the shrieks of a despairing old man" and conceives a sinister idea to transform them into "magnificent melodies." He erects a huge hollow copper bull in which he imprisons his subjects and enemies; he heats it with a scorching fire, but places reeds in the nostrils that change the cries of agony welling from within into pleasant music. The story

---

and Schiller at age 18, and Shakespeare, Byron, and Tennyson between ages 20 and 23. Only volumes 5 and 6 of this recent edition of the collected works will be cited henceforth in reference to Jacobsen's correspondence. All other references to his works in the original Danish will be to first editions or to the first edition of the collected works.

22. This and a host of other early poems and sketches by Jacobsen from 1865 onwards were first published posthumously in 1886, one year after the author's death. They were gathered and ed. Edvard Brandes and Vilhelm Møller, both close friends of Jacobsen. For the poem on the bull of Phalaris see J. P. Jacobsen, *Digte og Udkast* (Copenhagen, 1886), pp. 43–44. The same poem is published in J. P. Jacobsen, *Samlede Værker*, 1st ed., Morten Borup, ed. (Copenhagen: Gyldendal, 1928), vol. IV, pp. 35–36.

23. See Frederik Nielsen, *J. P. Jacobsen, Digteren og Mennesket: En Literær Undersøgelse* (Copenhagen: G. E. C. Gad, 1953), pp. 297–304.

comes originally from Lucian and is the same one with which Kierkegaard commences his "Diapsalmata." It is all but certain that the then nineteen-year-old Jacobsen received the inspiration for his poem from the "Diapsalmata," which would mean he had been reading Kierkegaard at least one year prior to 1867, the time he mentions in his letter.[24]

Other evidence from Jacobsen's early writings reveals a continuing preoccupation with themes from *Either/Or*. His *En begavet ung Mands Dagbog* (The diary of a gifted young man) (1867–68) has clear structural affinities with the "Diapsalmata." In fact in the course of writing one of the short paragraphs of the diary, he refers in a footnote to having heard something about Søren Kierkegaard that same afternoon.[25] Nor was this diary an isolated indication of an incidental interest in the "Diapsalmata." In one of his unpublished college notebooks marked by the heading "J. P. Jacobsen—1867, Botanica," Jacobsen misquotes a few lines from the "Diapsalmata"—perhaps deliberately—and calls the words nonsense: "My life is split into two conditions (or states): either I dream awake or I dream sleeping; either I wish awake and receive it as a dream, dreaming, or I receive as reality sleeping!—which is all nonsense!"[26]

The shift from a mythological setting for the 1866 Phalaris poem to an identification of the cruel tyrant with God the Father in the 1868 poem is significant. Jacobsen's renunciation of Christianity had become complete by the time he wrote the latter poem, yet exposure to Darwinian evolution was not the sole factor behind his early atheism. While a student of the natural sciences in Copenhagen in the late 1860s, Jacobsen also belonged to a group of students who shared literary and philosophical interests and lived at a student boardinghouse under the management of a spinster named Marie Zoffmann. The Zoffmann Circle, as they came to be known, consisted of Jacobsen, E. Fraenkel (1849–1918), who eventu-

---

24. This suggestion is made not by Fr. Nielsen but by Svend Ole Madsen in his book *J. P. Jacobsen—Virkelighed og Kunst. En Undersøgelse af den eksistentielle Erfarings transformering til Kunst* (Copenhagen: Akademisk Forlag, 1974), p. 78.

25. "En begavet ung Mands Dagbog" was published posthumously in 1886 by Edvard Brandes and Vilhelm Møller. For the reference to Kierkegaard see J. P. Jacobsen, *Digte og Udkast*, p. 17.

26. Quoted in Brita Tigerschiöld, *J. P. Jacobsen och hans Roman Niels Lyhne* (Göteborg: Elander, 1945), p. 58, esp. the footnote. The piece misquoted from the "Diapsalmata" reads: "My time I divide as follows: the one half I sleep; the other half I dream. I never dream when I sleep; that would be a shame, because to sleep is the height of genius." See Søren Kierkegaard, *Either/Or*, volume I (*KW*, III), ed. and trans. Howard V. Hong and Edna H. Hong (Princeton: Princeton University Press, 1987), p. 28.

ally became a celebrated neurophysiologist and wrote books on hypnotism (*Hypnotismen,* 1889) and homosexuality (*De Homoseksuelle,* 1908); Hans Sophus Vodskov (1846–1910), a later literary critic and historian of religion who was a disciple of Taine and Sainte-Beuve and translated Taine's four-volume history of English literature; and Poul Kierkegaard (1842–1915), the son of Bishop Peter Christian Kierkegaard and Søren's nephew. Of these, it was Poul Kierkegaard who first introduced Jacobsen and the others to the writings of Feuerbach in 1868. It was Darwin and Feuerbach who together defined the interests and shaped the outlook of the Zoffmann Circle.[27]

Poul began as a theology student in 1866, but quickly became a militant atheist under the combined influence of Max Stirner and Feuerbach and promptly left the Church. After a period of debauchery, during which he would spend time at a popular meeting place for students in Copenhagen called the "café des étudiants" drinking excessively and reciting aloud from Feuerbach and Max Stirner, Poul had a nervous collapse and was confined in 1872 to an asylum. That year Harald Høffding's study of German philosophy after Hegel appeared—*Filosofien i Tyskland efter Hegel*—and contained a detailed treatment of Feuerbach. Poul read it and became very excited. He then embarked on a translation of *Das Wesen des Christentums,* the first in Danish.[28] From an early age Poul showed signs of rebellion against the austere religious climate of the Kierkegaard family. In 1867 his mother wrote in a letter to her husband the bishop that their son was "without faith and besides, full of bitterness, sarcasm, blasphemous words and irreverently witty remarks."[29] Poul seemed to be

---

27. On the Zoffmann Circle see Sejer Kühle's article "Fra J. P. Jacobsens Kreds," in *Fund og Forskning i det Kongelige Biblioteks Samlinger,* 4 (Copenhagen, 1957), pp. 127ff. On Poul Kierkegaard see the detailed study by Ib Ostenfeld entitled *Poul Kierkegaard, En Skæbne. Og Andre Studier over Religion og Ateisme* (Copenhagen: Nyt Nordisk Forlag, 1957), esp. chap. III called "Frk. Zoffmanns Pensionat," pp. 36–48. Ostenfeld examines Poul's development in the context of the history and psychology of modern atheism. The second half of his book is devoted to an analysis of this atheism.

28. Kühle, "Fra J. P. Jacobsens Kreds," pp. 130 and 132. Ostenfeld, *Paul Kierkegaard,* pp. 16, 34, and 44–45.

29. Quoted in Ostenfeld, *Paul Kierkegaard,* p. 32; see also pp. 45–46. Kühle, "Fra J. P. Jacobsens Kreds," pp. 130–31, says the source of these words was Poul's cousin Henriette Lund. Ostenfeld learned from Carl Weltzer, author of *Peter og Søren Kierkegaard,* that during the three-year Schleswig-Holstein war with Prussia, the young Poul exhibited a morbid fascination with newspaper accounts of the battles and lists of dead Danish soldiers and would throw himself with gleaming enthusiasm and a sick appetite on the pages of the newspaper in order to find out how many had perished (Ostenfeld, p. 28).

deliberately defying the prominently visible—though markedly different—religiosities of both his father and his uncle. He once described his relationship to them as follows: "My uncle became either-or, my father became both-and, and I remained neither-nor."[30]

Being the oldest among the members of the Zoffmann Circle, Poul exercised a tangible influence on the others and acted, to a certain extent, as an authority figure.[31] It is not inconceivable that he imparted to Jacobsen some of his own personal hostility toward the religious orientation of his uncle Søren. According to some scholars, Poul's hard-nosed atheism may have inspired the title *En Kaktus springer ud* (A cactus springs up) of a series of poems and sketches that Jacobsen wrote between 1867 and 1870.[32] Another figure held in high esteem by Jacobsen and the other members of the Zoffmann Circle was Hans Brøchner, himself a freethinker and a Feuerbach specialist. The group followed with interest the successive phases of the "Tro og Viden" Controversy as they unfolded in the late 1860s, and their sentiments were clearly with Brøchner against Rasmus Nielsen.[33]

Jacobsen's writings from those early years are replete with images evocative of Kierkegaardian themes, yet aside from the case of the two Phalaris poems and our definite knowledge that he did read Kierkegaard, no conclusive instances of borrowing or direct influence can be documented. This early material has provided literary critics and specialists in comparative literature with ample opportunities for indulging in speculations about Kierkegaardian affinities. Some claim to have detected indirect Kierkegaardian "traces" in unpublished sketches written by the adoles-

---

Ostenfeld's thesis is that being a Kierkegaard and having manic-depressive tendencies to begin with, it was Poul's destiny to turn out the way he did: "His life history was a history of sickness, a destiny" (p. 12).

30. Quoted in Otto Holmgaard, *Peter Christian Kierkegaard, Grundtvigs Lærling* (Copenhagen: Rosenkilde og Bagger, 1953), p. 133. See also Johannes Hohlenberg, *Sören Kierkegaard*, trans. T. H. Croxall, p. 275. Both Holmgaard and Hohlenberg agree that Poul, though very gifted in philosophy, showed signs of schizophrenia and became mentally ill at a young age. His subsequent life was an utter waste and he lived as an oddity in Aalborg for years.

31. Ostenfeld, *Poul Kierkegaard*, p. 41.

32. Ibid., p. 40.

33. Kühle, "Fra J. P. Jacobsens Kreds," pp. 128–30. Tigerschiöld, *J. P. Jacobsen och hans Roman Niels Lyhne*, pp. 46–47, says that the moral influence of Kierkegaard and Ibsen on Jacobsen clashed with the impression he gathered from the acrimonious debates over "Tro og Viden."

cent Jacobsen as early as 1864, particularly those on the subject of the dichotomy of body and soul.[34] His immature reflections often turned to this topic during the period before he abandoned religious feelings altogether, and he wondered a great deal about the relations of sleep and dreams with death. It is possible that he was exposed peripherally to some of the theological debates about the unity and separation of body and soul that were bifurcations of the "Tro og Viden" Controversy, then just commencing. Kierkegaard's views on these issues were "in the air," and as with Ibsen, Jacobsen could have been stimulated by undefined impulses at a very young age. Upon reading Kierkegaard a little later, Jacobsen's rudimentary musings assume more concrete shape, which becomes apparent through the conflicts raging in most of his male heroes between their animal and spiritual natures. These conflicts continued to characterize his writings well after he became an atheist.[35]

Concern about man's bestial tendencies reveals another feature of Jacobsen's youth: his engrossment in the erotic. In one respect, Jacobsen was an erotic writer and poet before being anything else.[36] Here his reading of the first volume of *Either/Or* comes into play. The editors of the first edition of Jacobsen's complete works state unequivocally that a piece he wrote between 1869 and 1870 entitled *Erotiske Studier efter Biblen* (Erotic studies according to the Bible) was the result of his having read and pondered the "Diary of a Seducer."[37] In it he considers male-female relations before and after the Fall, and speculates about their carnal differentiation in light of the Adam and Eve story in Genesis. Similarly, his 1868 sketch *Et Kjærlighedsforhold* (A love affair) centers on the physical love between man and woman. From these two pieces, Jacobsen's view of women emerges and has an interesting resemblance to that of Johannes

---

34. See in particular Frédéric Durand's interesting, though highly speculative, work *Jens Peter Jacobsen ou la Gravitation d'une Solitude* (Paris: Faculté des lettres et sciences humaines de l'Université, 1968), p. 45.

35. See Jørgen Ottosen, *J. P. Jacobsens "Mogens"* (Copenhagen: Gyldendal, 1968), pp. 224–27, and pp. 282–91. The central theme of *Mogens* (1872) is the conflict in man's dual nature between the animal and the spiritual.

36. Peer E. Sørensen, "Fascination og Handling: et Essay omkring J. P. Jacobsens Noveller," in *Kritik* 14 (1970), p. 31.

37. See the introduction to volume III of J. P. Jacobsen's *Samlede Værker*, ed. Morten Borup (Copenhagen, 1927), pp. xiv–xv. See also Tigerschiöld, *J. P. Jacobsen och hans Roman Niels Lyhne*, p. 46; and Durand, *Jens Peter Jacobsen ou la Gravitation d'une Solitude*, pp. 74–75.

the Seducer. Unlike man, who is both body and spirit in close coordination, woman leans more in the direction of spirit. This incongruity leaves women vulnerable and causes them to fall in love with men (like Don Juan) who can easily manipulate them.

It has been suggested that this view has algolagnic (sado-masochistic) implications deriving, in part, from Jacobsen's own relations in late adolescence with a young woman named Anna Michelsen (1847–1924), the daughter of a doctor's widow whose household he used to frequent while a student in Copenhagen. Anna was greatly attached to Jacobsen and loved him deeply, whereas he felt indifferent toward her emotionally, considering her only as a friend. This caused her much suffering, and when she eventually became mentally ill and had to be committed to an asylum, Jacobsen was greatly saddened and disturbed. There is some evidence from marginal jottings in a book in Jacobsen's library that he placed his relation with Anna in the same category as Kierkegaard's with Regine.[38]

Some perspective is required lest the impression be given that the few instances mentioned thus far of direct Kierkegaardian influence on Jacobsen constituted a unique, or even a principal, source of inspiration for the young writer. Many of Jacobsen's early poems have a certain dreamy aspect about them and appear under the heading "dream." This fact reflected a propensity toward daydreaming in Jacobsen enhanced by

38. Frederik Nielsen pursues this question intricately and cites two notes in Jacobsen's copy of a book by Carl Gustav Estlander called *De bildende Konsternas Historia*, pp. 104 and 108, in which Jacobsen asks rhetorically whether Anna's sufferings are greater than his and then writes: "Had the exam not been so near I would write a poem . . . and I as a Kierkegaard and Regine. I am a tyrant also, you know—worse luck!" See Fr. Nielsen, *J. P. Jacobsen, Digteren og Mennesket*, pp. 65–66. Nielsen concludes that Jacobsen viewed Kierkegaard's relation to Regine in algolagnic terms, and his reading of Kierkegaard tempted him to play the role of the cynical seducer with respect to Anna. For more on Jacobsen and Anna see Kühle, "Fra J. P. Jacobsens Kreds," pp. 122–26. Interpretations of Jacobsen's relation to Anna have varied widely. Tigerschiöld regarded it as the basis for his general anxiety when it came to women (*J. P. Jacobsen*, pp. 32–41, and 79–81); Nielsen saw it as indicative of sado-masochistic tendencies in Jacobsen (pp. 167–68); a certain Hans Blüher detected a latent homosexuality or bisexuality [see his article from 1912 entitled "Niels Lyhne von J. P. Jacobsen und das Problem der Bisexualität," reprinted in Niels Barfoed, ed., *Omkring Niels Lyhne* (Copenhagen: Hans Reitzel, 1970), pp. 205–12]; and Ottosen psychoanalyzed the erotic content of Jacobsen's early poems as an indication of an extended puberty inhibition, due especially to an attachment to the mother (*J. P. Jacobsens "Mogens,"* pp. 297–303). See also Sven Ole Madsen, *J. P. Jacobsen—Virkelighed og Kunst*, pp. 17–18.

his readings in the poems and tales of Edgar Allan Poe. His fascination with the morbid and the macabre found its way into his poetry and some of his prose, where shadowy images and dream-like settings abound. Jacobsen was one of the inspirers of James Joyce's peculiarly delirious style, rich in symbolism.[39] In addition to Poe, a major influence on Jacobsen was Flaubert, whom Jacobsen may have read as early as 1872, and whose *Madame Bovary* (1856–57), which first appeared in Danish translation as *Fru Bovary* in 1874, provided ideas and stylistic impulses for Jacobsen's historical novel *Fru Marie Grubbe* (1876).[40] Other writers who left their mark on Jacobsen were H. C. Andersen, Ibsen, Bjørnson, Turgeniev, Stendhal, Sainte-Beuve, and Shakespeare.

The last two, plus a number of English authors, were read at the behest of H. S. Vodskov, who was particularly close to Jacobsen in the Zoffmann Circle. Vodskov is important in himself because of an essay he wrote on Kierkegaard in 1881, when the last installment of the journals covering the *Kirkekampen* period was published by Gottsched. Vodskov did not like *Øjeblikket,* but he did not follow the lead of other freethinkers who tried repeatedly to use it as a weapon in support of their own cause against religion. Seeing the entire *Kirkekampen* as an aberration in the overall development of Kierkegaard, he preferred to probe its roots in search of the causes for the mishap. He concentrated on the year 1849 and believed he had discovered the answer in a crisis in Kierkegaard's life at that point that deflected him from the course he had been following. Instead of continuing to write about Christianity and to expound on Christian prin-

---

39. See David Hayman, "A Portrait of the Artist as a Young Man and L'Education Sentimentale: The Structural Affinities," in *Orbis Litterarum* 19, no. 4 (Copenhagen, 1964), pp. 161–63, where the author says both Flaubert and Jacobsen supplied precedents for a significant number of the qualities of Joyce's *A Portrait of the Artist as a Young Man* (1916).

40. The list of scholars who have studied Flaubert's influence on Jacobsen is long and their documentation is long. Determining the earliest date of Jacobsen's exposure to *Madame Bovary* has been crucial for ascertaining the novel's influence on *Marie Grubbe.* See as examples Dot Pallis, "J. P. Jacobsen og Flaubert," in *Danske Studier* (1973), pp. 90–107; Durand, *Jens Peter Jacobsen ou la Gravitation d'une Solitude,* p. 172; and Tigerschiöld, *J. P. Jacobsen och hans Roman Niels Lyhne,* p. 123. Jacobsen followed Flaubert not only stylistically but also methodologically. Like Flaubert, he conducted detailed background research in historical sources for his novel and traveled around Europe gathering information and impressions. See H. G. Topsøe-Jensen, *Scandinavian Literature from Brandes to Our Day,* trans. Isaac Anderson (New York: American Scandinavian Foundation, W. W. Norton, 1929), p. 23; and Pallis, pp. 92–93.

ciples, Kierkegaard had decided to strive for "personal truth," which he would then embody in his own life. This, according to Vodskov, is where Kierkegaard went astray.[41]

Vodskov's interpretation of Kierkegaard's final years resembled Brandes's, with which he was familiar. Like Brandes, Vodskov was a student of Taine and Sainte-Beuve and applied their critical psycho-historical analysis to Kierkegaard; like Brandes also, he relied primarily on the journals and read into them retrospectively a preconceived scheme. Vodskov, however, was not a follower of Brandes or his "Modern Breakthrough," and he was averse to Brandes's revolutionary approach, opting instead for more gradual change. He was therefore unhappy when Jacobsen, his best friend, decided in 1872 to join the Brandes movement.[42]

In the same year, Jacobsen made the formal acquaintance of the two Brandes brothers, Georg and Edvard, who were impressed by the iconoclastic flavor of his articles on Darwinism. He had met Georg for the first time in 1869, but did not particularly attract his attention at the time.[43] Now, however, Brandes became excited about Jacobsen's version of nonconformity and desired to recruit him on the side of the new radicalism taking shape. Of the two brothers, Edvard became the more intimate friend of Jacobsen, and years later, wrote the following in appreciation of his atheism: "He struggled all his life in science and literary writing for one idea: the idea of proud godlessness, the pure irreligiosity, the atheism that removes all reservations."[44]

It should be stressed that, prior to Jacobsen's affiliation with the Brandes Circle, he had already formed his views on religion independently

41. Vodskov's essay, entitled "En Krise i Søren Kierkegaards Liv," first appeared in *Illustreret Tidende* 22 (Copenhagen, 1881), nos. 1128–30. It was reprinted in a collection of essays by Vodskov called *Spredte Studier* (Copenhagen, 1884), pp. 1–30. See also Aage Henriksen, *Methods and Results,* pp. 35–39.

42. For more on Vodskov see *DBL*, 2d ed., vol. 26, pp. 199–206. See also Oluf Friis, "Hans Sophus Vodskov som Litterær Kritiker i 1870'erne og 1880'erne," in *Festskrift til Vilhelm Andersen* (Copenhagen: Gyldendal Nordisk Forlag, 1934), pp. 235–50. On Vodskov and Jacobsen see Kühle, "Fra J. P. Jacobsens Kreds," p. 133. See also the published letters of Jacobsen to Vodskov, gathered and ed. Carl S. Petersen in *Tilskueren* (January–June 1911), pp. 213–29.

43. Frédéric Durand, "Les Rapports de Georg Brandes et de J. P. Jacobsen," in *Etudes Germaniques* (Paris, April–September 1953), p. 109.

44. See the foreword to Edvard Brandes's edition of his correspondence with Jacobsen, entitled *Breve fra J. P. Jacobsen,* 2d ed. (Copenhagen, 1899), p. liii. In the same foreword, Edvard writes disdainfully about Kierkegaard: "When Søren Kierkegaard wished to write for only one reader, that was certainly pure affectation: he intended with his one reader the entire public at large" (p. II).

and had read most of the key writings that were to inform the intellectual orientation of that Circle. As far back as 1868, in his *En begavet ung Mands Dagbog*, a brief statement dated April 4 reveals Jacobsen's then-firm atheism: "If there was a personal God and I believed in him, I would pray until the hair on his head would rise up. . . . But now I do not believe—and consequently I do not pray—but wish—receive nothing—but dream."[45] Feuerbach and Darwin were thus well known to Jacobsen long before he came across Brandes.[46] And so was Kierkegaard. This wealth of knowledge made Jacobsen a valuable asset to the newly formed group under Brandes's guidance that became known as the *Litteratursel-skabet*" (Literary Society) and used to assemble regularly at the famous Copenhagen restaurant "D'Angleterre" to discuss the current status and future of Danish literature. It also strengthened his position vis-à-vis Brandes, enabling him to resist toeing the Brandesian line all the way, and facilitating his eventual departure from the group. This autonomous disposition was resented by Brandes, whose letters to Jacobsen often betray a discourtesy bordering on outright indignation, in marked contrast to the deferential tone of Jacobsen's letters. Edvard had to intervene frequently in order to reconcile his brother with Jacobsen.[47] Brandes had reason to feel the way he did. Thanks to his patronage the hitherto little-known writer received some much-needed publicity and the opportunity to publish in Brandes's prestigious periodical *Det Nittende Aarhundrede*. It was partly at Brandes's urging that Jacobsen embarked on, and completed, his novel *Marie Grubbe*,[48] chapters of which first appeared in Brandes's publication, and the finished book was subsequently reviewed by Brandes in the January–February 1877 issue of the same publication. Brandes was also the first critic to provide readers with a detailed analysis of Jacobsen's entire literary output. This came in the form of an essay on Jacobsen in his *Det moderne Gjennembruds Mænd* [The Men of the "Modern Breakthrough"] published in 1883.[49]

45. J. P. Jacobsen, *Digte og Udkast*, p. 13.
46. Jacobsen was familiar with the broad lines of Darwin's theories as early as 1867. See Kühle, "Fra J. P. Jacobsens Kreds," p. 135; and Durand, *Jens Peter Jacobsen ou la Gravitation d'une Solitude*, p. 62.
47. Durand, "Les Rapports de Georg Brandes et de J. P. Jacobsen," pp. 108 and 111.
48. Ibid., pp. 111 and 113.
49. The essay has been reproduced in the section entitled "Danske Personligheder" in Brandes's *Samlede Skrifter*, vol. III (Copenhagen, 1900), pp. 3–72. The same year that Brandes wrote this essay, Gustaf af Geijerstam published in Stockholm his own appraisal of Jacobsen, in which he stressed, among other things, the importance of Flaubert for an

From hints in Jacobsen's correspondence throughout the 1870s with the Brandes brothers and other friends, it is clear that he continued to read, or at least to reflect on, Kierkegaard. To Edvard Brandes he writes in 1874 about the character Julian in Ibsen's *Emperor and Galilean* (1873): "[He] is a young teutonic man, who has read his Kierkegaard."[50] A couple of years later, in a letter to his friend Vilhelm Møller (written from Thisted, his hometown in Jutland, where he had moved after a deterioration in his health), Jacobsen tells of completing *Marie Grubbe* and of plans for a new book. He complains about his loneliness and his boredom, and laments melancholically: "All are getting married, while I must go my dark way alone." At the end he inquires whether Møller was the actual author of a recently published anonymous article, and adds that he found this hard to believe because of the presence of "some Søren Kierkegaard words" in the article. Møller, like Jacobsen, was a staunch Darwinist and atheist.[51] Writing to Edvard Brandes again in 1877, Jacobsen praises highly Brøchner's "Reminiscences" of Kierkegaard that had appeared a few weeks earlier in *Det Nittende Aarhundrede*. In his view the "Reminiscences" were the best thing on Kierkegaard that the periodical had published.[52] Finally, in an important letter to Georg Brandes that same year, Jacobsen discloses that he had just finished reading Brandes's book on Kierkegaard, "the man whom I always imagined having his lunch on his innermost thoughts and moods with his pen as his fork." He says the book made a particularly strong impression on him, more so than earlier lectures and treatises on Kierkegaard to which he had been exposed. By way of complementing Brandes, Jacobsen adds that every time he reads a new book by him he is convinced it is his best yet, only to see it surpassed by the next one. Immediately after finishing Brandes's book on Kierkegaard, Jacobsen writes that he turned to Goldschmidt's autobiographical reminiscences, *Livs Erindringer og Resultater,* which also appeared in 1877.[53]

---

understanding of *Marie Grubbe*. See Gustaf af Geijerstam, *Ur Samtiden, Literaturstudier med tre Porträtt* (Stockholm, 1883), pp. 91-120.

50. Letter from Jacobsen to Edvard Brandes dated August 7, 1874, in *Georg og Edvard Brandes: Brevveksling,* ed. Morten Borup, vol. II, p. 261.

51. Letter from Jacobsen to Vilhelm Møller dated December 6, 1876, in J. P. Jacobsen, *Samlede Værker: Romaner, Noveller, Digte, Breve,* vol. 5: "Breve: 1863-1877", pp. 153-55.

52. Letter from Jacobsen to Edvard Brandes dated March 14, 1877 in ibid., pp. 177-78.

53. Letter from Jacobsen to Georg Brandes dated May 2, 1877, in ibid., pp. 186-89. The translation of the quoted passage is by Wera Hildebrand, this author's Danish-language teacher at Harvard University.

A marginal preoccupation with Kierkegaard in the 1870s—as the few brief references just surveyed legitimately allow us to infer—would tend to lend credibility to some of the endless speculation regarding the presence of Kierkegaardian elements in Jacobsen's novel *Marie Grubbe*. A historian has to be cautious, however, in the absence of a clearly established connection. The parallels, for example, between the character of Sti Høg, the husband of Marie's sister, and Johannes the Seducer are compelling. At one point Høg is talking with Marie and declares:

> Know you not, madam, that there is in the world a secret society which I might call 'the melancholy company'? It is composed of people who at birth have been given a different nature and constitution from others, and yearn more and covet more, whose passions are stronger, and whose desires burn more wildly than those of the vulgar mob. . . . But the mob—what does it know of pleasure in grief or despair?[54]

The melancholy, the passion, the despair, the disdain for the "vulgar mob," as well as Høg's own voluptuous qualities, are all highly suggestive of wafts from Kierkegaard. The idea of certain people being singled out at birth for special natures probably derives indirectly from the current biological theories of inherited traits, with which Jacobsen was familiar, although an affinity with the notion of original sin after the Fall, as expounded in Kierkegaard's *Sickness unto Death,* and the idea of hereditary sin and guilt, as discussed in *Concept of Anxiety,* cannot be discounted. This is bolstered by the statement during a conversation early in the story to the effect that the sins of the fathers are visited upon the children.[55] Repeatedly throughout the book the phrases "fear and trembling" and "sickness unto death" are mentioned in various contexts.

It would not be surprising if Jacobsen did indeed have Kierkegaard in mind during the creation of *Marie Grubbe.* Much of his writing from those years explored what to him seemed to be the apparent futility and meaninglessness of existence. In a famous poem that appeared in 1874,

---

54. J. P. Jacobsen, *Marie Grubbe, A Lady of the Seventeenth Century,* 2d ed., trans. Hanna Astrup Larsen (Boston: Scandinavian Classics, 1975), pp. 146–47. Several scholars have made the connection between Sti Høg and Kierkegaard's seducer. See as examples Tigerschiöld, *J. P. Jacobsen och hans Roman Niels Lyhne,* p. 226; Johan Fjord Jensen, *Turgeniev i dansk Åndsliv* (Copenhagen: Gyldendal, 1961), p. 121; and Sven Møller Kristensen's "Marie Grubbe," in his *Digtning og Livssyn: Fortolkninger af Syv Danske Værker,* 2d ed. (Copenhagen: Gyldendal, 1960), p. 36.

55. Jacobsen, *Marie Grubbe,* p. 10. The reference to "a different constitution from others" in the quotation could point to Kierkegaard's crooked build and hunched back.

for instance, parts of which may have been written as early as 1870,[56] raw existential questions are posed rhetorically with typical Jacobsenian starkness and urgency:

> Why life?
> Why death?
> Why live, when after all we shall die?

His melancholy was accentuated in the mid-1870s upon his return to his hometown of Thisted on the Jutland heath. His failing health (tuberculosis) and his loneliness, surrounded as he was by the desolate expanses of land, sea, and sky, weighed oppressively on his heart. The terrible grandeur of nature and man's solitude in its midst have traditionally molded the Scandinavian spirit and accounted for its tenacity and ruggedness. Jacobsen's bleak surroundings were the same as those of the little shepherd boy Michael Kierkegaard, Søren's father. In this sense Jacobsen participated with Kierkegaard in a common source of gloom: their Jutlandish roots. Kierkegaard's works, when read by Jacobsen, had a particularly personal ring to them. This is even more true for those volumes of his journals covering his childhood years and relations with his father. The reference, mentioned earlier, to the sins of the fathers being visited upon the children undoubtedly stems from Jacobsen's knowledge of the source of Michael Kierkegaard's melancholy gleaned from his son's journals. These journals had all been published by the mid-1870s and were easily available to Jacobsen.[57]

The feeling in Jacobsen of a weariness with life, and the concurrent pessimism resulting from a youthful atheism that had hardened through the years, combined to produce his chief work—the remarkably modern novel *Niels Lyhne*. What Flaubert's Emma Bovary had been to *Marie Grubbe*, Kierkegaard was to *Niels Lyhne*. This was a Kierkegaard, however, who had capitulated to Darwin and Feuerbach, retaining only the outer husk of his solitary individualism. The hero, Niels, was the literary equivalent—with an added personal-existential dimension—of a Kierke-

---

56. See the poem "Arabesk til en Haandtegning af Michel Angelo" in J. P. Jacobsen, *Digte og Udkast*, pp. 155–59, especially p. 158.

57. A number of scholars have concentrated on the common Jutlandish background and shared melancholy of Jacobsen and Kierkegaard. See as examples Durand, *Jens Peter Jacobsen ou la Gravitation d'une Solitude*, pp. 23–25; and Walther Rehm, *Gontscharow und Jacobsen, oder Langweile und Schwermut* (Göttingen: Vandenhoeck & Ruprecht, 1963), pp. 103–6. See also Rehm's *Experimentum Medietatis: Studien zur Geistes-und Literaturgeschichte des 19. Jahrhunderts* (Munich: H. Rinn, 1947), pp. 184–239.

gaard minus faith in God, with all that such a character implied. In creating Niels, Jacobsen went one step beyond Brandes's abstract depiction of a despiritualized Kierkegaard to confront the concrete consequences for such an individual of his utter and frightening solitude.

Niels inhabits a world without God, one in which chance and the randomness of the accidental reign supreme. Heredity and environment have united to determine the makeup of his personality, a curious mixture of sensitivity, timidity, and introspection. From an early age he is surrounded by people who he feels can barely comprehend what he is all about; he resolves to endure strife and harsh misfortunes and "the martyrdom of being misjudged."[58] He oscillates between reality and dreamlike states and discovers, after repeated frustrations, the difficulties of exercising strong will power, decision, and action—what he calls appropriately "the leap."[59] At one point, during a conversation with his mother, Niels sounds a little like Ibsen's Brand as he resolves to fight for the noblest causes and never yield: "No compromise, mother!" he declares, "Every single work must be my best."[60] Niels's "all or nothing" tone, however, remains pure rhetoric and is not backed by action.

At an early age Niels overhears his aunt Edele rejecting the pathetic declarations of love made to her by Herr Bigum, the theology professor and philosopher who renounced his "eternal truths" in order to embrace the ideals of a Don Juan, only to be spurned by the woman he coveted. The experience causes Niels to shudder at life's cruelties, and an ominous feeling of terror grips him. When his aunt falls sick, he prays fervently for her recovery, but she soon dies and with her also dies his faith in God. From there the story proceeds to weave a complex tapestry of inner emotions, of hesitant relations with a number of women, of meditations on life, and of painful confrontations with death.

In addition to "the leap," a few specific indicators point in a Kierkegaardian direction. On more than one occasion, for instance, Jacobsen appears to be deriding philosophers who are system-builders. Herr Bigum, though a philosopher, enjoyed the advantage of not belonging to those "productive philosophers who find new laws and build new systems."[61] Again, in a comment on his friend Frithjof's study of Heiberg,

---

58. J. P. Jacobsen, *Niels Lyhne,* trans. Hanna Astrup Larsen (New York: American Scandinavian Foundation, 1919), p. 17.

59. Ibid., pp. 103 and 191.   60. Ibid., p. 120.

61. Ibid., p. 25.

Niels reflects: ". . . Frithjof, who had a good head for systems, and a broad back for dogmas, had read a little too much Heiberg, and had taken it all for gospel truth, never suspecting that the makers of systems are clever folk who fashion their systems from their books and not their books from their systems."[62] The abortive and often tragic relations Niels has with women, as well as his erotic images of his aunt Edele when he was little and the disillusioned marriages he observes around him as he gets older, are all tied with Jacobsen's ambivalent treatment of sexual themes in his life and in many of his writings. Having read fairly carefully *Either/Or,* where the erotic and marriage play a central role, and knowing some of the details pertaining to Kierkegaard's broken engagement, Jacobsen may well be drawing on this material for his novel. Admittedly, however, the connections here remain flimsy and largely speculative in the absence of more tangible links.

One issue on which Niels does not compromise is his atheism. In this he resembles a sort of inverted Brand, a despiritualized Kierkegaardian individualist. The few times when Niels does waver, he derives reassurance from his friend Dr. Hjerrild, a steadfast atheist who had become resigned to the continued presence of religion in the world. Hjerrild also acts as a restraint on Niels's overzealous animosity toward religion. It is futile to try and fight Christianity, Hjerrild tells him: "And how in the world can [one] get fanatic about a negation? Fanatic for the idea that there is no God!"[63] Hjerrild and Niels feel like pariahs on Christmas Eve when everyone else is celebrating, and even Hjerrild experiences a sad feeling of nostalgia at that time of year, but it quickly passes.

Jacobsen has customarily been regarded as a transitional figure between the early gropings of Brandes's "Modern Breakthrough" and the realism born of the spiritual malaise attending the *fin de siècle.*[64] In fact he is fully at home in the latter and looks ahead in anticipation of twentieth-century movements. *Niels Lyhne* was the culmination of his brief career and received praise from several intellectuals, including the already famous Ibsen.[65] Brandes, still bitter about a onetime protégé and subordi-

---

62. Ibid., p. 110.   63. Ibid., pp. 156–59.
64. See Alrik Gustafson's "Toward Decadence: Jens Peter Jacobsen," in his *Six Scandinavian Novelists: Lie, Jacobsen, Heidenstam, Selma Lagerlöf, Hamsun, Sigrid Undset* (Princeton: Princeton University Press, 1940), p. 92.
65. See letter from Ibsen to his publisher Frederik Hegel dated January 16, 1881 in *Letters of Henrik Ibsen,* trans. Laurvik and Morison, p. 336: "Jacobsen's book is a fine work in every respect. I venture to say that it is one of the very best of its kind which has

nate deserting the fold to attain independent stature, was reserved in his public admiration and continued to be critical.[66] On the whole, people in the 1880s were less excited about the novel than those of the following decade, which saw a general reaction against positivism accompanied by the onset of the enigmatic concept of the subconscious. Writing in 1897 for *Cosmopolis,* a commentator summed up as follows:

> "Niels Lyhne" has been called the Bible of young Scandinavia. And if we wish to grasp the peculiar, indefinable essence of the Northern mind, it is to this book we shall turn rather than to many that have won a wider European fame.... There is a touch of the "melancholy of eternity" upon it. It embodies, in a peculiar degree, the hopes and struggles, the dreams and disillusions of our century's end.[67]

Now, more than at any other time in the century, Kierkegaardian words like "anxiety," "despair," "suffering," and "fear and trembling," which appear over and over again throughout *Niels Lyhne,* were ringing with a poignant urgency in the ears of *fin de siècle* readers. The "twilight moods" evoked by the novel spoke directly to the weary ennui and the feeling of decay that many intellectuals were experiencing at the turn of the century: a form of alienation to which, in its extreme manifestations, the label "sickness unto death" would not be ill-suited. *Niels Lyhne* represents a rare literary bridge between Kierkegaard's writings, with their promise of spiritual solace amidst all the bleak human despair they so exquisitely portray, and the absurdism of "no exit" writers like Sartre and Camus. This is best illustrated in the novel's treatment of death. Niels attempts to impart to his wife Gerda the realities of life in its distressing arbitrariness. He does not conceal from her that the "truth of atheism" will seem "crushingly sad and comfortless" at the hour of death.[68] Gerda falls sick and dies, yet retains her faith in God to the end. Next, his son is struck by illness and suffers greatly before dying. In spite of himself, Niels is driven in desperation to prayer to "the God Who demands that every knee shall bend to Him in trembling, from Whom no flight is possible."[69] Nevertheless, death prevails. Once more, as with Ibsen's *Brand,* it is a

---

been written in our day." Jacobsen had made the personal acquaintance of Ibsen in 1878, while both were in Rome.

66. Durand, "Les Rapports de Georg Brandes et de J. P. Jacobsen," pp. 116–17.

67. E. F. L. Robertson, "A Danish Poet: J. P. Jacobsen," in *Cosmopolis,* VIII (1897), p. 358.

68. Jacobsen, *Niels Lyhne,* pp. 267–68.   69. Ibid., p. 276.

variation on the powerful motif of the Abraham story that lurks behind the climax of Jacobsen's novel. Niels regrets having weakened and turned to God for help. He enlists in the army and seeks refuge in "the monotony of training"—a move prefiguring Camus's Sisyphus.[70] He is mortally wounded while defending his country on the battlefield, and dies "the death— the difficult death."[71]

Niels Lyhne appeared at the beginning of a decade that saw a number of interesting, though not particularly spectacular, developments in Kierkegaard's reception in Scandinavia and Germany. In Denmark, where the journals had been published in full and the furor over Brandes's book was slowly settling, attention continued to be focused on Kierkegaard from a mainly theological perspective. The biographical-psychological impetus provided by the journals and Brandes was to bear fruit a little later. In 1883 Kierkegaard's name came up in a two-volume history of the Danish Church in the first half of the nineteenth century. He was mentioned in connection with Grundtvig and with the *Kirkekampen*.[72] In the same year an old friend of Kierkegaard from their college days in the 1830s, Andreas Listov (1817–89), wrote a book on Kierkegaard's understanding of Luther.[73] A few years later he published some articles on Kierkegaard's relation to Feuerbach and to Pascal. Associating Kierkegaard with these two thinkers was becoming increasingly fashionable.

Following on the heels of the last consignment of Kierkegaard's journals to make it to the printers came Martensen's three-volume autobiography in 1882 and 1883. In volumes two and three Martensen discusses his relation to Kierkegaard in conjunction with Nielsen's critical reaction to *Christelige Dogmatik* of 1849, and in the context of Kierkegaard's attack on Mynster, which precipitated the *Kirkekampen*. Not surprisingly, Martensen's assessment of Kierkegaard in both instances is anything but flat-

---

70. Ibid., p. 279. Sisyphus is actually mentioned on page 250 in connection with an earlier attempt by Niels to find pleasure and meaning in monotonous daily physical labor. See also Durand, *Jens Peter Jacobsen ou la Gravitation d'une Solitude*, p. 16 and 18 where parallels with Sartre's *Chemains de la liberté* and Camus's Sisyphus story and *La Peste* are drawn. Durand's article "Jens Peter Jacobsen et la France," in *Orbis Litterarum* 22 (1967), p. 282, elaborates on this.

71. Jacobsen, *Niels Lyhne*, p. 284.

72. See L. Koch, *Den Danske Kirkes Historie i det nittende Aarhundrede* (Copenhagen, 1883), volume II, pp. 147–50 and 186–87.

73. See Andreas Listov, *Morten Luther, opfattet af Søren Kierkegaard. Et historisk Lejlighedsskrift* (Copenhagen, 1883).

tering, and his tone in places betrays a rankling bitterness.[74] He depicts the steady deterioration in their relationship, from the early friendly days when Martensen taught Kierkegaard Schleiermacher's dogmatics, as presented in *Der christliche Glaube* (1821–22),[75] to the final rupture and the *Øjeblikket* articles. He claims he read only the first issue of *Øjeblikket*, which he calls "negative and desultory,"[76] and he defends the positions he took at the time, all of which are to be expected in an autobiography. He also takes a few parting shots at what he calls Kierkegaard's "ascetic caricature" of Christ and Christian living.[77]

One year later, in 1884, Mynster's son takes courage from Martensen's autobiography and publishes an essay on Kierkegaard that is predictably critical of his conception of Christianity and truth.[78] Both of these works, written by men with personal stakes in the issues they tackle, reignited the debate over Kierkegaard's final attack on the Church. A certain Niels Teisen (1851–1916), a Danish teacher and scholar of religion, saw fit to respond in 1884 to Martensen and Mynster's son with a sober tract in which he defended Kierkegaard's attack on the established ecclesiastical order, using Rasmus Nielsen's words to call it "a good deed."[79]

The radical and destabilizing nature of Kierkegaard's *Øjeblikket* articles was still strong thirty years after their inception, as evidenced by the writings of Martensen and the younger Mynster. These explosive articles had been discovered by the anti-religious forces of the 1870s associated with Brandes's "Modern Breakthrough," who put them to effective use against orthodoxy and the Church. In a curiously unexpected way, the same potency of these final polemical writings by Kierkegaard had a hand in advancing the political goals of liberals who were beginning to clamour loudly for greater democratization in Denmark. The case in point is Viggo Hörup (1841–1902), the journalist and founder in 1884 of the radical, socialist-leaning newspaper *Politiken*. Hörup was of peasant stock but

---

74. H. L. Martensen, *Af mit Levned* (Copenhagen, 1883), vol. II, pp. 134–49; and vol. III, pp. 12–23. Nielsen, too, receives harsh treatment, especially regarding the manner in which he used Kierkegaard to assault Martensen's book of 1849 and then turned to Grundtvigianism in later years.

75. Ibid., vol. I, p. 78.   76. Ibid., vol. III, pp. 16 and 20.

77. Ibid., vol. III, p. 22.

78. See C. L. N. Mynster, *Har S. Kierkegaard fremstillet de christelige Idealer—er dette Sandhed?* (Copenhagen, 1884).

79. See Niels Teisen, *Kort Indlæg i Sagen mellem S. Kierkegaard og H. L. Martensen: Et Lejlighedsskrift* (Copenhagen, 1884).

managed to study law and receive a degree. Being a child of the lower classes who had struggled and succeeded through education, he was bent on bringing about the emancipation of the peasants and workers. He had read Kierkegaard and was attracted by his nonconformity with respect to the religious authorities, and by his ironic style. He combined these with the social ideas of the French Revolution to create a powerful mixture. In the early 1870s Hörup joined the wider circle of young enthusiasts for Brandes's new program in literature. At their gatherings he would frequently bring up Kierkegaard in connection with social reform.

The 1880s in Denmark were marked politically by a highly conservative government that catered almost exclusively to the wishes of the king. Hörup felt that certain economic measures taken by the cabinet were resulting in injustices for the poor, and in 1884 he enlisted the pages of his newly established newspaper in the battle against the government. He employed all the polemical invective he could dredge up from Kierkegaard's writings, in particular *Øjeblikket*, and championed increased liberalization. He often quoted Kierkegaard directly, targeting not only the state but the Church and clergy as well. Ten years after *Politiken* began, a political agreement was reached among the various parties that eventually led in 1901 to the formation of Denmark's first liberal ministry. Hörup's dreams were starting to be realized at last. He joined this first liberal government but died a few months later.[80] It is ironic that the works of the politically conservative—even monarchist—Kierkegaard, who was by no means enamored of the press of his day, should have had an indirect hand in hastening the birth of liberal democracy in Denmark.

While the emphasis in Kierkegaard's reception throughout the 1880s in Germany remained, as in Denmark, largely theological, signs of a shift were beginning to emerge and would become more pronounced in the next decade. Germany, after all, was at the heart of European intellectual crosscurrents and interacting cultural trends, which generated competing political ideologies, philosophical outlooks, and artistic fashions. The feeling in theological circles of traditional religion coming increasingly under siege since mid-century persisted. The combined force of biblical higher criticism, new discoveries in science, and spiraling industrialization, exerted tremendous pressures on dearly held beliefs among German

---

80. On Viggo Hörup see F. J. Billeskov Jansen, "L'Heritage de Kierkegaard dans les Pays nordiques," in *Cahiers du Sud* 50, no. 371 (1963), pp. 22-23; see also J. Oskar Andersen, *Survey of the History of the Church in Denmark*, pp. 63-64.

Protestants and Catholics alike, the latter of whom were still reeling from the aftereffects of Bismarck's *Kulturkampf*. For the slowly growing popularity of Kierkegaard's works to spread beyond the narrow confines of a beleaguered theology and attain a broader intellectual appreciation, other trends threatening to eclipse their appeal had to be overcome. This could occur through an assimilation of these new trends or a displacement of them altogether, and neither course was an easy one. Naturally, a prerequisite was the availability of abundant and readily accessible translations. Another more difficult requirement was the presence of a receptive ambience, perhaps the result of a general crisis in the *Zeitgeist*—this in keeping with Kierkegaard's prediction that matters would have to get much worse before his writings received the serious consideration they deserved.

For the time being, however, the diligent labors of German translators dominated the scene, and busiest among them was Albert Bärthold. In 1881 he produced a translation of *Sickness unto Death* and four years later, in 1885, a second edition of his translation of "The Lilies of the Field" was issued. In 1886 he put out the first German translation of *Stages on Life's Way*. Simultaneously with these translations, Bärthold was immersed in his favorite Kierkegaardian theme: *Persönlichkeit* and its primacy for Christian life. He wrote three separate treatises—all published in Gütersloh—in an attempt to reinject the "ideal" of personality, as he called it, into the mainstream of contemporary theological discourse and cultural development. The first two addressed the question of the relevance of Christian truth in an age characterized by an unshakable faith in progress and impersonal collectives, yet one in which "a hunger after personality cries out."[81] Here, the criticism was directed, in part, at the compromising disposition of Protestant theologians eager to live comfortably in the world and ready to appease the socialists by watering down their Christian commitment to personality. An optimistic note was sounded, however, as Bärthold pointed repeatedly to signs of spiritual renewal and a return to authentic personal faith.

The last of these works, written in 1886, dealt entirely with Kierkegaard and constituted Bärthold's rebuttal to the criticisms and charges of Martensen, whose autobiography appeared in German translation in 1883–

---

81. Albert Bärthold, *Die Wendung zur Wahrheit in der modernen Kulturentwicklung* (Gütersloh, 1885), p. 40. See also Bärthold's *Was Christentum ist. Zur Verständigung über diese Frage* (Gütersloh, 1884).

84.[82] Apparently this translation, with its array of disparaging remarks about Kierkegaard, had aroused Bärthold's concern that an erroneous impression of his admired champion of individuality would spread in Germany. Upon reading the essay of the young Mynster against Kierkegaard, and then Teisen's subsequent retort, he decided to join the battle. His 1886 book, entitled appropriately *S. Kierkegaards Persönlichkeit in ihrer Verwirklichung der Ideale* (S.K's personality in his realization of the ideal) and dedicated to Barfod and Gottsched, was a reexamination of the concept of the "single individual" as embodied in Kierkegaard's own life and writings, in particular during the final years of the *Kirkekampen*. Bärthold polemicized not only against Martensen and Mynster but, as in the two earlier tracts, against the Church and the accommodative tendencies of theologians generally who were faced with an aggressive secularism. He called for an imitation of Christ through a return to the ideal of personality, so well illustrated by and in Kierkegaard. Interestingly, however, he referred again and again to Rasmus Nielsen as having been the faithful follower of the master, and one who would have benefited to a greater degree from Kierkegaard's idea of *Persönlichkeit* had their relationship not ended abruptly.[83] At times it seemed as though Bärthold was more concerned with Nielsen than with Kierkegaard; nevertheless, his analysis of their relationship was the first of its kind in German.

Through his writings, Bärthold served as a convenient theological link between Denmark and Germany in the 1880s. This latest work of his on Kierkegaard was reviewed in two German theological journals. *Theologischer Jahresbericht* gave a brief synopsis of the book without comment, whereas Paul Wetzel of *Theologische Literaturzeitung* sounded indignant at Bärthold's audacity in waging a polemic against eminent theologians like Martensen and Mynster; he scornfully added that such "enthusiasm" for Kierkegaard rendered any treatise on *Persönlichkeit* worthless.[84] The latter review was representative of the official line among German Protestant theologians at the time.

Other German translators besides Bärthold were at work in the 1880s. The decade saw a third edition in 1881 of Christian Hansen's 1862 transla-

---

82. See H. L. Martensen, *Aus meinem Leben*, volumes I-III, trans. Alexander Michelsen (Leipzig, 1883-84).

83. See Albert Bärthold, *S. Kierkegaards Persönlichkeit in ihrer Verwirklichung der Ideale* (Gütersloh, 1886), pp. 137-41.

84. See August Werner's review in *Theologischer Jahresbericht*, vol. 6 (Leipzig, 1887), p. 240. See also Paul Wetzel's review in *Theologische Literaturzeitung*, no. 1 (Leipzig, 1887), pp. 9-10.

tion of *For Self-Examination*, as well as the first appearance in 1882 of *Fear and Trembling* in German, provided by a certain H. C. Ketels, and a full translation in 1885 of both volumes of *Either/Or*. This last accomplishment was begun by Alexander Michelsen—a theologian in Hamburg and the same person who translated Martensen's autobiography—and completed upon his death by Otto Gleiss, who published it in Leipzig.[85] The most significant event, however, which was to influence the entire course of Kierkegaard translations into German for at least the next thirty years, occurred during the school year 1883-84 in Tübingen, when a theology student of J. T. Beck named Christoph Schrempf (1860-1944) read Hansen's translation of *For Self-Examination* and thereby discovered Kierkegaard.[86]

If Bärthold, the unsung pioneer of Kierkegaard in German, remains obscure and elusive, Schrempf is his exact antithesis: ostentatious, self-centered, and prolific, especially in his writing about himself. His collected works run to sixteen volumes and cover a wide array of subjects, the very diffuseness of which testifies to the eclecticism of their author and to the often erratic course of his intellectual development. Moreover, whereas Bärthold maintains a consistently sympathetic disposition toward Kierkegaard, Schrempf soon overcomes his initial enthusiasm as he allows himself to be sucked into the swirl of *fin de siècle* skepticism and malaise. The first casualties of this are his religious faith—tenuous from the start—and his affiliation with the Lutheran Church, which he renounces altogether. He enters the twentieth century an angry and unstable man, determined to snuff out any lingering traces in himself of conventional spirituality, yet unsure of what to replace it with or in which direction to head. The result was a nondescript kind of agnosticism, self-enclosed and egotistical, and given to much ink spilling.

All along, however, Schrempf never let go of Kierkegaard. In 1886, two years after his discovery of him, and while still under his strong spell,

---

85. See the foreword by Otto Gleiss to his joint translation with Alexander Michelsen of Kierkegaard's *Entweder-Oder. Ein Lebens-Fragment, herausgegeben von Victor Eremita*, in two parts (Leipzig, 1885), Part I, pp. v-vii. For a survey of reviews of this translation and other early German translations of works by Kierkegaard see the useful, though often inaccurate, article by Helen M. Mustard entitled "Sören Kierkegaard in German Literary Periodicals, 1860-1930," in *Germanic Review*, XXVI (April 1951), pp. 83-101. Most of the early German reviews were inconsequential.

86. Like Bärthold and Gottsched before him, Schrempf was a follower of J. T. Beck's theology, and like them he first bumped into Kierkegaard through Hansen's translation of *For Self-Examination*. He then read Bärthold's and Ketels's translations.

Schrempf reacted polemically to a review by Paul Wetzel in *Theologische Literaturzeitung* of Michelsen and Gleiss's translation in the previous year of *Either/Or*. Wetzel was a member of the Protestant theological establishment in Germany and a follower of Adolf von Harnack (1851–1930), the founder and editor of the *Theologische Literaturzeitung* and a Ritschlian liberal Protestant theologian then engaged in writing his grand opus, *Dogmengeschichte* (1885–90). There was a strong antipathy in Harnack's circle for the intermingling of philosophy and Christian theology that had been going on since the days of the early church. Harnack's work was an attempt to dehellenize the original message of the gospel and rid it of the metaphysical trappings acquired over the centuries. He was also doing this partly in order to escape the age's secular onslaught on religion. From the little that Wetzel knew of Kierkegaard, he formed an unappealing impression of a nonconformist renegade and a philosopher dabbling in Christianity. His review of *Either/Or*, like his review in the following year of Bärthold's book on Kierkegaard, was very negative, criticizing Michelsen on his unquestioning reverence for Kierkegaard and downplaying the importance of Kierkegaard for the German reading public.[87] Schrempf's response to Wetzel constituted his first article on Kierkegaard and demonstrated that already in the space of two years he had gained a broad knowledge of the works.[88]

After studying Danish, Schrempf produced in 1890 his first translation, consisting of *Concept of Anxiety* and *Philosophical Fragments* together under the devised title *Zur Psychologie der Sünde, der Bekehrung und des Glaubens* (On the psychology of sin, conversion, and faith). A few more translations followed some years later, and from 1909 to 1922 Schrempf acted as self-appointed general editor of the first German edition of Kierkegaard's *Gesammelte Werke* in twelve volumes, overseeing and contrib-

---

87. See Paul Wetzel's review of *Either/Or* in *Theologische Literaturzeitung*, no. 12 (Leipzig, 1886), pp. 279–82. Wetzel read the section on Kierkegaard in Strodtmann's 1873 book on Denmark, and mentions Strodtmann twice in his review.

88. Christoph Schrempf, "Sören Kierkegaard und sein neuester Beurteiler in der Theologischen Literaturzeitung" [1886], in *Gesammelte Werke*, ed. Otto Engel (Stuttgart: F. Fromann, 1935), vol. XII: "Auseinandersetzungen IV, Sören Kierkegaard, Dritter Teil," pp. 3–26. All subsequent references to Schrempf's writings will be to this edition of his complete works, accompanied by the original dates. Although this was Schrempf's first independent article on Kierkegaard, it was not the first mention of him in his writings. In 1884 Schrempf published a book called *Die Grundlage der Ethik* as his entry in a competition in the faculty of theology at Tübingen. His readings of Kierkegaard that year resulted in several references to him in this work. The book is published as volume XIV of the *Gesammelte Werke*.

uting to the translations in collaboration with Gottsched and Albert Dorner. It is in his numerous forewords and afterwords to these translations that Schrempf's changing attitudes toward Kierkegaard are most vividly mapped out. It is here also that one observes a certain cavalier and arbitrary quality in the way in which Schrempf treats his subject matter, which would have remained relatively benign were it not also employed in the preparation of the translations themselves. The consequences were deplorable for Kierkegaard's early introduction into Germany. In several instances—all well documented by later, more careful scholars who went out of their way to expose his errors and excesses—Schrempf took the liberty of trimming, altering, or restructuring the text to his liking, and even went so far as to declare in the foreword to his two-volume "biography" of Kierkegaard of 1927: "The critical question is not so much whether I have accurately translated my quotations, but whether I have properly selected them [!]"[89]

Schrempf's freewheeling approach to his duties as Kierkegaard's German translator, and his habit of constantly interposing himself and his opinions between Kierkegaard's text and the reader's independent judgment, have earned him a well-deserved notoriety among Kierkegaard specialists. Emanuel Hirsch, the new editor of *Theologische Literaturzeitung* and one of Germany's most competent twentieth-century experts on Kierkegaard, in a review of Schrempf's 1927 work provides specific examples of unwarranted comments about the translations that Schrempf interjects in his forewords. Schrempf, for example, calls *Fear and Trembling* "an entirely unsatisfactory work," and writes elsewhere that he was "poorly edified" upon reading the *Upbuilding Discourse* "Purity of Heart" because it made him discover that he did not possess a pure heart.[90] Eduard Geismar, another leading Kierkegaard scholar of the nineteen-twenties and thirties, also laments Schrempf's atrocious translations and overbear-

89. Schrempf, "Vorwort zu 'Sören Kierkegaard, eine Biographie' " [1927], in ibid., vol. XII, p. 446.
90. See the review of Schrempf's book by Emanuel Hirsch in *Theologische Literaturzeitung*, no. 23 (Leipzig, 1927), pp. 548–49. Otto Engel, Schrempf's editor and close friend, published an article in 1954 defending Schrempf's translations of Kierkegaard and attacking Hirsch. Some of his arguments about the "merits of inaccuracy" are nothing short of ludicrous. See Otto Engel, "Kierkegaard und seine deutschen Übersetzer," in *Stuttgarter Zeitung (Literaturblatt)*, Saturday, November 6, 1954. It is reproduced in Otto Engel, *Distanz und Hingabe: Philosophische und literarische Essays* (Stuttgart: F. Fromann, 1971), pp. 120–24. This collection of essays by Engel contains a wealth of information on Schrempf.

ing liberties, while Franz Josef Brecht, for his part, suggests half-seriously that Schrempf sought to present Kierkegaard in the way he "ought to have written," had German been his mother language![91] One writer summed the matter up facetiously as follows: "Schrempf was a translator with character, often with too much character [!]"[92]

Yet the most incensed among later translators was not a German at all. Walter Lowrie seized several opportunities to criticize Schrempf. According to Lowrie, there are "lovers" and there are "haters" of Kierkegaard among the scholars who have translated and written about him, and Schrempf clearly belongs to the latter group.[93] Schrempf was a pastor in the Lutheran Church who became convinced, after reading Kierkegaard, that he was not a Christian. He resigned from the pastorate and left the Church. He seemed never to have forgiven Kierkegaard for revealing to him his own unbelief, and since he had no source of livelihood after leaving the Church, Schrempf turned to the task of translating Kierkegaard and denouncing what he had translated.[94] Regarding the quality of the translations, Lowrie writes:

> It was the least of Schrempf's offenses that when he encountered a sentence or even a whole paragraph which he could not easily translate, or for some reason did not like, he simply omitted it—providing thereby a sure criterion for identifying translations of S. K. into various languages which are actually translations of Schrempf's translation by writers who have no knowledge of Danish.[95]

91. See Eduard Geismar's "Kierkegaard" in *Die Religion in Geschichte und Gegenwart: Handwörterbuch für Theologie und Religionswissenschaft*, III, ed. Hermann Gunkel and Leopold Zscharnack (Tübingen: J. C. B. Mohr, 1929), p. 750; and Franz Josef Brecht, "Die Kierkegaardforschung in letzten Jahrfünft," in *Literarische Berichte aus dem Gebiete der Philosophie* (Erfurt, 1931), p. 7. For a discussion of Schrempf and other German translators of Kierkegaard see Heinrich Getzeny, "Kierkegaards Eindeutung. Ein Beitrag zur deutschen Geistesgeschichte der letzten hundert Jahre," in *Historisches Jahrbuch*, vol. 76 (Munich, 1957), especially pp. 186-87.

92. Friedrich Hansen-Löve, "Der deutsche Sören Kierkegaard," in *Wort und Wahrheit* 7 (Vienna, 1952), pp. 624-25.

93. See the introduction to Lowrie's translation of Kierkegaard's *Stages on Life's Way* (Princeton: Princeton University Press, 1940), p. 14, the long footnote.

94. See Walter Lowrie's preface to *On Authority and Revelation (The Book on Adler)* (Princeton: Princeton University Press, 1955), pp. vi-vii.

95. Walter Lowrie, "Translators and Interpreters of Søren Kierkegaard," in *Theology Today* 12, no. 3 (October 1955), p. 318. During conversations this writer had with Niels Thulstrup on April 7, 1983, at the Søren Kierkegaard Biblioteket in Copenhagen, he termed Schrempf's translations "awful"; as an example of arbitrariness, he singled out in

Much as one might hesitate to use words like "megalomania" to account for Schrempf's conduct, one is left with little choice, not just based on his attitude toward Kierkegaard, but taking into consideration as well the voluminous size of his own writings and the frequent occurrence of the first person singular. Schrempf clearly aspired to be the Kierkegaard broker *par excellence* in the German-speaking world, and he wished to achieve this through both his translations and his personal *Auseinandersetzung* with Kierkegaard. He acknowledges openly his love-hate relationship with the man, stating that "an 'antipathetic sympathy and a sympathetic antipathy' binds me to him, which is nearly as strong as the antipathetic sympathy and sympathetic antipathy that binds me to myself."[96] In the 1890s Schrempf concentrated on Kierkegaard's polemical writings against the Church, with a view to employing them in his own personal struggle with the German Lutheran Church that he had turned his back on and in order to undermine organized religion in general. In this he resembled Brandes, except that Brandes never translated Kierkegaard and could always fall back on his status as a literary critic and as the leader of a new movement in literature to justify his agitational activity. Schrempf, however, had no excuse for his sloppy translations; furthermore, he did not possess the attributes of an original philosopher, which might have redeemed him somewhat.

Before closing the books on the 1880s it is worth mentioning a couple of developments pertaining to the still-limited English reception of Kierkegaard. In 1884 an English translation appeared of a German history of Scandinavian literature published four years earlier by a Danish literary historian named Frederik Winkel Horn. Horn devotes a page and a half out of his four-hundred-page survey to Kierkegaard. This "greatest thinker Denmark ever produced" is contrasted with Mynster, Clausen, and Martensen—all strictly theologians—as "the connecting link between theology and philosophy." His writings are "most striking and original" and "distinguished for their refined and brilliant dialectics combined with passionate enthusiasm." Beyond these general superlatives, Horn draws a passing parallel between Kierkegaard and Feuerbach, mentions the paradox and the "individual," touches in condensed fashion on the *Kirkekampen* and *Øjeblikket,* and lists the major works that, he concludes,

---

particular Schrempf's omission of the entire section at the beginning of *Concept of Anxiety* where Kierkegaard differentiates and classifies the various disciplines.

96. Schrempf, *Gesammelte Werke,* vol. XII, p. 440.

"exercised a powerful influence upon his [Kierkegaard's] contemporaries and sowed in many souls the seeds of true religion."[97] Being a history of literature, Horn's book would be expected to reach a larger German reading public than the usual theological treatise where Kierkegaard had thus far received the greatest exposure; yet the impact of such a brief and general account of Kierkegaard on both German and English readers can, for all practical purposes, be considered negligible. The interesting thing about the English translation is that it was published in Chicago, which made it accessible not only to the Scandinavian-Americans of the Midwest, but to anyone else there who wished to learn about the literature of Scandinavia.

Of potential significance for future Kierkegaard research in North America were the activities in the 1880s of professor Nels E. Simonsen (?–1959) of the Garrett Biblical Institute in Evanston, Illinois. As a second-generation Norwegian-American who had gone briefly to Christiania to do graduate studies, Simonsen felt fully at home in the New World and contributed to the creation of the educational curriculum of late-nineteenth-century Midwestern Norwegian-Danish schools. Following the waves of immigration earlier in the century, the Scandinavian-American communities were beginning to organize their lives and deepen their acquaintance with their newly adopted country, without diluting the strong linguistic and cultural ties that they still maintained with their original homeland. Most courses, therefore, continued to be taught in Dano-Norwegian well into the 1890s. This was true of the theology lectures and seminars given by the young Simonsen, who was particularly interested in Martensen's writings, but "not at the expense of Kierkegaard," as a friend of his once asserted. In fact Simonsen was discussing with his students the intricacies of the Martensen-Kierkegaard dispute over speculative theology, dialectics, Hegel, and the role of the individual as early as 1887, or even 1885.[98] Martensen's *Christelige Dogmatik* of 1849

---

97. Frederik Winkel Horn, *Geschichte der Literatur des Skandinavischen Nordens* (Leipzig, 1880), pp. 259–61. The English translations of the quotations come from F. W. Horn's *Literature of the Scandinavian North,* trans. Rasmus B. Anderson (Chicago, 1884), pp. 286–88.

98. Most of the information on N. E. Simonsen comes from Howard A. Slaatte's article "Kierkegaard's Introduction to American Methodists—A Tribute," in *The Drew Gateway,* XXX (Spring 1960), pp. 162–67; see esp. p. 162. See also Arlow W. Andersen, *The Norwegian-Americans,* p. 116; and Lewis A. Lawson, "Small Talk on the 'Melancholy Dane' in America," in *The Legacy and Interpretation of Kierkegaard,* vol. 8 of *Bibliotheca Kierkegaardiana,* p. 181. For a discussion of Kierkegaard in American religious thought

and his three-volume *Christelige Ethik* (1871-78), as well as selected works of Kierkegaard owned by Simonsen, were used in his classes in the late 1880s and beyond. With Simonsen, therefore, the dormant Kierkegaard of the nineteenth-century Midwestern prairies, transported in musty boxes across the ocean and left for years to gather dust on the shelves of countless Scandinavian-American clerical libraries, begins to see the light of day in anticipation of the avalanche of translations and studies in the following century.

In Europe the final decade of the nineteenth century was bustling with intellectual controversy, and new movements were straining to be heard and to carve out a niche for their views in the crowded marketplace of ideas. Philosophically, a rigid polarization was taking shape between an entrenched positivism and naturalism on the one hand, and a resurgent anti-intellectualism side by side with a neo-Kantianism on the other. This polarization had repercussions in every field, including the sciences, where in biology, for example, it took the form of a showdown between mechanism and vitalism. In theology there was a strong tendency among liberal Protestants of the Ritschlian school to perform two parallel maneuvers: to look back to a pristine early Christianity uncluttered by metaphysical props and to cater more openly to the socio-economic needs of the community as a response to the growing political challenges of socialism. For their part, Roman Catholics took their cue on social matters from Pope Leo XIII's 1891 encyclical *Rerum Novarum,* and the intellectuals among them were beginning to heed his call in *Aeterni Patris* of 1878 for a revival of the medieval scholastic attempt to harmonize faith and reason. The decade also witnessed the birth of the newly defined and segregated disciplines of psychology, sociology, and anthropology, as well as refinements in historical research and writing with a distinctively German emphasis on *Geistesgeschichte.*

The onset of the 1890s saw a continuation of the combined Scandinavian and German lead in the discovery and reception of Kierkegaard. The standard-bearers of Brandes's "Modern Breakthrough" had wished to relegate Kierkegaard to the bygone annals of romanticism, but not before they had plundered his works for everything that from a freethinker's perspective seemed worth salvaging. With the *fin de siècle* reaction against positivism and naturalism intensifying, a new door was opened

---

see Reidar Thomte, "Kierkegaard im amerikanischen religiösen Denken," in *Lutherische Rundschau* 5 (Zurich, 1955), pp. 147-57.

through which Kierkegaardian individualism could reenter and make its presence felt. There were others besides Kierkegaard, however, who would benefit from this new climate of ideas and moods—thinkers whose hitherto solitary indictments of their culture and its values suddenly seemed to strike a relevant chord in the psyche of a disillusioned age. Chief among these was Friedrich Nietzsche, and the swiftly rising vogue of his philosophy in the 1890s offered Kierkegaard's legacy some stiff competition.[99]

Brandes's 1888 lectures on Nietzsche at the University of Copenhagen were published the following year in *Tilskueren* (The Spectator) under the title "Aristocratic Radicalism," which was the term Brandes had coined to describe the new philosophy of his German friend and for which he had received in return the appreciative title "the Good European" from a very pleased Nietzsche.[100] At the end of *Ecce Homo* (written in 1888; published posthumously in 1908), Nietzsche acknowledged Brandes's efforts to promote his thought and contrasted them with the neglect he had suffered at the hands of his German compatriots.[101] In Brandes's

---

99. The literature on the early and meteoric coming into fashion of Nietzsche in the German-speaking world is extensive. William J. McGrath, in his *Dionysian Art and Populist Politics in Austria* (New Haven: Yale University Press, 1974), argues that Nietzsche's influence began in the 1870s among a group of Viennese student admirers that included Gustav Mahler and Victor Adler. The best study in English of Nietzsche's reception in Germany is Steven E. Aschheim's *The Nietzsche Legacy in Germany: 1890–1990* (Berkeley: University of California Press, 1992). For an analysis of the political implications of Nietzsche's reception in the 1890s in Germany see R. Hinton Thomas, *Nietzsche in German Politics and Society: 1890–1918* (London: Manchester University Press, 1983). For extracts from early German articles on Nietzsche see *Nietzsche und die deutsche Literatur*, 2 volumes, vol. I: "Texte zur Nietzsche-Rezeption, 1873–1963," ed. Bruno Hillebrand (München: Deutscher Taschenbuch-Verlag, 1978).

100. For Brandes's essay on Nietzsche see *Tilskueren,* August 1889, pp. 565–613. For an English translation see Georg Brandes, "An Essay on Aristocratic Radicalism," in his *Friedrich Nietzsche,* trans. A. G. Chater (London, 1914), pp. 3–56. In his letter to Brandes dated December 2, 1887, Nietzsche writes: "The expression 'Aristocratic Radicalism,' which you employ, is very good. It is, permit me to say, the cleverest thing I have yet read about myself." He then bestows on Brandes the title "a good European and missionary of culture." See p. 64 in the English translation of Brandes's book on Nietzsche.

101. "Ten years and no one in Germany has made it a question of conscience to defend my name against the absurd silence under which it has lain buried: it was a foreigner, a Dane, who was the first to possess sufficient refinement of instinct *and courage* for that, who inveighed against my supposed friends.... At which German university today would lectures on my philosophy be possible such as were given last spring by Dr. Georg Brandes in Copenhagen—who therewith once more proved himself a psychologist?" See Friedrich Nietzsche, *Ecce Homo: How One Becomes What One Is,* trans. R. J. Hollingdale (London, New York: Penguin, 1979), p. 124.

essay we come across a few instances where he mentions Kierkegaard, usually as a kindred individualist with Nietzsche. These are the earliest associations made between Kierkegaard and Nietzsche; however, Brandes makes it clear that Kierkegaard's individualism was intended to enhance Christianity rather than transcend it.[102]

Brandes's essay on Nietzsche elicited a critical response from a colleague in Copenhagen who was a philosopher in his own right. Harald Høffding wrote an article he entitled "Democratic Radicalism" in which he took Brandes to task for heaping unqualified praise on Nietzsche's conception of the superior individual—or Superman *(Übermensch)*—and on his critique of society from the standpoint of the will to power. Høffding argued that such an unquestioning acceptance by Brandes of this Nietzschean line of thinking would land him in self-contradiction, since it would ultimately undermine these very same liberal principles that he had always advocated and fought for. The article by Høffding started a controversy between the two men that played itself out in several newspaper articles during the remainder of that year and into 1890. Its details would be important for any investigation of Nietzsche's early reception in Scandinavia.[103] Two years later, in 1892, Høffding wrote what amounted to the first serious analysis of Kierkegaard's philosophy; this work would eventually serve as a primary channel for the transmission of his thought beyond Denmark.

At a young age Høffding read and was greatly captivated by Kierkegaard. Many years later he wrote in his memoirs: ". . . in my student years I deepened myself in Kierkegaard's writings."[104] In 1863–64 he read the religious works, and after struggling hard with Kierkegaard's understand-

---

102. See Georg Brandes, "An Essay on Aristocratic Radicalism," in *Friedrich Nietzsche*, p. 9; see also pp. 19, 20, and 28 for other references to Kierkegaard and Nietzsche.

103. For Høffding's essay in reply to Brandes entitled "Democratic Radicalism" see *Tilskueren,* November–December 1889, pp. 849–72. Both Brandes and Høffding refer in their writings to their controversy over Nietzsche. See Brandes's introduction, written in December 1899, to his correspondence with Nietzsche in his *Friedrich Nietzsche*, p. 60; see Harald Høffding's *Erindringer* (Copenhagen: Gyldendal, 1928), pp. 163–68. On the early history of Nietzsche's Scandinavian reception, which in large part is a treatment of the Brandes-Høffding controversy over Nietzsche in 1889–90 and its subsequent repercussions, see Horst Brandl, "Skandinavische Aspekte der Nietzsche-Rezeption," in *Nietzsche-Studien: Internationales Jahrbuch für die Nietzsche Forschung*, vol. 12, ed. Ernst Behler, Mazzino Montinari, Wolfgang Müller-Lauter, and Heinz Wenzel (Berlin and New York, 1983), pp. 387–418, especially pp. 396–406, which deal directly with the Brandes-Høffding debate.

104. See Høffding's *Erindringer*, pp. 24 and 44.

ing of Christianity he concluded that though basically sound, it was too idealistic. At that time Høffding, a student of classical languages and history, was growing increasingly interested in philosophy and theology. It was his reading of Kierkegaard, in particular the critique of dogmatic theology, that oriented him more in a philosophical direction and caused him to abandon ideas of pursuing theology.[105] Kierkegaard's depiction of the various types of human personality in different stages of development, and his emphasis on the need to become a "single individual" who lives life rather than thinks it, stuck with Høffding and played a central role in the subsequent formulation of his own philosophical views of man. On the extent of his early involvement with Kierkegaard and its lasting effects, Høffding wrote:

> Kierkegaard's problem accompanied me from my youth, determined the direction of my life, led me again and again to an intense perception of a multitude of relations and conditions, to a stricter examination of myself, to a fear of what did not possess personal truth [for me].[106]

He added that throughout the many changes in his life he continued to cling fast to Kierkegaard's principle of "truth is subjectivity," discovering its special meaning for his own personality.

Høffding matriculated under all three great professors dominating the philosophical scene at the University of Copenhagen in the 1860s—Nielsen, Brøchner, and Sibbern. He avidly absorbed Nielsen's lectures on the Kierkegaardian stages. Initially, during the early beginnings of the "Tro og Viden" Controversy, Nielsen exerted the strongest influence on him, and Høffding published a short essay in 1866 he called "Philosophie og Theologie," in which he essentially took a pro-Nielsen line and sought to justify the combination, in a single consciousness, of the two heterogeneous principles of faith and knowledge. In the same year Brandes's essay critical of Nielsen's dualism appeared, and Brandes later recalled how he and Høffding had started out on opposite sides of the debate.[107] It did

---

105. In a piece written in 1905 as a foreword to the second edition of his *Religionsfilosofi* of 1901, Høffding mentions Kierkegaard as the cause of his shift away from theology. See "Forord og Efterskrift til Min Religionsfilosofi, 1905" in his *Mindre Arbejder*, vol. II (Copenhagen: Nordisk Forlag, 1905), pp. 48–49 and 50–51.

106. Høffding, *Erindringer*, p. 50; see also 44–46 and 48–51.

107. Ibid., pp. 39–41, 45, and 57–60. For Brandes's view of Høffding during the "Tro og Viden" Controversy see his *Samlede Skrifter*, vol. XII, pp. 13–21. See also Erik Rindom, *Harald Høffding: Bidrag til Biografi og Karakteristik* (Copenhagen, 1913), p. 17. For the details of the "Tro og Viden" Controversy see Chapter 5 above.

not take long for Høffding to alter his position, and this occurred mainly upon his reading of Brøchner's *Problemet om Tro og Viden*. The book showed him the errors of Nielsen and proved, among other things, how un-Kierkegaardian Nielsen really was. Høffding came to regard Brøchner's book as a crucial turning point in the history of Danish philosophy. Another person who helped him overcome his Nielsen phase was Poul Kierkegaard. He was Høffding's fellow student and succeeded during their long talks in persuading him to abandon Nielsen's position. Høffding then left on a trip to Paris, where he was exposed to French positivism and English utilitarianism. In 1869, soon after his return to Copenhagen, he received his doctorate in philosophy.[108]

During the last years leading up to Brøchner's death in 1875, Høffding was the closest person to him intellectually and personally. Brøchner infused Høffding's philosophical outlook with a strong rationalist-monist streak. He also encouraged Høffding's study of the history of philosophy. The similarity of their views emerges in their mature attitudes toward Kierkegaard. He influenced both men intensely, yet neither ended by espousing his brand of Christianity—or any brand for that matter. They admired him as Denmark's greatest thinker while stopping short of endorsing his religious philosophy. They were not "haters," to use Lowrie's term. Høffding, however, arrived at this positive, though religiously uncommitted, view of Kierkegaard only after much internal wavering and largely through Brøchner's influence. In his earlier encounter with Kierkegaard, Høffding resembled Brandes in that, like him, he had passed through a religious period. In Høffding's case the prospect of being ordained a pastor was seriously entertained for a while, as his memoirs reveal.[109]

Høffding read Brandes's 1877 book on Kierkegaard and derived much stimulation from it. He expressed his feelings in a letter to Brandes: "Your book on S. Kierkegaard has interested me a lot and has set many things clear for me, which I had not until now understood." Of particular significance for him was Brandes's discussion of the "single individual," and

---

108. Høffding, *Erindringer*, p. 60. With the benefit of hindsight, Høffding does his best in his memoirs to put distance between himself and Nielsen by claiming that his 1866 essay had not been an uncritical endorsement of Nielsen's position. On the role played by Poul Kierkegaard see pp. 67 and 71–75, where Høffding gives an optimistic assessment of Poul's abilities as a thinker, although at the time he did sense an uncertainty about Poul's talents and future. See also P. A. Rosenberg, *Rasmus Nielsen*, p. 112.

109. Høffding, *Erindringer*, p. 57 and elsewhere throughhout the early memoirs.

his assertion that Kierkegaard was definitely on the road to becoming a freethinker. Høffding agreed that in this respect Kierkegaard had died too soon, because "rationalism cannot be said to have lain too far from his standpoint in *Øjeblikket*."[110] By nature and training, however, Høffding was not given to the kind of aesthetic analysis and literary criticism that characterized most of Brandes's writings. Although like Brandes he had mastered the critical theories of Taine and Sainte-Beuve and had imbibed the positivism of Comte, he preferred to employ a more philosophically rigorous German approach in his writing. Moreover, being a historian of philosophy as well, he was interested in tracing in his works the progression over time of ideas and schools of thought.

His 1892 book, entitled *Søren Kierkegaard som Filosof* (S.K. as philosopher), is no exception. It opens with a brief historical overview of the theological and philosophical situations in Kierkegaard's time as represented by Schleiermacher and Hegel respectively. Kierkegaard was profoundly influenced by both men, but ended by differing markedly from each. Høffding then looks at four Danish contemporaries of Kierkegaard who left their imprints on his intellectual development: Heiberg, Martensen, Sibbern, and Poul M. Møller. The last two in particular are shown to have influenced his early formulations of the central concepts of truth as subjectivity and of the paradox. Høffding's survey becomes the first of its kind to seriously assess the various thinkers and ideas contributing to Kierkegaard's philosophical formation, and to attempt to determine his place in the history of both Danish and European philosophy.[111]

In the chapter about Kierkegaard's personal development, Høffding keeps biographical narration to a minimum. He does, however, follow a Tainian approach and, like Brandes, fixes on an overriding personality feature that he regards as being responsible for much of Kierkegaard's conduct and thought. He rejects the Brandesian reverence/contempt dichotomy, and substitutes in its place depression or melancholy *(Tung-*

---

110. Letter from Høffding to Brandes dated January 21, 1878 in *Georg og Edvard Brandes: Brevveksling med nordiske Forfattere og Videnskabsmænd*, ed. Morton Borup, vol. I, p. 341.

111. See Harald Høffding, *Søren Kierkegaard som Filosof* (Copenhagen, 1892), pp. 5–27. Høffding also discusses Kierkegaard's indebtedness to Schelling and to Adolf Trendelenburg (pp. 54–58), and points to similarities between Kierkegaard's views of women and those of Schopenhauer (p. 141). According to Høffding, Kierkegaard's austere tendencies in later life and his severe standards that ran counter to the "natural needs" of man received a boost from his late reading of Schopenhauer.

sind).¹¹² Kierkegaard is dubbed the philosopher of melancholy with a propensity toward dialectical reflectiveness. Here the journals act as Høffding's main source of information and are frequently quoted.

The central portion of the book is a critical analysis of Kierkegaard's philosophy—his theory of knowledge, his ethics, the stages, and the leap. This is where Høffding's own rationalist positivism and monism assert themselves. He posits that there are two types of thinkers: those who proceed quantitatively, detecting rational links and retaining the overall continuum of thought, and those who take qualitative leaps and bounds, disrupting rational flow and breaking continuity. For Høffding, Kierkegaard clearly belonged to the latter.¹¹³ He himself, on the other hand, being a firm believer in the popular nineteenth-century idea of progress, would have classified his own approach under the former category. Thus Kierkegaard's "leap" *(Spring)* comes under heavy criticism in the book, as do his discrete stages. Høffding maintains that Kierkegaard was a psychologist of the first order, and he refers to *Concept of Anxiety* as proof of this. However, Kierkegaard is not interested in empirical or rational comprehension, but resorts instead to irrational means like the paradox and the leap in order to attain truth. Whenever Høffding speaks of the "irrational" in Kierkegaard, especially the paradox, it is with obvious exasperation.¹¹⁴ He claims that Kierkegaard lands himself in contradiction when he tries to have both an "either-or" and a "both-and," and cites in support of this the discrepancies between *Concept of Anxiety* and *Either/Or*.¹¹⁵ According to Høffding, Kierkegaard's psychology and his ethics are often at odds.

Another contradiction is allegedly detected by Høffding in Kierkegaard's concept of subjectivity. On one level Kierkegaard says that we truly know only what relates intimately to our personal existence, and that to exist means to be a "single individual." Truth, therefore, is subjectivity, i.e. truth "for me." Yet, on another level, he infuses this subjective truth with a definite objective content.¹¹⁶ Høffding discerns a tension in Kierkegaard between authority and subjectivity. This translates externally into the lack of a social ethical dimension, which also derives, in part, from his conservative politics and his respect for temporal authority.¹¹⁷

---

112. Ibid., pp. 31ff.
113. Ibid., pp. 70-72.
114. Ibid., pp. 73-74.
115. Ibid., pp. 76-77.
116. Ibid., p. 58, 63, and 67-68. See also pp. 98ff. on *den Enkelte* (the "single individual").
117. Ibid., p. 107.

In fact, as Høffding sees it, the ethical stage in Kierkegaard is a vanishing interlude between the real either-or: the aesthetic and the religious.[118] Stressing the leap at crucial transitional junctures, Kierkegaard deprives his ethics of any real content or ability to deal with concrete given problems.

By confusing Kierkegaard's category of subjectivity with crude subjectivism, Høffding was unmasking his own proclivity toward the latter. Ironically, this confusion manifested itself in the way in which he understood the relevance of Kierkegaard's statement "truth is subjectivity" for his own life. Subjectivity here seems to have implied a form of personal relativism for Høffding, which he clung to and ascribed to Kierkegaard. In so doing, Høffding represents an early philosophical precursor of the monumental misinterpretation—partly unknowing, partly deliberate—of Kierkegaardian subjectivity that characterizes certain varieties of twentieth-century existentialism.

The final section of his book treats the *Kirkekampen*. Høffding contends that the spiritual experience Kierkegaard had at Easter in 1848—of which he speaks in his journals—touched off an internal struggle in him about whether or not he was a "witness to truth," and that the attack on Mynster was merely an external projection of this inner crisis.[119] The break with the Church Høffding regards as further confirmation of the pervading tendency in Kierkegaard toward leaps, abrupt breaks, and discontinuities.[120] Kierkegaard was correct, admits Høffding, in detecting an absence of New Testament Christianity in the modern world; however, any attempt to hark back to the Christianity of the promised Kingdom will not do.[121] In light of the unfulfilled eschatology of early Christianity, the entire Christian message needs to be reinterpreted beyond the rigidities of dogma. Høffding concludes that Kierkegaard's disappointment with dogmas, coupled with his increased sympathy for Catholicism on one side and his acknowledgment of the insights of freethinkers like Feuerbach on the other, opens up a number of possibilities concerning the direction he might have taken had he lived longer. Høffding speculates at the end about the additional possibility that Kierkegaard might have

---

118. Ibid., pp. 107-9 and throughout the section entitled "Etik," pp. 70-126.
119. Ibid., pp. 128ff. and 134. Henriksen, *Methods and Results*, pp. 35-38, points to the similarities and differences between Høffding's and Vodskov's interpretations of Kierkegaard's spiritual crisis in the late 1840s.
120. Høffding, *Søren Kierkegaard*, p. 144.
121. Ibid., p. 155.

wished, like Tolstoy, to chart his own course, perhaps starting a new sect.[122] In formulating his discussion of the unfulfilled promises of the Gospels since the early centuries, Høffding appears to have overlooked Kierkegaard's comprehensive treatment of that very question in his *Philosophical Fragments*.

Reviews of the book in the Danish press were favorable though, on the whole, superficial. The reviewers did their best to avoid dealing with the intricacies of Høffding's philosophical analysis and critique of Kierkegaard's thought, probably because they realized their incompetence to do so. The writer in *Berlingske Tidende* was a little more specific than the others and supported Høffding on most points, especially his objections to Kierkegaard's weak social sensibility: "One rejoices over the fineness and clarity with which H. demonstrates that life is not [a matter of] isolated human beings, but [of] interacting ones."[123] *Dagens Nyheder* concentrated, for its part, on the differences between Høffding's book and its controversial predecessor by Brandes fifteen years earlier: "This 159-page treatise will stand in our literature as a valuable complement and corrective to the monograph by Dr. G. Brandes."[124] The "misleading tendency" and anti-religious quality of Brandes's book comes under fire in the review. Clearly the reviewer is displeased by the one-sided emphasis of Brandes's biographical-psychological treatment. However, beyond praising Høffding for his insights and his sense of balance, the review hardly tackles the philosophical arguments he advances and appears designed for the general reader. It passes mildly over Høffding's final claim that the New Testament Christianity to which Kierkegaard wished to return has become passé (*"forbi"*). This position is ascribed simply to Høffding's "humanistic view of life."[125] Finally, writing for *Politiken* a couple of months later, Oscar Hansen waxes lyrical throughout most of his review in an attempt to capture the mood evoked by Høffding's discussion of Kierkegaard's melancholy.[126]

More substantive reviews of Høffding's book had to wait a few years until it was translated into German. This occurred in 1896 at the hands

122. Ibid., pp. 158–59.   123. *Berlingske Tidende,* April 28, 1892.
124. *Dagens Nyheder,* April 25, 1892.
125. Høffding's remarks about Kierkegaard and Christianity stirred Niels Teisen to publish in 1893 a reflective essay on the subject. See his *Til Overvejelse, Anledning af Prof. Høffdings Bog om S. Kierkegaard* (Odense, 1893). Some years later, in 1903, Teisen published a book on Kierkegaard's significance as a Christian thinker; see his *Om Søren Kierkegaards betydning som Kristelig Tænker* (Copenhagen, 1903).
126. See Oscar Hansen's review in *Politiken,* July 3, 1892.

of Christoph Schrempf. Of the many German reviews it received, two in particular stand out among the rest. One of these was by the philosopher and virtual polymath Wilhelm Dilthey (1833–1911), who enjoys the distinction of being the earliest philosopher of world renown to have known about and studied Kierkegaard's thought. His review appeared in 1899 in *Archiv für Geschichte der Philosophie,* of which he was the editor, but his knowledge of Kierkegaard dates back at least to 1889. In that year Høffding contributed a twenty-five-page article in German to Dilthey's publication, in which he surveyed Danish nineteenth-century philosophy. Kierkegaard was among the roster of famous names discussed by Høffding, which also included Ørsted, Sibbern, Heiberg, Nielsen, and Brøchner. In the space of three pages allotted to Kierkegaard, Høffding focused mainly on his animosity toward idealism and the system-building of speculative philosophy, his concept of truth, and his emphasis on individual existence.[127] This article undoubtedly served to alert Dilthey to Kierkegaard, although it is more than likely that a voracious reader with his wide range of interests would have come across some of the early German translations by Bärthold and others. In any case, Dilthey read plenty of Kierkegaard in the intervening ten years between Høffding's article and his own review of Høffding's book. This is evident from the highly condensed and incisive critique he levels at the book, which indicates he was well versed in Kierkegaard's works. In fact he enumerates the various German translators of Kierkegaard at the beginning of the first part of his review, in which he examines Schrempf's and Dorner's 1896 translations of *The Point of View* and of all Kierkegaard's polemical articles pertaining to the *Kirkekampen.*

Dilthey is unsparing as he turns, in the second part of his review, to a consideration of Høffding's book on Kierkegaard. Not only is Høffding guilty of systematizing a thinker who, like Nietzsche, is averse to the artificiality of such endeavors, he also downplays the significance of the religious stage for Kierkegaard's entire outlook. The result is an erroneous interpretation of the other remaining stages that precede it. What is required, declares Dilthey, is a meticulous investigation of the various "life possibilities" *(Lebensmöglichkeiten)* that are yielded by the Kierkegaardian stages, and their import for personal existence. Such a "psycho-

---

127. See Harald Høffding, "Die Philosophie in Dänemark im 19. Jahrhundert," in *Archiv für Geschichte der Philosophie,* vol. II, ed. Wilhelm Dilthey and Ludwig Stein (Berlin, 1889), pp. 49–74; on Kierkegaard see pp. 65–68.

logical analysis" is wanting in Høffding's treatment. Nevertheless, Dilthey manages to find a few positive words to say about the book. Høffding's discussion of the intellectual climate in the Denmark of Kierkegaard's youth, for example, is termed "indispensable" for an understanding of his development. Also, the few biographical instances that Høffding dwells on constitute, according to Dilthey, "the best section of the book."[128] As a philosopher who occupied Hegel's chair at the University of Berlin from 1882 to 1905, and who had taken upon himself the gargantuan challenge of "ordering the human disciplines," Dilthey took a special interest in Kierkegaard's censure of the systematizers. And as a thinker who described his philosophy as "a philosophy of life," meaning the collective life of mankind, he was fascinated by Kierkegaard's ceaseless glorification of personal existence.[129]

The writer of the second review of Høffding's book, appearing in *Theologischer Jahresbericht* in 1897, was the young Protestant theologian Ernst Troeltsch (1865–1923), who like Dilthey was inclined toward social issues and would become increasingly preoccupied with the relativistic implications for Christianity of Dilthey's historical theories.[130] Troeltsch commences his short review by remarking about the yearly increase in the attention that Kierkegaard was receiving in Germany. The rest of the review is fairly straightforward, touching on Høffding's exposition of Kierkegaard's departure from speculative philosophy and dogmatic theology, and his critique of Christendom. As a young theology student, writes Troeltsch, Høffding experienced the tension posited by Kierkegaard between *Humanität* (humanity) and Christianity, and eventually decided to cast his lot with the former.[131] In other reviews from the same period of tracts on Kierkegaard, Troeltsch displays a growing critical displeasure with the basic Kierkegaardian theme of individuality. Refer-

---

128. See Wilhelm Dilthey's review of Høffding's book on Kierkegaard in *Archiv für Geschichte der Philosophie*, vol. XII (Berlin, 1899), pp. 358–60.

129. On Dilthey see H. P. Rickham, *Wilhelm Dilthey: Pioneer of the Human Studies* (Berkeley: University of California Press, 1979), pp. 9 and 42.

130. This is the problem of historicism, which caused much havoc among philosophers and theologians alike at the turn of the century. See H. Stuart Hughes, *Consciousness and Society: The Reorientation of European Social Thought, 1890–1930* (New York: Vintage Books, 1961), pp. 239–40. For a discussion of Dilthey, Troeltsch, and historicism see Carlo Antoni, *From History to Sociology: The Transition in German Historical Thinking*, trans. Hayden V. White (Westport, Connecticut: Greenwood, 1977).

131. See Troeltsch's review of Høffding's book in *Theologischer Jahresbericht*, vol. XVI (1896–97), pp. 539–40.

ences to Kierkegaard's "single individual" and the "leap of faith" show up from time to time in Troeltsch's later works.[132]

Høffding's list of personal acquaintances among German and other foreign professors and intellectuals was a long one. As he did much traveling in Germany and elsewhere, he became a prime disseminator of Kierkegaard at the turn of the century.[133] Unlike Brandes, Høffding kept returning to Kierkegaard in his writings and lectures following his book of 1892. Despite his disagreements with Kierkegaard on fundamental matters, he did not see his book as equivalent to a final dismissal of him, but instead repeatedly reevaluated his earlier positions and continued wrestling with the questions raised by Kierkegaard to the end of his life.[134] Many of his books, especially the histories of philosophy containing sections on Kierkegaard, were translated into other languages, notably German and English. His two-volume *Den nyere Filosofis Historie* (1894), for example, came out in English in 1900. The second volume had four pages on Kierkegaard, under the section dealing with philosophy in the north. They were basically a distillation of Høffding's 1892 book on Kierkegaard, including the author's criticisms of the leap, Kierkegaard's ethics, and his call for a return to New Testament Christianity.[135]

Among the more famous foreign acquaintances of Høffding was William James (1842-1910), who invited Høffding to visit Harvard University in 1904. There Høffding gave a lecture on what he called "pluralism," which aimed at dispelling the notion that existence in all its diversity could be subsumed under some grand intellectual system or design. In

---

132. See for example Troeltsch's review of Paul Graue's "Søren Kierkegaard's Angriff auf die Christenheit" (1898) in *Theologischer Jahresbericht*, vol. XVIII (1898-99), pp. 532-34. For references to Kierkegaard in Troeltsch's works see his *Zur religiösen Lage, Religionsphilosophie und Ethik*, in his *Gesammelte Schriften*, vol. 2 (Tübingen: J.C.B. Mohr, 1913), pp. 293-94; and *Der Historismus und seine Probleme* (vol. 1), in *Gesammelte Schriften*, vol. 3 (Tübingen: J. C. B. Mohr, 1922), pp. 53, 178, 307, and 311-12.

133. For an account of Høffding's travels in Europe in the 1880s and 1890s and the people he saw, see his *Erindringer*, pp. 136-84.

134. For a discussion of Kierkegaard's presence in Høffding's writings prior to and including his 1892 book, see Kalle Sorainen, "Kierkegaard und Høffding," in *Orbis Litterarum* 10, nos. 1-2 (Copenhagen, 1955), pp. 245-51.

135. See Harald Høffding, *A History of Modern Philosophy. A Sketch of the History of Philosophy from the Close of the Renaissance to Our Own Day*, in two volumes, 1st English ed., trans. from the German edition by B. E. Meyer (London and New York, 1900), vol. II, pp. 285-89. Another work by Høffding containing a short section on Kierkegaard and translated into English was his *A Brief History of Modern Philosophy*, 1st English ed. trans. from the 1905 German edition by Charles Finley Sanders (New York, 1912); see pp. 201-5.

the course of his talk he cited Kierkegaard in support of this position: "A Danish thinker, Søren Kierkegaard, has said, we live forward, but we understand backward."[136] This statement stuck in James's mind and was repeated in his principal work, *Pragmatism,* of 1907, as well as in other lesser writings.[137] Like other turn-of-the-century philosophers in Europe, James had arrived—independently of Kierkegaard—at a personalistic, non-determinist, and volitional view of life. Høffding's passing reference to Kierkegaard seemed to James to capture the radical difference between living and thinking, which most idealists and system-builders had lost sight of. James was in such a state of philosophical receptivity to ideas like Kierkegaard's that there is no telling what might have ensued had his fleeting exposure to them been rigorously pursued. Certainly the course of Kierkegaard's entry into Anglo-Saxon thought would have been altered drastically, or at least speeded up. We have no detailed records, beyond the few paragraphs in Høffding's memoirs, about the nature of the philosophical and psychological discussions he and James had when they first met in September 1904 on James's farm in New Hampshire.[138] Whether Kierkegaard came up in that meeting or in subsequent ones, and whether James ever got hold of Høffding's book on Kierkegaard—which he could have read in its German translation—remains unknown. Both events, however, appear unlikely.

James called Høffding "a good pluralist and irrationalist," adding, "I took to him immensely and so did everybody."[139] Yet Høffding, in reality, was less of a pluralist in the Jamesian sense than he was an outright relativist. In fact on spiritual matters, for example, Høffding would be better described as a monist. Moreover, his aversion to absolutes and to rational systems does not automatically render him an irrationalist. On the contrary, he was very much at home with the kind of positivist ratio-

---

136. See the published version of Høffding's lecture entitled "A Philosophical Confession," in *The Journal of Philosophy, Psychology, and Scientific Methods* 2 (February 16, 1905), p. 86. The citation from Kierkegaard occurs in his journals and is dated 1843; see *JP* 1030 (IV A164).

137. See William James, *Pragmatism,* part of *The Works of William James* series, textual editor Fredson Bowers (Cambridge, Massachusetts: Harvard University Press, 1975), p. 107. James also makes a similar reference in his *Essays in Radical Empiricism,* published posthumously in 1912.

138. Høffding, *Erindringer,* pp. 206–9 and 212–13.

139. Letter from William James to F. C. S. Schiller dated October 26, 1904, in *The Letters of William James,* in 2 volumes, ed. Henry James (Boston: Atlantic Monthly Press, 1920), vol. II, p. 216.

nalism that characterized the thinking of men like Brøchner and Brandes, with whose views he shared a lot in common. What emerges from all this is that Høffding was not a particularly coherent or clear thinker, and he is therefore not easy to classify. In this sense he fitted well with the anguished philosophical gropings of the *fin de siècle* and was simultaneously a good mirror of them.

Having turned away in his youth from religion to pursue philosophy and become a positivist, Høffding ultimately found little there that satisfied him, and consequently he sought refuge in the study of ethics, psychology, and the history of philosophy. Once infected with the bug of Kierkegaard, Høffding could not shake off a longing for that elusive extra ingredient that made a decisive *qualitative* difference in human life. Despite the total lack of evolutionary or genetic continuity that he observed in Kierkegaard's thought,[140] and despite his vehement critique of what he called Kierkegaard's "qualitative dialectic" that operates through leaps rather than progressive quantitative flow, Høffding strove for an accommodation between quality and quantity. This was apparent in a lecture on vitalism that he delivered on January 27, 1898, at a biological conference in Copenhagen. After opening with his usual historical survey of the literature on the vitalist-mechanist debate, Høffding argued in favor of a combination of both "tendencies," as he termed them, since they point to an inherent "doubleness" in man and cannot be separated.[141] This represented a significant concession to vitalism on the part of the "continuity-philosopher" Høffding essentially was. In connection with vitalism also, Høffding knew its principal philosopher Henri Bergson (1859–1941) and—as Bergson himself relates—pointed out to him around 1913 the similarities between his conception of time and that of Kierkegaard.[142]

The gist of Høffding's accommodationist position actually recalls distinct affinities with the philosophy of F. C. Sibbern, who was a major influence on Høffding's intellectual development. Indeed Høffding continued throughout his later life to write about, and ponder over,

140. Høffding, *Søren Kierkegaard som Filosof,* p. 89.
141. See Høffding's "Om Vitalisme," in his *Mindre Arbejder,* vol. I (Copenhagen, 1899), p. 50.
142. This information comes to us from Georges Cattaui, who received it through a personal conversation with Henri Bergson. See Cattaui's article "Bergson, Kierkegaard, and Mysticism," trans. Alexander Dru and published in *The Dublin Review,* ed. Algar Thorold, vol. 192, 97th year, no. 384 (London, 1933), note p. 71.

Sibbern's philosophical views. In the preface to the first volume of his *Mindre Arbejder* (Minor works), Høffding declared that he would like to be called Sibbern's disciple when it came to psychology.[143] For Høffding, as for Sibbern, the true philosopher was at once a psychologist, logician, and moralist, and interacted with other disciplines, including natural science, from this combined vantage point.[144] At various times it seemed as though Sibbern and Kierkegaard were tugging in opposite directions at Høffding's thought. In a 1923 essay on the two philosophers, Høffding contrasted Sibbern's open eye for harmony with Kierkegaard's passionate insistence on the absolute paradox; he was undeniably leaning in Sibbern's direction.[145] Even back in 1885, in an essay on Sibbern, Høffding maintained that he had thought through much more thoroughly than Kierkegaard the proposition that subjectivity is truth: "Kierkegaard gave this proposition far too narrow an application and execution."[146]

Noteworthy about the way in which Kierkegaard was being presented through Høffding at the turn of the century are the subjectivism and relativism marking the exposition. In the 1892 book and in later writings, Høffding implicitly and erroneously equated Kierkegaardian subjectivity with subjectivism. He drew a picture of Kierkegaard as a rebel against all absolutes and an advocate of indeterminacy, all of which amounted for Høffding to the relativizing of truth. This supposed Kierkegaardian concept of truth was in fact Høffding's own. Many in Denmark, Germany, and elsewhere who had their first acquaintance with Kierkegaard via Høffding were infected with this misconception. However, there may have been a beneficial side to all this with respect to Høffding's influence on Niels Bohr (1885-1962), a onetime student of his in the early 1900s and the father of the quantum theory in physics. Depending on where one stands in the ongoing lively debate over the extent of Kierkegaard's impact—directly and through Høffding—on Bohr, one can assess the solidity or tenuity of the threads presumed to link Kierkegaardian subjectivity, indeterminacy, and qualitative choices and leaps with Bohr's prin-

---

143. Høffding, *Mindre Arbejder*, vol. I, p. vi. See also Himmelstrup, *Sibbern*, pp. 123 and 171.

144. See Høffding's 1901 essay "Filosofien og Livet," in *Mindre Arbejder*, vol. II, pp. 8 and 11.

145. The essay is published in Høffding's *Religiøse Tænker* (Copenhagen, 1927); see p. 99.

146. Høffding, "Frederik Christian Sibbern," in *Mindre Arbejder*, vol. I, p. 97.

ciple of complementarity, and perhaps even with relativity in general.[147]

His differences with, and occasional distortions of, Kierkegaard notwithstanding, Høffding remained the leading expounder-propagator of Kierkegaard's thought in Denmark and abroad during the 1890s and early 1900s. For their parts, Schrempf and Bärthold were also active in Germany in the 1890s, but in differing ways. Schrempf's renunciation of his clerical vows and his dramatic departure in 1891 from service in the Lutheran Church in Württemberg caused a sensation throughout the land. One day, at a baptism service he was conducting, Schrempf decided to bring years of internal agonizing over his personal beliefs to an abrupt climax by refusing to recite the words of a ceremony he no longer believed in. He left the Church shortly thereafter, and was officially dismissed the following year. The event came to be known as "the Schrempf Affair" *(der Fall Schrempf)* and was written about extensively in theological journals and church periodicals, with many defending his action as a matter of conscience and applauding his display of honesty.[148] One of these was Bärthold, who quoted the opening words of Kierkegaard's twelfth *Fædrelandet* article of March 31, 1855, "What do I want? Quite simply, I want honesty," to describe Schrempf's situation. This came in an article for *Die Christliche Welt* that Bärthold entitled "Aus Kierkegaard zur

---

147. There is no dearth of literature on this topic. Max Jammer's *The Conceptual Development of Quantum Mechanics,* 2d ed. (New York: American Institute of Physics, 1989), makes a strong case in favor of Kierkegaardian influences on Bohr via Høffding. Jammer's book, originally published in 1966, was challenged by David Favrholdt in his article "Niels Bohr and Danish Philosophy," in *Danish Yearbook of Philosophy* 13 (1976), pp. 206–20. The debate was resumed with Jan Faye's vindication of Jammer's views regarding Høffding's role in his "The Influence of Harald Høffding's Philosophy on Niels Bohr's Interpretation of Quantum Mechanics," in *Danish Yearbook of Philosophy* 16 (1979), pp. 37–72; Favrholdt offered a rejoinder entitled "On Høffding and Bohr: A Reply to Jan Faye," in the same issue, pp. 73–77. Paralleling this debate is Lewis S. Feuer's *Einstein and the Generations of Science* (New York: Basic Books, 1974), which supports the argument that Kierkegaard, directly and through Høffding, had a substantial impact on Bohr's thinking and development. One has to be careful with Feuer's book, however, because it tends to make sweeping unsubstantiated statements based largely on the author's speculations and hunches.

148. On "the Schrempf Affair" see the essay by Otto Engel "Der Weg Christoph Schrempfs," in his *Distanz und Hingabe,* pp. 257–64; see also his essay "Christoph Schrempf," pp. 176–80. For Schrempf's writings on the matter see "Akten zu meiner Entlassung aus dem Württembergischen Kirchendienst" [1892]; "Eine Frage an die evangelische Landeskirche Württembergs" [1892]; and "Zur Pfarrersfrage" [1893] in his *Gesammelte Werke,* vol. I, pp. 99–170, 171–228, and 229–86 respectively.

Sache Schrempfs."[149] Bärthold admired the assertion of individuality involved in Schrempf's decision and recognized in it the hand of Kierkegaard; however, his endorsement did not lead him to follow suit. He was content to remain a pastor in the town of Halberstadt and continue to publish little essays on Kierkegaard in *Die Christliche Welt* that were of a spiritual and devotional nature.[150] For Bärthold, Kierkegaardian individuality led to an affirmation rather than a denial of faith.

What Bärthold did not suspect when he correctly identified Kierkegaard as the obvious source influencing Schrempf's action of 1891 was that a new player would soon enter the scene: Nietzsche. As Schrempf reveals many years later, he made his first acquaintance with Nietzsche's writings sometime around 1893, although he had heard of him back in 1886.[151] At the time he read Nietzsche, Schrempf was busy addressing the theology students at Tübingen in an effort to explain his recent confrontation with the Church. He exhorted them to follow his lead and called on each to examine for himself his "subjective position" regarding the truth or untruth of ecclesiastical dogmas.[152] The combination of Nietzsche's works and Kierkegaard's *Øjeblikket* articles, read and interpreted in a highly subjective-egotistical fashion, provided the fuel for Schrempf's dissent in the 1890s. Elements from the thought of both philosophers regarding the individual, his personality, and his motives in opposing his religious and cultural milieu blended to form Schrempf's new rebellious outlook. In addition to the articulation of his views through public preaching, Schrempf was doing a great deal of writing in the early- and mid-

149. See Albert Bärthold, "Aus Kierkegaard zur Sache Schrempfs," in *Die Christliche Welt*, ed. Martin Rade, no. 13 (Leipzig, March 23, 1893), pp. 293-95.
150. See for example his "Ein Jünger Jesu (Sören Kierkegaard)," and "Zur Bekanntschaft mit Sören Kierkegaard," in *Die Christliche Welt*, no. 14 (Leipzig, March 30, 1893), pp. 318-21, and no. 25 (Leipzig, June 15, 1893), pp. 595-97 respectively. The publication was an evangelical Lutheran one in whose pages many small articles on Kierkegaard appeared in the 1890s and the early twentieth century. Both Schrempf and Bärthold published in it.
151. See Schrempf's "Abrechnung mit Nietzsche" [1918] and "Mein Verhältnis zu Nietzsche" [1933-34], in his *Gessamelte Werke*, vol. 16, pp. 91 and 163 respectively. In 1918 Schrempf wrote another "Abrechnung" (settlement of accounts) with Kierkegaard; see vol. 16, pp. 55-91. In 1922 he wrote an entire book on Nietzsche, which in Schrempf's case is always a book on himself and whoever it is he is writing about; see his *Gessamelte Werke*, vol. 9, pp. 185-311.
152. Schrempf, "An die Studenten der Theologie zu Tübingen: Noch ein Wort zur Pfarrersfrage" [1893], in *Gessamelte Werke*, vol. 1, pp. 287-315, especially pp. 293-94.

1890s, with Kierkegaard as the inspiration for—and sometimes as the direct subject of—much of it. However, Schrempf's feeling about Kierkegaard at the time seemed to be that he had mostly addressed the symptoms of the sickness he wished to combat instead of the sickness itself.[153]

In his bid to get at the heart of that very "sickness," which he equated with organized religion and its rigid dogmas, Schrempf started, in October 1893 in Stuttgart, his own semi-monthly periodical under the arresting title *Die Wahrheit* (The truth). It continued until September 1897 and served not only as Schrempf's personal mouthpiece but as a convenient forum for a number of intellectuals, mostly with socio-political and literary interests, although some had philosophical and religious ones as well. The topics covered in its pages ranged from liberal church congresses and theological questions to discussions on socialism, social democracy, and anarchism. Specific political-ideological issues such as the nationality question, "Grossdeutschland," and the destiny of the German "Volk" were also treated. Many of its articles were of an exploratory and innovative genre, venturing into novel areas or addressing familiar themes in unconventional ways. Some of its essays could be accurately described as purely personal reflections. It had a definite flavor of religious heterodoxy about it and was considered progressive in its day.

The publication was indeed one of contrasts, presenting Kierkegaardian and Nietzschean *Persönlichkeit* alongside social and sociological themes. In this it reflected the existing *fin de siècle* tensions between the opposing tendencies of radical individualism and social collectivism. A number of articles on Nietzsche appeared in it, most written by the Berlin professor and noted Nietzsche enthusiast Alois Riehl (1844–1924). Riehl shared the early excitement in Germany over Nietzsche that people like Lou Andreas-Salomé, Peter Gast, Rudolf Steiner, and others were experiencing.[154] Also featured in *Die Wahrheit* was J. P. Jacobsen, whose *Niels Lyhne* had been translated into German in 1889. In an 1896 review of the book entitled "Ein Dichter der Sehnsucht," Jacobsen was

---

153. See his "Sören Kierkegaards Stellung zu Bibel und Dogma" [1891], in *Gessamelte Werke*, vol. 12, p. 98. Other writings in the early 1890s by Schrempf included "Natürliches Christentum: Vier neue religiöse Reden" [1893], patterned along Kierkegaard's *Upbuilding Discourses*. See vol. 2, pp. 85–202; see also the rest of this volume for further essays from the period.

154. In addition to his articles on Nietzsche in Schrempf's *Die Wahrheit*, Riehl published a book on him entitled *Friedrich Nietzsche: Der Künstler und der Denker* (Stuttgart, 1897).

compared to Nietzsche and called "Denmark's greatest stylist."[155] The combination of Nietzsche and Jacobsen in an iconoclastic periodical edited by Kierkegaard's soon-to-become chief German translator Schrempf was symptomatic of the bubbling intellectual unrest and dissenting spirit in *fin de siècle* Germany.

Among those contributing to *Die Wahrheit* were two eminent names in the history of sociology: Ferdinand Tönnies (1855-1936) and Max Weber (1864-1920). Tönnies wrote one piece on "Nationalgefühl" in 1895, and saw his critical work of 1897 on what he labeled the rising "Nietzsche-Kultus" reviewed negatively in the journal. Weber published in 1896 an article entitled "Die sozialen Gründe des Untergangs der antiken Kultur" (The social foundations of the decline of ancient culture).[156] It can be assumed that both men knew Schrempf, the editor of the journal, and read at least some of his articles, which may have included ones on Kierkegaard. In Weber's case, however, this conjectured early "exposure" did not amount to much initially. The lone reference to Kierkegaard in the 1920 edition of his *Die protestantische Ethik und der Geist des Kapitalismus,* which is absent from the first edition of 1904-5, is the result of later knowledge.[157] In Tönnies's case, no evidence exists to suggest any identifiable Kierkegaardian traces in his writings, although since the appearance of his celebrated book *Gemeinschaft und Gesellschaft* in 1887 he had increasingly pondered the relationship of the individual to the community. He also knew Høffding, who wrote an essay on his book in 1890 entitled "Social Pessimisme"; however, it is uncertain if Tönnies ever read Høffding's book on Kierkegaard.[158] On the whole, the sociologists of the 1890s, like their counterpart in theology, Troeltsch, showed little appreciation for any form of individualism, Kierkegaardian or otherwise.

The main ideological thrust of Schrempf's *Die Wahrheit,* especially during its later years 1895-97, expressed itself in an open and deliberate promotion of skepticism. Nietzsche and Kierkegaard served as convenient

155. See "Ein Dichter der Sehnsucht," by Carl Busse in *Die Wahrheit,* ed. Christoph Schrempf (Stuttgart, April 15 and May 1, 1896), pp. 40-53 and 77-84. The translator of *Niels Lyhne* into German was Marianne von Borch.

156. For Tönnies' piece see *Die Wahrheit* (November 1, 1895), pp. 65-72; and for Weber's article see *Die Wahrheit* (May 1, 1896), pp. 57-77.

157. For an English version of the Kierkegaard reference see Max Weber's *The Protestant Ethic and the Spirit of Capitalism,* trans. Talcott Parsons (New York: Scribner, 1958), p. 109.

158. See Høffding, "Social Pessimisme," in his *Mindre Arbejder,* vol. I, pp. 142-57.

tools in Schrempf's hands for this purpose. Under the banner of "the Truth," Schrempf now began to intensify his anti-clerical and anti-Church campaign, using whatever means lay at his disposal. In April 1895 he wrote an essay on Nietzsche's *Antichrist*, in which he portrayed Nietzsche as the one who had promised to be the long-awaited cleanser of Christianity, and who would purge it of the accumulated untruth of Christendom. Whatever could not withstand Nietzsche's purifying flames, wrote Schrempf, would be rejected as untruth. He concluded, however, that Nietzsche's ability to fill the post left vacant since Kierkegaard's death was proving to be a disappointment. The tranquillity of Christendom remained undisturbed and a new warrior for truth had to be found.[159]

At the time he wrote this short piece, Schrempf was busy with Dorner preparing a new German edition of Kierkegaard's last writings, which included the *Fædrelandet* and *Øjeblikket* articles, *For Self-Examination*, and *The Point of View*. Most of the material, except for *The Point of View*, was actually taken by Schrempf from previous German translations and only slightly amended. The collection appeared in 1896 under the provocative title *Sören Kierkegaards Angriff auf die Christenheit: agitatorische Schriften und Aufsätze, 1851–1855* (S.K.'s attack on Christendom: agitational writings and essays). Thus the "new warrior for truth" had finally arrived, and he turned out, not surprisingly, to be the same old one resurrected and presented in a new mantle intended to speak directly to the ecclesiastical authorities in Lutheran Germany. Schrempf expressed it as follows in his foreword to the translation:

> The [issue of] "the truth-witness" is the problem of the present, and especially in Germany. I know of no one who could have grasped, thought out and probed the problem of "the truth-witness" with such consciousness, energy and circumspection as S. Kierkegaard.[160]

Having deserted the Church and questioned his own faith repeatedly, Schrempf now was not exactly out to accomplish the "reform" and "purification" of Christianity. With this 1896 translation, which he partially

---

159. *Die Wahrheit* (April 1, 1895), pp. 18–31, esp. pp. 30–31 on Kierkegaard and Nietzsche. All of Schrempf's articles from *Die Wahrheit* appear in his *Gessamelte Werke*, vols. 2, 3, and 15.

160. See Schrempf's "Einleitung" to his and Dorner's translation of *Sören Kierkegaards Angriff auf die Christenheit: agitatorische Schriften und aufsätze, 1851–1855* (Stuttgart, 1896), pp. xiii–xiv.

intended as a self-vindication in the eyes of the Württemberg church authorities, Schrempf effectively joined the ranks of many before him who had wished to turn Kierkegaard's critique of established Protestant culture and its complacent self-deification into a critique of Christianity as such.[161] Throughout the succeeding years, the boundaries between Kierkegaard's despised Christendom and authentic Christianity would become very blurred for Schrempf.

The picture one inevitably tends to form of Schrempf during the 1890s, particularly in his relation to Kierkegaard, is a contradictory one: nonconformist, calculating opportunist, and sincere soul-searcher wrapped together. It is a picture of a spiritually confused and intellectually unstable man. At times we find him vigorously lamenting the limitations he sees as inherent in Kierkegaard's critique of the "sickness" in the established cultural and religious order; at other times he is bestowing lofty praise on Kierkegaard as the only person capable of fathoming and exposing the same sickness. Years later, in an essay he wrote on Schrempf, Høffding called him "a true thinker, in the sense that Socrates was one," and proceeded to examine his writings and the erratic intellectual development underlying them. Høffding's comparison dignifies Schrempf beyond what he deserves. Høffding states in his article that it was important for him to understand how someone who, like himself, had studied theology in his youth and interacted personally with Kierkegaard's thought went on to become a skeptic and a rebel against traditional religion. In contrast to Schrempf's prolonged and ever-changing entanglement with Kierkegaard, Høffding stresses the movement away from Kierkegaard that his own development soon led to. He did not take clerical vows only to break them a little while later.[162]

In the end, Schrempf's desire to find a justification for his own unbelief induced him to project that unbelief onto Kierkegaard. No one can be led to faith via Kierkegaard, argued Schrempf in his two-volume "biography" of 1927–28, because Kierkegaard himself was not convinced, but rather offended—a reference to Kierkegaard's "Possibility of Offense at Christ" in Part Two of *Sickness unto Death* and "The Offense" in Part Two of *Practice in Christianity*. Offense leads to irrational paradoxes,

---

161. See Schrempf's article entitled "Mein Skeptizismus," in *Die Wahrheit* (July 15 and August 1, 1895), pp. 207–15 and 234–39. Schrempf also dabbled in Buddhism in later years; see vol. 16 of the *Gesammelte Werke* for his writings on it.

162. Harald Høffding, "En Tysk Kierkegaardianer Christoph Schrempf," in *Tilskueren*, vol. 38, no. II (July–December 1921), p. 74.

he continued, which in turn breed despair, and this pushes the person toward the abyss . . . so he leaps and calls it faith in Jesus.[163] There is something to be said in favor of the scholar K. Olesen Larsen's opinion that despite the bizarre and often preposterous features of Schrempf's interpretation, he took Kierkegaard more seriously than most.[164] To conduct an *Auseinandersetzung*, no matter how peculiar, with someone for over forty years must indicate a certain level of seriousness. Yet this seriousness did not find expression in Schrempf's writings so much as it did in his obsessive and maverick individualism. He took to calling himself a "religious individualist,"[165] and although his individualism was fraught with egotistical subjectivism, it represented a powerful existential response to the unmistakable source of its inspiration: Søren Kierkegaard.

163. This is Schrempf's position in a nutshell. See his *Sören Kierkegaard: Eine Biographie*, vol. II: "Kierkegaard-Anticlimacus" [1928], in *Gesammelte Werke*, vol. 11, pp. 59, 64, 66, and 67–77.

164. See Vibeke Olesen Larsen and Tage Wilhjelm, editors, *Søren Kierkegaard Læst af K. Olesen Larsen*, vol. II of the *Efterladte Arbejder* (Copenhagen: G. E. C. Gad, 1966), pp. 239–48 and 259–60.

165. See Schrempf's address entitled "What We Want, A Confession, No Programme," reprinted from the General Report of the Fifth Universal Congress for Free Christianity and Religious Progress, Berlin 1910, pp. 3–13. Also attending this conference of liberal theologians was Ernst Troeltsch, who delivered a paper, "The Possibility of Free Christianity." As far as this writer could determine, this is the only piece by Schrempf to have been translated into English. It was made available in 1911 to English readers by Williams and Norgate of London, Sole Agents for Great Britain and the Colonies.

8. The Beginnings of Serious Reception in the German-Speaking World

There were various scatterings of Kierkegaardiana in the 1890s that coincided with the crucial activities of Høffding and Schrempf. The year 1894 saw the first translation of the "Diary of a Seducer" as an independent piece extracted from its proper context at the end of *Either/Or*, Part One. This marked the beginning of a trend to isolate the "Diary," usually for purposes of sensationalism, since it soon became apparent that the title's evocation of the image "Søren and sex" was a sure means of arousing curiosity and attracting readers. Interestingly, the 1894 translation was in Russian, with the title *Naslazdenie i dolg* (Pleasure and guilt), and was done by a certain P. G. Hansen. The "Diary" by itself was eventually to go through no fewer than thirty-four different editions in thirteen languages, in most cases with an erotically suggestive etching adorning the front cover. There followed a Swedish translation in 1902 and a German one in 1903, made by the writer and traveler Max Dauthendey (1867–1918), who was also an early German admirer of J. P. Jacobsen.[1]

---

1. See the fascinating article by Bradley R. Dewey entitled "Søren Kierkegaard's Diary of the Seducer: A History of Its Use and Abuse in International Print," in *Fund og*

Not all readers were entertained by what trickles of Kierkegaard they were receiving during the 1890s. Some intellectuals, particularly in Germany, were unhappy with the resurgence of individualism and made it a point to be vocal in their opposition. The main target of their displeasure was Nietzsche and his swift rise in popularity, but other perceived "individualists" like Ibsen and Kierkegaard were not spared. One of those reacting negatively to the Nietzsche vogue was Max Nordau (1849-1923), a Hungarian doctor, a Zionist pioneer, and a thorough-going positivist, who believed in scientific progress as a remedy for all social ills. Nordau's famous *Entartung* (Degeneration) of 1893 was an extended polemic against all forms of what he called "mysticism" and "ego-mania," from the Pre-Raphaelite painters of mid-Victorian England to Tolstoy, Ibsen, and Nietzsche of the *fin de siècle*. For Nordau these men and movements were sure signs of the decay of European culture. In the section on Ibsen, Kierkegaard is mentioned a couple of times as the playwright's spiritual father. It appears Nordau had read Brandes's essays on Ibsen in which associations with Kierkegaard are made. What is both interesting and amusing about the highly inaccurate crudities of Nordau's polemical treatise is the way in which they serve as typical indicators of the popular, second-hand misconceptions about little-known figures like Kierkegaard that were rampant in bourgeois intellectual circles in the 1890s. Kierkegaard suddenly becomes a "zealot" and a "theosophist" for Nordau, and Ibsen's *Brand* is a "silly piece" and a dramatic depiction of Kierkegaard's "crazy 'Either-Or.'" Even Brandes, the positivist and rationalist, does not escape Nordau's invective, which seems to know no limits. He is "one of the most repulsive literary phenomena of the century."[2] Brandes's reply came in the 1899 preface to the publication of his correspondence with Nietzsche, where he referred to Nordau as "a noisy German charlatan living in Paris."[3]

In Denmark of the 1890s, where Nordau-like trivializations of Kierkegaard had long since ceased to be acceptable to seasoned writers address-

---

Forskning i Det Kongelige Biblioteks Samlinger 20 (Copenhagen, 1973), pp. 137-57. See also Helen Mustard, "Sören Kierkegaard in German Literary Periodicals, 1860-1930," in *Germanic Review*, XXVI (April 1951), pp. 87-88.

2. See Max Nordau, *Degeneration,* trans. unknown (New York, 1895), pp. 357, 386, and 356 respectively.

3. Georg Brandes, *Friedrich Nietzsche,* trans. A. G. Chater (London, 1914), p. 60. For more on Nordau as a typical liberal bourgeois see Roy Pascal, *From Naturalism to Expressionism: German Literature and Society, 1880-1918* (New York: Basic Books, 1973), pp. 22-23.

ing an informed audience, three books appeared that followed the familiar biographical-psychological approach enunciated by Brandes in 1877. The first of these (in 1895) concentrated on Kierkegaard's childhood and school years, on the basis of a description of the young Søren written by his teacher and the headmaster of his school, Michael Nielsen.[4] The author, P. A. Heiberg (1864-1926), was attempting to reconcile Nielsen's sketch of a bright, outgoing, and carefree schoolboy with Kierkegaard's own self-assessments in his journals and in *The Point of View*, which portray a gloomy melancholy and a brooding, introverted nature. The question is potentially significant for any project to write a serious biography of Kierkegaard, and Heiberg discloses that his study is intended as a forerunner for precisely such a project.[5] He concludes that Kierkegaard at school deliberately cultivated an outward image of a jolly young fellow in order to conceal his inner melancholy. Beneath both these layers, however, Heiberg detects a deeper love of life, a pervading innocence, and a goodness that were the true hallmarks of Kierkegaard's character. In his extensive use of Kierkegaard's journals, Heiberg comes down hard on the sloppy features of Barfod's editing of the first edition.[6] This same Heiberg, in collaboration with V. Kuhr, would produce the second edition of the journals in sixteen volumes, starting in 1909.

The other two books, both from 1898, also displayed a heavy reliance on the journals and on the biographical-psychological method. P. A. Rosenberg's work was a straightforward biography matching events in Kierkegaard's personal development with various of his writings. Rosenberg's main point was that since Christianity was a religion with a definite social dimension, Kierkegaard's individualism fell dismally short of meeting its requirements. Both Kierkegaard's "single individual" and Nietzsche's "Superman" were for Rosenberg symptoms of anti-social biases peculiar to a certain group of thinkers.[7] Christian Jensen's work emphasized Kierkegaard's religious development. In his introduction Jensen lamented the scanty treatment that the Christian qualities of Kierkegaard's

---

4. For Michael Nielsen's testimonial see Steen Johansen, ed., *Erindringer om Søren Kierkegaard*, pp. 20-22 and 30-31; for the English version see *LD*, (*KW*, XXV), pp. 5-7.

5. P. A. Heiberg, *Bidrag til et Psykologisk Billede af Søren Kierkegaard i Barndom og Ungdom* (Copenhagen, 1895), p. 122. Heiberg actually wrote a number of psychological studies in later years of Kierkegaard's personal and religious development, but none of them constituted the detailed, full-length biography he had initially envisaged.

6. Ibid., footnote p. 68 (see p. 129).

7. P. A. Rosenberg, *Søren Kierkegaard: Hans Liv, Hans Personlighed og Hans Forfatterskab. En Vejledning til Studiet af Hans Værker* (Copenhagen, 1898), p. 207.

works had received among Danish writers. According to him, the poetic and the philosophical aspects of Kierkegaard were handled adequately by Brandes and Høffding respectively, yet "both depictions satisfy only poorly a Christian reader's desire for knowledge."[8] In Germany and in the other Scandinavian countries, he wrote, greater appreciation has been afforded Kierkegaard's religious side. J. T. Beck and his Tübingen pupils Bärthold and Gottsched are named, along with the Norwegians L. Dietrichson and F. C. Petersen and the Swede W. Rudin. Jensen's book aims to rectify the situation on the Danish front by chronicling the interrelation between the external events in Kierkegaard's life and his inner spiritual journey as gleaned from his meditations, writings, and deeds. By keeping critical analysis of Kierkegaard's Christianity to a minimum, the work resembles Rudin's book of 1880; however, its biographical thrust is unmistakably Brandesian. This Rudin/Brandes combination constitutes an odd methodological route to have been followed by Jensen in his book.

No appreciable Kierkegaardian ripples were generated beyond Denmark by these three studies.[9] Heiberg's subsequent labors on the journals and the few treatises that resulted from his researches earned him renown at home and throughout the North. Rosenberg and Jensen received a couple of local reviews, one of which was by the Grundtvigian Carl Koch, who had himself published in 1898 a series of lectures on Kierkegaard. Koch naturally favored Rosenberg over Jensen, since Rosenberg stressed the communal aspects of Christianity (which appealed to Grundtvigians) and generally displayed greater critical acumen than Jensen.[10]

Kierkegaard's reception began to make slow headway at the turn of the century in the English-speaking countries, but the isolated instances of impact remained few and far between. In North America it was not unusual throughout the 1890s to come across preachers and theology professors in the relatively insular Scandinavian-American communities of the Midwest who had read Kierkegaard. His works had become avail-

---

8. Christian Jensen, *Søren Kierkegaards religiøse Udvikling* (Copenhagen, 1898), p. iii.

9. A few of the earliest studies of Kierkegaard in English and French listed these works in their meager bibliographies. The catalog for Unamuno's library names Jensen's book among its holdings, which also included a copy of Schrempf's 1896 German translation of Høffding's book on Kierkegaard.

10. For Koch's review see *Dansk Kirketidende*, no. 51, December 18, 1898, pp. 820–23. For his lectures on Kierkegaard see Carl Koch, *Søren Kierkegaard, Tre Foredrag* (Copenhagen, 1898). See also the rather lusterless review of Rosenberg's and Jensen's books by C. N. Starcke in *Politiken*, May 2, 1899. For more on Heiberg, Rosenberg, and Jensen see Henriksen, *Methods and Results*, pp. 42–46, 48–50, 52–53, and 67ff.

able at various centers of learning such as Luther College and St. Olaf College, in addition to being scattered among private book collections. It was in the library of a pastor from Elk Point, South Dakota, the Reverend P. J. Reinertsen, that in 1894 an eighteen-year-old recent Norwegian immigrant came upon, and avariciously consumed, the works of Kierkegaard. This was Ole Edvart Rølvaag (1876–1931), undoubtedly the most celebrated writer of the Norwegian immigrant experience in America. Rølvaag had actually read *Either/Or* at a much younger age back in Norway, but he rediscovered Kierkegaard through his friendship with Reinertsen.[11] His study of Norwegian literature at St. Olaf also attracted him to Ibsen, who took his place alongside Kierkegaard as Rølvaag's other favorite writer.

The hardships of immigrant life, with the accompanying anxieties that resulted from being uprooted from one's native land and cast into the desolate wilderness of a strange and vast continent, weighed heavily upon Rølvaag throughout his life and became the principal sources of inspiration for the themes informing his literary writings. The struggle within the immigrant soul between a nostalgic yearning for the ancestral home and the immediate necessities and duties of coping with a rugged, new life and an uncertain future, provided fertile soil for the germination of Kierkegaardian ideas like anxiety, despair, radical personal choice, the difference between mere ethics and religious faith, and the particular versus the universal. This was poignantly true for the religious immigrant, and Rølvaag certainly was religious in the tradition of Norwegian Lutheranism.[12] In one work after another, Rølvaag treated the experience of immigrant solitude and alienation in the New World, infusing it with strong Kierkegaardian-Ibsenian content and a decidedly religious flavor.

---

11. See Harold P. Simonson, "Rølvaag and Kierkegaard," in *Scandinavian Studies* 49, no. 1 (January–March 1977), p. 67. See also Theodore Jorgenson and Nora O. Solum, *Ole Edvart Rølvaag, A Biography* (New York: Harper and Brothers, 1939), p. 147.

12. For a superb discussion of the uprooted lives and unsettled emotions of Norwegian immigrants to America and Rølvaag's own experience as one of them see Harold P. Simonson's *"Angst* on the Prairie: Reflections on Immigrants, Rølvaag, and Beret," in *Norwegian-American Studies* 29, published by the Norwegian-American Historical Association (Northfield, Minnesota, 1983), pp. 89–110. This writer owes much of his knowledge of Rølvaag to Professor Kristofer Paulson, with whom he had a long discussion on June 17, 1983, at the Søren Kierkegaard Library at St. Olaf College in Northfield under the direction of Howard V. Hong. Among the things gleaned from Professor Paulson was that most of the turn-of-the-century immigrant Norwegian intellectuals like Rølvaag were orthodox, not pietist, and belonged to the Norwegian Lutheran Church. This would explain Rølvaag's seeming lack of interest in Kierkegaard's last anti-ecclesiastical writings.

His *Amerika-Breve (Letters from America)* of 1912, for instance, which dealt with the relation of the immigrant to his newly adopted home and to that of his origin, appeared under a pseudonym, as if launched by a person who had supposedly received permission to publish a packet of letters from a mysterious writer. This fictitious device bears strong resemblance to the structure of *Either/Or*.[13] Yet the book that most embodies a blend of the spirit of Kierkegaard and Ibsen is Rølvaag's 1924 *I de Dage: Fortælling om Norske Nykommere i Amerika* (translated into English as *Giants in the Earth*). Each of the two main characters—a husband and wife immigrant couple—depicts a distinct Kierkegaardian stage. Per Hansa, the husband, can ascend only as far as the ethical and is thereby akin to Brand (and Judge William of *Either/Or* Part Two), while his wife Beret attains the religious by performing a teleological suspension of the ethical, as Abraham did. The story is one of constant tension between the two outlooks and is played out on the bleak American prairies.[14] Most of Rølvaag's books were translated into English and have been read avidly by second- and third-generation Scandinavian-Americans.

Interest in Ibsen among English readers was mounting at the turn of the century, and some critics were beginning to discern associations with Kierkegaard. Mabel Annie Stobart's 1899 article in the *Fortnightly Review* was the first of these; it was followed some years later by Angelo Rappoport's "Ibsen, Nietzsche, and Kierkegaard" in *New Age*.[15] Stobart published another essay in 1902 about *Either/Or*, which she opened with the lament that, had Kierkegaard been born in Germany, every cultured reader in England would have been familiar with his works as they already were "with those of the quasi-crazy prophet Nietzsche."[16]

Another person writing about Ibsen for the *Fortnightly Review* was James Joyce, who published in 1900 a long review of *When We Dead Awaken*, which Ibsen completed the previous year. The review said noth-

---

13. Jorgenson and Solum, *Ole Edvart Rølvaag, A Biography*, pp. 146–47.

14. Simonson, "Rølvaag and Kierkegaard," pp. 69ff. As a further example of influence from Kierkegaard, Simonson relates that on March 18, 1907, Rølvaag gave a lecture at St. Olaf College, where he had become a professor, entitled "What Is It to Will One Thing?" This choice of the New Testament text (James 4:8) was the same as that used by Kierkegaard in his *Purity of Heart Is to Will One Thing* (1847), and Rølvaag's treatment is identical to Kierkegaard's (Simonson, pp. 70–71). In addition to Kierkegaard's *Upbuilding Discourses*, Rølvaag was greatly influenced by *Either/Or* and *Fear and Trembling*.

15. See Chapter 4 above.

16. Mabel Annie Stobart, "The 'Either-Or' of Sören Kirkegaard [*sic*]," in *Fortnightly Review*, LXXI (London, January–June 1902), p. 53.

ing about Kierkegaard, even though Joyce must have read Stobart's 1899 article on Ibsen and Kierkegaard in the same periodical.[17] More significant, however, was that, in order to review Ibsen's recent play, Joyce had to have read it in the original Norwegian, since an English translation was still in preparation. This is in fact what Joyce did, and although his biographers are not fully certain about the degree of his proficiency in Norwegian at the turn of the century, they affirm that he knew enough to have read and mastered the play. Indeed, in 1901 Joyce wrote a letter in Norwegian to Ibsen on the occasion of his seventy-third birthday. Their mutual friend, William Archer, who was Ibsen's English translator, had put them in touch with each other.[18]

The importance of all this in the context of Kierkegaard's Anglo-Saxon reception is not readily apparent, and may actually be nonexistent. Details such as these are more suitable in an account of the much-documented influence of Ibsen on Joyce.[19] Yet scholars researching *Finnegans Wake* (begun in 1922, published in 1939), Joyce's famous stream-of-consciousness "epic," have discovered that it is made up of phrases from over forty languages, including the Scandinavian ones. At least six distinct instances of veiled references to Kierkegaard's name or to one of his works have been catalogued.[20] Although these curious finds probably indicate little

---

17. Arnold Goldman, *The Joyce Paradox: Form and Freedom in His Fiction* (London: Routledge & Keagan Paul, 1966), p. 65. Goldman speculates about Joyce's possible knowledge of Kierkegaard through Stobart's articles in the *Fortnightly Review* (pp. 65–68). For Joyce's review of Ibsen's play see James Joyce, "Ibsen's New Drama," in *Fortnightly Review*, LXVII (London, April 1900), pp. 575–90.

18. See Vivienne Koch Macleod, "The Influence of Ibsen on Joyce," in *PMLA*, LX (1945), p. 881. See also the continuation of Macleod's discussion in her "The Influence of Ibsen on Joyce: Addendum," in *PMLA*, LXII (1947), pp. 573–80.

19. Ibsen's *Brand* had a marked influence on Joyce's play *Exiles* (1918). B. J. Tysdahl, in his *Joyce and Ibsen: A Study in Literary Influence* (Oslo: Norwegian Universities Press, 1968), p. 76, dismisses out of hand any attempt at finding a Kierkegaardian influence, via *Brand*, on Joyce's uncompromising attitude toward the Roman Catholic Church as expressed both in his life and through the character of Stephen in *Stephen Hero* (1904–6) and *A Portrait of the Artist as a Young Man* (1916). Tysdahl's statement that "the only Kierkegaard that we can know for certain that Joyce knew is the one that is reflected in Ibsen's plays" (p. 139), concedes the possibility of Kierkegaardian transmission via Ibsen, which is discussed in Chapter 4 above.

20. James Joyce, *Finnegans Wake*, 201.31: "We won't have room in the kirkeyaard."; 246.01: "De oud huis bij de kerkegaard."; 281.26–27: "Enten eller, either or."; 336.02–03: "(enterellbo add all taller Danis)"; 388.02: "kirked into yord"; and 596.31: "sorensplit and paddypatched." See Dounia Bunis Christiani, *Scandinavian Elements of Finnegans Wake* (Evanston: Northwestern University Press, 1965), pp. 63–67. Andersen, Ibsen, and J. P. Jacobsen also find their way into the *Wake*.

more than Joyce's acquaintance with Kierkegaard's name and the titles of some of his works, they leave open the question as to whether, how much, and *when* Joyce might have read any Kierkegaard. The timing is the most interesting issue, because Joyce's early knowledge of Norwegian would have provided him access to Kierkegaard before any of his works appeared in English.

It has been asserted by one scholar that Kierkegaard's reputation in the early years of the century "was being kept alive in the English-speaking world only as footnotes to Ibsen."[21] This is only partially true. Some British clerics and theologians with a knowledge of German were taking notice of Kierkegaard independently of Ibsen, and the earliest among these was a Scotsman from Aberdeen named H. R. Mackintosh. In a one-page review of a recent German translation of Kierkegaard's *Two Ethico-Religious Discourses*, written in 1902 for *The Expository Times* of Edinburgh, Mackintosh echoes a commonly repeated refrain among the early non-Scandinavian commentators when he declares: "Had Kierkegaard written in German or (which is more difficult to imagine) French, his name would long ago have been a household word." He asks: "Will some one not translate a selection of his shorter pieces into English?" For Kierkegaard, says Mackintosh, "is not a man to be neglected without loss."[22]

English translations of Kierkegaard were still in the future, but the first full-length book on him in English appeared in 1908, written by Francis Fulford, rector of Turvey and formerly a scholar at Jesus College, Cambridge. Fulford evidently knew some Danish, since the sources he cites throughout and lists at the end include the Danish and Swedish editions of works by Brandes, Høffding, Jensen, Koch, and Rudin. He manages, in the space of seventy-five small pages, to provide an impressive overview of Kierkegaard interspersed with frequent translated quotations. The tone, however, betrays a typically British attitude of cringing at Kierkegaard's constant invocation of paradox as the central attribute of Christian faith. "No doubt in relation to the deep things of life, common sense has its frontier," admits Fulford, for "beyond it lies a territory which is none the less real because it is not under its rule." "But," he adds, "this thinker,

---

21. See Goldman, *The Joyce Paradox*, p. 64.
22. H. R. Mackintosh, "A Great Danish Thinker," in *The Expository Times*, XIII, ed. James Hastings (Edinburgh, 1902), p. 404. The German translation reviewed was by Julie von Reincke and entitled *Zwei ethisch-religiöse Abhandlungen* (Giessen, 1902). It had a foreword by Adolf von Harnack. In later years Mackintosh wrote more on Kierkegaard and devoted a chapter to him in his *Types of Modern Theology* (London: Nesbit, 1937).

one feels, would press back the boundaries, and enclose common sense within a too small domain. Kierkegaard starts from that which is beyond reason and too often makes it appear against reason."[23]

By the time an article appeared in the *Modern Language Review* of Cambridge University in 1914, written by the editor of the periodical J. G. Robertson, the first Danish edition of Kierkegaard's complete works had come out in fourteen volumes, Schrempf's German edition was fairly advanced, and work had already commenced on a second Danish edition of the journals. Robertson enumerates these sources at the outset of his article, along with the then-standard philosophical and theological studies of Kierkegaard, but he makes it clear that his focus is to be predominantly literary. His essay consists of little more than a survey of the works in correlation with the biographical highlights. Robertson relies greatly on Brandes, whose book he hails as "brilliant." His final conclusion is that Kierkegaard was a product of nineteenth-century romanticism and represented the perpetuation of the individualism associated with that literary movement.[24]

Two years after Robertson's article, on the other side of the Atlantic, a timely analytical piece on Kierkegaard's thought appeared in the *Philosophical Review*, written by the American who was to become Kierkegaard's foremost English translator and popularizer before Walter Lowrie took over—David F. Swenson (1876–1940). The story of Swenson's first acquaintance with Kierkegaard is related by his wife in the preface to a posthumous collection of her husband's essays. As a newly appointed professor of philosophy at the University of Minnesota in 1898, Swenson chanced upon a Danish copy of Kierkegaard's *Concluding Unscientific Postscript* in the library and read it straight through over the next twenty-four hours. He had never heard of Kierkegaard before and became very excited as a result of his new discovery. That fortuitous discovery determined the course of the rest of Swenson's life, most of which was devoted to translating and expounding Kierkegaard.[25]

23. Francis W. Fulford, *Sören Aabye Kierkegaard: A Study* (Cambridge, 1908), p. 67. Fulford is also critical of what he perceives as Kierkegaard's carelessness in quoting Scripture and his "fanciful" interpretations of it; see p. 63.

24. J. G. Robertson, "Sören Kierkegaard," in *Modern Language Review*, IX, no. 4 (October 1914), pp. 501 and 512-13. Robertson too links Ibsen's plays, especially *Brand*, with Kierkegaard; see p. 513.

25. See the preface to Lillian M. Swenson's edition of essays by David F. Swenson entitled *Kierkegaardian Philosophy in the Faith of a Scholar* (Philadelphia: Westminster, 1949), pp. 7–8.

The first substantive fruit of his serious study of Kierkegaard came in 1916 in the form of the aforementioned piece entitled "The Anti-Intellectualism of Kierkegaard." The title, writes Swenson, is inspired by "present-day currents of thought"—meaning those in 1916—and specifically by the activities of James and Bergson. He hastens, however, to caution against a simplistic and unqualified application of the term "anti-intellectual" to the philosophy of Kierkegaard, who displayed, in Swenson's words, a "rare combination of dialectical power with an imaginative and dramatic intuition."[26] While James and Bergson were the leading opponents in Swenson's day of rational self-sufficiency and intellectual reductionism, their critiques tended in his view to be excessively epistemological in orientation and lacked the Kierkegaardian call to decisive personal action. Swenson does a good job of illustrating Kierkegaard's rebuttals of an over-confident Hegelian faith in the supremacy of human logic. The method of "indirect communication," he says, so skillfully used by Kierkegaard, constituted a bold challenge to rational discourse. Moreover, his passionate advocacy of a "leap" was primarily intended to show the impossibility of *qualitative* logical transitions and to highlight the pervading contingency of reality. Here Swenson appears to be responding indirectly to Høffding's critique of the Kierkegaardian "leap" as constituting an abrupt and unwarranted break in progressive rational flow.[27]

The chronicle of Kierkegaard's early Anglo-Saxon reception would remain incomplete without a word on the Scottish theologian Peter Taylor Forsyth (1848–1921).[28] Although his importance came to rest on his solitary and outspoken protests against the excessive anthropomorphism of nineteenth-century liberal Protestant theology, Forsyth had his theological beginnings within that very tradition. After graduating at a very young age from Aberdeen University in 1869, he traveled to Germany, where he studied for one term under Ritschl in Göttingen. While there, he also received broad exposure to German theology and philosophy, which left its deep mark on his intellectual and spiritual formation. He

---

26. David. F. Swenson, "The Anti-Intellectualism of Kierkegaard," in *Philosophical Review*, XXV (July 1916), p. 567. The article reappears in a posthumous collection of writings on Kierkegaard by the author, edited by Lillian M. Swenson and entitled *Something about Kierkegaard* (Minneapolis: Augsburg, 1941), pp. 95–118.

27. Swenson had read both Høffding and Brandes on Kierkegaard in their German translations, which he mentions in his article.

28. This writer is indebted to Edna H. Hong for bringing to his attention in the summer of 1983 the importance of P. T. Forsyth in relation to Kierkegaard's impact on early-twentieth-century English theology.

was ordained in 1876 in Yorkshire, but soon experienced some friction with his orthodox superiors on account of his liberal views. Two years later, and for reasons not entirely clear, Forsyth underwent a complete reversal, renouncing his former interest in biblical criticism and turning to evangelism. At this point, neither the liberals nor the orthodox would take him in, and he consequently plotted his own course, which tended with the years to become highly kerygmatic and Christocentric.[29]

From 1901 until his death, Forsyth waged a veritable war against liberal Protestantism through a series of unsystematic theological works. His targets included the "Historical Jesus" school, the diverse manifestations of Kantian and Hegelian infusions into theology, the Unitarianism of James Martineau, Harnack's liberal Ritschlianism, and all tendencies spurred by Darwinism and positivism to place man rather than God at the center of theological discourse. His relative neglect in the history of modern English theology may be partially explained by the fact that few among his contemporaries were competent to respond to the attacks of one who was so versed in German philosophy. A secret source tapped by Forsyth for his crusade was the writings of Kierkegaard, which he read in Schrempf's German translations. In the preface to his book *The Work of Christ* (1910), for example, Forsyth quotes Kierkegaard speaking about his tactics in presenting authentic Christianity and refers to him as "that searching Christian genius Kierkegaard—the great and melancholy Dane in whom Hamlet was mastered by Christ."[30] In other works, Forsyth's arguments in favor of the total separateness of faith from the realm of ethics, his anti-Hegelian tirades, his strong Christological orientation centering on the Incarnation and salvation through the Cross, and his emphasis on the timeless value of Christ's redemptive act, all suggest distinct Kierkegaardian undertones.[31] It is ironic that such a staunch believer as Forsyth

---

29. See John H. Rodgers, *The Theology of P. T. Forsyth: The Cross of Christ and the Revelation of God* (London: Independent Press, 1965), pp. 1–8.

30. P. T. Forsyth, *The Work of Christ* (London: Hodder & Stoughton, 1910), p. xxxii.

31. See as examples Forsyth's *Principle of Authority* (1913) and *The Christian Ethic of War* (1916). See also the brief discussion of Forsyth and Kierkegaard in J. Heywood Thomas, "Influence on English Thought," in *The Legacy and Interpretation of Kierkegaard*, vol. 8 of *Bibliotheca Kierkegaardiana*, pp. 167–71. Thomas's article, though weak in many respects, manages to give a brief overview of Kierkegaard's English impact. For a brief, general survey of Kierkegaard's Anglo-Saxon reception in the period since the 1930s (i.e., beyond the scope of the present study) see Rev. Rodney A. Ward, "The Reception of Søren Kierkegaard into English," *Expository Times* 107, no. 2 (November 1995), pp. 43–47.

should have received his knowledge of Kierkegaard through the suspect Schrempf translations. Yet he put it to good use at a time when English acquaintance with Kierkegaard was less than rudimentary.

Just as Kierkegaard's early-twentieth-century Anglo-Saxon reception was characterized by its primitive nature and its paucity, so was his reception in France. There, too, the frequent tendency was to identify Kierkegaard with Ibsen's *Brand*. Every one of the half dozen or so French treatises on Kierkegaard from the 1890s and early 1900s makes this identification. In fact, one of these was specifically devoted to the study of the Kierkegaard-Ibsen relationship.[32] An 1893 article on Kierkegaard in the *Nouvelle Revue*, a journal that covered Scandinavian cultural developments among its many topics, called Ibsen and Bjørnson "his direct disciples." The writer specifically cited Brandes's work on Kierkegaard as a key source of inspiration. Brandes's views were being debated in French cultured and artistic circles during the 1890s in conjunction with a string of performances of plays by Ibsen.[33] After a brief biographical sketch in which the two main Christian institutions opposed by Kierkegaard—marriage and the Church—were mentioned and Kierkegaard's morality labeled "petty bourgeois," the writer of the 1893 article turned to Germany where, he said, the new generation was being increasingly attracted to Kierkegaard's austere prescriptions because it was fed up with materialism.[34]

The arena in which Kierkegaard first made his real entry into France was the university. In July 1897 a Frenchman of Danish descent, Victor Deleuran, submitted a thesis on Kierkegaard to the Protestant Faculty of Theology at the University of Paris. It was published in the same year. There was nothing spectacular about it, but as Deleuran states in his preface, the study was intended to familiarize the French public with Denmark's most outstanding thinker.[35] Contemporaneously, however, a

---

32. This is Maurice Muret's "Un Précurseur d'Henrik Ibsen; Soeren Kierkegaard," in *Revue de Paris* (July–August 1901), pp. 98–122; see also M. Prozor's "Un drame de Henrik Ibsen, *Brand*, drame philosophique," in *Revue des deux Mondes*, 4th period, 126 (Paris, 1894), pp. 129–61. See Chapter 4 above for more on these.

33. For a discussion of the crucial role played by Brandes's views on Kierkegaard and Ibsen in influencing the early French reception of Kierkegaard see Peter Kemp, " 'Le Précurseur de Henrik Ibsen': Quelques aspects de la découverte de Kierkegaard en France," in *Les Etudes Philosophiques*, number 2 (April–June 1979), pp. 139–50.

34. B. Jeannine, "Sören Kierkegaard, le moraliste danois," in *La Nouvelle Revue*, LXXXV, 15th year (1893), pp. 581 and 595–96.

35. Victor Deleuran, *Esquisse d'une Etude sur Soeren Kierkegaard* (Paris, 1897), p. 1. Deleuran's sources included all the major nineteenth-century Scandinavian and German writers on Kierkegaard.

spurious interest in Kierkegaard was surfacing at the Sorbonne. At the turn of the century, that university was still dominated by neo-Kantian and positivist currents, and the leading professors there could hardly be described as sympathetic to any writings of an overtly religious nature. A couple of these professors undertook, in the early 1900s, to delve into Kierkegaard with the express aim of exposing what to them were the "tragic" consequences of radical Christian commitment. Pascal had for a long time been suffering a similar fate at their hands. Henri Delacroix was the first of these and wrote in 1900 for the prestigious *Revue de Métaphysique et de Morale*. His attention had been drawn to Kierkegaard by the German translations of Brandes's and Høffding's books. In his article he denies Kierkegaard the title of philosopher, because Kierkegaard had chosen "the absurd, faith, and resignation" over "reason, science, and progress." More often than not, writes Delacroix, Kierkegaard stops at doubt, obscurity, and uncertainty, all of which suggest a man in despair.[36]

Three years later, in 1903, another Sorbonne professor of the same ideological persuasion as Delacroix came out with a long study of Kierkegaard's religious individualism for the *Grande Revue*. This was Victor Basch, whose analysis of Kierkegaard proved to be more sophisticated than Delacroix's, although they shared a similar anti-religious bias. A year earlier, the *Grande Revue* had published a piece by a certain Jules Hoch, which mentioned Max Stirner as a precursor of Kierkegaard's individualism, although the author did point out the obvious differences.[37] Basch takes up this theme of individualism in his article, calling Kierkegaard "the powerful inspirer of Ibsen, [and] the authentic precursor of Nietzsche"! Despite his aversion to all forms of religious feeling—"mysticism" as the positivists deprecatingly referred to it—Basch was able to appreciate the centrality of the religious sentiment for the type of individualism Kierkegaard had advocated, a "sentiment of the tragic problem of life and death."

---

36. Henri Delacroix, "Sören Kierkegaard: le christianisme absolu à travers le paradoxe et le désespoir," in *Revue de Métaphysique et de Morale* 8 (1900), pp. 459 and 475. Like others before him, Delacroix emphasizes the connection between Ibsen and Kierkegaard; see pp. 462, 469, and 483. On Delacroix and the early reception at the Sorbonne see the article by Pierre Mesnard, "Kierkegaard aux prises avec la Conscience Francaise," in *Revue de Littérature Comparée* 29 (1955), pp. 454-55.

37. See Jules Hoch, "Sören Kierkegaard," in *Grande Revue* 23 (September 1902), pp. 615-16. Hoch names Høffding as his principal source on Kierkegaard (p. 603), and like everyone else sees in Ibsen's *Brand* Kierkegaard "poetized and dramatized" (pp. 609-10 and 615).

In the end, however, it is hardly startling—though it is disappointing, given Basch's considerable knowledge and insight—to see him arrive at a subjectivist-egotist interpretation of Kierkegaard's religious individualism.[38] Once again, Kierkegaardian subjectivity is misread as subjectivism by one who himself lacked any notion of an objective, independent, external frame of reference.

Prior to the outbreak of the First World War, little of any significance was published on Kierkegaard in French besides the Sorbonne studies. Some short reviews of the second Danish edition of the *Papirer,* then in progress, appeared in the *Revue Critique d'Histoire et de Littérature,* written by a certain Léon Pineau.[39] Also, a theology candidate named Raoul Hoffmann wrote his thesis on Kierkegaard at the University of Geneva in Switzerland and had it published. The precise date of the publication is lacking; it was probably 1906 or 1907. Hoffmann's sources were mostly German, though his bibliographic list includes some Scandinavian and French works as well. His main concern was with the problem of religious certainty in Kierkegaard, and his major criticism was directed at the abolition of reason through the paradox and what he felt was an excessively one-sided Kierkegaardian individualism grounded firmly in the will.[40] Hoffmann's critique came from one who clearly wished to preserve room for the rational within theology; he exclaims at one point, "Yes, the theology that is most authentically Christian and truly pious is capable of existing without killing reason."[41] The book received enough notice to be translated into German in 1910, with a foreword by Hermann Gottsched.

It is worth mentioning that the Italians received their first taste of Kierkegaard in 1906 through the intellectual journal *Leonardo.* An article by Høffding in Italian on Kierkegaard and Hamlet appeared in that year in its pages, and the following year the journal carried translated excerpts from *Stages on Life's Way* done by Knud Ferlov, who eventually translated some Kierkegaard into French before settling permanently in

---

38. Victor Basch, "Un individualiste religieux, Sören Kierkegaard," in *Grande Revue* 27 (August 1903), pp. 281 and 315-17. On Basch see Mesnard, "Kierkegaard aux prises avec la Conscience Francaise," pp. 455-57.

39. See *Revue Critique d'Histoire et de Littérature,* 44, vol. 69, no. 6 (Paris, 1910), pp. 116-17; 45, vol. 71, no. 17 (1911), p. 337; 45, vol. 72, no. 52 (1911), pp. 514-15; and 47, vol. 76, no. 42 (1913), pp. 319-20.

40. See Raoul Hoffmann, *Kierkegaard et la Certitude Religieuse: Esquisse Biographique et Critique* (Geneva, 1907?), pp. 113-21.

41. Ibid., p. 119.

Italy.⁴² These smatterings of Kierkegaard, however, had a negligible effect on Italian readers.

While England, France, Italy, and Spain, in the first decade of the twentieth century, were just waking up to the importance of Kierkegaard, the German-speaking world had already been enjoying a modest head start. In fact the rest of non-Scandinavian Europe was obtaining its early knowledge of Kierkegaard largely through German translations and scholarship. The years preceding the war saw many short reviews and articles in a variety of German literary publications that commented on the new translations or touched on some aspect of Kierkegaard's writings.⁴³ German-speaking artists and writers who read these publications could not miss at least learning of Kierkegaard's name. A number of German books on Kierkegaard also made their appearance at this time, but only two, from 1909, are worth mentioning. One of these constituted the first full-length "intellectual biography" of Kierkegaard in German since Brandes's biographical work was translated in 1879. The author, O. P. Monrad, was a Danish philosopher-theologian who saw the need for a new biography in German to supplement the ongoing translations. His book is chronological, factual, and narrative, deliberately avoiding critical analysis; in his conclusion, Monrad flatly states: "We have delineated as objectively as possible the man and the author Kierkegaard. Criticism was not our task."⁴⁴ The reviews it received, including one in English, were all favorable. The English reviewer called it "pleasantly and interestingly—one might say daintily—written."⁴⁵ The other book of 1909 was a short study of Kierkegaard and romanticism that attempted—not without a measure of success—to show his intellectual affinities with early-nineteenth-century figures such as Schelling and Schopenhauer, as well as with later thinkers like Nietzsche and theologians like Ritschl.⁴⁶

42. See Harald Høffding, "Un discendente di Amleto, Søren Kierkegaard," in *Leonardo, Rivista d'idee* 4, nos. 2–3 (Firenze, April–June 1906), pp. 65–79. Høffding's *A History of Modern Philosophy*, with its section on Kierkegaard, came out in Italian translation in 1906; see *Storia della filosofia moderna,* trans. P. Martinetti (Milano, 1906). For a survey of the early Italian reception before the First World War see Franca Castagnino, *Gli Studi Italiani su Kierkegaard, 1906–1966* (Rome: Edizioni dell'Ateneo, 1972), pp. 5–11.

43. For a survey of these refer to Helen Mustard, "Sören Kierkegaard in German Literary Periodicals, 1860–1930," pp. 93ff.

44. O. P. Monrad, *Sören Kierkegaard: Sein Leben und seine Werke* (Jena, 1909), p. 133.

45. See the review by Richard Bell in *Review of Theology and Philosophy* 6 (1910), p. 306.

46. See Gerhard Niedermeyer, *Sören Kierkegaard und die Romantik* (Leipzig, 1909).

The heightened interest in Kierkegaard among Germans had a definite intellectual context. As a reaction against *fin de siècle* malaise, and partly as a direct consequence of it, new movements in art, literature, and poetry began to emerge and coalesce in pre-war Germany and Austria with a view to providing alternatives to the stifling determinism of the positivist-scientistic legacy, on the one hand, and Marxist socialism on the other. Symbolism and Expressionism were in the forefront of this reaction; they strove to liberate the human spirit through a reassertion of individuality, personality, and freedom and the reawakening of a sense of awe and wonder. This new aesthetic drive quickly joined forces with the philosophies of intuition already battling entrenched mechanistic conceptions in biology. Philosophically as well, a trend that would become known as the phenomenological movement was taking shape, principally through the early work of Edmund Husserl (1859–1938). It entailed "a return to the primary sources of direct intuition and to insights into essential structures derived from them . . . to put to use the great traditions of philosophy [e.g. Aristotle and the Greeks] with their concepts and problems."[47]

Several German and German-educated East European writers and intellectuals in the early twentieth century began to turn to Kierkegaard as a means of overcoming the constraints placed on individual freedom by the respective outlooks of naturalism, socialism, historicism, and a proliferating technologism. Each one of these intellectuals arrived at Kierkegaard in his own unique way, and interacted with his thought in an original manner. The resulting outcomes were diverse. To the ranks of this group belongs the young Hungarian Georg Lukács (1885–1971), who received his doctorate in philosophy in 1906 from the University of Budapest before proceeding to Germany where he studied under Georg Simmel in Berlin and Max Weber in Heidelberg.

Although exhibiting an interest in a variety of sociological and philosophical issues, while at the same time tending increasingly in a radical political direction, Lukács's overriding concerns during this early period of his formation continued to belong to the realm of aesthetics. This is mirrored in a series of essays he wrote between 1907 and 1910 that dealt

---

47. Quoted from the defining statement at the head of the *Jahrbuch für Philosophie und phänomenologische Forschung* in Herbert Spiegelberg, *The Phenomenological Movement: A Historical Introduction* (The Hague: Nijhoff, 1971), vol. I, p. 5. See also Roy Pascal, *From Naturalism to Expressionism*, pp. 26–27, 52–53, and 63–66.

with the question of the relation of form to life. One of these essays from 1909 was about Kierkegaard's broken engagement to Regine, which Lukács refers to as a "gesture" determining the entire course of Kierkegaard's life: "he built his whole life upon a gesture."[48] He openly admires Kierkegaard's "heroism" and "honesty" in desiring to match what Lukács calls "Form" to "Life," yet the attempt ultimately ends in failure and Kierkegaard's life, like his death, becomes a tragedy—with the "gesture" having been a "vain effort."[49]

Lukács, at this time, was immersed in the study of Marx's *Das Kapital* and Simmel's *Philosophie des Geldes* (1900). His growing perceptions of capitalism as a depersonalizing system and the noble class—to which his own family belonged—as a contemptible group with worthless values, produced in him a profound sense of the eclipsing of ethics in contemporary society. This state of affairs had serious implications for aesthetics, causing Lukács to adopt a tragic view of life that is vividly illustrated in his writings from the period, including the essay on Kierkegaard. He was not yet a full-fledged Marxist and did not join the Hungarian communist party until 1918. He was in that pre-Marxist phase when it still seemed meaningful to search for authentic personal self-fulfillment through art. Years later, he referred to himself in retrospect as having been at the time "a romantic anti-capitalist."[50] His idols up to the point when he became a communist were Ibsen, Tolstoy, Dostoevsky, Solovyev, Kierkegaard,

---

48. Georg Lukács, "The Foundering of Form Against Life: Sören Kierkegaard and Regine Olsen," [1909] in his *Soul and Form,* trans. Anna Bostock (Cambridge, Massachusetts: MIT Press, 1974), p. 28. The original essay in Hungarian first appeared in *Nyugat* 2 (1910), a journal that Lukács helped found. His essay, along with others from the period, came out subsequently as a collection in German. See "Das Zerschellen der Form am Leben: Sören Kierkegaard und Regine Olsen," in *Die Seele und die Formen* (Berlin, 1911), pp. 65–90.

49. Lukács, "Sören Kierkegaard and Regine Olsen," in *Soul and Form,* pp. 40–41. It is highly significant that in December 1907 Lukács met a young woman named Irma Seidler with whom he had a brief relationship that came to an end in 1908 when she married another gentleman. Thereafter they corresponded sporadically, and Lukács sent her copies of his essays from that period, including the one on Kierkegaard and Regine. He wrote her in 1911 asking that she agree to have the collection of essays he intended to publish dedicated in her name. She wrote back to thank him. Her marriage was apparently a very unhappy one and Lukács knew about it. In April of 1911 Irma committed suicide. The relationship of Lukács to Irma Seidler is explored thoroughly by Agnes Heller in her "Georg Lukács and Irma Seidler," in *Lukács Revalued,* ed. Agnes Heller (Oxford, 1983), pp. 27–62.

50. See the 1969 French version of the 1933 essay by Lukacs entitled "Mon chemin vers Marx," appearing in *Nouvelles Etudes hongroises* 8 (Budapest, 1973), pp. 80–81.

and Meister Eckart. Between 1915 and 1918 he organized in Budapest a discussion group called the "Sunday Circle" in which these literary and philosophical figures were read.[51] After becoming a communist, however, Lukács turned his doctrinaire critical apparatus against the heroes of his youth and repudiated them with a vengeance. Kierkegaard eventually came to signify for him a decisive factor in the formulation of the type of "irrationalism" that led to the rise of Hitler.[52] He continued his preoccupation with aesthetics during his communist period and attempted to construct a critical "Marxist aesthetic." His pre-1918 aesthetic writings have remained a source of interest for scholars studying the European intellectual climate in the early years of the century. In their day these essays exerted an influence on many of Lukács's friends, including Thomas Mann (1875-1955), who drew on them when writing *Der Tod in Venedig* (1913).[53] Although Mann read Lukács's 1909 essay on Kierkegaard, his name cannot justifiably be added to the list of pre-war Germans and East Europeans who knew Kierkegaard first hand and wrote about him. Such a knowledge came to Mann a little later.

Any number of sources could have served as the young Lukács's avenues to Kierkegaard. We know, for instance, that in 1905 he was associated with a theater group that was staging plays by Ibsen and Strindberg.[54] Kierkegaard's name might have come up in connection with these playwrights. Moreover, Lukács's discussion of "Diary of a Seducer" in his essay, as embodying the camouflage of the "gesture" with respect to Regine, meant that he had read it with care, probably in Max Dauthendey's 1903 translation. Furthermore, the *Neue Freie Presse* of Vienna published in 1904 a short article entitled "Sören Kierkegaards Verlöbnisbruch," which discussed his breaking of the engagement to Regine.[55] Yet

---

51. See Michael Löwy, *Georg Lukács: From Romanticism to Bolshevism* (London: NLB, 1979), pp. 39 and 88.

52. George Hunsinger, "A Marxist View of Kierkegaard: George Lukács on the Intellectual Origins of Fascism," in *Union Seminary Quarterly Review* 30, no. 1 (Fall 1974), p. 31. On Lukács and Marxism see Eugene Lunn, *Marxism and Modernism: An Historical Study of Lukács, Brecht, Benjamin, and Adorno* (Berkeley: University of California Press, 1982).

53. Löwy, *Georg Lukács: From Romanticism to Bolshevism,* pp. 100–101. On Mann see also Terence James Reed, *Thomas Mann: The Uses of Tradition* (Oxford: Oxford University Press, 1974).

54. See Béla Kiralyfalvi, *The Aesthetics of György Lukács* (Princeton: Princeton University Press, 1975), p. 5.

55. See J. V. Widmann, "Sören Kierkegaards Verlöbnisbruch," in *Neue Freie Presse* 14 (Vienna, 1904), p. 580.

the most significant source of Kierkegaard for Lukács was none of these. In his 1909 essay, Lukács mentions someone who had written about Kierkegaard "in unforgettable and unsurpassable terms," and who described Kierkegaard's relationship to Regine as having been "a poem."[56] This was Rudolf Kassner (1873-1959), to whom Lukács devoted an essay in 1908, and whose writings he read with great care.

Who was Rudolf Kassner? Moravian-born, German-educated, and Catholic, Kassner has been variously called philosopher, essayist, cultural critic, and physiognomist—this last appellation referring to his life-long interest in the pseudo-science of correlating apparent features and traits with hidden ones (in people or ideas). Kassner's contacts ranged broadly among Central and East European intellectuals, and he often served as a bridge among them. His knowledge of several languages facilitated this, and the role he played as critic and cross-cultural ambassador resembled that of Brandes before him. He traveled widely, wrote prolifically, translated writings of Dostoevsky, Tolstoy, and Cardinal Newman, and, in his early years at least, never seemed to lack enthusiastic readers and admirers.

In a late work from 1957 entitled *Der goldene Drachen,* Kassner relates how he first came by Kierkegaard.[57] It happened in 1899 while he was on vacation with a friend in the Harz district in Germany. He had completed a year of study in Berlin and was on his way back to Vienna. His friend, who remains unnamed, suggested they save some money by staying at a Protestant vicarage that he knew in the region. Never having been inside a Protestant vicarage before, Kassner's curiosity was aroused and he agreed. The son of their host pastor at the vicarage engaged them in lively conversation over meals and dropped the name of Kierkegaard, whose works he had been reading. Probing further, the inquisitive Kassner was given a copy of Schrempf's 1896 translation of Kierkegaard's last polemical articles against Christendom and the Church, *Angriff auf die Christenheit.* He began at once to read it in the shaded garden of the vicarage and became intensely absorbed in it.[58] Apparently that pastor's

---

56. Lukács, "Sören Kierkegaard and Regine Olsen," in *Soul and Form,* p. 30.

57. For much of the information on Kassner this writer is greatly indebted to Professor Herta Staub, 1983 president of the "Rudolf Kassner Gesellschaft" in Vienna. Through a long telephone conversation from Innsbruck with Professor Staub, followed by a detailed letter from her dated May 28, 1983, and rich in facts and sources on Kassner, this writer was provided with most of the clues he needed to pursue in order to complete the picture of Kassner's role in Kierkegaard's German reception.

58. Rudolf Kassner, *Der goldene Drachen: Gleichnis und Essay* (Zurich and Stuttgart: E. Rentsch, 1957), pp. 169-75.

son, who first introduced Kassner to Kierkegaard's writings, went on to become a pastor himself and married and had children. "He had given up," declares Kassner, "all the earlier ideas, those of martyrdom and blood-witness, of which so much is written in Kierkegaard's books." Kassner then proceeds to use the occasion to discuss another pastor—a fictitious one—and his relation to Kierkegaard: Ibsen's Brand, who, he says, "comes right out of Kierkegaard's *Either/Or*."[59]

Kassner's initial discovery of Kierkegaard prompted him to read more, so that before long he became something of an expert on the corpus. He identified personally with Kierkegaard's mysterious "Thorn in the Flesh," having, as a child, suffered a bout of polio that left him partially crippled. In 1902 he began to conduct a regular reading circle in the evenings at his home in Vienna to which many of his intellectual friends were invited. The readings included material from Kierkegaard, Dostoevsky, Tolstoy, Stefan George, and Rilke. Among those attending was Houston Stewart Chamberlain (1855–1927), who had become a close friend of Kassner and from whose racial theories Kassner eventually borrowed in order to construct his "science" of physiognomy.[60]

Kassner's principal contribution to the dissemination of Kierkegaard in the German-speaking world before the Great War came in the form of a 1906 article for the well-known literary journal *Die neue Rundschau*, entitled "Sören Kierkegaard—Aphorismen." Everybody in Germany who even remotely claimed a right to the epithet "intellectual," or made pretenses to being "cultured," read *Die neue Rundschau* of Berlin. Thus Kassner's article received broad exposure and was influential in introducing many—the truly gifted and the dilettantish alike—to Kierkegaard. It was this article that stimulated Lukács, for instance, to write his essays on Kassner and Kierkegaard respectively. Of the ten separate segments comprised by Kassner's article, the third, seventh, eighth, and tenth seem to have inspired Lukács the most. The third dealt with the engagement to Regine, which Kierkegaard had to break on account of his melancholy.[61] The seventh and eighth treated the aesthetic and ethical stages

---

59. Ibid., pp. 172 and 175–84.
60. See Rudolf Kassner, *Buch der Erinnerung* [1938–54], in *Sämtliche Werke*, ed. Ernst Zinn and Klaus E. Bohnenkamp (Pfullingen: Neske, 1984), vol. VII, pp. 142–43. See also William M. Johnston, *The Austrian Mind: An Intellectual and Social History, 1848–1938* (Berkeley: University of California Press, 1972), p. 331.
61. Rudolf Kassner, "Sören Kierkegaard—Aphorismen," in *Die neue Rundschau* 17, I–II (Berlin, 1906), pp. 518–21. The article reappeared in modified form on several occasions in later years, which testifies to its importance both as a statement of Kassner's views

respectively in Kierkegaard's own development, showing again that he could not marry because of his poetic nature, with its powers of imagination, and his sensuality.[62] In the final section, entitled "Die Form," Kassner writes that every great genius finds for himself a *"Form"* that embodies his ideals and distinguishes him from others: for Pascal it was the cloister; for Nietzsche, the Superman; for Plato, the Ideas; and for St. Francis, poverty. Kierkegaard's *"Form"* is the "single individual" with all his paradoxes.[63] Ultimately, concludes Kassner, Kierkegaard is an artist, "the greatest artist among all philosophers," and the supreme characteristic of his genius is his humor.[64]

Using Kassner's conceptual terminology from his 1906 article, Lukács a couple of years later analyzed critically the differences between a poet and a Platonist, in favor of the former. In his view Kassner was a Platonist—"one of the most Platonist writers in world literature today." On the other hand, Kierkegaard, though a rigorous dialectician, remained a poet: "Life for him became what writing is for the poet, and the poet hidden within him was like the tempting siren-song of life."[65] Lukács had clearly captured the essence of Kassner's emphasis on *"Form"*: its Platonic substructure and implications. Yet categorizing Kassner in a neat box is difficult to do. He belonged to that class of German writers whose frequent recourse to words like *"Form"* and *"Geist,"* which rested on layers of concealed meaning, often atop a bedrock of ambiguity, defies easy classification. One thing is certain, however: Kierkegaard's impact on Kassner was so powerful and lasting that it permeated all his thoughts and writings throughout the successive phases of his development. A piece he wrote in 1908 was given the conspicuous Kierkegaardian title *Melancholia: Eine Trilogie des Geistes.*[66] In his later writings on physiognomy, there are some telling references to Kierkegaard. At one point in his *Das physiognomische Weltbild* (1930), Kassner declares that the "single individual" *(Der Einzelne)* lies at the foundation of his physiognomical outlook, and that the term is taken originally from Kierkegaard, although its sense has undergone alteration.[67] In his book *Physiognomik* of 1932,

---

and for his German readers. It is included in the *Sämtliche Werke*, vol. II (1974), pp. 39–97. Subsequent page references are to the original 1906 version in *Die neue Rundschau*.

62. Ibid., p. 531; see pp. 528–33.   63. Ibid., pp. 539–41.

64. Ibid., pp. 514 and 542–43.

65. Georg Lukács, "Platonism, Poetry and Form: Rudolf Kassner," in *Soul and Form*, pp. 23–24 and 22–23 respectively.

66. See Kassner, *Sämtliche Werke*, vol. II (1974), pp. 177–372.

67. Ibid., vol. IV (1978), p. 408.

Kassner even uses the standard portraits and sketches of Kierkegaard to analyze his inward feelings from clues in his outward features such as "the full lips":

> Kierkegaard's youthful face and his mature face. How the full lips of the youth have become locked together in old age and now smack of the bitterness and the denial! . . . What despair despite all the genius and all the spirit of inwardness!"[68]

Yet Kassner's view of Kierkegaard is perhaps best summarized in a statement from a 1927 preface he wrote for a French translation of selections from Kierkegaard's journals, which echoes the opening sentences of his 1906 article for *Die neue Rundschau:*

> Kierkegaard was the last great Protestant. He can only be compared with the great founders of Protestantism—with Luther, with Calvin, and [he] towers high above all those who lie in between. The basic question for Kierkegaard was: How do I become a Christian? Only a Protestant, not a Catholic, should ask such a question. . . . The deepest and most original of Kierkegaard's works is his *Concept of Anxiety*, which can only be compared with Dostoevsky just as Kierkegaard himself ought to be placed next to the Russian writer. Both rank as equals and no other mind of the century surpasses them.[69]

For some people who know little about Kassner, he is usually associated with a great name in German poetry: Rainer Maria Rilke (1875–1926). Kassner and Rilke first met in late 1907 in Vienna at the request of Rilke, who had read something by Kassner and wished to discuss it with him. Kassner, for his part, had known of Rilke for some years and included occasional selections from his writings in the reading group he had held regularly since 1902 at his home. Much of our information about Rilke's personal life and acquaintances comes from his voluminous correspondence. In a letter from 1912 to his friend Lou Andreas-Salomé, Rilke dwelt briefly on Kassner, with whom he had become intimate after 1910. Following a description of his impressions at their first encounter, when it seemed to him as though Kassner's whole presence shone with bright radiance, Rilke wrote: "He is certainly—which he too would admit—a

---

68. Ibid., vol. V (1980), p. 149.
69. Ibid., vol. VI (1982), pp. 239–40. For similar comparisons with Luther and Dostoevsky see Kassner's 1906 article in *Die neue Rundschau*, p. 513. On Kassner and Kierkegaard see the published lecture by professor Steffen Steffensen of Copenhagen entitled "Kassner und Kierkegaard: Ein Vortrag," in *Orbis Litterarum*, XVIII, nos. 1-2, ed. Steffen Steffensen and Hans Sörensen (Copenhagen, 1963), pp. 80–90.

spiritual child of Kierkegaard. . . . I have an idea that what his 'melancholy' was for Kierkegaard, Kassner's infirmity is for him."[70]

Rilke undoubtedly read Kassner's 1906 article on Kierkegaard and had ample opportunity to discuss Kierkegaard with Kassner in the succeeding years. It was not Kassner, however, who first introduced Rilke to Kierkegaard's works. This occurred in 1901, when Rilke obtained a copy of a German translation of Kierkegaard's *Christian Discourses* (1848) that also contained an appendix of translated extracts about Kierkegaard from the reminiscences of his niece Henriette Lund (1829-1909). Lund had written these recollections in 1876 and printed the manuscripts privately in 1880 in a limited first edition, which was quickly sold out to family and friends. The recollections were not issued again until after her death in 1909; it appears, however, that Julie von Reincke managed to get hold of a Danish copy of the first edition and translated parts of it into German to be included as an appendix to her 1901 translation of *Christian Discourses*.[71] We learn of Rilke's acquaintance with these translations from a letter dated March 1, 1904, which he wrote from Rome to his Berlin-based publisher, Axel Juncker (1870-1952). The letter is worth quoting at some length:

> Around three years ago, I borrowed from someone—I cannot recall any more who it was—the German translation of a small biography of Soeren Kierkegaard. If I remember correctly, the biography was written by a sister of Kierkegaard [*sic*] and was very good. Now I should like to own this book in the same German translation; however, I know neither the publisher nor the translator, and cannot give you their names. If it is in your ability to buy this small book for me, please do so and send it to me. It will not be difficult for you to discover it. Perhaps you even know it? You would do me a loving service. (It might also be that the small biography of Kierkegaard I am talking

---

70. Letter from Rilke to Lou Andreas-Salomé dated February 7, 1912, in *Letters of Rainer Maria Rilke,* trans. Jane Bannard Greene and M. D. Herter Norton (New York: W. W. Norton, 1948), vol. II: 1910-26, p. 53. For more on Rilke's first meeting with Kassner see Gerhart Mayer, *Rilke und Kassner: Eine geistige Begegnung* (Bonn: H. Bouvier, 1960), p. 9.

71. See Søren Kierkegaard, *Ausgewählte christliche Reden,* trans. Julie von Reincke (Giessen, 1901). See pp. 121-58 for Henriette Lund's *S. Kierkegaards Familie und Privatleben,* taken originally, according to von Reincke, "from a little-known Danish manuscript by Sören Kierkegaard's niece, Miss K. [*sic*]." The Danish original by Henriette Lund was entitled *Erindringer fra Hjemmet* (Copenhagen, 1880). For those sections in Lund's work pertaining to Kierkegaard see Steen Johansen, *Erindringer om Søren Kierkegaard,* pp. 42-45, 118-39, 145, and 162-63. For extracts from Lund's work in English translation see Croxall, *Glimpses and Impressions of Kierkegaard,* pp. 47-77.

about exists as a preface to a little book that contains a translation of a series of K.'s sermons. . . .) Is there still nothing good by Kierkegaard published in German? There has appeared through the Insel publishers "Diary of the Seducer," which is a remarkable book worthy of great mention.[72]

Axel Juncker was quick to comply with Rilke's request and sent him the desired translation of *Christian Discourses* with Lund's reminiscences appended at the back. Juncker had been born in Copenhagen and was very knowledgeable about Scandinavian literature, which he actively sought to promote in Germany. He also wished to help advance the careers of aspiring young poets like Max Dauthendey (whose 1903 translation of "Diary of a Seducer" Rilke read) and Rilke himself.[73] Rilke was delighted to receive the book and wrote Juncker to thank him

> . . . for procuring that desired and obscurely written book on Soeren Kierkegaard; it already arrived in my hand about two weeks ago, was the precise one and is exceedingly dear to me. The sketches of this niece of Kierkegaard, which form the appendix, are very charming, as if written by a great poet. Do you know anything about this Miss Lund? One must also publish other papers of hers, if such papers are to be found; unless there is not much to be known and told. Is her name known in Denmark? Does one know about her—who she had been and what she had done?[74]

Rilke's resumption in 1904 of his earlier reading of Kierkegaard, as disclosed in this letter to Juncker, receives additional confirmation in a

---

72. Letter from Rilke to Axel Juncker dated March 1, 1904, in *Rainer Maria Rilke Briefe an Axel Juncker*, 1st published ed., ed. Renate Scharffenberg (Frankfurt: Insel-Verlag, 1979), pp. 117–18. This represents the earliest known instance of Kierkegaard's being mentioned by Rilke. To the knowledge of this writer, none of the scholars who have investigated the Rilke-Kierkegaard connection and researched the Rilke Archives alludes to this letter and its significance. Werner Kohlschmidt, who did research in the library of Clara Rilke (Rilke's wife) in Fischerhude, lists *Christian Discourses* among the works by Kierkegaard that Rilke read, but he provides no dates, does not discuss the circumstances of the reading, and makes no mention of Axel Juncker. See his *Die entzweite Welt. Studien zum Menschenbild in der neueren Dichtung* (Gladbeck: Freizeiten, 1953), p. 92.

73. Wolfgang Leppmann, *Rilke: A Life*, trans. Russell M. Stockman and Richard Exner (New York: Fromm International Publishing Corp., 1984), p. 161. This writer is indebted to Dr. Donald Fleming of Harvard University for bringing to his attention the name of Axel Juncker as a pivotal figure in the story of Rilke's initial encounter with Kierkegaard. For an extensive study of Rilke and Kierkegaard, see Rune Engebretsen *Kierkegaard and Poet-Existence with Special Reference to Germany and Rilke*, unpublished Ph.D. dissertation at Stanford University, May 1980.

74. Letter from Rilke to Juncker dated March 25, 1904, in *Briefe an Axel Juncker*, p. 129.

March 17 letter to Lou Andreas-Salomé in which he states simply: "I am reading Soeren Kierkegaard. And this summer I shall learn Danish so as to read him and Jacobsen in the original."[75]

In answer to Rilke's questions, Juncker wrote that Henriette Lund was still alive but very little known in Denmark, and that her biographical sketches of Kierkegaard appeared only once in Danish.[76] During the spring and summer of 1904 Rilke began to learn Danish, exactly as he had told Lou, and received much valuable assistance from Juncker, who was fluent in the language.[77] He wrote Lou again on May 12 informing her: "I am already beginning to learn Danish, chiefly so that I can read Jacobsen and various things of Kierkegaard in the original."[78] Rilke's fascination with Jacobsen dated back to his Munich days, in 1896–97, when his friend Jakob Wassermann (1873–1934) first drew his attention to Jacobsen's *Niels Lyhne*, as well as to Dostoevsky and Turgeniev.[79] Rilke then steeped himself in Jacobsen's works and eventually came to see the opposite course to that of Kierkegaard that Jacobsen's development had taken.[80]

By 1904 Rilke's affections for things Scandinavian were well established. That unknown "someone" from 1901, whose name Rilke could not recall in the March 1 letter to Juncker, and who had given him the translated works by Kierkegaard and Lund, could have been one of a number of friends who shared an interest in Scandinavian literature and culture. In the year 1900–1901, Rilke lived in Worpswede and Westerwede in Germany among various painters and writers whose cultural milieu was definitely northern European. Even Lou Andreas-Salomé,

---

75. Letter from Rilke to Lou Andreas-Salomé dated March 17, 1904, in *Selected Letters of Rainer Maria Rilke, 1902–1926*, trans. R. F. C. Hull (London: Macmillan and Co., 1946), p. 43. It used to be thought that this letter contained the earliest mention of Kierkegaard by Rilke, but the correspondence with Axel Juncker tells a different tale.

76. Letter from Juncker to Rilke dated March 31, 1904, in ibid., p. 265. Rilke's excitement about Henriette Lund did not abate quickly. After receiving confirmation from Juncker that she was still alive, though old and neglected, Rilke wrote him requesting her address in Copenhagen: "Her recollections of Kierkegaard have touched me profoundly. ... Do you know Miss Lund? Where she lives? Do you know her address?"—see Rilke's letter to Juncker dated April 26, 1904 (p. 134).

77. See the introduction to *Briefe an Axel Juncker*, p. 9.

78. Letter from Rilke to Lou Andreas-Salomé dated May 12, 1904, in *Letters of Rainer Maria Rilke*, vol. I: 1892–1910 (1945), pp. 160–61.

79. Leppmann, *Rilke: A Life*, p. 66. See also ibid., p. 144.

80. There is an abundance of literature on Rilke and Jacobsen, but for the most part its relevance lies outside the scope of the present study.

whom he first met in Wassermann's house, had a Danish-German mother and herself knew some Danish. Rilke also became friends with the Swedish writer Ellen Key, who accompanied him on part of a trip he took in the summer and fall of 1904 to Denmark and Sweden. While in Scandinavia, he continued to learn Danish and to read Jacobsen and Kierkegaard. He also began translating into German the letters of Kierkegaard to Regine and sent the proofs to Juncker for editing.[81]

On the whole, Rilke's early attraction to Kierkegaard seems to have resulted more from an interest in his life than in his philosophy or his Christian faith. With time, Rilke drew further away from traditional Christianity until by 1912 one could hardly call him a man of faith in the Christian sense. Much has been made of the obvious Scandinavian influences on his famous *Die Aufzeichnungen des Malte Laurids Brigge* (begun in 1904, completed in 1910), yet the determination of a clear *Kierkegaardian* influence per se continues to be elusive. This is not to say that it is totally absent, but scholars have generally found it easier to trace Jacobsen's impact on the work, for instance, than Kierkegaard's.[82] Having established beyond doubt that Rilke read some Kierkegaard in 1901, it now becomes possible to investigate the presence of Kierkegaardian traces in those works of his written between 1901 and March 1, 1904, the date of his earliest available written mention of Kierkegaard.

Rilke was not alone in having a particular fascination with Kierkegaard's personal life; Lukács, Kassner, and many others felt the same way during the pre-war years. It was therefore with great excitement that all

---

81. Regine died that same year, and Kierkegaard's letters to her were turned over, via Henriette Lund, to a certain E. Rohr, who translated them into German. Another translation was begun simultaneously by Raphael Meyer. Juncker sent Rilke copies of these same manuscript letters, because Rilke wished to translate them as well. Eventually, Rohr's and Meyer's translations were published but Rilke's remained among his private papers. He did not think it proper that his name appear on the translation alongside that of Kierkegaard. See Rilke's letters to Juncker from Sweden dated July 15, September 9, and October 16, 1904, in which his translation of Kierkegaard's letters to Regine is discussed (*Briefe an Axel Juncker*, pp. 150–54 and 157–58). See also *Sören Kierkegaards Verhältnis zu seiner Braut. Briefe und Aufzeichnungen aus seinem Nachlass,* trans. E. Rohr (Leipzig, 1904); and *Sören Kierkegaard und sein Verhältnis zu "ihr." Aus nachgelassenen Papieren,* trans. Raphael Meyer (Stuttgart, 1905). On Rilke's trip to Sweden see Leppmann, *Rilke: A Life,* pp. 194–202.

82. See as an example Borge Gedso Madsen's article "Influences from J. P. Jacobsen and Sigbjörn Obstfelder on Rainer Maria Rilke's 'Die Aufzeichnungen des Malte Laurids Brigge,'" in *Scandinavian Studies* 26, no. 3 (August 1954), pp. 105–14.

these young writers and poets greeted a 1905 translation of selections from Kierkegaard's journals by Hermann Gottsched. The title for the selections was chosen by Gottsched from an 1849 journal entry that read: "If someone wanted to publish my journals after my death, it could be done under the title: The Book of the Judge."[83] The selections spanned the years 1833 to 1855 and represented the first substantial edition of journal entries to appear in German.[84]

The *Buch des Richters*, as it was called, was procured and read by many intellectuals, in whose personal libraries it turned up after their deaths. Two prominent Viennese writers were among them: Arthur Schnitzler (1862-1931) and Hugo von Hofmannsthal (1874-1929). Both men had read Brandes on Kierkegaard, and Hofmannsthal certainly read Kassner. In his huge library, Hofmannsthal possessed several volumes by Kierkegaard, some of which he may have read as early as the mid-1890s. He owned a copy of *Buch des Richters* and quotes from it in his *Aufzeichnungen und Tagebücher* covering the years 1904 to 1921.[85] The journal selections were also read by those attending Kassner's regular reading circle.[86]

On none of the writers who read it did *Buch des Richters* make a greater impression than upon Franz Kafka (1883-1924). Like Rilke and the rest, Kafka's early interest in Kierkegaard was predominantly biographical, revolving mainly around his relations with Regine and the broken engagement, to which an entire section is devoted in *Buch des Richters*.[87] He writes in a diary entry dated August 21, 1913:

83. *JP* 6380 (X^1 A 239).
84. See *Sören Kierkegaard, Buch des Richters. Seine Tagebücher, 1833-1855 in Auszug*, trans. Hermann Gottsched (Jena and Leipzig, 1905).
85. See Hugo von Hofmannsthal, *Aufzeichnungen*, in *Gesammelte Werke*, vol. 14, ed. Herbert Steiner (Frankfurt, 1959), p. 141. See also Michael Hamburger, "Hofmannsthals Bibliotek, ein Bericht," in *Euphorion* 55, I (Heidelberg, 1961), pp. 19, 37, and 71-75. On Schnitzler and Hofmannsthal see also Wolfdietrich von Kloeden, "Einfluss und Bedeutung im deutsch-sprachingen Denken," in *The Legacy and Interpretation of Kierkegaard*, vol. 8 of *Bibliotheca Kierkegaardiana* (1981), pp. 54-55; and Steffen Steffensen, "Die Einwirkung Kierkegaards auf die deutschsprachige Literatur des 20. Jahrhunderts," in *Die Rezeption Søren Kierkegaards in der deutschen und dänischen Philosophie und Theologie* in *Text und Kontext*, 15 (special series), ed. Heinrich Anz, Poul Lübcke, and Friedrich Schmöe (Copenhagen and Munich, 1983), p. 213.
86. Rudolf Kassner, *Sämtliche Werke*, vol. VII, p. 143.
87. See the section entitled "Kierkegaard und Regine Olsen" in *Buch des Richters*, pp. 18-45.

Today I received Kierkegaard's *Buch des Richters*. As I suspected, his case is very similar to mine despite essential differences. At least he is on the same side of the world as myself. He corroborates me like a friend.[88]

The entry is the earliest known reference to Kierkegaard by Kafka and is curious since it suggests that Kafka had a knowledge of Kierkegaard prior to receiving the journal selections. At the time he read *Buch des Richters* in 1913, Kafka's feelings about commitment to his fiancée-to-be, Felice Bauer, were passing through an uncertain period. The following year Kafka became engaged to Felice, only to break the engagement less than twelve days later. He was reengaged to her in August of 1917, but he broke off that engagement as well in December after learning he had tuberculosis. Simultaneously, he resumed his reading of Kierkegaard.

Max Brod, Kafka's close friend and principal biographer, does not deny the importance that Kierkegaard assumed for Kafka during those years; but neither does he overemphasize it.[89] In fact in later writings Brod goes out of his way to highlight the differences between Kafka and Kierkegaard.[90] It is clear from a letter written to Brod in March 1918 that Kafka was then deeply absorbed in Kierkegaard's works, especially *Either/Or, Fear and Trembling,* and *Repetition*.[91] The problem of Abraham, as set forth by Kierkegaard, preoccupied Kafka intermittently thereafter. For him, Kierkegaard's interpretation of Abraham's faith and actions seemed to require a critique from a specifically Jewish standpoint, and toward the end of his short life he often pondered various aspects of such a critique.[92] Other themes in Kafka that bear a connection with

---

88. Franz Kafka, *Tagebücher: 1910–1923,* ed. Max Brod (New York: Fischer Taschenbuch Verlag, 1948), p. 318.

89. See Max Brod, *Franz Kafka, eine Biographie. Erinnerungen und Dokumente* (Prague: Heinr. Mercy Sohn, 1937), pp. 177 and 201.

90. See Max Brod, *Franz Kafkas Glauben und Lehre (Kafka und Tolstoi)* (Munich: K. Desch, 1948), pp. 32 and 34. Brod qualifies himself partially at one point when he admits that Kierkegaard's Christian thought did have a significant influence on Kafka (see p. 69).

91. Letter from Kafka to Max Brod dated mid-March 1918 in Franz Kafka, *Letters to Friends, Family, and Editors,* second edition, trans. Richard and Clara Winston (New York: Schoken Books, 1977), pp. 199–200. Kafka also mentions in this letter that he was reading Raphael Meyer's 1905 translation of Kierkegaard's letters to Regine (*Sören Kierkegaard und sein Verhältnis zu ihr*), which Rilke had also translated (see the earlier discussion on Rilke).

92. Not long after reading *Fear and Trembling* in 1918, Kafka wrote a short and pregnant piece he entitled simply "Abraham." In it he reveals a disagreement with the Kierkegaardian concept of "leap of faith" as applied to Abraham. In "the real Abraham," writes Kafka, "I can't see the leap." Abraham's predicament, he explains, is "logical and

Kierkegaard are "the transcendental" and its unreachable nature, the father-son relationship, the ethical versus the religious, and the problem of communication and misunderstanding.[93] No matter what the final verdict—if one is ever forthcoming—turns out to be regarding the degree of Kierkegaard's influence on Kafka, it will not be denied that what has since come to be known as the "Kafkaesque" in literature could only have been sharpened as a result of its creator's exposure to Kierkegaard's writings.

In the fall of 1913, a couple of months after receiving *Buch des Richters,* Kafka made the acquaintance of a self-styled thinker from the South Tyrol region named Carl Dallago (1869–1949). The meeting was arranged by Brod, who was a friend of Dallago. Through Dallago, in the succeeding years, Kafka was able to tap another source of Kierkegaard in the German-speaking world: the Innsbruck-based fortnightly cultural periodical *Der Brenner* (The burner), to which he subscribed and read on a regular basis. On the day of his first meeting with Kafka in the town of Nago, Dallago wrote as follows to his friend Ludwig von Ficker (1880–1967), the founder and lifelong editor of *Der Brenner:* "Today I met here the writer Kafka, a very nice man indeed whose literary creations are quite valuable." A couple of years before his death, Kafka gave a young friend of his an essay by Dallago on Kierkegaard (probably Dallago's *Der Christ Kierkegaards,* written in 1914 and published in 1922) along with some issues of *Der Brenner* containing translations from Kierkegaard's works.[94]

Who were Dallago and Ficker, and how did Kierkegaard's writings find their way into *Der Brenner?* What was the significance of this Aus-

---

no leap." Leaps and the like belong to "the other Abrahams," implying Kierkegaard's as well as any other nonbiblical portraits of the Father of the Faithful. See Franz Kafka, "Abraham," in *Parables and Paradoxes,* ed. Nahum N. Glatzer, trans. Clement Greenberger (New York: Schocken Books, 1958), pp. 41–45.

93. See Brian F. M. Edward, "Kafka and Kierkegaard: A Reassessment," in *German Life and Letters,* 20 (1967), pp. 218–25; and Jean Wahl, "Kierkegaard and Kafka," in *The Kafka Problem,* ed. Angel Flores (New York: Gordian Press, 1975), pp. 277–90.

94. For information on Dallago and Kafka this writer is indebted to conversations he had with Professor Allan Janik on April 9, 1982, in Cambridge, Massachusetts, and with Dr. Walter Methlagl, director of the *Brenner Archiv,* on May 20, 1983, in Innsbruck, Austria. The unpublished letter from Dallago to Ficker is dated October 10, 1913, and housed with the rest of Ficker's correspondence in the *Brenner Archiv* (henceforth *BA*). All subsequent references to unpublished *Brenner*-related material are courtesy of the *Brenner-Archiv* at the University of Innsbruck, and all translations from this material are this writer's unless otherwise indicated. For the reference to Kafka's possession of Dallago's essay and issues of *Der Brenner* see Gustav Janouch, *Conversations with Kafka: Notes and Reminiscences,* trans. Goronwy Rees (New York: F. A. Praeger, 1953), pp. 48 and 88.

trian journal for the twentieth-century German reception of Kierkegaard? Ficker originally conceived the periodical as a convenient platform for Dallago to air his intellectual and poetic views on a variety of subjects.[95] The periodical also served as a means to create for Ficker a suitable occupation as the editor of a cultural publication. Ficker, a native of Innsbruck and son of the legal historian Julius von Ficker, had tried his hand at law, art history, and even acting with no success. His friendship, beginning in 1905, with the gifted South Tyrolian poet Dallago, who was in search of a publisher,[96] led to the idea of establishing a journal that would feature the one and be managed by the other. The first issue came out in June 1910. The title chosen referred to the famous Alpine pass "Brenner" that leads to Dallago's cherished South Tyrol. This title was also inspired by another publication in Vienna, *Die Fackel* (The torch), whose editor, Karl Kraus (1874–1936), was something of a hero to Ficker and Dallago.[97]

Since 1899 Kraus had been waging a tireless campaign in the pages of *Die Fackel* against what he perceived to be a corrupt and duplicitous Viennese press. His powers of satire were unsurpassed, and the main target of this satire was the perfidious *feuilleton*, which artificially bridged the growing rift between art and life in *fin de siècle* Vienna, through a cheap display of French aestheticism. Viewed against the dark background of a crumbling Habsburg Empire, the rise of the congested urban metropolis, the uncontrolled spread of industrialization, and a pervasive decline in aesthetic standards, the press had definite social and ethical responsibilities to fulfill. Instead, it was participating with gusto in the general ritual of decay by committing the gravest of sins in Kraus's eyes: the disfigurement of language and its reduction to sheer chatter. By contrast, Kraus agonized over every comma and was a master of the German idiom and pun.[98] His hostility toward the press and his sensitivity to the issue

---

95. In a letter to his friend Robert Michel (a member of Hofmannsthal's circle) dated April 6, 1910 (*BA*), Ficker wrote that he had resolved to publish a bimonthly journal for the purpose of exchanging ideas with Dallago on the current artistic and intellectual mood.

96. In 1909 Dallago sent some samples of his writings to Axel Juncker for possible publication, but apparently Juncker was not impressed. See letter from Dallago to Ficker dated December 13, 1909 (*BA*).

97. Allan Janik, "Carl Dallago and the Early Brenner," in *Modern Austrian Literature* 11, no. 2 (1978), pp. 3–5. See also Walter Methlagl, "Ludwig von Ficker," in *Neue Österreichische Biographie*, vol. XVII (Vienna: Amalthea-Verlag, 1968), pp. 20–31.

98. On Kraus, the press, and language see Allan Janik and Stephen Toulmin, *Wittgenstein's Vienna* (New York: Simon and Schuster, 1973), pp. 14, 30–31, 68, 78, 87, 89, and 90.

of communication resonated favorably with Ficker and Dallago in Innsbruck. While the Viennese press tried its best to ignore Kraus, Ficker was alone in outspokenly praising him and trumpeting the virtues of *Die Fackel* in *Der Brenner*. Kraus responded by calling Ficker's journal "the only honest periodical in Austria."[99]

Kraus was no philosopher, and neither was Ficker or Dallago. All three believed more in living than in philosophizing. They were by no means isolated, however, from the philosophical tradition and its impact on contemporary intellectual currents. In Kraus's case it was Schopenhauer who played a crucial role in shaping his outlook, which tended to be very suspicious of German philosophical idealism and all types of unbridled rationalism. Schopenhauer and Tolstoy had become popular reading in turn-of-the-century Vienna.[100] Dallago, for his part, received a strict Catholic upbringing, but repudiated the Church and its teachings following a disastrous marriage. He opted for the simple life and took to nature, becoming a sort of latter-day version of Rousseau's "natural man." He also became a Nietzsche enthusiast for a time and knew Nietzsche's sister, to whom he had Ficker send copies of *Der Brenner*.[101] Other early recipients of *Der Brenner* included the Mann brothers Heinrich and Thomas.[102] Dallago read Ibsen in 1906 and Dostoevsky in 1911,[103] and he wrote an assortment of poems and essays during those years that appeared in *Der Brenner* after 1910. Both he and Ficker led unconventional lifestyles that raised many eyebrows around conservative Innsbruck. Dallago virtually preached free love, and Ficker lived openly for years with a woman named Paula Schlier before he finally married.

At its inception, *Der Brenner* catered exclusively to Tyrolian affairs and to Dallago's writings, but in 1911 Ficker began accepting contributions from a broad range of young writers and poets in the German-speaking world. An opposite development occurred in that year at the

---

99. Ibid., pp. 164–65 and 191. See also Gerald Stieg's excellent study of Karl Kraus's relationship with Ficker, Dallago, and others entitled *Der Brenner und die Fackel: Ein Beitrag zur Wirkungsgeschichte von Karl Kraus* (Salzburg: O. Müller, 1976), pp. 15–16.

100. Janik and Toulmin, *Wittgenstein's Vienna*, pp. 74 and 146–66.

101. Janik, "Dallago and the Early Brenner," pp. 2–3. Letters from Dallago to Ficker dated July 9, 1910, and September 30, 1912, discuss Frau Förster-Nietzsche (*BA*).

102. Heinrich Mann wrote Ficker thanking him for sending the first issue of *Der Brenner*. See letter from Heinrich Mann to Ficker dated August 3, 1910. See also letter from Thomas Mann to Ficker dated June 12, 1913 (*BA*).

103. Letters from Dallago to Ficker dated December 18, 1906, and October 21, 1911 (*BA*).

older *Die Fackel,* where Kraus stopped accepting any outside articles and thereafter wrote every issue himself.[104] Through Ficker's wide contacts and correspondence, *Der Brenner* quickly became a focal point of cultural and intellectual ferment. With time, it managed to attract the attention of some of the greatest names in twentieth-century thought. In addition to Ficker and Dallago, the inner core of the journal, which came to be known as the "Brenner Circle" *(Brenner-Kreis),* included a talented caricaturist named Max von Esterle (1870–1914), the poets Theodor Däubler (1876–1934) and Else Lasker-Schüler (1869–1945), and the famous Georg Trakl (1887–1914). In fact, Ficker is credited with having discovered Trakl, whose poetry appeared for the first time in *Der Brenner* beginning in May 1912. Also published in *Der Brenner* were the early poems and philosophical essays of Hermann Broch (1886–1951).[105] A degree of eclecticism characterizing the pre-war issues of the journal stemmed, in part, from Dallago's own shifting gallery of "heroes," to whom he referred sentimentally as the "pure men of olden times" *(Reine Menschen der Vorzeit):* Socrates, Jesus, Lao Tzu, Walt Whitman, and others. Despite a strong admiration for Nietzsche and a conscious emulation of his polemical techniques against the conventions of bourgeois society, Dallago refused to embrace his "will to power" or his Superman, and substituted in their place a "will to nature" and the Natural Man.[106] In 1914 Dallago discovered and added a new name to his roster of "pure men," one who was to dominate his thinking for years: Kierkegaard. For the next ten years, Kierkegaard exercised an enormous influence on the members of

104. After 1911, *Die Fackel* "became more and more a subjective diary of Kraus. In it he constantly held the world to account for its attitude toward him." See Wilma Abeles Iggers, *Karl Kraus, A Viennese Critic of the Twentieth Century* (The Hague: Martinus Nijhoff, 1967), p. 11.

105. Stieg, *Der Brenner und die Fackel,* pp. 48–52. On Däubler see also Walter Methlagl's article in *Die Furche,* March 25, 1967, pp. 77–78, and Werner Hellwig in *Faz,* March 30, 1965. On Broch see Paul Michael Lützeler, "Hermann Broch und 'Der Brenner,'" in *Untersuchungen zum "Brenner": Festschrift für Ignaz Zangerle zum 75 Geburtstag,* ed. Walter Methlagl, Eberhard Sauermann, and Sigurd Paul Scheichl (Salzburg: O. Müller, 1981), pp. 218–28.

106. On Dallago's *Weltanschauung* and his relation to Nietzsche see the unpublished doctoral dissertation of Walter Methlagl entitled *"Der Brenner": Weltanschauliche Wandlungen vor dem Ersten Weltkrieg,* at the University of Innsbruck, 1966 (*BA*), pp. 55–69. This vital source is indispensable for any serious investigation of the early development of *Der Brenner.* See also the published dissertation of one of Dallago's close followers, Hans Haller, who introduced Dallago in later life to Schopenhauer's works, entitled *Der südtirolische Denker, Carl Dallago: Die Mystik seines Schrifttums* (Innsbruck: Winkler, 1938), pp. 35–52; and Janik, "Carl Dallago and the Early Brenner," pp. 8–10.

the "Brenner Circle," and through the translations and commentaries carried in the pages of *Der Brenner*, on the German-speaking world at large.

It will be objected that by 1914 ten of the twelve volumes comprised by Schrempf's edition of the *Gesammelte Werke* had already appeared, and an assortment of other German translations was in circulation as well. Kierkegaard had become a familiar name to most German-speaking intellectuals of the *fin de siècle* generation. Hofmannsthal and Schnitzler read him, Kassner and Lukács wrote essays on him, while Rilke translated some of his letters. He even made his way surreptitiously into *Die Fackel*, where an early and unexpected reference to him occurred on July 23, 1906, in the context of an article entitled "Spiegel sterbender Welten" that concentrated on three books depicting the psychology of a particular cultural milieu and marking the end of an era (the death of a world): Petronius's *Satyrikon*, Huysmans's *Là-bas*, and the Marquis de Sade's *Juliette*. In the Huysmans section the author, Karl Hauer, speaks of the contrasts between the "heathen man" and the "Christian man" and names "Pascal and Kirkegaard [*sic*]" as representatives of the latter genre.[107] Given this degree of Kierkegaardian presence in German and availability to the German-speaking reader—it will be argued—what outstanding and original service could a provincial journal like *Der Brenner* still hope to render Kierkegaard's German reception?

The answer to all this is embodied in one person: Theodor Haecker (1879–1945). It is no exaggeration to say that the story of Kierkegaard and the "Brenner Circle" can best be understood as a function of this man's intellectual and spiritual odyssey. Haecker's personal *Auseinandersetzung* with Kierkegaard's thought had a decisive impact on the direction of his entire life, as well as on the fortunes of Kierkegaard's legacy in the German-speaking world. As Walter Methlagl has aptly summed it: "Among the possible channels through which Kierkegaard could have gained entry into the intellectual life of the German-speaking world, that inaugurated by Haecker in the 'Brenner' has had the most enduring impact."[108]

Haecker's association with *Der Brenner* did not begin until early 1914. Toward the end of the previous year, Ficker received from the Munich

---

107. Karl Hauer, "Spiegel sterbender Welten," in *Die Fackel*, ed. Karl Kraus, no. 207, July 23, 1906, p. 14.
108. Walter Methlagl, "Theodor Haecker und 'Der Brenner,' " in *Literaturwissenschaftliches Jahrbuch* 19 (Berlin, 1978), pp. 207–8.

publisher, Ferdinand Schreiber, a little tract entitled *Sören Kierkegaard und die Philosophie der Innerlichkeit,* written that year by one of Schreiber's employees. This was Theodor Haecker. Ficker, who had heard of Kierkegaard in 1912 from a friend named Robert Müller, passed the book on to Dallago.[109] Dallago read it, became excited about Kierkegaard, and urged Ficker to recruit the author for *Der Brenner.* Ficker complied and invited Haecker to join the "Brenner Circle" and contribute to the journal. Haecker accepted in January of the new year and thanked Ficker for his cordial invitation.[110] In March he wrote Ficker requesting that *Der Brenner* announce the forthcoming appearance in its pages of new translations of Kierkegaard's aesthetic, philosophical, and religious writings.[111]

It is not difficult to comprehend Dallago's spontaneous enthusiasm for Haecker's book on Kierkegaard, which was, significantly, the first work published by Haecker. In it he attempts to place Kierkegaard in the company of other great thinkers, both historical and contemporary (Dallago's *Reine Menschen*). By doing so, Haecker reveals the kinds of outlooks and their representative figures that had made the deepest impression on his own early development. According to Haecker, Kierkegaard belongs spiritually in the same league with Augustine and Pascal.[112] While the French have increasingly turned to rationalism since Descartes and Pascal the mathematician,[113] a contemporary Frenchman, Henri Bergson, stands out as the champion of the life of the spirit. In his struggle against the immanent philosophy of Haeckel and the monists, this "complete metaphysician [and] poet to learning" provides, in his philosophy of becoming and freedom, the best guide to Kierkegaard's thought.[114] What Bergson lacks, however, in terms of personal passion and inwardness [*Innerlichkeit*], Nietzsche makes up for. Both he and Kierkegaard realized the need for passionate inward commitment, and Nietzsche could

---

109. Müller belonged to the Vienna Circle and wrote some poetic essays for *Der Brenner*. He corresponded with Ficker before the war on a variety of literary topics and mentioned Kierkegaard and Dostoevsky in his letters. He took an interest in Scandinavian literature and wrote *Skandinavien-Essays,* which he sent to Ficker in 1912 for his impressions. Ficker himself visited Sweden that year (conversation with Walter Methlagl, Innsbruck, May 27, 1983). See letters from Müller to Ficker dated February 17, March 4, and December 4, 1912 (*BA*).

110. Methlagl, "Theodor Haecker und 'Der Brenner,'" p. 202. See letter from Haecker to Ficker dated January 21, 1914 (*BA*).

111. Letter from Haecker to Ficker dated March 30, 1914 (*BA*).

112. Theodor Haecker, *Sören Kierkegaard und die Philosophie der Innerlichkeit* (Munich, 1913), pp. 5–6 and 39.

113. Ibid., pp. 31–32.   114. Ibid., pp. 12–13.

easily have been the author of that section of Kierkegaard's *Two Ages* called "The Present Age," which anticipates, in Haecker's view, Nietzsche's theme of *Ressentiment*.[115]

In his discussion of Nietzsche, Haecker had in the back of his mind the ravages being perpetrated on religious faith, especially among the youth, by the ascending Nietzsche vogue. His strategy—the obverse of Brandes's earlier approach—was to soften, as much as possible, Nietzsche's anti-Christian posture by comparing him favorably with Kierkegaard and stressing his passion, his inwardness, his solitary suffering, and the "valiant and pure life" he lived, all of which, says Haecker, had more to do with Christianity than meets the eye. If only he had discovered Christian faith as Kierkegaard did, Nietzsche could have been the source of a tremendous spiritual rebirth.[116] Like Kassner, Haecker feels that Kierkegaard and Dostoevsky enjoy a special spiritual kinship. Both disclose the deepest secrets of the human soul from the standpoint of religious faith. Kierkegaard's *Concept of Anxiety* and *Sickness unto Death* in particular, and all of Dostoevsky's novels, constitute unrivaled explorations of the dark recesses of spiritual despair.[117] Kierkegaard is also compared to the later Tolstoy in that, like Tolstoy, he was concerned with *actually living* what he believed rather than merely writing about it.[118] Haecker also touches on Ibsen and Strindberg as having been influenced by Kierkegaard, and he makes allusions to Kant, whose philosophy in the *Kritik der reinen Vernunft* represented the greatest possible separation between the realms of thought and life.[119] Throughout Haecker's book, the criterion invoked repeatedly is "the degree of inwardness" exhibited by each one of the thinkers as he is compared with Kierkegaard: ". . . Inwardness is known and recognized only by inwardness," declares Haecker, and "the deeper an inwardness is, so much more ambiguous are its outer signs and manifestations."[120] Hence the need for indirect communication between people of authentic inwardness.

The book is important because it tells us a lot about Haecker and Kierkegaard both. We learn, for instance, that Haecker was familiar with Høffding's book on Kierkegaard, which he mentions in connection with his discussion of Kierkegaard's view of the ethical stage. Haecker agrees

---

115. Ibid., pp. 51–52.
116. Ibid., pp. 56–57.
117. Ibid., p. 34.
118. Ibid., pp. 47–49.
119. Ibid., pp. 45–47, 19, and 41 respectively.
120. Ibid., pp. 22, 26, and 27 respectively.

with Høffding that the ethical plays a scanty role in Kierkegaard's thought, but he believes that this is the way it should be. He laments the excessive prominence that the age was affording to the "ethical life" in itself when, according to Kierkegaard, it is only a momentary passageway to the religious.[121] By the time he sat down to write his book, Haecker had formed very definite ideas about Kierkegaard and had obviously read a great many of his works. In his view Kierkegaard had immortalized the Danish language, which meant that one had to learn Danish in order to seriously comprehend his writings. Haecker had done precisely that. He begins the book with an assault on all the writers and critics of the sixty years since Kierkegaard's death, whose treatments of Christianity and the spiritual life betray hardly any knowledge of Kierkegaard's works. He is dealt with in their writings only in the broadest of terms and assigned a vague Christian label. Were this not shameful, writes Haecker indignantly, it would be a joke.[122] His book follows none of the methodological prescriptions of previous critics. It is a sincere personal statement with an audible ring of existential urgency to it. Haecker's style is passionate and satirical in the best Kierkegaardian tradition. He emphasizes the need to view Kierkegaard in his many-sidedness as a complete personality who is at once a poet, an enthusiast, and a visionary, as Haecker calls him, and a fearsome dialectician backed by a powerful sense of humor—"one of the wittiest writers in world literature."[123]

Haecker makes a significant gesture in his book toward an illustrious contemporary by comparing him to Kierkegaard. This is Karl Kraus, in whom Haecker discerns a true Kierkegaardian who lives his ideas and has the courage to proclaim them publicly. Moreover, he is "the single greatest polemicist and satirist of our time," who alone understood Kierkegaard's terrible utterances about journalists and the press. Many of the essays in *Die Fackel,* writes Haecker, seem like continuations of the writings of Constantin Constantius (a Kierkegaard pseudonym), while others could easily belong to the erotic outbursts of the banquet scene in Kierkegaard's "In Vino Veritas" of *Stages on Life's Way,* or be counted among the sayings of Frater Taciturnus (a pseudonym in *Stages*).[124] Kraus delighted in these comparisons and published in *Die Fackel* the excerpts from Haecker's book that mentioned him. He then explained that he had not read anything by Kierkegaard.[125] Whether this was actually the case

---

121. Ibid., pp. 35 and 37.
122. Ibid., p. 6.
123. Ibid., p. 7.
124. Ibid., pp. 57–58.
125. See *Die Fackel,* no. 395, March 28, 1914, pp. 19–21.

is difficult to say. Kraus had certainly heard of Kierkegaard before reading Haecker, and he knew about Brandes, whom he despised and had referred to in 1906 as "one of the shallowest flatheads of the nineteenth century using profound-sounding words."[126] It is a fact, however, that in the wake of Haecker's comparison, Kraus did not cease to quote Kierkegaard's biting remarks on the press.[127]

Kraus's polemical style may not have been an imitation of Kierkegaard's, but Haecker's certainly was. It was also an attempt to imitate Kraus's own more subtle satire. Haecker's main biographer, Eugen Blessing, calls it a melancholy satire.[128] He says it is not easy for young people of the post-1945 generation to comprehend fully the satirical writings of Haecker from the period before and during the First World War. These satires were very closely bound to the time and milieu in which they arose.[129] Haecker, for instance, generally had a low opinion of psychoanalysts, language critics, and journalists (except Kraus and the "Brenner Circle"). For him, these people appeared as invariable skeptics and cynical corruptors of values, whose personal lives were totally severed from their armchair analyses. This sensitivity to *living*, as opposed to mere thinking, Haecker derived from Kierkegaard. It was primarily responsible for the melancholic ingredient in his satire. Furthermore, like Kraus he detected a massive conspiracy underway against language, authentic expression, and clarity. His reaction was to make fun of it. In his role as a cultural critic, Haecker constantly resorted to the weapon of satire in order to differentiate the genuine from the ungenuine, and to expose and ridicule the latter. For him satire was an autonomous art, and the basic notions he had of what constituted the comical, the ironical, and the satirical came directly from his readings of Karl Kraus and Kierkegaard.[130]

Little is known about Haecker's background and early years, or of the precise time and manner in which he came by Kierkegaard. He was born into a poor family in Württemberg, Swabia, where he grew up in humble, pietist surroundings. He had to disrupt his initial studies in order to

126. See *Die Fackel*, no. 212, November 23, 1906, p. 14.
127. See as examples *Die Fackel*, no. 418, April 8, 1916, p. 1; no. 455, January 18, 1917, pp. 22 and 93; no. 484, October 15, 1918, p. 143; and no. 521, January 4, 1920, pp. 7ff.
128. Eugen Blessing, *Theodor Haecker: Gestalt und Werk* (Nürnberg: Glock und Lutz, 1959), pp. 53-54.
129. Ibid., p. 35.
130. Ibid., p. 47. Satire pervades Haecker's writings from all periods. For examples of it see his *Satire und Polemik* (1922); *Über Humor und Satire* (1928); and *Dialog über die Satire* (1930).

work and support the family. His friendship with the Munich publisher Ferdinand Schreiber brought him some much-needed financial relief and allowed him to pursue a university education in Berlin. Before returning in 1905 to Munich, where he lived most of his life working for Schreiber and writing, Haecker attended in Berlin the lectures of Harnack, Troeltsch, Dilthey, and Virchow. In Munich between 1905 and 1911 he read Bergson and Husserl and sat in on the lectures of Max Scheler (1874-1928), who was busy expounding Nietzsche. Scheler's claim that Nietzsche had missed the true meaning of Christian love stuck in Haecker's mind. His study of Scheler and a personal acquaintance with him in 1910 helped to awaken in Haecker a love for philosophy, especially religious philosophy. This played a role in steering him toward Kierkegaard, although Scheler himself, whom Haecker once called "the last great philosopher," did not know Kierkegaard in the early 1900s and in fact mentions him very seldom in his later writings.[131] Other influences during Haecker's formative years came from his reading of Karl Kraus and from a thorough study he made of the theologies of the Swiss Carl Hilty (1833-1909) and the Swabian Johann Christoph Blumhardt (1805-80). These two theologians provided Haecker with early spiritual nourishment that eventually blossomed when he read Kierkegaard.[132]

Most scholars who are knowledgeable about Haecker, including the Haecker expert and Munich professor Curt Hohoff, agree that it was his fellow Swabian Christoph Schrempf who first introduced Haecker to Kierkegaard's works.[133] Haecker became sufficiently intrigued by his new

131. See John H. Nota, *Max Scheler: The Man and His Work* (Chicago: Franciscan Herald Press, 1983), pp. 1 and 88. Nota says that the works by Kierkegaard in Scheler's library—acquired after 1922—appear to have been very little used and read.
132. On Haecker's life and studies see Blessing, *Theodor Haecker*, pp. 264-65.
133. See Curt Hohoff, "Fruchtbare Keulenschläge: Dem Autor Theodor Haecker zum 100. Geburtstag," in *Rheinischer Merkur*, June 1, 1979. See also his *Unter den Fischen: Erinnerungen an Männer, Mädschen und Bücher, 1934-1939* (Wiesbaden: Limes, 1982), p. 115. The same association between Haecker and Schrempf is made in the following articles about Haecker: "Theodor Haeckers Schaffen im Innsbrucker 'Brenner' Kreis," in *Tiroler Tageszeitung*, April 6, 1965; "Innsbruck verschaffte seinem Wort Gehör: Theodor Haecker und 'Der Brenner'," by F. H. R. in *Dolomiten*, April 10, 1965; and "Theodor Haecker," by Friedrich Pfäfflin in *Die Furche*, June 12, 1965. In a letter to this writer dated May 17, 1983, Professor Curt Hohoff says that Haecker's natural reticence is partly to blame for the paucity of data at our disposal regarding his early encounter with Kierkegaard. He was a very taciturn and private person, who did not like to publicize personal affairs. Eugen Blessing mentions nothing about Schrempf in his biography.

discovery to take the next logical step and learn Danish. This he did initially with a view to reading Kierkegaard in the original, but he soon realized that the Schrempf translations were unfaithful to the Danish works. By then Haecker had become so captivated by Kierkegaard's spirituality that he resolved to produce his own translations to help repair the damage done by Schrempf. He selected for translation those works by Kierkegaard that Schrempf had either overlooked or deliberately ignored because of his apostasy. This usually meant the more explicitly religious writings such as the *Upbuilding Discourses*. There were other non-religious writings, however, that Schrempf had not touched and that appeared to Haecker to be very timely, in view of the decline in moral and cultural values that he saw everywhere around him. By 1913, the year in which he produced his first book on Kierkegaard, Haecker had become deeply suspicious of all forms of idealism and positivism, of socialism and the new sociologism, and of the unchecked rise in Nietzsche's popularity—in short, of modernism in all its aspects. He saw in Kierkegaard the perfect antidote for these dangerous and misguided trends. He was fighting a common enemy from the same trench as Kraus and the "Brenner Circle," and he chose to use as his weapons translations from Kierkegaard and Kierkegaardian-Krausian satire. It is essential to keep this in mind if one wishes to understand the role played by *Der Brenner*—in whose issues Haecker's translations and essays appeared—in the transmission of Kierkegaard to the German-speaking world before and after the First World War.

The year 1913 marked the centenary of Kierkegaard's birth, and this fact alone helped to precipitate a score of books and articles on or by him. It was not by accident that Haecker chose that very year to publish his *Sören Kierkegaard und die Philosophie der Innerlichkeit*. Also appearing in that year as part of the series Die Klassiker der Religion, put out by the Berlin-based publishers of Protestant religious classics, was an anthology of translated material from Kierkegaard prepared by a professor at the University of Lund named Edvard Lehmann. In addition to its wide circulation among a serious audience due, in part, to the respectability of the publishers, the significance of this volume lay in the fact that Kierkegaard now had come to be regarded as belonging to the mainstream of the Protestant religious tradition. The second mention of Kierkegaard in *Die Fackel* occurred in the same year, when Kraus published part of a letter to him from a certain Richard Moses Meyer in which it was written:

"Kierkegaard, the last great religious genius, and you [Kraus] keep me awake in a dull world."[134]

Upon accepting Ficker's invitation early in 1914 to publish in *Der Brenner*, Haecker set to work preparing his first Kierkegaard translations. These consisted of the third section in *Two Ages*, entitled "The Present Age," and an 1844 *Edifying Discourse* entitled "Thorn in the Flesh." Both choices are highly significant. As Allan Janik explains, the timeliness of "The Present Age," appearing as it did on the eve of the First World War, cannot be overemphasized. It had never before been translated and was now being presented by Haecker in a decidedly polemical context intended as a denunciation of the Viennese, Munich, and Berlin press; the "idle talk" of the liberals; and the "levelling process" of mediocrity in contemporary Austro-German society.[135] It appeared in two installments in *Der Brenner* on July 1 and 15, 1914, under the bold title "Kritik der Gegenwart" (Critique of the present).[136] Even bolder was the "Nachwort" that Haecker wrote for it, in which he took the opportunity to draw stark parallels between the situation that Kierkegaard was confronting in 1846 and the present deplorable state of affairs. Various liberal newspapers in Berlin and Vienna were singled out for scorn, as was the loathsome *feuilleton*. The language theorist and critic Fritz Mauthner (1849–1923), a particular obsession of Haecker, received his share of derision, while Georg Simmel, another undesirable, was dubbed an outright charlatan.[137] It is evident from Haecker's letters to Ficker during the second half of 1914 that he attached great importance to this Kierkegaard translation and was intensely interested in hearing about the repercussions, if any, that it and the accompanying "Nachwort" would have: "The interest in Kierkegaard will surely be aroused and in time the stirring of the public can be sensational."[138] With Kierkegaard's "Kritik der Gegenwart," excerpts

---

134. *Die Fackel*, no. 387, November 17, 1913, p. 17.

135. See the excellent article by Allan Janik entitled "Haecker, Kierkegaard, and the Early Brenner: A Contribution to the History of the Reception of 'Two Ages' in the German-speaking World," in *International Kierkegaard Commentary*, volume 14: "Two Ages," ed. Robert L. Perkins (Macon, Georgia: Mercer University Press, 1984), p. 191.

136. Søren Kierkegaard, "Kritik der Gegenwart," trans. Theodor Haecker in *Der Brenner*, IV, ed. Ludwig von Ficker (Innsbruck, 1914), pp. 815–49 and pp. 869–86.

137. Theodor Haecker, "Nachwort," in *Der Brenner*, IV, pp. 890 and 895–901.

138. See letters from Haecker to Ficker dated May 7 and June 2, 1914 (*BA*). Haecker also wrote Ficker asking that the translation of "The Present Age" appear eventually as a single tract put out by the "Brenner-Verlag." This occurred in 1922. See letter to Ficker dated April 28, 1914 (*BA*).

of new translations from Dostoevsky, and attacks on the liberal press, *Der Brenner* was moving in an unmistakably conservative direction, while at the same time becoming more focused and less eclectic. Haecker's Krausian crusade, carried on under the banner of Kierkegaard, was the driving force behind this new orientation.

For entirely different reasons, Haecker's choice of "Thorn in the Flesh" *(Pfahl im Fleisch)* bore significance. As a young man he was afflicted with a severe sinus infection and had to undergo an operation that left a visible deformity on his nose. This brought to an end his early hopes of pursuing a career in acting. Thus Haecker readily identified with Kierkegaard's reputed hunchback and general physical frailty once he had discovered his writings and read about his life. He joined Kassner and a string of other "cripples" who were ushering in the era of personal physical identification with Kierkegaard—a particular existential disposition that is not an inconsequential facet of his modern reception. Kafka in 1918 plunged into Kierkegaard's works upon learning he had contracted tuberculosis, and the association with Kierkegaard's physical infirmity was not lost on Karl Kraus, who had a delicate build and suffered from a congenital curvature of the spine. In Kraus's case, this did not deter him from making piercing jokes about the physical ailments and disfigurements of his adversaries.[139] With Haecker, however, the identification ran deep and assumed the intended religious connotations of "Thorn in the Flesh" from 2 Corinthians 12:7. It also acted as inspiration for the title of an essay on Kierkegaard that he wrote later in life and that was published posthumously in 1947: *Der Buckel Kierkegaards* (K. the cripple).[140]

Barely two weeks after *Der Brenner* published the second installment of Haecker's translation of "The Present Age," Europe found itself at war. A crisis of colossal proportions for individuals and nations alike was unfolding, with momentous consequences for Kierkegaard's legacy. The long-anticipated crisis was at hand that would open the floodgates

---

139. Iggers, *Karl Kraus*, p. 36.
140. Haecker's translation of Kierkegaard's *Upbuilding Discourse* under the title *Der Pfahl im Fleisch* appeared with a foreword in *Der Brenner*, IV (May 15, 1914), pp. 691–712, and 797–814. For a study of the various extant portraits and sketches of Kierkegaard and accounts of his outward appearance by contemporaries who knew him, see Rikard Magnussen, *Søren Kierkegaard set Udefra* and the accompanying volume *Det Særlige Kors: Efterskrift til Bogen: Søren Kierkegaard set Udefra* (Copenhagen: Munksgaard, 1942).

through which Kierkegaard's vivid depictions of the individual's state of anxiety and despair were to leave their indelible mark on the rest of the century. Many of the century's greatest thinkers would read Kierkegaard in the coming years through Haecker's translations appearing in *Der Brenner,* and also published separately by the "Brenner-Verlag."

One of these was Ludwig Wittgenstein (1889–1951), who wrote to Ficker just before the war requesting his help in the disbursement of part of his inheritance to talented young poets and writers. Apparently Wittgenstein had heard of *Der Brenner* from Kraus's journal; he was a strong admirer of Kraus. Ficker agreed to cooperate and saw to it that Trakl, Rilke, Dallago, Haecker, and several others received certain portions of the money.[141] Wittgenstein continued for years to correspond with Ficker and tried unsuccessfully to interest Ficker in publishing his first book, *Tractatus Logico-Philosophicus,* through the "Brenner-Verlag": "On the other hand, I think I can say that if you print Dallago, Haecker, etc., *then* you can also print *my* book."[142] He undoubtedly read Haecker's Kierkegaard translations and the adjoining commentaries in *Der Brenner* during those years, although just how Kierkegaard figured in his early philosophizing—if indeed he did—remains a matter of much dispute and speculation.[143] Wittgenstein became sufficiently acquainted with Kierkegaard's thought, however, to have remarked once to one of his students, Maurice Drury, that Kierkegaard was "By far the greatest philosopher of the nineteenth century."[144] Another of his students reports that Wittgenstein esteemed Kierkegaard highly and "referred to him with something of awe in his expression, as a 'really religious' man."[145] Coming

---

141. See Allan Janik, "Wittgenstein, Ficker, and 'Der Brenner'," in C. G. Luckhardt, ed., *Wittgenstein: Sources and Perspectives* (Ithaca, New York: Cornell University Press, 1979), pp. 163 and 167. See also in the same book Wittgenstein's letters to Ficker, trans. Bruce Gillette, ed. Allan Janik, pp. 82–98.

142. Letter from Wittgenstein to Ficker dated December 4, 1919, in ibid., p. 96.

143. Allan Janik maintains that the final "ethical" section of Wittgenstein's *Tractatus* derives inspiration from Kierkegaard, among others—Tolstoy, Augustine, Schopenhauer, Kant, and Kraus. Wittgenstein's insistence that ethical values are incommunicable through direct language, says Janik, is very Kierkegaardian. See Janik and Toulmin, *Wittgenstein's Vienna,* pp. 11, 14–16, 27–28, 31, 66, 93, 117, 176–78, 191, 194–98, and 200. See also Janik, "Wittgenstein, Ficker, and 'Der Brenner,' " p. 177.

144. For Drury's testimony see *Ludwig Wittgenstein: Personal Recollections,* ed. Rush Rhees (Totowa, New Jersey: Rowman and Littlefield, 1981), pp. 102–4. See also Michael P. Gallagher, "Wittgenstein's Admiration for Kierkegaard," in *The Month* 39 (January–June 1968), pp. 43–49.

145. Norman Malcolm, *Ludwig Wittgenstein: A Memoir* (London: Oxford University Press, 1958), p. 71.

from Wittgenstein, who was not known to have read much classical philosophy or to have liked a great deal of what he did read, these statements are remarkable.

With the onset of the war, Wittgenstein enlisted for duty and was sent to the eastern front. Members of the "Brenner Circle," including Ficker and Trakl, also fought in the war. Work on the periodical became irregular and eventually came to a halt. Three months into the war the news arrived that Trakl, who was stationed in Krakow, had died in the hospital. It transpired later that his death had been suicide. The war had greatly depressed him and compounded earlier miseries from which he had suffered. Trakl's death profoundly shook the "Brenner Circle" and also affected Wittgenstein, who was on his way to meet him for the first time but arrived too late.[146] Ficker and the rest decided to issue a *Brenner-Jahrbuch* in 1915 dedicated to the memory of Trakl and containing his last poems. After this, *Der Brenner* did not come out again until 1919. Haecker selected and translated an *Upbuilding Discourse* by Kierkegaard from 1845 entitled "At a Graveside" for inclusion in the 1915 volume. It belonged to those writings that Schrempf had bypassed, and, thanks to Haecker, it was now making its debut in German on the occasion of Trakl's death. Haecker also contributed a polemical piece of his own that he called "Der Krieg und die Führer des Geistes" (The war and the leaders of the mind), in which he unleashed the wrath of his satire on a number of intellectuals who regularly contributed to the liberal press, accusing them of nothing short of responsibility for the war.[147]

As part of his continuing attempts to locate and translate hitherto untouched material from Kierkegaard, Haecker began to draw up plans for tackling Kierkegaard's neglected thesis on irony, as well as virgin selections from the journals. As usual, his primary problems were financial, and he wrote to Ficker in September 1914 asking him to find a rich person willing to finance the translation and publication of *Concept of Irony*.[148] In the same letter Haecker reflected on the war in the spirit of

---

146. Janik, "Wittgenstein, Ficker, and 'Der Brenner,'" pp. 168–69. See also Wittgenstein's letters to Ficker on Trakl in *Wittgenstein: Sources and Perspectives,* pp. 86–88.

147. Theodor Haecker, "Der Krieg und die Führer des Geistes," in *Brenner-Jahrbuch,* V (1915), pp. 130–87.

148. Much to his dismay, Haecker never got around to translating *Concept of Irony.* The task was accomplished in 1929 by Wilhelm Kütemeyer, who was self-taught in Danish. Kütemeyer wanted to imitate Haecker and become the principal transmitter of Kierkegaard into German. He wrote Ficker on May 4, 1927 (*BA*), asking whether his translation of *Concept of Irony,* which he sent with the letter, could be published by the "Brenner-

Kierkegaard's "The Present Age": "I sometimes have the desire to be out on the front because I believe that life there is still worthier and more tolerable than here where the babble and the idle talk [*Geschwätz*] has become even more disgusting than in peace time."¹⁴⁹ In another letter to Ficker he speaks of the relevance of "Kritik der Gegenwart" for the war and how he had sensed this when he chose it for translation.¹⁵⁰ As the *Brenner-Jahrbuch* was about to appear in late 1915, Haecker wrote to Ficker requesting that a copy be sent "to professor Dr. Christoph Schrempf in Esslingen, Württemberg."¹⁵¹ Haecker was obviously proud of his translations and essays and wished Schrempf to know that he had a competitor with very different philosophical views. The correspondence with Ficker breaks off toward the end of 1915 and does not resume until 1919.

The war years brought about fundamental changes in the outlooks of both Haecker and Dallago, causing them to begin a gradual drift apart. This marked the beginnings of a split in the "Brenner Circle" that would become permanent with time. At the center of the growing divergence in Haecker's and Dallago's views were their contrasting attitudes toward Kierkegaard. After being led to Kierkegaard through Haecker's 1913 book, Dallago began to get more and more absorbed in his works, ordering book after book and devouring them instantly. Among the books he also acquired was Monrad's 1909 biography of Kierkegaard. His passion for Kierkegaard grew to a feverish pitch at times and was expressed unreservedly in his letters to Ficker. After reading *Either/Or*, for example, he wrote: "I now know 'the Diary of the Seducer' and it is certainly something extraordinary in its peculiarity, spirit, courage, depth, [and] inspiration."¹⁵² He repeatedly referred to Karl Kraus in connection with Kierkegaard,¹⁵³ and it soon became apparent that Kierkegaard was fast

---

Verlag." Ficker politely declined, so Kütemeyer went ahead and published it elsewhere. When Haecker found out that someone had translated the work and published it before him, he became very angry and wrote Ficker a long letter dated October 22, 1929 (*BA*), in which he attacked Kütemeyer's translation and entire approach to Kierkegaard. This writer is indebted to Dr. Methlagl for this information and for showing him a copy of Haecker's letter to Ficker.

149. Letter from Haecker to Ficker dated September 29, 1914. See also letter from Haecker to Ficker dated December 16, 1914, in which he announces his intention to translate Kierkegaard's journals (*BA*).

150. Letter from Haecker to Ficker dated January 1, 1915 (*BA*).

151. Letter from Haecker to Ficker dated September 24, 1915 (*BA*).

152. Letter from Dallago to Ficker dated February 19, 1914 (*BA*).

153. See letter from Dallago to Ficker dated February 23, 1914 (*BA*).

supplanting Nietzsche as Dallago's principal idol. Kierkegaard's works contained "a greater concentration of power than is found in Nietzsche's,"[154] and he "is like a new standard of values for men. I allow his writings to work [slowly] on me."[155] The work that eventually captured most of his attention was *Øjeblikket*, which he read in March 1914. During that year he wrote an essay on Kierkegaard that remained unpublished until 1922, and in it he spoke with enthusiasm about "Der Augenblick."[156] Dallago spent much of the rest of his life drawing on Kierkegaard's last writings in order to attack the Catholic Church, and concomitantly celebrating his own bohemian version of Kierkegaardian individualism.

While Dallago prepared his assault on Catholicism, using Kierkegaard as the spearhead, Haecker was gradually moving closer to the Catholic Church and at the same time becoming increasingly critical of his earlier unqualified embrace of Kierkegaard. The road to Rome began for Haecker in 1917 when he first read John Henry Newman. He was led to Newman after reading about him in a work by Baron Friedrich von Hügel (1852-1925), in which the author proudly acknowledged Newman's influence on his own development: "But further back than all the living writers and friends lies the stimulation and help of him who was later on to become Cardinal Newman. It was he who first taught me to glory in my appurtenance to the Catholic and Roman Church, and to conceive this my inheritance in a large and historical manner."[157] Significantly, in the same year that he began to read Newman, Haecker embarked on a translation of Kierkegaard's *Book on Adler* (written in 1847 but never published in Danish as a separate work until 1984). Haecker had come across it as he was going through Kierkegaard's journals and making selections for his prospective translation. His attention was immediately arrested by its style, which in many respects was a continuation of Kierkegaard's scathing critique of his age begun in 1846 in *Two Ages,* and by

---

154. Letter from Dallago to Ficker dated March 31, 1914 (*BA*).
155. Letter from Dallago to Ficker dated June 10, 1914 (*BA*).
156. See Carl Dallago, *Der Christ Kierkegaards* (Innsbruck: Brenner-Verlag, 1922), pp. 33ff.
157. Baron Friedrich von Hügel, *The Mystical Element of Religion as Studied in Saint Catherine of Genoa and Her Friends,* vol. I (London, 1909), p. xv. Von Hügel makes several references to Kierkegaard in his two-volume work; see vol. I, pp. xiii and xvii, and vol. II, pp. 287-88 and 345-46. Haecker, however, is sure that Hügel had not read Kierkegaard, but only Høffding's book on him. See Haecker's 1924 essay entitled "Sören Kierkegaard" in his *Christentum und Kultur* (Munich: J. Kosel & F. Pustet, 1927), note p. 66.

the central issue it tackles: the question of authority in religious matters. The issue of authority had of late been weighing increasingly on Haecker's mind, and was given additional impetus by his reading of Newman. It was the question of authority, more than anything else, which had led Newman to leave the Church of England and convert to Catholicism.

In the *Book on Adler,* Kierkegaard treats the crucial question of the authenticity of individual claims to divine revelation and the authority on which they rest. In *Two Ethico-Religious Essays,* which Kierkegaard published in 1849, the section of the book titled "On the Difference between a Genius and an Apostle" states that, whereas reflection was the domain of the genius, revelation was that of the apostle, who, by virtue of this fact, spoke with religious authority. Authority, therefore, is the decisive qualitative difference between a genius and an apostle, and a person possessing divine authority is known by the "possibility of offense" that he occasions.[158] Several points in Kierkegaard's discussion struck Haecker as worthy of contemplation. For one thing, Kierkegaard in his book repeats what he says in the preface to every one of his *Upbuilding Discourses,* namely that he himself speaks "without authority."[159] He also stresses throughout the need for obedience to the authority of the established order, declaring that "disobedience is the secret of the religious confusion of our age."[160] Moreover, the elect or *"extraordinarius,"* as he is called—a third category alongside the genius and the apostle—must be willing paradoxically to make himself repulsive and to sacrifice himself out of love for the established order.[161] Presumably, Kierkegaard wrote this in anticipation of the role he himself would play a few years hence in the *Kirkekampen* vis-à-vis the established order. At last it seemed to Haecker that he had grasped an important distinction in Kierkegaard's corrective attitude toward the official Church and the ecclesiastical au-

---

158. See Søren Kierkegaard, *Fear and Trembling; The Book on Adler,* trans. Walter Lowrie with an introduction by George Steiner (New York: Alfred A. Knopf, 1994), pp. 131–32 and 201.

159. Ibid., p. 206. See also *Postscript (KW,* XII.1), pp. 272–73, and *For Self-Examination (KW,* XXI), p. 17, for similar declarations by Kierkegaard that he speaks "without authority."

160. Kierkegaard, *Fear and Trembling; The Book on Adler,* pp. 139 and 211. Not included in this edition are Kierkegaard's own author's prefaces (two in number). See the earlier edition of Kierkegaard's *The Book on Adler,* trans. Walter Lowrie as *On Authority and Revelation (The Book on Adler), or a Cycle of Ethico-Religious Essays* (Princeton: Princeton University Press, 1955), p. xviii.

161. *Fear and Trembling; The Book on Adler,* pp. 155–56.

thorities: Kierkegaard's final attack on these was done *out of love* for them and not as a sign of rebellion or rejection of religious authority. What Kierkegaard was out to eliminate was the concept of a *state-Church*, which is precisely what Newman had objected to in the Anglican Church before becoming a Catholic. Haecker had thus arrived at a diametrically opposite conclusion about Kierkegaard's final outburst from that of Dallago.

Haecker set to work translating the *Book on Adler*, which appeared in 1917 under the title *Der Begriff des Auserwählten* (The concept of the elect) because Haecker wished to avoid mentioning Adler by name. Appended to it was a long "Nachwort" in which Haecker recanted everything he had hitherto written that could be construed as undermining the Church as the repository of truth. In keeping with the spirit of Kierkegaard's critical thrusts against "an age of confusion" and of "cowardly, effeminate religiosity,"[162] Haecker also employed his own brand of satire aimed at his favorite contemporary targets. This time people like Brandes and Schrempf did not escape his polemics—Brandes's book being labeled a piece of "deplorable mischief," and Schrempf being characterized as "the purest of the rebellious pastors."[163] In his discussion of the question of authority it is evident that Haecker had already become firmly committed to a belief in the Church as possessing the final word on matters of doctrine and faith.[164]

Yet for more than three years following this translation, Haecker grappled with Kierkegaard's writings in his attempt to synthesize them with ideas and views he was receiving from his continued readings in Newman. Specifically, it was Newman's *Grammar of Assent*, which Haecker translated into German in 1921, that provided him with a new insight into the harmony of faith and reason, grace and nature, and the Church and culture. He did his best to search for those elements in Kierkegaard that supported such scholastic harmonies, and his desire to combine Kierkegaard and Newman guided his selections of entries from Kierkegaard's journals that he intended for translation.[165] These appeared first in 1922 in *Der Brenner*, and were published the following year by the "Brenner-

---

162. Ibid., p. 247.
163. Theodor Haecker, "Nachwort" to his translation of Kierkegaard's *Der Begriff des Auserwählten* (Hellerau: J. Hegner, 1917), pp. 338–39 and 369.
164. Ibid., pp. 361ff.
165. Conversation with Allan Janik on April 25, 1984, in Cambridge, Massachusetts. See also Methlagl, "Theodor Haecker und 'Der Brenner,' " p. 210. Haecker's selections reveal a lot about his own spiritual development at the time he made them.

Verlag" in two volumes entitled *Die Tagebücher*. On a personal level, Haecker was searching all this time for a satisfactory answer to the question: who can guarantee the truth for me? Finally, in 1921, he converted to Catholicism. Kierkegaard had poignantly raised the question of authority for Haecker, and in the end it was John Henry Newman who resolved it.[166]

After becoming a Catholic, Haecker did not abandon Ficker and *Der Brenner*. It soon became apparent to him, however, that the growing differences between his views and those of Dallago were fast becoming irreconcilable, which made it very difficult for them to continue publishing in the same periodical. He complained to Ficker, for instance, about Dallago's designation of the Church as "a murderess" *(eine Mörderin)* in a long essay from 1921 entitled "Augustine, Pascal und Kierkegaard."[167] In this essay Dallago openly used Kierkegaard to assault the Catholic Church and to oppose Haecker's position.[168] Despite this, Haecker kept sending Ficker translations from Kierkegaard and Newman for *Der Brenner*. Ficker felt embarrassed about Dallago's conduct but was pleased that Haecker decided to stick with *Der Brenner*.[169] Ficker was of the opinion that the post-war periodical should aim to present a wide range of views on cultural and religious issues. With time, however, Ficker and Dallago parted ways, and the early bond that had grown between them and resulted in the birth of *Der Brenner* was dissolved for good.

A new figure joined the "Brenner Circle" in 1919 after Haecker brought him to Ficker's attention.[170] This was Ferdinand Ebner (1882-1931), a Catholic philosopher concerned mainly with the pneumatology of words. His book *Das Wort und die geistigen Realitäten* was first published in 1921 by the "Brenner-Verlag." Ebner is interesting because he can be regarded as the earliest Catholic philosopher to recognize the importance

---

166. On Haecker's relation to both Kierkegaard and Newman see Werner Becker, "Der Überschritt von Kierkegaard zu Newman in der Lebensentscheidung Theodor Haeckers," in *Newman-Studien*, vol. 1 (Nürnberg-Bamberg-Passau, 1948), pp. 251-70. On Kierkegaard's and Newman's views of the state-Church see Cornelio Fabro, "Le Problème de l'Eglise chez Newman et Kierkegaard," in *Revue Thomiste*, no. 1 (January-March 1977), pp. 30-90.

167. Letter from Haecker to Ficker dated April 23, 1921 (*BA*). See Carl Dallago, "Augustine, Pascal und Kierkegaard," in *Der Brenner*, VI (1921), p. 701.

168. See, for example, Dallago, *Der Brenner*, VI, p. 676.

169. In a letter to his friend Alfred Eicholz dated October 17, 1921 (*BA*), Ficker wrote that he thought very highly of Haecker for remaining with *Der Brenner* after becoming a Catholic.

170. Letter from Haecker to Ficker dated July 25, 1919 (*BA*).

of Kierkegaard and to be deeply influenced by him. This came about through his readings of Haecker's translations and essays in *Der Brenner* as early as 1914, five years before he joined the group.[171] During the war years, Ebner became increasingly disenchanted with Max Scheler's thought and moved even closer to Kierkegaard.[172] In the foreword to his book of 1921 he writes that Kierkegaard and Dostoevsky exercised a major impact on the ideas of the book.[173] These ideas represent Ebner's original formulation of the I-Thou relationship, based chiefly on the first chapter of the Gospel of St. John that speaks of Christ as the Word of God, but also drawing upon Kierkegaard's subject-object dialectic as presented in the religious framework of the individual's personal relation to God. Rivka Horwitz has demonstrated convincingly that Ebner's concept of "I and Thou" was the source of the same idea in the philosophy of Martin Buber (1878–1965), who, as it turns out, was reading *Der Brenner* after the war ended.[174] Thus Buber, through *Der Brenner*, was exposed in his early years not only to Ebner's philosophy but to Kierkegaard's as well. Ebner's enthusiasm for Kierkegaard reached its peak in the early 1920s when he wrote in his diary: "The reality of spiritual life came into the world with Christ: with the Paradox. What our time needs: Kierkegaard and once again Kierkegaard."[175] Eventually, however, Kierkegaard became submerged in the labyrinths of Ebner's linguistic pneumatics.

171. Kierkegaard and Haecker are mentioned repeatedly in Ebner's diaries from 1914 onwards. See as examples Ferdinand Ebner, *Schriften*, vol. II: "Tagebücher" (Munich: Kösel-Verlag, 1963), pp. 585–86, entries dated October 9 and 22, 1914; p. 589, entry dated January 20, 1915, in which he says he read "Kritik der Gegenwart"; p. 591, entry dated April 29, 1915, when he read Haecker on Kierkegaard; and p. 638, entry dated June 29, 1916. Further entries suggest he was reading Kierkegaard in other translations as well, probably Schrempf's. H. Roos is wrong when he says in his *Søren Kierkegaard og Katolicismen* (Copenhagen: Munksgaard, 1952), pp. 8–9, that it was Ebner who "exercised a great influence on Haecker," who then learned Danish to translate Kierkegaard. Roos's slight book (58 pages) is the only available independent treatment of the crucial subject of Kierkegaard and Catholicism.

172. See Ebner, *Schriften*, vol. II, pp. 623–24 and 627–28, entries dated May 5, 6, and 7, 1916. See also p. 605, entry dated February 27, 1916, in which Ebner says that the spirit of Haecker and Kierkegaard is nearer to his own than is Scheler's.

173. Ibid., vol. I, pp. 79–80.

174. See Rivka Horwitz, *Buber's Way to I and Thou: An Historical Analysis and the First Publication of Martin Buber's Lectures "Religion als Gegenwart"* (Heidelberg: Schneider, 1978), pp. 171–72. See also Horwitz's article "Ferdinand Ebner als Quelle von Martin Bubers 'Ich und Du,' " in *Untersuchungen zum "Brenner": Festschrift für Ignaz Zangerle zum 75 Geburtstag*, pp. 283–93.

175. Ebner, *Schriften*, vol. II, p. 527, entry dated June 9, 1921. Ebner has been called the "Austrian Kierkegaard," who lived his life "in the shadow of Kierkegaard." See Robert

Haecker's preoccupation with Kierkegaard did not diminish following his conversion, but it took on a different form. He now became more critical of certain features in Kierkegaard's thought that were clearly out of step with a Catholic outlook. In a 1922 essay written as an afterword to his translation of one of the *Upbuilding Discourses* from 1851, Haecker expresses dismay at Kierkegaard's weak sense of community, which hindered his ability to grasp the significance of "the visible Church and the Sacraments." His excessive individualism distanced him from the Church. Kierkegaard was also too passionate at times and often treated the things of this life too cavalierly.[176] Haecker was speaking as one who, through Newman and the neo-scholastics, had arrived at a degree of harmony between culture and Church, the natural and the supernatural, the temporal and the eternal, that made some of Kierkegaard's radical critiques—for which he had once had such enthusiasm—now appear to him very one-sided and extreme. Haecker, however, carefully cautions against interpreting Kierkegaard's individualism as license for subjectivism and egotism.[177] He clearly perceived this as a mounting danger in certain post-war readings of Kierkegaard; as time would tell, he was only too correct. It was precisely Kierkegaard's emphasis on subjectivity that had raised for Haecker the question of authority in the first place, causing him ultimately to seek the answer in Catholicism, where man, as a harmonious unity of intellect, will, and feelings, was in touch with a firm source of authority *outside* himself.

An investigation of the Catholic Haecker's attitudes toward Kierkegaard, as expressed in a number of essays on him after 1921, could make a fascinating study in itself. He continued his attempts to appropriate for Catholicism as many of the elements of Kierkegaard's genius as possible, while at the same time pointing out the difficulties and incompatibilities. He rejected, for example, Kierkegaard's Abraham, calling him "a philosophic myth" and not a true representation of the Abraham of the Old Testament, Father of the Faithful. On the other hand, Haecker found

---

Braun, "Der österreichische Kierkegaard," in *Die Literarische Tat*, June 25, 1965; and Walter Nigg, "Ein Leben im Schatten Kierkegaards: zu Ferdinand Ebners Briefen," in *Neue Zürcher Zeitung*, July 29, 1966. On Ebner see also Johnston, *The Austrian Mind*, pp. 217-20.

176. Theodor Haecker, "Søren Kierkegaards Altarreden" [1922], published in his *Christentum und Kultur* (Munich: J. Kosel & F. Pustet, 1927), pp. 129-30. Alexander Dru translated the essay in 1930 and published it seven years later. See Theodor Haecker, *Søren Kierkegaard*, trans. Alexander Dru (London: Oxford University Press, 1937), p. 63.

177. Ibid., pp. 128-29; Dru's translation, pp. 62-63.

Kierkegaard to be at his spiritually most profound in the *Upbuilding Discourses,* which he translated with joy.[178] Over and over, Haecker warns of the dangers of interpreting Kierkegaard's subjectivity as subjectivism. Although, according to Haecker, Kierkegaard's "Truth is Subjectivity" lies essentially outside the main course of development of western philosophy, Kierkegaard does manage, through his insistence on subjectivity, to bring in as never before for philosophical consideration the person of the thinker himself.[179] Haecker in fact devotes a long essay in 1932 to a critical consideration of Kierkegaard's concept of truth. Here the mature Haecker, fully at home in his Thomistic *philosophia perennis,* treats critically Kierkegaard's notions of paradox and subjectivity.[180] The anxieties and uncertainties of the lonely Kierkegaardian leap have given way for Haecker to the unperturbed serenity of Newman's assent. It is not surprising, therefore, that Haecker refused in later life to publish a second edition of his first 1913 book on Kierkegaard.

As a newcomer to Catholicism, Haecker was initially viewed with considerable suspicion that only slowly abated. Despite launching in his book *Satire und Polemik* (1922), a bitter attack on the liberal Protestantism of his early mentors Harnack, Troeltsch, and others, Haecker did not escape the indignation of Catholic critics who saw him as an upstart with no genuine Catholic roots. One of these critics, writing in December 1922 in *Literarischer Handweiser,* condemned Hecker's *Satire und Polemik* as gruff and crude polemics. What Haecker lacks, in the unimpressed writer's view, is the dimension of Christian love. He is a raving fanatic and, like Kierkegaard, resembles Tertullian: "The Lord is not encountered through raging assaults, and so long as Haecker excitedly and impatiently delivers his blows and [fights] his battles in this manner on behalf of the Catholic Idea, we become compelled to reserve such a judgment for him."[181] This same writer, back in 1913 in a negative article on Kierkegaard that he wrote for the Catholic journal *Hochland,* described Kierkegaard

---

178. Theodor Haecker, "Sören Kierkegaard" [1924], published in *Christentum und Kultur,* pp. 75–76 and 77–78 respectively; see Dru's translation, pp. 16 and 18.

179. Haecker, ibid., pp. 82–83 and pp. 85–87; Dru's translation, pp. 22–23 and 25–27.

180. See Theodor Haecker, "Der Begriff der Wahrheit bei Sören Kierkegaard" [1932], published in his *Opuscula: Ein Sammelband* (Munich: Kösel-Verlag, 1949), pp. 155–223. David R. Law, in his discussion of Kierkegaard's concept of truth, lists this work by Haecker as belonging with those scholarly treatments that regard Kierkegaard as a subjectivist. See his *Kierkegaard as Negative Theologian,* p. 91.

181. See Johannes Mumbauer, "Die neuen Tertulliane (Sören Kierkegaard und Theodor Haecker)," in *Literarischer Handweiser* 58, no. 12 (December 1922), p. 549.

as "one of the greatest but also the most unfortunate geniuses of all time."[182] The suspicion that greeted Haecker in Catholic circles in the early 1920s derived, in large part, from his association in people's minds with Kierkegaard.

What helped Haecker to gain gradual acceptance among Catholics was a friendship he developed with Karl Muth (1867–1944), the influential editor of *Hochland,* who favorably reviewed Haecker's *Satire und Polemik,* arguing that the times called for the kind of anger displayed in Haecker's polemics.[183] Haecker began to work for Muth in the 1920s and to publish in *Hochland.* At the same time, his continued interaction with *Der Brenner* was instrumental in transforming it into a Catholic periodical during the 1930s, after Ficker, who had been baptized a Catholic, returned to Catholicism in 1932. Many of the lesser figures revolving around the periodical also converted to Catholicism.

One cannot as yet speak of a "Catholic theological reception" of Kierkegaard in the 1920s, but with the acceptance of Haecker and his growing numbers of Catholic readers, there came forth a few individuals who followed his lead in attempting to claim Kierkegaard for the Catholic tradition, and to express Kierkegaardian insights in Catholic terms. Most notable among these was the Jesuit Erich Przywara, whose book *Das Geheimnis Kierkegaards* (1929) revolved around the provocative suggestion that Kierkegaard had actually been a Catholic without knowing it.[184] On the surface this seems laughable, but it represents a radical way of raising the legitimate question of Kierkegaard's relation to Catholicism, both historically as regards his own acquaintance with it, and theologically in terms of affinities between his positions and Catholic doctrine.

Haecker's impact on the development of Kierkegaard scholarship must

---

182. Mumbauer, "Sören Kierkegaard," in *Hochland,* X (1913), p. 184.

183. See Muth's review in *Hochland,* XX (1922–23), pp. 95–100. It was Muth who managed to secure Haecker's release from jail in 1933 after he was arrested by the Nazi authorities for attacking the philosophy of National Socialism in one of his articles. During the Second World War, Haecker hid the manuscripts of his journals in Muth's house for fear they might fall into the hands of the Gestapo. It was fortunate that he did this, because in 1944 his Munich home was completely destroyed, along with his library and all his papers, from a bomb dropped during an Allied air raid.

184. See Adolf Darlap, "Die Rezeption S. Kierkegaards in der Katholischen Theologie," in *Text und Kontext* (Copenhagen and Munich, 1983), pp. 225–38. This writer is also indebted to a conversation with Professor Darlap at his home in Mühlau near Innsbruck on May 7, 1983.

not be overlooked. Emanuel Hirsch of Germany took a lively interest in Haecker's translations and reviewed many of them for theological journals. In 1923 there appeared the first set of Kierkegaard translations in the English-speaking world. They were assorted selections made by a professor of Germanic languages named Lee M. Hollander, who translated from the German edition of Schrempf. This Schrempf-inspired debut notwithstanding, Haecker's influence managed to find its way to England as well, where his work caught the attention of Alexander Dru, who became one of the leading translators of Kierkegaard into English. Dru converted to Catholicism and was so captivated by Haecker's writings that he translated Haecker's essays on Kierkegaard along with his wartime journals from the years 1939–45. He even tried to arrange a meeting in the summer of 1930 in Italy between Haecker and Walter Lowrie, but it did not materialize.[185] Dru's appreciation of Haecker led him to write about his importance both as translator of Kierkegaard and as a thinker in his own right.[186]

Through Theodor Haecker, Kierkegaard entered *Der Brenner* and found his way into the lives of those making up the "Brenner Circle." Through this periodical he shone with a new face on the German intellectual scene, a face that had hitherto been obscured by the Schrempf Kierkegaard. We know that Martin Heidegger (1889–1976) subscribed to *Der Brenner* beginning in 1911, became an ardent admirer of the poetry of Georg Trakl, and became a good friend of Ficker in later years. We also know from a letter written to Ficker by a young student of Husserl, Hans Jaeger, that Husserl read *Der Brenner* regularly and enjoyed Haecker's essays. Similarly, Karl Jaspers (1883–1969) read *Der Brenner* in its early years, with the result that his landmark analysis of key Kierkegaardian categories appeared in 1919 under the title *Psychologie der Weltanschauungen*. In all these thinkers the *Brenner* Kierkegaard served to heighten a sense of crisis that eventually found expression in a variety of ways in

---

185. See Walter Lowrie's article entitled "How Kierkegaard Got into English," appended to his translation of Kierkegaard's *Repetition* (Princeton: Princeton University Press, 1941), p. 190.

186. See Alexander Dru, "Haecker's Point of View: Notes on the History of Existentialism," in *The Downside Review* 67 (Exeter, 1949), pp. 260–75; and his "On Haecker's 'Metaphysik des Gefühls,' " in *The Downside Review*, 68 (Exeter, 1950), pp. 35–45. See also his introduction to his translation of Haecker's *Journal in the Night* (London: Harvill Press, 1951), pp. xi–xlvi.

their philosophies: Heidegger's *"Gerede"* (idle talk) in *Sein und Zeit* (1927); Husserl's view of the crisis in western science; and Jaspers's critique of modernity.[187]

At the same time, and independently of *Der Brenner*, Kierkegaard stood at the center of a revolution in Protestant theology after the First World War—principally through his influence on the early Karl Barth (1886–1968). The "Theology of Crisis," or "Neo-Orthodoxy" as it came to be known, was a radical reaction against the liberal Protestantism of the Ritschlian and Harnackian variety. It was anchored firmly in Kierkegaard's repudiation of nineteenth-century speculative theology, in his dialectic of the temporal and the eternal, and in his Scripture-grounded Christocentric faith. Although the later Barth altered his previous Kierkegaardian course, there is no denying the fact that his pivotal *Der Römerbrief*, especially the second edition of 1922, would have been inconceivable without Kierkegaard.[188]

Thus, by the mid-1920s, the beginnings of Kierkegaard's serious reception in the German-speaking world were underway at last.

187. See Allan Janik, "Haecker, Kierkegaard, and the Early Brenner," pp. 220–22. See also Methlagl, "Theodor Haecker und 'Der Brenner,' " pp. 207–8. On Heidegger's early knowledge of Kierkegaard through *Der Brenner* see John van Buren, *The Young Heidegger: Rumor of the Hidden King*, part of the Studies in Continental Thought series, gen. ed. John Sallis (Bloomington and Indianapolis: Indiana University Press, 1994), esp. pp. 150–56. See also John D. Caputo, "Kierkegaard, Heidegger, and the Foundering of Metaphysics," in *International Kierkegaard Commentary, Fear and Trembling and Repetition*, ed. Robert L. Perkins (Macon, Ga.: Mercer University Press, 1994), pp. 201–24.

188. On Barth and Kierkegaard see Egon Brinkschmidt, *Sören Kierkegaard und Karl Barth* (Neukirchen-Vluyn: Neukirchener Verlag, 1971).

Conclusion

Haecker's confrontation with the problem of authority in Kierkegaard in the years immediately following the First World War, and the substantial alteration that ensued in the course of his life, opened a new and more complex phase in the history of Kierkegaard's reception. The decisive impact of Kierkegaard's thought on the rise of the existential movement in European philosophy during the 1930s and 1940s, on Heidegger's ontological philosophy with its phenomenological roots, on Protestant Neo-Orthodoxy, and eventually on Catholic theology as well, including Neo-Thomism—this all belongs to the new phase. In a sense the truly exciting part of the story is just beginning where this study terminates. The purpose from the start has been to provide a thorough thematic and chronological examination of Kierkegaard's early or "pre-reception" reception, leading up to those momentous, twentieth-century developments at the core of which he stands.

In Kierkegaard's case, a workable recipe for any serious reception of his thought would require that a number of ingredients and conditions be simultaneously in place: a favorable *Zeitgeist,* preferably the result of prolonged malaise culminating in a profound crisis on the personal-spiritual level; the presence of a few exceptional minds capable of penetrating his insights and fastening upon the essence of his thought; the availability of adequate translations into at least some of the major European languages; as few prejudicial vestiges and methodological predeterminations as possible; and finally, the absence of any attitude of deliberate malice. Throughout the seventy or so years between Kierkegaard's death and the appearance of Heidegger's *Sein und Zeit,* the conjunction of all these factors was never complete and the consequent receptions were invariably truncated. Since the appearance in 1919 of Karl Jaspers's *Psychologie der Weltanschauungen,* followed by *Sein und Zeit* eight years later, a sustained, deeper, more extensive, and generally more meaningful interaction with Kierkegaard's thought has occurred in diverse forms; however, even here, one-sidedness and prejudice did not vanish, so that the question becomes: Is such a thing as a unified and all-encompassing view of Kierkegaard in his totality attainable? Given the varied and unsystematic nature of his thought as an unalterable constant, along with the fact that he has served different personal, literary, intellectual, philosophical, and theological purposes for different people, the answer is probably negative. It may well be that, in the nature of the case, Kierkegaard was conducive to the fragmentation of his own legacy.

Existentialism emerged out of an emphasis on the primacy of individual-personal existence over against collective existence or pure abstract thought. This emphasis is grounded more than anything else in Kierkegaard's "single individual," a fundamental category underlying all his writings. The meaning of serious reception is precisely that such fundamental categories become the operative focus for the responsible thinkers of an age. During the period covered in the present study, those few individuals of outstanding intellectual stature who were exposed to Kierkegaard's thought did not achieve this required level of seriousness, even though in most cases, and despite the cursory nature of the encounter, they managed to fathom crucial aspects of his thought. Dilthey comes to mind as an example. Kierkegaard's basic outlook on man ran so radically counter to the prevailing positivist currents of thought in the nineteenth century, and received such stiff competition from certain growing movements like the various philosophies of the will, that matters had to run their course before the particular novelty of his insights and orientation could begin to exercise the desired impact on major thinkers. Simply put, there was a lack of cooperation from the *Zeitgeist* throughout the nineteenth century. There is no telling what would have happened had Nietzsche read Kierkegaard. The same is true for Freud, who knew nothing about Kierkegaard. Sometimes the encounters that did not take place are as significant as those that did.

Although on the whole the "transmitting agents" during the period from 1855 to 1925 were relatively minor figures, they exhibited at least one Kierkegaardian trait: they allowed their personal lives to be affected by their reading of Kierkegaard, especially the religious writings. Thus they reacted *existentially* to his thought, and this alone credits them with a significant degree of seriousness and depth. Whether it was Brandes during his brief youthful religious crisis, or Høffding as he entertained the option of pursuing theology and becoming a clergyman, or Schrempf in his lifelong preoccupation with the consequences of *Øjeblikket* for his own personal faith and relations with the Church, or Haecker's anguished wrestling with the issues raised in *The Book on Adler* and their impact on his life, in every instance Kierkegaard pushed the individual concerned to take certain life decisions that usually proved to be critical for his overall development. Even Rasmus Nielsen's life, which at one time was described by Kierkegaard as lacking in passion and personal commitment, experienced a radical change beginning in 1849, when he first came in contact with Kierkegaard's works. Despite his subsequent departure from Kierkegaard on the question of faith and knowledge, Nielsen remained for years obsessed with his ideas. Only Brøchner, whose admiration for Kierkegaard never abated, was untouched existentially by his religious views.

Of the many Scandinavian and German literary figures who developed an interest in Kierkegaard, none has been more instrumental in furthering his reception than Ibsen, even though his actual relationship to Kierkegaard remains ironically the most ambiguous of all. Nevertheless, an early association of the two stubbornly lodged itself in the popular mind, so that each helped to promote the dissemination of the other. This was particularly true at the turn of the century. At that time also several German-speaking poets and writers were being drawn to Kierkegaard primarily through the story of his broken engagement. Ever since the publication of his private journals and Brandes's pioneering biographical-psychological treatment, certain features of Kierkegaard's life have served as convenient entries to his thought. This was as it should be for Kierkegaard the "single individual," yet more often than not those very same biographical components became a hindrance to a detached assessment of his thought and instead exclusively monopolized people's attention. The results bordered on the dramatic and included a series of sentimental attempts to reenact the engagement episode, conscious emulations by rebellious types of the final attack on the Church, personal identifications with physical infirmities, and parallel father-son interactions.

An overview of Kierkegaard's early reception shows that it proceeded amidst much strife at nearly every juncture. Kierkegaard became a bone of contention between atheists and believers, freethinkers and theologians, rationalists and romantics, and some of his writings, like *Øjeblikket*, produced a string of religious controversies. In most of these controversies, however, the level of both the criticism and the support of his views was characteristically crude. The criticism was largely agitational in nature, while the support rarely ventured beyond enthusiastic praise and apologetics to engage in any rigorous analysis. Moreover, the overtly critical writings usually saw the light of day in a new language under decidedly polemical circumstances: Schrempf translated *Øjeblikket* in 1896 in order to use it in his fight against the Lutheran Church in Württemberg; Haecker intended his 1914 translation of "The Present Age" as a denunciation of liberalism in Austria and Germany.

A discernible tendency toward extremism, which only increases in magnitude with time, is evident among the various early interpreters of Kierkegaard's thought. Subjectivity is readily transmuted into subjectivism; the rigid limits Kierkegaard set on reason become license for irrationalism and anti-intellectualism; the paradox gives way to absurdism; Kierkegaard's faith is labeled "mysticism"; his critique of Christendom is fashioned into a convenient tool in the hands of anti-religious activists. This extremism has prompted some in more recent times to take another careful look at Kierkegaard's writings to see if the seeds of misconception and abuse do not originate there. Certain modern critiques of Kierkegaard stem from such reevaluations: Buber's interpersonal philosophy based on the I-Thou relation, Berdyaev's Russian Orthodox notion of *sobornost* (religious community), and the parallel Catholic emphasis on the community of the faithful represent three examples of direct responses to the potential excesses of radical Kierkegaardian individualism. Could it be, it is asked, that Kierkegaard's failure to sound a loud and clear warning against misinterpreting his category of subjectivity as an easy pathway to subjectivism-egotism left that category vulnerable to the kind of abuse it has generated? Perhaps, it is felt, "the corrective" himself now requires a corrective—to be advanced in a spirit of which he would fully approve.

Bibliography

In researching this project I was aided by the two massive bibliographies of Kierkegaard compiled by Jens Himmelstrup and François Lapointe. The first is by far the more comprehensive and accurate of the two, although by Himmelstrup's own admission even it remains incomplete for the period it covers up to 1962. The second Danish edition of Kierkegaard's complete works, *Søren Kierkegaards Samlede Værker,* was used whenever necessary, particularly in cases where an English translation of a work in question is lacking. Similarly, in the case of the journals, the second Danish edition, *Søren Kierkegaards Papirer,* was the main reference in those few cases where there was no available English translation of journal entries. In all other cases the standard English translations of the works were cited. Care was taken to refer, whenever possible, to the new series of translations still in the process of coming out under the general heading: *Kierkegaard's Writings,* edited by Howard V. Hong.

Aage Kabell's *Kierkegaardstudiet i Norden* served as a useful guide to the diverse newspaper and periodical articles pertaining to the *Kirkekampen*. These articles were obtained and read at the University Library and the Royal Library in Copenhagen, and constitute the bibliographic backbone of Chapter 3. Many of them were written anonymously or using pseudonyms. The anonymous ones are listed alphabetically according to name of newspaper, periodical, or article. Those having pseudonyms as authors are listed in a straightforward alphabetical manner except in the few cases where the pseudonym in question is an abbreviation, such as "Uk-d," for instance, when the *last* letter ('d' in this case) is the key to alphabetizing. For biographical information about the various participants in the *Kirkekampen,* and about other, more obscure Danish and Norwegian figures making their appearance at different points in the story, recourse was had to the *Dansk Biografisk Lexicon* in both editions and to the *Norsk Biografisk Leksikon.* Two sourcebooks of documents, Johansen's *Erindringer om Søren Kierkegaard* and Croxall's *Glimpses and Impressions of Kierkegaard* (in English translation), were consulted frequently. The first is an excellent collection of sketches and recollections of a variety of features of Kierkegaard's life, written by friends, family members, and other contemporaries. The editor provides extensive commentary in the back. The second, though less professional and containing several errors and factual inaccuracies, provides the only available English translations (available as this book goes to press) of such vital documents as Hans Brøchner's "Reminiscences" and Henriette Lund's "Recollections."

Primary Sources

Works of Kierkegaard in Danish

Bladartikler. Edited by Rasmus Nielsen. Copenhagen, 1857.
Af Søren Kierkegaards Efterladte Papirer. Vols. I–VIII. 1st ed. Edited by H. P. Barfod and H. Gottsched. Copenhagen, 1869–81.
Søren Kierkegaards Samlede Værker. Vols. I–XIV. 1st ed. Edited by A. B. Drachmann, J. L. Heiberg, and H. O. Lange. Copenhagen: Gyldendal, 1901–6.
Søren Kierkegaards Papirer. Vols. I–XI^3. 2d ed. Edited by P. A. Heiberg, V. Kuhr, and E. Torsting. Copenhagen: Gyldendal, 1909–48.
Søren Kierkegaards Samlede Værker. Vols. I–XV. 2d ed. Edited by A. B. Drachmann, J. L. Heiberg, and H. O. Lange. Copenhagen: Gyldendal, 1920–36.

Selected Works of Kierkegaard in German Translation

Søren Kierkegaard. *Ausgewählte christliche Reden.* Translated by Julie von Reincke. Giessen, 1901.
Sören Kierkegaards Verhältnis zu seiner Braut. Briefe und Aufzeichnungen aus seinem Nachlass. Translated by E. Rohr. Leipzig, 1904.
Sören Kierkegaard und sein Verhältnis zu "ihr". Aus nachgelassenen Papieren. Translated by Raphael Meyer. Stuttgart, 1905.
Sören Kierkegaard. Buch des Richters, Seine Tagebücher, 1833–1855 in Auszug. Translated by Hermann Gottsched. Jena and Leipzig, 1905.
Søren Kierkegaard. *Die Tagebücher.* Vols. I–II. Translated by Theodor Haecker. Innsbruck: Brenner-Verlag, 1923.

Works of Kierkegaard in English Translation

Early Polemical Writings. Vol. I of *Kierkegaard's Writings.* Edited and translated by Julia Watkin. Princeton: Princeton University Press, 1990.
The Concept of Irony: With Constant Reference to Socrates. Translated by Lee M. Capel. Bloomington, Indiana: Indiana University Press, 1965.
The Concept of Irony, With Continual Reference to Socrates. Vol. II of *Kierkegaard's Writings.* Edited and translated by Howard V. Hong and Edna H. Hong. Princeton: Princeton University Press, 1989.
Johannes Climacus or De Omnibus Dubitandum Est, and A Sermon. Translated by T. H. Croxall. Stanford: Stanford University Press, 1958.

Either/Or (vols. I and II). Vols. III and IV of *Kierkegaard's Writings*. Edited and translated by Howard V. Hong and Edna H. Hong. Princeton: Princeton University Press, 1987.
Eighteen Upbuilding Discourses. Vol. V of *Kierkegaard's Writings*. Edited and translated by Howard V. Hong and Edna H. Hong. Princeton: Princeton University Press, 1990.
Fear and Trembling; Repetition. Vol. VI of *Kierkegaard's Writings*. Edited and translated by Howard V. Hong and Edna H. Hong. Princeton: Princeton University Press, 1983.
Philosophical Fragments; Johannes Climacus. Vol. VII of *Kierkegaard's Writings*. Edited and translated by Howard V. Hong and Edna H. Hong. Princeton: Princeton University Press, 1985.
The Concept of Anxiety. Vol. VIII of *Kierkegaard's Writings*. Edited and translated by Reidar Thomte and Albert B. Anderson. Princeton: Princeton University Press, 1980.
Three Discourses on Imagined Occasions. Vol. X of *Kierkegaard's Writings*. Edited and translated by Howard V. Hong and Edna H. Hong. Princeton: Princeton University Press, 1993.
Stages on Life's Way. Vol. XI of *Kierkegaard's Writings*. Edited and translated by Howard V. Hong and Edna H. Hong. Princeton: Princeton University Press, 1988.
Concluding Unscientific Postscript. Vols. XII.1 and XII.2 of *Kierkegaard's Writings*. Edited and translated by Howard V. Hong and Edna H. Hong. Princeton: Princeton University Press, 1992.
The Corsair Affair, and Articles Related to the Writings. Vol. XIII of *Kierkegaard's Writings*. Edited and translated by Howard V. Hong and Edna H. Hong. Princeton: Princeton University Press, 1982.
Two Ages: The Age of Revolution and the Present Age, A Literary Review. Vol. XIV of *Kierkegaard's Writings*. Edited and translated by Howard V. Hong and Edna H. Hong. Princeton: Princeton University Press, 1978.
Upbuilding Discourses in Various Spirits. Vol. XV of *Kierkegaard's Writings*. Edited and translated by Howard V. Hong and Edna H. Hong. Princeton: Princeton University Press, 1993.
Works of Love. Vol. XVI of *Kierkegaard's Writings*. Edited and translated by Howard V. Hong and Edna H. Hong. Princeton: Princeton University Press, 1995.
On Authority and Revelation (The Book on Adler), or a Cycle of Ethico-Religious Essays. Translated by Walter Lowrie. Princeton: Princeton University Press, 1955.
Fear and Trembling; The Book on Adler. Translated by Walter Lowrie with an introduction by George Steiner. New York: Alfred A. Knopf, 1994.
Crisis in the Life of an Actress, and Other Essays on Drama. Translated by Stephen D. Crites. New York: Harper Collins, 1967.
The Sickness unto Death. Vol. XIX of *Kierkegaard's Writings*. Edited and translated by Howard V. Hong and Edna H. Hong. Princeton: Princeton University Press, 1980.
The Point of View for My Work as an Author. Edited by Benjamin Nelson and translated by Walter Lowrie. New York: Harper and Row, 1962.
Armed Neutrality and An Open Letter. Edited and translated by Howard V. Hong and Edna H. Hong. Bloomington, Indiana: Indiana University Press, 1968.
Practice in Christianity. Vol. XX of *Kierkegaard's Writings*. Edited and translated by Howard V. Hong and Edna H. Hong. Princeton: Princeton University Press, 1991.
For Self-Examination; Judge for Yourself! Vol. XXI of *Kierkegaard's Writings*. Edited and translated by Howard V. Hong and Edna H. Hong. Princeton: Princeton University Press, 1990.

Attack upon "Christendom." Translated by Walter Lowrie. Princeton: Princeton University Press, 1944.
Letters and Documents. Vol. XXV of *Kierkegaard's Writings.* Edited by Howard V. Hong and Edna H. Hong. Translated by Henrik Rosenmeier. Princeton: Princeton University Press, 1978.
Søren Kierkegaard's Journals and Papers. Vols. I–VII. Edited and translated by Howard V. Hong and Edna H. Hong, assisted by Gregor Malantschuk. Bloomington, Indiana: Indiana University Press, 1967-78.

Other Primary Works

"A." "Et Angreb paa Biskop Mynster." *Dagbladet,* December 21, 1854.
"Æsculap." *Kjøbenhavnsposten,* December 24, 1854.
Andersen, Hans Christian. *Dagbøger: 1825–1875.* Vols. I–XII. Edited by Kåre Olsen and H. Topsøe-Jensen. Copenhagen: G. E. C. Gad, 1971-77.
———. *Deres Broderligt Hengivne: Et Udvalg af Breve fra H. C. Andersen.* Edited by Niels Birger Wamburg. Copenhagen: Gyldendal, 1975.
———. *Fairy Tales.* Translated by Jean Hersholt. New York: Heritage Press, 1942.
———. *Mit Livs Eventyr.* Vols. I–II. Edited by H. Topsøe-Jensen. Copenhagen: Gyldendal, 1951.
———. *Shorter Tales.* Translated by Jean Hersholt. New York: Heritage Press, 1948.
———. *The Story of My Life.* Translator unknown. New York, 1871.
Andresen, Andreas Daniel. *Dr. Søren Kierkegaards falske Paastande,* I–III. Copenhagen, 1855-56.
Anonymous. *Aftonbladet,* May 23, 1877.
———. *Aftonbladet,* July 24, 1880.
———. "En Antikritik." *Fædrelandet,* October 22, 1859.
———. *Berlingske Tidende,* July 27, 1859.
———. *Berlingske Tidende,* June 29, 1880.
———. *Berlingske Tidende,* April 28, 1892.
———. *Christianiaposten,* no. 152 (1859).
———. "Die Dänische Staatskirche. Der Angriff Sören Kierkegaards." In 13 parts in *Kopenhagener Zeitung,* January 24, 28, and 31; February 4, 7, 11, 14, and 18; March 6, 10, 17, and 31, 1856.
———. *Dagbladet,* October 12, 1855.
———. *Dagbladet,* November, 14, 1855.
———. *Dagbladet,* September 21 and 22, 1859.
———. *Dagbladet,* March 25, 1873.
———. *Dagens Nyheder,* April 25, 1892.
———. "Dr. Søren Kierkegaards Dødsfald." *Dagbladet,* November 21, 1855.
———. *Dannevirke,* July 12, 1855.
———. "Etats européens—Le Danemark. Questions religieuses." *Annuaire des deux Mondes, Histoire génerale des divers états.* Vol. VI, p. 489. Paris, October 20, 1856.
———. *Fædrelandet,* November 12, 1855.
———. *Flensburger Zeitung,* May 11, 1859.
———. *Flyveposten,* October 5, 1855.
———. *Flyveposten,* November 16, 1855.
———. *Flyveposten,* July 24, 1857.

———. *Holbæk Amts Avis*, January 3, 1855.
———. "Et Indlæg i den Kierkegaardske Strid." *Dagbladet*, October 2, 1855.
———. "Kierkegaard." In *Encyclopedia Britannica*, 11th edition. Vol. 15, p. 788. London, 1910–11.
———. "Den Kierkegaardske Strid." *Dagbladet*, April 25, 1855.
———. *Kjøbenhavnsposten*, December 23, 1854.
———. *Kjøbenhavnsposten*, August 23, 1855.
———. *Kjøbenhavnsposten*, October 18, 1855.
———. *Kjøbenhavnsposten*, November 13, 1855.
———. *Kjøbenhavnsposten*, November 21, 1855.
———. *Lolland-Falsters Stiftstidende*, January 31, 1855.
———. "Mod S. Ks 'aphoristiske' artikler i 'Fædrelandet.' " *Kjøbenhavnsposten*, May 12, 1855.
———. *Morgenbladet*, December 15, 1876.
———. *Morgenposten*, November 14, 1855.
———. *Morgenposten*, November 20, 1855.
———. *Morgenposten*, April 4, 1856.
———. *Neues Repertorium für die theologische Literatur und kirchliche Statistik*. Vol. II, copy 1, pp. 44–48. Berlin, April 1845.
———. *Øre-Sund*. Vol. 1, no. 47 (November 22, 1857).
———. "Et Rygte om S. Kierkegaard." *Kjøbenhavnsposten*, September 5, 1855.
———. "Samtaler i Præstens Huus over Dr. S. Kierkegaards 'Øjeblikke.' " *Pilegrimen*. Edited by M. A. Sommer. 1st year, nos. 25–40 (1860).
———. "S. K. og Hans polemiske Modstandere." *Dannevirke*, January 11, 1855.
———. *Stockholms Dagblad*, November 16, 1880.
———. "Taler Dr. Søren Kierkegaard ikke om sig selv?" *Flyveposten*, June 4, 1855.
———. *Theologischer Jahresbericht*. Edited by Wilhelm Hanck. Vol. 10, no. 8, pp. 386–87. Wiesbaden, 1875.
"B", *Dagbladet*, December 22, 1854.
Bärthold, Albert. *Die Bedeutung der ästhetischen Schriften Sören Kierkegaards, mit Bezug auf G. Brandes: "Sören Kierkegaard, ein literarisches Charakterbild."* Halle, 1879.
———. "Zur Bekanntschaft mit Sören Kierkegaard." *Die Christliche Welt*, no. 25 (Leipzig, June 15, 1893), pp. 595–97.
———. *Einladung und Aergerniss. Biblische Darstellung und christliche begriffsbestimmung von Sören Kierkegaard*. Halberstadt, 1872.
———. "Ein Jünger Jesu (Sören Kierkegaard)." *Die Christliche Welt*, no. 14 (Leipzig, March 30, 1893), pp. 318–21.
———. "Aus Kierkegaard zur Sache Schrempfs." *Die Christliche Welt*, no. 13 (Leipzig, March 23, 1893), pp. 293–95.
———. *Lessing und die objective Wahrheit*. Halle, 1877.
———. *Noten zu Sören Kierkegaards Lebensgeschichte*. Halle, 1876.
———. *S. Kierkegaards Persönlichkeit in ihrer Verwirklichung der Ideale*. Gütersloh, 1886.
———. *Sören Kierkegaard, Eine Verfasser-Existenz eigner Art: Aus seinen Mittheilungen zusammengestellet*. Halberstadt, 1873.
———. *Aus und über Sören Kierkegaard. Früchte und Blätter*. Halberstadt, 1874.
———. *Zur theologischen Bedeutung Sören Kierkegaards*. Halle, 1880.
———. *Was Christentum ist. Zur Verständigung über diese Frage*. Gütersloh, 1884.

———. *Die Wendung zur Wahrheit in der modernen Kulturentwicklung*. Gütersloh, 1885.

Basch, Victor. "Un individualiste religieux, Sören Kierkegaard." *Grande Revue* 27 (August 1903), pp. 281–320.

Beck, Andreas Frederik. *Darmstädter Allgemeine Kirchenzeitung*, September 22, 1855.

———. *Darmstädter Allgemeine Kirchenzeitung*, January 31, 1856.

———. *Deutsche Jahrbücher für Wissenschaft und Kunst*, nos. 222 and 223 (Halle, September 17 and 19, 1842), pp. 885–88 and 889–91, respectively. Edited by Arnold Ruge.

———. *Fædrelandet*, May 29 and June 5, 1842.

———. "Martensen und Kierkegaard." *Nordisches Telegraph*, II, no. 89 (June 14, 1850), pp. 1095–96.

———. "Übersichtliche Darstellung des jetzigen Zustandes der Theologie in Dänemark." *Theologische Jahrbücher*, vol. 3 (Tübingen, 1844), pp. 497–536. Edited by E. Zeller.

Bell, Richard. *Review of Theology and Philosophy* 6 (1910), pp. 304–8.

Bigeon, Maurice. *Les Révoltés Scandinaves*. Paris, 1894.

Bjørnson, Bjørnstjerne. *Kamp-Liv, Brev fra Aarene 1879–1884*. Vols. I–II. Edited by Halvdan Koht. Oslo: Gyldendal, 1932.

Bloch, Jørgen Victor. *Dansk Kirketidende*, no. 27 (June 17, 1855), pp. 436–40.

———. *Fædrelandet*, February 13, 1856.

———. *Guds Kirke er bygget for Evigheden: Et kirkeligt Vidnesbyrd mod Dr. S. Kierkegaard*. Odense, 1855.

———. "I Anledning af 'Forslaget' til Dr. S. Kierkegaard." *Fædrelandet*, April 24, 1855.

———. "Ikke Navnet, men Sagen!" *Berlingske Tidende*, June 1, 1855.

Bøgh, Erik. *Søren Kierkegaard og St. Sørens-Dyrkelsen*. Copenhagen, 1870.

Boisen, F. E. " 'Dannevirke' og Dr. S. Kierkegaard." *Dannevirke*, April 11, 1855.

Boisen, L. N. "Indlæg i Sagen: S. K. contra 'det bestaaende.' " *Dansk Kirketidende*, no. 20 (May 6, 1855), pp. 313–17.

Brandes, Georg, "Aristokratisk Radicalisme." *Tilskueren*, August 1889, pp. 565–613.

———. *Correspondance de Georg Brandes*. Vols. I–VI. Edited by Paul Krüger. Copenhagen: Rosenkilde og Bagger, 1952–66.

———. *Dualismen i vor nyeste Philosophie*. Copenhagen, 1866.

———. *Friedrich Nietzsche*. Translated by A. G. Chater. London, 1914.

———. *Georg Brandes' Breve til Forældrene: 1859–71*. Vols. I–III. Edited by Morten Borup. Copenhagen: C. A. Reitzel, 1978.

———. *Georg Brandes og Emil Petersen, en Brevveksling*. Edited by Morten Borup. Copenhagen: Lademann, 1980.

———. *Georg og Edvard Brandes: Brevveksling med nordiske Forfattere og Videnskabsmænd*. Vols. I–VIII. Edited by Morten Borup. Copenhagen: Gyldendal, 1939–42.

———. *Henrik Ibsen and Bjørnstjerne Bjørnson*. Translated by Jessie Muir. New York, 1899.

———. *Hovedstrømninger i det nittende Aarhundredes Litteratur*. Vol. I: *Emigrantlitteraturen*. Copenhagen, 1872.

———. *Hovedstrømninger i det nittende Aarhundredes Litteratur*. Vol. II: *Den romantiske Skole i Tydskland*. Copenhagen, 1873.

———. *Levned*. Vols. I–III. Copenhagen: Gyldendal, 1905–8.

———. *Reminiscences of My Childhood and Youth.* Translator unknown. New York: Arno Press, 1906.
———. *Samlede Skrifter.* Vols. I–XVII. Copenhagen: Gyldendal, 1899–1910.
———. *Søren Kierkegaard: En Kritisk Fremstilling i Grundrids.* Copenhagen, 1877.
———. *Sören Kierkegaard: Ein literarisches Charakterbild.* Translated by Adolf Strodtmann. Leipzig, 1879.
Bremer, Fredrika. *Brev.* Vols. I–IV. Edited by Klara Johanson and Ellen Kleman. Stockholm: Norstedt, 1917.
———. *Hertha.* Stockholm, 1856.
———. *Hertha.* Translated by Mary Howitt. New York, 1856.
———. *Homes of the New World: Impressions of America.* Vols. I–II. Translated by Mary Howitt. New York, 1853.
———. *Lif i Norden.* Stockholm, 1849.
———. *Life in the North.* Translated by Mary Howitt for *Sartain's Union Magazine of Literature and Art.* Vol. VI (Philadelphia, January–June 1850), pp. 157ff. and 329ff.
Brøchner, Hans. *Fædrelandet,* December 20, 1856.
———. *Problemet om Tro og Viden, en historisk-kritisk Afhandling.* Copenhagen, 1868.
———. *Om det Religiøse i dets Enhed med det Humane.* Copenhagen, 1869.
"-r" [Hans Brøchner]. "Om Søren Kierkegaards Virksomhed som religiøs Forfatter." *Fædrelandet,* December 1, 1855.
———. *Et Svar til Professor R. Nielsen.* Copenhagen, 1868.
Busse, Carl. "Ein Dichter der Sehnsucht." *Die Wahrheit* (Stuttgart), April 15 and May 1, 1896, pp. 40–53 and 77–84. Edited by Christoph Schrempf.
"C." *Dagbladet,* December 28, 1854.
Claëson, Kristian Theodor. *Skrifter.* Vols. I–II. Stockholm, 1860.
Collett, Camilla. *Amtmandens Døtre.* Christiania, 1855.
Croxall, T. H. *Glimpses and Impressions of Kierkegaard.* London: Welwyn Herts-J. Nisbet, 1959.
"D." *Dagbladet,* February 20, 1855.
"Uk-d." "Dr. S. Kierkegaards Kamp." *Dannevirke,* April 7, 1855.
———. "Grundtvigianerne—S. Kierkegaard: Strøtanker." *Dannevirke,* April 28, 1855.
———. "Kirkespørgsmaalet i Kongeriget." *Dannevirke,* July 20, 1855.
Dallago, Carl. "Augustine, Pascal und Kierkegaard." *Der Brenner,* VI (1921), pp. 641–734. Edited by Ludwig von Ficker.
———. *Der Christ Kierkegaards.* Innsbruck: Brenner-Verlag, 1922.
Delacroix, Henri. "Sören Kierkegaard: le christianisme absolu à travers le paradoxe et le désespoir." *Revue de Métaphysique et de Morale* 8 (1900), pp. 459–84.
Deleuran, Victor. *Esquisse d'une Etude sur Soeren Kierkegaard.* Paris, 1897.
Dietrichson, Lorentz. *Indledning i Studiet af Danmarks Literatur i vort Aarhundrede: Literærhistoriske forelæsninger holdne i Uppsala vaarterminen.* Uppsala, 1860.
Dilthey, Wilhelm. *Archiv für Geschichte der Philosophie,* XII (Berlin, 1899), pp. 358–60. Edited by Wilhelm Dilthey.
Due, Christopher. *Erindringer fra Henrik Ibsens Ungdomsaar.* Copenhagen, 1909.
Ebner, Ferdinand. *Schriften.* Vols. I–III. Munich: Kösel- Verlag, 1963–65.
"f." *Lolland-Falsters Stiftstidende,* February 14, 1855.
Feuerbach, Ludwig. *The Essence of Christianity.* Translated by George Eliot. New York: Harper, 1957.

Ficker, Ludwig von, ed. *Der Brenner.* Vols. I–XVIII. Innsbruck: Brenner-Verlag, 1910–15 and 1919–54.

———. Unpublished Letters to and from Ludwig von Ficker at the *Brenner-Archiv*, University of Innsbruck, under the direction of Walter Methlagl.

Forsyth, P. T. *The Work of Christ.* London: Hodder and Stoughton, 1910.

Fulford, Francis W. *Sören Aabye Kierkegaard: A Study.* Cambridge, 1908.

Garnett, R. *The Saturday Review of Politics, Literature, Science and Art*, vol. 47 (London, February 15, 1879), pp. 219–20.

Goldschmidt, Meïr. *Livs Erindringer og Resultater.* Vols. I–II. Copenhagen, 1877.

Gosse, Edmund. *Two Visits to Denmark.* London, 1911.

Grässe, Johan Georg Theodor. *Geschichte der Poesie Europas und der bedeutendsten aussereuropäischen Länder vom Anfang des 16. Jahrhunderts bis auf die neueste Zeit.* Leipzig, 1848.

Grove, Peter Vilhelm. *Thurah og Søren Kierkegaard. Nogle Bemærkninger af en theologisk Student.* Copenhagen, 1855.

Grundtvig, Nikolai Frederik Severin. "Om en christelig Skilsmisse fra Folke-Kirken." *Dansk Kirketidende*, no. 49 (December 2, 1855), pp. 797–801.

Haecker, Theodor. *Der Buckel Kierkegaards.* Zurich: Thomas, 1947.

———. *Christentum und Kultur.* Munich, 1927.

———. "Der Krieg und die Führer des Geistes." *Brenner-Jahrbuch*, V (1915), pp. 130–87.

———. "Nachwort" to his translation of Kierkegaard's *Der Begriff des Auserwählten*, pp. 334–421. Hellerau: J. Hegner, 1917.

———. *Opuscula: Ein Sammelband* [includes "Über Humor und Satire" (1928), and "Dialog über die Satire" (1930)]. Munich: Kösel-Verlag, 1949.

———. *Satire und Polemik, 1914–1920.* Innsbruck: Brenner- Verlag, 1922.

———. *Søren Kierkegaard.* Translated by Alexander Dru. London: Oxford University Press, 1937.

———. *Sören Kierkegaard und die Philosophie der Innerlichkeit.* Munich: J. F. Schreiber, 1913.

———. "Vorwort" to his translation of Kierkegaard's *Der Pfahl im Fleisch* in *Der Brenner.* Vol. IV (May 15, 1914), pp. 691–712 and pp. 797–814. Edited by Ludwig von Ficker.

Hamilton, Andrew. *Sixteen Months in the Danish Isles.* Vols. I–II. London, 1852.

Hansen, Oskar. *Politiken,* July 3, 1892.

Hansen, P. *Noter til Dr. G. Brandes' "Søren Kierkegaard."* Christiania, 1877.

Hauch, Johannes Carsten. *H. C. Oersteds Leben.* Translated from the Danish by H. Sebald. Spandau, 1853.

Hauer, Karl. "Spiegel sterbender Welten." *Die Fackel*, no. 207 (July 23, 1906), pp. 1–21. Edited by Karl Kraus.

Heegaard, Sophus. *Om Intolerance.* Copenhagen: Gyldendal, 1878.

———. *Prof. Rasmus Nielsens Lære om Tro og Viden.* Copenhagen, 1867.

Heiberg, P. A. *Bidrag til et Psykologisk Billede af Søren Kierkegaard i Barndom og Ungdom.* Copenhagen, 1895.

Helveg, Fr. "Søren Kierkegaard og Nutiden." *Nordisk Månedskrift for folkelig og Kristelig Oplysning*, II (1877), pp. 293–94.

Helweg, Hans Frederik. "Dr. S. Kierkegaards og Bibelens Beskrivelse af den Christne Tro." *Dansk Kirketidende*, no. 29 (July 1, 1855), pp. 457–72.

———. "Hegelianismen i Danmark." *Dansk Kirketidende*, no. 51 (December 16, 1855), pp. 827–33.
———. "Et Ord om Thurahs Riimbrev." *Dagbladet*, October 26, 1855.
Herrig, Hans. *Magazin für die Literatur des Auslandes*. Vol. 48 (1879), pp. 105–8.
Heuch, Johan Christian. *Dr. G. Brandes' Polemik mod Kristendommen*. Christiania, 1877.
———. *Luthersk Ugeskrift*, no. 5 (Christiania, February 8, 1877), pp. 103–12.
———. "Sören Aaby Kierkegaard." *Zeitschrift für die gesammte lutherische Theologie und Kirche*, 25th year (Leipzig, 1864), pp. 295–309.
Hoch, Jules. "Sören Kierkegaard." *Grande Revue* 23 (September 1902), pp. 603–22.
Høffding, Harald. *A Brief History of Modern Philosophy*. Translated by Charles Finley Sanders. New York, 1912.
———. "Demokratisk radicalisme." *Tilskueren*, November–December 1889, pp. 849–72.
———. "Un discendente di Amleto, Søren Kierkegaard." *Leonardo, Rivista d'idee* 4, nos. 2–3 (Firenze, April–June 1906), pp. 65–79.
———. *Erindringer*. Copenhagen: Gyldendal, 1928.
———. *A History of Modern Philosophy. A Sketch of the History of Philosophy from the Close of the Renaissance to Our Own Day*. Vols. I–II. 1st English ed. Translated from the German edition by B. E. Meyer. London and New York: Macmillan & Co., 1900.
———. *Mindre Arbejder*. Vols. I–III. Copenhagen: Nordisk Forlag, 1899–1913.
———. "A Philosophical Confession." *The Journal of Philosophy, Psychology, and Scientific Methods* 2 (February 16, 1905), pp. 85–92.
———. "Die Philosophie in Dänemark im 19. Jahrhundert." *Archiv für Geschichte der Philosophie*, II (Berlin, 1889), pp. 49–74. Edited by Wilhelm Dilthey and Ludwig Stein.
———. *Søren Kierkegaard som Filosof*. Copenhagen, 1892.
———. "En Tysk Kierkegaardianer Christoph Schrempf." *Tilskueren* 38, no. II (July–December, 1921), pp. 73–80.
Hoffmann, Raoul. *Kierkegaard et la Certitude Religieuse. Esquisse Biographique et Critique*. Geneva, 1907?
Hofmannsthal, Hugo von. *Gesammelte Werke*. Vols. I–XV. Edited by Herbert Steiner. Frankfurt: S. Fischer-Verlag, 1945.
Horn, Frederik Winkel. *Geschichte der Literatur des skandinavischen Nordens*. Leipzig, 1880.
———. *Literature of the Scandinavian North*. Translated by Rasmus B. Anderson. Chicago, 1884.
Howitt, Mary Botham. *An Autobiography*. Vols. I–II. Edited by Margaret Howitt. Boston and New York, 1889.
Howitt, William and Mary. *The Literature and Romance of Northern Europe: Constituting a Complete History of the Literature of Sweden, Denmark, Norway and Iceland, with Copious Specimens of the Most Celebrated Histories, Romances, Popular Legends and Tales, Old Chivalrous Ballads, Tragic and Comic Dramas, National and Favourite Songs, Novels, and Scenes from the Life of the Present Day*. Vols. I–II. London, 1852.
Hügel, Baron Friedrich von. *The Mystical Element of Religion as Studied in St. Catherine of Genoa and Her Friends*. Vols. I–II. London, 1909.
Ibsen, Henrik. *Brand*. Translated by Michael Meyer. New York: R. Hart-Davis, 1960.
———. *Letters of Henrik Ibsen*. Translated by J. N. Laurvik and M. Morison. New York: Duffield and Company, 1908.
———. *Love's Comedy*. Translated by C. H. Herford. Chicago, 1900.

———. *Peer Gynt*. Translated by Michael Meyer. Garden City, N.Y.: Doubleday, 1963.
———. *When We Dead Awaken*. Translated by Michael Meyer. London: R. Hart-Davis, 1960.
Jacobsen, Jens Peter. *Breve fra J. P. Jacobsen*. 2d ed. Edited by Edvard Brandes. Copenhagen, 1899.
———. *Digte og Udkast*. Edited by Edvard Brandes and Vilhelm Møller. Copenhagen, 1886.
———. *Marie Grubbe, A Lady of the Seventeenth Century*. 2d English ed. Translated by Hanna Astrup Larsen. Boston: Scandinavian Classics, 1975.
———. *Niels Lyhne*. Translated by Hanna Astrup Larsen. New York: American-Scandinavian Foundation, 1919.
———. *Samlede Værker*. 1st ed. Vols. I-V. Edited by Morton Borup. Copenhagen: Gyldendal, 1924-29.
———. *Samlede Værker: Romaner, Noveller, Digte, Breve*. Vols. 5 and 6: *Breve: 1863-1885*. Edited by Frederik Nielsen. Copenhagen: Rosenkilde og Bagger, 1973-74.
Jaeger, Henrik. *Henrik Ibsen, 1828-1888, A Critical Biography*. Translated by William Morton Payne. Chicago, 1890.
James, William. *The Letters of William James*. Vols. I-II. Edited by Henry James. Boston: Atlantic Monthly Press, 1920.
Jeannine, B. "Sören Kierkegaard, le moraliste danois." *La Nouvelle Revue*, LXXXV, 15th year (1893), pp. 578-96.
Jensen, Christian. *Søren Kierkegaards religiøse Udvikling*. Copenhagen, 1898.
Jörg, Joseph Edmund. "Dr. Kierkegaard und seine Kritik des protestantischen Kirchenthums." In *Geschichte der Protestantismus in seiner neuesten Entwicklung*. Vol. 2: *Die Schwärmerkirche und ihre Bedingungen*, pp. 336-50. Freiburg, 1858.
———. "Streiflichter auf die neueste Geschichte des Protestantismus: Die religiöse Bewegungen in den scandinavischen Ländern." *Historisch-politische Blätter für das Katholische Deutschland* 38 (Munich, 1856), pp. 1-30.
Johansen, Steen, ed. *Erindringer om Søren Kierkegaard*. Copenhagen: C. A. Reitzel, 1980.
Joyce, James. *Finnegans Wake*. New York: Viking Penguin, 1982.
———. "Ibsen's New Drama." *Fortnightly Review*, LXVII (London, April 1900), pp. 575-90.
Kafka, Franz. *Letters to Friends, Family, and Editors*. 2d English ed. Translated by Richard and Clara Winston. New York: Schoken Books, 1977.
———. *Parables and Paradoxes*. Edited by Nahum N. Glatzer. Translated by Clement Greenberger. New York: Schocken Books, 1958.
———. *Tagebücher: 1910-1923*. Edited by Max Brod. New York: Fischer Taschenbuch Verlag, 1948.
Kassner, Rudolf. *Der goldene Drachen: Gleichnis und Essay*. Zurich and Stuttgart: E. Rentsch, 1957.
———. *Sämtliche Werke*. Vols. I-X. Edited by Ernst Zinn and Klaus E. Bohenkamp. Pfullingen: Neske, 1969-91.
———. "Sören Kierkegaard—Aphorismen." *Die neue Rundschau* 17, I-II (Berlin, 1906), pp. 513-43.
Keppler, P. *Literarische Rundschau* 5 (1879), pp. 184-86.
Koch, Carl. *Dansk Kirketidende*, December 18, 1898, pp. 820-23.
———. *Søren Kierkegaard, Tre Foredrag*. Copenhagen, 1898.

Koch, L. *Den Danske Kirkes Historie i det nittende Aarhundrede.* Vols. I-II. Copenhagen, 1883.
Koch, P. C. *Dannevirke,* April 12, 1855.
———. *Dannevirke,* July 12, 1855.
Kofoed-Hansen, H. P. *Dr. S. Kierkegaard mod Dr. H. Martensen.* Copenhagen, 1856.
———. *S. Kierkegaard mod det bestaaende.* Copenhagen, 1857.
Kraus, Karl, ed. *Die Fackel,* no. 212 (November 23, 1906), p. 14; no. 387 (November 17, 1913), p. 17; no. 395 (March 28, 1914), pp. 19-21; no. 418 (April 8, 1916), p. 1.
Kroman, K. "Hans Brøchner." In *Dansk Biografisk Lexicon.* 1st ed. Vol. III, pp. 202-6. Copenhagen: Gyldendal, 1889.
"L." "En Karrikaturtegning af Dr. S. Kierkegaard." *Berlingske Tidende,* December 22, 1854.
J. L. *Flyveposten,* December 27, 1854.
"En Lægmand." "Kan Dr. phil. Søren Kierkegaards Angreb paa Biskop Mynsters Eftermæle kaldes 'en god gjerning'?" *Lolland-Falsters Stiftstidende,* January 25, 1855.
"En Lægmand." "Et Ord i den Kierkegaardske Sag." *Flyveposten,* April 16, 1855.
Lange, Thomas. *Riimbrev til 'defensor fidei' alias stud. theol. Thurah.* Copenhagen, 1855.
Lindenberg, H. *Theologische Literaturzeitung* 3, no. 8 (Leipzig, 1878), pp. 186-87.
———. *Theologische Literaturzeitung* 5, no. 24 (Leipzig, 1880), pp. 594-95.
Listov, Andreas. *Morten Luther, opfattet af Søren Kierkegaard. Et historisk Lejlighedsskrift.* Copenhagen, 1883.
Lukács, Georg. "Mon Chemain vers Marx." *Nouvelles Etudes hongroises* 8 (Budapest, 1973), pp. 77-92.
———. *Die Seele und die Formen.* Berlin, 1911.
———. *Soul and Form.* Translated by Anna Bostock. Cambridge, Massachusetts: MIT Press, 1974.
Lund, Henriette. *Erindringer fra Hjemmet.* Copenhagen, 1880.
Lund, Henrik. "Min Protest: Hvad jeg har sagt og ikke sagt." *Fædrelandet,* November 22, 1855.
———. "I næste Øjeblik—hvad saa? En Opbyggelig Tale—Samtiden anbefalet til Overveielse." *Fædrelandet,* November 26, 1855.
Lysander, Albert Theodor. "Søren Kierkegaard, Litterärhistorisk teckning." *Tidskrift för Litteratur,* no. 10 (Uppsala, 1851), pp. 227-52.
Mackintosh, H. R. "A Great Danish Thinker." *The Expository Times,* XIII (Edinburgh, 1902), p. 404.
———. *Types of Modern Theology.* London: Nesbit, 1937.
Martensen, Hans Lassen. *Af Mit Levned.* Vols. I-III. Copenhagen, 1882-83.
———. "I Anledning af Dr. S. Kierkegaards Artikel i 'Fædrelandet' nr. 295." *Berlingske Tidende,* December 28, 1854.
———. *Aus meinem Leben.* Vols. I-III. Translated by Alexander Michelsen. Leipzig, 1883-84.
———. *Breve.* Vols. I-III. Edited by Bjørn Kornerup. Copenhagen: G. E. C. Gad, 1955.
———. *Den Christelige Dogmatik.* Copenhagen, 1849.
———. *Den Christelige Ethik.* Vols. I-III. Copenhagen, 1871-78.
———. *Christian Dogmatics. A Compendium of the Doctrines of Christianity.* Translated from the German edition by William Urwick. Edinburgh, 1866.
———. *Om Tro og Viden, et Lejlighedsskrift.* Copenhagen, 1867.
Møller, Christen. *Sædmanden,* 50 (Copenhagen, December 12, 1880), pp. 794-800.

Møller, Poul Martin. *Efterladte Skrifter.* 3d ed. Vols. I–VI. Copenhagen, 1855–56.
Monrad, O. P. *Sören Kierkegaard: Sein Leben und seine Werke.* Jena, 1909.
Mumbauer, Johannes. "Die neuen Tertulliane (Sören Kierkegaard und Theodor Haecker)." *Literarischer Handweiser,* 58, no. 12 (December 1922), pp. 545–50.
———. "Sören Kierkegaard." *Hochland,* X (1913), pp. 184–94.
Muret, Maurice. "Un Précurseur d'Henrik Ibsen; Soeren Kierkegaard." *La Revue de Paris* (July–August 1901), pp. 98–122.
Mynster, F. L., and G. Schepelein. *Biskop Otto Laubs Levnet.* Part I: 1855–82. Copenhagen, 1886.
"-d-n." *Dannevirke,* October 22, 1855.
"N-n." "Forslag til Hr. Dr. S. Kierkegaard." *Fædrelandet,* April 3, 1855.
Niedermeyer, Gerhard. *Sören Kierkegaard und die Romantik.* Leipzig, 1909.
Nielsen, Rasmus. *Evangelietroen og den moderne Bevidsthed.* Copenhagen, 1849.
———. "En god Gjerning." *Fædrelandet,* January 10, 1855.
———. *Om "Den gode Villie" som Magt i Videnskaben.* Copenhagen, 1867.
———. *Grundideernes Logik.* Vols. I–II. Copenhagen, 1864 and 1866.
———. *Om Hindringer og Betingelser for det aandelige Liv i Nutiden.* Copenhagen, 1868.
———. "Til Høivelbaarne Høiærværdige Biskop Martensen: Et Spørgsmaal." *Fædrelandet,* January 16, 1855.
———. *Hr. Prof. Brøchners filosofiske Kritik gjennemset.* Copenhagen, 1868.
———. "Ide og Virkelighed." *For Ide og Virkelighed* (Copenhagen, 1869), pp. 1–39. Edited by R. Nielsen, B. Bjørnson, and R. Schmidt.
———. "Karakter og Villie." In *For Ide og Virkelighed,* edited by R. Nielsen, B. Bjørnson, and R. Schmidt, pp. 489–517. Copenhagen, 1872.
———. *Paa Kierkegaardske "Stadier": Et Livsbillede.* Copenhagen, 1860.
———. *Mag. S. Kierkegaards "Johannes Climacus" og Dr. H. Martensens "Christelige Dogmatik", en undersøgende Anmeldelse.* Copenhagen, 1849.
———. *Philosophiske Propædeutik i Grundtræk.* Copenhagen, 1857.
———. *Religionsphilosophie.* Copenhagen, 1869.
———. "Om S. Kierkegaards 'Mentale Tilstand.'" *Nordisk Universitets-Tidsskrift,* IV (Copenhagen, 1858), pp. 1–29.
Nietzsche, Friedrich. *Ecce Homo: How One Becomes What One Is.* Translated by R. J. Hollingdale. London and New York: Penguin, 1979.
———. *Nietzsche: A Self-Portrait from His Letters.* Edited by Peter Fuss and Henry Shapiro. Cambridge, Massachusetts: Harvard University Press, 1971.
Nordau, Max. *Degeneration.* Translator unknown. New York, 1895.
Ørsted, Hans Christian. *Aanden i Naturen.* Vols. I–II. Copenhagen, 1850.
———. *Breve fra og til Hans Christian Ørsted.* Edited by Mathilde Ørsted. Copenhagen, 1870.
———. *The Soul in Nature, with Supplementary Contributions.* Translated from the German edition by Leonora and Joanna B. Horner. London, 1852.
Ørum, Jacob Christian Martin. "Forespørgsel til Pastor J. Paludan-Müller i Aalborg." *Dansk Kirketidende,* nos. 7–8 (February 25, 1855), pp. 142–44.
———. *Om Forholdet imellem Søren Kierkegaard og Luther: Iagttagelser af en Lægmand.* Copenhagen, 1858.
———. *Sandhedsvidnestriden.* Copenhagen, 1856.

———. "Om S. Kierkegaards 'Øjeblikke.' " *Dansk Kirketidende,* no. 45 (November 4, 1855), pp. 742–44.
"2pp." "Nr. 120 af 'Fædrelandet' 1855." *Kjøbenhavnsposten,* May 30, 1855.
Paludan-Müller, Caspar. *Berlingske Tidende,* December 30, 1854.
Paludan-Müller, Jens. Dr. *Søren Kierkegaards Angreb paa Biskop Mynsters Eftermæle.* Copenhagen, 1855.
———. "Dr. Søren Kierkegaards Indøvelse i Christendom." *Nyt Theologisk Tidsskrift* 6 (1855), pp. 318–405.
Pape, W. "S. Aa. Kierkegaard: Skizze seines Lebens und Wirkens." *Der Beweis des Glaubens,* 14 (Gütersloh, 1878), pp. 169–89.
Petersen, Fredrik Christian. *Luthersk Kirketidende.* New series II (Christiania, January 15, 1870), pp. 56–57.
———. *Morgenbladet,* January 23, 30; February 6, 13, 27; and March 6, 1870.
———. Dr. *Søren Kierkegaards Christendomsforkyndelse.* Vols. I–III. Christiania, 1877.
Pineau, Léon. Reviews of the 2d Danish ed. of Kierkegaard's *Papirer* in *Revue Critique d'Histoire et de Littérature,* 44, vol. 69, no. 6 (Paris, 1910), pp. 116–17; 45, vol. 71, no. 17 (1911), p. 337; 45, vol. 72, no. 52 (1911), pp. 514–15; and 47, vol. 76, no. 42 (1913), pp. 319–20.
Preus, Caroline Dorothea Margrethe (Keyser). *Linka's Diary: On Land and Sea, 1845–1864.* Edited and translated by Johan Carl Keyser Preus and his wife Diderikke Margrethe, née Brandt. Minneapolis: Augsburg Publishing House, 1952.
Prozor, M. "Un drame d'Henrik Ibsen, 'Brand', drame philosophique." *Revue des deux Mondes,* 4th period, 126 (Paris, 1894), pp. 129–61.
Quehl, Ryno. *Aus Dänemark.* Berlin, 1856.
Rilke, Rainer Maria. *Briefe an Axel Juncker.* Edited by Renate Scharffenberg. Frankfurt: Insel-Verlag, 1979.
———. *Letters of Rainer Maria Rilke.* Vols. I–II: 1892–1926. Translated by Jane Bannard Greene and M. D. Herter Norton. New York: W. W. Norton, 1945–48.
———. *Selected Letters of Rainer Maria Rilke, 1902–1926.* Translated by R. F. C. Hull. London: Macmillan & Co., 1946.
Robertson, J. G. "Sören Kierkegaard." *Modern Language Review,* IX, no. 4 (October 1914), pp. 500–513.
Rølvaag, Ole Edvart. *Amerika-Breve fra P. A. Smevik til hans far og bror i Norge.* Minneapolis: Augsburg Pub., 1912.
———. *Giants in the Earth.* Translated by Lincoln Colcord. New York: Harper, 1929.
———. *The Third Life of Per Smevik.* Translated by Ella Valborg Tweet and Solveig Zempel. Minneapolis: Dillon Press, 1971.
Rosenberg, P. A. *Søren Kierkegaard: Hans Liv, Hans Personlighed og Hans Forfatterskab. En Vejledning til Studiet af Hans Værker.* Copenhagen, 1898.
Rudin, Waldemar. *Sören Kierkegaards Person och Författarskap, ett Försök.* Stockholm, 1880.
"A. S." *Fædrelandet,* July 30, 1880.
Scharling, C. E. *Nyt Theologisk Tidsskrift,* 8 (Copenhagen, 1857), pp. 203–4.
Scharling, Henrik. "Søren Kierkegaard og Grundtvig." *Dansk Tidsskrift for Kirke- og Folkeliv, Literatur og Kunst,* I (Copenhagen, 1870), pp. 3–28.

Schiødte, A. F. *Om de dialektiske Grundbegreber hos Søren Kierkegaard*. Copenhagen, 1874.
Schrempf, Christoph. "Der Antichrist (Fr. Nietzsche)." *Die Wahrheit*, April 1, 1895, pp. 18–31. Edited by Christoph Schrempf.
———. *Gesammelte Werke*. Vols. 1–16. Edited by Otto Engel. Stuttgart: F. Fromann, 1930–40.
———. "Mein Skeptizismus." *Die Wahrheit*, July 15 and August 1, 1895, pp. 207–15 and 234–39. Edited by Christoph Schrempf.
———. "What We Want, A Confession, No Programme." An Address delivered by Professor Christof [sic] Schrempf of Stuttgart and reprinted from the General Report of the Fifth Universal Congress for Free Christianity and Religious Progress, pp. 3–13. Berlin, 1910.
Sibbern, Frederik Christian. *Breve til og fra F. C. Sibbern*. Vols. I–II. Edited by C. L. N. Mynster. Copenhagen, 1866.
———. *Meddelelser af Indholdet af et Skrift fra Aaret 2135*. Vols. I–III. Copenhagen, 1858–72.
———. *Speculativ Kosmologie med Grundlag til en Speculativ Theologie*. Copenhagen, 1846.
Starcke, C. N. *Politiken*, May 2, 1899.
Stilling, P. M. *Om den indbildte Forsoning mellem Tro og Viden med særligt Hensyn til Martensens "Christelige Dogmatik."* Copenhagen, 1850.
Stobart, Mabel Annie. "The 'Either-Or' of Sören Kirkegaard [sic]." *The Fortnightly Review*, LXXI (London, January–June, 1902), pp. 53–60.
———. "New Lights on Ibsen's 'Brand.'" *The Fortnightly Review*, LXVI (August 1899), pp. 227–39.
Strindberg, August. *Brev*. Vols. I–XV: *Brev, 1858–1907*. Edited by Torsten Eklund. Stockholm: A. Bonnier, 1948–76.
———. *Inferno*. Translated by Claud Field. New York: G. P. Putnam's Sons, 1913.
———. *Jäsningstriden: En Själs Utvecklingshistoria*. Stockholm, 1886.
———. *Samlade Skrifter*. Vols. 1–55. Edited by Albert Bonnier's publishing house. Stockholm: A. Bonnier, 1912–20.
Strodtmann, Adolf. *Das geistige Leben in Dänemark. Streifzüge auf den Gebieten der Kunst, Literatur, Politik und Journalistik des skandinavischen Nordens*. Berlin, 1873.
Swenson, David F. "The Anti-Intellectualism of Kierkegaard." *Philosophical Review*, XXV (July 1916), pp. 567–86.
Teisen, Niels. *Kort Indlæg i Sagen mellem S. Kierkegaard og H. L. Martensen: Et Lejlighedsskrift*. Copenhagen, 1884.
———. *Om Søren Kierkegaards betydning som Kristelig Tænker*. Copenhagen, 1903.
———. *Til Overvejelse, Anledning af Prof. Høffdings Bog om S. Kierkegaard*. Odense, 1893.
Thoresen, Magdalene, *Breve fra Magdalene Thoresen: 1855–1901*. Edited by Jul. Clausen and P. Fr. Rist. Copenhagen: Gyldendal Nordisk Forlag, 1919.
Thurah, Christian Henrik. *Hvorfor netop saaledes? Præmisserne i Sagen C. H. Thurah contra Dr. S. Kierkegaard*. Copenhagen, 1855.
———. *Mester Jakel. En Dyrehavs-Scene, gjengivet efter Virkeligheden*. Odense, 1855.
———. *Riimbrev til Johannes Forføreren alias Dr. Søren Kierkegaard*. Copenhagen, 1855.

Tönnies, Ferdinand. "Nationalgefühl." *Die Wahrheit,* November 1, 1895, pp. 65-72. Edited by Christoph Schrempf.
Troeltsch, Ernst. *Gesammelte Schriften.* Vols. I-IV. Tübingen: J. C. B. Mohr, 1912-25.
———. *Theologischer Jahresbericht,* vol. XVI (Leipzig, 1896-97), pp. 539-40.
———. *Theologischer Jahresbericht,* vol. XVIII (Leipzig, 1898-99), pp. 532-34.
Unamuno, Miguel de. *Perplexities and Paradoxes.* Translated by Stuart Gross. New York: Philosophical Library, 1945.
———. *The Tragic Sense of Life in Men and Peoples.* 1st English ed. Translated by J. E. Crawford Flitch. London: Macmillan & Co., 1921.
Vodskov, Hans Sophus. "En Krise i Søren Kierkegaards Liv." In *Spredte Studier,* pp. 1-30. Copenhagen, 1884.
Weber, Max. *The Protestant Ethic and the Spirit of Capitalism.* Translated by Talcott Parsons. New York: Scribner, 1958.
———. "Die sozialen Gründe des Untergangs der antiken Kultur." *Die Wahrheit,* May 1, 1896, pp. 57-77. Edited by Christoph Schrempf.
Werner, August. *Theologischer Jahresbericht,* vol. VI (Leipzig, 1887), p. 240.
Wetzel, Paul. *Theologische Literaturzeitung,* no. 12 (Leipzig, 1886), pp. 279-82.
———. *Theologische Literaturzeitung,* no. 1 (Leipzig, 1887), pp. 9-10.
Widmann, J. V. "Sören Kierkegaards Verlöbnisbruch." *Neue Freie Presse* 14 (Vienna, 1904), p. 580.
Wittgenstein, Ludwig. "Letters to Ludwig von Ficker." Translated by Bruce Gillette and edited by Allan Janik. In C. G. Luckhardt, ed., *Wittgenstein: Sources and Perspectives,* pp. 82-98. Ithaca, N.Y.: Cornell University Press, 1979.
"X." *Fædrelandet,* January 18, 1855.
———. "Om Sandhedsvidnestriden." *Lolland-Falsters Stiftstidende,* January 1, 1855.
"xy." "Protest med Mere til C. H. Thurah." *Christianiaposten,* March 20, 1856.
Zahle, Peter Christian. *Til Erindring om Johan Georg Hamann og Søren Aabye Kierkegaard.* Copenhagen, 1856.
Zeuthen, F. L. B. *Et Par Aar af mit Liv.* Copenhagen, 1869.
———. *Polemiske Blade imod Dr. Søren Kierkegaard,* I-III. Copenhagen, 1855.

Secondary Sources

Aall, Anathon. *Filosofien i Norden: Til Oplysning om den Nyere Tænknings og Videnskaps Historie i Sverige og Finland, Danmark og Norge.* Christiania: J. Dybwad, 1919.
Aarnes, Sigurd Aa. *Søkelys på Amtmandens Døtre.* Oslo: Universitetsforlag, 1977.
Ahlenius, Holger. "Sören Kierkegaard, en dansk och en svensk diskussion." *Vår Lösen* 20 (Stockholm, 1929), pp. 82-87.
Allgemeine Deutsche Biographie, vols. 1-56. Published by the Historische Kommission bei der Königl. Akademie der Wissenschaften. Berlin and Leipzig: Duncker & Humblot, 1875ff.
Andersen, Arlow W. *The Norwegian-Americans.* Boston: Twayne Publishers, 1975.
Andersen, J. Oskar. *Survey of the History of the Church in Denmark.* Copenhagen: O. Lohse, 1930.
Andersen, Vilhelm. *Tider og Typer, af Dansk Aands Historie.* Vol. II: *Goethe.* Copenhagen: Gyldendal, 1916.
Anonymous. "Theodor Haeckers Schaffen im Innsbrucker 'Brenner' Kreis." *Tiroler Tageszeitung,* April 6, 1965.

Antoni, Carlo. *From History to Sociology: The Transition in German Historical Thinking.* Translated by Hayden V. White. Westport, Connecticut: Greenwood, 1977.

Anz, Heinrich, Poul Lübcke, and Friedrich Schmöe, eds. *Die Rezeption Søren Kierkegaards in der deutschen und dänischen Philosophie und Theologie* in *Text und Kontext*, 15, special series. Copenhagen and Munich, 1983.

Arildsen, Skat. *Biskop Hans Lassen Martensen, Hans Liv, Udvikling og Arbejde.* Copenhagen: G. E. C. Gad, 1932.

———. "Protesten ved Søren Kierkegaards Begravelse." In *Kierkegaardiana,* vol. VIII, pp. 80–102. Copenhagen, 1971. Edited by Niels Thulstrup.

Aschheim, Steven E. *The Nietzsche Legacy in Germany: 1890–1990.* Berkeley: University of California Press, 1992.

Asmussen, Eduard. *Entwicklungsgang und Grundprobleme der Philosophie Rasmus Nielsens.* Flensburg: Laban & Larsen, 1911.

Barth, Karl. *Protestant Theology in the Nineteenth Century: Its Background and History.* Translated by Brian Cozens and John Bowden. Valley Forge, Pennsylvania: Judson Press, 1973.

Becker, Werner. "Der Überschritt von Kierkegaard zu Newman in der Lebensentscheidung Theodor Haeckers." *Newman-Studien* 1 (Nürnberg-Bamberg-Passau, 1948), pp. 251–70.

Bergsøe, Clara, *Camilla Collett, et livsbillede.* Copenhagen, 1902.

———. *Magdalene Thoresen, Portrætstudie.* Copenhagen, 1904.

Berlin, Isaiah. *The Magus of the North: J. G. Hamann and the Origins of Modern Irrationalism.* Edited by Henry Hardy. New York: Farrar, Strauss and Giroux, 1993.

Betz, Werner. "Andersen und Kierkegaard." In *Festschrift für Walter Baetke.* Edited by Kurt Rudolf et al. Weimar: Böhlau, 1966.

Beyer, Harald. *A History of Norwegian Literature.* Translated by Einar Haugen. New York: New York University Press for the American-Scandinavian Foundation, 1956.

———. *Søren Kierkegaard og Norge.* Christiania: H. Ascheoug, 1924.

———. "Søren Kierkegaard og Svensk Litteratur." *Kirke og Kultur* 56, no. 8 (Oslo, October 1951), pp. 500–504.

———. "Søren Kierkegaards betydning for Norsk Aandsliv." *EDDA: Nordisk Tidsskrift for Litteraturforskning,* vol. XIX, tenth year, copy 1 (Christiania, 1923), pp. 1–208. Edited by Gerhard Gran and Francis Bull.

Billeskov Jansen, F. J. " 'Aanden i Naturen': H. C. Ørsteds naturmetafysiske system." In *Oversigt over det Kongelige Danske Videnskabernes Selskabs Virksomhed,* pp. 127–37. Copenhagen, 1970–71.

———. "L'Héritage de Kierkegaard dans les Pays nordiques." *Cahiers du Sud* 50, no. 371 (Marseilles, April–May, 1963), pp. 18–27.

Bjarnason, Loftur L. "Categories of Søren Kierkegaard's Thought in the Life and Writings of August Strindberg." Unpublished doctoral dissertation at Stanford University, 1951.

Blessing, Eugen. *Theodor Haecker: Gestalt und Werk.* Nürnberg: Glock und Lutz, 1959.

Blüher, Hans. "Niels Lyhne von J. P. Jacobsen und das Problem der Bisexualität." In *Omkring Niels Lyhne,* edited by Niels Barfoed, pp. 205–12. Copenhagen: Hans Reitzel, 1970.

Brandell, Gunnar. *Strindberg in Inferno.* Translated by Barry Jacobs. Cambridge, Massachusetts: Harvard University Press, 1974.

Brandl, Horst. "Skandinavische Aspekte der Nietzsche-Rezeption." In *Nietzsche-Studien: Internationales Jahrbuch für die Nietzsche Forschung,* vol. 12, edited by Ernst Behler,

Mazzino Montinari, Wolfgang Müller-Lauter, and Heinz Wenzel, pp. 387-418. Berlin and New York, 1983.

Brandt, Frithiof. "Søren Kierkegaard: Hans tre hoved-optagelser—Hvorfor er han saa verdensberømt?" *Politiken,* November 10, 1955.

———. *Den Unge Søren Kierkegaard.* Copenhagen: Levin & Munksgaard, 1929.

Brandt, Frithiof, and Else Rammel, *Søren Kierkegaard og Pengene.* Copenhagen: Levin & Munksgaard, 1935.

Braun, Robert. "Der österreichische Kierkegaard." *Die Literarische Tat,* June 25, 1965.

Brecht, Franz Josef. "Die Kierkegaardforschung in letzten Jahrfünft." In *Literarische Berichte aus dem Geiste der Philosophie,* pp. 5-35. Erfurt, 1931.

Bredsdorff, Elias. *Hans Christian Andersen: The Story of His Life and Work, 1805-1875.* New York: Scribner, 1975.

———. "H. C. Andersen og Søren Kierkegaard." *Anderseniana,* 3rd series, volume III, 4 (Odense, 1981), pp. 229-54.

Brinkschmidt, Egon. *Sören Kierkegaard und Karl Barth.* Neukirchen-Vluyn: Neukirchener Verlag, 1971.

Brod, Max. *Franz Kafka, eine Biographie. Erinnerungen und Dokumente.* Prague: Heinr. Mercy Sohn, 1937.

———. *Franz Kafkas Glauben und Lehre (Kafka und Tolstoi).* Munich: K. Desch, 1948.

Brun, Jean. "Feuerbach et Kierkegaard." *Cahiers du Sud* 50, number 371 (Marseilles, April-May 1963), pp. 34-43.

Brun, Lyder. "Professor Fredrik Petersen." in *Norsk Teologisk Tidsskrift* 10, 4th series (Oslo, 1939), pp. 65-70.

Caputo, John D. "Kierkegaard, Heidegger, and the Foundering of Metaphysics." In *International Kierkegaard Commentary, Fear and Trembling and Repetition,* pp. 201-24. Edited by Robert L. Perkins. Macon, Ga.: Mercer University Press, 1994.

Castagnino, Franca. *Gli Studi Italiani su Kierkegaard, 1906-1966.* Rome: Edizioni dell' Ateneo, 1972.

Cattaui, Georges. "Bergson, Kierkegaard, and Mysticism." Translated by Alexander Dru in *The Dublin Review.*, vol. 192, 97th year, no. 384 (London, 1933), pp. 70-78.

Christensen, Erik M. "Guldalderen som idéhistorisk periode: H. C. Ørsteds optimistiske dualisme." In *Guldalder Studier: Festskrift til Gustav Albeck.* Edited by Henning Høirup, pp. 11-45. Aarhus: Universitetsforlag, 1966.

Christensen, Villads. *Peripatetikeren Søren Kierkegaard.* Copenhagen: Graabrodre Torvs Forlag, 1965.

Christiani, Dounia Bunis. *Scandinavian Elements in Finnegans Wake.* Evanston: Northwestern University Press, 1965.

Christiansen, C. "H. C. Ørsted som Naturfilosof." *Oversigt over det Kongelige Danske Videnskabernes Selskabs Forhandlinger,* no. 4 (Copenhagen, 1903), pp. 473-93.

Collins, James. *The Mind of Kierkegaard.* Chicago: H. Regnery, 1953.

Crites, Stephen. "The Author and the Authorship: Recent Kierkegaard Literature." *Journal of the American Academy of Religion* 38, no. 1 (March 1970), pp. 37-54.

Crouter, Richard E. "Kierkegaard's Not-So-Hidden Debt to Schleiermacher." *Journal of the History of Modern Theology* 1 (1994), pp. 205-25.

Dansk Biografisk Lexicon. 1st ed., volumes I-XIX. Edited by C. F. Bricka. Copenhagen, 1887-1905.

———. 2d ed., volumes 1-27. Edited by Poul Engelstoft. Copenhagen: J. H. Schultz, 1933-44.

Dewey, Bradley R. "Søren Kierkegaard's Diary of the Seducer: A History of Its Use and Abuse in International Print." *Fund og Forskning i Det Kongelige Biblioteks Samlinger* 20 (Copenhagen, 1973), pp. 137-57.

Downs, Brian. *Ibsen: The Intellectual Background.* London: At the University Press, 1946.

———. *A Study of Six Plays by Ibsen.* Cambridge: Cambridge University Press, 1950.

Drachmann, A. B. "Brandes og Søren Kierkegaard." *Tilskueren,* no. 2 (1912), pp. 148-53.

———. "Søren Kierkegaards Papirer, I." *Tilskueren,* no. 1 (January-June 1910), pp. 141-60.

Dru, Alexander. "On Haecker's 'Metaphysik des Gefühls.'" *The Downside Review* 68 (Exeter, 1950), pp. 35-45.

———. "Haecker's Point of View: Notes on the History of Existentialism." *The Downside Review* 67 (Exeter, 1949), pp. 260-75.

———. "Introduction" to his translation of Haecker's *Journal in the Night* (London: Harvill Press, 1951), pp. xi-xlvi.

Dunicliff, Joy. *Mary Howitt: Another Lost Victorian Writer.* London: Excalibur Press, 1992.

Dupré, Louis. *A Dubious Heritage: Studies in the Philosophy of Religion after Kant.* New York: Paulist Press, 1977.

———. *Kierkegaard as Theologian: The Dialectic of Christian Existence.* New York: Sheed and Ward, 1963.

Durand, Frédéric. "Jens Peter Jacobsen et la France." *Orbis Litterarum* 22 (1967), pp. 272-82.

———. *Jens Peter Jacobsen ou la Gravitation d'une Solitude.* Paris: Faculté des lettres et sciences humaines de l'Université, 1968.

———. "Les Rapports de Georg Brandes et de J. P. Jacobsen." *Etudes Germaniques* (Paris), April-September 1953, pp. 106-17.

Edward, Brian F. M. "Kafka and Kierkegaard: A Reassessment." *German Life and Letters* 20 (1967), pp. 218-25.

Eitrem, H. *Ibsen og Grimstad.* Oslo: H. Aschehoug, 1940.

Elrod, John W. *Kierkegaard and Christendom.* Princeton: Princeton University Press, 1981.

Emmanuel, Steven M. *Kierkegaard and the Concept of Revelation.* Albany: State University of New York Press, 1996.

Engel, Otto. *Distanz und Hingabe: Philosophische und literarische Essays.* Stuttgart: F. Fromann, 1971.

Erichsen, Valborg. "Søren Kierkegaards betydning for Norsk Aandsliv." *EDDA: Nordisk Tidsskrift for Litteraturforskning,* volume XIX, tenth year, copy 2. Edited by Gerhard Gran and Francis Bull (Christiania, 1923), pp. 209-429.

Fabro, Cornelio. "Le Probleme de l'Eglise chez Newman et Kierkegaard." *Revue Thomiste,* no. 1 (January-March 1977), pp. 30-90.

Fasel, Oskar A. "Observations on Unamuno and Kierkegaard." *Hispania* 38 (1955), pp. 443-50.

Favrholdt, David. "On Høffding and Bohr." *Danish Yearbook of Philosophy* 16 (Copenhagen, 1979), pp. 73-77.

———. "Niels Bohr and Danish Philosophy." *Danish Yearbook of Philosophy* 13 (Copenhagen, 1976), pp. 206-20.

Faye, Jan. "The Influence of Harald Høffding's Philosophy on Niels Bohr's Interpretation of Quantum Mechanics." *Danish Yearbook of Philosophy* 16 (Copenhagen, 1979), pp. 37–72.

Fenger, Henning. *Georg Brandes et la France: La Formation de son Esprit et ses Gouts Littéraires, 1842–1872,* volume VIII. Paris: Faculté des lettres et sciences humaines de l'Université, 1963.

———. *Den Unge Brandes: Miljø, Venner, Rejser, Kriser.* Copenhagen: Gyldendal, 1957.

Feuer, Lewis S. *Einstein and the Generations of Science.* New York: Basic Books, 1974.

Fitzpatrick, Mallary, Jr. "Kierkegaard and the Church." *Journal of Religion* 27 (1947), pp. 255–62.

Friis, Oluf. "Hans Sophus Vodskov som Litterær Kritiker i 1870'erne og 1880'erne." In *Festskrift til Vilhelm Andersen,* pp. 235–50. Copenhagen: Gyldendal Nordisk Forlag, 1934.

Gallagher, Michael P. "Wittgenstein's Admiration for Kierkegaard." *The Month* 39 (January–June 1968), pp. 43–49.

Geismar, Eduard. "Kierkegaard." In Hermann Gunkel and Leopold Zscharnack, eds., *Die Religion in Geschichte und Gegenwart: Handwörterbuch für Theologie und Religionswissenschaft,* III, pp. 747–51. Tübingen: J. C. B. Mohr, 1929.

Gerdes, Hayo. *Der geschichtliche biblische Jesus oder den Christus der Philosophen: Erwägungen zur christologie Kierkegaards, Hegels und Schleiermachers.* Berlin: Verlag Die Spur, 1974.

Getzeny, Heinrich. "Kierkegaards Eindeutschung. Ein Beitrag zur deutschen Geistesgeschichte der letzten hundert Jahre." *Historisches Jahrbuch* 76 (Munich, 1957), pp. 181–92.

Gill, Jerry H. "Kant, Kierkegaard, and Religious Knowledge." *Philosophy and Phenomenological Research* 28 (1967), pp. 188–204.

Goldman, Arnold, *The Joyce Paradox: Form and Freedom in His Fiction.* London: Routledge & Kegan Paul, 1966.

Gouwens, David J. *Kierkegaard as Religious Thinker.* Cambridge: Cambridge University Press, 1996.

Green, Ronald M. *Kierkegaard and Kant: The Hidden Debt.* Albany: State University of New York Press, 1992.

Gustafson, Alrik. "Toward Decadence: Jens Peter Jacobsen." In his *Six Scandinavian Novelists: Lie, Jacobsen, Heidenstam, Selma Lagerlöf, Hamsun, Sigrid Undset,* pp. 73–122. Princeton: Princeton University Press, 1940.

Haller, Hans. *Der südtirolische Denker, Carl Dallago: Die Mystik seines Schrifttums.* Innsbruck: Winkler, 1938.

Halverson, Wendell Q. "Ibsen and Kierkegaard," in *Union Seminary Quarterly Review* 2 (November 1946), pp. 13–17.

Hamburger, Michael. "Hofmannsthals Bibliotek, ein Bericht." *Euphorion* 55, I (Heidelberg, 1961), pp. 15–76.

Hansen, Ernst Fr. "Søren Kierkegaard og Danmarks Genius i Verdenslitteraturen." *Kristeligt Dagblad,* June 8, 1933.

Hansen, Holger. "Søren Kierkegaard og Danmark." *Berlingske Aftenavis,* September 6, 1940.

Hansen, P., ed. *Illustreret Dansk Litteraturhistorie.* 2d ed., volumes 17–24, numbers 41–49 (Copenhagen, 1902).

Hansen, Søren Gorm. *H. C. Andersen og Søren Kierkegaard i Dannelseskulturen.* Copenhagen: Medusa, 1976.
Hansen-Löve, Friedrich. "Der deutsche Sören Kierkegaard." *Wort und Wahrheit* 7 (Vienna, 1952), pp. 624-26.
Hayman, David. "A Portrait of the Artist as a Young Man and L'Education Sentimentale: The Structural Affinities." *Orbis Litterarum* 19, no. 4 (Copenhagen, 1964), pp. 161-75.
Heiberg, Hans. *Ibsen: A Portrait of the Artist.* Translated by Joan Tate. London: Allan & Unwin, 1969.
Heilmann, Ernst. *Søren Kierkegaards hidtil fortiede testamentariske Villie angaaende hans literære Efterladenskaber.* Copenhagen: Bertelsen, 1909.
Heller, Agnes. "Georg Lukács and Irma Seidler." In *Lukács Revalued,* edited by Agnes Heller, pp. 27-62. Oxford: Oxford University Press, 1983.
Heller, Otto. *Henrik Ibsen: Plays and Problems.* Boston and New York: Houghton & Mifflin, 1912.
Hellwig, Werner. *Faz,* March 30, 1965 (on Theodor Däubler).
Hems, John M. "Abraham and Brand." *Philosophy,* XXXIX (April 1964), pp. 137-44.
Henriksen, Aage. *Methods and Results of Kierkegaard Studies in Scandinavia: A Historical and Critical Survey.* Publications of the Søren Kierkegaard Society, vol. I. Copenhagen: Munksgaard, 1951.
Hertel, Hans, and Sven Møller Kristensen, eds. *The Activist Critic: A Symposium on the Political Ideas, Literary Methods and International Reception of Georg Brandes.* Copenhagen: Munksgaard, 1980.
Hillebrand, Bruno, ed. *Nietzsche und die deutsche Literatur.* Volume I: *Texte zur Nietzsche-Rezeption, 1873-1963.* Munich: Deutscher Taschenbuch-Verlag, 1978.
Himmelstrup, Jens. *Sibbern, en Monografi.* Copenhagen: J. H. Schultz, 1934.
———. *Søren Kierkegaard International Bibliografi.* Copenhagen: Nyt Nordisk Forlag, 1962.
Hirsch, Emanuel. *Theologische Literaturzeitung,* no. 23 (Leipzig, 1927), pp. 548-49.
Høirup, Henning. *Grundtvigs Syn paa Tro og Erkendelse, Modsigelsens Grundsætning som Teologisk Aksiom hos Grundtvig.* Copenhagen: Gyldendal, 1949.
Hohlenberg, Johannes. *Sören Kierkegaard.* Translated by T. H. Croxall. New York: Pantheon, 1954.
Hohoff, Curt. "Fruchtbare Keulenschläge: Dem Autor Theodor Haecker zum 100. Geburtstag." *Rheinischer Merkur,* June 1, 1979.
———. *Unter den Fischen: Erinnerungen an Männer, Mädschen und Bücher, 1934-1939.* Wiesbaden: Limes, 1982.
Holm, Søren. *Filosofien i Norden før 1900.* Copenhagen: Munksgaard, 1967.
Holmgaard, Otto. *Extaticus: Søren Kierkegaards sidste Kamp, derunder hans Forhold til Broderen.* Copenhagen: Nyt Nordisk Forlag, 1967.
———. *Peter Christian Kierkegaard, Grundtvigs Lærling.* Copenhagen: Rosenkilde og Bagger, 1953.
Hong, Howard V. "Kierkegaard Interpretation and the Genetic Fallacy." An undated and unpublished essay, courtesy of the author in June 1983.
———. "The Kierkegaard Papers." *Tri-Quarterly,* no. 16, (Fall 1969), pp. 100-123.
Hornby, Richard. *Patterns in Ibsen's Middle Plays.* Lewisburg; Bucknell University Press, 1981.
Horwitz, Rivka. *Buber's Way to I and Thou: An Historical Analysis and the First Publication of Martin Buber's Lectures "Religion als Gegenwart."* Heidelberg: Schneider, 1978.

Hovde, B. J. *The Scandinavian Countries, 1720–1865: The Rise of the Middle Classes.* Vols. I–II. Boston: Chapman & Grimes, 1943.
Hude, Elizabeth. *Fredrika Bremer og Hendes Venskab med H. C. Andersen og andre Danske.* Copenhagen: G. E. C. Gad, 1972.
Hughes, H. Stuart. *Consciousness and Society: The Reorientation of European Social Thought, 1890–1930.* New York: Vintage Books, 1961.
Hultberg, Helge. "Kierkegaard og Rasmus Nielsen." *Kierkegaardiana,* vol. XII, pp. 9–21. Copenhagen, 1982. Edited by Niels Thulstrup.
Hultgren, Gunnar. "Mysteriet Kierkegaard." *Vår Lösen* 31 (Stockholm, 1940), pp. 317–26.
Hunsinger, George. "A Marxist View of Kierkegaard: George Lukács on the Intellectual Origins of Fascism." *Union Seminary Quarterly Review* 30, no. 1 (Fall 1974), pp. 29–40.
Iggers, Wilma Abeles. *Karl Kraus, A Viennese Critic of the Twentieth Century.* The Hague: Martinus Nijhoff, 1967.
Jammer, Max. *The Conceptual Development of Quantum Mechanics,* 2d ed. New York: American Institute of Physics, 1989.
Janik, Allan. "Carl Dallago and the Early Brenner." *Modern Austrian Literature* 11, no. 2 (1978), pp. 1–17.
———. "Haecker, Kierkegaard and the Early Brenner: A Contribution to the History of the Reception of 'Two Ages' in the German-speaking World." In *International Kierkegaard Commentary,* vol. 14: "Two Ages," edited by Robert L. Perkins, pp. 189–222. Macon, Ga.: Mercer University Press, 1984.
———. "Wittgenstein, Ficker, and 'Der Brenner.' " In *Wittgenstein: Sources and Perspectives,* edited by C. G. Luckhardt, pp. 161–89. Ithaca, N.Y.: Cornell University Press, 1979.
———, ed. "Wittgenstein's Letters to Ficker." Translated by Bruce Gillette and published in *Wittgenstein: Sources and Perspectives,* edited by C. G. Luckhardt, pp. 82–98. Ithaca, N.Y.: Cornell University Press, 1979.
Janik, Allan, and Stephen Toulmin. *Wittgenstein's Vienna.* New York: Simon and Schuster, 1973.
Janouch, Gustav. *Conversations with Kafka: Notes and Reminiscences.* Translated by Goronwy Rees. New York: F. A. Praeger, 1953.
Jensen, Johan Fjord. *Turgeniev i dansk Åndsliv.* Copenhagen: Gyldendal, 1961.
Jørgensen, Carl, *Søren Kierkegaards Skuffelser.* Copenhagen: Nyt Nordisk Forlag, 1967.
Jørgensen, P. P. *H. P. Kofoed-Hansen med Særligt Henblick til Søren Kierkegaard.* Copenhagen: Gyldendal, 1920.
Johnson, Howard A., and Niels Thulstrup, eds. *A Kierkegaard Critique.* New York: Harper Collins, 1962.
Johnston, Brian. *To The Third Empire: Ibsen's Early Drama.* Minneapolis: University of Minnesota Press, 1980.
Johnston, William M. *The Austrian Mind: An Intellectual and Social History, 1848–1938.* Berkeley: University of California Press, 1972.
Jolivet, Regis. *Introduction to Kierkegaard.* Translated by W. H. Barber. New York: Dutton, 1946.
Jorgenson, Theodore, and Nora O. Solum. *Ole Edvart Rølvaag, A Biography.* New York: Harper and Brothers, 1939.
Kabell, Aage. *Kierkegaardstudiet i Norden.* Copenhagen: H. Hagerup, 1948.
Kallmoes, Poul. *Frederik Christian Sibbern, Træk af en Dansk Filosofs Liv og Tænkning.* Copenhagen: Munksgaard, 1946.

Kaufmann, Walter. Introduction to Kierkegaard's *The Present Age*. Translated by Alexander Dru, pp. 9–29. New York: Harper Collins, 1962.
Kemp, Peter. " 'Le Précurseur de Henrik Ibsen.' Quelques aspects de la découverte de Kierkegaard en France." *Les Etudes Philosophique*, no. 2 (April–June 1979), pp. 139–50.
Kiralyfalvi, Béla. *The Aesthetics of György Lukacs*. Princeton: Princeton University Press, 1975.
Kirchhoff-Larsen, Christian. *Den Danske Presses Historie*. Vols. I–III: 1827–1866. Copenhagen: Levin & Munksgaard, 1942–43.
Kirmmse, Bruce. *Kierkegaard in Golden Age Denmark*. Bloomington & Indianapolis: Indiana University Press, 1990.
Kjær-Hansen, Ulf. *Søren Kierkegaards pressepolemik: Søren Kierkegaards Meninger om Dagpressen*. Copenhagen: Berlingske Forlag, 1955.
Koch, Carl. *Søren Kierkegaard og Emil Boesen, Breve og Indledning med et Tillæg*. Copenhagen: Schonberg, 1901.
Koch, Hal, and Bjørn Kornerup, eds. *Den Danske Kirkes Historie*. Vols. I-VIII. Copenhagen: Gyldendalske Boghandel, 1950–66.
Kohlschmidt, Werner. "Rilke und Kierkegaard." In his *Die entzweite Welt. Studien zum Menschenbild in der neueren Dichtung*, pp. 88–97. Gladbeck: Freizeiten, 1953.
Koht, Halvdan. *The Life of Ibsen*. Vols. I–II. Translated by Ruth Lima McMahon and Hanna Astrup Larsen. New York: B. Blom, 1931.
Kristensen, Sven Møller. "Georg Brandes Research: A Survey." *Scandinavica* 3, no. 2 (November 1964), pp. 121–32.
———. "Marie Grubbe." In his *Digtning og Livssyn: Fortolkninger af Syv Danske Værker*. 2d ed., pp. 30–56. Copenhagen: Gyldendal, 1960.
Kühle, Sejer. *Berlingske Aftenavis*, February 24, 1943.
———. "Fra J. P. Jacobsens Kreds." *Fund og Forskning i det Kongelige Biblioteks Samlinger* 4 (Copenhagen, 1957), pp. 120–37.
———. "Sören Kierkegaard und die Frauen." *Orbis Litterarum* 10 (1955), pp. 118–29.
La Chesnais, P. G. "Ibsen Disciple de Kierkegaard?" *EDDA: Nordisk Tidsskrift for Litteraturforskning* 34 (Oslo, 1934), pp. 355–410.
Lamm, Martin. *Strindberg och Makterna*. Stockholm: Svenska Kyrkans diakonistyrelses Bokförlag, 1936.
Lapointe, François H. *Sören Kierkegaard and His Critics: An International Bibliography of Criticism*. Westport, Connecticut: Greenwood Press, 1980.
Law, David R. *Kierkegaard as Negative Theologian*. Oxford: Clarendon Press, 1993.
Lawson, Lewis A., ed. *Kierkegaard's Presence in Contemporary American Life: Essays from Various Disciplines*. Metuchen, New Jersey: Scarecrow, 1970.
Lee, Amice. *Laurels and Rosemary: The Life of William and Mary Howitt*. London: Oxford University Press, 1955.
Lehmann, Ed. "Deux réformateurs du Protestantisme danois: Kierkegaard et Grundtvig." *Revue d'Histoire et de Philosophie Religieuses* 11 (1931), pp. 499–505.
Leppmann, Wolfgang. *Rilke: A Life*. Translated by Russell M. Stockman and Richard Exner. New York: Fromm International Publishing Corp., 1984.
Lindhardt, P. G. *Konfrontation*. Copenhagen: Akademisk Forlag, 1974.
———. *Søren Kierkegaards Angreb paa Folkekirken*. Aarhus: Aros, 1955.
Livingston, James C. *Modern Christian Thought: From the Enlightenment to Vatican II*. New York: Macmillan, 1971.

Lønning, Per. "Kierkegaard's 'Corrective'—a Corrective to Kierkegaardians?" *Liber Academiæ Kierkegaardiensis Annuarius.* Volumes I-IV: 1979–81. Edited by Alessandro Cortese and Niels Thulstrup (Copenhagen, 1982), pp. 105-19.

———. "Kierkegaard's 'Paradox.' " *Orbis Litterarum* 10 (Copenhagen, 1955), pp. 156–65.

Löwith, Karl. "On the Historical Understanding of Kierkegaard." *Review of Religion* 7 (March 1943), pp. 227–41.

Löwy, Michael. *Georg Lukács: From Romanticism to Bolshevism.* London: NLB, 1979.

Lowrie, Walter. "How Kierkegaard Got into English." Appended to his translation of Kierkegaard's *Repetition,* pp. 177–212. Princeton: Princeton University Press, 1941.

———. Introduction to his translation of Kierkegaard's *Stages on Life's Way,* pp. 3–16. Princeton: Princeton University Press, 1940.

———. *Kierkegaard.* London and New York: Oxford University Press, 1938.

———. Preface to *On Authority and Revelation (The Book on Adler),* pp. v-xiv. Princeton: Princeton University Press, 1955.

———. *A Short Life of Kierkegaard.* Princeton: Princeton University Press, 1970.

———. "Translators and Interpreters of Søren Kierkegaard." *Theology Today* 12, no. 3 (October 1955), pp. 312–27.

Lucas, F. L. *The Drama of Ibsen and Strindberg.* New York: Macmillan, 1962.

Lübcke, Poul. "F. C. Sibbern: Epistemology as Ontology." *Danish Yearbook of Philosophy* 13 (Copenhagen, 1976), pp. 84–104.

Lund, Mary Graham. "The Existentialism of Ibsen." *The Personalist,* XLI (summer 1960), pp. 310–17.

Lunn, Eugene. *Marxism and Modernism: An Historical Study of Lukács, Brecht, Benjamin, and Adorno.* Berkeley: University of California Press, 1982.

McGrath, William J. *Dionysian Art and Populist Politics in Austria.* New Haven: Yale University Press, 1974.

Mackey, Louis. *Kierkegaard: A Kind of Poet.* Philadelphia: University of Pennsylvania Press, 1971.

Macleod, Vivienne Koch. "The Influence of Ibsen on Joyce." *PMLA* 60 (1945), pp. 879–98.

———. "The Influence of Ibsen on Joyce: Addendum." *PMLA* 62 (1947), pp. 573–80.

Madsen, Borge Gedso. "Influence from J. P. Jacobsen and Sigbjörn Obstfelder on Rainer Maria Rilke's 'Die Aufzeichnungen des Malte Laurids Brigge.' " *Scandinavian Studies* 26, no. 3 (August 1954), pp. 105–14.

Madsen, Svend Ole. *J. P. Jacobsen—Virkelighed og Kunst. En Undersøgelse af den eksistentielle Erfarings transformering til Kunst.* Copenhagen: Akademisk Forlag, 1974.

Magnussen, Rikard. *Det Særlige Kors: Efterskrift til Bogen: Søren Kierkegaard Set Udefra.* Copenhagen: Munksgaard, 1942.

———. *Søren Kierkegaard Set Udefra.* Copenhagen: Munksgaard, 1942.

Malantschuk, Gregor. *The Controversial Kierkegaard.* Translated by Howard V. Hong and Edna H. Hong for the Kierkegaard Monograph Series. Edited by Alastair McKinnon. Waterloo, Ontario: Wilfred Laurier University Press, 1980.

———. "Søren Kierkegaard og naturvidenskaberne." *Kristeligt Dagblad,* October 22, 1951.

Malcolm, Norman. *Ludwig Wittgenstein: A Memoir.* London: Oxford University Press, 1958.

Mayer, Gerhart. *Rilke und Kassner: Eine geistige Begegnung.* Bonn: H. Bouvier, 1960.

Mesnard, Pierre. "Kierkegaard et la Conscience Française." *Revue de Littérature Comparée* 9 (1955), pp. 453–77.
Methlagl, Walter. *"Der Brenner": Weltanschauliche Wandlungen vor dem Ersten Weltkrieg.* Unpublished doctoral dissertation at the University of Innsbruck, 1966 (courtesy of the *Brenner-Archiv*).
———. *Die Furche,* March 25, 1967 (on Theodor Däubler).
———. "Ludwig von Ficker." In *Neue Österreichische Biographie,* volume XVII (Vienna: Amalthea-Verlag, 1968), pp. 20–31.
———. "Theodor Haecker und 'Der Brenner.' " *Literaturwissenschaftliches Jahrbuch* 19 (Berlin, 1978), pp. 199–216.
Methlagl, Walter, Eberhard Sauermann, and Sigurd Paul Scheichl, eds. *Untersuchungen zum "Brenner": Festschrift für Ignaz Zangerle zum 75 Geburtstag.* Salzburg: O. Müller, 1981.
Meyer, François. "Kierkegaard et Unamuno." *Revue de Littérature Comparée* 29 (1955), pp. 478–92.
Meyer, Michael. *Henrik Ibsen.* Vol. I: *The Making of a Dramatist, 1828–1864.* Vol. II: *The Farewell to Poetry, 1864–1882.* Vol. III: *The Top of a Cold Mountain, 1883–1906.* London: R. Hart-Davis, 1967–71.
Michalson, Carl, ed. *Christianity and the Existentialists.* New York: Scribner, 1956.
Mitchell, P. M. *A History of Danish Literature.* 2d ed. New York: Kraus Thomson Organization, 1971.
Möhring, Werner. "Ibsens Abkehr von Kierkegaard." *EDDA: Nordisk Tidsskrift for Litteraturforskning,* volume XXVIII, 15th year (Christiania, 1928), pp. 43–71.
Møller, A. Egelund. *Søren Kierkegaard om Politik.* Copenhagen: Forlaget Strand, 1975.
Montén, Karin Carsten. "Zur Rezeptionsgeschichte Fredrika Bremers in Deutschland." In *Scripta Minora,* edited by Berta Stjernquist, pp. 5–109. Lund, 1976.
Mosfjeld, Oskar. *Henrik Ibsen og Skien: En Biografisk og Litteratur-Psykologisk Studie.* Oslo: Gyldendal, 1949.
Mustard, Helen M. "Sören Kierkegaard in German Literary Periodicals, 1860–1930." *Germanic Review,* XXVI (April 1951), pp. 83–101.
Nelson, E. Clifford, ed. *A Pioneer Churchman: J. W. C. Dietrichson in Wisconsin, 1844–1850.* Translated by Malcolm Rosholt and Harris E. Kaasa. New York: Norwegian-American Historical Association by Twayne Publishers, 1973.
Neue Deutsche Biographie. Vols. I–XVII. Published by the Historische Kommission bei der Bayerischen Akademie der Wissenschaften. Berlin: Duncker & Humblot, 1953–93.
Neue Österreichische Biographie, 1815–1918. Vols. I–XVII. Edited by Anton Bettelheim. Vienna: Amalthea-Verlag, 1957–70.
Nielsen, Frederik. *J. P. Jacobsen, Digteren og Mennesket: En Literær Undersøgelse.* Copenhagen: G. E. C. Gad, 1953.
Nigg, Walter. "Ein Leben im Schatten Kierkegaards: zu Ferdinand Ebners Briefen." *Neue Zürcher Zeitung,* July 29, 1966.
Nolin, Bertil. *Georg Brandes.* Boston: Twayne Publishers, 1976.
———. *Den Gode Européen, Studier i Georg Brandes' idéutveckling 1871–1893.* Stockholm: Svenska Bokförlaget, 1965.
Norris, Christopher. "Fictions of Authority: Narrative and Viewpoint in Kierkegaard's Writing." In his *The Deconstructive Turn: Essays in the Rhetoric of Philosophy,* pp. 85–106. London: Methuen, 1983.

Norsk Biografisk Leksikon. Vols. I–XVIII. Edited by Einar Jansen, Paulus Svendsen, and Jonas Jansen (edited initially by Edvard Bull, Anders Krogvig, and Gerhard Gran). Christiania/Oslo: H. Aschehoug, 1923–1977.

Nota, John H. *Max Scheler: The Man and His Work.* Chicago: Franciscan Herald Press, 1983.

O'Connor, D. T. "Schleiermacher and Kierkegaard: The Odd Couple of Modern Theology." *Religion in Life* 41 (1972), pp. 8–17.

Olesen Larsen, Vibeke, and Wilhjelm Tage, eds. *Søren Kierkegaard Læst af K. Olesen Larsen.* Vol. II of the *Efterladte Arbejder.* Copenhagen: G. E. C. Gad, 1966.

Ostenfeld, Ib. *Poul Kierkegaard, En Skæbne. Og Andre Studier over Religion og Ateisme.* Copenhagen: Nyt Nordisk Forlag, 1957.

Ottosen, Jørgen. *J. P. Jacobsens "Mogens."* Copenhagen: Gyldendal, 1968.

Pallis, Dot. "J. P. Jacobsen og Flaubert." *Danske Studier* (1973), pp. 90–107.

Palmer, Donald D. "Unamuno's Don Quijote and Kierkegaard's Abraham." *Revista de Estudios Hispànicos* 3 (1969), pp. 295–312.

Pascal, Roy. *From Naturalism to Expressionism: German Literature and Society, 1880–1918.* New York: Basic Books, 1973.

Paston, George. "William and Mary Howitt." In his *Little Memoirs of the Nineteenth Century.* Freeport, N.Y.: Books for Libraries Press, 1969.

Perkins, Robert L. "Søren Kierkegaard's Library." *American Book Collector* 12 (1961), pp. 9–16.

Pfäfflin, Friedrich. "Theodor Haecker." *Die Furche,* June 12, 1965.

Pletsch, Carl. "The Self-Sufficient Text in Nietzsche and Kierkegaard." In *The Anxiety of Anticipation,* ed. Sima Godfrey, pp. 160–88. No. 66 in the biannual series Yale French Studies. New Haven, 1984.

Poll, Maria. *Edmund Jörgs Kampf für eine christliche und grossdeutsche Volks- und Staatsordnung.* Paderborn: Ferdinand Schöningh Verlag, 1936.

Przywara, Erich, S.J. *Das Geheimnis Kierkegaards.* Munich and Berlin: R. Oldenbourg, 1929.

Qvist, Gunnar. *Fredrika Bremer och Kvinnans emancipation: Opinionshistoriska studier.* Göteborg: Läromedelsförlaget, Akademiförlaget, 1969.

F. H. R. "Innsbruck verschaffte seinem Wort Gehör: Theodor Haecker und 'Der Brenner.' " *Dolomiten,* April, 10, 1965.

Rappoport, Angelo S. "Ibsen, Nietzsche, and Kierkegaard." *New Age,* III (1908), pp. 408–9 and 428–29.

Rasmussen, S. V. *Den Unge Brøchner.* Copenhagen: Gyldendal, 1966.

———. "Hans Brøchner." In *Dansk Biografisk Lexicon.* 2d ed. Vol. IV, pp. 286–92. Copenhagen: Gyldendal, 1934.

Reed, Terence James. *Thomas Mann: The Uses of Tradition.* Oxford; Oxford University Press, 1974.

Rehm, Walther. *Gontscharow und Jacobsen, oder Langweile und Schwermut.* Göttingen: Vandenhoeck & Ruprecht, 1963.

———. "Jacobsen und die Schwermut." In his *Experimentum Medietatis: Studien zur Geistes- und Literaturgeschichte des 19. Jahrhunderts,* pp. 184–239. Munich: H. Rinn, 1947.

Rhees, Rush, ed. *Ludwig Wittgenstein: Personal Recollections.* Totowa, New Jersey: Rowman and Littlefield, 1981.

Rickham, H. P. *Wilhelm Dilthey: Pioneer of the Human Studies.* Berkeley: University of California Press, 1979.
Rindom, Erik. *Harald Høffding: Bidrag til Biografi og Karakteristik.* Copenhagen: Gyldendal, 1913.
Robertson, E. F. L. "A Danish Poet: J. P. Jacobsen." *Cosmopolis,* VIII (1897), pp. 346-58.
Rodgers, John H. *The Theology of P. T. Forsyth: The Cross of Christ and the Revelation of God.* London: Independent Press, 1965.
Rohde, H. P., ed. *Auktionsprotokol over Søren Kierkegaards Bogsamling.* Copenhagen: Det Kongelige Bibliotek, 1967.
Roos, H. *Søren Kierkegaard og Katolicismen.* Copenhagen: Munksgaard, 1952.
Rosenberg, P. A. *Rasmus Nielsen: Nordens Filosof.* Copenhagen: K. Schonberg, 1903.
Rubow, Paul V. *Georg Brandes' Briller.* Copenhagen: Levin & Munksgaard, 1932.
―――. "Georg Brandes og Hans Lærere." In *Studier fra Sprog- og Oldtidsforskning,* pp. 3-24. Copenhagen, 1924.
Rygnestad, Knut. *Johan Christian Heuch: Apologet og Stridsmann.* Trondheim: Globus Forlag, 1966.
Sato, Toshihiko. "Scandinavian Literature in Japan." *Scandinavica* 4, no. 1 (May 1965), pp. 16-26.
Scharling, C. I. *Grundtvig og Romantiken: belyst ved Grundtvigs Forhold til Schelling.* Copenhagen: Gyldendal, 1947.
Schoeps, Hans Joachim. "Über das Frühecho Søren Kierkegaards in Deutschland." *Meddelelser fra Søren Kierkegaard Selskabet* 3, no. 2 (Copenhagen: Munksgaard, 1951), pp. 93-100.
Schorske, Carl E. *Fin-de-Siècle Vienna: Politics and Culture.* New York: Alfred A. Knopf, 1980.
Seidlin, Oskar. "Georg Brandes." *Journal of the History of Ideas,* III (October 1942), pp. 415-42.
Selmer, Ludvig (Gabriel Fredrik). "J. C. Heuch i Kamp mot Vantroen." In *Norsk Teologisk Tidsskrift.* Vol. 9, 4th series (Oslo, 1938), pp. 186-202.
―――. *Professor Fredrik Petersen og Hans Samtid.* Oslo: Land og Kirke, 1948.
Simonson, Harold P. "'Angst' on the Prairie: Reflections on Immigrants, Rølvaag, and Beret." *Norwegian-American Studies* 29 (Northfield, Minnesota, 1983), pp. 89-110.
―――. "Rølvaag and Kierkegaard." *Scandinavian Studies* 49, no. 1 (January-March 1977), pp. 67-80.
Sjöstedt, Nils Åke. *Søren Kierkegaard och Svensk Litteratur: från Fredrika Bremer till Hjalmar Söderberg.* Göteborg: Elander, 1950.
Slaatte, Howard A. "Kierkegaard's Introduction to American Methodists—A Tribute." *The Drew Gateway,* XXX (Spring 1960), pp. 161-67.
Sletten, Klaus. *Christopher Bruun: Folkelæraren—Stridsmannen.* Oslo: Gyldendal, 1949.
Sløk, Johannes. *Kierkegaard: Humanismens Tænker.* Copenhagen: C. A. Reitzel, 1978.
Smith, Ronald G. "Kierkegaard's Library." *Hibbert Journal* 50 (1951), pp. 18-21.
Sørensen, E. "Fascination og Handling: et Essay omkring J. P. Jacobsens Noveller." *Kritik* 14 (1970), pp. 22-38.
Sørensen, Villy. *Schopenhauer.* Copenhagen: G. E. C. Gad, 1969.
Sorainen, Kalle. "Kierkegaard und Høffding." *Orbis Litterarum* 10, no. 1-2 (Copenhagen, 1955), pp. 245-51.

Spiegelberg, Herbert. *The Phenomenological Movement: A Historical Introduction.* 2d ed. Vols. I–II. The Hague: Martinus Nijhoff, 1971.
Spink, Reginald. *Hans Christian Andersen and His World.* London: Thames and Hudson, 1972.
Stamm, Eugen. *Konstantin Frantz, 1857–1866: Ein Wort zur Deutschen Frage.* Berlin and Leipzig: Deutsche Verlag, 1930.
Steen, Ellisiv. *Diktning og Virkelighet: En Studie i Camilla Colletts Forfatterskap.* Oslo: Gyldendal, 1947.
Steffensen, Steffen. "Kassner und Kierkegaard: Ein Vortrag." *Orbis Litterarum* 18, no. 1–2 (Copenhagen, 1963), pp. 80–90.
Stieg, Gerald. *Der Brenner und Die Fackel: Ein Beitrag zur Wirkungsgeschichte von Karl Kraus.* Salzburg: O. Müller, 1976.
Sturzen-Becker, Ragnar. *Oscar Patrick Sturzen-Becker (Orvar Odd).* Vol. I. Stockholm, 1911.
Swensen, David F. *Kierkegaardian Philosophy in the Faith of a Scholar.* Edited by Lillian M. Swenson. Philadelphia: Westminster, 1949.
———. *Something about Kierkegaard.* Edited by Lillian M. Swensen. Minneapolis: Augsburg, 1941.
Tammany, Jane Ellert. *Henrik Ibsen's Theatre Aesthetic and Dramatic Art: A Reflection of Kierkegaardian Consciousness—Its Significance for Modern Dramatic Interpretation and the American Theatre.* New York: Philosophical Library, 1980.
Tandberg, Jens. *Biskop Heuchs Liv og Virke.* Christiania, 1905.
Tavuchis, Nicholas. *Pastors and Immigrants: The Role of a Religious Elite in the Absorption of Norwegian Immigrants.* The Hague: Martinus Nijhoff, 1963.
Taylor, Mark C. *Journeys to Selfhood: Hegel and Kierkegaard.* Berkeley: University of California Press, 1980.
———. *Kierkegaard's Pseudonymous Authorship: A Study of Time and the Self.* Princeton: Princeton University Press, 1975.
Thomas, R. Hinton. *Nietzsche in German Politics and Society: 1890–1918.* London: Manchester University Press, 1983.
Thompson, Josiah, ed. *Kierkegaard: A Collection of Critical Essays.* New York: Anchor Books, 1972.
Thomte, Reidar. "Kierkegaard im amerikanischen religiösen Denken." *Lutherische Rundschau* 5 (Zurich, 1955), pp. 141–57.
Thulstrup, Marie Mikulova. "Kierkegaard og naturvidenskaben." *Kierkegaardiana,* vol. VIII, pp. 53–63. Copenhagen, 1971.
———. *Kierkegaard og Pietismen.* No. 13 in the series Søren Kierkegaard Selskabets Populære Skrifter. Copenhagen: Munksgaard, 1967.
Thulstrup, Niels. *Kierkegaard's Relation to Hegel.* Translated by George L. Stengren. Princeton: Princeton University Press, 1980.
Thulstrup, Niels, and Marie Mikulova, eds. *Bibliotheca Kierkegaardiana.* Vols. 1–12. Copenhagen: C. A. Reitzel, 1978–83.
Tigerschiöld, Brita. *J. P. Jacobsen och hans Roman Niels Lyhne.* Göteborg: Elander, 1945.
Topsøe-Jensen, H. G. *Scandinavian Literature from Brandes to Our Day.* Translated by Isaac Anderson. New York: American-Scandinavian Foundation and W. W. Norton, 1929.
Tysdahl, B. J. *Joyce and Ibsen: A Study in Literary Influence.* Oslo: Norwegian Universities Press, 1968.

Valdés, Mario J. and Maria Elena de. *An Unamuno Source Book: A Catalogue of Readings and Acquisitions with an Introductory Essay on Unamuno's Dialectical Enquiry.* Toronto: University of Toronto Press, 1973.

Van Buren, John. *The Young Heidegger: Rumor of the Hidden King.* In Studies in Continental Thought Series. Bloomington and Indianapolis: Indiana University Press, 1994.

Vidler, Alec R. *The Church in an Age of Revolution: 1789 to the Present Day.* London: Penguin Books, 1961.

Wahl, Jean. *Etudes Kierkegaardiennes.* Paris: Aubier, 1938.

———. "Kierkegaard and Kafka." in *The Kafka Problem.* Edited by Angel Flores, pp. 277–90. New York: Gordian Press, 1975.

Ward, Rodney A. "The Reception of Søren Kierkegaard into English." *Expository Times* 107, no. 2 (November 1995), pp. 43–47.

Wamberg, Niels Birger, ed. *Deres Broderligt Hengivne: Et Udvalg af Breve fra H. C. Andersen.* Copenhagen: Gyldendal, 1975.

Webber, Ruth House. "Kierkegaard and the Elaboration of Unamuno's 'Niebla.'" In *Hispanic Review* 32 (1964), pp. 118–34.

Wellek, René. *A History of Modern Criticism, 1750–1950.* Vol. IV: *The Later Nineteenth Century.* New Haven: Yale University Press, 1965.

Weltzer, Carl. "Omkring Søren Kierkegaards Disputats." *Kirkehistoriske Samlinger* 6, 6th series (Copenhagen, 1948–50), pp. 284–311.

———. *Peter og Søren Kierkegaard.* Vols. I–II. Copenhagen: G. E. C. Gad, 1936.

Wieselgren, Greta. *Fredrika Bremer och Verkligheten: Romanen Herthas tillblivelse.* Stockholm: Norstedt, 1978.

Witt-Hansen, Johs. "H. C. Örsted, Immanuel Kant, and the Thought Experiment." *Danish Yearbook of Philosophy* 13 (Copenhagen, 1976), pp. 48–65.

Wood, Forrest, Jr. "Kierkegaardian Light on Ibsen's Brand." *The Personalist* 51 (1970), pp. 393–400.

Woodring, Carl Ray. *Victorian Samplers: William and Mary Howitt.* Lawrence, Kansas: University of Kansas Press, 1952.

Index

The name Søren Kierkegaard in the titles of certain works listed below is usually abbreviated as S.K.

Abelard, Peter, 269n. 214
Abraham, ix, xix, 155–56, 195, 231, 248, 251, 263, 306, 344, 366, 366n. 92, 388
Absolute Paradox. *See* paradox; Christ
Absurd, the, 167, 177, 199, 200, 210, 252, 305, 351, 396
Adam, 33, 295
Adler, Viktor, 318n. 99
Aftonbladet, 53, 122, 122n. 166, 239, 264, 276
Alas, Leopoldo (*pseud*. Clarin), 285n. 3
America, xviii, 56, 58–59, 60, 62, 63, 63n. 66, 72–76, 79, 249, 316–17, 329, 342–44, 347
Andersen, Hans Christian, xii, xviii, 4, 7–17, 34–36, 39, 40, 42, 45, 55, 60, 61, 64, 73n. 92, 77, 123n. 168, 124, 124n. 174, 147, 169, 175, 229, 229n. 64, 236, 256, 273–74, 284n. 2, 297, 345n. 20; *At Være Eller Ikke Være?* (To Be, or Not to Be?), 16, 175; *En Comedie i det Grønne* (An Open-air Comedy), 13; *Kun en Spillemand* (Only a Fiddler), 7–9; *Lykkens Galoscher* (The Galoshes of Fortune), 11–12, 12n. 38, 35n. 124; *Mit Livs Eventyr* (The Fairy Tale of My Life), 9; *Nye Eventyr* (New Fairy Tales), 10; "The Snail and the Rose Bush," 14–15, 273–74; *I Sverrig* (In Sweden), 36

Andreas-Salomé, Lou, 334, 360, 363–64
Andresen, Andreas Daniel, 104, 128, 129
Anselm, Saint, 209
Antichrist, 99
Aquinas. *See* Thomas Aquinas, Saint
Archer, William, 151, 345
Aristophanes, 108, 162
Aristotle, 32, 354
Armed Neutrality, 94n. 54, 226
"At a Graveside." *See Upbuilding Discourses*
atheism, xxi, 15, 98n. 70, 126, 127, 134, 175, 234, 239, 258, 276, 281, 290, 292, 293n. 27, 294, 295, 298, 299, 300, 302, 304, 305, 396
Auden, W. H., 156n. 65
Augustine, Saint, ix, 82n. 13, 91, 172, 173, 372, 380n. 143, 386
authority, apostolic, 111–12
authority in religious matters, 384–86, 388, 393

Baader, Franz von, 42n. 143
Bärthold, Albert, xii, 220–21, 225–28, 231–32, 267–74, 275, 276, 277–78, 279, 283, 309–10, 311, 311n. 86, 312, 326, 332–33, 342; *Aus und über S.K. Früchte und Blätter*, 227–28; *Die Bedeutung der ästhetischen Schriften S.K.s*,

425

273-74; *Einladung und Aergerniss. Biblische Darstellung und christliche Begriffsbestimmung von S.K.*, 221; *Einubung in Christentum*, 271; *Noten zu S.K.s Lebensgeschichte*, 268; *S.K., Eine Verfasser-Existenz eigner Art: Aus seinem Mittheilungen zusammengestellt*, 225-27; *S.K.s Persönlichkeit im ihrer Verwirklichung der Ideale*, 309-10; *Zur theologischen Bedeutung S.K.s*, 277; *Von den Lilien auf dem Felde und den Vögeln unter dem Himmel*, 267; *Was Christentum ist. Zur Verständigung uber diese Frage*, 309, 309n. 81; *Die Wendung zur Wahrheit in der modernen Kulturentwicklung*, 309, 309n. 81; *Zwölf Reden von S.K.*, 267
baptism. *See* infant baptism
Baptists, 117, 219
Barfod, Hans Peter, 211-17, 218, 221, 224, 240, 241, 247, 260, 261, 268, 271, 272, 273, 310, 341; *S.K.s Efterladte Papirer*, 216-17, 247, 260, 272, 277, 352
Barth, H. G. D., 175
Barth, Karl, 220, 220n. 32, 286n. 7, 392, 393
Basch, Victor, 351
Bauer, Bruno, 269n. 216
Bauer, Felice, 366
Beck, Andreas Frederik, 17, 18-19, 47, 49-50, 71, 127, 131
Beck, Johann Tobias, xx, 220, 221n. 33, 225, 261, 271, 274, 311, 311n. 86, 342
Beckett, Samuel, 163
Berdyaev, Nicolai A., 396
Bergson, Henri, 287, 330, 348, 372, 376
Berling, Carl, 87n. 25
Berlingske Tidende, 29, 86, 87n. 25, 90, 91, 96, 99, 118n. 148, 129, 138, 238, 325
Bible, 23, 79, 92, 93, 98n. 68, 100, 101, 103, 104, 109, 114, 117, 118, 123, 157n. 67, 160, 167, 183, 195, 213, 219, 232, 235, 244, 248, 252, 253, 260, 265, 276, 290, 295, 305, 308, 324, 325, 328, 344, 347n. 23, 349, 387, 388, 392
Bille, Carl Steen Andersen, 86n. 24, 107n. 111
Billeskov Jansen, F. J., 12n. 38, 88, 289
Binzer, H. F., 91n. 40
biographical-psychological approach, the, 141, 217, 218, 245, 258, 263, 273, 274, 280n. 253, 281, 283, 306, 325, 341, 395
Bismarck, Otto Eduard Leopold von, 309
Bjørnson, Bjørnstjerne, 145, 159, 164-65, 236, 239, 256n. 167, 264, 265-66, 287, 288, 297, 350; *Beyond Our Power*, 165
Blessing, Eugen, 375
Blicher, Steen Steensen, 55
Bloch, Jørgen Victor, 99-101, 104, 119n. 154, 129
Blumhardt, Johann Christoph, 376

Bøgh, Eric, 217-18, 282, 282n. 257
Böklin, Per Johan, 64n. 69
Börne, Ludwig, 255
Boesen, Emil, 47, 47n. 20, 48, 105-06, 216
Bohr, Niels, 331-32
Boisen, Frederik Engelhart, 119, 119n. 151
Boisen, L. N., 109-10
Bonald, Louis Gabriel Ambroise, 238
Bonaparte, Napoleon, 249n. 146
The Book on Adler, xv, 383-85, 395
Borchsenius, Otto, 239
Boström, C. J., 177
Botten-Hansen, Paul, 147
Brahe, Tycho, 32n. 115, 230, 236
Brandes, Edvard, 239, 291n. 22, 298-99, 300
Brandes, Georg, xii, xix-xx, 145, 148, 148n. 40, 150, 151n. 45, 164, 165, 166-67, 169, 183-85, 186, 187, 201, 209, 228-41, 243, 245-60, 263-64, 266-68, 271, 273-82, 283-84, 285, 287, 288, 290, 298, 299, 300, 303, 304-5, 306, 307, 308, 315, 317, 318-19, 320, 321, 322, 325, 328, 330, 340, 341, 342, 346, 347, 348n. 27, 350, 351, 353, 357, 365, 373, 375, 385, 395; "Aristocratic Radicalism," 318-19; his "Modern Breakthrough" in literature, 232, 237, 239, 259, 290, 298, 304, 307, 317; *Dualismen i vor nyeste Philosophie*, 183, 235-36, 252; *Henrik Ibsen and Bjørnstjerne Bjørnson*, 148n. 40; *Hovedstrømninger i det nittende Aarhundredes Litteratur*, 237-38, 247n. 136; *Impressions* (First, Second, & Third), 148, 148n. 40, 151n. 45, 166; *Det moderne Gjennembruds Mænd*, 299; *Det nittende Aarhundrede*, 239, 241, 299, 300; *Den romantiske Skole i Tydsland*, 238; *S.K: En Kritik Fremstilling i Grundrids*, 240, 245-52, 284, 300, 321; *Foragt* (contempt), 246; *Pietet* (reverence), 246
Brecht, Franz Josef, 314
Bremer, Fredrika, xii, 54, 55-68, 69, 70, 71, 73n. 92, 75, 247, 248n. 137; *Hertha*, 63-66, 69; *Lif i Norden* (Life in the North), 56-57, 57n. 51, 59, 60, 122-23
Brenner Circle, xii, 370, 371, 372, 375, 377, 381, 382, 386, 391
Bretteville, Lodovica de, 31
Broch, Hermann, 370, 370n. 105
Brod, Max, 366, 367
Brøchner, Hans, 127-28, 133, 134, 189-96, 198, 201, 204, 205, 208, 209, 210, 233, 236n. 94, 238n. 101, 241-45, 276, 278, 282, 294, 300, 320, 321, 326, 330, 395; *Om det Religiøse i dets Enhed med det Humane*, 198; *Problemet om Tro og Viden, en historisk-kritisk Afhandling*, 190-96, 198, 204, 236n. 94, 321; "Reminiscences," 242-45, 276, 278, 300

Brøndsted, Peter Oluf, 17
Brorson, Hans Adolph, 117n. 146
Bruun, Christopher Arnt, 150, 151n. 47, 152–53, 156, 158, 265
Buber, Martin, ix, xii, 387, 396
Buch des Richters (The Book of the Judge), 365–67
Buddhism, 337n. 161
Buffon, George-Louis Leclerc Comte de, 36
Bultmann, Rudolf Karl, 281
Byron, (George Gordon) Lord, 248, 290n. 21

Caesar, 110, 249n. 146
Calvin, John, 360
Camus, Albert, 305, 306, 306n. 70
Carlyle, Thomas, 267
Carus, Carl G., 37, 37n. 128, 38, 39, 40
Catholicism, xxi, 30, 80, 82, 111n. 128, 115, 119n. 154, 131–32, 250, 287, 288, 317, 324, 357, 360, 369, 383–86, 387n. 171, 388–90, 391, 396
Chamberlain, Houston Stewart, 358
Chamisso, Adalbert von, 34n. 120
Chateaubriand, François-Auguste-René de, 238, 247n. 136
chatter, 12, 249, 368, 378, 382, 392
Christ, 15, 16, 24, 41, 86, 90, 103, 104, 106, 106n. 107, 112, 118n. 150, 157n. 67, 177, 199–200, 219, 251, 257, 263, 270, 289, 307, 310, 337, 338, 349, 370, 387
"Christ's Judgment upon Official Christianity," 122n. 167
Christendom, 5, 63, 80n. 5, 82–83, 84, 93, 99, 101, 118, 119n. 154, 121n. 160, 125, 136, 159, 220, 231, 251, 327, 336, 337, 357, 396
Christian, 2, 16, 23, 24, 30, 41, 42, 57, 58, 65, 80, 81, 86, 89, 91, 92, 96, 97, 97n. 64, 98n. 70, 99, 99n. 74, 100n. 76, 102, 103, 104, 106, 107, 109, 110, 112n. 131, 113, 116, 117, 118, 119n. 151, 120, 134, 137, 157, 163n. 86, 165, 168, 176, 185, 195, 202, 224, 227, 230, 231, 233, 249, 251, 255, 256, 256n. 167, 258, 263, 265, 268, 270, 274, 275, 276, 280, 281, 297, 307, 309, 312, 314, 324, 325n. 125, 341, 342, 346, 349, 350, 351, 352, 360, 364, 366n. 90, 373, 374, 376, 389
Christian Discourses. See *Upbuilding Discourses*
Christiania (later Oslo), 114, 116, 121n. 160, 147, 149n. 42, 152, 175, 188, 202, 202n. 120, 204, 239, 240, 256, 260, 261, 262, 316
Christianiaposten, 113, 140, 150
Christianity, 5, 6, 29, 37, 41, 44, 52n. 38, 81, 82, 83, 85, 90, 92, 93, 95, 96, 97n. 64, 100, 101, 103, 104, 108, 109, 110, 112, 113, 113n. 135, 114, 117, 118, 119n. 151, 120, 122, 126, 130, 131, 134, 138, 142, 150, 151, 157, 158n. 68, 171, 177, 179, 185, 191, 198, 201, 222, 230, 231, 233, 237, 240, 244, 251, 252, 253, 258, 260, 263, 264, 284, 289, 291, 292, 297, 304, 307, 312, 317, 319, 320, 321, 324, 325n. 125, 327, 328, 336, 337, 341, 342, 349, 364, 373, 374
"Church party," the, 99, 102, 109, 109n. 118, 113, 118, 134
Claëson, Kristian, 177–78
Clausen, Henrik Nicolai, 100n. 76, 315
Collett, Camilla, 68–71, 75, 167n. 101; *Amtmandens Døtre* (The governor's daughters), 69–70, 167n. 101
Collett, Peter Jonas, 68, 70n. 84
Collin, Jonas, 15
comic, the. *See* humor
communism, 355, 356
Comte, Auguste, 239, 258, 322
The Concept of Anxiety, 4, 8n. 25, 15, 27, 101n. 82, 205, 234n. 88, 301, 312, 314n. 95, 323, 360, 373
The Concept of Irony, 14, 17, 18, 20, 21, 21n. 69, 26, 47, 49, 49n. 30, 53, 94, 111, 247n. 136, 381–82
Concluding Unscientific Postscript, 4n. 12, 27, 50, 50n. 34, 52n. 38, 94, 127, 128, 154, 162n. 83, 174, 178, 184, 189, 191, 192n. 81, 205n. 133, 226, 226n. 53, 231, 232, 234, 263, 270, 275, 285, 285n. 6, 347
Condillac, Étienne Bonnot de, 36
Copenhagen, xii, xviii, xxi, 2, 7, 17, 18, 19, 20, 21, 23, 34, 34n. 120, 43, 45, 48, 53, 54, 55, 56, 57, 57n. 51, 58, 63, 68, 69, 76, 84, 86, 89, 89n. 34, 106, 114, 117, 118, 120, 121, 121n. 160, 122, 124, 126, 130, 138n. 6, 139, 147, 147n. 35, 162, 163, 164, 180, 202, 213, 215, 217, 225, 228, 237, 238, 240, 245n. 127, 251, 254, 260, 264, 270, 271, 291, 292, 293, 296, 299, 314n. 95, 318, 319, 320, 321, 330, 360n. 69, 362, 363
corrective, xix, 81, 81n. 10, 82, 82nn. 11&12, 89, 89n. 35, 110n. 120, 133, 223, 231, 274, 277, 278, 325, 384, 396
Corsair Affair, xviii, 2, 53, 54, 57, 71, 77, 84, 91n. 40, 120, 134, 137, 138, 216, 221, 240–41, 245n. 127, 247, 247n. 133, 250–51, 269, 270
Crawfurd, Miss, 146, 146n. 31
credo quia absurdum. *See* paradox
Crisis in the Life of an Actress, xv, 162
Crites, Stephen, 163

Däubler, Theodor, 370, 370n. 105
Dagbladet, 86n. 24, 87, 107, 118n. 150, 121, 138, 164, 230, 231, 238, 265

Dallago, Carl, 367–70, 372, 380, 382–83, 385, 386; *Der Christ Kierkegaards*, 367; *Reine Menchen der Vorzeit*, 370, 372
Danish Lutheran Church. *See* state-Church
Dannevirke, 118–19, 126, 130n. 193
Dansk Kirketidende, 109, 110, 111, 112, 113, 197
Darlap, Adolf, 390n. 184
Darwin, Charles, 36, 166n. 95, 167, 239, 249, 255, 258, 288, 290, 290n. 21, 292, 293, 298, 299, 299n. 46, 300, 302, 349; *Descent of Man*, 290; *Origin of Species*, 167, 290
Dauthendey, Max, 339, 356, 362
David, Christian Georg Nathan, 84
Davidsen, Jacob, 89n. 34
deconstruction, 140n. 12
deism, 166
Delacroix, Henri, 351
Deleuran, Victor, 350
Der Brenner, xi, xii, xxi, 367–72, 377–79, 380, 385–89, 390, 391, 392
Descartes, René, 22n. 71, 287, 372
"Diary of a Seducer," xi, 11, 47n. 18, 55, 69–70, 104, 105n. 100, 106n. 107, 134, 161, 162, 230, 238, 245, 284n. 1, 286, 295, 301, 339, 356, 362, 382
Dickens, Charles, 146
Die Fackel, 368–71, 374, 377
Dietrichson, J. W. C., 72, 73, 74
Dietrichson, Lorentz H. S., 142, 275, 342
Dilthey, Wilhelm, 326–27, 376, 394
Dinesen, Isak (Karen Blixen), 70
Don Juan, 162, 269, 296, 303
Dorner, Albert, 313, 326, 336
Dostoevsky, Feodor, ix, 284, 355, 357, 358, 360, 360n. 69, 363, 369, 372n. 109, 373, 379, 387
Drachmann, A. B., 214n. 12, 280n. 252
Drachmann, Holger, 239
dreams, 292, 292n. 26, 295, 296–97, 299, 303
Drewsen, Viggo, 14, 15
Dru, Alexander, 391
Drury, Maurice, 380
Due, Christopher, 146

Ebner, Ferdinand, 386–87; the "I-Thou" relationship, 387, 396
ecclesiastical authorities, xix, 78–79, 80, 82, 96, 134, 266, 384–85
Eicholz, Alfred, 386n. 169
either-or, xix, 11, 53n. 41, 103–4, 106n. 107, 115, 116, 136, 153, 153n. 51, 294, 323, 324, 340
Either/Or, 10, 11, 47, 47n. 18, 55, 55n. 45, 56, 61, 66n. 74, 67, 68, 70, 77, 105n. 100, 121n. 160, 122n. 165, 128, 130, 137, 146–47, 148, 151, 156n. 64, 161, 162, 165, 226n. 53, 230, 232n. 81, 234n. 88, 247, 247n. 136, 248, 248n. 140, 263, 285n. 6, 286, 291, 292, 295, 304, 311, 312, 323, 339, 343, 344, 358, 366, 382
electromagnetism, 17, 31–32
Encyclopedia Britannica (eleventh edition), 154n. 55
Engel, Otto, 313n. 90
Enlightenment, the, 238
Epicureanism, 92
epistemology, 2, 46, 208
erotic, the, 295, 296n. 38, 304, 339, 374
Esterle, Max von, 370
Eve, 295
evil, 198
evolution, 36–37, 40, 45, 166n. 95, 167, 183, 201, 239, 249, 287, 292
existentialism, x, xii, xvii, xx, xxi, 38, 42n. 143, 49, 50n. 34, 101n. 82, 167, 168, 172, 178, 179, 191, 194n. 86, 207, 208, 209, 266, 278, 281, 286n. 7, 290, 302, 324, 338, 374, 379, 393, 394, 395
Expressionism, 354

Fædrelandet, 4, 18, 19, 63, 82, 84, 85, 86, 88, 90, 90n. 36, 91, 95, 97, 98, 100, 101, 102, 113, 118, 119, 121, 124, 127, 129, 129n. 191, 139, 195, 225, 226, 227, 242, 259, 277, 332, 336
faith, x, xix, 16, 23, 24, 29, 30, 31, 36, 37, 39, 76, 94n. 55, 98n. 70, 101n. 82, 111, 111n. 128, 113, 115, 116, 131, 155, 157, 166n. 95, 171–93, 195–99, 201–2, 204–210, 213, 231, 235, 252, 261, 264–65, 266, 269, 270, 271, 273, 285, 293, 303, 305, 309, 311, 312, 317, 320, 323, 324, 328, 333, 336, 337, 338, 346, 348, 349, 351, 366, 366n. 92, 373, 385, 389, 392, 395, 396
fascism, 287
fate, 179
Fear and Trembling, ix, 61, 156, 156n. 64, 181n. 29, 231, 232, 232n. 81, 248, 263, 285, 285n. 6, 311, 313, 344n. 14, 366, 366n. 92
Ferlov Knud, 352
Feuerbach, Ludwig, 5, 6, 7, 127, 134, 189–91, 195, 198, 231, 235, 243, 244, 274, 290, 293, 294, 299, 302, 306, 315, 324; *Das Wesen des Christentums*, 6–7, 231, 243, 293
feuilleton. *See* press
Fichte, Johann Gottlieb, 23, 46, 204
Ficker, Julius von, 368
Ficker, Ludwig von, xii, 367–72, 378, 380, 381, 386, 390, 391
fin de siècle, xx, 290, 304, 305, 311, 317, 330, 334, 335, 340, 354, 368, 371

First World War, xi, xvii, xx, 154n. 60, 352, 353n. 42, 358, 375, 377, 378, 379, 382, 392, 393
Flaubert, Gustave, 297, 297nn. 39&40, 299n. 49, 302; *Madame Bovary*, 297, 297n. 40, 302
Fleming, Donald, x, xii, 362n. 73
Flensburger Zeitung, 139
Flyveposten, 89, 89n. 34, 108, 111, 118n. 148, 121, 129
Förster-Nietzsche, Elisabeth, 369, 369n. 101
Fog, B. F., 97n. 64
For Self-Examination, 41, 87, 95n. 57, 115, 121n. 160, 122n. 167, 219, 232n. 81, 271, 275n. 241, 311, 336
Forsyth, Peter Taylor, 348–50
Fortnightly Review, 154, 344
Fraenkel, E., 292–93
Francis, Saint, 359
Francke, August Hermann, 117n. 146
freedom, ix, 37, 80, 112, 113, 160, 172, 173, 199, 238, 247, 249, 250, 263, 287, 354, 372
French Revolution, 308
Freud, Sigmund, 394; Freudian psychoanalysis, 281
From the Papers of One Still Living, 8, 13, 232n. 81
Fulford, Francis, 346–47

Garnett, R., 267
Gast, Peter, 334
Geijerstam, Gustaf af, 288, 289n. 16, 299n. 49
Geismar, Eduard, 313
George, Stefan, 358
German philosophical idealism. *See* Fichte; Hegel; Schelling
Giødwad, Jens F., 84
Gleiss, Otto, 311, 312
God, ix, 2–3, 10, 15, 16, 24, 25, 30, 36, 37, 37n. 128, 38, 40, 41, 45, 58, 64, 65, 74, 81, 98, 100, 101, 103, 106, 110, 113, 115, 116, 142, 155, 156, 157n. 67, 175, 179, 185, 195, 199, 200, 201, 250, 257, 263, 270, 275, 277, 289, 291, 292, 299, 303, 304, 305, 306, 387
Göransson, Zacharias, 177, 289
Goethe, Johann Wolfgang von, 29, 32, 38, 233, 248, 249n. 146, 269, 290
Goldschmidt, Meïr, xviii, 57, 58, 216, 221, 240–41, 245, 245n. 127, 300
"The Gospel of Suffering," 61, 251
Gosse, Sir Edmund, 259, 259n. 175
Gottsched, Hermann, 271–72, 277, 297, 310, 311n. 86, 313, 342, 352, 365
Grässe, Johan Georg, Theodor, 55

Greece, ix, 101n. 82, 108, 187, 247, 248, 354
Grieg, Edvard, 287
Grimm, the Brothers, 11n. 34
Grove, Peter Vilhelm, 107
Grüne, J. P. M., 88n. 29
Grundloven (the great liberalizing law) of 1849, 80
Grundtvig, N. F. S., 16, 18, 23–25, 31, 44, 45, 50, 56, 61, 72, 73, 80, 81, 86n. 24, 99, 99n. 74, 101n. 80, 102, 104, 107, 108, 108n. 114, 109, 109n. 118, 110, 111–13, 114, 118, 119, 119n. 154, 129, 165, 174, 175, 197, 197n. 101, 201, 204, 206, 212, 213, 235, 236, 244, 306, 307n. 74, 342
Gude, Ludvig Jacob Mendel, 99
Guizot, François-Pierre-Guillaume, 185–86

Habsburg Empire, 368
Haeckel, Ernst, 239, 372
Haecker, Theodor, xii, xxi, 371–91, 393, 395, 396; "Kritik der Gegenwart," 378–79, 382; *Satire und Polemik*, 375n. 130, 389–90; "S.K.s Altarreden," 388–89; *S.K. und die Philosophie der Innerlichkeit*, 372–74, 377, 389
Haller, Hans, 370n. 106
Hamann, Johann Georg, 129, 269n. 216
Hamilton, Andrew, 76–77; *Sixteen Months in the Danish Isles*, 76
Hamilton, Jane, 77
Hamilton, William, 77
Hansen, Christian, 219, 271, 310–11
Hansen, Oscar, 325
Hansen, P. G., 339
Hansen, Peter, 145, 158, 260
Harnack, Adolf von, 312, 346n. 22, 349, 376, 389, 392
Hartmann, Eduard von, 167, 249
Harvard University, x, xii, xiii, 300n. 53, 328, 362n. 73
Hauch, Johan Carsten, 22, 30, 236
Hauer, Karl, 371
Hauge, Hans Nielsen, 72–73, 78, 114, 150, 260
Hazlitt, William, 267
Heegaard, Sophus, 184, 264
Hegel, Frederik, 145, 266n. 200, 304n. 65
Hegel, Georg Wilhelm Friedrich, 5, 7, 8, 9, 13, 17, 17n. 58, 20n. 66, 27, 27n. 90, 30, 36, 44, 45, 46, 55, 61, 71, 83, 94, 102, 111, 130, 147, 147n. 33, 167, 171, 172, 173, 174, 179, 181, 182, 183, 184, 186, 189, 190, 192, 194, 194n. 87, 195, 197, 198, 199, 202, 202n. 121, 205, 207, 208, 209, 210, 220, 222, 233, 234, 235, 243, 263, 287, 293, 316, 322, 327, 348, 349, 369

Hegelian. *See* Hegel (G. W. F.)
Heiberg, Johan Ludvig, 17, 17n. 58, 44, 55, 57, 69, 147, 162n. 82, 235, 243, 303–4, 322, 326
Heiberg, Johanne Luise, 147, 162
Heiberg, P. A., 341, 341n. 5, 342
Heidegger, Martin, ix, xii, 391–92, 393, 394
Heine, Heinrich, 255, 290
Heloise (wife of Abelard), 269n. 214
Helveg, Fr., 282n. 257
Helweg, Hans Friedrich, 108, 111
Henriksen, Aage, 215, 275
Hertz, Henrik, 11, 55
Heuch, Johan Christian, 175–78, 256–59, 264–66, 275
Hilty, Carl, 376
Hirsch, Emanuel, 313, 391
historicism, 327n. 130, 354
Hitler, Adolf, 356
Hoch, Jules, 351
Hochland, 389–90
Høffding, Harald, xx, 239, 241, 293, 319–32, 335, 337, 339, 342, 346, 348, 348n. 27, 351, 351n. 37, 352, 373–74, 383n. 157, 395; "Democratic Radicalism," 319; *Filosofien i Tyskland efter Hegel*, 293; *Mindre Arbejder*, 331; *Den nyere Filosofs Historie*, 328; *S.K. som Filosof*, 322–25, 326–28, 329, 331
Hörup, Viggo, xi, 307–8
Hoffmann, Raoul, 352
Hofmannsthal, Hugo von, 365, 368n. 95, 371
Hohoff, Curt, 376, 376n. 133
Holberg, Baron Ludvig, 162
Holland Circle, 147
Hollander, Lee M., 391
Holy Spirit 90, 199
homosexuality, 293, 296n. 38
Hong, Edna H., xi, xii, xv, 76n. 99, 348n. 28
Hong, Howard, V., xi, xii, xv, 13, 280–81, 343n. 12; "genetic fallacy" in S.K. interpretation, 280, 280n. 253
Horn, E. F. B., 202, 202nn. 120&121
Horn, Frederik Winkel, 315–16
Horneman, J. W., 33
Horwitz, Rivka, 387
Howitt, Mary Botham, 57n. 51, 59–68, 68n. 78, 77; *The Literature and Romance of Northern Europe*, 61–62
Howitt, William, 59, 60, 61, 62, 77
Hügel, Baron Friedrich von, 383, 383n. 157
Hultberg, Helge, 200
humor, 2, 18, 19, 100, 231, 244, 268, 359, 374, 375
Husserl, Edmund, 354, 376, 391–92
Huysmans, Joris-Karl, 371; *Là-bas*, 371
Hvoslef, Frederik Waldemar, 75
hypnotism, 293

Ibsen, Hedvig, 150, 158
Ibsen, Henrik, xix, xx, 143–70, 228, 228n. 61, 239, 254n. 164, 260, 284, 284n. 2, 285, 285n. 3, 286, 287, 290, 294n. 33, 295, 297, 300, 303, 304, 304n. 65, 305, 340, 343, 344, 345, 347n. 24, 350, 351, 351nn. 36&37, 355, 356, 358, 369, 373, 395; and Norwegian nationalism, 149; and Scandinavianism, 149; *Brand*, xix, 143, 148, 149, 149n. 41, 150 56, 159–60, 164–67, 285, 305, 340, 345n. 19, 347n. 24, 350, 351n. 37; *Agnes*, 151n. 47, 156; Alf, 155; Brand, 145, 145n. 27, 149–61, 165, 169, 285, 303, 304, 358; Einar, 151n. 47, 156n. 65, 157; *Catiline*, 145; *A Doll's House*, 167; *Emperor and Galilean*, 149n. 43, 166n. 97, 300; Julian, 300; *An Enemy of the People*, 148n. 40, 159, 159n. 75; Dr. Stockman, 159n. 75; *Ghosts*, 167; *Hedda Gabler*, 167; *Love's Comedy*, xix, 143, 143n. 20, 148, 149, 160–61; *Peer Gynt*, xix, 149, 160–61; Peer Gynt, 158, 161; *When We Dead Awaken*, 168, 344; Irene, 168; Rubek, 168; Stensgaard (*The League of Youth*), 158
idle talk. *See* chatter
immortality, 16, 34, 235, 287
indeterminacy, 331–32
indirect communication, 2, 14, 51–52, 93n. 48, 94, 94n. 54, 95, 137, 139, 163, 176, 178, 225, 226, 246, 248, 348, 367, 373, 380n. 143
individualism, 16, 36, 50, 79, 113, 117, 131, 137, 150, 158–60, 161, 172, 177, 178, 179, 187, 192, 197, 202, 208, 222–23, 225, 226, 231, 235, 249–51, 281, 287, 302, 303, 304, 310, 315, 316, 318, 319, 326, 327, 333, 334, 335, 338, 340, 341, 347, 351–52, 354, 380, 383, 387, 388, 395, 396. *See also* "single individual"
infant baptism, 104, 104n. 97, 115, 116, 190, 200
inherited guilt, 167, 250, 301, 302
Innsbruck, xi, xii, 367, 367n. 94, 368, 369, 372n. 109
inwardness, 27, 154, 154n. 54, 192, 231, 278, 360, 372, 373
Ipsen, Christine Margaretha, 46
irony, 19, 20, 26, 40, 50, 51–52, 52n. 38, 53, 133, 140, 168n. 103, 237, 243, 246, 251, 257, 259, 266, 268, 270, 308, 381
Isaac, 155

Jacobsen, Jens Peter, xii, xx, 167, 239, 290–306, 334–35, 339, 345n. 20, 363, 364; *En begavet ung Mands Dagbog*, 292, 299; *Erotiske Studier efter Biblen*, 295; *Marie Grubbe*, 297, 299, 299n. 49, 300, 301, 302; Marie, 301; Sti Høg, 301; *En Kaktus springer ud*, 294; *Et Kjærlighedsforhold*, 295; *Mogens*,

Index 431

295n. 35; *Niels Lyhne*, 290, 302–6, 335, 335n. 155, 363; on death, 305–6; Gerda, 305–6; Dr. Hjerrild, 304; Niels, 302–6; "Phalaris," 291; "Saa er nu da Jorden en Kobbertyr," 291
Jacobsen, P. V., 11
Jaeger, Hans, 391
Jaeger, Henrik, 150–51
James, William, 287, 328–29, 348
Janik, Allan, 367n. 94, 378, 380n. 143, 385n. 165
Janus, 180
Jaspers, Karl, xii, 391–92, 394
Jensen, Christian, 341–42, 346
Jesus. *See* Christ
Jörg, Joseph Edmund, xi, 131–32
Johannes Climacus, or De Omnibus Dubitandum Est, 268
Johannes the Seducer. *See* "Diary of a Seducer"; pseudonyms
Johnson, Gisle, 115–16, 175, 260–61, 262, 266
Joyce James, 297, 297n. 39, 344–46
Judaism 81, 232, 256–59, 366, 366n. 92
Judge For Yourself! 41, 239
Juncker, Axel, 361–64, 368n. 96

Kafka, Franz, 365–67, 379; the Kafkaesque, 367
Kant, Immanuel, ix, 22, 22n. 71, 46, 171, 172, 172n. 3, 182, 203–4, 204n. 128, 208, 317, 349, 351, 373, 380n. 143
Kassner, Rudolf, xii, 357–61, 364, 365, 371, 373, 379; *Der goldne Drachen*, 357; physiognomy (a pseudo-science), 357–59; "S.K.-Aphorismen," 358–59, 360
Kaufmann, Walter, 282n. 256
Ketels, H. C., 311, 311n. 86
Key, Ellen, 234n. 86, 364
Kierkegaard, Michael, 302
Kierkegaard, Peter Christian, 49, 61, 62, 74n. 94, 102, 123, 128, 137, 211–15, 262, 272n. 229, 293
Kierkegaard, Poul 293–94, 321, 321n. 108
Kierkegaard, Søren: Berlin, trip to, 47–49; *Bladartikler*, 130; death of, 3, 4, 12, 49, 64, 94, 105–6, 111, 113, 120–24, 125, 127, 135, 136, 142, 143, 144, 163, 173, 174, 176n. 12, 178, 181, 195, 208, 211, 212, 214, 215, 222, 242, 252, 253, 283, 322, 336, 355, 374; his dissertation (or thesis): *see Concept of Irony*; and drama, 144, 162–63, 169–70, 285, 348; his engagement: *see* Olsen, Regine; father, relations with, xix, 12, 13, 83, 86, 90, 217, 238, 244, 246, 247, 247n. 133, 248n. 140, 249, 250, 251, 268, 269, 273, 301, 302, 367, 396; journals and papers of, xix, 2, 3, 6, 13, 27,

29, 31, 32, 38, 39, 41, 56, 57, 58, 59, 82, 85, 88, 93, 105, 127, 162, 173, 179, 211–19, 221–22, 224, 238, 240, 241, 245, 260, 261, 262, 266, 268, 270, 271–72, 273, 275, 277, 279, 280–81, 284, 288, 297, 298, 302, 306, 323, 324, 341, 342, 347, 360, 365, 381, 383, 385–86, 395; politics of, 85, 125, 237n. 97, 308, 323; and science, 27, 29, 32–34, 36–42, 174, 255; women, attitude to, 56–59, 66–67, 70, 71, 76, 322n. 111
Kierkegaard, Søren, reception of: Anglo-Saxon, xx, 57n. 51, 59–61, 64–66, 76–77, 154, 154nn. 55 and 60, 259n. 175, 267, 315–16, 328–29, 342, 342n. 9, 344–50, 391; Catholic, xii, xxi, 131–32, 287, 389–90; French, xx, 129–30, 144n. 23, 287–88, 342n. 9, 350–53; general, xvii–xviii, 19, 19n. 65, 20, 23, 52, 132–35, 136–39, 142–43, 163, 206–7, 209, 219, 240, 279, 280–81, 319, 328, 379, 393–96; German, xi, xii, xix, xx, 17–19, 47–48, 49, 50–52, 54–55, 71, 124–27, 131–32, 139–40, 175–78, 211, 219–221, 223, 225–32, 266–74, 277–78, 279, 283, 306, 308–15, 316, 327, 332, 335, 342, 353–92; Italian, xx, 352–53; Jewish, xii, 284, 366, 366n. 92, 387; Norwegian, xi, 53, 68–71, 113–17, 123, 140, 260–64; philosophical, 322–25, 326–27; Scandinavian, x, xi, xii, xviii, xix, 17, 52, 78, 122, 123, 130, 130n. 194, 142, 143, 144, 164, 209, 255, 275, 279, 283, 306, 342; Scandinavian-American, xi, xii, xviii, 72–76, 316–17, 342–44; Slavic, 284; Spanish, 284–87; Swedish, xi, xii, 53–68, 71–72, 122–23, 177–78, 274–77, 288–90; theological, xviii, xx, 4, 18, 31, 49–52, 71, 88, 90, 91, 92, 93, 103, 104, 110, 111, 174–87, 198–99, 201–5, 219–20, 221–22, 225–28, 268, 271, 276, 278, 306–7, 310, 346, 348–49
Kirkekampen, xvi, 63–64, 86, 87, 91, 93, 96, 98, 101, 102, 104n. 97, 109, 109n. 118, 111–14, 117, 118n. 150, 120–22, 122n. 165, 126–30, 132, 133, 135, 136, 138, 139, 142, 150, 173, 174, 176, 180, 180n. 25, 187, 203, 204n. 128, 206, 207, 208, 212, 221–25, 227, 272, 274, 275, 276, 283, 288, 297, 306, 310, 315, 324, 326, 384
Kjøbenhavnsposten, 6, 84, 88, 88n. 29, 98, 108, 121
Knight of Faith, 155, 231, 285n. 6
Knight of Infinite Resignation, 156n. 65
knowledge, xix, 23, 24, 31, 36, 38, 94n. 55, 173, 174, 176, 180–93, 196–99, 201–2, 204–8, 235, 270, 271, 320, 323, 395
Koch, Carl, 342, 346
Koch, Peter Christian, 118n. 147, 119, 130n. 193
Kofoed-Hansen, Hans Peter, 130–31, 236, 288

Kolderup-Rosenvinge, Jens Laurids Andreas, 25, 34
Kopenhagener Zeitung, 126–27, 131
Kraus, Karl, 368–70, 374–80, 382
Kütemeyer, Wilhelm, 49n. 30, 381n. 148
Kuhr, V., 341
Kulturkampf, 309

Lammers, Gustav Adolph, 114–17, 134, 150–52, 158, 260, 274
Lange, Julius, 233–34, 234n. 86
Lange, Thomas, 107
Lao Tzu, 370
Lasker-Schüler, Else, 370
Lassalle, Ferdinand, 239, 249
Laub, Otto, 221–22
leap of faith. *See* faith
Lehmann, Edvard, 377
Lehmann, Orla, 69, 84, 85
Leibniz, Gottfried Wilhelm, 190, 222
Lessing, Gotthold Ephraim, 230, 270
Levin, Israel, 10
Lie, Jonas, 236
The Lily in the Field and the Bird in the Air, 121n. 160, 122n. 167, 309
Lindberg, Niels, 197
Lindenberg, H., 271, 278n. 249
Linka. *See* Preus, Caroline Dorothea Margrethe (Keyser)
Listov, Andreas, 306
Löwith, Karl, 134
Lowrie, Walter, xv, 314, 321, 347, 391
Lucas, F. L., 145–46, 146n. 28
Lucian, 292
Lukács, Georg, 354–59, 364, 371
Lund, Henriette, 293n. 29, 361–64
Lund, Henrik, 123–24, 125, 211, 212, 213, 231n. 6
Lund, Johan Christian, 211
Lund, Peter Wilhelm, 32, 33, 37, 42n. 143
Luther, Martin, 6, 30, 82n. 12, 89, 89n. 35, 91, 132, 139, 306, 360, 360n. 69; Lutheranism, xviii, xx, 30, 78, 79, 82, 95, 111n. 128, 115, 117, 131, 159n. 74, 165, 175, 256, 261, 287, 288, 311, 314, 315, 332, 333n. 150, 336, 343, 343n. 12, 396
Luther College, xi, 76n. 99, 343
Lysander, Albert Theodor, 71–72, 77, 275

Macintosh, H. R., 346, 346n. 22
Mackay, John A., 286n. 7
Mahler, Gustav, 318n. 99
maieutic, 14n. 45; agents, xxi; purpose, 14
Maistre, Joseph de, 238
Malantschuk, Gregor, 6, 67

Mann, Heinrich, 369, 369n. 102
Mann, Thomas, 356, 369, 369n. 102
Marheineke, Philipp Konrad, 48, 48n. 24, 102
Martensen, Hans Lassen, 17n. 57, 21, 44, 56, 57, 58, 61, 63, 64, 71, 72, 81, 83, 90–91, 92, 93, 94, 96, 97, 97n. 64, 98, 98n. 67, 99, 99n. 73, 100n. 76, 101n. 81, 102, 103, 106, 109, 111, 112n. 131, 122, 123n. 168, 131, 174, 175, 178, 179, 180, 183, 185–87, 190, 193, 197, 200, 201, 202, 203, 207, 208, 212, 216, 221, 222, 223, 225, 226, 227, 228, 263, 270, 274, 275, 306–7, 309–10, 315, 316–17, 322; *Af Mit Levned*, 98, 307, 309–10; *Christelige Dogmatik*, 56, 58, 71, 92, 174, 178, 200, 212, 223, 306–7, 316; *Christelige Ethik*, 222–23, 228, 317; *Om Tro og Viden, et Lejlighedsskrift*, 185–87
Martineau, James, 349
martyr, 86, 87, 89, 90–92, 152, 225, 251, 289, 303, 358
Marx, Karl, 5, 6, 83n. 14; "Kein Berliner," 6, 354, 355, 356
mass society, 287
Mauthner, Fritz, 378
mechanism, 288, 317, 330, 354
Meister Eckart, 356
melancholy, 218, 247, 250, 251, 262, 268, 269, 285, 290, 291, 300, 302, 305, 322–23, 325, 341, 349, 358, 361, 375
Methlagl, Walter, xii, 367n. 94, 371, 372n. 109, 381n. 148
Meyer, Edvard, 89n. 34
Meyer, Michael, 146, 153, 164
Meyer, Raphael, 364n. 81
Meyer, Richard Moses, 377–78
Michaelsen, Anna, 296, 296n. 38
Michel, Robert, 368n. 95
Michelsen, Alexander, 311, 312
Mill, John Stuart, 167, 228n. 61, 237, 239, 247, 258
miracle, 37n. 128, 38, 41, 186, 201, 203, 213, 235
modernism, 377
Møller, Christen, 278n. 250
Møller, Peter Ludvig, 11, 53, 57, 240
Møller, Poul Martin, 5n. 14, 7, 7n. 24, 8, 8n. 25, 12, 43, 44n. 2, 322
Møller, Vilhelm, 290n. 21, 300
Molbech, Christian Knud Frederik, 54–55, 128, 239, 241, 242
Molière (Jean-Baptiste Poquelin), 162
The Moment (or Instant), 50, 101–2
monism, 184, 194, 196, 321, 323, 329, 372
Monrad, M. J., 202, 202n. 121
Monrad, O. P., 353, 382
Morgenbladet, 202, 255–56, 262

Mormons, 101, 101n. 80, 113
Mozart, Wolfgang Amadeus, 162
Müller, Robert, 372, 372n. 109
Muth, Karl, 390, 390n. 183
Mynster, C. L. N., 307, 310
Mynster, Jakob Peter, 25n. 84, 30, 31, 61, 63, 77, 80, 81, 83, 86, 87, 87n. 27, 88–93, 95, 96, 102, 110, 112, 112n. 131, 119, 120, 121, 130, 134, 176n. 12, 221–22, 224, 225, 227, 244, 260, 306, 310, 315, 324
mystery, 187–89, 193, 198–201, 203, 207, 208
mysticism, 166
myth, 62, 169

Nathanson, Mendel Levin, 87n. 25
National Socialism, 390n. 183
nationalism, 18, 81, 85, 112, 113, 114, 149, 176n. 13
nature, 22–23, 24, 25, 28, 29, 30, 32, 33, 38, 40, 41, 194, 194n. 87, 199, 244, 302, 369, 385
Naturphilosophie. *See* Schelling
Neander, Johann August Wilhelm (David Mendel), 61, 102
Neo-Orthodoxy. *See* Barth, Karl
Neo-Thomism. *See* Thomas Aquinas, Saint
New Testament. *See* Bible
Newman, John Henry (Cardinal), 357, 383–86, 388; *Grammar of Assent*, 385
Newtonian physics, 22n. 71
Nielsen, Frederik, 291, 296n. 38
Nielsen, Michael, 341
Nielsen, Rasmus, xix, 18, 18n. 62, 21, 93–97, 111, 120, 120n. 157, 129, 130, 147, 174, 178–210, 212, 213, 213nn. 6 & 8, 214, 214n. 12, 215, 226, 227, 232, 234, 235, 236n. 94, 239, 243, 253, 261, 270, 275, 276, 294, 306, 307, 307n. 74, 310, 320, 321, 326, 395; dualism of, 179–80, 181–83, 184, 186, 188, 189, 193, 195, 196, 197, 199, 202, 203, 204, 207, 209, 253, 320; *Evangelietroen og den moderne Bevidsthed*, 178, 213; *Grundideernes Logik*, 182–83; *Om Hindringer og Betingelser for det aandelige Liv i Nutiden*, 188–89; "Om S. Kierkegaards 'Mentale Tilstand',"180; *Paa Kierkegaardske "Stadier": Et Livsbillede*, 181n. 29; *Religionsphilosophie*, 198–201
Nietzsche, Friedrich, ix, xx, 140, 249, 250, 253–54, 284, 287, 288n. 14, 318–19, 326, 333, 333n. 151, 334–35, 336, 340, 341, 344, 351, 353, 359, 369, 370, 370n. 106, 372–73, 376, 377, 383, 394; early reception in Scandinavia, 319, 319n. 103; *Antichrist*, 336; *Ecce Homo*, 318; *Ressentiment*, 373; "Superman," 319, 341, 359, 370; "will to power," 370

Nordau, Max, 340, 340n. 3
Nordic spirit, 62, 79, 114, 158–59, 160, 169, 290, 302, 305
Norwegian Lutheran Church. *See* state-Church
Novalis (*pseud*. G. F. P. von Hardenberg), 238

Oehlenschläger, Adam Gottlob, 23, 23n. 75, 45, 56, 145n. 24
Oehlenschläger, Sophie, 45–46, 46n. 12
Øjeblikket, 4, 54, 63, 64, 65, 68, 91, 100n. 78, 101, 101n. 81, 102, 105, 110, 112–17, 122, 122n. 167, 123–28, 131, 134, 142, 150, 151, 175, 184, 219, 227, 232n. 81, 240, 251, 252, 252n. 157, 257, 261, 263, 265, 274, 275, 283, 298n. 16, 297, 307, 308, 315, 322, 333, 336, 383, 395, 396
Øre-Sund, 130, 130n. 193
Öresundposten, 54n. 42
Ørsted, Albertine, 45, 46
Ørsted, Anders Sandoe, 21, 22, 23, 25, 25n. 84, 26, 36, 45, 46, 83, 224
Ørsted, Hans Christian, xii, xviii, 4, 17, 19, 20, 21–37, 40, 41, 42, 44, 45, 46, 46n. 14, 49, 55, 59, 59n. 58, 94, 130, 174, 184–85, 194, 199, 326; *Aanden i Naturen* (*The Soul in Nature*), 26–32, 36, 41, 59, 184
Ørsted, Sophie, 35, 35n. 122
Ørum, Jacob Christian Martin, 110–11, 128, 132, 133
Old Testament. *See* Bible
Oldenburg, Th. W., 74n. 94
Olesen Larsen, K., 338
Olsen, Regine, xix, xxi, 13, 21n. 69, 46, 47, 47nn. (17,18,20), 137, 138, 161, 168, 216, 247–48, 250, 251, 269–70, 272, 274, 296, 296n. 38, 304, 355, 355n. 49, 356–57, 358, 364, 364n. 81, 365, 366n. 91, 395, 396
"On the Difference between a Genius and an Apostle," 288, 384
On My Work as an Author, 94n. 54, 127, 139, 225, 226, 226n. 55
"On the Occasion of a Wedding." *See* *Upbuilding Discourses*
An Open Letter, 94n. 54, 225
Orvar Odd (*pseud.*). *See* Sturzen-Becker, Patrick

Paludan-Müller, Caspar, 91
Paludan-Müller, Jens, 92–93, 100n. 76, 110
pantheism, 45, 49, 79, 166, 194, 222, 233, 235
Pape, W., 275, 275n. 242
paradox, xix, 50, 51, 98n. 70, 101n. 82, 108, 111n. 128, 115, 116, 136, 172, 173, 177, 179, 181, 184, 187, 188, 188n. 65, 189, 192, 196, 198–200, 202, 204, 205, 205n. 133, 206, 208,

209, 210, 245, 252–53, 263, 270, 278, 315, 322, 323, 331, 337, 346, 352, 359, 384, 387, 389, 396
Pascal, Blaise, ix, 13, 230, 255, 267, 278n. 250, 287, 306, 351, 359, 371, 372, 386
passion, 38, 81, 84, 137, 164, 172, 179, 187, 189, 192, 244, 246, 268, 287, 301, 315, 331, 372, 373, 374, 388, 395
Paul, Saint, 126, 289
Paulli, Just Henrik, 57
Paulson, Kristofer, 343n. 12
personality, xxi, 193, 278, 309–10, 334, 354
Petersen, Clemens C. M., 201–2
Petersen, Emil, 229n. 62, 264n. 194, 277
Petersen, Frederik Christian (Danish; prof. of Greek), 17
Petersen, Frederik Christian (Norwegian; prof. of theology), 260–64, 265, 265n. 198, 274, 275, 276, 277, 278, 283, 342
Petronius, 371; *Satyrikon*, 371
Phalaris, 291–92, 294
phenomenology, 172–73, 354, 393
Philosophical Fragments, 27, 50–51, 52n. 38, 101n. 82, 192n. 81, 234n. 88, 312, 325
philosophy of intuition. *See* vitalism; phenomenology
philosophy of language, 140n. 12, 205n. 133
pietism, 78–79, 113, 114, 115, 117, 150, 158, 165, 202, 260, 278, 343n. 12, 375
Pineau, Léon, 352
Plato, 32, 32n. 115, 187, 359
Plitt, Gustav, 177n. 17
Ploug, Carl, 84, 236, 259
pneumatology, 386
Poe, Edgar Allan, 297
The Point of View for My Work as an Author, 3n. 9, 52, 93, 94n. 54, 137–42, 153, 163, 176, 181, 225, 226, 231, 232n. 81, 262, 268, 274, 275, 326, 336, 341
Politiken, xi, 307–8, 325
Pope Leo XIII, 317; *Aeterni Patris* (1878), 317; *Rerum Novarum* (1891), 317
positivism, 40, 198, 200, 207, 232, 249, 255, 279, 287, 305, 317, 321, 322, 323, 329, 330, 340, 349, 351, 354, 377, 394
Practice in Christianity, 72, 82, 92, 100, 113, 115, 121n. 160, 122n. 167, 129, 165, 221, 251, 270, 271, 275n. 241, 337
Pre-Raphaelites, 340
present age, the, 137, 137n. 2, 138, 141, 150, 160, 207, 210, 248–49, 261, 263, 264, 279, 287, 288, 309, 312, 318, 374, 378–79, 382, 383, 385, 393, 394, 396
press, the, 84, 85, 101, 113–14, 117, 124, 133, 138, 142, 227, 276, 308, 368, 374, 375, 378, 379, 381

Preus, Caroline Dorothea, Margrethe (Keyser), 72–76, 79n. 1
Preus, Herman Amberg, 72, 73, 74, 74n. 94, 79n. 1
progress, idea of, 35, 40, 309, 323, 340, 351
Protestantism, 30, 78, 80, 89, 95, 117, 121, 131–32, 159, 160, 185, 278, 287, 309, 310, 312, 317, 327, 337, 348, 349, 350, 357, 360, 377, 389, 392, 393
Proudhon, Pierre-Joseph, 144n. 23
providence, 36, 138, 179, 275
Prussia, 124, 125, 126, 149, 212, 237, 293n. 29
Przywara, Erich, 390
pseudo-Kierkegaard. *See* Nielsen, Rasmus
pseudonyms, 1–2, 3n. 5, 11, 41, 47, 52n. 38, 56, 58, 61, 67, 76, 95, 111, 137, 139, 162, 162n. 82, 163, 176n. 12, 189, 226, 226n. 53, 231, 246, 248, 260, 268, 269, 270, 274, 295–96, 301, 344, 374
"Purity of Heart is to Will One Thing." *See Upbuilding Discourses*

quantum physics, 331–32
Quehl, Ryno, xi, 124–26, 131

Rappoport, Angelo, 344
Reincke, Julie von, 346n. 22, 361
Reinertsen, P. J., 343
relativism, 178, 194n. 86, 324, 327, 329, 331
Renan, Joseph Ernest, 144n. 23, 237
Repetition: An Essay in Experimental Psychology, 61, 161, 234n. 88, 237n. 99, 289, 366
Riehl, Alois, 334, 334n. 154
Rilke, Clara, 362n. 72
Rilke, Rainer Maria, xii, 358, 360–64, 366n. 91, 371, 380
Ritschl, Albrecht, 278, 312, 317, 348, 349, 353, 392
Ritter, Johan Wilhelm, 22n. 71
Robertson, J. G., 347
Rølvaag, Ole Edvart, xii, 343–44
Rohr, E., 364n. 81
romanticism, 28, 68, 71, 79, 149, 166, 230, 232, 237, 238, 317, 347, 353, 355, 396
Rosenberg, P. A., 180n. 24, 341, 342
Rousseau, Jean-Jacques, 369
Rudelbach, Andreas Gottlob, 226–27
Rudin, Waldemar, 274–78, 283, 342, 346
Ruge, Arnold, 6; *Anekdota*, 6, 7; *Deutsche Jahrbücher für Wissenschaft und Kunst*, 18
Rydberg, Viktor, 265, 266n. 199

Sade, Comte Donatien-Alphonse-François Marquis de, 371; *Juliette*, 371
sado-masochism, 296

Index 435

St. Olaf College, xi, xii, xiii, 76n. 99, 343, 343n. 12, 344n. 14
St. Simonians, 62
Sainte-Beuve, Charles-Augustin, 237, 246n. 132, 293, 297, 298, 322
Salmonsen, C. J., 229n. 62
Sars, Ernst, 258
Sartre, Jean-Paul, 163, 194n. 86, 281, 305, 306n. 70
satire, 84, 368, 374, 375, 375n. 130, 377, 381, 385
Scharling, C. E., 174n. 7, 180
Scharling, Henrik, 204
Scheler, Max, xii, 376, 376n. 131, 387, 387n. 172
Schelling, Friedrich Wilhelm Joseph von, 22, 23, 24, 46, 48, 48n. 24, 49, 49n. 27, 61, 62, 102, 190, 199, 222, 237n. 99, 322n. 111, 353
Schiller, (Johann Christoph) Friedrich von, 290n. 21
Schiødte, A. F., 204-5, 208, 209
schizophrenia, 294n. 30
Schlegel, August Wilhelm von, 23
Schlegel, Friedrich von, 23, 238, 247n. 136
Schlegel, Johan Frederik, 272
Schleiermacher, Friedrich Ernst Daniel, 5, 23, 46, 61, 102, 172, 185, 190, 220, 307, 322; *Der christliche Glaube*, 307
Schleswig-Holstein, 118, 118n. 147; 125, 126, 139, 229, 237, 293n. 29
Schlier, Paula, 369
Schmidt, P. C. Rudolf, 201, 235-36, 239
Schnitzler, Arthur, 365, 371
Schopenhauer, Arthur, 5, 167, 249, 287, 322n. 111, 353, 369, 370n. 106, 380n. 143
Schreiber, Ferdinand, 372, 376
Schrempf, Christoph, xx, xxi, 311-15, 326, 332-38, 339, 342n. 9, 347, 349, 350, 357, 371, 376, 377, 381, 382, 385, 391, 395, 396
Schulerud, Ole Carelius, 146
Schwarz, Karl, 177
science, xviii, 22, 23, 24, 26, 27, 29, 32-39, 166, 171, 173, 174, 175, 180, 182, 184, 186, 195, 198, 199, 200, 201, 205, 235, 237, 238, 256, 288, 292, 298, 308, 317, 331, 340, 351
science fiction 223-25
scientism, 39, 256
Scott, Sir Walter, 146
Scribe, Augustin-Eugène, 162
Scripture. *See* Bible
Second World War, 221n. 33, 390
Seidler, Irma, 355n. 49
Seidlin, Oskar, 250
Selmer, Ludvig, 262
sex. *See* the erotic

Shakespeare, William, 145, 148, 162, 249n. 146, 290n. 21, 297; Hamlet, 349, 352; *Julius Caesar*, 145
Shelley, Percy Bysshe, 239
Shouw, Joakim Frederik, 33
Sibbern, Frederik Christian, 17, 19, 20, 21, 21n. 69, 25n. 84, 43-49, 61, 92, 94n. 52, 130, 223-25, 243-44, 320, 322, 326, 330-31
The Sickness Unto Death, 77, 176, 234, 234n. 88, 301, 309, 337, 373
Siesby, Gottlieb, 89n. 34
Simmel, Georg, 354, 355, 378
Simon Stylites, 56, 64, 123n. 168, 247
Simonsen, Nels E., 316-17
sin, 27, 37, 176, 183, 234, 250, 264, 298, 301, 302, 312
"single individual," xxii, 57, 81, 99, 113, 116, 121, 137, 138, 159n. 75, 176, 202, 230, 231, 249, 251, 257, 263, 270, 281, 310, 315, 320, 321, 323, 323n. 116, 328, 333, 341, 359, 394, 395. *See also* individualism
Socrates, xxi, 14, 14n. 45, 19, 38, 108, 139, 247, 270, 281, 287, 337, 370
Solovyev, Vladimir, 355
Sommer, M. A., 142
Sophocles, 162
Sorbonne, the, 351-52
South Tyrol, 367, 368, 369
Spang, Peter, J., 48
Spencer, Herbert, 239, 258
Spener, Philipp Jacob, 117n. 146
Spinoza, Baruch, 189, 190, 194, 222, 233, 235, 287
spiritualism, 154n. 60
Stael, Mme. de (Anne-Louise-Germaine), 238
stages, xxi, 47n. 17, 67, 93, 116, 137, 155-57, 168, 176, 226, 230, 245, 270, 320, 323, 326, 344, 358, 367, 373
Stages on Life's Way, 53, 56, 66n. 74, 156n. 65, 163, 181n. 29, 232n. 81, 245, 309, 352, 374
state-Church, xv, xvi, xviii, 4, 63-64, 78-85, 88, 93, 100, 101, 101n. 80, 109n. 118, 112, 114, 115, 116, 117, 119, 120, 121, 123, 123n. 170, 124n. 173, 125, 131, 134, 260, 265, 288, 385, 386n. 166
Staub, Herta, 357n. 57
Steffens, Heinrich, 28, 48, 48n. 24, 79, 102
Steiner, Rudolf, 334
Stendhal (Marie-Henri Beyle), 297
Stilling, Peter Michael, 174
Stirner, Max, 293, 351
Stobart, Mabel Annie, 154, 154n. 60, 169, 344
Stoicism, 92
Strauss, David Friedrich, 6, 17, 18, 19, 127, 189-90, 195, 235, 244, 269n. 216, 274; *Die christliche Glaubenslehre*, 127, 189-90

Strindberg, August, xi, xx, 165, 166, 284, 287, 288–90, 373; *Inferno*, 288–89; *To Damascus*, 289
Strodtmann, Adolf, 228–32, 237, 253, 266, 312n. 87
Strodtmann, Henriette (Gerda), 228–29
Sturzen-Becker, Patrick (*pseud.* Orvar Odd), 53–54, 71, 77
subjectivism, 159n. 75, 160, 177, 193–94, 194n. 84, 204, 243, 281, 324, 331, 333, 338, 352, 388, 389, 389n. 180, 396
subjectivity, 27, 154, 171, 172, 174, 177, 181, 182, 192, 193–94, 194n. 84, 202, 202n. 121, 206, 231, 263, 269, 270, 320, 322, 323, 324, 331, 352, 388, 389, 396
Sunday Circle, 356
Swenson, David F., 347–48
Swenson, Lillian M., 347
syphilis, 228n. 61

Taine, Hippolyte, 184, 237, 239, 246n. 132, 258, 293, 298, 322
Tegnér, Elaias, 64
Teisen, Niels, 307, 310, 325n. 125
teleological suspension of the ethical, 156, 344
Tennyson, Alfred Lord, 290n. 21
Tersteegen, Gerhard, 117n. 146
Tertullian, 173, 389
theosophy, 340
"This Must Be Said; So Let it Now Be Said," 65, 101, 122n. 167
Thomas Aquinas, Saint, ix, 172, 209, 209n. 136, 389; *philosophia perennis*, 389
Thomsen, Julie, 241n. 108
Thoresen, Magdalene, 147–48, 236
"Thorn in the Flesh," 248, 358, 378, 379
Thorsen (nineteenth-century archivist, University Library, Copenhagen), 213
Thue, Henning Junghans, 53
Thulstrup, Niels, 314n. 95
Thurah, Christian Henrik, 11, 11n. 35, 104–9, 111, 114n. 136, 120n. 155, 122n. 165, 124n. 174
Tieck, Johann Ludwig, 23, 238
Tönnies, Ferdinand, 335
Tolstoy, Lev Nikolayevich, 325, 340, 355, 357, 358, 369, 373, 380n. 143
Trakl, Georg, 370, 380, 381, 391
translations (of works by, or material on, S.K.): English, 59–61, 64–65, 315–16, 328, 346, 347; French, 288, 352, 360; German, xx, 18, 125, 126, 131, 139, 177, 211, 219–21, 223, 225–28, 231–32, 254, 266–67, 269, 270–71, 273, 284, 309–15, 325–26, 328, 329, 335, 336, 339, 347, 351, 365, 367, 371, 376–77, 378, 380, 381–82, 383, 385, 388, 389, 391, 396;
Italian, 352, 353n. 42; Russian, 339; Spanish, 286; Swedish, 122, 274–75, 284, 339
Trendelenberg, Adolf, 322n. 111
"Tro og Viden," xix, 173, 175, 178, 182, 188, 190, 194, 195, 197, 198, 200, 201, 203, 203n. 122, 204, 205, 207, 208, 209, 210, 211, 212, 213, 214, 235, 236, 244, 259, 261, 270, 278, 294, 294n. 33, 295, 320, 320n. 107
Troels-Lund, Troels Frederik, 25–26
Troeltsch, Ernst, 327–28, 335, 338n. 165, 376, 389
"Truth is subjectivity." *See* subjectivity
tuberculosis, 302, 366, 379
Tübingen, xx, 18, 220, 221n. 33, 261, 271, 311, 312n. 88, 333, 342
Turgeniev, Ivan Sergeyevich, 297, 363
Two Ages: The Age of Revolution and the Present Age, A Literary Review, 287, 373, 378, 382, 383
Two Discourses at the Communion on Fridays. See *Upbuilding Discourses*
Two Upbuilding Discourses (1843). See *Upbuilding Discourses*

Unamuno, Miguel de, xx, 284–87, 342n. 9
Unitarianism, 349
Upbuilding Discourses, 47, 61, 73, 75n. 96, 95n. 59, 121n. 160, 122n. 167, 129, 137, 165, 203, 225n. 50, 226, 251, 267, 313, 334n. 153, 344n. 14, 346, 361, 377, 381, 384, 388, 389

Valhalla, 62
Verne, Jules, 35
Vienna Circle, 372n. 109
Vinet, Alexander, 278n. 250
Virchow, Rudolf, 376
vitalism, 287, 317, 330, 354
Vodskov, Hans Sophus, 293, 297–98, 324n. 119
Voltaire (Francois-Marie Arouet), 166, 255

Die Wahrheit, 334–36
Wallin, J. O., 65
Wassermann, Jacob, 363, 364
Weber, Max, 335, 354
Welhaven, Johan Sebastian, 68, 69, 70n. 84
Werder, Karl W., 48, 48n. 24
Wergeland, Henrik, 68, 145n. 24
Wergeland, Nicolai, 68
Wetzel, Paul, 310, 312
Whitehead, Alfred North, ix
Whitman, Walt, 370
Wiehe, Hanna, 148
will, 153–54, 155, 160, 179, 189, 193, 195, 199, 250, 303, 319, 329, 352, 394

Winterl, J. J., 22n. 71
Winther, Christian, 55, 69
"witness to the truth" (*Sandhedsvidne*), 83, 86, 87, 89–92, 95, 109, 110, 112, 224–25, 324, 336, 358
Wittgenstein, Ludwig, 205n. 133, 380–81
women, emancipation of, 62–63, 63n. 66, 66–67, 68–71
Works of Love, 75, 77, 113, 121n. 160, 147, 261
Wulff, Henriette, 11, 124n. 174

Xenophon, 19

Zahle, Peter, Christian, 129
Zeitgeist. See present age
Zeuthen, F. L. B., 102–4, 109, 128, 203
Zionism, 340
Zoffman Circle, 292–93, 294, 297
Zoffman, Marie, 292
Zoller, Edmund, 55

Receiving Søren Kierkegaard was composed in Bulmer by WorldComp, Sterling, Virginia; printed on sixty-pound Natural Smooth and bound by Braun-Brumfield, Inc., Ann Arbor, Michigan; and designed and produced by Kachergis Book Design, Pittsboro, North Carolina.

B
4377
.M36
1996